INTER/MEDIA

INTER/MEDIA

Interpersonal Communication in a Media World

THIRD EDITION

Edited by

GARY GUMPERT and ROBERT CATHCART

Queens College of the City University of New York

New York / Oxford

OXFORD UNIVERSITY PRESS

1986

Oxford University Press

Oxford New York Toronto

Delhi Bombay Calcutta Madras Karachi
Petaling Jaya Singapore Hong Kong Tokyo
Nairobi Dar es Salaam Cape Town
Melbourne Auckland

and associated companies in
Beirut Berlin Ibadan Nicosia

Published by Oxford University Press, Inc.,
200 Madison Avenue, New York, New York   10016

Oxford is a registered trademark of Oxford University Press

Library of Congress Cataloging-in-Publication Data
Main entry under title:
Inter/Media: interpersonal communication in a media
   world.
   Bibliography: p.
   1. Mass media—Addresses, essays, lectures.
2. Interpersonal communication—Addresses, essays, lectures.
3. Interpersonal relations—Addresses, essays, lectures.
I. Gumpert, Gary. I. Cathcart, Robert S.
P91.25.I48 1986 302.2'34 85-18811
ISBN 0-19-503737-5 (pbk.)

Printing (last digit): 9 8 7 6 5 4 3 2 1

Printed in the United States of America
on acid-free paper

Preface

The first edition of Inter/Media was motivated by our desire to uphold a thesis: that the traditional division of communication study into interpersonal, group and public, and mass communication is inadequate because it ignores the pervasiveness of media. The first edition focused on the connection of interpersonal and mass communication by juxtaposing essays. The second edition added original contributions of colleagues who recognized and accepted the premise of connection. This edition continues our effort to expand and update the concept of mediated interpersonal communication. It maintains that media and interpersonal communication are not only connected but symbiotic.

We, as editors, recognized and attempted to deal with the complexities of this topic. Developments since the publication of the previous edition indicate even further intricacies, particularly in the realms of business and education. Telecommunications serve an increasingly important role as the force and effect of the computer as a medium leaves its mark on every aspect of human communication. An additional factor should be noted: the recognition of the media-interpersonal connection is not limited to American scholars. We have become aware that a considerable group of international scholars are studying the affects of mediation upon personal communication. In the first edition Jan-Erik Nordlund of Sweden and Elihu Katz of Israel contributed essays. In the second edition Karl Erik Rosengren and Sven Windhal added material. In this edition the international flavor is extended with the addition of essays by Peter Moss and Christine Higgins of Australia, Anthony Smith of England, and a new essay by Elihu Katz and Tamar Liebes. Ten original essays are introduced for the first time in the third edition. In total, this volume includes nineteen essays specifically written for Inter/Media.

We wish to thank James Danowski, Elihu Katz and Tamar Liebes, Linda Linderman, James Lull, Peter Moss, Anthony Smith, Sari Thomas, Charles Turner, and Elizabeth White who wrote original essays for this edition as well as those who contributed essays to the first two volumes. We are heartened by the support of such esteemed colleagues and encouraged in our efforts to stimulate insight into this important aspect of human communication.

Flushing, N.Y.
January 1986

G.G.
R.S.C.

Contents

INTER/MEDIA

Drawing by Lorenz; Copyright 1971. The New Yorker Magazine, Inc.

MICHAEL J. ARLEN

Cameras in Command

I have a friend who is a bachelor from time to time and who at present resides in an enormous new apartment building, constructed of pale-blue brick and named after a Wagner heroine, that has a video camera mounted in each of its elevators. These cameras are not the swiveling kind, such as may be found in giant drugstores, whose roving eye scans the cosmetics counter and magazine rack and garden-accessories display with the rhythmic, inquisitorial, and easily outwittable manner of a Mr. McGregor searching his lettuce patch for Peter Rabbit. The cameras in my friend's elevators make no such claim to restless curiosity. Instead, they are stationary, sure of themselves, each fixed in place upon a little shelf high in the left rear corner of the elevator, with its lens pointing more or less directly at the front of the car, although I've noticed, riding up to and down from my friend's apartment in the company of other residents of the Wagnerian building, that we all generally tend to flatten ourselves ever so casually against the back of the elevator; out of sight, as it were, if not out of mind. It is a tendency, one might add, that affords an endearing example of mutual trust among urban strangers, for if our elevator group some afternoon should happen to contain a burglar-rapist-maniac he would clearly be able to wreak his dreadful havoc upon the rest of us unobserved by the vigilant though farsighted camera, his depredations as well as our gallant struggles unrecorded on the downstairs monitor screen, which is situated next to the mail room in the lobby and is supposed to be monitored by Raoul, the doorman: a descendant of a past more spiritual and humanistic than our own cool, Japanese electronics culture, who thus passes most of his time on a stool near the air vent just inside the front door, discussing night life with delivery boys and giving unsound advice to Haitian domestics.

I've thought of these elevator cameras every so often, not only last summer, when I used to drop by my friend's place fairly frequently, but this fall and winter, as the Iranian crisis prolonged itself (as the newscasters say) into its second and third month, because in certain ways they seem so representative, so emblematic, of the camera era that we are all living in. For some time, that is, we have been surrounded by camera images, and in the past decade we have started to actually live by them: to revere what the camera reveres, to see what the camera sees, to be guided by what the camera shows us. Long ago, in 1930, Christopher Isherwood wrote in *A Berlin Diary:* "I am a camera with its shutter open, quite passive, recording, not thinking." Such a lovely sentence, but how quaint and inexact and literary (dread modern pejorative!) it sounds today, in the context of the camera's looming and forceful presence in our midst. With what irony does Isherwood's tender phrase "quite passive" echo in the years that have seen the rise of photojournalism, *The March of Time,* paparazzi, *60 Minutes,* and the dialectics of *auteur* cinema and the young filmmakers. And now there is Iran: Iran, Day 67 or 76—for the networks seem to have discovered the pleasures of linear time, with the result that each night's report has been introduced by a logo to remind us of the consecutive, or perhaps Newtonian, nature of the event. Or possibly it is not so much the pleasures of linear time which have been discovered as the homespun satisfactions of fidelity; that is, for many years network news departments have been wearing themselves thin in the service of a kind of hyperactive news promiscuity, careening from crisis to crisis, setting up their cameras at a new trouble spot before the rubble has been cleared away from the last one, so that now, having decided to *stick with the story,* they have been covering it with the relentless predictability of a Don Juan who has decided to stay home for a few evenings. Was any man ever so consistently, so regularly, so admirably *at home* as this fellow? Day after Day, night after night, the networks have brought us the news from the streets of Teheran, even when there was no news, or when what there was of it had been more or less produced by the host nation for the purposes of worldwide television coverage.

Such fidelity to an important news event is a fine thing, to be sure; nor is steadfastness in covering a television beat such a commonplace occurrence that one should be impatient for a return to the old promiscuity. But what has obtained in our Iranian coverage, for the most part, seems less a matter of steadfastness of thought or action than a matter of rigidity of camera view. Let us even take this small thought a step further and say what has surely been in the minds of many persons over the past sixty-seven or seventy-six Iranian days: that there appear to have been two sets of prisoners taken in the Iranian crisis. Most explicitly and affectingly, of course, there are the fifty or so men and women of the American Embassy who are being held hostage in Teheran; apparently, they are not being physically brutalized, but they are being held against their will, are not free to go, and are presumably being compelled, or at least encouraged, to channel their thoughts along lines selected by their captors. Not altogether dissimilarly, the American news audience (decidedly more comfortable but also, while not actually brutalized, not entirely free to go either, and with its conscious thoughts being shaped by its captors) has been held captive by the TV cameras. One could say that it is the network news organizations that own the cameras and direct their placement, but in a sense the network news organizations have been held captive, too. The cameras are in command, as they have been so often in recent history. Cameras, for example, largely determined the selection of the American President, Jimmy Carter, who is trying to deal with the Iranian crisis, and though cameras didn't exactly topple the Shah, a close cousin of the camera—the cassette tape recorder—brought the Ayatollah Khomeini to power, and cameras have most certainly been determining the shape of the hostage crisis, both on the Iranian side and on our own. The mighty Wurlitzer of "the news" supposedly speaks with many voices, many *words*—the words of newscasters and voice-over correspondents and government spokesmen trying to describe the situation and define their views of it—but the single, focusing message that the public has lately received has been the camera's message: the belligerent, chanting, menacing Iranians in the streets of Teheran outside our Embassy. In earlier times, when people lived in oral or print eras, they could be focused and controlled by slogans (like "God for Harry! England and St. George!") or print messages (as from Tom Paine or Harriet Beecher Stowe). In the late nineteen-thirties, as Christopher Isherwood was to discover, whole nations could be rallied and controlled by loudspeakers and radio: a distanced version of the human voice, yet one that became even more powerful than the real thing. Now it is the camera that provides our points of reference, our focus. Indeed, our sense of great events has become so overwhelmingly visual—Mrs. John F. Kennedy reaching out across the back of that car in Dallas—that many people (whose forebears were doubtless once as widely deprived of man-made imagery and color as their progeny are now inundated by them) appear to believe that the visual plane is the only plane that life itself happens on. Consider, for instance, those fragments from the vast network news coverage of Vietnam, which were never really stories as such (those reiterated glimpses of helicopters landing, of men fanning out in the tall grass, of distant flames and puffs of smoke and napalm, of Westy Westmoreland in his little cap, and of visiting dignitaries touring the war zone), but which come down to us as *scenes:* symbolic messages of the war, even more powerful and haunting, I think, than the exaggerated flourishes of such recent epics as *The Deer Hunter* and *Apocalypse Now* (though, alas, not quite so "real").

For most of the public, Vietnam *was* those scenes, and is remembered not only through them but in terms of them; lately, they have passed as actual experience into the moviemakers' own cameras. Then came the "boat people," who had *their* scenes: capsizing hulks and heartrending waifs. Then the Cambodians, though the starving and decimated Cambodians unfortunately lacked both cameras and scenes; there were print reports and articles and some pictures of Mrs. Carter at refugee camps in Thailand, but no *scenes*. And now the Iranians and the hostages: our nightly glimpse of Teheran. For many years it must be recalled, our cameras unsuccessfully visited Iran: nodding politely at the Shah, who would usually dress up for the occasion (as if dressing up produced a scene!); or going to sleep over the Shah's land-reform program; or waking up somewhat over the Shah water-skiing (the Shah in a bathing suit; not a scene, either); and simply going out to lunch at the mention of repression (no scene here) or SAVAK (there is such a thing as *too much* of a scene) or the power of the Muslim priesthood (be serious; how can there be a scene about priests; old, bearded priests?). But now the cameras are back and are presumably happy, for they finally have their Iranian scene: the mobs in the streets outside the Embassy. At first, who would have thought it? Such an unlikely film location: the outside of a captured embassy, with the presumed subject of the story inside and out of sight! The network news directors couldn't have hoped for much: eventually, maybe a small war, of course, or, better still, a little armed conflict, with those far-off planes and tiny puffs of smoke; but, if not armed conflict, then what? The usual nothing. That only goes to show you what network news directors know, or ayatollahs, for that matter, because, though Khomeini certainly knew a lot about tape recorders and cassettes, maybe as much as Oriana Fallaci (since it was by cassette that he transmitted the Good Word from the suburbs of Paris to the Muslim faithful in Iran), he couldn't have really known that much about cameras, about what our cameras would see. The young Iranian activists, however, were quick to see what our cameras saw, and so began to speak to *them,* commune with the cameras. At this point, the network news directors, remembering their solemn journalistic mission and also the expensive reportorial talent on their payrolls, dispatched their heavy hitters to Iran: Mike Wallace to Qum! But why should the Iranians bother with the heavy hitters when they could speak directly to our cameras?

It was a dilemma, admittedly; a modern dilemma. By this time, virtually everyone disliked the Iranians. The government disliked the Iranians. The citizens disliked the Iranians. The news directors, being citizens too, certainly disliked the Iranians. But the cameras loved them. The cameras and the Iranians were pals. Of course, the Iranians didn't get the affection of the cameras for nothing. They had to put in a day's work now and then: raise the old fist, chant the old chant, march the old march down to the gates of the Embassy compound. But it was worth it, because of the scene. An interesting point, too, is that it wasn't what you would call a surefire, terrific scene. It didn't leap out at your from the pages of the script and say: Film me, young filmmaker. It was more the kind of scene you don't really notice at first, while you're blocking all the other, really important scenes; but then afterward, in the notorious cutting room, when the celebrated *auteur* film editor is telling you that none of the other really important scenes work, you suddenly notice: Hey, man, *this* is the really big scene. All those swarthy faces, all those hands and arms, all those beards. No matter that there's no fancy dialogue, no exploding ammo dumps, no little planes in the sky. This one *works*. It all sort of flows together, naturally cinematic, and, besides, you can hang things on it, cut to the subplot: cameo appearances by the Foreign Minister of the moment, attacking the criminality of our foreign policy; or nice Mr. Waldheim, of the United Nations, huddled in the back of his car; or even, now and then, a glimpse of the old Ayatollah, sitting on his carpet up in Qum murmuring "Rosebud" into a blank tape cassette. The only problem with the scene, I guess, is that it's incomplete; it lends to leave things out. It lacks the hostages, for one thing, though that's rather to be expected, considering the circumstances. Mostly, I imagine, it lacks *information*. Who are those people in the streets, anyway? Who are these militants (referred to as "students" on television, presumably in the spirit of palship) who hold our people prisoners in our Embassy? What did the Shah do, good or bad, that made a number of Americans happy to watch him water-skiing and a large number of Iranians want to kill him? There are many more questions that might be asked and could be answered, even on television, but to ask and answer them would doubtless detract from the scene, make it unworkable. The cameras would begin to blink their eyes in ambivalence and confusion, and sulk, and lose their pleasure, and leave Iran again.

So the moral, if there is one, is that we must probably learn to live with our cameras, at least for the time being (whether they are mounted in elevators or in drugstores or in wars or in political conventions or in Teheran), and learn to understand the scenes and images they choose to bring us. Only God's love, as the saying goes, is complete. I should point out, though, that my friend in the blue-brick building has been burgled twice since July—nothing really serious, if you know what I mean: his cuff links and Cuisinart the first time, his stereo speakers the second time—and has been giving serious thought to moving to a different neighborhood and a less contemporary building, with bars on the windows and one of those Prisoner of Zenda locks on the front door. He says that he will miss Raoul, who is of the opinion that both heists were inside jobs, but he won't miss the cameras that always pretended to be looking after him but never told him what he really needed to know. The trick now, one imagines, is to figure out which neighborhood to move to.

Introduction

This book is about the way we communicate with each other face to face, while at the same time being influenced by the media. It is a book about the inextricable relationship between media and interpersonal communication.

The book grew out of our experience over the years, trying to learn and teach about the mass media and about the uses and functions of interpersonal communication. We became concerned that our students were not being exposed to the larger, truer picture of the human communication process, and began to assemble the kinds of articles and research studies which would reveal how interpersonal and media worlds are intertwined. We present them to you along with our ideas about the significance of this relationship for human communication.

The Impact of Media

We begin this exploration with the belief that the acceleration of media (technological innovation) has had an impact on all our relationships. The new media have altered our patterns of communication just as surely as the Ice Age changed the contours of the land. When we can be there as Egyptian President Anwar Sadat steps from an airplane and shakes hands with Israeli Prime Minister Menachem Begin; when an astronaut walking on the moon can converse with us across 180,000 miles as easily as talking with a next-door neighbor; when we can telephone a friend or relative in Australia via a communication satellite, our world has been changed and so have we. Time and space, man's age old barriers, have been erased and each of us lives with this new reality. When our concepts of time and space are altered, our perception of reality shifts. Knowledge and truth take on different dimensions. Our symbols have new or added meanings. And, our notions of self and other are affected. The very stuff of human communication is changed.

The modern electronic media have affected what we know, who and what we talk about, who talks to us, and who listens. Our knowledge and store of information have been immeasurably increased. The most rural, isolated coal miner can speak knowledgeably about cancer or the Russian Flu, certainly knows what goes on inside a modern hospital, and knows what Rome looks like from the steps of the Vatican. Our ability to sustain communication is almost unlimited. Every member of our family is only seven touch tones and fifteen seconds away. Every driver on the road within eight miles is a "good buddy." Any doctor, nurse, or repairperson is in continual contact with his or her home base through an electronic umbilical carried on the belt. Our ability to consume communication is awesome. On a given weekday afternoon, three hundred and eighty thousand women and men in New York City alone consume *Ryan's Hope*. On Superbowl Sunday almost seventy million Americans watch this pageant of masculine violence. In any given month, almost every man, woman, and child in the United States will be exposed to a "Big Mac" commercial. Let there be a skyjacking in Italy or a riot in Soweto, South Africa, and within minutes half of the world's population will be tuned in. It must follow that our notions of self and other, source and receiver, channel and message have been affected.

The Media-Interpersonal Gap

It is our intention, through this collection of readings and original essays, to begin to bridge the gap that has existed in the study of mediated communication and interpersonal communication. We have tended in the past to treat the mass media as isolated phenomena having little to do directly with interpersonal communication, and we have dealt with interpersonal communication as though mass media did not exist. Too often the study of mass media has been from a commercial and technological viewpoint having little or nothing to do with the whole process of human communication. To a large extent, the study of interpersonal communication has concentrated on the relationship between two persons without regard for the media environment which contains that relationship.

This is understandable when we see how the academic study of human communication has evolved over the past seventy-five years. There have been created a number of separate disciplines such as journalism, public speaking, broadcasting, group dynamics, film theory, rhetoric, each dealing with particular aspects of human communication. This artificial division was necessary in order to deal with the complexities of communication and to identify suitable areas for research and training. What has been lost in this quest for territory and identity are the inherent connections which make human communication an on-going process. For example, the nexus of media and interpersonal communication has been overlooked. We have come to know and understand the technology of media, the art of media as performance, the regulatory problems of the media and the public, the economics of the mass media, and the professional possibilities for employment in the media. We have explored the relationship of self and other, of verbal and nonverbal communication, of personal and social space, of disclosure and feedback in interpersonal encounters. What has been underemphasized is the whole of the communication process: a process in which each part affects the other part and no one part can be fully understood apart from the whole. It is our intent in this book to emphasize the connections; to restore a perspective that has been overlooked in the acceleration of technology and the collision with face-to-face communication.

We want to make clear at the outset that it is not our purpose to suggest another, newly demarcated territory for communication study replete with its own experts. We firmly believe that the social scientist, the historian, the philosopher, the dramatist have all contributed immensely to our understanding of the communication process. We have found that there exists a great reservoir of materials that provide insights into the significant relationship of media and interpersonal behavior. From this vast array of writings and research we have selected a number of readings which we believe will help you understand and more accurately assess your communicative behavior in this media world. Our purpose has been to select from the widest range of disciplines in order to juxtapose ideas that reveal processes and that enable us to appreciate the ambiguities and subtleties that characterize our mediated relationships.

This volume asks you to examine your interpersonal relationships as reflected and infected by the media of mass communication. We are concerned with more than the media of television, although there is no escaping the fact that television is now the dominant influence in our lives. We want you to think about all the media you are dependent on and all the ways you use and are used by media. More specifically, we are asking you to attempt to look critically at yourself and your interpersonal relationships, while analyzing the communications media that surround you, and to make connections with your intrapersonal and interpersonal behavior.

The Reflexive Problem

We are all somewhat defensive about our media habits because there has always been a great deal of negativism associated with the advent of each medium. You can hear the negative comments all around you: Popular music can corrupt you! Newspapers, books, and magazines can arouse you! Films can give you unreal expectations! Television can turn your brain to jello!

It has been fashionable to blame the mass media for the ailments of our society. You have been told that the media are to blame for the growth of pornography and violence. Political parties blame the media when they lose an election. There may be, of course, some truth to these charges. But the point is that the media do receive a great deal of criticism and we all feel somewhat guilty about our dependence on media. It is hard, for example, not to be concerned about television viewing when Marie Winn writes in *The Plug-in Drug:*

> Its use and overuse may be seen as symptoms of other modern ills: alienation, de-humanization, apathy, moral vacuum. Or one can regard the television set as a pathogen, a source of such symptoms.[1]

In 1938 it was a different medium that we were warned about:

> This passive state is increasing because people are depending more and more on the radio, etc., for their entertainment and knowledge of world affairs. They are becoming too passive and being passive they will be more easily led. Where they will be led depends on the viewpoint of those who control the channels of information. If people neglect to see for themselves they will be unable to cure the evils they see.[2]

Despite doubts and warnings, no medium has been eliminated and we have all adjusted our lives, or have had them adjusted, to functioning with each medium while still harboring some doubts about its effects.

While we may enjoy hearing and making our own criticism of media content and effects, criticism of our personal utilization of media is much more threatening. We can all judge various media performances: "I don't like the record;" "The film was great," "She's a terrific comedian." It is more difficult to admit we really enjoy watching *Family Feud;* that we want to see closeups of violence on TV and in films; that some of our attitudes about sex have been formed by the media; that we would rather listen to our favorite DJ than talk with someone riding in the car with us.

The task of looking at ourselves objectively while we are in the midst of the very circumstances we are examining presents great problems. Can we be thoughtful and analytical about how we are being manipulated by the media *while* we are being manipulated? It is difficult to be reflective about an activity while we are part of that activity because we lack psychological space in which to make an examination. When asked to look at ourselves, particularly in reference to our media activities, we tend to become protective of our behavior and attitudes even though we do have a vague sense of dissatisfaction.

Some degree of psychological distance is necessary if we are to become critics of our face-to-face and media behaviors. Detachment can be developed only to the degree that we can gain perspective on, as well as gain some knowledge about, the process in which we are enmeshed. Perhaps an analogy would be helpful. An actor on the stage must engage in real, interpersonal communication as the character being portrayed. The actor must put himself into this role completely, without reservations, and interact with the other characters in a truly involved way if the play is to be effective. Yet, to understand what is happening in a play as it develops its own life, the actor must maintain some detachment or distance from the role he is playing. Actors learn to do this through years of training, but they can also stop the play or step into the wings and look at it from a "real world" perspective. And when the play is finished, they can leave the reality of make-believe and return to the reality of everyday existence. It would be easier if we, like the actor, could stop the media world and reflect on it and ourselves; but we can't. We have to learn how to look at ourselves and our relationships while we are interacting with others. This book is designed to help you step back and look—to help you gain some psychological space for a perspective on yourself and the media that connects you to the world and to others.

The Media, the Mass, and the Individual

You may think perhaps that we are overstating the case with regard to the pervasiveness of media influence on ourselves and our interactions with others. Try the following nonscientific experiment: meet a friend and interact with that person in your usual manner, but keep a part of yourself detached. Maintain a sense of objectivity. Answer the following questions: (1) How many times did some media language get into the conversation? ("That turns me off.") (2) How many media intrusions occurred during the conversation? (Posters and neon signs across the street, someone walking by playing a radio or tape recorder.) (3) How dependent was your interaction on media? ("I'll phone you right after *Dick Cavett*.") (4) How much media content was fed into your exchanges? ("He's an Archie Bunker if ever I saw one.")

We could go on, but you get the idea. Self-identity is formed by the media as well as by interpersonal acts. As explained earlier, one reason for this is that we have been conditioned to think negatively about the impact of media, just as we have been trained to take very seriously our face-to-face relationships with parents, teachers, friends, and coworkers. Another, and perhaps more subtle, reason is related to how we define the media and how we define ourselves. Most textbook definitions of the media explain them as a means of transmission: a channel for carrying a message to an audience. The definition usually carries with it the concept of a mechanism of impersonal reproduction that intervenes between the source and a mass audience. The term "mass," however, is not intrinsic to media. It is a characteristic of only some media, such as the electronic media, that are extremely efficient delivery systems for bringing messages to huge, undifferentiated audiences. Any of today's "mass" media could be utilized for "non-mass" purposes, such as point-to-point communication, e.g., a "ham" radio operator talking to a friend on the other side of the world. Because they are efficient, cheap, and relatively unrestricted means of reaching a great number of people quickly, the electronic media and the daily newspapers of the United States have come to be thought of as mass media. In this case, mass media are those complex institutions that distribute content to potential customers as a means of economic gain. While it might be interesting to debate the values of American institutions of media versus those of other nations, it is more important to recognize what this has meant for our attitudes toward mass media and what influence it has had on mass culture.

There is also a reluctance to examine our relationship to the mass media due in part to our negative attitude toward mass culture. Fostered by those who claim that the masses enjoy (or consume) a culture significantly different from that enjoyed now or in the past by the elite members of society, the feeling is that the culture made available to the masses is poorer in both the content and quality. When cultural objects are transmitted and diffused through the mass media, they are thought to be affected by this act of transmission, by their marketability, and by the size of the market. This attitude toward mass culture has influenced all of us. We don't like to think that we enjoy things that are low class—that we are being herded into a mass audience just to be sold a product. We have been taught that we are individuals; that we make our own decisions about whom to associate with and about how to spend our money. We never think of ourselves or our friends as part of the "mass." To be involved with the mass media is to be faceless, to be part of the herd. We want to think of ourselves as unique individuals and we want to be perceived on that level. Ironically, the mass media never address the mass. Rather, they appeal to numerous individuals, none of whom see themselves as part of the mass. Most of us prefer the romantic version of life where we alone control our destinies, choose our relationships, decide for ourselves what we want to hear and see, and above all, where we each create a life full of warm and affectionate personal relationships. The romantic vision says that all these "true" and "real" relationships exist outside the realm of media. The reality is that our relationships coexist and interact with the media as well as with others on a face-to-face basis. While we worship face-to-face interaction, it is very probable that everyone who reads this has a telephone, and would be quite unhappy without that instrument, which has done so much to alter face-to-face relationships. Think about the actuality of our family relationships when the TV set is on for a period of six-and-a-half hours each day. What used to occur during that time in pre-TV days? You probably have your own radio and your own stereo. Your car undoubtedly has a radio, maybe even a tape deck and a CB. If you made a media inventory you would discover that an extraordinary amount of time each day is taken up with mediated communication. Just the time alone that we devote to media must have a profound effect on our interpersonal relationships. Moreover, the process is cyclical. The media are dependent on us to alter our relationships to accommodate the media, and the media in turn present us with a picture of our altered relationships. The media-interpersonal helix reverberates throughout our society. We cannot help but dwell upon our own images. We must learn how to develop enough psychological space to see which image is which.

The Uses of This Book

We have just pointed out the complexities, difficulties, and threatening aspects of examining our own interpersonal behavior in a media world. We believe, however, that there are ways to develop an awareness and an understanding of the processes of mediated communication and their effects on us.

First, it is necessary to juxtapose appropriate interpersonal concepts with media concepts. To do this we have divided our study into four sections—"The Interpersonal and Media Connection," which presents the framework for the interpersonal and media interface and the research that supports it; "Media and Interpersonal Intimacy," which considers the technological identities of the media and relates those properties to our search for intimate contacts; "Reality and Media Perception," which shows how the intrinsic nature of media influences the way we perceive ourselves and our environment; "Media Values and Interpersonal Roles," which examines the connection among roles, values, and media.

An essay introduces each section to provide a perspective from which to view and relate the readings in the section. Each essay should provide you with (1) an understanding of the linkage between the two concepts being examined; (2) a construct in which to fit the significant ideas from each reading; and (3) a stimulus to an analysis of your own interpersonal behavior and media involvements.

Finally, the readings are arranged in each section so that they can unfold a view of media as part of our personal world of communication. In addition, we provide an alternate table of contents that groups the readings according to a source-message-channel-receiver model of communication. This arrangement emphasizes the interaction of media with each component of the communication process. The readings in their original presentations were not necessarily used to reveal the relationships that we are trying to uncover, but in each case the author of the reading recognized (either explicitly or implicitly) the interconnectedness of media and interpersonal behavior. Not all the pieces take the same approach. Some present a unique perspective on media, while others reveal unique aspects of a particular medium. In every reading, however, there is something to make us more aware and self-critical. At the end of the book is an extensive list of references that will guide you to other books, articles, and research reports pertinent to the study of media and interpersonal communication.

The arrangement of essays reflects the authors' attempt at providing a structure or pattern that will give some perspective on the complexities of our modern media world. The forty pieces here are not a continuum nor do they neatly explain the authors' point of view as an introductory textbook might. Some are theoretical, some are reports of social scientific research, some are anecdotal, and others are polemical. Some touch lightly on the issues while others explore deep sociological problems. What all of them have in common is a fundamental awareness that media are pervasive and inseparable from our personal worlds. Each essay offers some insight into the ways our notions of self, other, family, community and environment are being altered by our interactions with the media. Most importantly, none accept that the media are simply a vast entertainment industry with little import for the tasks and crises that fill our personal worlds.

Readers' interests and needs may dictate other arrangements of these essays. Some may want to read as a unit all those essays dealing with the impact of television; others may wish to concentrate on those essays that reveal the information functions of media. The four groupings we have are not unique nor does each essay fit neatly into a category like "values" or "reality," but taken as a whole they all reveal the importance of our media connections and the inevitability of interpersonal and media interactions.

In reading these essays, what is important is not that a select group of them tells you something about the affects of media on interpersonal intimacy or societal values, but rather that you read them with the kind of psychological distance that will enable you to see new relationships with the media and altered patterns of socialization. We caution you not to fall into the trap of believing that television is the only medium with which to be concerned. Accept that you are a participant in a vast and varied media-communication system. You are not exempt from the influences of the media even if you tell yourself that you use the media only for entertainment. Nor is it helpful to think of the media as some gigantic monster forcing people to believe and act in ways they do not want. Bell Telephone might be a huge, impersonal conglomerate, but it does not make you use the telephone to talk over the latest soap opera episode with your friends. We are suggesting that you accept what is patently true; that we all make use of media technology to facilitate daily living and that the media serve a variety of functions in our society. We recommend that you use these readings to better understand the functions of media and the uses that we all make of them. We hope that you will become more aware that as we make increased use of the media, our interpersonal relationships are changed just as surely as our use of the automobile and electric light changed our homes, our architecture, our industries, and our cities. It is not necessary to begin this book at the beginning. We are using the print form to examine events, concepts, and processes that are not linear. Enter the book through any section that interests you and continue until you return to where you began.

Notes

1. Marie Winn, *The Plug-in Drug: Television, Children and the Family* (New York: The Viking Press, 1977), p. 215.
2. Tim Madden, "The Passive State," *The Weekly Review* (May 5, 1938), p. 147.

1
The Interpersonal and Media Connection

Traditionally human communication has been viewed as a speaker saying something to a listener. Even though there have been tremendous variations on this simple theme of sender-message-receiver, it has served throughout the centuries as our basic interpersonal communication model. In classical antiquity Socrates presented the dialogue—questioner, answerer—as the ideal way to advance learning and thought. Aristotle utilized the speaker-message-audience or actor-performance-audience model in all his writings about the uses and effects of human communication. With the development of the alphabet and systems of writing, there was applied this same configuration—writer, message, reader. Even with the development of the printing press, radio, film, and television, we have continued to look upon human communication as basically one human being directing words and gestures at another human being.

There have been more intricate models of human communication developed, especially in this century, but all serve similar functions: (1) they permit us to make predictions based upon a description of the communication process, (2) they indicate the relationships of components found within the process, (3) they facilitate our understanding, and (4) they generate research. Some of the more well-known models are the Shannon and Weaver mathematical model (encoder-transmitter-noise-receiver-decoder), which is concerned with how information is sent and received; the Berlo model (sender-message-channel-receiver), which is concerned with the makeup and relationship of each element in the process; the Westley-MacLean model (A transmits something about an object X through C to B), which focuses on the gatekeeping aspect of C as well as the nonpurposiveness of some of A's messages; and the Lasswell model (who says what through which channels to whom with what effects), which is concerned with how effects are produced and controlled. All models and all theories of human communication begin with an acceptance of the basic act and process whereby two human beings are able to symbolize internal and external states and transmit and receive signs and signals of those states. No matter whether the model and its theory concentrate on the nature of the symbolizing process, or the means by which signs are transmitted, or how symbols affect and are affected by the human senses, it is assumed that the "simple" face-to-face communicative act is *the*

This cartoon originally appeared in *Saturday Review*, January, 1971.

act of communication and contains all the necessary elements of human communication.

To engage in face-to-face communication requires: a language; a set of meanings; a process of encoding and decoding signals; a means of transmitting and receiving symbols; a channel or medium to carry the signals from one individual to another; an understanding of the rules or grammar entailed; awareness of the social norms and psychological states involved in such an act; and an implicit agreement about behaviors appropriate to the communication act. In other words, everything that is necessary to communicate can be found in the face-to-face or interpersonal communication model. Furthermore, complex acts of human communication such as group communication, or a speaker addressing an audience, or an editor writing a magazine article, are only variations of this basic process and not different in kind. When people talk with each other in groups they are still communicating face-to-face in dyads, but with added rules governing the flow of conversation and with more complicated feedback procedures. The public speaker addressing a large audience makes use of all the same processes of language and gesture, of grammar and syntax as does the interpersonal communicator, but is limited in the amount and type of feedback that can be received; the audience is limited in what it can hear and see, and how it can respond. Nevertheless, all parties, especially the speaker, attempt to make the communicative act as similar as possible to the interpersonal one by compensating for the limitations such as speaking more slowly, projecting more, using enlarged gestures, etc. The writer writing a magazine article faces even greater limitations because of the lack of direct and immediate

"I fell in love with you the first time I heard your message on the answering machine."
Drawing by Koren; © 1978. The New Yorker Magazine, Inc.

feedback, because of the added effort of reading and translating alphabetic symbols, because of the lack of vocal cues, and because of the lack of control over the setting in which the communication act is completed. But even in the case in which the receiver may not be physically present, every effort is made within the limits of written communication to make the communicative act as close an imitation as possible of the face-to-face one. Alphabetic letters which approximate spoken sounds are employed, as are punctuation marks which substitute for vocal pauses and inflections, styles of writing which reveal the persona of the communicator are employed, and language which can make the communication seem more or less intimate. All these make the written communication a derivation of face-to-face communication.

Every type of human communication, from face-to-face to mass communication, is still basically an interpersonal communicative act. This does not mean there is no need to study or understand communicative acts other than interpersonal, but rather that all human communication is, in the final analysis, interpersonal. Also, we do not mean to imply that all human communication is simple or just like ordinary conversation, but that all the necessary components as well as complexities of communication exist in the interpersonal communicative act and as such provide a touchstone for measuring all communication. Whatever communication does to relate us to our universe—to relate individual to individual, and to produce the "humanizing" process—must in some way be related to that basic communicative act in which one human interacts with another.

Mediated Interpersonal Communication

The great technological advances of the nineteenth and twentieth centuries brought about what has come to be known as "mass communication." With the invention of the telegraph, the telephone, the gramophone, the camera, and finally radio, television, and film, human beings have been able to expand the fundamental interpersonal communicative act into an instantaneous, public dissemination of messages on an almost unlimited scale. Never before has a speaker or source of a message been able to reach so many receivers with so many sense modalities as can now be achieved by the use of the electronic media. Today a speaker can instantly engage in several million interpersonal communicative acts simultaneously through electronic channels. The only component missing from the traditional dyadic model is instant feedback. (Feedback here includes smell, touch, and body heat.)

That a communicator can reach a mass audience over time and space is not new. Marshall McLuhan refers to the invention of the printing press in 1450 as the beginning of mass communication, but man's attempt to extend the senses and bridge time and space with his communications began long before in prehistory. The use of smoke signals and the beating of drums have long been utilized as ways of extending the "voice" of the communicator over distance. Cave paintings and hieroglyphic writings were early attempts at bridging time so that messages could be preserved and the voice of the sender could be heard by later generations. In other words, human beings have always engaged in the activity of extending and expanding the simple face-to-face communicative act. It is only in the last hundred years that technology has been developed to almost perfectly replicate the interpersonal dyadic communicative act over time and space. This phenomenal extension of communicative potential has naturally produced great changes in our use of media and in the effect that can be achieved. We have now an overwhelming communications industry and have produced an explosion of information. These changes have not only produced jobs and commerce, they have also created questions about the meaning and impact of mass communication. Scholars and researchers have attempted to answer those questions. New theories of communication have been forthcoming and new communication models have been developed to account for these extensions. In the last fifty years, mass communication has emerged as a discipline within the academic community.

Stages in the Growth of Mass Media

General interest in the media of mass communication has followed a pattern similar to that of other types of technological advances. First, the new medium (telegraph, photograph, motion picture) is viewed as a toy—something to be played with or owned by the rich or the eccentric—something that society could get along just as well without. At that stage, the medium is not taken seriously by scholars and researchers, nor is it considered to have social or political significance by the general public. There are, of course, those who make "wild" and sometimes accurate predictions about the future impact of the medium, as well as those individuals who point out what foolishness it is. A common source of jokes about photography in the nineteenth century was the discomfort it caused the subject to sit still for so long and the flash powder that frightened the horses.

The next stage of interest and involvement is concerned with the techniques of the phenomenon. People want to know how it works and they marvel at how its effects are achieved. The early days of radio and television were marked by public displays and demonstrations showing the workings of a microphone, the inside of a vacuum tube, the parts of a TV camera. Now the medium has become "commercialized"; that is, it has developed to where it can be an aid in promoting commerce both in terms of selling the medium to the public and using the medium to sell products. At this stage, "schools" are created to train technicians to make the necessary components of the camera, transmitter, receiver, etc., and to train the personnel who will produce for the medium—cameramen, programmers, directors, scriptwriters, and support personnel. This is usually a stage of accelerated growth, and as a result of that growth, business leaders and politicians become concerned with the advantages groups might gain through the use of the medium. They begin to devise ways to control its growth and use, usually in the name of protecting the public who are viewed as helpless victims ensnared by the magic of the new medium. The media of the nineteenth and twentieth centuries introduced the need for governmental or self-regulation because of the public's "interest, convenience, and necessity" (a phrase later incorporated into the 1934 Federal Communication Commission Act). The desire to regulate leads to questions about how the medium affects the general public and what the role of the innovation should be. This in turn produces experts who study and predict the effects of the media. The results of these studies feed public debate, which usually centers around whether the new medium will destroy established institutions and corrupt the nation's youth. Well into the 1930s numbers of preachers argued that it was a sin to see a motion picture. In the 1920s there were cartoons that depicted radio listeners with enlarged ears and atrophied eyes. In the 1970s public officials cited television as the main cause of violence in our society.

The third stage of media usage and involvement can be labeled the "artistic" stage. At this point the medium has been institutionalized, has survived its critics, and has legitimized its functions. Award systems are established by the institution in recognition of its own contributions to society. Distinctions are made among schools that train technicians of the media and those that instruct the future performers and directors of the media in its proper use. To do the latter requires that the medium have a history or tradition, agreed-upon standards of excellence, and a secure place in the shaping of attitudes, beliefs, and values. By this stage, the public, the business sector, and the politicians have accepted the medium as an unquestioned part of the system and have usually forgotten the earlier predictions of doom and gloom. It is characteristic of young people at this stage to assume that the particular medium has always been present and that there is no choice about whether to use it or not. Furthermore, it is characteristic of academicians at this stage to argue whether the medium is a social science, a fine art, or a practical art; and to study it and teach about it accordingly.

There is a fourth stage in the development of most media and that is the one where the medium has become so much a part of the scheme of things that much of the public is unaware of how dependent it is. The medium comes to be accepted as "natural" as running water, electricity, and automobiles, and it fulfills a need that the medium itself helps to create. People no longer consider whether they need the medium, but the fear of being disconnected from the medium becomes a major concern, as when the telephone goes dead or the television set is in the repair shop.

At this stage people begin to anticipate the next technological advance in the life of the medium, like those now who are concerned with two-way television where the viewer can respond directly to the TV performer, or the videophone where communicators can be seen as well as heard. It is a time when scholars begin to look at the medium as an integral part of human activity and try to develop models and theories which incorporate the medium into whatever "system" they are studying, e.g. sociology, psychology, history, communication. Researchers no longer consider the medium as something separate or alien to be examined as though it were from another universe, but view it as part of the human condition. This book is part of that fourth stage.

Theories and Models of Mass Communication
It should not be necessary to point out that the four stages discussed are not mutually exclusive. It is possible that one stage continues long after the advent of the next stage. There are probably some people who still consider TV a luxury toy having nothing to do with the important aspects of life, just as there are people who are still enamored of its techniques and wonder how, and with grave suspicion, a "live" picture can be transported over thousands of miles of space into someone's home. There are also academicians who believe that the study of mass communications has little or nothing to do with the way human beings organize or think or how they talk to each other.

While we have suggested four stages in the evolution of a medium, the total picture is far more complex because media do not exist alone but in association with other media. No one medium develops separately, but in conjunction with its audiences and with other media as well. The interaction of media, audience, and society creates a complexity in which the four stages of evolution are sometimes hidden.

Early studies, particularly of the broadcasting media, concentrated on how the media shaped or influenced the response of its listeners and viewers without recognizing the various stages of development of a given medium or the milieu in which that medium arose. Researchers tended to look at the mass media as singular sources sending forth messages to a passive mass of individual receivers who were directly manipulated by the message. Their investigations focused on persuasive strategies utilized in media messages, on the numbers of audience members reached by the message, and on the resultant change in attitudes and beliefs. This resulted in a one-step model of mass communication where there were no recognized intervening variables between the medium and the individual receiver. It was held that if the media employed the correct persuasive strategies and controlled the exposure situation, then the individual receiver could be manipulated by the message. There was little regard for social structure, group influence, peer pressure, or other sources of information and influence. In these studies it was assumed that mass communication had little or nothing to do with interpersonal communication and vice versa.

When media became institutionalized, the research became more sophisticated and concentrated on the behavior of persons exposed to the mass media. It was discovered that individual audience members were influenced simultaneously by a variety of media and by opinion leaders who frequently relayed, reinforced, and interpreted the media content. The resultant two-step flow model of mass communication effects was very useful in bringing to media theory the important role of face-to-face communication. It was no longer assumed that the media audience was either passive or an undifferentiated mass, but that it was made up of groups of interacting people dependent on opinion leaders for much of their response to mass media messages. There was, at this point, the recognition of a direct connection between interpersonal communication and mass communication.

Further research along this line led to the "multi-step" flow model which included sequential effects of messages over time, gatekeeping, opinion leadership, and interpersonal communication. It was found that communication flowed not only from opinion leaders to followers, but from followers to leaders, and from followers to followers, all of which has to be accounted for in explaining media effect. Much of the media industry itself, however, has continued to rely on linear models of mass communication flow. The usual industry model holds that the most effective media message is the one that reaches the largest number of persons with minimum delay and holds them long enough to be manipulated by the advertisement. Some experts in the media industry have recognized a different version of the two-step model. In this model, the first step in selling a product is to capture the largest number of receivers available through the vehicle of entertainment or news. The second step is to deliver a direct and appealing pitch for the advertiser's product. Many in the media industry have yet to recognize the complexities of mass communication and the relationship with interpersonal communication.

A Systematic Model of Mass and Interpersonal Communication

Those in the fourth stage of media involvement have begun to look at the mass media as part of a *total system,* a system which includes all the ways that human beings receive and process information; symbolize thoughts, feelings, and experiences, encode messages; send, retrieve, and preserve messages; and the ways these functions relate to the sociocultural context. In a systems model, mass communication cannot be viewed as an external force manipulating passive receivers, nor can interpersonal communication be examined apart from the mediated communication that surrounds and involves each individual in the social environment. A systems theory of human communication assumes that all message inputs—verbal, nonverbal, firsthand or mediated, and purposeful or accidental—affect the internal states of the individual and help shape the message outputs from the individual to others (interpersonal behaviors) as well as the messages one sends to oneself (intrapersonal behaviors).

A systems model of communication shifts attention away from concern primarily with how the source manipulates messages or controls the effects, as in the speaker-message-receiver model. It goes beyond a multi-step or gatekeeper model, with its focus on channels of communication and diffusion of information, to focusing attention on how each component of the model *functions* in making the entire communicative system work. Receivers or audiences are considered an active part of the system, utilizing all the channels, mediated as well as interpersonal, to meet individual and societal needs. In turn, receivers influence the entire system by their messages and behaviors that become part of the inputs that influence attitudes and behaviors of those who create messages for the mass media. It requires that media and channels of communication be viewed as having distinct forms and structures which shape the messages carried and in turn influence those who produce the mediated messages as well as those who receive them. A systems theory looks at human communication as an ongoing process interacting with all the other elements in human existence, ever changing to meet the needs of human beings who must by nature communicate with each other and respond to changes in their environment. A systems approach does not seek to "blame" one component of the communication system for the effects produced, nor does it resist or reject innovation in human communication. Rather it attempts to explain how the system functions. In such an approach the mass media cannot be considered a technical monster manipulating helpless human beings, nor can it be pretended that human beings can communicate in face-to-face situations without being influenced by the mass media which surround them. We contend that mass communication and interpersonal communication are of a piece, and that we have a great deal at stake in learning how these two important aspects of human communication interrelate.

In the readings that follow, a number of leading theorists of mass media and interpersonal communication examine the connections in the human communicative system. Each one is saying something about how we use and become dependent on our media of communication. They explore the reasons for the supposed dichotomy between "real" and "pseudo" communication, i.e., face-to-face conversation and interposed media conversation. They explain that although communication stimuli are processed as information by the human individual, that what we bring to this process, the context in which we receive it, and the form that it takes, produces different results. They point out, also, that the change in technologies of communication, such as the shift from print channels of information to electronic channels, alters the way we think about the world and see our place in it. As the information flow increases, we have to change the way we organize and respond to that information. We now see and hear hundreds of mediated images a day, but we also see and hear the images of our immediate, directly sensed environment. What do we do with all this information? How do the amount and form of this new media information, along with the traditional information, influence what we talk about and with whom we interact?

In this section we address questions about the media-interpersonal connection with essays which offer both theoretical and conceptual explanations and answers. We begin by presenting the case for a new typology which will account for mediated interpersonal communication. The following essays explain how we use all sources of information to help us in our daily lives and how the uses we make of it shape our intra- and interpersonal communications. What emerges is a theory that contends that mass media and interpersonal communication are part of a dynamic interactive system, no part of which can be separated or removed from the other. This theory can be cast in the form of a model that relates our social system to our media of communication and our individual uses of media to our need for socialization.

ROBERT CATHCART and GARY GUMPERT

Mediated Interpersonal Communication: Toward a New Typology

In this essay we introduce the concept of "mediated interpersonal communication" and suggest that it be included in the typology of human communication. We define it as a general category of communication that includes any situation in which a technological medium is introduced into person to person communication. We describe four types of communication which fit into this category and we explain how each of these mediated communication acts accounts for our uses of media in a much more functional way than does the more traditional explanations of types of mass communication. We propose that media of communication be introduced into all definitions of human communication and we argue that the more typical division of communication study into interpersonal, group and public, and mass communications is inadequate to account for contemporary communications because it ignores the central role of media.

In 1962 Franklin Fearing offered four generalizations about situations in which human communication takes place:

1. They are situations in which human beings enter into certain strategic relationships with each other or with their environment.
2. They are situations the central characteristic of which is the production and utilization of signs, symbols, and symbolic acts.
3. They are situations which provide a maximal opportunity through the use of signs and symbols for the sharing of experience, achievement of goals, gaining of insights and, in general, mastering one's environment.
4. The sign or symbols material used in these situations is subject to the perceptual processes of the individuals involved.[1]

We cite this not as the preferred way of looking at communication, but rather as descriptive of the research interests of communication scholars. It is interesting and provocative that nowhere in this situational map can "media" be located as an important component of human communication. The same is true for accepted definitions of communication. For example, communication is "the process by which an individual (the communicator) transmits stimuli (usually verbal) to modify the behavior of other individ-

From *Quarterly Journal of Speech*, vol. 69 (1983), 267–77. Permission granted by *Quarterly Journal of Speech* and the Speech Communication Association.

uals (the audience)."[2] Or, "Communication: the transmission of information, ideas, emotions, skills, etc. by the use of symbols-words, pictures, figures, graphs, etc."[3] Definitions, particularly those used in the study of speech communication, have minimized the role of media and channel in the communication process. The focus has been on the number of participants, source and receiver relationships, and forms and functions of messages. The media of communication have been accepted, more or less, as fixed or neutral channels for the transmission of messages among participants.[4] It is difficult to find an interpersonal communication text or resource book which treats the subject of media as a significant factor.[5] The role of media in personal communication has, by and large, been overlooked.

Mass communication scholars have exhibited a concern with the individual's interaction with the mass media. Robert K. Merton, Joseph Klapper, and Wilbur Schramm have analyzed the effects of mass media on the individual. In 1962 Elihu Katz and Paul Lazarsfeld wrote *Personal Influence: The Part Played by People in the Flow of Mass Communication.*[6] The subtitle is significant for it indicated the authors' emphasis on the role of the individual in the mass communication process rather than on the role media plays in shaping interpersonal behavior. Despite this orientation, most definitions of "mass communication" fail to take into account the influential role of media in interpersonal communication. A definition which holds that mass communication connotes all mass media of communication in which a mechanism of interpersonal reproduction intervenes between the speaker and the audience makes "medium" synonymous with "mass communication." Such a definition does not suffice because it overlooks the role of the media in interpersonal interaction. *All media are not mass media.* Any so called mass medium can be used for point to point transmission, e.g., "ham radio," and any point to point medium can be used to reach a mass audience, e.g., "junk mail." Mass communication refers to a specific utilization of medium; a circumstance of communication in which a medium replicates, duplicates, and disseminates identical content to a geographically wide spread population. Therefore, the term "media" does not characterize a distinct type of communication because it does not account for or suggest its use. In the typology of human communication, "media" should not be relegated solely to the category "mass communication," nor should it be excluded from the other categories: interpersonal communication, group communication, and public communication.

To bridge the definitional gaps and reconcile the role of media in human communication, the following should be added to Fearing's generalizations:

1. There are interpersonal situations which require media for the purpose of communication.

2. The media are part of a complex of variables that influence behaviors and attitudes.
3. The content of media is both a reflection and projection of interpersonal behaviors.
4. An individual's self image and its development is media dependent.

If these claims accurately reflect the realities of media and human interaction then we would argue that what is needed is a new typology which will include media technology. The new typology should incorporate the traditional concepts of communication with the role of the technological media.

I

Any typology which overlooks pervasive, potent media functions and connections ignores an increasingly significant and complex aspect of human communication. It must be recognized that even intrapersonal communication is media involved. Intrapersonal communication refers to that internal dialogue that occurs between the "I" and the "me"—the dual processing system where information received from outside is processed through the ego to form a self-image.[7] It is generally accepted that there can be no sense of self without interaction with others, i.e., without role taking and feedback which corrects or verifies the outcomes of internal dialogues.[8] Obviously, television, radio, and film provide feedback which reinforce, negate and/or verify an individual's self-image.[9] Portraits developed in novels, magazines, and newspapers have long served in the formulation and reinforcement of socially acceptable and unacceptable self-images.[10]

Of increasing importance are photographs and recordings in the intrapersonal dialogue. The photograph creates and reflects socially desirable images. Voice and video recordings are being utilized to check self-image as well as improve one's projected image.[11] What makes this significant is the complete credulity with which persons accept photographs and recordings as unimpeachable portrayals of reality, often overriding interpersonal responses.[12]

Intrapersonal communication has traditionally been referred to as non-observable internalized dialogue which occurs in all humans. The medium of recording materializes that dialogue bringing the internal more in line with the external, thereby altering the way the individual processes information during intrapersonal communication. There is a growing reliance upon media technology for self-assessment and image formation. This alone would call for research to determine the role media play in creating the "significant other."

II

Interpersonal communication refers to dyadic interaction which takes the form of verbal and nonverbal exchanges between two or more individuals, consciously aware of each other, usually interacting in the same time and space, performing interchangeable sender-receiver roles.[13] Through the interpersonal communication process people maintain and adjust their self-image, relate to others, cooperate in decision making, accomplish tasks, and make order of their environment. All acts of communication emerge from the need of two humans to connect symbolically. The dyad serves as the paradigm of human communication. Michael Schudson, in an examination of the dyadic model, claims that "we have developed a notion that all communication *should* be like a certain model of conversation, whether that model really exists or not,"[14] and "the ideal is not one concocted by social scientists. Rather it is a widely shared ideal in contemporary American culture which social science has uncritically adopted."[15]

Humans have always sought mechanical means of extending and enhancing face to face communication to efficiently serve needs for security, socialization, collectivization, and fantasy. The result has been the permanentizing and electrifying of the channels of communication which make possible the reproduction of human communication over time and space. Each new technology not only extended the reach of human communication, it also altered the ways in which humans related to information and to each other.[16] If, however, it is maintained that mediated communication is synonymous with interpersonal communication, i.e., adds only neutral channels of transmission, it will not be understood how media have altered interpersonal connections. It is time, therefore, to expand the traditional typology to include *"mediated interpersonal communication."* A number of scholars have recognized the need. Gerald R. Miller states:

> I will argue . . . that mass communication messages potentially affect interpersonal relationships in even more fundamental, pervasive ways which at this writing have received relatively little research attention. Specifically, I will propose that the media often: (1) exert a powerful impact on people's initial perceptions of other interpersonal transactions; (2) influence the manner in which information about other transactions is processed and interpreted; and in many cases (3) distract persons from gathering the kind of information they need to relate effectively in interpersonal settings.[17]

Robert K. Avery and Thomas A. McCain point out that "the placement of intrapersonal communication and mass communication at opposite ends of a single continuum has resulted in masking the multifaceted nature of the differences among types of communicative encounters."[18] They state that radio phone-in talk shows are a form of interpersonal communication with unique characteristics. They conclude that, "the examination of interpersonal and media encounters must continue. Research on personal junctures with media and others needs careful description and understanding." [19]

The term "mediated interpersonal communication" is a general category referring to any situation where a technological medium is introduced into face to face interaction. It includes:

1. *interpersonal mediated communication:* telephone conversations, letters, CB radio, electronic mail, audio and video cassettes.
2. *media simulated interpersonal communication:* para-social interactions, broadcast-teleparticipatory communication, etc.
3. *person-computer interpersonal communication:* computers utilized as interpersonal proxies.
4. *unicommunication:* the utilization of such artifacts as T-shirts and bumper stickers for interpersonal interaction. [20]

Interpersonal mediated communication refers to any person-to-person interaction where a medium has been interposed to transcend the limitations of time and space. A technology is interposed between and is integral to the communicating parties. The interposed medium determines the quantity and quality of information and also shapes the relationships of the participants. [21] For example, a handwritten or typed letter can facilitate a personal relationship over distance, but the time it takes to transport the message along with the lack of immediate feedback alters the quality and quantity of information shared. The time factor also alters the relationship between the two participants. More significantly, interpersonal written communication differs from face-to-face communication because it requires mastery of a secondary coding system—written language—and a knowledge of the conventions of that medium. The fact that written communication can be stored and retrieved makes the exchange context-free and permanent. Consequently, there are things that can be said face-to-face that could never be put into writing.

Communication mediated by the personal letter is but one of several forms of interpersonal mediated communication. The telephone also transcends space—it allows us to carry on conversations in an essentially private and intimate manner far beyond the reach of the unmediated human voice. [22] Telephoning, however, utilizes only one sensory channel, and this limits the amount and quality of information transmitted. One has to compensate for the lack of nonverbal signals, which in turn, lowers predictability and makes for less control.

The widespread use of interposed interpersonal communication such as letter writing and telephoning has altered face-to-face relationships. For example, we do not have to leave the confines of our dwellings to maintain relationships over distance.[23] Face-to-face contact with the people in the street and marketplace can be avoided. The eyes, nose, and tongue can be protected from unwanted stimuli. Physical contact is eliminated even though telephone company ads suggest that we "reach out and touch someone." In addition, the telephone is altering proxemic norms. Edward Hall established that Americans maintain carefully proscribed interpersonal distances and that violation of spacial norms is risky.[24] The telephone alters interpersonal spacial relationships. Telephonic conversation always takes place at a socially "intimate" distance. The other person's voice is literally next to our ear—the distance at which, according to Hall, the sense of sight is not nearly as important as touch, smell, and the feel of bodily warmth. Perhaps this is why, at times, the telephone can be so threatening. It invades intimate space, but denies us most of the sensory means of communication control and verification present in intimate situations.

Other interposed media such as "CB" and "ham radio," audio and video cassettes (utilized for one-to-one communication), computers (used to connect two or more people) can be categorized as interpersonal mediated communication.[25] They share with face-to-face communication the characteristics of interchangeability of sender-receiver roles, immediacy of feedback, and use of unrestricted codes. They differ from interpersonal communication in the lack of privacy and communication control—whatever message is sent is available to all receivers—making the information more *public* than private. This tends to transform the sender of a message into a *performer*, placing emphasis on messages which entertain or carry general public information. The association of audio and video tape with radio and television broadcasting further suggests public performance, deemphasizing verbal content, and, at the same time, limiting intimacy.

III

The ambiguity of private and public communication suggests another variation of mediated interpersonal communication: *media simulated interpersonal communication*. This phenomenon was first explored by Horton and Wohl in their analysis of "para-social interaction."[26]

> In television, especially, the image which is presented makes available nuances of appearance and gesture to which ordinary social perception is attentive and to which interaction is cued. Sometimes the "actor"—whether he is playing himself or performing in a fictional role—is seen engaged with others; but often he faces the spectator, uses the mode of direct address, talks as if he were conversing personally and privately. The audience, for its part, responds with something more than mere running observation; it is, as it were, subtly insinuated into the program's action and internal social relationships and, by dint of this kind of staging, is ambiguously transformed into a group which ob-

serves and participates in the show by turns. The more the performer seems to adjust his performance to the supposed response of the audience, the more the audience tends to make the response anticipated. This simulacrum of conversational give and take may be called *para-social interaction*.[27]

Para-social interaction is a staple of mass media "personality" shows. The main ingredient is the illusion of intimacy created by the media personality through imitation of the gestures, conversational style, and the informal milieu of the face to face interaction. The audience members know the performer in the same way they know their friends; by observation and interpretation of gestures, voice, conversations, and actions. The celebrity program is designed to coach the audience into making personal judgments. Audience members report that they know these personalities better than their friends and neighbors. Though designed and controlled by media programmers and broadcast to a relatively undifferentiated audience, the para-social interation is not one-sided. The audience members are not passive observers of a skilled performance. Rather, they make appropriate responses to the personality's performance; they join into the joking, teasing, praising, admiring, gossiping and telling of anecdotes. When they play this answering role, they are doing exactly the things that lead to friendship and intimacy. As Horton and Wohl point out, "the relationship of the devotee to the persona is . . . of the same order as, and related to, the network of actual social relations. . . . As a matter of fact, it seems profitable to consider the interaction with the persona as a phase of the role-enactments of the spectator's daily life."[28] The broadcast audience's need for intimacy and the ability of performers to simulate face-to-face interaction explains in part the success of such personalities as Don MacNeil, Arthur Godfrey, Jack Paar, Phil Donahue, and Johnny Carson.

In the case of para-social interaction, though, there can be only the illusion of intimacy and friendship. The sender and receiver roles are sharply separated and *never* interchange. This form of communication is highly institutionalized and control is not in the hands of either the sender or the receiver but is pre-planned by media specialists who design and orchestrate the interaction. Though the audience member is aware that several million others are watching and interacting at the same time, the interaction seems intimate because the performer discloses personal information which is associated with intimacy. It seems private because the listener/viewer agrees to react as though the disclosure was made by a close friend in a face-to-face situation.[29]

The importance of simulated mediated interpersonal communication is two-fold. One, it functions as a substitute for face-to-face relationships. It is less demanding for some people to work out a close relationship with

Johnny Carson than with their next-door neighbor. The "para-social friend" is always predictable, never unpleasant, always sympathetic, never threatening. In other words, there are no challenges to the audience member's self esteem, nor limits on his or her ability to respond appropriately. Two, media producers of para-social interaction set up unreal expectations which lead many people to feel that their own interpersonal relationships are inadequate because the para-social relationship is based upon an ideal of face-to-face communication which is seldom achieved in practice. This leads to increased feelings of alienation and a greater reliance upon mass media for interpersonal satisfaction.

Closely related to para-social interaction and an important part of media simulated interpersonal communication is the radio talk show or what we call "broadcast teleparticipatory media." In a study of the talk radio phenomenon, Robert K. Avery and Donald G. Ellis point out that the exchange of messages between a call-in listener and talk radio host "creates a pattern of talk which defines a symbol system for the interactants. That is, social reality is uniquely defined by the interactants, and hence becomes significant to the communication process."[30] A later study by Avery and McCain states:

> After reviewing the results of several talk radio shows, one might easily come to the conclusion that although the communication patterns between a call-in listener and a talk radio host reveal numerous similarities to the face to face encounter the unique characteristics imposed by this communication setting afford a special context that needs to be considered in order to develop a complete understanding of this particular media-person transaction.[31]

It is significant that radio talk show conversation is more a public performance than a private and interrelational act. Despite its public aspect, the phone-in part of talk radio is carried on as though it were a private telephone conversation. The radio host is quite aware that the conversation is part of a public performance and one that must be handled and manipulated well if it is to be commercially viable. At the same time, the majority of the audience never call the talk show host but vicariously participate in the host-caller interaction much like neighbors who listen in on the telephone party line to learn what is going on and identify with one of the parties. For the non-caller the interaction serves an important non-threatening function; coaching the listener for future media-person and face-to-face conversations. The listener-caller selects a favorite radio host and interacts on a daily basis in much the same way that all of us select friends to interact with face-to-face. For the phone-in audience the radio talk show provides a relatively safe environment in which members can contact important public personalities, giving them status and a feeling of connection. The willingness of the "personality" to come into the home as a companion, listening to the caller and providing assurance that beliefs and values are shared, simulates interpersonal interaction.

Similar to para-social interaction, broadcast teleparticipatory interaction represents a form of simulated interpersonal communication. Unlike telephone talk, sender-receiver roles are relatively fixed, there is little or no relational development, and the communicative code is restricted-implicit rather than unrestricted-implicit. Even on phone-in shows featuring psychologist hosts where callers often disclose intimate sexual information, both interactants follow carefully proscribed restricted language codes more suitable for public forums than the more unrestricted intimate codes of personal telephoning. Avery and Ellis report that callers never forget who is in control of the interaction.[32] Callers know they can be cut off if they are boring, too bizarre, too emotional, too aggressive, etc. If they do not please the host, who acts as interpreter and gatekeeper of what is interesting and acceptable to the audience, they will be stopped by disconnection.

Broadcast teleparticipatory media are viewed as entertainment by those in control of the program. They shape the public perception of an ideal interpersonal performance. The seven second tape delay technology makes source control absolute. Programmers can bleep out anything they think should not be heard, making the conversation "safe" for all participants. The exercise of this control teaches the audience the restricted code of "public" interpersonal communication; rewarding those who can perform the "ideal" intimate communication with the host. It is this public aspect, along with the placing of control in the hands of an unseen, unknown source, that establishes broadcast teleparticipatory interaction as a distinct type of mediated interpersonal communication. Research by Avery, Ellis, McCain and others verifies that this is a firmly established and growing mode of interaction, one which many Americans are dependent upon for supplementing and/or substituting for daily face-to-face interaction

IV

The *person-computer interpersonal encounter* represents another facet of "mediated interpersonal communication." It includes any situation in which one party activates a computer which in turn responds appropriately in a graphic, alphanumeric, or vocal mode (or combinations thereof) thereby establishing a sender/receiver relationship.[33] In the computer-person interaction the computer is programmed by a person, but that person is not the sender or receiver of the message. The human partner interacts not with the computer programmer, but with the computer program. Ithiel de Sola Pool points out that prior to the introduction of the computer every communication device "took a message that had been composed by a human being and (with some occasional loss) delivered it unchanged to another human being. The computer for the first time provides a communication device by which a person may receive a message quite different from what any human sent. Indeed, machines may talk to each other."[34]

Although person-computer transactions simulate dyadic communication, the process and the alternatives are predetermined. The human partner activates the computer, but once the encounter has begun the computer program controls the communication. To compensate for the loss of control we anthropomorphize the computer; i.e., give it human qualities. The human partner can then "role play" a face-to-face interaction because all the components of dyadic communication exist, except that one of the partners is a machine.

Not all human-computer contacts, however, are characterized by this particular interactive quality. The person-computer mediated encounter should be contrasted with the situation in which one communicates *through* a computer rather than *with* a computer. "Electronic mail," for example, represents a change of medium (paper to display screen) in which the computer is interposed. In this case the computer is a high speed transmitter of what is essentially a written message. The person-computer mediated encounter, on the other hand, always involves direct dialogue between individual and computer.

V

In 1975, Gumpert described "communication from one to many of values prescribed by associations in the environment through various non-electronic media. Uni-communication is a type of mediated interpersonal behavior."[35]

Uni-communication is that communication mediated by objects of clothing, adornment, and personal possessions—houses, automobiles, furniture, etc.—which people select and display to communicate to others their status, affiliation, and self-esteem. It includes, also, more explicit messages like imprinted T-shirts, jackets, and caps, as well as bumperstickers, armbands, and buttons.

Communicating something about one's status and role through clothing and personal possessions is, of course, an ancient and well established mode of communications.[36] Personal possessions—everything from the exterior and interior design of homes to a pair of Gucci loafers—can and do take on symbolic functions which impart implicit information to others and reenforce one's self-image. What has received little attention is how this attenuated, symbolic interaction operates as a form of mediated interpersonal communication. What makes it interpersonal is that it is self-disclosing and it produces sender-receiver relationships. The item displayed can serve one or more purposes and establish one or more relationships. For example, it can reveal group affiliation (wearing a Masonic ring), mark one's status (driving a white Mercedes Benz 450 SL), identify a role (carrying a brief case), and express support for or rejection of established values and institutions (wearing a Star of David, displaying orange colored, spikey hair). The fact that a single item of attire can have multiple meanings makes it useful in establishing a variety of relationships. A studded black leather vest with "Hells Angels" inscribed can serve to identify, reject, boast, etc., depending upon the context and the receiver's response. Unicommunication is extremely helpful for informing people of status, role, and affiliation in situations where face-to-face interaction is difficult and possibly risky.

What makes uni-communication important in an updated communication typology is an expanded function brought on by the mass media of communication and the mass distribution of "pop" symbols. Increasingly, individuals in all levels of society are making explicit messages out of these symbols and transmitting them to mass audiences. Wearing a T-shirt imprinted with "No Nukes" makes use of a utilitarian item of clothing to "broadcast" a message to any and all who come close enough to read the words and view the person displaying them. The bumper sticker, "Jesus Saves," makes use of an automobile, which is both a means of transportation and a symbol, to carry an additional and more explicit message to fellow drivers.

Such messages ordinarily do not originate with the person displaying them. Rather, they are mass produced and distributed by groups who are campaigning for certain causes. The persons displaying these messages become part of the campaign as well as part of the transmission system. This makes unicommunication different from other forms of interpersonal interaction. It communicates affiliation with a group or suggests a social role rather than making an individual statement. Uni-communication facilitates stimulus generalization rather than stimulus discrimination.[37] Receivers respond to the attached symbols and the individual as one entity; deriving different messages depending on the receiver's perceptions of the affiliate group or social role. Uni-communication discloses how the displayer views her or himself in affiliation with others rather than in relationship to an individual receiver.

Receivers of uni-communication are confronted by the message in situations where face-to-face interaction is neither expected nor desired. There is, however, a response and an interaction. The response is like the reaction to a billboard or a poster. We may not want to see it or read it, but the fact that it comes into our view draws our attention, makes us read, and we are forced to respond. The response is to the person as part of the message—with hostility, or anger, or admiration, or identification. It is an interpersonal interaction. Seldom is there any immediate, verbal feedback. Similar to the para-social and other mediated interactions, communication is carried on at a distance even though each person may be within social speaking range. The receiver decides what the message means and works out an appropriate verbal scenario. The sender has in mind a message, or maybe several messages, which may or may not coincide with the messages being formulated by receivers. Each is satisfied that something has been communicated. Each has been involved in a personal communicative inter- action. Senders have made a statement—one which says something about who they are and how they feel. Receivers respond as though the message was directed at them as individuals. The fact that this same interaction is replicated thousands of times all over the nation (made possible by both mass distribution and mass media), creates a kind of national interpersonal dialogue about values, roles, and status.

We believe that uni-communication serves important interpersonal func- tions in our society. A study of it would tell us something about how we communicate and with whom in an increasingly impersonal environment where long established institutions of social interaction are undergoing change. For example, we have created public places like "discos" and "sin- gles" bars to serve courtship and match-pairing functions once exclusively the domain of the home and the church. These places exist to promote in- terpersonal relationships. In such places, the communication process is aided by the kinds of clothing and jewelry worn which become explicit messages to others concerning one's status, one's availability, and one's feeling about the kinds of interactions one desires. We point this out as only one area of potential research into a type of mediated communication which has been ignored.

In summary, there may be other types of mediated interpersonal com- munication which we have not recognized. There are, of course, other forms of communication which need to be placed in an updated communication typology. The mediated political campaign is one example. The printed magazine or journal distributed to a select audience which is part of a spe- cialized network, what Gumpert has called "mini-communication,"[38] is another example. We could go on, but the point is that a typology which compartmentalizes thought and research and prevents investigations of im- portant types and forms of human communication cannot be tolerated. We are quite convinced that the traditional division of communication study into interpersonal, group and public, and mass communication is inade- quate because it ignores the pervasiveness of media. We propose that media be incorporated in definitions of communication and that we begin to realign our research to account for the significant impact of media.

Notes

1. Franklin Fearing, "Human Communication," in Lewis Anthony Dexter and David Manning White, eds., *People, Society, and Mass Communications* (New York: The Free Press, 1953), p. 42.

2. C. I. Hovland, I. L. Janis, and H. H. Kelly, *Communication and Persuasion* (New Haven: Yale University Press, 1953), p. 12.

3. B. Berelson and G. Steiner, *Human Behavior* (New York: Harcourt Brace, and Jovanovich, 1964), p. 527.

4. See, for example, David K. Berlo, *The Process of Communication* (New York: Holt, Rinehart and Winston, 1960), p. 31, who states that "Channel is a medium, a carrier of messages." Also, Frank E. X. Dance and Carl E. Larson, *The Functions of Human Communication* (New York: Holt, Rinehart and Winston, 1976), which makes no mention of media as channel or medium as a variable.

5. In developing the first edition of *Inter/Media: Interpersonal Communication in a Media World* (New York: Oxford University Press, 1979), we were unable to find textbooks which treated media as a significant variable in interpersonal communication. See, for example, Dean C. Barnlund, *Interpersonal Communication: Survey and Studies* (New York: Houghton Mifflin Co., 1968); Joseph A. De Vito, *The Interpersonal Communication Book* (New York: Harper and Row, 1977); Gerald M. Phillips and Nancy Metzger, *Intimate Communication* (Boston: Allyn and Bacon, 1976); and John Stewart and Gary D'Angelo, *Together: Communicating Interpersonally* (Reading: Addison Wesley, 1975).

6. See Wilbur Schramm, *The Process and Effects of Mass Communication* (Urbana: University of Illinois Press, 1954); Joseph T. Klapper, *The Effects of Mass Communication* (New York: Free Press, 1960); and Robert K. Merton, "Patterns of Influence: A Study of Interpersonal Influence and Communication Behavior," in P. F. Lazarsfeld and F. N. Stanton, *Communication Research* (New York: Harper, 1949); Elihu Katz and Paul F. Lazarsfeld, *Personal Influence: The Part Played by People in the Flow of Mass Communication* (New York: The Free Press, 1955).

7. For a discussion of the sense of self as the individual "I" and the "Me" as social sttitudes, see George Herbert Mead, *Mind, Self and Society* (Chicago: University of Chicago Press, 1934).

8. Duncan claims that, "The self and society originates and develops in communication," H. D. Duncan *Communication and Social Order* (New York: Bedminster Press, 1962), p. 76. B. Aubrey Fisher explains, "Dialogue implies the expression of self and the development of mutual understanding (that is, congruence) along with the development of self through social interaction. . . . And the concept of role taking allows for the individual to discover and develop self through social interaction." *Perspectives on Human Communication* (New York: Macmillan Publishing Co., 1978), p. 179.

9. See Michael Novak, "Television Shapes the Soul" in L. L. Sellars and W. C. Rivers, eds. *Mass Media Issues* (New York: Prentice Hall, 1977).

10. See Virginia Kidd, "Happily Ever After and other Relationship Styles: Advice on Interpersonal Relations in Popular Magazines," *Quarterly Journal of Speech,* 61 (1975); and James Lull, "The Social Uses of Television," *Human Communication Research,* 6 (1980).

11. The widespread use of audio and video recordings to improve the image of politicians, beauty contestants, salespersons, etc., is documented in newspaper and magazine articles. See, for example, "Rose Queen Prepares for the Pageant," *Los Angeles Times,* December 27, 1981, B-3; and "Cops Go High Tech for Fiesta, Plan Second Year of Taping," *Santa Barbara Journal,* March 15, 1981, p. 14.

12. For a discussion of the effects of photographs on perceptions of reality see, Susan Sontag, *On Photography* (New York: Farrar, Straus and Giroux, 1973).

13. We are using the term "interpersonal communication" in its generic sense, emphasizing function rather than relationship. Our approach is similar to that of Donald P. Cushman and Robert T. Graig: "Interpersonal communication systems are distinguished from other general levels in terms of function, structure, and process, but primarily in terms of function. . . . A well-defined interpersonal system is necessarily a *small* system—paradigmatically a dyad. . . . Relationship issues like affection and openness, and processes of development, presentation, and validation of self-conceptions seems necessary in view of the basic function of the interpersonal systems." See Donald P. Cushman and Robert T. Graig, "Communication Systems: Interpersonal Implications" in Gerald L. Miller, ed., *Explorations in Interpersonal Communication* (Beverly Hills: Sage Publications, 1976), p. 46.

14. Michael Schudson, "The Ideal of Conversation in the Study of Mass Media," *Communication Research,* 5 (1978), 323.

15. Schudson, p. 323.

16. For a discussion of the symbiotic relationship between technology and communication from a historical perspective, see Walter Ong, *Interfaces of the Word: Studies in the Evolution of Consciousness and Culture* (Ithaca: Cornell University Press, 1977); and Marshall McLuhan, *The Gutenberg Galaxy* (Toronto: University of Toronto Press, 1962).

17. Gerald R. Miller, "A Neglected Connection: Mass Media Exposure and Interpersonal Communicative Competency," in G. Gumpert and R. Cathcart, eds., *Inter/Media: Interpersonal Communication in a Media World,* 2nd ed., (New York: Oxford University Press, 1982), p. 50.

18. Robert K. Avery and Thomas A. McCain, "Interpersonal and Mediated Encounters: A Reorientation to the Mass Communication Process," in G. Gumpert and R. Cathcart, *Inter/Media: Interpersonal Communication in a Media World,* 2nd ed., p. 30.

19. Gumpert and Cathcart, p. 39.

20. While the categories listed under the concept of "mediated interpersonal communication" can be demonstrated, the classification labels should be considered "in progress."

21. In comparing mediated interpersonal communication and interpersonal communication we will utilize the following basic characteristics of interpersonal communication: (1) it is transmitted through multiple channels. Sight, smell, touch, and taste operate as receiving channels. (2) It is spontaneous and evanescent. It cannot be recreated. (3) Feedback is immediate and continuous. (4) Interchangeable sender-receiver roles provide maximum control of content. (5)

There is unlimited channel capacity and no production costs. (6) It utilizes implicit and restricted audio-verbal and audio-visual codes which make for privacy and intimacy. (7) Psychological as well as sociological and anthropological information is generated and processed. (8) Basic skills and conventions are learned informally at an early age, usually in non-institutional settings.

22. For an extensive analysis of the influence of the telephone, see Ithiel de Sola Pool, ed., *The Social Impact of the Telephone* (Cambridge: M.I.T. Press, 1977). For a discussion of the significance of letter writing as verbal expression, see Walter J. Ong, *The Presence of the Word* (New Haven: Yale University Press, 1967).

23. The electronic relationship and its implications for the future is one of the primary issues examined by Alvin Toffler, *The Third Wave* (New York: William Morrow and Company, Inc., 1980). Melvin M. Webber examines a related notion when he proposed "non-place communities." See *Explorations into Urban Structure*, edited by Melvin M. Webber *et al.* (Philadelphia: University of Pennsylvania Press, 1971).

24. Edward T. Hall, *The Hidden Dimension* (New York: Doubleday & Co., 1966), pp. 113–130.

25. See Bert Cowlan, "A Revolution in Personal Communications: The Explosive Growth of Citizens Band Radio," in G. Gumpert and R. Cathcart, *Inter/Media: Interpersonal Communication in a Media World* (New York: Oxford University Press, 1979), pp. 116–21. See Sherry Turkle, "Computer as Rorschach," *Society*, 17 (1980).

26. Donald Horton and R. Richard Wohl, "Mass Communication and Para-Social Interaction: Observation on Intimacy at a Distance," *Psychiatry*, 19 (1956), 215–29.

27. Horton and Wohl, p. 215.

28. Horton and Wohl, p. 228.

29. Horton and Wohl, p. 219.

30. Robert K. Avery and Donald G. Ellis, "Talk Radio as an Interpersonal Phenomenon," in G. Gumpert and R. Cathart, p. 112.

31. Avery and McCain, p. 37.

32. Avery and Ellis, p. 113.

33. For an overview of person-computer interactions, see Hollis Vail, "The Home Computer Terminal: Transforming the Households of Tomorrow," *The Futurist*, December 1980. For a more general discussion of microcomputers, see Christopher Evans, *The Micro Millennium* (New York: The Viking Press, 1979).

34. Ithiel de Sola Pool, "Forward" to *The Coming Information Age: An Overview of Technology, Economics, and Politics* by Wilson P. Dizard, Jr. (New York: Longman, 1982), pp. xi–xii.

35. Gary Gumpert, "The Rise of Uni-Comm," *Today's Speech*, 23 (1975), 34.

36. For an historical analysis of the symbolic nature of clothes, see Anne Hollander, *Seeing Through Clothes* (New York: The Viking Press, 1976).

37. See Gerald R. Miller, "A Neglected Connection: Mass Media Exposure and Interpersonal Communication Competency," pp. 51–53, for a discussion of generalization and discrimination responses in interpersonal communication.

38. Gary Gumpert, "The Rise of Mini-Comm," *Journal of Communication*, 20 (1970), 280–90.

On the Mass Media and Mass Communication: Notes Toward a Theory

It is necessary to understand the meaning of terms such as "media," "mass communication," "mediated communication," and "interpersonal communication." Adequate definitions help clarify the processes and concepts central to the study of human communication. Lee Thayer provides some operational definitions that clarify the "basic dynamic" of mass communication, i.e., the uses to which each of us put the media and their fare. He describes five major ways we use the mass media and the resultant effects upon the media themselves. Perhaps you have always thought of the mass media as affecting people—most persons do. Try the opposite: what are your *uses* of media?

Some Preliminary Definitions

Definitions do not make a theory, of course. But some preliminary redefinitions of terms consistent with the preceding analysis may help to set the stage for an alternative conceptual framework.

Media

By the term *media,* we should be referring to *all* of the means—all of the devices, technologies, etc.—utilized for acquiring, storing, transporting, displaying "messages" (i.e., codified data). The human ear is thus a medium, as are human languages.[1] The microscope and the telescope are media. A piece of parchment, like the wall of an inhabited cave, when used to inscribed "messages," is also a medium. Most of the popular media are compounded: radio requires not only the devices which broadcast and which receive codified signals, but the natural "medium" of "air waves." Historically, the most ubiquitous and significant of all of the media have been people themselves: people may be utilized, or utilize themselves, as a *means* of storing, transporting, acquiring, or displaying "messages" presumed to have some potential relevance or meaningfulness for others.

There are many ways of categorizing media. Some we take ourselves to (e.g., museums and churches), others are more portable (e.g., radio, photographs). Some can be privately utilized (e.g., books); others are necessarily more public (e.g., circuses[2]). Some are simple (e.g., the human ear, the newspaper); others are compound (e.g., roads and highways, which are

From *Beyond Media: New Approaches to Mass Communication,* edited by Richard W. Budd and Brent D. Ruben. (Rochelle Park, N.J.: Hayden Book Co., 1979). Reprinted by permission.

used to transport people, who store and transmit "messages," and television, which displays people talking to each other by telephone). But the essential point is that the media include *all* means of acquiring, storing, transporting, or displaying "messages."

Communication Messages and Mass Communication Messages

A communication message is one which is addressed to a specific person or to specific persons who are functionally related to the source in some way. A mass communication message is of the sort: to whom it may concern; the addressees are essentially anonymous; and a mass communication message neither implies nor requires a personal relationship, even though the conventional uses to which people put the media or media fare over time establishes a reciprocal relationship, a special form of "institutionalization" which will be discussed below. A piece of mail addressed to John Jones by a friend or a legitimate creditor is a communication message. A piece of mail in his mail box addressed to "Occupant" or to "John Jones" from someone unknown and unrelated is a mass communication message. By its nature, a television network cannot transport communication messages; it can transport only mass communication messages. The telephone and telegraph systems, like the postal system, can transport either kind of message. The ultimate distinction between the two is this: a communication message involves two or more people reciprocally, and in terms of their relationship; a mass communication message is of the sort: to whom it may concern; it is impersonal in the sense that either or both the source and the consumer are anonymous.

A weakness of existing formulations is the typical assumption that non-mediated (e.g., "face-to-face") communication is always personal, while mediated communication is generally impersonal. A letter or telephone call between friends is certainly mediated; but it can be extremely personal. On the other hand, the ritual pleasantries we exchange at cocktail parties, although "face-to-face," are typically impersonal, such "messages" as "The weather has certainly been unusual," or "Hello, how are you?" can be addressed to anyone who cares to listen; they are therefore essentially impersonal, in the manner of "to whom it may concern."

Communication Media and Mass Communication Media

Whether a given medium is a communication medium or a mass communication medium therefore depends entirely upon how it is used. By their nature, some are more "usable" one way than the other. For example, the print and electronic media may lend themselves more to the transport and display of mass communication messages. While the major use of the telephone is for the transport of communication messages, it can be used the other way too. Film may be used to transport a movie to be viewed by millions; or it can be used to capture a special moment having special meaning for only one or two people—as when an absent lover sends a picture of himself. Memos between two principals of the "Watergate affair" may have been a communication medium prior to the investigation; but, if read by others, they become a mass communication medium.

So the distinction between the two is neither a dichotomous nor a mutually exclusive one. Entertainment media typically become more specialized over time by the uses to which their audiences put them. Specialized media having specifiable audiences are somewhere in the middle of the continuum from the exclusively personal to the indiscriminately impersonal.

Any means of storing or transporting or displaying what people say is a communication medium. The distinction is not in the technologies used, but in the uses to which they are put. Using two-way television for personal conversations in lieu of using the telephone doesn't alter the devices used: it merely alters their use.

Communication Networks and Mass Communication Networks

A much more important distinction, theoretically, is that between a communication network and a mass communication network. A communication network emerges from people talking to each other about matters that make a difference to them. It connects or links people functionally "in series." A mass communication network is superimposed or overlaid on existing communication networks (*viz.*, social structure) to the extent made possible by the available technology. It networks or connects people nonfunctionally "in parallel." *What is* and *what matters*—indeed, all human reality, all human values—are products of communication networks. There is more to be aware of in our physical and social environments than we could possibly be aware of; there is more to be known than we can possibly know. One function of a communication network is to sort out what we need to be aware of from what we don't, and what we need to know from what we don't. The mass media and their fare are ultimately no more than a part of our social environment. What aspects of that fare we need to be aware of depends generally upon who we talk to; what we need to know of what is provided by a mass communication network depends generally upon the communication networks to which we belong. In a free society, the relationship between people and the mass communication media is the same as that between people and their communication media—adaptive, emergent, and evolving. Therefore, the more subcultures (communication networks) there are in a given society, and the more heterogeneous they are, the more "selectivity" there is or the more specialized the mass communication media become. The demise of *Life* was but one of a long list of examples in recent U.S. history of what happens when a "something-for-everyone" medium fails to adapt to changing social conditions. Would the disciples of the cause → effect approach want to argue in this case that the "effect" of *Life* was to kill its audience?

Mediators

A mediator is someone who, intentionally or not, mediates for others some world, some domain of existence, some knowledge, etc., which is presently or permanently inaccessible to those others. Parents are, of necessity, mediators of the adult world for their children. Teachers are, by choice, mediators of knowledge and value for their pupils; priests are the mediators of other worlds for their parishioners, as movie and television and stage stars are for their followers, as sports or music celebrities are for their publics, as reporters and broadcasters are for their audiences, and as scientists are for laymen.

The nature of the relationship between a mediator and his constituency is such that what he says or how he acts about those inaccessible worlds he is mediating cannot be directly verified by those who, by necessity or by choice, comprise that constituency. Whether what we take to be public beliefs about "the Establishment" or about "Hollywood" are well-grounded or not cannot be decided by direct inspection. They can be validated only in communication with other persons, and these are typically other members of the same constituency. Whether a given public's image of the President is truly "accurate" cannot in fact be determined; it is acceptable as "true" to me or to you to the extent that its relevance to others confirms that image. "Is it true? Is it true that President Kennedy was shot?" was the question that was asked of millions by millions. There were, of course, the radio and television and newspaper "reports." But did the event in fact occur? And, if so, what does it *mean*? When we cannot see for ourselves, and often even when we can, we can determine the truth and the relevance and the *human* meaning of something or some event only by talking to each other. What the child's mother or teacher tells him about sex may be interesting; but is it *true*? For this, most children must turn to their peers.

Mediators may create, in what they say or what they do, some possibilities. But the social significance and the social reality—whether of Vietnam or Santa Claus—has to be created by those for whom given social realities have reliable social utility. Thus the distinction between "reality" and myth is a blurred one. The beliefs and opinions of various publics about Vietnam, like the beliefs and opinions of various publics about the sex lives of movie stars, emerge not directly out of what our mediators of those worlds say and do, but out of the ways in which we talk to other people about those worlds. The assumption made—whether by reporters or researchers or parents or preachers—that what we say as mediators of an inaccessible world determines the image that people will have of it, or the opinions they will develop about it, is a grossly naive one. The opinions and images that various publics hold of mediated worlds are products not of what mediators say, but of the ways in which their constituents come to talk about what those mediators say.

It will occasionally be useful to distinguish two kinds of mediators. There are *instrumental* mediators—those who perform their function more or less anonymously. There are also *consummatory* mediators—those who mediate other worlds for us by embodying those other worlds. The local weather forecaster reports the weather news; Jane Fonda *is* news. An instrumental mediator is one *through* whom we are enabled to see or vicariously experience other worlds which are at least at that moment inaccessible to us. A consummatory mediator is one *in* whom we see and vicariously experience those other worlds. The consummatory mediator is a celebrity; the instrumental mediator is a functionary. The two are not mutually exclusive; many mediators, for example parents, function as a little of both. But, in the extreme, the distinction is useful. For example, the industries which arise around the revelation of the lives of celebrities may be economically far more important than what the celebrity actually does. For example, the President of the United States has a fixed salary. But the time and money invested in reporting on and reading and hearing and talking about the President undoubtedly runs to many times what the President makes.

Consummatory mediators are *institutionalized*—taken together with their constituencies and the beliefs and images that their constituencies have of them, the whole is as much a social institution as any other. Bob Hope is an American institution; can you imagine how difficult it would be for most people to take him seriously at the opening of his regular "specials"? Or how difficult it would be for us to accept Doris Day as a serious character actress? Or to accept the Pope as a practical joker? Or one's own parents as being lascivious?

The Basic Dynamic

The basic dynamic in the phenomena of mass communication, the pivotal mechanism out of which all else evolves, is not the technology, awesome as that has become. Nor is it the "message," or the implicit culture imparted in the "content" of the media. Nor is it the "effects" which the media are purported to have. The basic mechanism inheres in the *social and personal uses* to which people put the media and their fare.[3] It is this basic dynamic which any relevant theory of mass communication will have to be based upon.

The historically and theoretically significant phenomenon, and the measurable and explicable one, is not that of the "effects" of the media on people, but that of the effects *on* the media of the *uses* to which people put the media and their fare.[4] Books, as such, have had no measurable effect upon people, for example; but the uses to which books have been put by people have altered the structure of that industry over the years, and have had identifiable social and human consequences. So it has been with radio, and with movies and museums and the greeting card and recording industries. The change and evolution of mass communication systems in the context of particular societies, and the change and evolution of particular human societies networked by certain kinds of mass communication systems having certain kinds of characteristics: these are matters of central theoretical importance. And they can be validly approached only from this point of departure: that the basic dynamic is the uses to which people put the media and their fare. All the rest is incidental to this.

The producers and distributors of mass communication messages can and do use the media for the transportation and display of those messages. But in the same way that "I love you" has no relevance for the people involved apart from the ways in which it is taken into account by people. And our ways of taking mass communication messages into account hinge generally upon the personal and social uses to which they can be put.

Uses of the Mass Media and Their Fare

The uses to which people put the mass media and their fare, in approximately descending order of importance or magnitude, are these:

1. The primary use to which people put the media and their fare is that of providing something to talk about in ritual, non-vital encounters with other people. The more complex and the more mobile a society, the more frequent are such encounters, and hence the more functional the media and their fare. Betrand de Jouvenel wrote:

> The more society is mixed, the more a man needs to know what to expect of the unlike-seeming stranger. He needs security for and against the behavior of another.[5]

Using media fare as something to talk about provides just this kind of security. People who live in relatively non-complex, non-mobile societies have little occasion to use the media and their fare in this way, except perhaps for the purpose of talking to an occasional tourist or anthropologist from this culture! Thus having a radio or a television has a quite different meaning for such people than it does for us. A businessman drawn into a casual conversation with a tourist in a Hong Kong bar will need to know the current ball standings, the current "front page news," the names of the characters in the currently "in" TV programs (e.g., Archie Bunker), or something of that sort which would serve as a basis for the conversation. Wherever you go today, whether to your own village or shopping center, or to any of the world's cities, it will be possible to talk with almost anyone about current news events or media celebrities, in the same way that we use talk about the weather to ease through such ritual encounters. And the fact that people can talk to each other without threat using media fare as a basis has some very real consequences for what media producers can and cannot do, as we shall see below. So this primary use that people make of media fare—that it gives them something to talk about—is not trivial; it is, in fact, of major theoretical import.

2. The second use to which people put the mass media and their fare, in order of importance or magnitude, is as the central component of personal identity or reality *rituals*. There are two aspects of this use that deserve attention. First, more than is often recognized, the routinization of our lives around certain regular, predictable happenings on a day-to-day basis is crucial to the maintenance of a sense of personal identity. The marking of time by certain rituals is common to people in every culture. Those who have the media available for such rituals can use them in this way: I know it's Saturday (or whenever) because "All in the Family" is on tonight. "You know I don't like to talk in the morning until after I've had a chance to look at the paper." There is "travelling music" and special traffic news during commuters' hours, silence in church, the indestructibility of Little Orphan Annie, the unchanging pulchritude of Daisy Mae, and the "profundity" of Peanuts. There is the "six o'clock news" which reliably comes on at six o'clock and structures that end of the day. There is knowing what to expect in the latest issue of your favorite magazine, with only the details to be filled in. And there is listening to (but not hearing) the "top forty" pop records over and over again for several days in a row. And so on. We need to know that we're in a structural and predictable world, and that the world is as we remembered or expected. The media and their fare can go far toward providing such props for our personal identity rituals.

There is another aspect to the ritual uses of the media and their fare. To the extent that we have our sense of being "in" the world through being like "others" and doing as "others" do, we will feel constrained to attend to the media and their fare according to our beliefs about how "others" are attending to the media and their fare. To the extent that we believe "everyone else" takes a daily newspaper, and to the extent that being like "everyone else" is vital to our own sense of being "in" the world, we will go through the ritual of "taking" a daily newspaper. If large numbers of people believed that "everyone else" attended a museum once a week, more people than now do so would go through the ritual of attending a museum. Suffering the nth repetition of a "top ten" tune being played that day, young people are no longer hearing it; they are performing a ritual—one which keeps each one tacitly in touch with all the "others."

Thus there comes to be a structuring of the media and their fare more or less consistent with the structure of the lives of those who use them in similar ritualistic ways. We speak of "curling up" with a good book. And most people comprehend the image of watching the late night television shows over one's bare feet. There are sermons on Sunday, but rarely any lectures. People go to see movies that other people are going to see, with likely little or no thought as to real personal preferences. Expressions like "Would you believe?" become public rituals.

In a complex society, these rituals are more and more frequently identification rituals for those who belong to the same "epistemic communities" or the same "interest groups" or the same "communication networks." But there are still some which are more national in scope. What adults in the U.S. do not feel a stirring of emotion when witnessing a colorful street parade? In 1973, what American could afford not to know *something* about the Watergate "scandal," even though he may have had no vital interest in it one way or the other?

All such rituals in which we engage the media and their fare provide us a sense of reality, and of being "in" the world with others, which is the only way we *can* be "in" the world. What is real to people, and what is indispensable to their sense of being "in" the world is of fundamental theoretical importance. The fact that what is real to people and what is indispensable to their sense of being "in" the world more and more involves ritual uses of the media and their fare makes it no less important.

3. The third use to which people put the media and their fare is the *mythical*. There are three levels at which this use of the media and their fare can be observed.

First, because no "recipes" for living are given in man's genes—as they are totally or largely given for all of the other creatures of the earth—these "recipes" have to be created and perpetuated in some way. No one of us can for long go without a feeling that our way of living is reasonable, just, proper, and "right." Whether in matters of morality, esthetic sensitivity, value, ideology, or of just everyday comportment, we need to be able to find in our social and/or physical surroundings some regular confirmation for our own "recipes" for living. All cultural and subcultural "recipes" for living are like myths: they are created and sustained by tacit covenant[6] and behavior. They are not absolute. Nor is there any ultimate test of their "rightness" beyond self-affirmation. To the extent that such cultural or subcultural "recipes" for living are functional and operative, they must be pervasive in that culture or subculture. Those "recipes," or aspects of them, must pervade what the members of that culture or subculture do and do not do, the manner in which they do and do not behave, the way they invent and deploy their artifacts and technologies, the stories they tell and the generic beliefs they hold, and so on. Thus, to the extent there are operative cultural "recipes" for living, they will be, covertly or overtly, intentionally or inadvertently, built into the fare of the mass media.[7] And we will sense them there; we will find there confirmation of the "recipes" for living by which we are guided, and we will find there alternative recipes for living, some of which may be feasible, as well as others we can only fantasize about. We may be surprised to learn that the Russian people are not that much different from us. But most of us can only fantasize about the "recipes" by which native islanders of the South Seas or the "beautiful people" of the "jet set" live.

Second, there are many aspects of our human existences which can be explained *only* by metaphor or myth. Humans are by nature the only creatures on earth who must explain the inexplicable. How are we to explain just what we are, where we came from, where we are going? How are we to comprehend death? Or life? Or love? These are questions whose ultimate and absolute answers must seemingly be always just out of reach. What we don't or can't know, we make up; myths undergird the existences or people of every culture.[8] Watts defined myth as follows: "Myth is to be defined as a complex of stories—some no doubt fact, and some fantasy—which, for various reasons, human beings regard as demonstrations of the inner meaning of the universe and of human life."[9] Again, to the extent these myths are cultural, they will necessarily be pervasive, and largely covert or tacit. Those who create and produce the fare of the mass media will not be able to avoid imbuing what they do with cultural myth. And those who consume the media and their fare will not be able to avoid finding in that fare some confirmation—or disconfirmation—of the "recipes" upon which their ways of seeing and knowing and being are based.

Third, neither of these mythical uses of the mass media and their fare is limited to "content." To the contrary, it seems altogether likely that the "deeper" and hence the more influential myths are sensed not in the "content" of the myriad of "messages" and "stories" to which the average person in the U.S. subjects himself every day, but in their individual structure and their aggregate patterning.[10] For example, it has been suggested that advertising (always good news) represents heaven, juxtaposed with "the news" (almost always bad news) which represents hell. The "story" which embodies the cultural myth of the western hero is not to be found so much in the plot or even in the theme, but in the structure of the action. And there is presently some research into the structure of the total pattern of television programming as being the mythically important aspect of television.[11] Whatever the outcome of these more contemporary approaches to the study of myth, it is clear that the most fundamental cultural myths are codified in the *patterns* of the things we say and do, and that being socialized into one culture rather than another means that we are empowered to "read" the patterns of our own culture and thus nurture those guiding and orienting myths within ourselves. To the extent that these patterns or "structures" get codified in the media or their fare, people will be able to "read" them there, and to use them for the purposes to which all cultural myths are put.

4. People use the fare of the mass media also for the purpose of providing varied experiences. In their book, *The Functions of Varied Experience,* Fiske and Maddi conclude that there are three broad positive functions of variation in experience: (a) it contributes to the normal development and to the normal functioning of organisms; (b) it is sought out for its own sake; and (c) it is one factor contributing to the affective state of human beings.[12] Some of this seeking out or "tuning in" may derive from pure curiosity—from a sheer curiosity to know what's "there" or what's "going on." Such curiosity may or may not be socially-inspired, may or may not be expected to produce socially-useful experiences or knowledge. But, just as the laboratory rat which explores a maze out of curiosity, then learns how to "run it" in order to reach food at the other end, the varied experience that one has in exploring the fare of the mass media out of curiosity becomes a part of that person and therefore has potential utility for personal ritual or as social currency.

Perhaps the major impetus behind this particular use of the fare of the mass media, however, is that of *compensation.* Although we all work out individual patterns, our psychological and social equilibrium depends upon compensating for too much, *or too little,* uncertainty, chance, risk, variety, etc.[13] There are many activities which we can turn to for such compensation: drinking, wilderness vacations, hobbies, eating, travelling, etc. To achieve that pattern of stimulation which, intuitively at least, seems "right" to use individually, we turn to what is available. The more available the fare of the mass media, the more possibilities there are for more people to use the media and their fare to compensate for too much, or too little, uncertainty, chance, riskiness, variety, etc., in the balance of their lives. This use of the media and their fare is related to people's individual life patterns, and not to any particular set of demographic factors, such as age or income level. A highly paid executive might be as bored with his everyday life as a housewife might be with hers. Yet their compensatory uses of media fare, or of any other compensatory activities, are not a function of "boredom" as such, but of the total life patterns of the two particular individuals. The fact that it is presumed to be "manly" in the U.S. to be interested in certain sports should not, therefore, be viewed as "mass" compensation or as a sufficient explanation of why more men than women watch professional football on television; different viewers may be putting this "same" fare to different uses. Or, to take another, perhaps too obvious example, the subscribers and readers of *Playboy* magazine do not constitute a homogeneous audience, except perhaps in a very naive microeconomic sense. Different subscribers and readers put *Playboy* to different uses. Some may use it as a status prop; others for purpose of phantasy; still others as a basis for confirming "nonconventional" values; and so on. It makes considerable theoretical difference whether we differentiate audiences by use rather than, for example, age or geographic location or social position, as is customarily done.

All audiences and all consumer aggregates of media fare are thus self-selecting. If a medium or one of its products were to be said to have an "effect" on people, it would have to have that "effect" on a *random* sampling of people. If the "effect" is discernible only in the case of a self-selected audience or consumer aggregates, the direction of the "effect" is the other way around. It is the *uses* to which people put the media and their fare that differentiates audiences and consumer aggregates, not demographic "variables" and not the "content" of that fare or the static "personality characteristics" of the people involved.

5. People make other uses of the media and their fare, certainly. A television set may be used as a status symbol; a head-set radio to isolate oneself from the rest of the world aurally; a library as a place to sleep or meet; a particular stereo amplifier or a trip to a particular art gallery for prestige; a highway as a challenge; a book to press leaves or a newspaper to wrap garbage; a particular magazine dropped on a suburban coffee table for snob appeal; a greeting card to hide indifference or inarticulateness; and so on and on. The "hardware" can be put to many diverse uses, in the same way that the "software" can be put to many diverse uses by people in the context of their personal and social existences.

People do use the media as a source of information for purchases they are going to make, have just made, or might make. There is the housewife whose primary use of the newspaper is that of clipping supermarket or other sale ads. There is the fellow who carefully reads advertisements for a certain Chevrolet automobile or a certain tour because he has just bought one. And there are those who use certain media as a source of information about next fall's or next spring's fashions—whether in clothing, party-giving, travel, reading, or office decor.

People use the media as a source of information about work- or hobby- or leisure-time-related interests. There is the executive who scans particular newspapers for news and ideas pertinent to his company. There are those who have a low attention threshold for ideas about golfing or wood-working or skydiving or mink-breeding or baby-raising or car repair, whatever the medium. And there are those who gain access to diffused subcultures like recreational vehicle owners by paying attention to media fare on that subject.

Some people may use media fare for educational purposes. This is not related to enterprises like "educational television," which serves mainly the purposes of those who make their living in it, or in related industries (e.g., "educational technology," which is a euphemism for all kinds of products and services that are sold primarily to schools and to "educators" and not to students). Rather, this refers to the *systematic* use of the media as a means of carrying out one's own educational plans and goals. Someone who could not afford books, for example, might set out to become an Elizabethan scholar by using the public libraries. Or, one might invest his time in media fare on the basis of his intent to become an expert on public affairs. It has been said that only about 15 percent of the people in the U.S. *can* learn from books. Whether it is the same 15 percent who *could* learn from television or from museums, or some other 15 percent of the people, remains to be determined. In any case, this use of the media is relatively minor.

And people do, of course, sometimes use media fare for purposes of pure entertainment. But in the overall view, this is also a relatively minor use of media fare, contrary to much popular belief. For a media experience to be used as sheer entertainment, it would have to remain personal. The experience would have to be the end in itself. When one talks to others about media fare, he is using it not only as "entertainment," but for social purposes or ends as well; and the latter may be the more important. We may "enjoy" a movie; but most people sooner or later talk to others about the movie's relevance, its "truth," its artistry, its "meaning," or its quality relative to other movies made by the same director or producer. Americans give considerable lip service to the value of communication "work" over communication "play." Regardless, almost, of how we may individually use television fare, we find it easy to agree that there should be "better" television programs. When you ask people how "good" television is in their part of the country or their part of the world, they will most likely describe to you the public affairs programs, the documentaries, the different ethnic programs, and the like. But if you ask them what they in fact "watch," you hear a different description. Given the alternative, a majority of Britons seem to prefer cops-and-robbers shows to ballet, domestic comedy to news analysis. Even so, there is no basis for assuming that "Gunsmoke" is entertainment and that a documentary is not. People can use either one in many ways. And it is these uses which define mass communication systems, mass communication audiences, and future alternatives, not arbitrary form or "content" classifications.

The several uses of the media and their fare described here do not exhaust the possibilities, of course. Nor are such uses mutually exclusive. One may put media fare to several uses simultaneously. And consumer uses of media fare are not always obvious or specific. We may not even be aware of the uses to which we put the media and their fare. And certainly the importance of one use relative to another may change over time. Nevertheless, for all such reservations and qualifications, the key to any empirically-sound theories or generalizations about mass communication lies not in the "effects" which the media have on people, but in the uses to which people put the media and media fare.

Institutionalization of Media and Media Fare

The uses to which people put the media and media fare have consequences for the future possibilities of those media and their fare. This is a condition of social life, it is a condition of social order. From a casual friendship to the largest, most complex human society, there must be order, structure. And this order or structure comes from the reliable expectations people have about how other people are going to behave. It comes from being able to depend upon what one expects, whether of other people, of oneself, or of things. Out of necessity for their own continuity, people base their lives on the dependability of their conceptions of the world. How we conceive of tables and cabbages may be as important socially as how we conceive of ideas and kings. The only difference is that, as far as we know, it doesn't make any difference to the table how we conceive of it. But it does make a difference to other people how we conceive of them. If other people don't behave according to our expectations, we have no way of relating to them. And this is as true for every other person as it is for us.

For example, someone in a community who has come to be known as the "town gossip" over a period of time will be expected by people who "know" this to continue providing "the gossip." If for some reason the "gossip's" resources dry up, or if he or she wishes to change from that expected role in the community, it will be at the considerable peril of losing the security of a known role and a reliable set of expectations; and this would threaten the psychological continuity of those people who had these expectations as much as it would the psychological continuity of the one "known" as the "gossip." Our expectations of others over time serve to *institutionalize* our relationships with them. It happens with husbands and wives. They come to expect certain behaviors of one another, and these expectations function as real constraints on the other. Husbands and wives *institutionalize* their relationships with each other. Or, consider the case of Joe Namath: it is conceivable that he could revert to a withdrawing, family-man type of role if he wanted to; but who could accept that image immediately beyond those who didn't already "know" who he is? We who "know" him have *institutionalized* him. We get impatient quickly with an automobile we have come to expect to start easily; we have more patience with one which we are less familiar with, in the same way that we have less patience with the unexpected behavior of others we "know" well than we would have with the unexpected behavior of strangers. We want the world to fit our expectations of it, and most of us are ready most of the time to exert whatever influence we can to *make* the world fit our expectations of it, for good or ill, right or wrong.

It is so for all humans in all human societies, and it is so in our relationships with the media and their fare. The crux of the matter is this: The conventional uses to which the media and media fare are put by people *over time* constitute an *institutionalization* of those media and of that fare. That is, when the uses to which people put particular media and particular fare become an integral part of their everyday lives, or an integral part of the basis on which people relate to each other over time, then those media and that fare have become institutionalized. When we can take our expectations for granted, we are relying upon a social institution. Joe Namath is a social institution, in much the same way that "the news" is a social institution; what we get is what we expect, and what we expect is what we get.

Consider ball game scores or stock market reports. If it becomes conventional for people to use this information as a basis for starting or sustaining a conversation (in a bar, a subway or train, or barber shop, etc.), then such "knowledge" has social utility. And this social utility can be exploited by an enterprising mediator. A Picasso exhibit may draw some who are just curious; but what makes such an exhibit economically feasible or practical are those for whom "knowing about" and talking about Picasso and his paintings has social utility—i.e., those who can be expected to *use* the occasion as a basis for talking to each other, or in some other way having social currency. The daily or hourly repetition of the top ten popular tunes provides listeners with something they can use: it confirms their expectations and hence serves as a kind of identity ritual. Then there is "the news." For the most part, "the news" has to be what people expect; it has to provide assurance that what they are talking about is what they should be talking about, because it is what "people" are talking about. Anything truly novel or "new" and unexpected has unknown social currency; perhaps none. Thus broadcasting or printing much that is really "new" or unexpected or unassessable in terms of its social currency would be an extremely high-risk venture, both for the broadcaster or editor, and for the consumer. Neither the economics nor the politics of the mass media can stand very much real "news." You can bet that the ABC, CBS, and NBC evening "news" will cover the same "news" in essentially the same order. This is due to no conscious conspiracy. The more people who get the same "news," even on different channels, the more assurance we can have as individuals that we really got "the news"—and that what we now "know" about what is going on is what we *need* to "know."

Examples are legion. The central theoretical issue, however, is this: The conventional ways in which people over time come to use places and people and ideas and things—including media and media fare—constitute a mutual constraint on both producer and consumer, both source and audience.[14] The producer is constrained to deploy the media and to produce that fare which people have a use for, when and where and how they have come to use the media and their fare. And users are reciprocally constrained by the ways in which particular personal and social "usefulnesses" are built into and out of the particular media and media fare available. This reciprocally-constraining system is never perfect, of course. The producer may misinterpret user interest or expectation. Or, the producer may be moved, for whatever reason, to produce something which he thinks people *ought* to have available. The producers of media fare do not live by bread alone, any more than do the consumers. Sometimes they simply experiment. These and other "imperfections" on the producer's side keep the system from being perfect. So, too, do users upset the inertia in the system. People are sometimes "obstinate."[15] They don't always react to media fare in the way even seasoned producers of that fare expect them to react. People may not always pay attention to what would be in their own best interest. Sometimes people will listen to what they "ought" to know about; and sometimes they won't. And, as consumers of the media and their fare, people are sometimes apparently just "fickle." Just when they seem to have taken a program or a feature or a new celebrity or some "current event" to their hearts, the affair may be over as quickly and as inexplicably as it started, and they begin to warm up to some new celebrity or some new cause[16] or Social Issue or some new feature. Even "Peanuts" no longer has the same appeal to the same people it once had, and "Star Trek" and the original "Laugh In" are now history. The "ecological crisis" has apparently given way to the "energy crisis" and this to the "Watergate crisis." Just as there are fashions in the way bathrooms are used, there are fashions in the usefulness of media fare. There are those people who don't know what they want in the fare of the media, simply because they are uncertain about the social currency it might have for them. Sometimes users don't go at all for the obvious. On other occasions they go overboard for the inobvious in what they buy or use. Who would have predicted the "hoola hoop" craze? Thus there are a great many imperfections in this reciprocally-constraining system, and this contributes to its continuous evolution and change. The mutual constraints which tend to "close" the system and to bring it into the perpetual equilibrium of perfect redundancy also provide for the dialectics of change. People want the security of the familiar and the routine and the predictable. But they also want the stimulation of the unfamiliar, the nonroutine, and the unpredictable. We want sameness; but we want some variety and change too—in our media fare as in other aspects of our lives.

The reaction of people to something truly novel cannot, of course, be predicted. And what is at work in the emergence or the decline of a current public fashion—whether in topical interests or clothes or media fare—is a set of variables so complex, so self-determining, that the particulars cannot be predicted. In the same way that the most accurate prediction we can make of tomorrow's weather is that it will be the same as today's, the most reliable prediction anyone can make about public tastes in media fare tomorrow is that they will be the same as today. This is why there is so much imitation and redundancy in programming, advertising, book publishing, songwriting, and so on. It is not that the producers conspire to present more of the same or similar media fare. It is that nothing succeeds like success. Except within very minor variations on already institutionalized themes, programs, formats, etc., the producers of media fare cannot predict what will appeal to consumers, and sometimes not even then. So when something seems to be "going," people get on the bandwagon, producer and consumer alike. An art exhibitor has some basis for calculating the appeal of a Renoir exhibit. He has no basis for predicting the public appeal of a totally unknown painter (unless, of course, there is already an audience institutionalized around the value of going only to exhibits of unknown painters, which happens). This is not "crassness" on the part of the exhibitor. He is constrained as much by the system as are those to whom he exhibits. People go to a Renoir exhibit because other people go. They don't go to the exhibits of painters to which no one else goes. This is as true in those nations where the media and the arts are mainly tax-supported as it is in the U.S., where they are not. The exhibitor might be a philanthropist, however; he might undertake to exhibit the work of unknown painters simply because he believed it would be "good" for people to look at something different for a change. But if no one came, then no one else would come; and our altruistic exhibitor would thereby be jeopardizing the future possibilities of the very work he wanted to make known.

These are not trivial matters. All of this is in the nature of the conditions of everyday social life. These conditions are not different elsewhere simply because of a different political or economic suasion. The constraints of social institutionalization are real, and they are significant. *Any* sensed threat to an institutional relationship—any threat to the conventional uses (or non-uses) to which people put other people and the artifacts of their environment—is a threat not just to that relationship. It is a threat to the very existences of the people involved, sometimes minor, sometimes major. Every human existence hinges upon the conventional, institutionalized relationships that obtain between and among individuals in their environments over time. Without these, we could not have human existence as we know it. So when we speak of the institutionalization of, for example, a television star, we are not talking about whimsy. We are talking about the fundamental stuff of social life. And that is not trivial. In the same way that social order depends upon the reliable continuity of most of the people of that society, the reliable continuity of every individual depends upon social order. And the ways in which we institutionalize media fare as a part of that predictable social order is just as important to our existences as the conventional uses to which we put other people and the other artifacts of our environment.

What could be more traumatizing than to discover one day that everything one "knew" about what-is-going-on had no social currency at all, that what one "knew" seemed totally irrelevant to what everyone else was talking about, and that what everyone else was talking about seemed strange and without any personal relevance? The fact that this does not occur gives ample evidence of the underlying social processes at work. What has personal or social utility for us establishes real constraints on what it is feasible or possible for the producers of media fare to provide us. And what is provided places limits on what can be found in media fare having personal or social utility.

We create these mutually-constraining systems through our conventional uses of the media and media fare over time. The uses to which people put the media and media fare in their everyday personal and social activities serve to institutionalize particular media and particular media fare in particular ways. The time and the place and the manner of institutionalization of media and media fare can no more be predicted than can the time and place and manner of genetic mutation. The specifics of social evolution are as indeterminable as are the specifics of biological evolution. In a totally controlled society, which could exist only hypothetically, the "controllers" might well concern themselves with the achievement of wanted "effects" and with the elimination of unwanted "effects" of the media and media fare. But in a free or "open" society, these are matters which emerge from the social behavior of people in the course of their everyday lives. They are not matters to be decided for them and imposed upon them.

Thus it is that in a free or "open" society the theoretical point of entry is that of the institutionalization of the uses to which people put the media and media fare.

● ● ●

The Proliferation of Publics

The greater the variety of alternative media or media fare, the more audiences there will emerge. And, the more audiences or publics there are, the more alternative possibilities there are for the media and for media fare. But this differentiation is essentially from within. It is not unlike the literacy problem. Producing and distributing more different kinds of books will not necessarily increase the literacy of a society-at-large. But it will go hand in hand with a further differentiation of the existing book-reading public into several specialized audiences, with some attributing more "significance" or value or usefulness to biographies, others to fiction, others to documentaries, and so on. Or, to take another example: the more conflicting political points of view made available to a public, the more fragmented that public will likely become. Not all of the alternatives offered will "catch on," but those that do will be given the legitimacy of an audience, and that audience the security of having its differentiated beliefs confirmed and legitimized. What is measurable is that where the media and their fare are more heterogeneous, publics proliferate—and conversely. This raises some intriguing questions about the relationship between the rate of proliferation of publics and social order.

Media Alternatives and Social Order

The more real alternatives there are for people in a given society, the more internally differentiated that society will be. And the more differentiated publics there are in a society, the more possibilities there are for additional variety in ideas, things, tastes, fashions, etc. Where there may have been but one guiding ideology or world-view in earlier societies, one could be either for it or against it. Because he was not *for* the dominant world-view of his time, Galileo was presumed to be *against* it. Where there are alternative world-views espoused by different publics within the same society, one has some choice of which publics to subscribe to. When there was but one type of sword, one either liked it or did not. When a different kind of sword was introduced, there could be factions; there were undoubtedly fights and skirmishes between those who were convinced that the one was better than the other. When there was but one kind of music, or when there was but one music celebrity at a time, it was difficult to get into an argument about which was best; today one can overhear such arguments everywhere. In the early days of television, there was little talk about how "bad" it was; people even sat around watching the test pattern. We may suffer now in the U.S. the consequences of too many alternatives. There could not be differences of opinion if there were not real alternatives for people.

Perhaps what distresses some of the more "intellectual" critics of our present situation is the range of the alternatives, the scope of the choices becoming available to more and more people. Of course television could be "better." It could be "better" in France, too, and in Japan and England. But the question is, better *for whom?* We "intellectuals" *know* that a revered ballet is "better" television fare than a quiz show. We "intellectuals" *know* that a higher ratio of social documentaries to "escape" fare on television would raise social consciousness and improve the lot of people in the process. But we have no evidence of this. Is our dogma less irrational than any one else's? Contrary to current folklore—and this is generally how we deal with the popular media these days, from the current folklore about it—there is some evidence that there is more public affairs broadcasting on television in the U.S. than in England.[17] The B.B.C. may not be the end-all for everyone.

People seek the security of the familiar; but people also seek the stimulation of the novel. The normal individual needs the comfort of the expected; but he also needs the perturbation of the unexpected. We all need certainty. Couple this with the institutionalization of the things we use and the people we see and the talk we engage in every day, and we have that certainty. But we also need variety. Couple this with the technological inventiveness and the affluence of a society such as that of the U.S., and we have that variety, whether in can openers, home music amplifiers, automobiles, spectacles, or television fare.

The more real alternatives there are for people in mass media fare, the more the society becomes differentiated. Yet the more differentiated the society becomes, the more utility there is in the fare of the mass media as a basis for social integration on another level. Another paradox. It is not unlike the process of socialization itself, through that process, we mold new members into cogs that fit the existing social machinery. But through that same process we also necessarily foster and nurture their individuality.

The apparent need that people have to differentiate themselves into smaller communities having interests, values, tastes, beliefs, etc., different from other such communities has led in the past to a specialization of the media. *Life,* in attempting to be *something* to *everyone,* failed, as had many other such magazines in the years since World War II. While most of the general "mass" circulation magazines have declined and disappeared, a great many new specialized periodicals have emerged. As such specialization increases, there is a parallel increase in the need for something which would contribute to communication *between* the increasingly specialized or differentiated audiences. Certain media fare—such as "the news," as already suggested—can be used in this way.

In his recent book, *World Communication: Threat or Promise?,* Colin Cherry raises the issue in this way: threat *or* promise?[18] In free societies, if unimpeded by well-intentioned but misguided policy-making, the continuing increase in alternative media and media fare is *both,* both threat *and* promise. It has been both since the first troubadour wandered into a remote village.

And this raises some intriguing questions about the ultimate compatibility of *mass* media and democracy. In his essay *On Liberty,* John Stuart Mill wrote that "The individual must be protected . . . against the tyranny of the prevailing opinion and feelings. . . ." To the extent there are many specialized worlds, not one general one, the individual would thus be protected. But if government policy requires that all television programming, for example, as well as all stations, be "balanced," how are we to maintain our separate worlds?[19]

An approach such as this raises a great many such questions. They cannot all be answered here, if at all. The challenge is that we must learn to think both more substantively and creatively about these issues. Hopefully the approach outlined here makes some small contribution to the possibilities for doing so.

Notes

1. On Languages as media, see Marshall McLuhan, "Myth and Mass Media," in H. A. Murray (ed.), *Myth and Mythmaking* (Boston: Beacon Press, 1968). On the "languages" of the media, see E. Carpenter, "The New Languages," in E. Carpenter and M. McLuhan (eds.), *Explorations in Communication* (Boston: Beacon Press, 1960).
2. See Paul Bouissac, "Poetics in the Lion's Den: The Circus Act as a Text," *Modern Language Notes,* 86:6 (December) 1971.
3. This was the gist of Katz's paper on mass communication research in 1959, and others have argued in this direction, with apparently little or no "effect". In response to the question of what makes a book sell, Charles Darwin replied to Samuel Butler, "Getting talked about is what makes a book sell."

4. This is of course true of all human inventions and artifacts. The wheel as such had no social effects; it was and is the uses to which wheels are put that have had social and human consequences.

5. In *The Art of Conjecture* (New York: Basic Books, 1967).

6. On the relevance of the concept of covenant for this kind of inquiry, see J. F. A. Taylor, *The Masks of Society: An Inquiry into the Covenants of Civilization* (New York: Appleton-Century-Crofts, 1966).

7. For a view of the role of one kind of fare—literature—in this regard, see ch. 5, "Literature and Society," of Leo Lowenthal, *Literature, Popular Culture, and Society* (Englewood Cliffs, N.J.: Prentice-Hall, 1961).

8. See, e.g., J. Campbell, *Myths to Live By* (New York: Viking, 1972); J. G. Frazer, *The Golden Bough* (New York: Macmillan, 1922); O. E. Klapp, *Heroes, Villains, and Fools* (Englewood Cliffs, N.J.: Prentice-Hall, 1962). For a contemporary analysis of the "mythic" function of mass entertainment, *c.f.* E. Morin, *The Stars* (New York: Grove Press, 1960).

9. Alan W. Watts, *Myth and Ritual in Christianity* (London: Macmillan, 1954).

10. *Cf.* Claude Lévi-Strauss, "The Structural Study of Myth," in T. A. Sebeok (ed.), *Myth: A Symposium* (Indiana University Press, 1955); and Roland Barthes, *Mythologies*, Trans. Annette Lavers (New York: Hill & Wang, 1972). For a general overview of the "Structuralist" approach, see Richard T. De-George, *Structuralists: From Marx to Lévi-Strauss* (New York: Anchor Books, 1972). *Cf.* Mircea Eliade, *Myth and Reality* (New York: Harper, 1963).

11. E.g., R. C. Schmidt, "The Mythic Structure of Television Programming," Meeting of the International Communication Association, Montreal, April 1973.

12. Donald W. Fiske and Salvatore R. Maddi, *Functions of Varied Experience* (Homewood, Ill.: Dorsey, 1961), p. 13. If it seems paradoxical that people need both sameness and variety in some dialectical mixture, then it may be.

13. One might compare this with the concepts of *communication-pleasure* and *communication-pain* suggested by the psychiatrist T. A. Szasz in *Pain and Pleasure* (New York: Basic Books, 1957), and extrapolated by William Stephenson in *The Play Theory of Mass Communication* (University of Chicago Press, 1967); but I believe there is more than just "pain" and "pleasure" involved.

14. In "The Communicator and the Audience," *Journal of Conflict Resolution,* 2:1 (1958), pp. 67–77, Raymond Bauer proposes, on the basis of experimental evidence, that (a) images of the audience affect the communicator, and (b) users commit sources to a position.

15. *Cf.* R. A. Bauer, "The Obstinate Audience," *loc. cit.*

16. On the phenomenon of Social Issues in general, with the issue of our ecology as the exemplar, see L. Thayer "Man's Ecology, Ecology's Man," *Main Currents in Modern Thought,* 27:3 (January-February 1971), pp. 71–78.

17. E.g., Karen Possner, "A Comparison of a Week of Television Programming in New York and London," University of Iowa, School of Journalism, (unpublished ms., 1972).

18. (London: Wiley-Interscience, 1971).

19. On the necessity of isolating populations to optimize evolutionary health and vigor, see Garrett Hardin, *Nature and Man's Fate* (New York: Rineheart, 1959). A "global village" as a criterion for the species reflects the hubris and the myopia of technologism.

STEVEN H. CHAFFEE

Mass Media and Interpersonal Channels: Competitive, Convergent, or Complementary?

Which would you prefer? A first-hand account of an event from a friend or media coverage of the event? If you needed advice about an overcharge on an automobile repair bill would you ask an acquaintance or call the consumer reporter at the television station? Are Ann Landers and Abigail better sources of information about personal problems than members of your family? Steven Chaffee is concerned with answers to such questions and what they reveal about our reliance on mass and interpersonal channels of information. He finds that there has been created a false competition between mass and interpersonal channels wherein we are led to believe that most people prefer interpersonal to media information. His thorough review of research and his careful analysis reveals that no such polarity exists. Rather, the accessibility of a channel and the likelihood of finding desired information through it are the main determinants for our choice of source of information.

An act of communication is a transaction between persons and can be described from either's point of view. Different questions and different answers are produced from each perspective. Compare:

Who (source)	Who (receiver)
Says what	Hears what
To whom (receiver)	From whom (source)
Via which channel	Via what channels
With what effect?	For what purpose?

The first of these models is the classic formulation of communication research by Harold Lasswell.[1] It envisions the act of communication from the viewpoint of the source of a message, and the questions for study unfold in sequence. The source creates a message, which is sent through some channel to an audience upon which it may exercise some effect. The second model examines the process from the other end. The initial "Who" in this formulation is the audience member, or receiver. The emphasis is on what is received (rather than what was sent), and the ultimate question concerns the purposes the information serves for the person (rather than its influence imposed on him). This is the general approach taken in the

This article was written expressly for the Second Edition of *Inter-Media*. Copyright © 1982 by Steven H. Chaffee.

study of information-seeking, and of needs and gratifications served by the mass media.[2]

Neither model is the "correct" one, and even both models taken together fail to state many important questions we might ask about communication. This paper will focus on an element that is common to both models, the question of communication channels. In the first model, the source confronts a choice among a number of ways of conveying the message. It may be written or printed and delivered on paper, or spoken and sent via electronic means, or stated directly to the intended audience. These are commonly referred to as print, electronic, and interpersonal channels; print and electronic transmission are usually studied as mass media, although they can also be used in one-to-one communication, as in the case of a letter or telephone call. Specific questions about channel selection are often conceived from the source's point of view: "Can we most effectively reach our audience via television, the newspaper, or personal contact?" "To what extent will a media campaign be counteracted by messages from other people close to the audience member?" "What can be done to neutralize the impact of interpersonal communication?" These problems in manipulative uses of communication have built a body of knowledge called "administrative research."[3]

From the second, receiver-oriented perspective, the distinctions among channels, and even between channel and source, are much less salient. We do not ordinarily think of the channels through which we get our information about the world as in competition with one another, nor do we differentiate clearly between a person who generates a message ("source") and one who relays a message that was created elsewhere ("channel"). We would often find it demeaning to consider ourselves objects of "persuasion," or even of "influence"; these are source-oriented concepts. A great deal of research on people's reception of information has, nevertheless, been geared toward assessing the relative efficacy of various channels. The purpose of this paper is to analyze what goes on between people who are parties to communication transactions in a society with many mass media channels and where people upon occasion engage heavily in interpersonal discussion as well.

Basic Assumptions and Terms

Conclusions drawn from any single perspective are likely to be misleading in our attempts to comprehend the outlines of the overall process of social communication. A number of different viewpoints need to be examined, drawing on studies of different kinds of social behavior, if we are to piece together a coherent picture.

An empirical study tells us only *what has been* the case under a specific set of circumstances. We need to compare studies that find different results under different circumstances to get an idea of the range of possibilities. For example, studies on some topics of persuasion have concluded that the possible impact of communication is very limited because a campaign has not brought about much change. This empirical observation is mistaken for an estimate of theoretical potential. Social conditions vary from time to time and place to place, and we should expect that communication—often called the basic social process—should vary accordingly. Research on advertising in the midst of affluence, for example, is no sure guide to its potential in an underdeveloped country or at a time of severe recession. Studies of a presidential campaign may tell us little about getting a local referendum passed. Surveys showing that people rarely discuss foreign events are not likely to apply when a war has just erupted in the Middle East. Only when we find similar results across a wide variety of social conditions should we begin to consider generalizations.

Accessibility and Flow

The sources one consults for information, and thus the seeming "influences" on one's behavior, are determined mainly by (a) their accessibility; and (b) the likelihood that they will contain the information one might be seeking. Accessibility is the more pervasive factor, involving variation in both the source's and the receiver's behaviors: how frequently does a message's source contact the person via a given channel? And how easy is it, physically or psychologically, for the would-be receiver to consult an information source via a given channel? The second question comes up less often, because much of the information flowing through society simply comes to us whether we seek it or not. Indeed, in modern society it takes a fair amount of effort to avoid receiving messages from a number of channels.

Convergence and Complementarity

The relationship between mass media and interpersonal sources is not clearcut. While different channels may be competitive from a sender's viewpoint, they are more likely to be convergent or complementary when viewed from a receiver's perspective. Convergence occurs when different channels provide the same or overlapping messages. This is the usual case, and it serves to increase a person's confidence in such messages. In the rarer case of divergence—when different sources provide contradictory information—one's belief in the message is called into question. This is a question of "credulity" regarding the correctness of one's information, and often results in seeking convergent information on one side or the other from additional sources. Although there have been many studies devoted to the inherent "credibility" of various channels, we shall see that there is little evidence that people make such a judgment about a channel; few of these studies have been conducted under conditions of divergent information from supposedly competing channels. Instead, a hypothetical situation is posed, one that rarely if ever occurs; example: "If you got opposite news reports from newspapers and television, which would you believe?"

Complementary relationships between channels occur when information is carried in one but not another, or when a person who lacks access to one channel gets information from another. Ordinarily the choice of channels is not a matter of great moment to an individual; information is received, or sought, from the most accessible source. Motivation to seek information is aroused mainly in the rare instance when a person contemplates a change in behavior or a personal decision and sees a risk of adverse consequences if the choice is not a wise one.[4] In such a case, one might reasonably seek information from several accessible channels, seeking convergence, with little regard to whether the channel is a mediated or personal one "at the mouth."

Channel Competition: The Conventional Wisdom

It has become conventional in communication theory to assume that interpersonal channels are more persuasive than mass media. This is the wisdom passed on as a policy generalization to professional communicators responsible for conducting campaigns on behalf of candidates, products, causes, and the like. It seems to stem from attempts to interpret receiver-based data from field surveys in terms of the source-oriented effects model. As will become evident, there are conditions under which communication via mass media is more effective—for the purposes of either source or receiver—and other conditions under which interpersonal channels are preferable. Because human communication is a continuous process over a series of different situations, statistics that sum across many events over time can be a poor guide for anticipating what will occur under specific circumstances. Nonetheless, it is important to know what statistical generalizations have been drawn, as a first step in breaking down the conventional wisdom based upon them. The following observations ought to be accounted for by any theory of social communication:

1. In the study of adoption of innovations, mass media tend to predominate in making people aware of the innovation, but by the time an individual decides to adopt it most of his communication about it is interpersonal.[5]

2. A person's social contacts tend to be with others who are similar to him in demographic characteristics, and also in terms of social values, political opinions, economic resources, etc. In homespun words, "Likes talk to likes"; in fancier terminology, conversations are mostly "homophilic," not "heterophilic." [6]

3. A message from a source that is untrustworthy or that lacks expertise on the topic is less likely to be accepted than is information from an expert source or one with no reason not to be truthful. [7] (Channel differences, and divergent messages, are not ordinarily examined in this research; comparisons are made of the degree of belief in a single message propagated through either media channels of varying expertise and trustworthiness or interpersonal sources that differ in these respects.)

The Homophily-Credibility Explanation

An interconnected set of social psychological processes has been inferred to tie the empirical observations to the conclusion that interpersonal channels are more effective than mass media. Perhaps the most central of these presumed relationships is the one between channel-receiver similarity or homophily, and the degree of credibility the receiver attributes to a channel. [8] Interpersonal contacts, the reasoning runs, are homophilic and therefore credible; consequently the messages they deliver should be accepted. Messages from the impersonal mass media are not readily believed, because channel-receiver heterophily (or non-homophily) implies lower credibility. A media message could be learned, but only tentatively accepted until corroborated via a homophilic personal channel. Decision or action, then, would be withheld pending interpersonal discussion.

Although this explanation would be consistent with the empirical findings noted above, and while it describes processes that do occur under certain limited conditions, there is considerable evidence to suggest that it does not account for the general case.

First, credibility is not a stable attribution that a person assigns consistently to a channel. Several studies have shown that credibility is highly situational, in that it can be modified significantly by sending the person a message that is different from the one expected. [9] Nor is credibility a singular dimension of judgment; in one analysis it was found to fragment into forty-one different factors. [10] The most important factors are expertise, which is an attribute of a source rather than a channel per se, and trustworthiness, which a receiver likewise attributes to the source rather than the channel as a rule. (The source-channel distinction is of course often blurred even in mass communication, as in the case of the widely trusted "anchor man" on a network newscast.)

When a message has been sent, as in a persuasion experiment, the source's expertise and trustworthiness may indeed govern its acceptance. But this does not particularly mean that these factors are important in a person's handling of channels of information, or day-to-day acceptance of information from them. It is likely that untrustworthy sources of competing intentions could, if they provided convergent information, be collectively at least as believable as would one, or even two, more trusted sources.[11] For example, if opposing candidates for office agree in their accounts of a recent event, this common interpretation is probably no less credible than if it had been transmitted by the AP and/or UPI without attribution to either source.

When information is sought, source expertise is probably an important criterion, although not so important as is channel accessibility. This distinction between accessibility as an interaction between receiver and channel, and expertise as an attribute of a source is critical with respect to mass media—channels in which inexpert reporters and editors gather and cross-check information from more expert sources. In interpersonal communication, the person might consult either an expert source, such as a "cosmopolite" or a technical specialist, or he might consult a close peer.[12] Almost by definition, a lay person's relationship to an expert will be heterophilic, and to a peer more homophilic. This leads to the interesting prediction that the expertise dimension of source credibility should be *negatively* related to interpersonal channel homophily when people consult experts directly. Put another way, there is more to learn from people who are different than from people who are a lot like oneself. In diffusion research, this paradox is called "the strength of weak ties," referring to the fact that contacts between dissimilar people are rare ("weak") but when they occur they are more likely than other contacts to result in information transfer ("strength").[13]

Several studies demonstrate that homophilic interpersonal networks often carry highly inaccurate information, much of it internally inconsistent.[14] People seem to sense this. For instance, when President John F. Kennedy was shot, the news was so rapidly disseminated that some 90 percent of U.S. citizens had heard about it before he died.[15] One study found that 44 percent of those who first heard about it via television completely believed it; but only 24 percent believed the news when they heard it first from even a good friend.[16] A 1978 Utah survey of dissemination of the revelation that black members of the Mormon church would henceforth be eligible for ordination produced similar findings.[17] This surprising but happy news traveled so rapidly that 94 percent heard about the day it was announced. Of those who first heard interpersonally, 63 percent doubted it enough to seek confirmation; of those who learned of it via television, only

39 percent checked it further before accepting it as accurate. Confirmation was sought predominantly from media, not interpersonally. A study of reactions to the Watergate scandals of early 1973, when the veracity of the charges against the Nixon administration was still very much in doubt, found that other people were believed less often than *any* mass media channel of Watergate news.[18]

Most studies that report positive correlations between channel use and source credibility involve topics on which there is very little interpersonal message flow.[19] Several surveys have reported null or even negative correlations between channel use and credibility; generally interpersonal communication has been more prevalent in these cases.[20]

The simple assumption that homophilic sources are more effective was directly contradicted in an advertising experiment in Hong Kong.[21] Five ads were prepared in two dialects: Cantonese, which was the regional dialect and therefore presumably homophilic, and Mandarin, a northern Chinese dialect traditionally associated with the elite class. Recall of content from the ads was greater among those who had read the Mandarin (heterophilic) versions, and among older subjects, at least, the products themselves were rated more favorably after the Mandarin ads than the Cantonese ads. This result could be easily explained on the basis of, say, status appeal, but it does not jibe at all with a homophily-breeds-credibility explanation of message reception and acceptance.

The Frequency Criterion

Two convergent bodies of research are often cited to support the general conclusion that interpersonal contacts are more persuasive than media channels. In keeping with the actuarial nature of communication research conducted from the sender's viewpoint, both rely on frequency as the criterion for inferring impact. By far the more thoroughly investigated of these two has been the diffusion of innovations, where the statistical conclusion can scarcely be in doubt. The second is the study of influence in election campaigns, where the evidence is much more limited and questionable.

Diffusion research is ordinarily conducted in rural, traditional societal settings, where a "modern" innovation is being presented for possible adoption. In such situations there are usually a few relatively more "modern" people, who more readily learn of and adopt the innovation; these people are also more cosmopolitan, in that they have both personal and media contacts outside the immediate locale.[22] Later adopters (called "laggards" by program sponsors impatient with delays in the adoption process) are more likely to rely on interpersonally transmitted information. Media channels are less accessible to them (for such reasons as illiteracy and poverty), and by the time they have heard much about the innovation there are plenty of other people in the area who know a lot about it so interpersonal sources are highly accessible. We should expect, then, that their channels will be primarly interpersonal by the time they hear about and adopt the innovation.[23]

These findings do not, however, lead inevitably to the conclusion that interpersonal channels are *preferred* by the poor and illiterate, nor that "modern" people are quick to adopt life-style changes on the basis of a media message alone. A variety of studies show that the more educated strata delay longer in making the decision to change their behavior.[24] For instance, a survey of 500 Taiwanese women found that those who were younger and more educated were better informed about family planning, discussed it more with their husbands, were more likely to consult specialists in clinics and hospitals, got more information from television and other media, and were more likely to adopt a family planning method.[25] Similarly, during a disease inoculation program in Honduras, a comparison was made of "instantaneous" vs. "protracted" deciders.[26] The first group consisted of those who had first heard of the inoculation on the day they came to get their shots. The "protracted" decision group, i.e., people who had heard about it before the day they came for shots, were both more literate and more likely to have discussed it with other people.

In general, then, the distinguishing features of more educated people include (1) a disinclination to adopt an innovation precipitately; and (2) a tendency to take control of their communication environment by seeking additional viewpoints via accessible channels to informed sources before making a personal decision. Whether the channels of contact with those sources are direct or mediated apparently makes no difference in terms of either the credence given the information or its influence on the decision made. The statistical tendency for less educated people to adopt innovations later is probably due to their becoming aware much later; they apparently spend less time between the points of awareness and adoption. Both these time-lag differences would be due to their lower levels of relevant communication and information handling.

The fallacy of using frequency of use as a criterion for evaluating either the effectiveness or the attractiveness of a channel can be demonstrated by a few raw data comparisons. In the diffusion of news, for instance, there are large differences from one news item to another in the percentage who learn of it interpersonally. Unexpected, dramatic, and important items are often heard from others who are relaying the news: the death of leaders like Franklin D. Roosevelt[27] and Chiang Kai-Shek,[28] the assassinations of the Kennedys,[29] the shooting of Gov. George Wallace,[30] and (in a Harvard student survey) the resignation of Vice President Spiro T. Agnew.[31] These and other studies consistently find that it is the younger, college-educated person who is most likely to *tell others* of news he has heard.[32] But there is also a lot of news that doesn't seem important enough to pass on. Examples include a major papal encyclical (heard of interpersonally by just 2 percent)[33] and the political assassinations of George Lincoln Rockwell, Medgar Evers, and Malcolm X (each 3 percent).[34] Timing of events also determines where one learns news. In 1967 President Lyndon B. Johnson announced that he would not run for re-election on an evening telecast to which almost all households were tuned in. So even though it aroused a lot of discussion only 5 percent first heard about it interpersonally.[35] Obviously these huge differences in frequency of interpersonal reception are no indicator of people's channel preferences. They are due to such structural and environmental factors as timing and newsworthiness as judged by potential interpersonal disseminators of the news.

Election campaign research has, since the classic 1940 Erie County study, been widely thought to demonstrate the superiority of interpersonal over mass communication as a social influence.[36] Examination of the original data, however, reveals that the media—even in that pretelevision era— were judged more powerful by most voters. A majority cited either radio or newspapers as the most important single source in making their voting decisions, and two-thirds found each of these media helpful.[37] About one-half of those who changed their voting intentions during the campaign cited something learned from either the newspaper or radio as the main reason.[38] On the other hand, less than half mentioned any personal contact as an influential source, and less than one-fourth considered an interpersonal source as the most important one.[39] Apparently the emphasis on interpersonal influence emanating from the Erie County study was due more to the contrast between these figures and the researchers' expectations for far more dramatic evidence of media impact. Figures from the 1948 Elmira study are not appreciably different, and yet the stress on interpersonal influence persisted in the interpretations drawn.[40] Subsequently the same research group undertook a concerted study of personal influence across a wider variety of topics.[41] As the authors reported, 58 percent of the reported opinion changes "were apparently made without involving any remembered personal contact, and were, very often, dependent upon the mass media."[42]

Since those are the studies repeatedly cited as basic evidence on the question of media vs. interpersonal influence, one might be tempted to take them at face value and conclude that mass media communication is more persuasive. But just as frequency of use is not a valid criterion for inferring higher credibility or preference for a channel, neither is recalled influence a valid criterion for concluding that one channel *is capable of* achieving stronger effects than another. Mass media, when they carry information relevant to a decision facing the person, seem to have some advantages. Media reports represent professional reporting, editing, and verification processes, and probably for that reason are on the average more believed. Far more important, the media are more amenable to control—by both the sender and the receiver—for various purposes. Sources can to a great extent determine what information they will release via the media. Receivers expect the media to provide them with certain kinds and amounts of information in a relatively coherent package. But wise users of information rarely rely on mass media alone; they do well to check with experts, compare notes with peers, and otherwise attempt to validate media content for themselves before acting upon it. This is what we find better-educated receivers doing, in all kinds of situations. The question of which channel reaches a person first, or where a person turns for information when he needs it, does not tell us much of importance about the people involved.

Getting and Giving Information

General statements about communication behavior can be addressed more directly in terms of what people do rather than their orientations toward channels. The static concept of "interpersonal channels" slightly masks the fact that people are actively doing several things with the information flowing from mass media. They are both asking and telling one another about it, often with a good deal of personal interpretation and opinion mixed in. Only as an outgrowth of these behaviors of asking and telling (sometimes after being asked) is there an interpersonal dissemination of information; this is the transaction that carries the possibility of personal influence as a communication process. A small research literature has, almost by inadvertence, built up on each of these specific interpersonal behaviors. We know a few things about the kinds of people involved, and their motivations, in each specific role in interpersonal dissemination: finding out, telling, asking, and being asked.

Motivations in Disseminating Information

Recommunication of messages to others appears to be at least as important as is intrapersonal use of information by the individual, as an explanation for mass media consumption. That is, many people seem to gather news and other media content largely for the purpose of passing it on to others. In studies of self-reported "gratifications" of media use, this interpersonal motive tends to be rated low; there may be some social undesirability associated with so commonplace a purpose. But it is a strong correlate of information seeking.[43] Becker found in two studies that interpersonal utility motives predicted attention to and knowledge of political news more strongly than did measures specifically related to knowledge-acquisition motivations.[44] Another survey found requests for partisan campaign materials higher among people who expected to be discussing the election.[45] The phenomenon is not limited to political topics. Adolescents' information-seeking regarding both symphony music and popular music, for example, is strongly related to the existence of others with whom this type of music is discussed.[46]

A number of explanations have been suggested to account for this tendency to use mass media in anticipation of interpersonal communication. It is a time-honored notion in sociology that people seek social approval and stature by appearing to be well informed.[47] One study concluded that it was "obvious how this use of the newspaper serves to increase the reader's prestige among his fellows."[48] Listening to popular music is a way in which adolescents who perform poorly in school can gain compensating peer approval.[49] Another motivation, more difficult to isolate empirically, is simply to have a basis for initiating a desired interaction—"small talk" or "breaking the ice."[50] There are also other-centered, altruistic motivations. It is possible that a person would seek, or at least pass on, information for the benefit of other people who might need it. This was one self-reported reason for interpersonal dissemination within a "distance running community" of the accidental death of a famous runner.[51] People also talk about the news simply for the opportunity to express their opinions about it.[52]

But the motivation that dominates the research literature, and probably the real world as well, is to have information that can be used in the service of interpersonal influence attempts. In election surveys especially, those who report that they try to persuade others to support their candidate are consistently found to be the heaviest consumers of news media.[53] This includes both discussions with friends and family, and writing letters to public officials—another, less personal, attempt at political influence.[54]

A modest study using a quite different method gives us some idea of the extent to which media content is employed in interpersonal influence. Students in a college class were assigned to keep records on conversations they overheard in public places.[55] Not only was information from news media frequently cited in support of overheard arguments, but this was more often the case when the target person expressed a change in opinion (i.e. when persuasion was apparently successful). Politics, which constitutes the bulk of news media content, is the dominant topic in this connection; 76 percent of conversations dealing with political topics included media references, compared with only 40 percent of other conversations.

Argumentative discussion does not necessarily reflect a strong motivation on the part of one person to influence another, of course. News events create new demands on a person for an ordered construction of the world; much of conversation may consist of people comparing their separate constructions of reality, and perhaps modifying them. The important fact is that the media "set the agenda" of much interpersonal communication.

Asking as a Transaction

Neither information nor influence attempts flow in one direction. A number of studies have found that the predominant interpersonal pattern is *exchange,* in that most people who try to persuade others are themselves likely to be targets of similar attempts.[56] And as has already been noted here, those who seek information are also inclined to pass it along to others. Researchers have not ordinarily looked at communication transactions from the viewpoint of each party separately. In an interpersonal transaction, if one person is *asking* for information, the other person is *being asked.*

Little specific attention has been given to the phenomenon of being asked for information, or even for opinion. We know from experimental studies of small, task-oriented groups that *opinions are given* more often than information, whereas *information is sought* more often than opinion.[57] Messages of both types are sent much more often than they are requested. A few studies give us at least a preliminary picture of the relationship between those who request information and those who respond to such requests. Where asking is concerned, we cannot distinguish clearly between information and opinion; more researchers have been interested in opinion flow, and that is the type of request they have typically examined. (From the viewpoint of the asker this is probably not terribly important, since much of information-seeking is evaluative and active seekers are usually comparing viewpoints from different perspectives. To ask for an opinion may well be the predominant and most enriching mode of eliciting information flow interpersonally.)

One survey specifically measured a person's likelihood of being asked for opinion—aside from his being motivated to influence someone else. Those who were asked their opinions ("opinion leaders") were more likely to be active members of organizations, to regularly read news magazines and newspapers, and to discuss public affairs.[58] Targets of personal information requests have the characteristics we should expect of informational channels: they are accessible for discussion and are likely to have information due to their heavy media use.

The profile of askees is more complicated then that, though. One analysis separated people who tried to influence someone else ("talkers") from those who made no such effort but who were nevertheless asked their opinions ("passive leaders").[59] The talkers were more informed than were the passive leaders, although both groups were much better informed than other people. In another study, giving advice about shopping was not significantly correlated with either attempted influence or media exposure.[60] (Influence attempts and media use were, as in other studies above, strongly intercorrelated.) A survey in Chile found no appreciable demographic difference between people who were asked their opinions on current problems and others; the nondistinguishing variables included income, class, education, occupation, and age.[61] The unique characteristic of the askees was that, when asked by the interviewer for an opinion (about local newspapers), they were four times as likely to express one as were other respondents.

It is the asker-askee relationship that, when separated from influence attempts, seems to be the homophilic one. Those of whom opinions are requested, and who otherwise do not volunteer their views or exercise persuasive designs on their listeners, are indeed demographically similar to their interaction partners. They are a bit more attentive to the media, a bit more informed, and do answer questions when the occasion arises. But these homophilic relationships are more involved in the flow of information than in any active influence process, and it is not clear that these are especially informative transactions. (Whether askers purposely seek homophilic informants, or simply seek informants locally and therefore find homophilic ones, cannot be determined from the data available.)

Seekers of information (and opinion), on the other hand, appear to be quite different from other people. An extensive review of studies of exposure to information[62] found that people tend to seek out viewpoints they have not yet heard—whether they agree with the opinions expressed or not—when those viewpoints would be useful to know about. Other strong predictors of voluntary exposure to information are education (and correlated social class), and a previous history of exposure to the same topic.[63] Taking these characteristics as a group produces a sensible generalization: potentially useful information is most likely to be sought by a person who knows enough (about the subject) to recognize deficiencies in his knowledge.

Subsequent research has borne this out in various ways. A survey of people who sought published information (about civil defense) found that these seekers had already been more informed about the subject than were other people.[64] Predictably too, they were more likely to ask others about it, and to be themselves asked for such information. A field experiment in which some people were mailed a brochure (on lawn care) had the effect of stimulating them to seek further information from expert sources.[65] A survey dealing with family planning found a positive correlation between socioeconomic status and interpersonal acquisition of *rare* information about birth control, but a negative association between SES and consultation of interpersonal sources regarding methods that were widely diffused.[66] People with a greater range of social skills are probably more able to exploit the resources in their local information environments. Mass communication about a subject seems to stimulate people's interest, which in turn leads to further communication of various kinds.

Opinion-seeking is a bit different from information-seeking, and the people who specifically seek (without giving) opinions appear to be more dependent than those who actively search for information and offer their own opinions. For example, people who say they are more likely than others to ask for voting advice during an election campaign tend to be young, and low in political interest, knowledge, and party identification.[67] They rely more on TV for news than do those who give or share opinions with others. Opinion-seeking, it should be remembered, is not a very common behavior, although when it occurs the opinion expressed may prove quite influential.

Overview

The underlying theme of this essay has been its focus on variabilities in the flow of communication due to both structural factors and micro-social relationships. The point of view has necessarily shifted back and forth between those of the separate parties to various types of communication transactions. People who assume the role of either a source (e.g., a communication campaign) or a channel communicator (e.g., a reporter or editor) can be more effective if they understand what goes on at the "other end of the line," rather than try to plan their efforts according to a mechanistic design based upon faulty generalizations. People who participate in social communication in other roles (e.g. expert, teacher, or persuader) likewise need to see the process from a more Olympian perspective, one that considers the total communication environments that other people construct and utilize.

Normally the mass media and the people in our daily settings serve complementary roles for most of us. We absorb a great deal of information from both kinds of channels. Only on a topic of unusual importance or concern are we likely to go out of our way either to seek information or to pass it on to others. The giving of information is often associated with attempts to influence others. When we seek information it is often for corroboration or comparison with prior constructions of reality, and we seek it through those channels that are most accessible to us and are likely to have something additional to say on the subject. Whether these are media or interpersonal channels depends largely on the topic, timing, and immediate accessibility. We can also count on others to bring us news of very important and unanticipated events, and often to give us their opinions whether we ask for them or not. While the professionalized mass media are on the average more reliable sources of information, they are not always accessible. Inaccessibility can be a psychological condition; many people, for example, are not accustomed to using libraries or other information archives.

There are also certain topics on which the mass media carry little or no information; other people may be our best sources on matters of taste or local fashion, or on very personal problems. When we turn to other people for information, we are most likely to seek it either from an expert source, or from an "interpersonal channel," which is to say a person who is well versed on the topic either through contact with an expert or from the mass media. Those who bring us information without our even asking for it tend to be well informed on the topic, but they are likely also to have persuasive intentions toward us.

In general, then, while daily social interaction is largely homophilic, instances of acquisition of information about the world beyond our immediate lives are not. When complementary channels present divergent or dubious information, the most likely result is that the person will seek further information from other channels. For most people, especially those who are poorly educated or otherwise unprepared to consult media and expert sources directly, there are more accessible interpersonal channels than formal channels to consult. Social communication consists of an ongoing series of transactions between people and the channels that bring them information, not a finite competition among these channels. The traditional concept of a directional "two-step" or "multi-step" flow fails to capture the cyclical and reciprocal nature of this process.

The most likely "effect" of communication, we might conclude, is further communication. The more one knows about a topic, the more one tries to find out and the more skilled one is in that effort. The more contact we have with people we would not normally interact with, the more we learn. The more people talk with one another about information from the mass media, the greater is the total impact of the media on social action.

Notes

1. Harold D. Lasswell, "The Structure and Function of Communication in Society." In Lyman Bryson (ed.), *The Communication of Ideas* (New York: Harper and Row, 1948), pp. 37–51.

2. Jay G. Blumler and Elihu Katz (eds.), *The Uses of Mass Communications* (Beverly Hills: Sage Pubns., 1974).

3. The term "administrative research" was coined by Paul F. Lazarsfeld, a pioneer in the field. This usage should not be confused with the pejorative application of the term to all empirical mass communication research by critical writers who are unversed in empirical scholarship.

4. Raymond A. Bauer, "The Obstinate Audience: The Influence Process from the Point of View of Social Communication." *American Psychologist* (1964) 19: 319–28.

5. Everett M. Rogers with F. Floyd Shoemaker, *Communication of Innovations* (New York: Free Press, 1971). See especially pp. 255–58.

6. *Ibid.* "Homophilic" literally means liking the same things, and "heterophilic" means liking different things; the terms have latterly been generalized to mean, roughly, "similar" and "different." Also see Steven H. Chaffee, "The Interpersonal Context of Mass Communication." In F. Gerald Kline and Phillip J. Tichenor (eds.), *Current Perspectives in Mass Communication Research* (Beverly Hills: Sage Pubns., 1972), pp. 95–120.

7. This finding is well established in experimental literature dating from Carl I. Hovland, Irving L. Janis, and Harold H. Kelley, *Communication and Persuasion* (New Haven: Yale University Press, 1953) Ch. 2.

8. The line of reasoning outlined here is oversimplified in comparison with the best theoretical literature. Rogers and Shoemaker (*op. cit.,* note 5) view homophily and credibility as parallel factors that both predict success by change agents (pp. 240–46). They note that commercial change agents, while they can encourage trial of an innovation, are not as persuasive as peers (or noncommercial change agents) because they lack credibility. Later, Rogers found that change agents were judged most credible by those with whom they worked most frequently (*Modernization Among Peasants,* New York: Holt, Rinehart & Winston, 1969, pp. 184–86), but also that media credibility had little relationship to media effects upon modernization. Katz suggests that peer interpersonal communication is mainly important for "legitimation" of information received from less credible sources. Elihu Katz, "The Social Itinerary of Technical Change." In Wilbur Schramm and Donald F. Roberts (eds.), *Process and Effects of Mass Communication, Rev. Ed.* (Urbana: University of Illinois Press, 1971), pp. 761–97. Many writers stress that a limitation on the effectiveness of mass media is their impersonality and distance from the individual receiver, but this makes the media more useful for some audiences (*see* Chaffee, note 6).

9. Don D. Smith, "Some Effects of Radio Moscow's North American Broadcasts." *Public Opinion Quarterly* (1970–71) 34: 539–51. Harold B. Hayes, "International Persuasion Variables are Tested Across Three Cultures," *Journalism Quarterly* (1971) 48: 714–23. Vernon A. Stone and Thomas L. Beell, "To Kill a Messenger: A Case of Congruity." *Journalism Quarterly* (1975) 52: 111–14.

10. Michael W. Singletary, "Components of Credibility of a Favorable News Source." *Journalism Quarterly* (1976) 53: 316–19.

11. Florangel Z. Rosario, "The Leader in Family Planning and the Two-Step Flow Model." *Journalism Quarterly* (1971) 48: 288–97.

12. On the distinction between "cosmopolite" and "localite" channels (sources), see Rogers and Shoemaker, *op. cit.,* note 5, pp. 258–59.

13. Everett M. Rogers, "Network Analysis of the Diffusion of Innovations." In Daniel Lerner and Lyle Nelson (eds.), *Communication Research—A Half-Century Appraisal* (Honolulu: University Press of Hawaii, 1977). William T. Liu and Robert W. Duff, "The Strength in Weak Ties." *Public Opinion Quarterly* (1972) 36: 361–66.

14. Niels G. Roling, Joseph Ascroft, and Fred Wa Chege, "The Diffusion of Innovations and the Issue of Equity in Rural Development." *Communication Research* (1976) 3: 155–70. F. Jane Marceau, "Communication and Development: A Reconsideration." *Public Opinion Quarterly* (1972) 36: 235–45.

15. Bradley S. Greenberg, "Diffusion of News of the Kennedy Assassination." *Public Opinion Quarterly* (1964) 28: 225–232.

16. Thomas J. Banta, "The Kennedy Assassination: Early Thoughts and Emotions." *Public Opinion Quarterly* (1964) 28: 216–24.

17. Edwin O. Haroldsen and Kenneth Harvey, "The Diffusion of 'Shocking' Good News." *Journalism Quarterly* (1979) 56: 771–75.

18. Alex S. Edelstein and Diane P. Tefft, "Media Credibility and Respondent Credulity with Respect to Watergate." *Communication Research* (1974) 1: 426–39.

19. Richard F. Carter and Bradley S. Greenberg, "Newspapers or Television: Which Do You Believe?" *Journalism Quarterly* (1965) 42: 29–34. Bradley S. Greenberg, "Media Use and Believability: Some Multiple Correlates." *Journalism Quarterly* (1966) 43: 665–70. Lee B. Becker, Raymond A. Martino and Wayne M. Towers, "Media Advertising Credibility." *Journalism Quarterly* (1976) 53: 216–22. Eugene F. Shaw, "Media Credibility: Taking the Measure of a Measure." *Journalism Quarterly* (1973) 50: 306–11.

20. Hilde Himmelweit and Betty Swift, "Continuities and Discontinuities in Media Usage and Taste: A Longitudinal Study." *Journal of Social Issues* (1976) 32: 133–56. Jack M. McLeod, Ramona R. Rush, and Karl H. Friederich, "The Mass Media and Political Knowledge in Quito, Ecuador." *Public Opinion Quarterly* (1968–69) 32: 575–87. Chaffee, *op. cit.*, note 6.

21. Luk Wah-shing, "Measurement of the impact of dialect in print media advertising copy." M.B.A. thesis, Chinese University of Hong Kong, 1973. Abstracted in Godwin Chu (ed.), *Research on Mass Communication in Taiwan and Hong Kong* (Honolulu: East-West Center Communication Institute, 1977) pp. 106–7.

22. Rogers and Shoemaker, *op. cit.*, note 5.

23. Steven H. Chaffee, "The Diffusion of Political Information." In Chaffee (ed.), *Political Communication* (Beverly Hills: Sage Pubns., 1975), Ch. 3.

24. This is presumably because they are gathering more information, not because they are slow to make up their minds. Time itself is an ambiguous variable in field studies.

25. Chia-shih Hsu, "The Response of Taipei Housewives to the Family Planning Campaign." *Mass Communication Research* (Taipei, Taiwan, 1974) 14: 1–73. Abstracted in Chu, *op. cit.*, note 21.

26. Nan Lin, "Information Flow, Influence Flow and the Decision-Making Process." *Journalism Quarterly* (1971) 48: 33–40.

27. Richard J. Hill and Charles M. Bonjean, "News Diffusion: A Test of the Regularity Hypothesis." *Journalism Quarterly* (1964) 41: 336–42.

28. Christopher Y. Chao, "Sources and Diffusion of an Important Event: A Study of Public Reactions to the News of President Chiang's Death." *Mass Com-*

munication Research (Taipei, Taiwan, 1975) 15: 11–44. Abstracted in Chu, *op. cit.*, fn. 23.

29. Sheldon G. Levy, "How Population Subgroups Differed in Knowledge of Six Assassinations." *Journalism Quarterly* (1969) 46: 685–98.

30. David A. Schwartz, "How Fast Does News Travel?" *Public Opinion Quarterly* (1973–74) 37: 625–27.

31. Gary Alan Fine, "Recall of Information About Diffusion of a Major News Event." *Journalism Quarterly* (1975) 52: 751–55.

32. M. Timothy O'Keefe and Bernard C. Kissel, "Visual Impact: An Added Dimension in the Study of News Diffusion." *Journalism Quarterly* (1971) 48: 298–303. Asghar Fathi, "Diffusion of a 'Happy' News Event." *Journalism Quarterly* (1973) 50: 271–77.

33. John B. Adams, James J. Mullen, and Harold M. Wilson, "Diffusion of a 'Minor' Foreign Affairs News Event." *Journalism Quarterly* (1969) 46: 545–51.

34. Levy, *op. cit.*, note 29.

35. Irving L. Allen and J. David Colfax, "The Diffusion of News of LBJ's March 31 Decision." *Journalism Quarterly* (1968) 45: 321–24.

36. Paul F. Lazarsfeld, Bernard Berelson, and Hazel Gaudet, *The People's Choice* (New York: Columbia University Press, 1944).

37. *Ibid.*, Chart 35. The exact total was 51 percent, with 38 percent citing a radio message and another 23 percent something read in a newspaper.

38. *Ibid.*, Chart 39.

39. *Ibid.*, Note 1 to Chapter XV.

40. Bernard R. Berelson, Paul F. Lazarsfeld and William N. McPhee, *Voting* (Chicago: University of Chicago Press, 1954).

41. Elihu Katz and Paul F. Lazarsfeld, *Personal Influence* (Glencoe: Free Press, 1955).

42. *Ibid.*, p. 142.

43. Steven H. Chaffee and Fausto Izcaray, "Mass Communication Functions in a Media-Rich Developing Society." *Communication Research* (1975) 2: 367–95.

44. Lee B. Becker, "Two Tests of Media Gratifications: Watergate and the 1974 Election." *Journalism Quarterly* (1976) 53: 28–33, 87.

45. Steven H. Chaffee and Jack M. McLeod, "Individual vs. Social Predictors of Information-Seeking." *Journalism Quarterly* (1973) 50: 237–45.

46. Peter Clarke, "Tennagers' Coorientation and Information-Seeking About Pop Music." *American Behavioral Scientist* (1973) 16: 551–66; "Children's Responses to Entertainment." *American Behavioral Scientist* (1971) 14: 353–70.

47. Robert Merton, *Social Theory and Social Structure* (New York: Free Press, 1949), pp. 406–9. Charles Wright, "Functional Analysis and Mass Communication." *Public Opinion Quarterly* (1960) 24: 605–20.

48. Bernard Berelson, "What 'Missing the Newspaper' Means." In Paul F. Lazarsfeld and Frank Stanton (eds.), *Communications Research, 1948–1949* (New York: Harper, 1949), p. 119.

49. Roger L. Brown and Michael O'Leary, "Pop Music in an English Secondary School System." *American Behavioral Scientist* (1971) 14: 401–14.

50. Chaffee, *op. cit.*, note 6. Walter Gantz and Sarah Trenholm, "Why People Pass on News: Motivations for Diffusion." *Journalism Quarterly* (1979) 56: 365–70.

51. Walter Gantz, Sarah Trenholm, and Mark Pittman, "The Impact of Salience and Altruism on Diffusion of News." *Journalism Quarterly* (1976) 53: 727–32.

52. Gantz and Trenholm, *op. cit.,* note 50.

53. Jerome D. Becker and Ivan L. Preston, "Media Usage and Political Activity." *Journalism Quarterly* (1969) 46: 129–34.

54. *Ibid.*

55. Saadia R. Greenberg, "Conversations as Units of Analysis in the Study of Personal Influence." *Journalism Quarterly* (1975) 52: 128–31.

56. Verling C. Troldahl and Robert C. Van Dam, "Face-to-Face Communication About Major Topics in the News," *Public Opinion Quarterly* (1965–66) 29: 626–34. Lloyd R. Bostian, "The Two-Step Flow Theory: Cross-Cultural Implications," *Journalism Quarterly* (1965–66) 29: 626–34. Lloyd R. Bostian, "The Two-Step Flow Theory: Cross-Cultural Implications," *Journalism Quarterly* (1970) 47: 109–17. Garrett J. O'Keefe, "Interpersonal Communication in Political Campaigns," paper presented to Midwest Association for Public Opinion Research, Chicago, November 1979.

57. Robert F. Bales, "How People Interact in Conferences," in Alfred G. Smith (ed.), *Communication and Culture* (New York: Holt, Rinehart and Winston, 1966), pp. 94–102.

58. Verling C. Troldahl and Robert C. Van Dam, "A New Scale for Identifying Public-Affairs Opinion Leaders," *Journalism Quarterly* (1965) 42: 655–57.

59. John W. Kingdon, "Opinion Leaders in the Electorate," *Public Opinion Quarterly* (1970) 34: 256–61.

60. Herbert Hamilton, "Dimensions of Self-Designated Opinion Leadership and Their Correlates." *Public Opinion Quarterly* (1971) 35: 266–74.

61. Roy E. Carter Jr. and Orlando Sepulveda, "Some Patterns of Mass Media Use in Santiago de Chile," *Journalism Quarterly* (1964) 41: 216–24.

62. David O. Sears and Jonathan L. Freedman, "Selective Exposure to Information: A Critical Review," *Public Opinion Quarterly* (1967) 31: 194–213.

63. *Ibid.*

64. Verling C. Troldahl, Robert Van Dam, and George B. Robeck, "Public Affairs Information-Seeking from Expert Institutionalized Sources," *Journalism Quarterly* (1965) 42: 403–12.

65. Verling C. Troldahl, "A Field Test of a Modified 'Two-Step Flow of Communication' Model," *Public Opinion Quarterly* (1966–67) 30: 609–23.

66. Liu and Duff, *op. cit.,* note 13.

67. O'Keefe, *op. cit.,* note 56.

S. J. BALL-ROKEACH and MELVIN DeFLEUR

The Interdependence of the Media and Other Social Systems

Do the media control the system or does the system control the media? Are we as individuals dependent upon or independent of the media? Ball-Rokeach and DeFleur point out that these contrasting positions are misleading because society, the individual, and the media are interdependent. In this essay they describe the relationship among media, society, and the individual as one of mutual needs. They point out, however, that modern industrialized and urbanizd society has made us all dependent on media for information, for social correlation, and for value clarification because we no longer have a close knit social system to meet thse needs. To account for media affects they have provided a model based upon their theory of interdependence. It might be interesting to see if you can relate this theory of interdependence to Chaffee's ideas about media uses and Ruben's systems approach.

How do modern governments communicate to their citizens, and how do corporations communicate to their potential customers? They cannot rely solely or even primarily on interpersonal communication to inform, activate, or persuade the millions of individuals and thousands of organizations and groups that they must somehow reach. Political, economic, and other large systems in modern societies thus come to depend upon the mass media for these communication links. In other words, the media control information and communication resources that political, economic, and other systems need in order to function effectively in modern complex societies.

But, as we know, the mass media are not all powerful. The media depend upon resources controlled by the political, economic, and other social systems, resources that the media need in order to function effectively. We can describe these relationships of mutual need between the media and other social systems with the concept of interdependence. Relationships between the media, on the one hand, and other large social systems, on the other, are interdependent because neither could attain its respective goals without being able to use the other's resources. Interdependence is the social glue binding the media to the other social systems of modern society.

We can illustrate such interdependence by briefly examining the relationships between the media and the political, economic, and other sys-

From *Theories of Mass Communication,* 4th ed., by Melvin L. DeFleur and Sandra Ball-Rokeach. Copyright © 1966, 1970, 1975, and 1982 by Longman Inc. Reprinted by permision of Longman Inc., New York.

tems in American society. What, for example, are the goals of the economic or the political system that most clearly require the use of media resources, and what media goals most clearly require the use of the political and economic systems' resources?

Media and Economic Relations

The goals of the economic system that are contingent upon media information resources include (1) inculcation and reinforcement of free enterprise values; (2) establishing and maintaining linkages between the producer or seller and the consumer that inform the consumer about what products are available and that stimulate consumers to purchase those products; (3) controlling and winning internal conflicts, such as between management and unions, or conflicts that develop with external organizations, such as regulatory agencies. The well-being of the economic institutions would be seriously threatened if, for some reason, the media attacked basic values that justify the free enterprise system. The economic system could not operate effectively if the media did not provide massive advertising links between producers, distributors, and consumers. The media in American society are also essential tools in economic conflict. Corporations need public support, and decision-maker cooperation can be activated by convincing people via media messages of the validity of the corporation's position in struggles with federal agencies, environmentalists, tax authorities, and so forth.

On the other hand, the goals of the media are contingent upon the resources of the economic system. Such goals include (1) profit from advertising revenue; (2) technological development to reduce costs and compete effectively by having the most advanced products; (3) expansion via access to banking and finance services; as well as access to international trade.

We can see that the media and the economic system depend upon each other's resources to attain rather basic goals of survival and prosperity. Such interdependence not only gives rise to stable relations that are essential to a smooth-running free enterprise consumer society but, as we shall see later in this chapter, these relations also shape the economic roles of the media for individuals in our society.

Media and Political System Relations

The goals of the political system that are contingent upon the resources of the media include (1) inculcation and reinforcement of political values and norms, such as freedom, equality, obedience to the law, and voting;

(2) maintenance of order and social integration, as, for example, in creating value consensus or generating processes of public opinion formation and resolution; (3) organization and mobilization of the citizenry to carry out essential activities, such as waging war or conducting an election; (4) controlling and winning conflicts that develop within political domains, such as "Watergate," or that develop between the political system and other social systems, such as between politics and religion with regard to the separation of church and state. The media goals of profit, technological development, and expansion are contingent on political system resources that include (1) judicial, executive, and legislative protection and facilitation, such as First Amendment guarantees, licensing, and anti-trust laws; (2) formal and informal information resources required to cover the news, as, for example, in access to press conferences and off-the-record comments; (3) revenue that comes from political advertising, tax writeoffs, or subsidies. The Fourth Estate (or people's watchdog on government) role of the media may create conflict between the media and various parts of the political system. These periodic conflicts do not alter the more basic fact that neither the media system nor the political system could survive and prosper without the fundamental cooperation of the other. This cooperation is based upon their interdependence.

Media and Other Social System Relations

The interdependencies between the media and the political and economic sectors of our society are central to our understanding of the role of the media in American society and in the lives of individual Americans. We should, however, briefly illustrate the media's interdependent relations with such other social systems as the family, religion, education, and the military. In general, these relations are more lopsided or asymmetric, because more of the goals of the family, religious, educational and military systems are contingent on the information resources of the media than the other way around. The goals of the family system, for example, that are contingent on media resources include (1) inculcation and reinforcement of such values as family security; (2) recreational and leisure; (3) coping with everyday problems of child rearing and marriage, as well as coping with financial and health crises. In contrast, only the media profit goal implicates family system resources; namely, the resource of family members to decide to be or not to be consumers of media products. Similarly, several goals of the religious system are, at least in part, contingent on media resources; inculcation and reinforcement of religious values, transmitting the religious message to the masses, and successfully competing with other religious or nonreligious philosophies. The media, however, depend only to some extent upon the religious system to attain profit from religious organizations' purchase of space or air time.

Like family and religious systems, the goals of the educational system that are contingent on media resources include value inculcation and reinforcement and waging successful conflicts or struggles for scarce resources. They also include the unique goal of knowledge transmission as, for example, in media public affairs and "educational" programming. Media goals contingent on the resources of the educational system are limited to such specific pragmatic concerns as access to expert information and being able to hire personnel trained in the educational system. Finally, the goals of the military system that are contingent on media resources include value inculcation and reinforcement; waging and winning conflicts; and specific organizational goals such as recruitment, mobilization, and intelligence. The goals of the media contingent on military system resources are limited to access to insider or expert information.

Implications for Individuals

The web of interdependencies between the media and the social systems we have discussed is a critical background factor for understanding why social analysts regard the media as a central feature of modern society. This web of interdependencies is also a critical background factor for understanding why and how individuals use, and are thus likely to be affected by, the media. We can summarize this point with the proposition that the dependencies that individuals *can have* on the media are determined, in large part, by this web of interdependent relations between the media and other social systems. How, for example, can we account for the following observations: Individual Americans depend upon media resources to attain the individual goals of being an informed citizen; making voting decisions; learning about new developments in recreation; medicine, and fashions; relaxation and entertainment; coping with economic problems and making consumption decisions; and a multitude of other goals. Should we say that it has something to do with the personality of Americans in general or of some subgroup of Americans? The answer is clearly no. It is rather the media's interdependent relations with other social systems that determine the media's societal roles and therefore determine the ways in which Americans *can* use the media. Individuals cannot control or determine the kinds of media messages disseminated any more than they, as individuals, can control the kinds of messages that are not disseminated. As individuals, we encounter the media as an ongoing system that has established relations with other systems. These, in turn, largely determine what messages will and will not be disseminated. This is why we say that the media's interdependent relations with other social systems shape the nature and scope of how individuals can depend on the media.

What individuals actually do with the media, as opposed to the range of possible uses, is affected by their individual and social characterizations. Because of the peculiar media-political system relation in America, for example, all Americans could depend on the media for a variety of political information that would not be available in other societies (such as the USSR), where the media-political system relation is different. But some individual Americans are more interested than others in political affairs, and so this individual difference affects how much people actually take advantage of or develop dependencies upon the media for political information.

Media System Dependency and Media Effects

As we have seen from our discussion of interdependence, it is not necessary to subscribe to either the more naive assumptions of mass society theories or unsophisticated accusations that there are media conspiracies to conclude that the media influence many important aspects of our lives. Rather, we assume that the ultimate basis of media influence lies in the nature of the interdependencies between the media and other social systems and how these interdependencies shape audience relationships with the media. Indeed, we propose that the nature of the tripartite audience-media-society relationship most directly determines many of the effects the media have on people and society.

The degree of audience members' dependence on media information is a key variable in understanding when and why media messages alter their beliefs, feelings, or behavior. We have suggested that audience dependency on media information is a ubiquitous condition in modern society. One finds it in settings ranging from specific goals, (e.g., finding the best buys at the supermarket) to more general or pervasive goals (e.g., obtaining information that will help maintain a sense of connectedness and familiarity with the social world outside one's neighborhood). We can classify the numerous ways in which audience members are dependent on the media system to satisfy their information goals into the needs to understand one's social world, the need to act meaningfully and effectively in that world, the need for play, sheer expressive satisfaction, or for escape from daily problems and tensions. The greater the need, and consequently the stronger the dependency, in such matters, the greater the likelihood that the information supplied will alter various forms of audience cognitions, feelings, and behavior.

As societies develop more complex and intense interdependencies with the media, and as the quality of media technology improves, the media provide more and more unique information-delivery services for members of the audience. In the American society, for example, the media are presumed to provide several unique services. They operate as a Fourth Estate delivering information about the actions of government; they serve as the primary signaling system in case of emergencies; they constitute the principal source of the ordinary citizen's conceptions of national and world events; they provide enormous amounts of entertainment information for fantasy-escape.

Some of the media's information-delivery services are more essential than others for individual well-being. Providing national sports coverage to residents of small towns is probably a less central service than providing them with information about national economic or political decisions that strongly affect their lives. It can be hypothesized that the greater the number and centrality of the specific information-delivery services provided by a medium, the greater the audience dependency on that medium.

The second condition in which dependency is heightened occurs when a relatively high degree of change and conflict is present in a society. Forces operating to maintain the structural stability of a society always coexist with forces geared toward conflict and change. The relative distribution of forces for stability or for change varies over time and place. Societies undergoing modernization, for example, experience high levels of conflict leading to rapid change until societal adaptations are made that reduce conflict and promote structural stability. Social conflict and social change usually involve challenges to established institutions, beliefs, or practices. When such challenges are effective, established social arrangements become, to one degree or another, inadequate as frameworks within which members of a society can cope with the situation. People's dependence on media information resources is intensified during such periods. This is a joint consequence of the reduced adequacy of their established social arrangements and the media's capacity to acquire and transmit information that facilitates reconstruction of arrangements. We can hypothesize, therefore, that in societies with developed media systems, audience dependency on media information increases as the level of structural instability (societal conflict and change) increases.

These basic propositions of dependency theory can be summarized as follows: The potential for mass media messages to achieve a broad range of cognitive, affective, and behavioral effects will be increased when media systems provide many unique and central information-delivery services. That potential will be further increased when there is a high degree of structural instability in the society due to conflict and change. We need to add, however, the idea that altering audience cognitive, affective, and behavioral conditions can feed back in turn to alter both society and the media. This

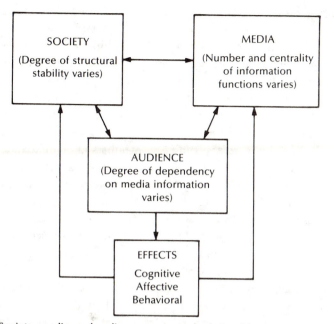

Figure 1 Society, media, and audience: reciprocal relationships.

is what was meant by a tripartite relationship between media, audience, and society. The general relationships implied in these propositions are presented in diagrammatic form in Figure 1.

What kinds of effects are we alluding to? They are effects that are not easily detected in laboratory experiments or in before-after studies of people who have been exposed to specific messages. We are referring to the enlargement of people's belief systems that new media bring; to the formation of attitudes toward a constant flow of new topics; to subtle shifts of individual and collective sentiment that may not be seen in the actions of individuals; and to a number of other society-wide changes. We believe that these changes come about mainly because of the persistent, sometimes intense, audience dependencies on media system information resources.

Cognitive Effects

Cognitive effects are distinct from effects on overt behavior, but the two are clearly related. This section makes a reference to people's feelings of ambiguity, their attitudes, beliefs, and values.

Ambiguity

The creation and resolution of *ambiguity* serves as the first example of a cognitive alteration effect that is particularly likely to receive the attention of investigators working from a dependency model. Ambiguity is a problem of either insufficient or conflicting information.[1] Ambiguity can occur because people lack enough information to understand the meaning of an event or because they lack adequate information to determine which of several possible interpretations of an event is the correct one. Research evidence shows that when unexpected events occur, such as natural disasters or the assassination of a political leader, many people first become aware of them through mass media information channels.[2] When the initial information gathered and delivered by the media is incomplete, feelings of ambiguity are created whereby audiences members know that an event has occurred, but do not know what it means or how to interpret it. More information will probably be sought in attempts to resolve such ambiguity. In many instances, the only source for that information is the mass media. The ambiguity resulting from incomplete or conflicting media reports will probably be resolved by more complete information subsequently delivered by media to their audiences. In such cases, the media's role in ambiguity creation and resolution is relatively easy to see.

What is perhaps harder to see, but what may have more sociopolitical significance, is the extent to which people are dependent on the media for continuous or ongoing ambiguity resolution. People living in times of rapid social change, in settings marked by relative instability or social conflict, or confronted with specific situations in which something unexpected has occurred will often experience ambiguity. Such ambiguity is usually stressful. Ambiguity can be resolved in a matter of seconds where media information delivery is adequate; it can persist for days, months, or even years in the absence of such media information.

Thus, *dependency* on the media for resolution of ambiguity is easy to understand. When people become heavily dependent upon the mass media for the information they need to resolve ambiguity, the defining or structuring effect of mass-mediated information is considerable. The media do not have the power to determine uniformly the exact content of the interpretations of "definitions of the situation" that every person constructs. But by controlling what information is and is not delivered and how that information is presented, the media can play a large role in limiting the range of interpretations that audiences are able to make.

Examination of the essential roles played by the media in periods of modernization suggests that the media clearly have such a role in the reconstruction of social reality.[3] Persons living in societies undergoing change from traditional to industrial forms experience pervasive ambiguity. This ambiguity is particularly acute during the period between their psychological unhitching from traditional customs, values, and world views and their adoption of more modern versions. The utility of having relatively standardized information packaged and transmitted via media by those agencies seeking to promote and control the modernization process has long been recognized. Control over such media information delivery is essential precisely because of the need to control how people resolve ambiguity.

Attitude Formation

Another cognitive effect that can be particularly common when audiences rely heavily upon media information resources to keep up with their changing world is *attitude formation*. During any year or decade in recent history, numerous instances of media-initiated attitude formation can be found. Publics have formed new attitudes about such events as speed limits, environmental problems, energy crises, specific wars, religious cults, and political corruption. New attitudes are continually being formed as various persons gain the public eye. Modern society presents a constant parade of new political figures, religious leaders, sports personalities, scientists, and artists. There is also a seemingly endless variety of social movements toward which orientations must be worked out. Even physical objects become the focus of attitude formation. These can include new household gadgets, clothing, birth-control devices, car safety mechanisms, and innovations in communication technology. The media push a never-ending flow of such events, issues, objects, and persons into public attention. People work out their feelings toward them as they confront this flow.

The media are not monolithic in their influence on such attitudes. The selectivity processes emphasized in earlier perspectives undoubtedly play a role in the attitude formation process. Likewise, local community opinion leaders selectively channel people's attention to events and influence the content or intensity of the attitude formed. Nevertheless, these psychological and social processes probably play more of a role in determining the *specific* content and intensity of the attitudes formed than they do in determining which events, people, or objects are likely to become candidates for attitude formation.

Agenda-Setting

Another cognitive effect centers around the media's role in *agenda-setting*. Neither individuals nor their opinion leaders control the selection activities of the media that sort among potential topics for presentation or among available sets of information about those topics. Moreover, even though the media deliver information on a broad range of topics, people have neither the time nor the energy to form attitudes and beliefs about everything. They must select some more limited set of topics and issues about which to concern themselves. It is out of this set of necessities that the effect of agenda-setting takes place.[4] We need to understand two major features of this process. First, why is there a considerable similarity in the agenda of concern regarding certain topics among members of the media audience? Second, in spite of such instances of similarity, why do members of the public who attend to the media show numerous differences in their agendas of concern regarding media-presented topics?

This seeming dilemma between tendencies toward both uniformity and differences in personal agendas can be resolved quite simply. Not all persons respond uniformly to media-presented information on a given topic; this has been understood by social scientists since the early formation of the individual differences perspective. People select material from the media in somewhat predictable ways that are related to their personality characteristics, problems, and needs. This does not mean that media audiences show no uniformities, however. We noted earlier that the social categories perspective permitted predictions to be made about differences in media habits because a given set of people were located at a similar point in the social structure (e.g., older, white, farmers in the Midwest vs. younger, black, industrial workers in urban areas).

From the individual differences and social categories perspectives come hypotheses concerning the agenda-setting effects of the media. To be certain, specific individuals will set their personal agendas in relation to their unique background of prior socialization, experience, and personality structure. However, the society produces broad strata of people with sufficient uniformity of social circumstances that they share many problems and concerns in greater or lesser degree in spite of individual differences. In our society, for example, many people are wage earners with limited monetary resources to obtain their mass-produced necessities. In this sense they are *alike* regardless of their personality differences; they share a concern over such matters as rising prices, taxes, unemployment, and other economic matters that can quickly alter their standard of living. These override their individual differences. Thus, when the media present information of importance on economic matters, these topics can be expected to be placed high on their agendas of concern.

Where individual differences play an important role in agenda-setting is with respect to topics that are less tied to such social locations. Animal lovers of any social category will be likely to attend to and respond strongly to media-delivered stories of mistreatment of animals. People of all walks of life who enjoy fishing are likely to include in their agendas new policies of the Fish and Game Department.

Agenda-setting, in other words, is an interactional process. Topics are sorted by the media for presentation to the public. Information about those topics is selectively assembled and selectively disseminated. The public then sorts out their interest and concern with this information as a function of both their individual differences in personal makeup and their location in societal strata and categories. Out of this system of variables and factors emerges a list of topics to which varying numbers of people give differential assignments of importance. That list is the agenda of the media audience as a whole.

Enlargement

Still another cognitive effect that occurs in a media-dependent society is the expansion of people's systems of *beliefs*. Charles H. Cooley long ago used the term "enlargement" to refer to the idea that people's knowledge and belief systems expand because they learn about other people, places, and things from the mass media.[5] This idea can be more specifically explained by examining what Altman and Taylor call the "breadth" dimension of belief structure.[6] Beliefs are organized into categories. These categories, pertaining to religion, family, politics, and so forth, reflect the major areas of a person's social activity. The breadth dimension refers to the number of categories in a belief system and how many beliefs are found in each category. Belief systems can be broadened (enlarged) by either increasing the number of categories or the number of beliefs in a given category. For example, the vast amount of new information about ecological matters disseminated by the media in recent years has surely fostered the enlargement of people's beliefs about everything from automobiles to Baggies, from babies to compacters, and so on. These can be incorporated into existing opinions, attitudes, and values concerning free enterprise, recreation, work, religion, and the family. By their constant surveillance and presentation of aspects of the changing social and physical world we live in, the media broaden their audiences' belief categories and enlarge their belief systems.

Values

The final cognitive effect that needs consideration is the media's impact on *values*. Values may be defined as very basic beliefs that people hold about either "desirable and states of existence" (e.g., salvation, equality, freedom) or "preferred modes of conduct" (e.g., honest, forgiving, capable).[7] Only under rare conditions would we expect mass media information to be able singlehandedly to alter such basic beliefs.[8] Mass-mediated information can, however, play an important part in creating the conditions for *value clarification*. One way that the media facilitate value clarification is by presenting information that precipitates *value conflict* within audience members. For example, the recent civil rights and ecology movements not only received broad media coverage but also involved fundamental value conflicts. Civil rights movements posed a conflict between individual freedom (e.g., property rights) and equality (e.g., human rights). Ecology movements bring economic values into conflict with aesthetic and survival values.

Most people did not, however, have the interest, inclination, or information necessary to see these issues as value conflicts. Mass-mediated information, in the form of reports of statements made by movement leaders or in the form of interpretations of the movement's motives and actions, usually includes identification of the underlying value conflicts. Once the value conflicts inherent in such movements are posed and clarified by the media, audience members are moved to articulate their own value positions.[9] This articulation can be painful because it can force a choice between mutually incompatible goals and the means for obtaining them. For action to take place, however, choices must be made. In the process of trying to decide which is more important in a particular case, general value priorities become clarified. Thus, the media indirectly have had a cognitive impact on members of their audiences.

Affective Effects

Affective processes are those we generally refer to in terms of various categories of feelings and emotions. Human beings like and dislike; they fear, hate, love, and are amused by various features of their environment. In a society that has developed a considerable dependency on its media for information, affective change in people can be anticipated when the media deliver such information. The impact of media messages on an audience's feelings and emotional responses is one of the least explored kinds of effects. Nevertheless, a limited body of writing on the matter makes some suggestions.

Desensitization

It has been hypothesized that prolonged exposure to violent media content has a "numbing" or *desensitization* effect.[10] Such effects may promote insensitivity or the lack of a desire to help others when violent encounters are witnessed in real life. Along a similar line, Hyman has pointed out that social scientists have not paid attention to the effects of violent media content on audience *sentiments*.[11] There is some evidence to suggest that the level of physiological arousal caused by exposure to audiovisual portrayals of violence does decline over time. But such evidence is no substitute for the kind of direct research on emotional responses that Hyman is calling for.

Fear and Anxiety

Fear, anxiety, and trigger-happiness are illustrations of affective effects that could be researched. For example, prolonged exposure to news messages or even TB dramas that portray cities as violence-ridden jungles may increase people's fear or anxiety about living in or even traveling to the city.[12] In a state of anticipation of the worst, city residents or visitors may be emotionally triggered to respond violently to others' actions. These effects may be particularly likely for residents of nonmetropolitan areas who depend largely on the media for information about what's going on in the cities, and who have little firsthand experience with city life.

Actually, almost all media effects could be examined in terms of their affective dimension. For example, the affective element of attitude formation can have serious social consequences. In periods of intense social conflict the police may form a number of attitudes from media characterizations about groups with which they have to deal. If media-derived attitudes contain affective elements such as *anger, hostility,* and *frustration,* it may retard the ability of the police to keep their cool when the encounter actually comes. Exactly this pattern developed in 1968 in Chicago during the disruptions of the Democratic National Convention.

Morale and Alienation

Morale and alienation serve as the final examples of the kinds of alterations in audience affect that can result from media messages. Klapp has proposed that in societies in which the mass media play central communication roles, the nature of media information has substantial effects on people's morale and level of alienation.[13] The reason why can be found in the pioneering writings of Emile Durkheim.[14] The sense of collective well-being and "we feeling" that promotes morale and combats alienation is a fragile product of successful social relations that cannot be developed or maintained without effective communication systems. A key element in that effective communication is the presence of regular and positive information about the groups and categories to which people belong, such as their society, community, profession, or ethnic group. People who rely on mass media systems as a primary source of information about their groups and categories can thus experience changes in morale and level of alienation when there are notable changes in the quantity or quality of the information delivered by the media about those collectives. According to this line of reasoning, any number of groups including women, blacks, native Americans, or even Americans generally would be expected to undergo increased or decreased morale and changes in level of alienation as the nature of media messages about them underwent change.

Behavioral Effects

Overt action is, of course, the kind of effect that interests most people. Changes in attitude, belief, and affective states are interesting as well, but it is the degree to which they influence overt action that makes them important. Of the numerous effects of media messages on behavior that could be considered, we have chosen to discuss *activation* and *deactivation*.[15]

Activation

Activation refers to instances in which audience members do something that they would not otherwise have done as a consequence of receiving media messages. As already suggested, activation may be the end product of elaborate cognitive or affective effects. For example, people may engage in *issue formation* or *issue resolution* as a consequence of attitudes they have formed and feelings they have developed. Take as an illustration, people whose primary contact with the contemporary women's movement is via the media. They may initially react to movement leaders' allegations of "sexism" with ambiguity, perhaps not even knowing what the term means. The problem of resolving ambiguity and the stress that accompanies it gain a high place on their cognitive agenda. Resolution of ambiguity leads to the formation of new attitudes and feelings about sexual equality and the women's movement. The culmination of this chain of effects is a felt need to act. Once established, the need to act is transformed into overt action by public expression of these new attitudes and feelings, thereby participating in issue formation. Subsequent media information, such as an announcement of a protest in support of a proposal made by a women's group, may further activate people to join the protest, while others may be activated to organize a counterprotest. These overt actions become part of the issue resolution process.

So much attention has been given to the undesirable behavioral consequences of television content that it might be well to mention briefly one socially desirable behavioral effect. Stein and Friedrich's research suggests that TV viewers may be activated to engage in both prosocial and antisocial behavior.[16] Subjects in their research who viewed a popular children's show *(Mr. Rogers)* increased their level of cooperative activity over several weeks of exposure. Those subjects exposed to violent content, on the other hand, increased their level of aggressive activity. Thus the research showed that both *cooperation* and *aggression* may be activated, depending on the nature of the television message received.

Research conducted in the 1940s suggests that media messages may activate altruistic economic behavior. Merton examined how a radio marathon featuring a well-known singer of that era (Kate Smith) activated large numbers of people to buy war bonds.[17]

Deactivation

In many instances, such as voting and consumption, deactivation, or what people would have otherwise done but which they *don't* do as a consequence of media messages, can be as important as what they are activated to do. Yet deactivation effects have not received as much research attention. *Not* voting and *not* consuming provide two examples of deactivation effects that could be examined. As shown in our discussion of interdependency, most people are heavily dependent on the media for information about state and national political contests and about the state of the economy. Political campaigns have not only become longer but have also depended more and more on the media to communicate to voters. Such campaigns may not change many established attitudes toward the contestants. They might, however, elicit affective responses, such as overwhelming boredom, disgust, or the cognitive assessment that it makes no difference who wins. These inner states can culminate in nonvoting or the deactivation of people's intention to vote.

In like manner, when media messages help to create an affective state of fear about one's own and the nation's economic future or the belief that a depression is unavoidable, people may *not* buy stocks, new cars, certain foods, or a multitude of other products that they would have otherwise bought. This would actually have the effect of deepening a recession by too much deactivation of consumption behavior.

Notes

1. S. J. Ball-Rokeach, "From Pervasive Ambiguity to a Definition of the Situation," *Sociometry* 36, no. 3 (September 1973): 378–89.
2. See, for example, Paul B. Sheatsley and Jacob J. Feldman, "The Assassination of President Kennedy," in R. Evans, *Readings in Collective Behavior* (Chicago: Rand-McNally, 1969), pp. 259–83.
3. Daniel Lerner, *The Passing of Traditional Society* (New York: Free Press, 1959).
4. For a discussion of the various ways in which the term agenda-setting has been used, see Jack McLeod, Lee Becker, and James Byrnes, "Another Look at the Agenda-Setting Function of the Press," *Communication Research* 1 (April 1974): 131–66.
5. Charles Cooley, *Social Organizations* (New York: Scribner's, 1909).
6. Irwin Altman and Dalmas A. Taylor, *Social Penetration* (New York: Holt, Rinehart & Winston, 1973), pp. 15–20.
7. Milton Rokeach, *The Nature of Human Values* (New York: Free Press, 1973).
8. See Sandra Ball-Rokeach, Milton Rokeach, and Joel Grube, *Influencing Political Beliefs and Behavior Through Television* (forthcoming), for an example of such rare conditions.
9. See Sandra Ball-Rokeach and Irving Tallman, "Social Movements as Moral Confrontations with Special Reference To Civil Rights," in *Understanding Human Values: Individual and Societal,* ed. M. Rokeach (New York: Free Press, 1979).
10. For example, see Frederich Wertham, *Seduction of the Innocent* (New York: Holt, Rinehart & Winston, 1954); and A. Rosenthal, *Thirty-eight Witnesses* (New York: McGraw-Hill, 1964).

11. Herbert Hyman, "Mass Communication and Socialization," *Public Opinion Quarterly* 37, no. 4 (Winter 1973): 524–40.
12. George Gerbner, Larry Gross, Michael Morgan, and Nancy Signorielli, "The Mainstreaming of America: Violence Profile No. 11," *Journal of Communication* 30 (Summer 1980): 10–29.
13. Orrin Klapp, *Currents of Unrest* (New York: Holt, Rinehart and Winston, 1972).
14. Durkheim, *Division of Labor in Society.*
15. For an earlier discussion of activation effects, see Otto N. Larsen, "Social Effects of Mass Communication," in *Handbook of Modern Sociology*, ed. Robert E. L. Faris (Chicago: Rand McNally, 1964), p. 348.
16. Aletha Stein and Lynette Friedrich, "Television Content and Young Children's Behavior," in *Television and Social Behavior* (Washington, DC.: Government Printing Office, 1971), 2:202–317.
17. Robert Merton, *Mass Persuasion: The Social Psychology of a War Bond Drive* (New York: Harper, 1946).

ELIHU KATZ and TAMAR LIEBES

Decoding *Dallas:* Notes from a Cross-Cultural Study

This essay addresses the question of how to explain the apparent ease with which American made television programs cross over into other cultures and are so readily understood and accepted. To answer this question the authors assembled fifty groups of viewers representing different languages and different cultures and studied the ways these groups "made sense" of episodes of *Dallas.* They found that people everywhere bring their own experiences to bear in analyzing the storyline and through conversation with others they incorporate these interpretations into their own culture. The authors concluded that television viewing is a negotiation process involving the story on the screen, the culture of the viewers, and the interpersonal exchanges among the viewers.

There seems to be growing support for that branch of communications research that asserts that television viewing is an active and social process. Viewing takes place at home, and, on the whole in the presence of family and friends. During and after a programme, people discuss what they have seen, and come to collective understandings. It is via such understandings, we believe, that the messages of the media enter into culture. We are suggesting, in other words, that viewers see programmes, not wallpaper; that programmes do not impose themselves unequivocally on passive viewers; that the reading of a programme is a process of negotiation between the story on the screen and the culture of the viewers; and that it takes place in interaction among the viewers themselves.[1]

This perspective raises a question about the apparent ease with which American television programmes cross cultural and linguistic frontiers. Indeed, the phenomenon is so taken for granted that hardly any systematic research has been done to explain the reasons why these programmes are so successful. One wonders how such quintessentially American products are understood at all. The often-heard assertion that this phenomenon is part of a process of cultural imperialism presumes, first, that there is an American message in the content or the form; second, that this message is somehow perceived by viewers; and third, that it is perceived in the same way by viewers in different cultures.

This article originally appeared in *Intermedia,* vol. 12, no. 3, May 1984. It has been revised for this volume.

Consider the worldwide success of a programme like *Dallas*. How do viewers from another culture understand it? A common sense reply might be that such programmes are so superficial that they are immediately understood by all: they portray stereotyped characters, visualised conflict, and much repetition. But this cannot be the whole of it. One cannot so simply explain the diffusion of a programme like *Dallas* by dismissing it as superficial or action-packed. In fact, at least as far as kinship structure is concerned, the story might be considered quite complex. Neither can it be understood without words; there is very little self-explanatory action. And there are American mores and cinematic conventions to grapple with.

Alternatively, perhaps the programme is only little understood. In many countries, American television programmes are aired as a by-product of the purchase of American television technology—equipment, spare parts, and programmes all arrive in the same package—and viewers may be satisfied to watch the lavish productions without paying much attention to their meaning. But this is also unlikely. Even children who do not understand the meanings intended by the producer, understand *something,* and shape what they think they are seeing in the light of their experience with life and with the conventions of the medium.

We are suggesting, similarly, that people everywhere bring their experience to bear in the decoding process and seek the assistance and confirmation of others in doing so. Some of these experiences are universal: deep structures such as kinship relations or relations between id and superego. Other experiences are more culturally differentiated by society and community and constitute more selective frames for interpreting the program and, possibly, for incorporating it into their lives. Incorporation, we think, is filtered by group dynamics—in conversations with significant others—and can be done in a variety of ways: by affirmation or negation of the moral of a story, for example, or through identification with a character, or by some more critical judgment.

Social Dynamics of Meaning-Making: An Empirical Approach

To observe these processes in action, we have undertaken a programme of empirical research. We assembled 50 groups of three couples each—an initial couple invites two others from among their friends—to view an episode from the second session of *Dallas,* and to discuss it with us afterwards. These focus groups were of lower-middle class, with high school education or less, and ethnically homogeneous. There were ten groups each of Israeli Arabs, new immigrants to Israel from Russia, first and second generation immigrants from Morocco, and kibbutz members. Taking these groups as a microcosm of the worldwide audience of *Dallas,* we are comparing their readings of the programme with ten groups of matched Americans in Los Angeles. The discussion following the programme takes approximately one hour and is guided by a rather open interview guide for focus groups. The discussion is recorded, and it is followed by a brief individual questionnaire that asks participants to indicate whether and with whom they normally view and discuss the programme.

If we are correct in our assumption about the social process of reading *Dallas*, the method we have chosen enables us to simulate and "sample" the high moments of this process. The post-discussion questionnaire, as well as a preliminary inspection of some of the protocols, provide evidence that the programme is viewed in the company of others and is widely discussed; there are repeated allusions in the focus groups to such discussions. Of course, we cannot prove that interpretation is altogether dependent on such interaction, or precisely how pervasive every day television talk might be. Even if we have overstated the "necessary" and pervasive aspects of such interaction, the method of focus group discussion provides a very close look at the social dynamics of meaning-making. People seem to express themselves very freely.

Of course, it is true that the statement of any individual in a group may be influenced by the statements—even the presence—of the others, and may well be different from what it might have been in a personal interview. But that's the point: if our assumption about the normality of the social reading of television is correct, it is precisely these group-influenced thoughts and statements in which we are interested.

Two other caveats need to be mentioned. This particular study cannot provide a conclusive answer to the question of whether American programmes are read with greater ease than programmes from other countries. Nor can we generalise easily from *Dallas,* or its genre, to other American genres. So we cannot say with certainty that *Kojak* or *I Love Lucy* are processed in similar ways, cognitively or socially. These questions require complex and costly comparative research for which we are not yet prepared. What we are doing is complicated enough. We are attempting to sample the interaction of small groups of different languages and cultures during and after the viewing of a television programme that has been imported from outside their own culture and language, in an effort to identify the ways in which meaning and possible relevance is ascribed to the programme.

A different way of stating our problem is to say that we are interested in the critical apparatus marshalled by lower-middle-class groups of varying ethnicity while sitting in front of the television screen. Again, we find ourselves in the midst of an almost unspoken debate over the activity level of television viewers and their conceptual powers. Most scholars and critics don't seem to give the common viewer much credit; yet, occasional research and some theories suggest that there is a native critical ability possessed even by the most unschooled viewer. One recent empirical study dares to suggest that lower-class viewers may be *more* articulate than well-educated ones in analysing popular television programmes.[2]

If we restate our basic concern in these terms, we are asking, in effect, how the viewer analyses content or performs his own structural analysis of a programme like *Dallas*. The group discussion, then, may be analysed as ethno-semiological data, in which the readings of the viewers may be compared to those of critics and scholars who have analysed the programme. Since the effects attributed to a TV programme are often inferred from content analysis alone, it is of particular interest to examine the extent to which members of the audience absorb, explicitly or implicitly, the messages which critics and scholars allege that they are receiving.

However one approaches the problematics of the study, we are, in effect, asking two basic question: how do viewers make sense of *Dallas?*; and does viewer understanding differ in different cultures? To translate these questions into research operations, we ask, first of all, what happened in the episode, inviting group members to address the narrative sequence and the topics, issues and themes with which the programme deals.[3]

We pay particular attention to the ways in which these issues are discussed. For example, *Dallas* raises value questions about family life, living by the rules, loyalty, money vs happiness, civilisation vs "the frontier," the invasion of the family by business, and vice versa. Which of these issues will be raised in the group discussion, and what concepts will be invoked to discuss them? Are these concepts taken from: universal forms (deep structures)? Tradition? Personal experience? TV genres?

We are also interested in viewers' perceptions of the message of the programme. Do they perceive that the programme proposes a correlation—positive or negative—between money and happiness? Do they agree that business is destroying the family, or vice versa? Do they feel that the programme takes sides between the id and the superego? Do they feel that the programme is about American decadence or American ascendance?

In addition to the analysis of issues and messages, we ask a second sort of question: how much "critical distance" can be discerned between the group discussions and the television screen? Thus, some groups will "gossip" about the characters as if they were real people, analysing their motivations in everyday terms. At the other extreme, certain groups will discuss attributes and actions as "functions" in a dramatic formula, groping, as critics do, towards a definition of the genre to which *Dallas* belongs. At this level of how "real" the characters and situations are thought to be, we ask whether they apply equally to all or only to "them," or to who "they" are: Texans? Americans? First World?

Yet another level of analysis is embedded in the sequences of conversation. Can one perceive in the interchange among group members a direction—some "progress"—towards a shared reading? Are there identifiable "outcomes" in the course of mutual help in understanding a character or an episode? Is there agreement or disagreement over whether an action is justified? Is there debate over whether a certain character or situation "could happen here"? What are the patterns of such processes of consensus-building or meaning-making? It is too early for us to answer these questions definitively. Nevertheless, we wish to share some very preliminary observations about this social process of meaning-making based on impressions from preliminary analysis of the Israeli cases.

Mutual Aid in Interpretation

First, let us look at an example of a statement which reflects the process of mutual aid in the making of meaning. During the viewing of the programme itself, group members fill in information for friends who missed the previous episode, remind each other about the past performances of certain characters who have been absent, explain motivations for actions, and prepare each other for a coming "surprise" or "unpleasantness." Consider the case of an illiterate middle-aged Morrocan woman named Ziviah conversing with her fellow-group members, including her husband, her sister, her sister's husband and a friend:

SALAH: [about Dusty]. "It's not clear whether or not he can have children."

MIRIAM: "They talked about it in court [in the last episode]."

SALAH: "Why does she [Sue Ellen] live with him? That's strange."

MIRIAM: "Why? Because she's suffered enough. What do you mean, 'why'?"

ZIVIAH: "Where's their father? Why don't we ever see him?"

MIRIAM: "I think the father is dead."

ZIVIAH: "That's what they say."

ZARI: "He died a few weeks ago, and it hardly matters."

ZIVIAH: [indicating the screen] "That's Bobby's wife. She's dying to have a child."

MIRIAM: "No, she's in a mental hospital now."

ZIVIAH: "Oh yes, yes, that's right."

YOSEF: "Really?"

ZIVIAH: "Yes, yes."

SALAH: "She's in a hospital now?"

MIRIAM: "A mental hospital."

But groups can reinforce each other not only in accurate exegesis of a test; they can also contribute cumulatively to a misreading. This process is particularly interesting when the distorted interpretation derives, apparently, from the attempt to incorporate a segment of the story into a familiar pattern of culture. Thus, in the following exchange, an Arabic group finds it culturally compatible to assume that Sue Ellen, having run away with the baby from her husband, JR, has returned to her father's home rather than to the home of her former lover and *his* father:

GEORGE: "He's trying to monopolise all the oil in order to destroy Sue Ellen's father. He wants to use it to pressure . . ."

WILLIAM: "Sue Ellen's father."

INTERVIEWER: "Sue Ellen's father? Is that right?"

WILLIAM: "Wasn't that Sue Ellen's father that was with him?"

HYAM: "Yes, Sue Ellen's father; that's him."

INTERVIEWER: "Where was Sue Ellen at the time?"

HYAM: "She's staying at her father's."

The previous example deals less with meaning, perhaps, and more with simple information. Let us look at an example of the way in which social interaction clarifies meaning. This is from a group of new immigrants from Russia, who know only a little of the English of the original and only a little more of the Hebrew of the subtitles. Yet here they are conversing in Russian, about Americans in Texas, on Israeli television. The issue is why the court gave custody of the baby to the mother, Sue Ellen, rather than to JR.

LIUBA: "Justice has a lot to do with it."

MISHA: "What justice? It was the medical certificate [attesting to the impotence of the man with whom Sue Ellen is living] that helped, not justice."

MILE: "No, it's justice, not the medical certificate, that helped her to win."

SOFIA: "It was proven that Sue Ellen left him not to go to another man but to a sick man whom she was going to help at a difficult moment, and that was the decisive factor in the court's decision."

MISHA: "Nothing would have helped without the certificate."

MILE: "Misha, he's not potent, this new husband of hers."

LIUBA: "She didn't go to a lover, but to . . ."

MILE: "Remember, he can't have any more children. So it's justice."

MISHA: "What justice? It's the medical certificate."

MILE: "You're wrong."

ALL: "You're wrong. It's about justice."

Mutual Aid in Evaluation

Additionally, there are arguments about how things *should* have turned out. Some members of the group think well of the outcome of an issue raised in the programme, while others disagree. Thus the group also sits in judgment of the values of the programme, or at least brings its own values into open debate. Here is an example of this process from a group of Moroccan Jews, most of whom are already rather well integrated into Israeli society. The subject of this conversation is why Miss Ellie refuses to be JR's accomplice in the kidnapping of the baby:

ZEHAVA: "She [Miss Ellie] knows how it feels to be a mother. If her own son were taken away how would she feel? She would feel it keenly. She doesn't want others to suffer that way."

YOSSI: "You're talking as a mother. How about talking like a father?"

ZEHAVA: "That's my opinion, and that's what I said. Let me explain to my husband. He's saying, 'Why should the father be the only one to suffer? Why should we be defending only the mother?' My answer is that the mother gave birth to the child and suffered for him. She loves him better than the father because the child is her flesh. A father is a father; ok, so he loves his child."

MACHLUF: "And not of his flesh? Isn't the father a partner in the child?"

ZEHAVA: "The child's from his seed, but not of his flesh."

MACHLUF: "What do you mean his seed and not his flesh?"

ZEHAVA: "It's not the same thing. She suffered at the time of birth, and not the father."

MACHLUF: "Don't they have half and half in the child . . . ? In the government you [women, feminists] say you want 50%, but you really mean you want 75%."

Another episode from this same group goes even further in questioning the wisdom of social arrangements for allocating and administering justice. Some members of the group insist that justice is too narrow in its focus. If only the judge had taken account of the whole of Sue Ellen's questionable past or the fact of her running off with the child, instead of focussing on her purity of soul, he would have awarded custody of the child to JR:

YOSSI: "The kind of justice we just saw is called dry law. It's a kind of impersonal law, without people. Who says that the court had to decide that the child should stay with its mother? It's only a coincidence that her friend can't go to bed with her or give her a child. She shouldn't have been unfaithful, and the court shouldn't have given her custody of the child."

Such arguments are not limited to taking sides over issues within the programme. A theme in the programme as a whole is sometimes interpreted or evaluated against an opposite position which is embedded in the culture of the viewing group. Thus, one of the members of this same Moroccan group spoke eloquently, in liturgical rhetoric, of how much he did not feel allied to the values of *Dallas:*

MACHLUF: "You see I'm a Jew who wears a skullcap and I learned from this series to say, 'Happy is our lot, goodly is our fate' *(Psalms)* that we're Jewish. Everything about JR and his baby, who has maybe four or five fathers, who knows? The mother is Sue Ellen, of course, and the brother of Pam left, maybe he's the father . . . I see that they're almost all bastards . . ."

A similar sort of rejection of the perceived message of *Dallas* can be found in a kibbutz group:

SARAH A: "When I see them, I only pity them."

AMALIAH: "I live better than they do."

SARAH A: "And I tell myself, how terrible it would be if I were one of them."

AMALIAH: "With all that they have money, my life style is higher than theirs."

But rejection is by no means the universal reaction. The groups we have examined so far are not so quick as the two just cited to reject the material values in *Dallas.* Indeed, even the groups that do reject them at one point in the discussion may reconsider at some other point. More typical, perhaps, is the following exchange from a group of North Africans in a semirural cooperative settlement:

MIRIAM: "Money will get you anything. That's why people view it. People sit at home and want to see how it looks."

SALAH: "These are special people. Somehow they get it all, and we don't."

ZIVIAH: "Right."

JOSEPH: "Everybody wants to be rich. Whatever he has, he wants more."

ZARI: "Who doesn't want to be rich? The whole world does."

MIRIAM: "Wealth also makes an easy life."

ZIVIAH: "It's the best thing."

Personalization vs Objectification: Dimensions of Critical Distance

It is clear from these examples that people are discussing and evaluating not only the issues of the Ewing family but the issues in their own lives. Indeed, much of the discussion in groups focuses on problems of conflict between the sexes, normative vs anomic family relations, money vs happiness, loyalty vs opportunism, and the like. Some of the discussants clearly use the programme to discuss themselves and their conflicts. Others do so less freely. This may turn out to be one of the important differences between the ethnic groups; namely, how much critical distance is maintained throughout the discussion. Here is an example of personal soul-searching triggered by the programme:

SARAH A: "When they tried to kill him [JR], her behaviour was simply . . . I don't know what to call it. How could she, suddenly . . . ? It's true you feel guilty, so you worry about a person. But suddenly to love him? . . . That seems put on. So what? Because I feel guilty, I should suddenly sell myself? sell my personality?"

Consider the following—from a Russian group—in comparison:

SIMA: "I'm surprised by his [JR's] attitude to his father. He must be feeling that his father is superior to him financially, as a businessman. What we see in the course of the programme is that he is constantly telling his father, 'Father don't worry, the boy will come home, don't worry, everything will be all right,' as if he were giving a report to his father, as if he were bowing down to him."

MARIK: "In my opinion, he has inferiority feelings toward his father . . ."

MISHA: "He's a very complex person . . . He has many contrasts. One can't say that such a person is very positive, although he does have certain positive qualities. I can't say that business for such a person, and his ambitions for achieving his goals, are negative. Without such qualities he couldn't work and make money, and making money is his profession."

MARIK: "Agree."

SIMA: "For him, everything is divided according to priorities, according to their importance. In business, let's say everything has to be organised. In a family, there has to be an heir. Everything as it should be."

INTERVIEWER: "Do you mean without emotion?"

SIMA: "I wouldn't say without emotion. Maybe yes. It seems to me that he wants his son not because he loves him; he's not so devoted to him. He simply knows that's the way it should be. He knows that he's his father's heir. I believe that he's living according to his father's code."

The more systematic analysis on which we are now engaged suggests that the several ethnic groups do differ, as we suspected, in degree of critical distance. Certain groups use the programme "referentially," that is, they relate the narrative to real life. Others speak much more analytically, or "poetically," relating to the dramatic construction of the story rather than to its reality.[4] The groups that specialise in referential statements are the Arabs and the Moroccan Jews; culturally, they are probably most distant from *Dallas*. The most purely poetic is the Russian group, who have much to say about genre, dramatic conflict, and the like. While the Oriental groups and the Russians may be said to specialise in one mode on account of the other—talking either about life or about genre—the American kibbutz groups seem to be more flexible, speaking both critically and referentially.

While the groups differ in the extent of their use of poetic and referential statements, the form of referential statements also appears to distinguish among the groups. Thus, when discussing the relationship of the program to real life, the Russians exceed all the others in their use of abstract or universal categories such as "businessmen" or "women" or "Americans." The others talk much more in terms of we-groups. Moroccans and Arabs do this more seriously, while Americans and kibbutz members do so more playfully, as if they were "trying on" the roles of the different characters of *Dallas,* imagining how wonderful or awful it might feel to be in their place.

While poetic statements are surely more distant than referential ones, it is not immediately clear that referential statements about general categories such as "businessmen" or "Americans" are less involved than references to oneself or one's we-group. In other words, it is possible that relating the program to broad categories of persons may imply a belief in the reality and generalisability of the program that is not necessarily present in talking about the relation of the program to oneself. If more generalised is more distant, then the Russians are the most distanced group, leading both in the proportion of poetic statements and in the proportion of referential statements that allude to abstract categories of people. According to the same calculus, the Arabs would rank least distant, or most involved.

Yet, for all of their differences, there are interesting similarities between the Russian and Arab groups. Not only are they more "specialised" (in the ratio of poetic to referential) than the other groups, and more "serious" (compared to the more playful role-takings of the Americans and kibbutzniks), they are also more "evaluative." Both groups tend to prefer the rhetorics of evaluation (good/bad) to the rhetorics of interpretation. The Arabs use evaluation in their referential statement, the Russians do so in their poetic statements.

Because we are still in the midst of analysing these very complex protocols of the focus group conversations—a mere sampling of which is reproduced here—it is too early to propose anything as pretentious as conclusions. Nevertheless,

1. We are impressed by the sophisticated ways in which very common people discuss these stories. Clearly, they understand the broad outlines of the narrative; clearly they know the structure of the relations among the characters, their emotions and motivations, and are able to articulate at least some of the central themes.
2. There is evident selectivity in what is discussed. The importance of family far outweighs the importance of business, as we expected. Less sophisticated groups sometimes use kinship terms to identify the characters.

3. Issues discussed include "success," "loyalty," "honour," "money and happiness," sex roles, the functions of children, and many others. Topics raised in the programme are generalised in the discussions so that they refer to generic human problems or immediate personal issues. The feeling of intimacy with the characters, expressed in many of the groups, has a "gossipy" quality which seems to facilitate an easy transition to discussion of oneself and one's close associates. It is likely that the continuous and indeterminate flow of the programme, from week to week, in the family salon invites viewers to invest themselves in fantasy, thought, and discussion. The social distance between the Ewing family and the rest of the world seems far less important than one might have thought. Unhappiness is the great leveller.[5]

4. Altogether, we feel strongly supported in our hypotheses that the viewing process is active and social—perhaps even among those who vigorously deny it. The discussion frequently alludes to what discussants said last week or last month. This social process surely contributes to the ease of understanding (and sometimes to misunderstanding) and to the making of meaning and evaluation. Anthropologists agree, even when survey statistics do not.[6]

5. The focus group method has proved very satisfactory. Discussions of television programmes, as simulated in these groups, appear to constitute a forum for the discussion of basic social issues and themes. They liberate people to say playfully—among their peers—what they might say seriously only in situations of crisis or conflict. It seems unlikely that these statements would be evoked in reply to an individual questionnaire or interview.

6. Groups appear to differ in what we call "critical distance," that is, the extent to which characters and issues are generalised or personalised, and the extent to which statements about the program refer to the structure of the story or to "life." Certain ethnic groups switch easily from discussing the story to discussing life; others keep their distance. Certain groups generalise the program to abstract social categories such as "women" or "Americans"; others implicate themselves more directly.

7. What seems clear from the analysis, even at this stage, is that the non-Americans consider the story more real than the Americans. The non-Americans have little doubt that the story is about "America"; the Americans are less sure, and are altogether more playful in their attitudes toward the programme.

8. Hegemonic theorists will find it easy to interpret the reactions of both acceptors and rejectors of the values in *Dallas* as establishment messages. If the money and muscle of the Ewings is an invitation to the fantasies of social mobility and the supposed "American way," then

identification with the *Dallas* characters will serve the purpose. But what about those who see in *Dallas* only a reminder of how much better off they are without power? It takes only the slightest agility to see that this is even more hegemonic. It is a message to stay down, and enjoy the better of the possible worlds, letting the unhappy few take care of the rest.

Notes

This is a revised and expanded version of our paper, "Once Upon a Time, in Dallas," that appeared in *Intermedia*, vol. 12, no. 3, 1984, 28–32. It includes findings from a draft paper, "Cross-Cultural Readings of *Dallas*: Poetic and Referential Statements," presented to the International Television Studies Conference, British Film Institute, summer 1984. The project is based jointly at the Annenberg School of Communications, University of Southern California, and the Hebrew University of Jerusalem, and we wish to thank the Trustees of the Annenberg Schools, Inc., and Dean Peter Clarke for their support.

1. Here we are in disagreement with others who believe that the unit of television viewing is better conceptualised as background, or as a "strip" that cuts through an evening's viewing or as a pervasive barrage of messages about society that is embedded in all of prime time. Our argument is simply that certain programmes—some more than others—are identified by viewers as discrete stories, and that such viewing entails attention, interpretation, evaluation, and perhaps social and psychological consequences. For recent, relevant writings on the "active" audience, see Philip Palmgreen, "The Uses and Gratifications Approach: A Theoretical Paradigm," in Robert Bostrom, ed., *Communication Yearbook*, VIII, Beverly Hills, CA: Sage, 1984; Dave Morley, *The Nationwide Audience*, London: BFI, 1980; and W. Anthony Collins, "Cognitive Processing and Television Viewing," in Ellen Wartella and J. Whitney, eds., *Mass Communication Review Yearbook*, 4, 1983, Beverly Hills, CA: Sage.

2. W. Russell Neuman, "TV and American Culture. The Mass Medium and the Pluralistic Audience," in *Public Opinion Quarterly*, 46, 1982, 471–487.

3. In their paper, "Television as a Cultural Forum: Implications for Research," in *Quarterly Review of Film Studies*, 8, 1983, 48–55, Horace Newcomb and Paul Hirsch argue that television is a "forum," presenting viewers with issues that need to be resolved. Their content analysis identifies three levels: topics, issues and themes.

4. See Roman Jacobson, "Linguistics and Poetics," in R. and F. de George, eds., *The Structuralists from Marx to Lévi-Strauss,* New York: Anchor Books, 1980. Larry Gross makes a similar distinction between "attributional" and "inferential" readings. The first connects the programme to parallels in real life, and the second (realising the constructedness of the event) infers the producer's intentions. See "Life vs Art: The Interpretation of Visual Narratives," a lecture on US-Hungarian Interaction in Literature. Hungarian Academy of Sciences, 1983. The classic statement, of course, is Roman Jakobson.

5. Content analysis finds that American prime-time family programmes consistently offer this message of consolation for those who can't make it up. See Sari

Thomas and Brian P. Callahan, "Allocating Happiness: Television Families and Social Class," in *Journal of Communication,* 32, 1982, 67–77.

6. Anthropologists are trying to show that survey research on the frequency of television talk is missing the active but subtle interpretations of programmes and applications to relevant issues that go on during and after viewing. See Jennifer Bryce and Hope Jensen Leichter, "The Family and Television: Forms of Mediation," in *Journal of Family Issues,* 4, 1983, 309–328.

ELIZABETH S. WHITE

Interpersonal Bias in Television and Interactive Media

Do you believe that television and radio are valuable aids to interpersonal communication because they provide people with interesting things to talk about? Are you fearful that computer conversations with banks, businesses, etc. will replace human contacts? White examines the research that supports these two diverse positions and concludes that using an interpersonal communication model as the only paradigm for measuring the uses and effects of media is not a fruitful approach for determining the functions of media in our society. She contends that all technological media are integrated into our lives in ways that are compatible with our existing needs.

Many people assume that a fruitful way to study the effects of mass communication is to compare its attributes to those of interpersonal communication. Michael Schudson (1978) noted that when such comparisons are made, mass communication is said to fail to match the "world of rich and complicated interaction" of the idealized view of conversation. "We are not really interested in what face-to-face communication is like," Schudson says, "rather, we have developed a notion that all communication should be like a certain model of conversation, whether that model really exists or not" (p. 323).

The concept of television and interactive technologies as equal or superior to interpersonal communication—or just totally different from it—is an uncomfortable one for many mass communication theorists, as evidenced by two popular but disparate lines of research. Both groups of researchers repeatedly compare television and new technologies with interpersonal conversation. On one hand, implicit in the writings of many "uses and gratifications" researchers concerned with parasocial interaction, is the complaint that the media are not living up to their part of the interpersonal bargain: even though the viewer interacts with television characters parasocially, that "relationship" is doomed. Television, after all, cannot provide feedback to each individual viewer. In an effort to compensate for the inferior quality of this relationship, "uses and gratifications" researchers provide an interpersonal utility category as one of the reasons for watching television; i.e., one of the motivations for watching television is its potential usefulness in future interactions with other people. Their conclusion: television is potentially undersirable because, although often chosen as a functional alternative to interaction with other people, it is not enough like face-to-face interaction.

Conversely, researchers studying the effects of new interactive technologies—such as videotex, interactive cable television, and computer conferencing—are fearful of the capability of television and technology to act as too able a substitute for face-to-face conversation. Instead of conducting meetings and bank transactions and shopping with other people, these researchers believe that users of new forms of interactive technologies will speak only with computers. Their conclusion: television is potentially undersirable because it may too readily become an able substitute for face-to-face-interaction.

This article cites somes examples illustrating each of these lines of thought with the purpose of showing that neither one offers a fruitful approach for studying media uses and effects. Researchers adhering to the first point of view have consistently been unable to prove harmful effects from the preference of television over interpersonal contact. Researchers studying new technologies usually learn that interactive systems are about as mysterious as a telephone and, in the cases of computer conferencing, tend to promote camaraderie among individuals who would otherwise have been unaware of each other. Both perspectives often place media use in an interpersonal model when other paradigms would be more appropriate in evaluating audience uses and media effects.

The Interpersonal Comparison

There is a great deal of evidence to suggest that interpersonal comparisons pervade and bias mass communication theories and methods. This is especially true in uses and gratifications researchers' constant legitimizing of television content by proclaiming its usefulness in future interpersonal interactions. Carey and Krieling (1974) note that this may have begun with the necessity to elevate television to a level worthy of interpersonal use. Television's value could not be argued for on traditional grounds of aesthetic merit. Therefore researchers abandoned the mass art/class art form of argument and instead conceded that it probably was mass art; this was useful because it facilitated interpersonal discussion. According to Carey and Kreiling:

> This feat is accomplished through various rhetorical strategies, including the argument that much of what appears to be escape is not really, or not entirely, because it has social utility functions or contributes to "incidental learning" or socialization. Mendelsohn (1966) makes explicit the assumption that mass

culture consumption is escapist or dysfunctional only when it totally severs the individual from his everyday world . . . uses and gratifications researchers seem intent on showing that it is typically true only of "isolated," "abnormal," and "maladjusted" people. Turned around, Mendelsohn's proposition implies that the consumption of cultural products is . . . approved when it has a payoff or utility external to the experience of consumption itself (p. 232).

According to this yardstick, the worth of a particular television program is frequently gauged according to its ability to provide viewers with information they could use to succeed interpersonally. Whether providing them with things to talk about or contributing to more general processes of socialization, the television viewing experience must appear to have some social value. The implication of this approach is that television viewing takes on positive meaning when discussed interpersonally and that it becomes especially useful when people can use it as something to talk about. Although no one would dispute the fact that people discuss television programs with their friends, equating this discussion with other *reasons* for watching is problematic. The interpersonal utility gratification (television gives me things to talk about with others) is more likely a by-product of viewing than a reason.

In his study of British schoolchildren, for example, Greenberg (1974) did not find justification for an interpersonal utility function when the children were asked to generate reasons for why they watched television. Greenberg nevertheless took the liberty of including interpersonal utility items, anyway. He wrote that "there was no spontaneous indication by the youngsters that a reason for watching television was to talk about the programs with peers, family, or anyone else. Believing strongly that this was nevertheless a reason for watching television, we developed an index of frequency of conversation with others . . . this index emerged in strong relationship to each of the independent functions" (p. 88). Greenberg saw this as evidence that talking with others about television pervaded other motivations for watching. However, the finding that interpersonal utility functions "pervade" the others may more likely be proof of their consequential relationships to more dominant functions which actually are reasons for watching.

Other researchers have adopted a compensatory model of sources for need satisfaction. They reasoned that if the opportunity for interpersonal contacts decreased, for example, then people would turn to television to fill the void. In a study of media use among the elderly, Swank conversely found that as the social world became less accessible, people in the sample depended less, not more, on media sources for gratification. She concluded that television and other media were not considered as adequate substitutes for interpersonal interactions when those relationships were no longer available (Swank, 1979). However, the reference to television as a substitute is typical of many studies. Its implication is that people require a certain degree of interpersonal interaction and that the means for achieving that goal are fairly interchangeable. The fact that television is used when interpersonal opportunities fail affirms its status as inferior to normal conversation. In a study of media interaction, Nordlund (1978) began with similar expectations and reached a similar conclusion:

> We would have expected to find positive associations between neuroticism and amount of mass media exposure, and negative associations between social interaction and variety of leisure activity, on the one hand, and mass media exposure, on the other. The underlying supposition is that a neurotic disposition, limited opportunities for social interaction, and limited leisure activity would lead to greater usage of the mass media, often for compensatory purposes. In fact the anticipated associations do occur, but they are neither particularly strong nor reach customary levels of statistical significance (p. 181).

Another example of television use as a compensatory mechanism is a conclusion drawn by Tan, studying how heavy users react to the loss of television.

> There seems to be some validity to the notion of the "narcotizing dysfunction" attributed by Lazarsfeld and Merton to all of the mass media, but more recently attributed primarily to television. This view suggests that people who watch TV a lot become inactive social participants, since they spend a large portion of the time that could be spent in social interaction before the TV set. Respondents did spend more time with other people in social activities when TV was not available (Tan, 1977, p. 378).

Although subjects did increase the time spent with friends from 1.20 hours per day, when television was available, to 1.96 hours, when it was not, they doubled the time spent with other media (newspapers, magazines/books, and radio/record/tape listening) and even increased the daily time spent on household chores (from 1.37 to 1.68 hours). In addition, adults said that they missed the news most of all during their experimental week without television. Movies followed in the list of priorities, followed by only 13 percent of the sample who said that they missed television's companionship function. The researcher, however, defined that function very broadly, using statements such as "habit," "noise," and "to pass the time" as measurements.

Results from these studies exemplify what Carey and Kreiling claim is the functionalist orientation: requiring television viewing to be related to external processes in order to acquire meaning. These processes are most often interpersonal interactions and television is faulted if it appears to displace these contacts and praised according to its ability to facilitate discussion. For example, gratification which allows viewers to watch television out of habit or escape is considered to be negative. Carey and Kreiling note that "some actions are not purposive, but instead are engaged in for their own sake, or for what was earlier called, following Dewey, their consummatory value" (p. 245). They suggest that it may be typical of "persons in a utilitarian culture to dismiss the reality of things in themselves and to treat them instead in terms of their consequences" (p. 233).

In addition to dealing only with purposive functions of the mass media, most gratification statements are so general that they depend upon a tie-in to other communication functions for their meaning. This interpretation has its place, but it should not be the only way the uses of television are interpreted. Placing television in the context of interpersonal communication means that television will be judged by interpersonal criteria. Since we have few conventions for evaluating television itself, we try to fit it into another category for which evaluative criteria exist. Researchers often hypothesize that television is a substitute for interpersonal interaction and judge its success according to how well it "stands in" for a real person—for example, the degree of parasocial interaction the viewer experiences with television characters. *Never* will a conversation be perceived as a substitute for television viewing and judged on its ability to offer those positive qualities attributed to television: nonthreatening fantasy or reality exploration, entertainment, or information acquisition.

Researchers also seem to be arbitrarily determining parameters for how much interpersonal contact is desirable. Some studies assume that more interpersonal contact is always better, regardless of the other circumstances present in an individual's life. By their yardstick, a student living in a dormitory and having a variety of conversations throughout the day and night might receive a more favorable ranking for interpersonal well-being than someone living in a quiet environment with a few close friends. There is also little recognition of the value of not communicating at times. It may be more beneficial to a married couple's relationship, for example, for them to sit wordlessly through an episode of *Family Feud* together at the end of a hard day than to try to engage each other in meaningful dialogue. Watching a television show which will be neither discussed nor remembered may be the cheapest, most relaxing, and most available option around.

Finally, a different problem with studying television only within an interpersonal framework is the tendency to ignore the areas in which it is powerful. To study newscasters as "friends"—as many uses and gratifications researchers suggest—is to overlook the credibility attributed to those friends by their appearance on television. Ed Asner of *Lou Grant* has received and accepted many offers to speak before journalism groups as an authority on newsgathering. To study Asner's role as that of an interpersonal companion is to miss the point that by appearing on television, he can exert a different kind of influence, one that cannot be assessed with an interpersonal paradigm.

The Fears About Technology

Jon Bradshaw has written an article entitled "The Shape of Media Things to Come," designed to provide a warning that drastic changes will occur in everyone's interpersonal relationships. Imagining himself in the future, the author speculates:

> The home had now become a total environment—the ultimate cocoon—and life, its bemused inhabitants believed, was terribly modern. More important, an intimate dialogue had been initiated between man and the machine. The computer had eliminated the merely mechanical (p. 585).

The theme of this article is not unlike that of many popular essays, television programs, and academic studies; the new, interactive technologies will provide so many services via computer to home and office that individuals will become dangerously privatized, drawing too much information and, hence, companionship from their keyboards and television screens.

In *The Republic of Technology* (1978), Daniel Boorstin has noted that he, too, believes the new communications technologies will insulate and isolate individuals from one another.

> While technology seems to bring us together, it does so only by making new ways of separating us from one another. The One World of Americans in the future will be a world of 250 million private compartments . . . the home of private television sets, each twinking in a different room for a different member of the family . . . Each of us will have his personal machine, adjusted, focused, and preselected for his private taste. CB radio now has begun to provide every citizen with his own broadcasting and receiving station. Each of us will be in danger of being suffocated by his own tastes (p. 10).

Two themes resurface in these and other examples of the antitechnology literature. First, individuals will necessarily prefer interacting with machines rather than other people, and they will generally do so without being in the presence of others. Second, for this phenomenon to occur, new technologies like interactive cable television and videotex will be owned by most people, presumably without regard to whether or not they consciously perceived a need to purchase and use them. The available research, on the other hand, suggests that interactive systems has specialized applications, that these applications are often educational or financial, and that they either put disparate groups of people in contact with each other or replace mundane interactions with strangers. There is also evidence that interactive technologies are diffusing very slowly through the general population, and many changes in individual communication and consumer behavior will have to occur before these technologies become popular and affordable.

For the purposes of classifying research, interactive technologies can be differentiated from each other in several different ways. Two-way cable systems allow individuals or groups to communicate with each other using face-to-face and/or voice-to-voice mediated dialogue. A user of a videotex or computer data service, on the other hand, interacts only with the TV screen or computer terminal to retrieve requested information in typewritten form. A hybrid of these services is the computer conference, which permits participants to send electronic mail to each other for immediate response or perusal at a later time. If researchers are to determine harmful effects, it would seem that they must find indications of inhibited interpersonal contact within face-to-face technologies, or, if used in educational programs, evidence of inferior learning and consumer dissatisfaction. Or, they must find that acquisition of videotex service substantially decreases opportunities for interpersonal relationships by taking up too much of the user's free time, that it fulfills the same functions as conversation, or that it decreases communication competence.

However, research on two-way systems used for instructional purposes, Warner's Qube cable system, and videotex and teleconferencing systems suggests that quite the opposite is true. Although the interactive systems have been used in only a few instances, the findings of audience uses of two-way capability have disclosed that it creates opportunities for interpersonal interaction and even increases interpersonal skill. A few examples of the uses of two-way television and some preliminary studies of the applications of videotex and teleconferencing indicate that the role of new technologies in the lives of most people is either a minor or beneficial one.

The National Science Foundation (NSF) was curious enough about the potential of two-way television to fund three studies in the mid 1970s. One system linked senior citizens of Reading, Pennsylvania, and the agencies that served them. Interactive television terminals were initially located in one multiservice center and two senior citizen housing projects, with responses becoming so positive that converters were installed in the private homes of 117 elderly people. Still later, a regular cable channel began carrying the programs so that 35,000 local cable subscribers could view them and participate by telephone.

Observers of the Reading project stated that "citizens and elected officials . . . gained skill in communicating over the course of the project. Participants became more adept at expressing their opinions and giving information as well as more assertive in stating their positions." The executive director of the program noted that "the senior citizens for whom the system was originally created have taken to it; they use it as they do the telephone to keep in touch with the city and its agencies and each other" (Page, 1978, p. 4).

The other two NSF projects focused on two-way television as an educational vehicle. In Rockford, Illinois, a 12-lesson course in prefire planning was administered to the city's fire department. In Spartanburg, South Carolina, one set of programs was administered to adults who had not completed their high school education. Another program was delivered to parents interested in the principles of child development. Interactive cable was an effective educational tool in both projects. Two-way television was found to be more effective than comparable one-way television in teaching cognitive information, with evidence of learning remaining for at least six months after the experience. The participants themselves assessed two-way television more favorably than one-way, and considered it equal to live instruction. The Spartanburg system, in particular, had great success with its capability for exchanging prearranged signals with the students at home, indicating confusion, boredom, or a desire to ask questions.

In a more recent study, Fredin (1983) studied some of the links between interactive television systems and interpersonal communication. Schools in the Rockford, Illinois, area were divided into interactive and one-way television groups and both were compared with a control group in which nothing was done. Programs about teaching different kinds of subjects were shown to the television groups, with the interactive group having the capability to answer multiple choice questions during the programs and receive feedback on the number of other viewers who gave the correct answer. Interviews were conducted with teachers after the viewing experiment in order to determine, among other things, whether the two-way system produced a wider diversity of ideas and communication. Interestingly, the interactive system increased the diversity of new ideas within groups, but the increase was regulated by the structure of interpersonal communicatioh within groups. Fredin concluded that "new communication systems can affect the relationship between interpersonal communication and the development of new ideas, but the new systems will not simply overwhelm the relationship" (p. 578). Interpersonal communication again seems to be enhanced, rather than discouraged, by the availability of two-way technology.

Although these earlier forays into the use of interactive technologies were largely educational and technological experiments, more recent adaptations of two-way services have centered on business and professional applications. Several studies have assessed a variety of dimensions of user satisfaction with video, audio, and computer teleconferencing. The focus is less on stretching the capabilities of a new technology and more on stretching a budget; individuals want to save commuting costs by doing work at home and companies hope to cut down travel costs by implementing teleconferences as a means of information exchange.

Regardless of their expectations, researchers have generally discovered that some of the newer technologies may displace other media but that face-to-face interpersonal communication plays a specific role in professional relations and will not be replaced by computers or other forms of mediation. After observing 13 research groups in an 18-month computer conferencing study, Johansen and DeGrasse (1979) found that computer use might substitute for mail and some telephone use but could actually lead to increased travel as new working relationships developed. Philips (1984) studied transcripts from three computer conferences and noted that, while some aspects of communication and group dynamics were certainly altered, "there appears to be a sense of successful interpersonal contact, as well as a good deal of . . . 'overt sociability.' . . . The written mode forces participants to be outright in expressing good feelings, and the general 'mood' of these conferences is undeniably amiable and filled with humor, metaphorical language, and friendliness" (p. 853).

A synthesis of the findings on audio teleconferencing done by Fowler and Wackerbarth found it more effective than fact-to-face meetings on several dimensions. More opinion change occurs when audio only is the method of delivery; in negotiating, the side with the strongest case is more effective than in face-to-face meetings; audio partners are rated as more trustworthy; and participants feel that they are more attentive to what is said. Communication in person has its advantages. However, since only around 30 percent of all business meetings actually require in-person appearances, audio-only conferencing has its own pragmatic place in business communication (p. 251).

While these studies have concentrated on interactive technologies which allow mediated face-to-face interaction, prophesies of doom also surround the use of videotex and computer data services. For example:

> If we accept the notion that in many developed nations computers will become a key fixture in homes of the future, offering opportunities for shopping without having to deal with the uncooperative sales clerk; for obtaining stock information and dealings without having to listen to the suggestions made by a broker as he attempts to influence our behavior; and, most importantly, for developing many basic educational skills and recreational opportunities through software utilized by very young children, opportunities for developing relationships skills could be significantly restricted. . . . If the members of any culture spend too much time staring into a box (television, video game, terminal, etc.), personalities will narrow, people will become ineffectual, and violence will increase. If members of a society do not plan their interaction or miss the opportunities for personal and social fulfillment, the very society is in danger (Salem and Gratz, 1983, pp. 31–32).

Several factors are not considered in this line of argument. First, the videotex technology has been in use since at least 1970 and has not exactly taken the consumer market by storm. There is speculation that videotex simply will not go over well with a large audience and that its applications will be for specialized businesses or small specialized groups (Carey, 1982). Knight-Ridder's Viewtron videotex project was canceled in late 1984 (after one year of operation) with losses of $17 million and only 2800 subscribers. And, although a subscriber to videotex services has access to banking and stock market information and up-to-the minute news, in the words of one media writer, "the average person probably doesn't go to the bank more than once a week, gets all the news he wants from newspapers and broadcasters and doesn't necessarily give a whit about the stock market" "Another Woe for Videotex").

There is also evidence that people will use interactive services only when the interpersonal interactions replaced by those services are not important to them. Dozier, Hellweg, and Ledingham (1984) studied the banking and shopping functions of an interactive cable system in order to determine the level of interest of consumers in these services and whether or not consumers would miss the contact with people that these electronic transactions replaced. Sixty-two percent of the individuals polled said, if home banking were possible, that they would not miss contact with other people in the bank at all; only 16 percent said that they would miss it a lot (p. 832). (Interestingly, when demographic characteristics of the respondents were studied, no differences were found in gender, education, or income among those indicating that they would feel a "social loss" if interactive services were used for banking.) The study concluded that "videotex banking services are of interest to those who do not view normal banking transactions as important social activities" and that "individuals who fear social loss are not interested in . . . potential banking services" (p. 834). Whether or not the relationship is causal, the study adds support to this article's contention that all new technologies will be integrated into the lives of individuals only if they are compatible with existing needs in their lives.

Finally, there are economic indicators in all areas of communications technology that suggest that the antitechnologists' arguments may be overemphasized. Television ratings take a dive during the summer because viewers prefer to spend time outside, go on vacation, and generally tear themselves away from their television screens. The video game industry is in serious financial trouble because its appeal seems to have run its course among its young clientele. Several home computer manufacturers have gone out of that business because consumers are not willing to make the commitments of time and money to integrate them into their private lives. Interactive cable systems, while appreciated once in place, have remained experimental ventures and have never made any money. Now, cable companies with the newest franchises are backing out of their optimistic agreements to install interactive systems.

When we look at research, we should remember Schudson's point: that we may tend to look too favorably on interpersonal conversations when in reality many of our interactions are mundane and ritualistic. When transactions that used to be conducted interpersonally are taken over by machines, we should ask ourselves whether or not this is a difference that makes a difference and be prepared to support out assertions with evidence.

ROBERT K. AVERY and THOMAS A. McCAIN

Interpersonal and Mediated Encounters: A Reorientation to the Mass Communication Process

What are the differences between an interpersonal encounter and a media-person encounter? Are these communication interactions basically the same? Is the only real difference the lack of immediate feedback? Although many scholars hold that the introduction of a medium only slightly alters the communication process, Robert Avery and Thomas McCain contend that media-person encounters are inherently different from interpersonal ones. They rest their case on the differences found in sensory potential, control over the exchange, and knowledge of the source. To demonstrate these differences they examined talk-radio call-in shows, which seem like interpersonal encounters but actually are a unique media phenomenon.

It was a typical family room: television set blaring in the corner, homework strewn this way and that, Dad reading the newspaper and trying to share every tidbit with a noncaptive audience. Kids watching—playing, not watching or listening—listening—arguing—watching but not listening—Dad talking to kids—kids not listening—Dad reads—Dad goes to the TV, turns it off.

DAD: "What do you want to do anyway, watch TV or communicate?"

SON: "You mean watching TV isn't communication?"

DAD: "No, it's not the same."

SON: "I guess you're right. I'd rather watch TV now, OK?"

People who watch television and read newspapers generally view these forms of communication differently than they do talking to someone. Why and how mass communication and interpersonal communication are different is a more complicated issue than would appear at first glance.

The purpose of this essay is to explore these differences between interpersonal transactions (those people have with one another) and transactions people have with the mass media. The perspective of the essay is receiver oriented; that is, it seeks to define some differences between the interpersonal communication process and the media-person process, from the vantage point of the viewer, listener, or reader. Further, it argues that there are a host of factors in this media-person encounter that may inherently prohibit the audience member from forming a transactional relation-

This article was written expressly for the second edition of *Inter/Media*. Copyright © 1982 by Robert K. Avery and Thomas A. McCain.

ship with a media source. As the dialogue between Dad and Son suggests, we can have transactional relationships with our fathers, but never with a television set.

The first portion of the essay addresses an orientation held by many communication scholars (including at one time the authors of this piece) that the differences between the process of mass communication and interpersonal communication are but differences in degree. Schramm's position is typical: "On the whole the similarities between the processes of mass and interpersonal communication are far greater than the differences."[1] By narrowly focusing on a single aspect of the mass communication process, the media-person encounter, it is hoped that continued thinking on this topic will be stimulated, as we believe it is an important issue. Three factors that are related to distinguishing media-person encounters from interpersonal encounters must be addressed from the perspective of the receiver: technology and sensory integration, receiver control of the source, and receiver knowledge of the source. Each of these three factors should be viewed as a dimension of a larger process; in many cases they operate independently of one another. It is our position that the placement of intrapersonal communication and mass communication at opposite ends of a single continuum has resulted in masking the multifaceted nature of the differences among types of communicative encounters. The following three propositions will be dealt with individually: (1) The technology of mass media messages inherently limits the sensory integration potential for receivers; (2) Receivers of mass media have no functional control over media sources; (3) Receivers of mass media messages have only limited or imaginary knowledge of media sources. Finally, the process of talk radio is examined as an example of why we need to study media-person encounters carefully from new perspectives.

I. The Technology of Mass Media Messages Inherently Limits the Sensory Integration Potential for Receivers. The human system is a homeokinetic one; that is, it is self-stimulating and self-perpetuating. Human sensory modalities are not dormant sensors waiting to be stimulated and affected by objects in the environment. Instead, the perceptual systems of the human body are searching systems, actively and constantly scanning the environment for information appropriate to the needs of the information processor.[2]

Seven modalities are of particular importance to those interested in the process of communication. These modalities are important because they have been isolated as systems that are handled by the brain in differential fashion according to their unique attributes. They have been labeled *audio verbal, audio nonverbal, visual verbal, visual pictoral, olfactory, tactile* and *taste.* One of the objectives of the human information processor is to achieve sensory integration from and between the various modalities; to gain an understanding of a phenomenon by receiving complimentary information about the perceived object from varying modalities. As Travers notes, "the full *experience* of the environment requires that redundant information be experienced through the different perceptual systems."[3] When an object is perceived that is lacking in information from one of the modalities, past experience from similar objects is used by the human system in order to gain a more complete understanding of the object. For example, if all a person knows about a particular object in the environment is the word "cat" spoken by someone (audio verbal), a vague picture as to the nature of that feline is brought to mind. If he or she hears the word cat and can hear the animal purr or meow (audio nonverbal), the receiver has a more complete idea as to the nature of the animal. If a person could see the cat in all its furriness (visual pictoral) and see C-A-T spelled out, along with the purr and the spoken word, the complimentarity of the modalities begins to reduce even more uncertainty as to the nature of the animal. To really understand the cat, however, you would need to touch its fur (tactile), smell its litter box (olfactory), and perhaps lick its coat (taste). Then you would have even more complete sensory integration, and significantly less uncertainty as to what the cat is all about.

Interpersonal encounters can provide the maximum of sensory integration potential, for the participants afford interaction among living organisms that move, speak, emit paralinguistic cues, have texture, odor, and taste. The modalities of the receiver constantly scan the other participant in an interpersonal encounter, seeking to integrate information from the varying sensory sources. This is simply not possible when listening to the radio, watching television, or reading the newspaper. The media-person encounter is inherently a different phenomenon.

Media are the result of technology. It may be useful to define media as unique combinations of potential sensory integration constrained by their technology. Technology has enabled the combining of potential cross modality checking with definite limiting parameters. Each of the media includes in every message the potential use of a specific number of modality stimuli. For example, of the seven sensory modalities individuals use to scan the environment and reduce uncertainty, newspapers offer information that can be processed by only two modalities—visual verbal and visual pictoral. These are the only modalities manipulable by a newspaper source. Radio offers audio verbal and audio nonverbal stimulation, while television holds the potential for providing four sensory stimuli—visual verbal, visual pictoral, audio verbal and audio nonverbal. Television and film offer more potential for sensory integration than either newspapers or radio, due to the technologies of each medium. However, all media generally have less potential for sensory integration than does an interpersonal encounter.

The technological constraints on sensory integration potential result in a different task for the information processor in a media encounter than he or she finds in the interpersonal setting. People must either supply the missing sensory data from their past experience or "know" the object in question based on "incomplete" sensory data. While interpersonal encounters are often lacking in sensory integration as well, it is the participants and the social situation that determine and constrain the extent of sensory data available. In short, the potential for total integration is always present in the interpersonal setting, but in the media-person encounter, technology inherently inhibits this potential.

II. Receivers of Mass Media Messages Have Little or no Functional Control over Media Sources. Feedback is an element in almost every communication model. It is a concept borrowed from cybernetics and engineering to help describe the human communication process. What is critical to our understanding of this element is that, functionally, feedback serves as a control device. Positive and negative feedback (in a cybernetic sense) provide information to the system as to how the system is reaching its goal. Feedback in a human communication sense is traditionally defined as the responses of a receiver to a source's message. This element is critical for human communication because feedback tells the source how his or her message is being processed. Most writers of human communication would have little problem with Burgoon and Ruffner's delineation of feedback:

> The receiver may smile, frown, sigh, yawn, wiggle, nod the head in disagreement, and make a variety of verbal answers. These cues let the source know whether his or her message is being received; *they are one of the most powerful means of control the receiver has.*[4] (emphasis added)

In order to understand the transactional nature of communication, we must recognize the extent to which participants can control the communicative situation. Some people refer to this as reciprocity. Feedback enables participants (both source and receiver) to adjust and change in order to fit the needs of self and coparticipants. Feedback is important to the extent that change in the message encoding and decoding process is facilitated. It is feedback that informs the participants in a communicative transaction whether a genuine sharing of personal experience is taking place. The functional consequences of this constrained feedback in the media-person encounter constitute the critical factor that distinguishes it from interpersonal communication.

Audience members learn quickly in their media-person encounters that they are unable to control the sources of mass media messages. No matter how much the mass media audience members wiggle, talk, frown, or smile, the media message does not adjust or change. Mass media technology limits an audience member's direct interaction with a media source in the vast majority of encounters with the media. This is a phenomenon substantially different from the experiences of interpersonal encounters that people have with one another. Letter writing, phone calling, or turning the TV set off are not the same as nonverbally or verbally *correcting* or *guiding* other participants in a transaction.

In order for media transactions to be more similar to interpersonal transactions, the audience member must perceive an opportunity to control what he or she sees and hears during the transaction itself. Without this opportunity the audience member can only use media messages as a source of information and as topics for communicative transactions with others over whom they can exercise some control. New technology, especially interactive cable, may change this. When audience members are able to interact and correct or change the course of the media message during the transmission, then an interpersonal encounter may be approximated.

The fact that audience members have little or no functional control over the nature of the communicative transaction due to technology and the structure of mass media industries, makes mass media encounters substantially different from encounters people have with each other.

III. Receivers of Mass Media Messages Have only Limited or "Imaginary" Knowledge of Media Sources. A receiver in any communicative transaction brings to the encounter two kinds of orientations or predispositions. The first is an orientation toward the topic or subject of the transaction. Every individual orients to topics with varying degrees of prior knowledge, experience, and attitudes. These predispositions are the result of past experience the participants have had with the topic under consideration. The second orientation is, of course, toward the other participant, or source. The perceived credibility of the other involved in any transaction is similarly based on past experiences in communicative encounters. Some communication scholars refer to the process a person goes through during the communicative enterprise as "co-orientation." They argue that a person interprets messages and carries on a communicative transaction by continually co-orienting, or adjusting, to both topic and other.

A number of factors concerning receivers' orientations toward media sources make the co-orientations toward media sources unique and substantially different from the interpersonal encounters people have with one another.

1. The concept of media source is vague and highly variant to most receivers. Viewers of television programs or readers of newspapers have at best a vague notion as to the source or originator of these messages. Is the source the producer, editor, writer, actor, television station, network, the newspaper owner? Perhaps it is all of them. People engaged in media encounters perceive media sources in a highly varied manner. Some viewers of *Dallas* think J.R. is the source and orient to the character. Others may orient to Larry Hagman the actor; some may consider the series producer to be the source, while others might perceive it to be the local network affiliate. The important point is that in media encounters the receiver is faced with far more variation as to the possible source of the message than in interpersonal encounters. Interpersonally, people have fewer choices in perceiving who the source of the message "really" is.

2. Technology limits the kinds of sensory data people may obtain about media sources. People do not know media sources as the result of total sensory integration. Receivers can only imagine or project how Dan Rather feels, smells, or tastes. These sensory data are not available to them. It is even more constrained for newspaper readers and radio listeners. All sorts of missing sensory data demand that people compensate for this lack in a variety of ways. For instance, millions of people attend rock concerts in order to see the stars perform. Even though the audio is often inferior to that available on a good stereo, the experience of seeing the performers, feeling the vibrations, and smelling the array of human odors, all contribute to a more complete and usually more satisfying understanding of the music. Generally speaking, fans frequently appreciate artists' records more if they have "seen" them perform. In other words, people desire maximum sensory integration in order to co-orient to both topic and source (music and performer). Technology inherently limits the information people have about media sources. This is in sharp contrast to the kinds of sensory data available in the interpersonal encounter.

3. Receivers of media messages tend to be functionally illiterate as to how media sources manipulate their credibility. It is not our intent to summarize how perceived credibility can be controlled by a source. What is important to recognize is that the presentation of media sources requires message forms decidedly different from interpersonal message forms. Television requires that camera shots be taken to represent the "reality" of the source. Newspapers print in varying type faces and sizes. The media industries encode their thinking in a stylized and limiting form in order to present to potential receivers, sources of varying credibility. For example, research has shown that such things as camera angle and image size effect the perceived credibility and attractiveness of media sources.[5]

Most television viewers have little difficulty in determining the good guys from the bad guys. This is true (though more difficult) even when the sound is turned off and only the pictures are present. And yet audience members are often at a loss as to *how* they know who's good and bad. The conventions and methods employed by media sources to manipulate and control the projected images requires specialized knowledge about such things as lenses, editing, lighting, image size, music, camera movement, color, and a host of other technical and esthetic factors. Most participants in media encounters are functionally illiterate when it comes to decoding the grammar of visualization and presentation. Because of this, the knowledge people have of media sources is often based on experiences and forms that are importantly different from those used by interpersonal sources to present themselves.

4. Media sources are assigned status by receivers due to their mere appearance in the media. Lazarsfeld and Merton referred to this phenomenon as status conferal.[6] People who appear in the media tend to enjoy higher credibility and status because they have been "chosen" to appear before large numbers of people. This credibility bestowed on media sources confounds the relationship in the co-orientation process people have in the media-person encounter.

While there may be other factors that influence the knowledge receivers have of media sources compared with interpersonal sources, these four, collectively, appear to make these differences substantial.

We have argued here that media-person encounters differ substantially from interpersonal encounters along three dimensions. First, interpersonal encounters allow for more sensory integration potential than any of the mass media. Second, because receivers in media encounters have no functional control of media sources like that which is available in interpersonal encounters, the concept of feedback in the two contexts is more than a difference of degree. Finally, the knowledge a receiver may have of a media source is inherently limited by technology and ranges of experience. This renders the co-orientation people have with topic and source to be different for media encounters than it is for interpersonal ones.

IV. Implications for Understanding the Mass Communication Process. Our argument for a conceptual reorientation to the media-person encounter is supported by contemporary social scientists who are calling into question the American norm for judging successful interpersonal communication. According to communication educators, and any one of a host of interpersonal communication texts, effective interpersonal communication has a number of "universal" characteristics. These elements of good conversation have been described in a variety of ways, but sociologist Michael Schudson has summarized the American "conversation ideal" in the following five statements:

1. continuous feedback between two people in a face-to-face setting;
2. multichannel communications: one not only hears the conversational partner but sees and touches him or her;
3. spontaneous utterance: the content of the conversation is unique and created on the spot;
4. the same person acts at once as sender and receiver of messages;
5. the norms of the conversation are egalitarian: whatever rules of speaking (like alternation of speakers) govern one govern the other.[7]

Just as Schudson and his colleagues effectively argue that these characteristics have no universal significance across cultures, it is our position that in order to better understand mass communication we should abandon this set of characteristics as the basis for describing and evaluating the media-person interaction.

By developing an entirely new "communication ideal" for the media-person encounter which is based upon the technological and functional realities of the mass media, we can begin to understand mass communication within the context of its own norms and standards, rather than those imposed by demarcations along a single continuum. To assume that an interpersonal paradigm provides an appropriate framework for the understanding of mass communication forces us to accept the basic premise that for many kinds of human interaction, the mass media are simply inferior. However, if our conceptual orientation focuses on the realities of the media-person interaction, we begin to recognize new functional alternatives that may have been previously hidden by the standards and ideals of the interpersonal perspective.

One line of inquiry that has provided new insights into the media-person encounter is research dealing with two-way or talk radio.[8] The very fact that the interaction between call-in listeners and talk radio hosts more closely approximates the characteristics generally attributed to interpersonal communication enables us to begin bridging the gap in our understanding of face-to-face and media-person encounters.

Consistent with our growing dependence on mediated information, there exists today a general feeling among many individuals that we are becoming less and less informed about matters of central importance to our daily lives. Of equal concern to many is the belief that we are frequently unable to express our own opinions to those people who are in positions of authority and decision-making power. Individuals who face additional barriers to interpersonal relationships due to poor health, physical disability, or geographic isolation have an even greater need to seek out alternative communication channels, especially those created by the electronic media.

Within this context, the interpersonal character of talk radio is especially significant. Talk radio is one of the few public media that allow for spontaneous interaction between two or more people. The exchange of messages between a call-in listener and a talk radio host creates a pattern of talk that defines a symbol system for the interactants. That is, social reality is uniquely defined by the interactants, and hence becomes significant to the communication process.

After reviewing the results of several talk radio studies, one might easily come to the conclusion that although the communication patterns between a call-in listener and a talk radio host reveal numerous similarities to the face-to-face encounter, the unique characteristics imposed by this communication setting afford a special context that needs to be considered in order to develop a complete understanding of this particular media-person transaction.

The on-air presence of the talk radio host on a regular basis permits the listener to form a variety of opinions about this person who is known only by his/her voice. The opportunity to witness the interaction patterns between the host and other callers without any personal threat to the listener enables him/her to prepare for a future media-person encounter. Even before the listener makes the conscious decision to initiate contact with the host, the impersonality of the medium allows the listener to use the information gleaned from the medium to facilitate interaction with others, or to simply reinforce or expand existing ideas.

One of the reasons that the two-way format has proved more successful on radio than television is that the interaction is enhanced by the absence of the visual pictoral and visual verbal modalities. What might be considered by some as a technological limitation of the radio medium actually contributes to this form of media-person interaction. In-depth interviews with selected call-in listeners revealed that not being able to see or even know what the host looked like (and vice versa) contributed greatly to the listener's level of relaxation and satisfaction with the media encounter.

Although the listening patterns of those who follow talk radio reveal a fairly faithful allegiance throughout the broadcast day, the vast majority of call-in listeners communicate directly with only one or two of the half-dozen hosts employed by a station. Analysis of the interaction patterns between caller and host revealed that the majority of the conversations are spent reinforcing the opinions or positions of the interactants. The conclusion drawn from these findings is that talk radio functions to expose listeners to a variety of opinions and issues, but listeners are seldom willing to engage in interaction with hosts who hold a competing position. Even though callers selected hosts who shared a common perspective, interviewees frequently noted that they never forgot who was in control of the interaction. For some, being cut off for whatever reason represented a form of chastisement and humiliation that they found difficult to accept.

We hope that these examples drawn from talk radio research will serve to support the position that media-person encounters differ significantly from interpersonal encounters, even in the case of a highly specialized mass medium that embodies many of the characteristics of personal conversation. The talk radio listener is both constrained and aided by the technology of radio broadcasting and telephonic communications. When a listener initiates contact with the talk radio host, he/she must remember that the interaction remains completely under the control of the host, who can terminate the conversation at any time. Similarly, the caller's knowledge and understanding of the talk host and the radio station he/she represents are generally limited to the level of information that has been transmitted by the station to its listening audience.

The suggestion that we need to reconsider a media-person paradigm for understanding the mass communication process is not offered at the expense of the well-established interpersonal model. The early two-step flow and subsequent multi-step flow theories of information diffusion provide ample support for the critical importance of an interpersonal orientation to some aspects of the mass communication process. Rather than discard one conceptualization in favor of the other, the interpersonal and media-person models should be viewed as companion orientations. One cannot fully understand the meaning of the media without recognizing that media-person encounters are but one aspect of a much larger process. People's subsequent talk about the media, as well as their conversation with others during media encounters, must obviously be taken into account.

One final issue regarding this broad topic needs to be raised. Do receivers use an interpersonal model of communicative expectations when they encounter the media? Do people use a media model of communicative expectation when they engage in interpersonal transactions? Or, do people have one model of expectations for media encounters and another for interpersonal ones? Part of the answer to these questions may be uncovered in terms of age and differential experiences with the media. It may well be the case that people who developed their communicative style and expectations in a pre-television and pre-technological time approach media encounters and interpersonal encounters far differently than do those born in the television and technology milieu of today. Because of this, the examination of interpersonal and media encounters must continue. Research on personal junctures with media and others needs careful description and understanding.

"So what do you want to do anyway, watch TV or communicate?"

Notes

1. W. Schramm, "The Nature of Communication Between Humans," in *The Process and Effects of Mass Communication*, eds. W. Schramm and D. Roberts (Urbana: University of Illinois Press, 1971), p. 50.
2. J. Gibson, *The Senses Considered as Perceptual Systems.* (Boston: Houghton Mifflin, 1966).
3. R. M. W. Travers, *Man's Information System.* (Scranton: Chandler Publishing Company, 1970), p. 9.
4. M. Burgoon and M. Ruffner, *Human Communication.* (New York: Holt, Rinehart and Winston, 1977), p. 82.
5. T. A. McCain, J. C. Chilberg, and J. J. Wakshlag, "The Effect of Camera Angle on Source Credibility and Attraction," *Journal of Broadcasting,* 21:35–46 (Winter 1977).
6. P. F. Lazarfeld and R. K. Merton, "Mass Communication, Popular Taste, and Organized Social Action," in *The Communication of Ideas*, ed. T. Bryson (New York: Harper, 1948).
7. M. Schudson, "The Ideal of Conversation in the Study of Mass Media," *Communication Research,* 5:320–329 (July 1978).
8. R. K. Avery, D. G. Ellis, and T. W. Glover, "Patterns of Communication on Talk Radio," *Journal of Broadcasting,* 22:5–17 (Winter 1978).

A Neglected Connection: Mass Media Exposure and Interpersonal Communicative Competency

All of us need information to communicate effectively. We need information to understand other people's attitudes and outlooks, likes and dislikes, interests and motivations, if we are to interact and communicate successfully. Where do we obtain this needed information and how do we process it? Quite obviously we acquire it through personal interaction and the mass media. How we process and use it depends on whether the information is cultural, sociological, or psychological. Gerald Miller explains what each type of information does to help us better predict the outcomes of our communication efforts. He examines the essential function of psychological information in interpersonal communication and contrasts this with media's overwhelming reliance on cultural and sociological information. Miller argues that heavy doses of media messages may inhibit our ability to relate interpersonally.

Communication researchers are certainly no strangers to issues concerning the interface between the mass media and interpersonal communication. The "two-step flow" studies of Lazarsfeld, Katz, and their associates (e.g., Katz and Lazarsfeld, 1955; Lazarsfeld, Berelson, and Gaudet, 1944) are of ancient vintage, and almost all students of communication are aware that media influence is not injected directly into the cognitive and affective veins of message recipients but rather is administered in oral doses by opinion leaders plying their trade in interpersonal settings. Turning from issues involving social influence per se to the question of why persons expose themselves selectively to media content, the uses and gratifications approach to media consumption (Blumler and Katz, 1974) emphasizes that media communications can be used for such purposes as achieving social contact (Nordenstreng, 1970) or acquiring information to be used in interpersonal transactions (Katz, Guervitch, and Haas, 1973). Unquestionably, much of the conversational grist for interpersonal dialogues is ground at the media mill, with such dialogues ranging in sophistication from the disjointed exchanges of several teenagers debating the relative merits of currently popular punk rock groups to the studied analyses of a particular *New York Times* editorial or CBS public affairs program performed by two or more like-minded members of the intellectual community.

This article was written expressly for the second edition of *Inter/Media*. Copyright © 1982 by Gerald R. Miller.

Though these previously established relationships are of substantial import, I will argue in this chapter that mass communication messages potentially affect interpersonal relationships in even more fundamental, pervasive ways which at this writing have received relatively little research attention. Specifically, I will propose that the media often: (1) exert a powerful impact on people's initial perceptions of other interpersonal transactants; (2) influence the manner in which information about other transactants is processed and interpreted; and in many cases (3) distract persons from gathering the kind of information they need to relate effectively in interpersonal settings. While my position falls somewhat short of McLuhan's (1964) cryptic "the medium is the message," at least as I understand this dictum, it does posit that consumption of media messages and expectations regarding interpersonal relationships are woven together in a complex relational fabric.

Some Conceptual Groundwork

A conceptualization of interpersonal communication developed by Mark Steinberg and me (Miller and Steinberg, 1975; Miller and Sunnafrank, 1982) provides the grounds for my argument. We began with the assumption that whenever people communicate with each other, they make predictions about the possible consequences, or outcomes, of their messages. Stated differently, message making does not occur haphazardly; rather, communicators purposively weigh the available message alternatives, including the option of sending no message, and select the alternative or alternatives expected to yield the most favorable outcomes. Naturally, the degree of cognitive involvement in prediction making varies from one situation to another: in certain situations, such as job interviews or oral examinations for graduate degrees, much conscious rehearsal and evaluation occurs; in other situations, such as greeting or leave-taking exchanges, prediction may occur at such a low level of awareness as to be almost synonymous with perception. Nevertheless, predictions are made in the latter situations, a fact that is most vividly underscored on those rare occasions when the predictions are disconfirmed.

Unless a random decision process is assumed—and in a few cases, this assumption may be justified because of the complete absence of relevant data; e.g., people sometimes speculate how they would communicate with aliens from other planets—prediction making requires information. Three types of information assist communicators in determining the probable outcomes of their messages.

First, a communicator's predictions about probable message outcomes may be grounded in *cultural information*. Knowledge about people's culture—its language, dominant values, myths, and prevailing ideology—often permits prediction of probable responses to certain messages. To illustrate this process, consider a widely aired perfume advertisement of several years ago. The commercial stressed that this particular perfume "interacts with normal body chemistry" to produce a unique fragrance for each wearer. The advertisement's potential appeal—in marketplace parlance, its effectiveness in persuading viewers to buy perfume—rested on the premise that members of our society assign a high value to individuality. Thus, the commercial sought to curry product conformity by focusing on individuality and uniqueness, a logical absurdity yet a potentially persuasive message based largely on cultural-level prediction making.

Sociological information may also provide the primary grounds for prediction making. Knowledge of others' membership groups, as well as the reference groups to which they aspire, allows communicators to make predictions about probable responses to numerous messages. Again, media advertising abounds with messages relying heavily on sociological information. The once popular practice of adorning patent medicine commercials with actors garbed in white medical coats sought to capitalize on the credibility conferred by many persons on this particular professional group. Advertisements for life insurance, toothpaste, and numerous other products and services rest on sociological-level predictions associated with the amorphous membership groups labeled "parents" and "spouses." Examples of messages grounded in sociological predictions are numerous; in fact, of the three types of information discussed herein, sociological information is probably used most frequently in arriving at predictions about message outcomes.

Predictions derived from both cultural and sociological information are founded on a process of *stimulus generalization;* i.e., the communicator abstracts a set of characteristics common to most members of a group and then assumes that any given individual or individuals belonging to that group will manifest these characteristics. As a result, cultural and sociological predictions are inevitably subject to error, since some individuals are certain to deviate from the majority of the group. All Americans do not value individuality and all parents do not place a high premium on their children's dental health or their family's economic security.

The third type of information used in prediction making differs markedly from the two types discussed thus far. Though our usage is more restricted than is typically the case, Steinberg and I call the third type *psychological information.* Such information departs drastically from sociological and cultural information because it directs attention at another person's prior learning history, particularly as it *varies* from the learning histories of other persons. To put it differently, cultural and sociological predictions rest on a view of individuals as undifferentiated role occupants, whereas psychological prediction treats people as individuals (Berger, Gardner, Parks, Schulman and Miller, 1976). Moreover, predictions based on psychological information are akin to a process of *stimulus discrimination;* i.e., the communicator seeks to determine how particular persons differ from others of common cultural and sociological lineage. Such an approach can, in principle, produce error-free prediction; though as a matter of fact, predictive perfection probably occurs seldom, if ever, since communicators need considerable personal information to make totally accurate psychological predictions.

Steinberg and I posit that interpersonal communication is characterized by frequent reliance on psychological prediction-making. Initial transactions are, perforce, largely impersonal, relying primarily on cultural and sociological information as guides to message making. *If* the transactants continue the relationship, *if* they are motivated to seek psychological information, and *if* they have the needed skills to acquire it, the relationship becomes increasingly interpersonal. Thus, the crux of our conceptualization of interpersonal communication can be stated as follows: *when predictions about communicative outcomes rely heavily on cultural and/or sociological information, the communicators are engaged in impersonal communication; when predictions are heavily grounded in psychological information, the communicators are engaged in interpersonal communication.*

Implications for the Media/Interpersonal Interface

Both the nature of the three types of information and my previous examples underscore the fact that mass media transactions are impersonal. In seeking to appeal to large, heterogeneous audiences, media communicators necessarily rely on cultural and sociological information when selecting among message alternatives. Some predictive error is inevitable and expected; no media message can ever hope to be effective with every potential recipient. In a sense, the hallowed ratings provide a quantitative index of success in predictive accuracy and relative reduction of error. Furthermore, while my prior examples were drawn from media advertising appeals, it should be obvious that the same strategy of prediction underlies all media messages. Characters in television or radio dramas are cultural and sociological stereotypes designed to appeal to the majority of viewers: though they differ in skin pigmentation, George Jefferson and Archie Bunker, Bill Russell and Rick Barry,[1] or Lea Thornton and Jessica Savitch,[2] are highly similar cultural and sociological creations who embody a number of widely shared American values and reflect commonly held stereotypes about certain membership and reference groups. Phrases such as, "All the news that's fit to print," or, "And that's the way it is, Monday, November 12, 1979," are most accurately translated to mean, "Based on cultural and sociological predictions, these are the items of news expected to appeal to, or capture the interest of, the reading and viewing public." Thus, though this chapter may be of considerable interest to some of this book's readers, it can safely be predicted that the effort I have devoted to it today will not be mentioned on tonight's CBS News or in tomorrow's *New York Times*—unless, of course, something quite dramatic and totally unexpected occurs while I am working on it.

Given their communicative objectives, the media's approach to prediction making is perfectly sensible. Still, it can be asked how consumption of media messages influences people's perceptions of others as well as their habitual ways of processing and interpreting information in face-to-face settings. Assuming the validity of such learning theory constructs as *transfer* and the previously mentioned *stimulus generalization,* the following fundamental proposition seems quite defensible: *extensive exposure to media messages predisposes persons to view other people as undifferentiated role occupants—simplistic cultural and sociological caricatures—rather than individuals.* This proposition stems from the likelihood that heavy doses of media messages contribute to the development of cognitively simple information processors who are conditioned to think in terms of stimulus generalization rather than stimulus discrimination. Hence, I am not primarily concerned with the persuasive impact of the media—except in its broadest, most pervasive sense—nor am I preoccupied with whether or not mass media make us more violent or more licentious creatures. Rather, I am disturbed by the possibility that the mass media inhibit our ability to relate interpersonally to each other; that they create sets, expectations, and thinking habits which hinder us in dealing with others in our daily environment *as individuals.*

It should be stressed that, depending on how broadly the term is defined, not all media are equally guilty of encouraging simplistic cultural and sociological stereotyping. Great novels and plays are often treasured because of their intricate, insightful, and individualistic character development: Captain Ahab is much more than just the commanding officer of a merchant whaling ship and Willy Loman is certainly not just another traveling salesman. Even in these cases, however, the notion that great drama and literature reveal identifiable universals of temperament and behavior suggests that the major goal of the author is to stimulate her or his readers or viewers to engage in stimulus generalization—to lump people together in terms of one or two general characteristics. Upon turning to the typical dramatic fare served up by television and popular magazines, any semblance of careful development of individual traits and personality attributes vanishes; rather, as mentioned earlier, viewers and readers are served a diet of uncomplicated cultural and sociological caricatures.

Numerous research questions are suggested by the position I have outlined above. For example, my viewpoint suggests that an inverse relationship exists between frequency of media exposure and the number of attributes assigned to others in one's personal environment; i.e., it implies that heavy media exposure inhibits the development of cognitively complex information processors. This possibility could be tested by employing a measure of cognitive complexity, such as Kelly's (1955) Rep Test, and correlating scores with reports of amount of time spent attending to media messages. Or alternatively, since problems associated with inferring causality can be raised regarding the preceding approach, measures of cognitive complexity could be obtained from individuals following varying amounts of media exposure, an experimental procedure which permits less ambiguous interpretation of causal linkages.

In a similar vein, it can also be hypothesized that frequency of media exposure is inversely related to the ability to make psychological-level predictions. Recently, several colleagues at Michigan State University (e.g., Bundens, 1980) have commenced developing procedures that permit tests of people's ability to use cultural, sociological, and psychological information in arriving at predictions about others' responses. Presently, Mark deTurck and I (1981) are devising a paper-and-pencil test designed to tap respondents' relative predilections to think in terms of stimulus generalization or stimulus discrimination. By taking advantage of these procedures and measurement tools, a variety of studies dealing with possible relationships between amount of media exposure and interpersonal communicative competency can be carried out.

Apart from possible influences of actual media content, I would suggest that the time spent consuming media messages detracts from people's opportunities and abilities to move their relationships to a more interpersonal plane. As the conceptualization developed herein implies, gathering psychological information demands considerable time and energy. When the television set, the radio, or the print media consistently intrude on people's chances for face-to-face dialogue, the likelihood of obtaining the necessary data base for psychological-level predictions is slim. Research that examines the abilities of relational partners with varying amounts of media consumption to make accurate predictions about each other's message responses should permit increased understanding of the possible intrusion of media on interpersonal relationships.

I have painted an extensive picture for future research in very broad brush strokes. Permit me a final observation about the potential utility of my conceptual perspective. It has always seemed to me that much research on media effects suffers from being pitched at too low a level of abstraction: interest is typically directed at isolating the effects of some particular kind of media message content, rather than identifying a set of overarching propositions or constructs capable of embracing diverse media content areas. My perspective posits that all media messages, whether a thirty-second advertisement on network television, a pornographic movie, a violent episode of "Hill Street Blues," or a 6:30 network news item, share a primary reliance on cultural and sociological information and prediction making. If it can be shown that differences in the extent to which persons are exposed to this common antecedent result in systematic variations in person perception and processing of personal information, we will be in a position to make wider generalizations about the impact of the media on face-to-face relationships.

As my remarks in this chapter clearly emphasize, I believe that mass media and interpersonal communication are psychologically interconnected in very fundamental ways, that the influence of one domain pervades communicative activities in the other. To avoid misunderstanding, I must stress that I see nothing inherently insidious or threatening about the mass media: they are designed to fulfill consensually agreed upon societal functions and they generally accomplish this goal admirably. Still, if we are to recognize the oft-endorsed objective of improving the quality of our interpersonal relationships, we must understand the impact of the media on the interpersonal arena. My concern is best captured by this statement from one of my earlier papers:

> The most calamitous possible effect of increased reliance on mediated communication lies in people's diminished ability to function and relate as individuals, and even more important, in their subsequent failure to satisfy basic human needs that are served by interpersonal contact. To say this in no way demeans the important gains that can be realized by improved and expanded communication technology; rather, it underscores the necessity of maintaining a balanced perspective between the social benefits to be reaped from advances in mediated communication systems and the individual rewards gained from face-to-face encounters. (Miller, 1977, 190).

Notes

1. Indeed, while this chapter was being written, an unfortunate cultural-level prediction has clouded the future effectiveness of the Russell and Barry sports broadcasting team. I refer, of course, to the incident in which Barry responded to a picture of Russell by asserting that he could immediately recognize him because of his "watermelon grin," a vivid example not only of failure to use psychological information in prediction making but also an illustration of inept cultural-level prediction.

2. A recent amusing story appearing in the *Detroit Free Press* contends that the esoteric, sophisticated names used by most women network reporters—"Jessica," "Lea," "Leslie," "Andrea," etc.—represent an instance of poor prediction making. The writer argues that most viewers prefer the "old shoe" names of male reporters—"Walter," "John," "Dan," "Bob," etc.—and contends there will never be a successful woman anchor person until she adopts a name such as "Nellie" or "Martha." Whether accurate or not, the story again underscores the centrality of cultural and sociological prediction to the enterprise of creating media messages.

BRENT D. RUBEN

Intrapersonal, Interpersonal, and Mass Communication Processes in Individual and Multi-Person Systems

This chapter from the book *General Systems Theory and Human Communication* links all communication, from intrapersonal to mass, as one continual process in which the individual comes "to know and be" in relationship to the world. Brent Ruben contends we cannot study and understand one form of human communication apart from all other kinds of human communication. Each form is part of a complex network of functionally interrelated communication acts in multi-individual systems. The basic function of this network is information processing. Ruben considers "information" to be all the inputs and outputs that flow through the human communication system producing the thoughts, feelings, and actions that we label as human. If you understand and accept Ruben's systems theory, you should be able to relate all the ideas presented in this collection of readings to a general system of human communication.

For communication study, one of the particularly significant contributions of C. West Churchman is his application of the concept of functionality. In *The Systems Approach,* Churchman differentiates between what might be termed *functional analysis,* which he contends is essential to the development of a systems orientation, and *descriptive analysis* which he believes is antithetical to system thinking. To make clear the difference, Churchman uses the automobile as an example. Where a descriptive analysis of an auto begins by listing the parts: wheels, axles, alternator, frame, and so on, analysis of function proceeds instead by considering how automobiles are used—what they are for.[1] The strength of this paradigm when applied to human communication study is that it draws one's attention to the predominantly descriptive traditions reflected in the majority of definitions of communication, while at the same time suggesting an alternative approach.

Descriptive Analysis in Human Communication Thought

That communication has been conceived of primarily in terms of "how-it-works" becomes apparent from even a most cursory consideration of the

From *General Systems Theory and Human Communication,* edited by Brent D. Ruben and John Y. Kim. (Rochelle Park, N.J.: Hayden Book Co., 1975). Reprinted by permission.

history of thought about the phenomenon. Since Aristotle set forth his concept of rhetoric, communication has primarily been examined in descriptive, component-oriented fashion:

> Since rhetoric exists to affect the giving of decisions . . . the orator must not only try to make the argument of his speech demonstrative and worthy of belief, he must also make his own character look right and put his bearers, who are to decide, into the right frame of mind.[2]

With his concern for a person who speaks, the speech to be given, and the person who will listen, Aristotle underscored in *Rhetoric* the same elements of communication as do most contemporary descriptions.

The descriptive mode of analysis was also evident in the classical portrayals of communication advanced by Lasswell,[3] Shannon and Weaver,[4] and Schramm,[5] whose models focus generally upon the same components as did Aristotle.[6] Lasswell,[7] of course, posited the well-known "*Who* said *what* in *which channel* to *whom* with *what effect*," and Shannon and Weaver[8] listed source, transmitter, signal, receiver, and destination as primary ingredients in their analytic scheme which was intended to characterize communication in mathematical terms. Similarly, Schramm[9] referenced the elements of source, encoder, signal, decoder, destination.

The more elaborate "two-step flow" paradigm advanced by Katz and Lazarsfeld[10] evidenced a similar descriptive focus. In that definition, communication was conceived of in terms of messages flowing from impersonal sources to opinion leaders who in turn influenced nonleaders through interpersonal means. Riley and Riley[11] provided a scheme which integrated aspects of previous models yet maintained a primarily descriptive component orientation, though giving some attention to sociological processes, structures, and functions.

The models provided by Westley and MacLean,[12] and Berlo[13] were intended to focus more upon communication as a *process*,[14] and particularly the Westley-Maclean[15] model better accommodated the communicative implications of non-purposive behavior than had previous characterizations. Broadened in application and increased in sophistication, these two pervasive models further reflected, and no doubt contributed significantly to, the penchant for descriptive portrayal of communication.

Speech-communication schemes, while often considering more elements, have maintained a predominantly descriptive focus. Barker and Kibler[16] provide a useful compilation of the variety of dimensions in terms of which writers in speech communication have chosen to characterize and examine communication. Their list includes: verbal and nonverbal communication; interpersonal, intrapersonal, group, mass and cultural communication; oral and written communication; formal and informal communication; intentional and unintentional communication; and logical and emotional communication.[17]

Brooks,[18] in like manner, presents a taxonomy of communication which focuses upon verbal, interpersonal, nonverbal, dyadic, and small group communication, and utilizes the basic Lasswellian paradigm of an initiator, message, and recipient(s). Samovar and Mills[19] offer a model which also stresses the elements of encoder, message, channel, and receiver. Miller,[20] Becker,[21] and Hasling[22] similarly conceptualize communication descriptively in terms of a speaker, messages, and listener(s).

In mass communication, descriptive analysis and consequent emphasis upon specific components has perhaps been more pronounced than in the writings on speech-communication.[23] The "how-it-works" orientation has been manifest in the tendency to focus upon the technology of the mass media as if it were the same as the mass communication *phenomenon*. One finds, for example, the terms mass media and mass communication used more or less interchangeably in Barnouw,[24] Stephenson,[25] and DeFleur.[26] This same descriptive focus leads other popular authors to fail to differentiate conceptually between mass communications (messages), and mass communication. This is the case, for example, in Schramm;[27] Emery, Ault and Agee;[28] and Rivers, Peterson and Jensen.[29]

Typically stressing *channel*—and sometimes *message*—as opposed to *source* and *receiver,* such schemes for conceiving of communication (and mass communication) have both reflected and reinforced the descriptive orientation.

The writings of journalism, taken to a generic level of analysis, indicate a similar proclivity for descriptive analysis, although the focus is generally more upon the *message* than *source, channel,* or *receiver.* Hohenberg,[30] Brown,[31] and Charnley[32] are examples. The literature of persuasion, whether approached from speech, social psychology, or mass communication evidences this pattern also, as Miller and Burgoon[33] suggest by implication. The works of Rosnow and Robinson,[34] Bettinghaus,[35] and Rogers and Shoemaker[36] are illustrative.

Clearly, there has been a great deal of attention devoted to models explaining how *communication works.* Like the definition of the automobile in terms of its parts and how they work together, communication has been characterized largely by focusing upon *source, message, channel,* and *receiver* and operational interactions between them.

What is noticeably lacking are models of the phenomenon which utilize functional analyses of the sort Churchman suggests. Few researchers who conceive themselves (and are conceived by others) to be in the field of communication appear to be focusing their efforts in any direct fashion toward an exploration of the *functions* of communication—what it is for, and how it is used.

Functional Analysis in Human Communication Thought

There are no doubt various explanations for this imbalance. Some would argue that the attention given to descriptive analysis indicates the lack of appropriateness, validity, and/or utility of functional modes of characterization. Others would point out that findings of descriptive analysis seem to have a clearer relevance for communication practitioners (e.g., journalists, speakers, librarians, writers, announcers, managers, information system managers, counselors) and that directions of scholarship in the field have been impacted centrally by a desire for finding which will help the practitioner on an operational level. Others have suggested that the shape and direction of scholarship in communication has come about more by default—through socialization and homogenization of individuals entering the field—than by conscious choice.

For these and perhaps other reasons many—if not most—of those contributions which are most central to characterizing human communication in functional terms, have been provided by individuals whose work falls outside the boundaries of "the field" as it is generally defined in reviews of the literature in many major journals and volumes.

One such source of analysis of function in human communication is provided in the works of Berger,[37] Luckman,[38] Holzner,[39] and McHugh,[40] whose research focus upon the social origins of information and knowledge and functions of the informational relationships between the individual and social reality.

Other sociologists, including Goffman,[41] Duncan,[42] and Blumer,[43] have provided particularly useful analysis for understanding communication in terms of its social functions.

Another pertinent area is general semantics with its focus upon the functions of information for science and reality mapping. The work of Korzybski,[44] Johnson,[45] and Brown,[46] are especially relevant here.

Additionally, the general semanticists' interest in human information ecology has in many respects been complemented by work on the role of communication in human adjustment of Rogers;[47] Ruesch;[48] Bateson;[49] Watzlawick, Beavin, and Jackson;[50] Grinker,[51] Shands,[52] Speigel,[53] and Quill.[54]

Still another source of input for functional research on human communication and individual behavior comes from a group of scholars with a psychological background. The writings of Thayer;[55] Allport;[56] Church;[57]

Kelley;[58] Maslow;[59] Schroder, Driver and Streuffert;[60] and Lindsay and Norman[61] are among these contributions.

Other works, by individuals often not centrally associated with communication, and yet especially useful for conceiving of communication in functional terms, have been provided by Delgado,[62] Young,[63] Laszlo,[64] and Smith,[65] relative to the neurophysiological, biological, epistemological, and cultural functions of information for man.

Given this wide-ranging diversity, it is apparent that a functional approach to human communication would have, of necessity, a multi-disciplinary heritage. And to the extent that one seeks to develop a system paradigm that meets the criteria suggested by von Bertalanffy, Boulding, and Rapoport, as well as by Churchman, the framework must be valid and useful in cross-disciplinary application.

As a foundation for such a conceptualization of communication and communication systems, J. G. Miller's[66] view of information processing as one of two basic processes of living systems is especially valuable. Building on this notion, communication can be meaningfully defined as *the process of information metabolism,* and understood to be of parallel importance to living organisms as the processes involved in the metabolism of matter-energy. In this light, communication can be regarded as essential to the birth, growth, development, change, evolution, and survival or death of all that is human.[67]

To further refine one's scheme for categorizing the processes of information metabolism, and hence communication, the concept of *symbol* is important.[68] There are, for man, but two sorts of possible exchanges with the environment: those involving bio-physical transactions and those involving symbolic transactions. And in a number of instances the two operate conjunctively. While man is clearly not the only living organism that processes information about his milieu, nor is he the only animal who can be said to utilize language, man alone has the capacity for inventing, accumulating, and attaching meanings and significance—through symbols—to the entirety of his biophysical and social environment and to himself.

Unlike other non symbol-using animals, man uniquely has the capacity and the necessity of accumulating information cast in the form of knowledge, behavior and culture for diffusion to and inculcation among his contemporaries and members of subsequent generations. Further, unlike other non symbol-transacting animals, man alone has the capacity and therefore the necessity of acquiring membership in the various social collectivities upon which he depends solely through the identification and internalization of the significant symbols of the social unit.

The study of communication systems is, therefore, logically understood as the study of the role of symbols, symbolization, and symbol internaliza-

tion in the creation, maintenance, and change of all human individual and multi-individual organization.

In order to develop a communication system paradigm, it is therefore necessary to develop a scheme for categorizing information-metabolizing structures in terms of the symbolic processes involved. For present purposes, the first such classificatory unit will be labelled the *individual system* and the second, the *multi-individual system.*[69] In considering the former, the focus of this chapter will be upon what can be termed the *intrapersonal functions of human communication.* Examination of the multi-individual system will center on the *interpersonal and socio-cultural functions of human communication.* The processes at the first of these levels of analysis will be termed *personal communication,* and those at the second level, *social communication.*

Personal Communication

Personal communication can be thought of as sensing, making sense of, and acting toward the objects and people in one's milieu. It is the process by which the individual informationally fits himself in (adapts to and adapts) his environment.

As the individual organizes himself in and with his milieu, he develops ways of comprehending, seeing, hearing, understanding, and knowing his environment. Largely as a consequence of this process, no two individuals will view the objects or people in their environment in the same way.

What an individual becomes is therefore a function of having organized himself in particular ways with the objects and people in his milieu. Allport[70] describes this fundamental process of personality development as becoming. General semanticists refer to this process as abstracting and speak of it in terms of a mapping of the territory.[71] Thayer refers to this as in-formation.[72] In a neuro-physiological context one could think of personal communication as a process of intracerebral elaboration of extracerebral information.[73] Berger[74] characterizes the process as internalization.

From a variety of disciplinary viewpoints then, personal communication can be conceived of as that active process by which the individual comes to know and be in relationship in his world. Unlike lower animals who are genetically organized with their environments in relatively fixed and determinant ways, man must organize himself.[75] He can and must invent his rules for attaching significance and meaning to his milieu and the people in it. It is man's organize-ability which would seem to most clearly distinguish him from lower organisms, and which here serves to clarify the nature of *personal* communication.

The necessary condition for these complex adaptive functions may be termed *reality integration,* and understood to be a most basic and essential information metabolizing function of personal communication. It is simply that function which allows and compels the individual to organize himself with—to come to know, to map the territory—his milieu, and therefore to become what he is and will be.

Personal communication, and the *reality integration function* can be categorized based upon the particular adaptive functions subserved. Such a classification includes: (1) biological adaptation; (2) physical adaptation; (3) interpersonal adaptation; (4) sociocultural adaptation.

Biological Integration

Through personal communication an individual develops, maintains, and alters the knowledge and "maps" necessary for his biological functioning. He comes to understand procreation and with whom, where, when, and under what circumstances it is appropriate. With regard to the processes involved in the metabolism of matter-energy, he comes to know what, when, where, and how to eat and excrete wastes. Through personal communication the individual learns about those aspects of his physical and biological environment which may threaten his well-being as a living system. He also comes to understand what data he must gather, how the data are to be processed, and how decisions are to be made in order to avoid collision with other structures; some of which are stationary, and others having patterns and rates of movement he must discern.[76] Personal communication functions also to enable the development and assertion of the individual's identity and territoriality as a human creature distinct from, and yet dependent upon, all others of the species. This occurs through the use of symbolic and geographical distancing utilizing a wide range of symbolic markers such as beach blankets, houses, autos, clothes, perfumes, hair stylings, and so on.

Physical Integration

Personal communication also functions to enable the individual to develop, maintain, and alter his explanations of the *nonhuman objects* in his environment. For present purposes, it is meaningful to distinguish between physical matter which is contrived and that which is noncontrived. Within the category of contrived objects are those nonliving things which man has created, like cars, tools, buildings, furniture, and processes like sawing, lawn-mowing, writing, and so on. Personal communication also enables the individual to develop and maintain understandings of physical properties and processes such as the atmosphere, metabolism, geological structures, evolution, rivers, communication, plants, animals, living/dying as well as other substances and processes generally assumed not to be human in origin.

Interpersonal Integration

One increasingly popular research area regards the functions of personal communication through which the individual comes to conceive of people—himself and others. It is this function of personal communication that enables the individual to know who he thinks he is, what he is like and who and what others in his milieu are about.

Sociocultural Integration

One of the least familiar, yet centrally important functions of personal communication relates to the symbolic reality systems of the various multi-person organizations in which all individuals operate. It is through personal communication that the individual comes to know what is informationally and behaviorally expected of him if he is to participate in such collectivities as friendships, passengers on an elevator, families, clubs, fraternities, religious sects, political parties, professional and vocational groups, societies, and so on.

Personal communication functions to enable the individual to internalize, symbolically, the accepted organizational truths, operating principles, habits, norms, rituals, protocol, conventions, explicit and implicit goals, required competencies, ethical standards, laws, rules, and so on. He learns what most people seem to say, what most people seem to do, how they dress, and where he fits.

Of particular importance also is the learning personal communication affords relative to the accepted modes of explanation. In an organization of social scientists, for example, "science" provides the explanatory framework which one must learn. In another organization, a "religious" mode of explanation may be more popular.

A related function of personal communication regards an individual's symbol internalization of prescribed and prohibited behaviors, which are both implicit and explicit in nature. The individual learns the nature and price of membership, "the coinage of the realm," [77] the significant and sacred symbols, flags, words, behaviors and the consequences of failure to posture oneself in an organizationally consistent manner.

At the level of analysis of the individual system then, personal communication operates such that the individual is able to identify and internalize through symbolic information processing those biological, physical, interpersonal, and sociocultural realities necessary for him to adapt in his environment.

Social Communication

Social communication is the process underlying *intersubjectivization,* a phenomenon which occurs as a consequence of public symbolization and symbol utilization and diffusion. It is through this information metabolism process that the world we know is defined, labeled, and categorized, our knowledge of it shared and validated, and our behavior toward it and one another regularized and regulated. It is through this same process that multi-person organization, social order, control and predictability are achieved.[78] The most basic transaction of social communication is two or more individuals organizing with one another, knowingly or not, in an effort to adapt to or adapt their environment.[79]

Because of the nature of human communication—and personal communication—achieving this goal requires active participation in the invention, construction, and maintenance of a plethora of overlapping and non-overlapping organizations.[80] Organization through social communication varies from the relatively simple informational-behavioral interdependency patterns man creates and perpetuates with other passengers riding an elevator, to the extremely complex and varigated organization necessary to the emergence, continuity, and evolution of a society.

Clearly then, the specific consequences of social communication may vary greatly from one multi-person organization to the next in terms of complexity and function. The basic information metabolizing processes by which these organizations are initiated and maintained, however, do not. When people organize with one another, in an elevator, a friendship, or a society, they discover, create, and share informational and behavioral realities.[81] In so doing, the whole they define together becomes more than a simple sum of the parts. This discovery, creation, sharing, socialization process can be termed intersubjectivization. Were there no intersubjective reality structures, there could be no multi-person organization. Thus "values," "norms," "knowledge," and "culture" may all be viewed as instances of intersubjectivated realities, defined and diffused through social communication.

Considered in this light, reality definition, standardization, and diffusion can be viewed as both necessary and sufficient conditions for social organization and joint-adaptation, and may be understood to be the primary function of social communication. The process of social communication can be further delineated in terms of particular biological, physical, and socio-cultural functions.

Biological Definition

Through social communication, multi-individual organizations define, label, and standardize information-behavior patterns relative to a wide range of human biological functions. Intersubjectivizations, variously termed knowledge, norms, and rituals that relate to sexual and reproductive practices, food consumption and excretory functions, medical care and medication are exemplars. It is not the intention to detail specifics in each case here, and it is adequate simply to note the rather obvious point that within multi-person systems rather specific socially defined legal, medical, and normative guidelines are constructed and shared with regard to where, under what conditions and with whom sexual relations are appropriate. Similarly, conventions are created and maintained with regard to conventions of food procurement, preservation, and preparation as well as excretion. It is also clearly through social communication that both organic and psychological illness and health are defined, and labels created, agreed upon and attached to what are conceived to be maladies.[82] It is this same process by which strategies for treatment are invented, tested, applied or discarded, and validated.

Additionally, it is through social communication that both explicit and implicit rules for locomotion—time-place movement—are developed, standardized, and diffused. Rules for passing oncoming pedestrians and cars on the right rather than left, as well as conventions governing right-of-way, pedestrian crosswalks, and red lights on street signs are examples.

It is also through social communication that the concepts of personal space and protection and differentiation from the environment are defined and institutionalized, and methods for marking and separating territories invented and regularized.[83] Architecture plays a central role with regard to the institutionalization of this social communication function. The nature and placement of construction, size, accessibility, and location of boundaries within physical structures exemplify the process and consequences of intersubjectivization.[84] Related also are multi-individual system conventions as to whom and under what conditions several persons can appropriately inhabit a single structural domain, and customs developed pertaining to the use of boundaries (e.g., walks, windows, doors) to isolate or protect individuals within one dwelling (or portion of a dwelling) from individuals in another portion of that dwelling or another structure.

Physical Definition

Intersubjectivization with regard to geophysical and biophysical substances in an important function of social communication. It is through social communication that informational-behavioral orientations relative to substances like granite, telephones, water, and books, as well as plants and animals are defined, standardized, classified, and those intersubjectivizations perpetuated and validated.

Social communication functions such that biophysical and geophysical substances and processes are classifiable in a systematic taxonomical framework in which each substance is defined in terms of constituent subclasses and is itself categorized as one component of the next larger encompassing classification.[85] It is through these same processes that biophysical and geophysical phenomena like evolution or metabolism are discovered, defined, and shared. It should be noted also that the instruments by which these and other biophysical and geophysical definitions are validated are themselves products of social communication and standardization, as with the rock-hardness scale or the Richter Scale.

A distinct function of social communication is the invention, production, marketing, utilization, and validation of technological devices, manufactured products, and consumer goods in general.[86] Thus, social communication is as critical to the production and definition of books, automobiles, or typewriters as it is to systems for the metaorganization of information about them.[87]

Sociocultural Definition

It is through social communication that sociocultural patterns essential to the functioning of all multi-person systems are defined, standardized, and diffused. While specific consequences in terms of complexity and goals will vary from one multi-person unit to the next—from an organization consisting of passengers on an elevator, to a friendship, family, club, business organization, professional group, or society—the fundamental information metabolizing processes and often the functions subserved remain constant. Informational-behavioral patterns related to roles, rules, language-use patterns, values, habits, norms, appropriate jargon, protocol, ethics, aesthetics and even requisite vocational competencies are created, shared, and perpetuated through social communication.

Social communication performs another critical socio-cultural function involving the establishment and maintenance of particular organizational truths, operating principles, or belief structures around which a multi-person system is formed. It is also through social communication that a characteristic mode of explanation for the events that beset members of the collectivity are created, implemented, and validated. Religion and science each exemplify the notion of mode of explanation in the sense suggested here.[88] For each multi-person system, social communication allows for the creation, utilization, and institutionalization of significant symbols such as flags, trademarks, political campaign posters and buttons, dress or any organization-specific insignias which function to identify and differentiate one multi-person system from another.

Another critically important sociocultural function of social communication relates to the enabling of transactions between members of a system. It is through social communication that social currency, and hence an economy, becomes possible. Without intersubjectivization and hence shared concepts of intrinsic value, comparative value, and symbolic value, neither a barter system nor a token-utilizing economic system is achievable. Further, these same economic functions may be said to be subserved in even the simplest multi-person systems such as friendships, where the coinage of the realm—the means of transaction—may be understood to be language and nonverbal symbols rather than more familiar monetary markers.

Mass Communication

The institutionalization, by multi-person systems, of the processes by which informational-behavioral patterns are diffused and perpetuated, may be termed *mass communication*. Such a definition, it should be noted, suggests that the mass communication process is neither media centered, nor purposive in the sense most definitions imply. Rather, mass communication is conceptualized in terms of function served rather than mode of transmission, size or nature of an audience, or goals of a communicator.

Thusly viewed, mass communication is an aspect of social communication; it serves the diffusion function necessary for intersubjectivization. By this definition, restaurants, schools, churches, supermarkets, highways, the clothing industry, and political campaigns are defined as mass communication institutions along with the mass media, theatre, museums, art galleries, and libraries in that all serve a reality diffusion and intersubjectivization function. A related function of mass communication pertains to the perpetuation function, which may be thought of in terms of time and space binding.[89] Through the institutionalization of diffusion processes, informational-behavioral realities are perpetuated across time, geographical distances, new members of multi-person systems, and new generations.

Transactions

Social communication, it has been said, is fundamental to the definition, categorization, and standardization of information-behavioral patterns; mass communication is essential to their diffusion; personal communication to the manner in which they are sensed, made sense of, and acted upon by the individual. Clearly, these three functions are not accomplished by independent activities, but rather operate in a continuous, interpenetrating, transactional fashion.

● ● ●

The information metabolizing functions of informational-behavioral *definition, standardization, diffusion,* and *integration* are as basic to the *in-*

dividual–multi-individual suprasystem, as sensing, making sense of, and acting toward are to the individual system and defining, standardizing, and diffusing are to the multi-person system. Implied is that what an individual becomes and can become is largely a consequence of how he or she organizes with the informational-behavioral patterns and demands of his or her milieu. Implied also is that the patterns with which the individual organized are consequences of the activities of multi-person system information metabolizing processes, which in turn, are a consequence of the social synthesis of the individual behaviors of its constituent members. Thus . . . society can be viewed as a multi-person communication system and understood to be defined and perpetuated by the behaviors of citizens. Information necessary for the individual citizens to adapt is provided by the multi-person system and digested and acted upon by the individual citizens, such as to continually redefine the society for themselves and one another. . . .

Conclusion

This, then, is the basic paradigm. In sum, the perspective developed provides a view of human enterprise as a complex network of functionally interrelated individuals in multi-individual systems, who, through the information metabolizing processes of intrapersonal, interpersonal and mass communication, enable and constrain, satisfy and frustrate, create and destroy, change and not, in all that is human.

The view of communication systems which emerges draws heavily on many fundamental open systems concepts, particularly multi-lateral causality, equi-finality, multi-finality, functionality, dynamic stabilization, organic growth and change, and interdependent, hierarchically ordered levels of organization. Basic notions of symbolic interaction, general semantics, transactional psychology, and sociology of knowledge are also heavily utilized.

While far from comprehensive in its present form, the paradigm would seem also to satisfy the systems criteria of cross-disciplinary validity and interdisciplinary applicability, and in this sense may serve as an outline for the subsequent development of more elaborate and detailed operational models.

Notes

1. C. West Churchman, *The Systems Approach,* New York: Delacorte, 1968.
2. This point is presented and discussed by Richard F. Hixson, "Mass Media: An Approach to Human Communication," *Approaches to Human Com-*

munication, Richard W. Budd and Brent D. Ruben, eds., Rochelle Park, N.J.: Hayden Book Co. (Spartan), 1972.

3. Harold D. Lasswell, "The Structure and Function of Communication in Society," *The Communication of Ideas*, Bryson Lyman, ed., Institute for Religion and Social Studies, 1948. Reprinted in *Mass Communications*, Wilbur Schramm, ed., Urbana, Ill.: University of Illinois Press, 1960, 1966, pp. 117–130.

4. Claude Shannon and Warren Weaver, *The Mathematical Theory of Communication*, Urbana, Ill.: University of Illinois Press, 1949.

5. Wilbur Schramm, "How Communication Works," *The Process and Effects of Mass Communication*, Wilbur Schramm, ed., Urbana, Ill.: University of Illinois Press, 1960, 1966, pp. 3–26.

6. This point is discussed by John Hasling, *The Message, The Speaker, The Audience*, New York: McGraw-Hill, 1971, pp. 2–3.

7. Harold D. Lasswell, "The Structure and Function of Communication in Society," p. 225.

8. Claude Shannon and Warren Weaver, *The Mathematical Theory of Communication*, Urbana, Ill: University of Illinois Press, 1949. *See also* Donald K. Darnell, "Information Theory: An Approach to Human Communication," *Approaches to Human Communication*, Rochelle Park, N.J.: Hayden Book Co. (Spartan), 1972.

9. Wilbur Schramm, "How Communication Works," *The Process and Effects of Mass Communication*, Wilbur Schramm, ed., Urbana: University of Illinois Press, 1960, 1966, pp. 3–26.

10. Elihu Katz and Paul F. Lazarsfeld, *Personal Influence*, New York: Free Press, 1960. *See also* earlier work of Paul Lazarsfeld, Bernard Berelson, and Hazel Gaudet, *The People's Choice*, New York: Columbia University Press, 1944, 1948. Discussion by Bernard Berelson, "Communication and Public Opinion," *The Process and Effects of Mass Communication*, Wilbur Schramm, ed., 1954, 1965, pp. 343–356, and Elihu Katz, "The Two-Step Flow of Communication," *Mass Communications*, Wilbur Schramm, ed., pp. 346–365.

11. John W. Riley, Jr. and Matilda White Riley, "A Sociological Approach to Mass Communication," *Sociology Today*, Robert K. Merton, Leonard Broom and Leonard S. Cottrell, Jr., eds., Basic Books, 1959. *See* "Sociology: An Approach to Human Communication," *Approaches to Human Communication*, Rochelle Park, N.J.: Hayden Book Co. 1972.

12. Bruce H. Westley and Malcolm S. MacLean, Jr., "A Conceptual Model for Communication Research," *Journalism Quarterly*, Vol. 34, 1957, pp. 31–38.

13. David K. Berlo, *The Process of Communication*, New York: Holt, Rinehart and Winston, 1960.

14. An excellent discussion of the status of "process" in conceptualizations of communication is provided in "Communication Research and the Idea of Process," by David H. Smith, *Speech Monographs*, August 1972. Smith argues that most models of communication which have purported to integrate the process concept have generally failed in their attempts.

15. The Westley-MacLean model is referenced in most contemporary communication volumes. *See* for example, discussion in *Communication—The Study of Human Interaction*, C. David Mortensen, New York: McGraw-Hill, 1972. An excellent critical discussion of the Westley-MacLean, Berlo, and other popular models of communication provided by John Y. Kim in "Feed-

back and Human Communication: Toward a Reconceptualization," an un-published doctoral dissertation, University of Iowa, 1971.

16. Larry L. Barker and Robert J. Kibler, *Speech Communication Behavior,* Englewood Cliffs, N.J.: Prentice-Hall, 1971.

17. Ibid. pp. 3–8.

18. William D. Brooks, *Speech Communication,* Dubuque, Iowa: W. C. Brown, 1972.

19. Larry A. Samovar and Jack Mills, *Oral Communication,* Dubuque, Iowa: W. C. Brown, 1968, 1972, pp. 3–5.

20. Gerald R. Miller, *An Introduction to Speech Communication,* Indianapolis, Ind.: Bobbs-Merrill, 1972, p. 58. *See also* Gerald Miller, "Speech: An Approach to Human Communication," *Approaches to Human Communication,* Rochelle Park, N.J.: Hayden Book Co., 1972.

21. Samuel L. Becker, "What Rhetoric (Communication Theory) Is Relevant for Contemporary Speech Communication?" presented at the University of Minnesota, 1968, Spring Symposium on Speech-Communication.

    A presentation of the model with discussion is also provided in C. David Mortensen, *Communication—The Study of Human Interaction,* New York: McGraw-Hill, 1972, pp. 46–48.

22. J. Hasling, *The Message, the Speaker, The Audience,* New York: McGraw-Hill, 1971, pp. 3–5.

23. It is interesting to note that although descriptive component-oriented analysis predominates in both speech and mass communication, there is remarkably little evidence of conceptual cross-fertilization between these disciplines despite some rather obvious philosophical and operational similarities.

24. Erik Barnouw, *Mass Communication,* New York: Holt, Rinehart and Winston, 1956. That mass communication is understood to be defined in terms of the mass media (channel component) is suggested by the subtitle of this volume: "Television, Radio, Film, Press." The point is underscored in Section 1 entitled "The History of Mass Communication," which consists of the following chapters: "The Paper Tide," "The Moving Image," "Signals in the Air," and "Of Words and Mousetraps."

25. William Stephenson, *The Play Theory of Mass Communication,* Chicago: University of Chicago Press, 1967. Stephenson begins Chapter 1, "Two New Theories of Mass Communication Research," as follows:

> From its beginnings, in 1924 or so, mass communication theory has concerned itself primarily with how the mass media influence the attitudes, beliefs, and actions of people. There was little evidence up to 1959, however, that the mass media had any significant effects on the deeper or more important beliefs of people . . .
> . . . it is the thesis of this book that at its best mass communication allows people to become absorbed in *subjective play.* People read newspapers, magazines, and paperbacks in vast numbers, and there are ever increasing audiences for movies, radio, records, and television.

26. Melvin L. DeFleur, *Theories of Mass Communication,* New York: McKay, 1966, 1970. While DeFleur argues initially that mass communication is a special case of communication, five of the eight chapters in the volume focus on the mass media.

27. Wilbur Schramm, *Mass Communication*, Urbana, Ill.: University of Illinois Press, 1960, 1966.

On page 3, Schramm says:

> When did mass communication begin? The date usually given is that of the beginning of printing from movable metal type, in Western Europe in the fifteenth century, but the roots are much earlier and the flowering much later.
>
> The *mass media* are the resultant forces set in motion when groups of manlike animals first huddled together against the cold and danger of primitive times. . . . In Korea, where they had paper, ink and metal type first, conditions were not ripe for the growth of *mass communication;* in Western Europe, when Gutenberg began to print, society was more nearly ready to develop *the new device.* (italics added)

The volume includes sections on "The Structure and Function of Mass Communications" which consists of articles by Lasswell, Lerner, Breed, and others about the structure and function of *mass communication* as a process.

In other sections, such as "The Development of Mass Communications," Schramm seems clearly to be referring to the development of the *mass media.* In yet another section, "Responsibility for Mass Communication," references are to *messages.*

28. Edwin Emery, Philip H. Ault, and Warren K. Agee, *Introduction to Mass Communications*, New York: Dodd, Mead, 1960, 1965, 1970. Of the 18 chapters in the volume, 13 are devoted to the mass media.

29. William L. Rivers, Theodore Peterson, and Jay W. Jensen, *The Mass Media and Modern Society*, New York: Holt, Rinehart, and Winston, 1971. On page 16, the authors state:

> Today one can more correctly speak of "mass communications" than of "journalism" when referring to media other than newspapers and magazines. In a sense, of course, every *communication* uses some medium, is committed to some channel for transmission. The letterhead or sheet of notepaper in correspondence, the sound waves utilized in conversation—these are channels or media. But in *mass communication,* a whole institution becomes the message carrier—a newspaper, a magazine, a broadcasting station . . .
>
> The term *mass communication* has sometimes been defined in two ways: *communication by the media* and *communication for the masses.* *Mass communication,* however, does not mean communication for everyone. (italics added)

The term "mass media" is used in the book to refer to channel, source, message, and sometimes receiver(s), as well. Included in the volume, for example, are chapters entitled "The Media as Persuaders" and "The Media as Informers and Interpreters."

30. John Hohenberg, *The Professional Journalist*, New York: Holt, Rinehart, and Winston, 1960, 1969.

31. Lee Brown, "Journalism: An Approach to Human Communication," *Approaches to Human Communication*, Rochelle Park, N.J.: Hayden Book Co. (Spartan), 1972.

32. Mitchell V. Charnley, *Reporting*, New York: Holt, Rinehart, and Winston, 1959, 1966.
33. Gerald R. Miller and Michael Burgoon, *New Techniques in Persuasion*, New York: Harper and Row, 1973, pp. 1–3.
34. Ralph L. Rosnow and Edward J. Robinson, *Experiments in Persuasion*, New York: Academic Press, 1967.
35. Erwin P. Bettinghaus, *Persuasive Communication*, New York: Holt, Rinehart, and Winston, 1968.
36. Everett M. Rogers and E. Floyd Shoemaker, *Communication of Innovations*, New York: Free Press, 1971. A related discussion is provided by Everett Rogers in *Communication and Social Change*, Rochelle Park, N.J.: Hayden Book Co.
37. Peter L. Berger and Thomas Luckmann, *The Social Construction of Reality*, Garden City: Doubleday, 1966 and Peter L. Berger in *The Sacred Canopy*, Garden City: Doubleday, 1969.
38. Peter L. Berger and Thomas Luckmann, *The Social Construction of Reality*, Garden City: Doubleday, 1966.
39. Burkart Holzner, *Reality Construction in Society*, Cambridge, Mass.: Schenkman, 1966.
40. Peter McHugh, *Defining the Situation*, Indianapolis, Ind.: Bobbs-Merrill, 1968. The central concepts undergirding the frameworks of Berger Luckmann, Holzner, and McHugh are reflective of the contributions of Schutz, Sorokin, Scheler, Mannheim, and Durkheim to the study of epistemology and the "sociology of knowledge."

    A discussion of their work and of the sociology of knowledge in general, is provided by Robert Merton in *Social Theory and Social Structure*, New York: Free Press, 1949, 1957, 1968, pp. 510–562. *See also* Werner Stark, *The Sociology of Knowledge*, London: Routledge and Kegan Paul, 1958, 1960, 1967, and W. J. H. Sprott, *Science and Social Action*, London: Watts, 1954, 1961.
41. Of the contributions of Erving Goffman, *Relations in Public*, New York: Basic Books, 1971; *Interaction Ritual*, Garden City: Doubleday, 1967; *The Presentation of Self in Everyday Life*, Garden City: Doubleday, 1959; and *Strategic Interaction*, Philadelphia: University of Pennsylvania, 1969, are most particularly relevant.
42. Hugh D. Ducan, *Symbols in Society*, London: Oxford University, 1968; *Communication and Social Order*, Oxford University, 1962; and *Symbols and Social Theory*, New York: Oxford University, 1969.
43. Herbert Blumer, *Symbolic Interactionism*, Englewood Cliffs: Prentice-Hall, 1969. Portions appear as "Symbolic Interaction: An Approach to Human Communication," *Approaches to Human Communication*, Rochelle Park, N.J.: Hayden Book Co., 1972.
44. Alfred Korzybski, *Science and Sanity*, Lakeville, Conn.: International Non-Aristotelian Library, 1933, 1948. *See also* discussion by Richard W. Budd, in "General Semantics: An Approach to Human Communication," *Approaches to Human Communication*, and *Communication: General Semantics Perspectives*, Lee Thayer ed., Rochelle Park, N.J.: Hayden Book Co., 1970.
45. Wendell Johnson, *People in Quandaries*, New York: Harper, 1946 and *Coping With Change* (Wendell Johnson and Dorothy Moeller), New York: Harper and Row, 1972.

46. Roger Brown, *Words and Things,* New York: Free Press, 1958, 1968.
47. Of Carl Rogers many contributions, *On Becoming a Person,* Boston: Houghton-Mifflin, 1961, and *Encounter Groups,* New York: Harper and Row, 1970, are particularly relevant as input for analysis of function in communication.
48. Major summary contributions of Jurgen Ruesch include *Communication: The Social Matrix of Society* (with Gregory Bateson), New York: Norton, 1951, 1968; *Nonverbal Communication* (with Veldon Kees), Stanford: University of California, 1956, 1972; *Therapeutic Communication,* New York: Norton, 1961; and *Disturbed Communication,* New York: Norton, 1957, 1972.
49. Major summary contributions of Gregory Bateson include *Communication: The Social Matrix of Society* (with Jurgen Ruesch), New York: Norton 1951, 1968; and *Steps to an Ecology of the Mind,* New York: Ballantine Books, 1972.
50. Paul Watzlawick, Janet Beavin, and Don D. Jackson, *Pragmatics of Human Communication,* New York:: Norton, 1967.
51. Roy R. Grinker, Sr., *Toward a Unified Theory of Human Behavior,* New York: Basic Books, 1956, 1967.
52. Harley C. Shands, *Thinking and Psychotherapy,* Cambridge, Mass.: Harvard University Press, 1960.
53. John Spiegel, *Transactions,* New York: Science House, 1971.
54. Quill, William G., *Subjective Psychology,* Rochelle Park, N.J.: Hayden Book Co., 1972.
55. Major summary contributions of Lee Thayer especially relevant for functional analysis of communication: *Communication and Communication Systems,* Homewood, Ill: Irwin, 1968; "Communication—*Sine Qua Non* of the Behavioral Sciences," *Vistas in Science,* D. L. Arm, ed., Albuquerque: University of New Mexico, 1968; *Communication: Concepts and Perspectives,* Rochelle Park, N.J.: Hayden Book Co., 1967; *Communication: Theory and Research,* Springfield, Ill.: Thomas, 1967; "Communication and the Human Condition," prepared for the VII Semana de Estudios Sociales "Mass Communication and Human Understanding" Instituto de Siencias Sociales, Barcelona, Spain, November, 1969; "Communication and Change," *Communication and Social Change,* Rochelle Park, N.J.: Hayden Book Co., "On Communication and Change: Some Provocations," *Systematics,* Vol. 6, No. 3, December, 1968; "On Human Communication and Social Development," presented at the first World Conference on Social Communication for Development, Mexico City, March, 1970.
56. Gordon W. Allport, *Becoming,* New Haven: Yale University, 1955.
57. Joseph Church, *Language and the Discovery of Reality,* New York: Vintage Books, 1961.
58. George A. Kelly, *A Theory of Personality,* New York: Norton, 1955, 1963.
59. Abraham H. Maslow, *Toward a Psychology of Being,* New York: Van Nostrand, 1968, and *Motivation and Personality,* New York: Harper and Row, 1954, 1970.
60. Harold M. Schroder, Michael J. Driver, and Seigfried Streufert, *Human Information Processing,* New York: Holt, Rinehart, and Winston, 1967.
61. Peter H. Lindsay and Donald A. Norman, *Human Information Processing,* New York: Academic Press, 1972.
62. José M. R. Delgado, *Physical Control of the Mind,* New York: Harper and

Row, 1969, portions of which appear as "Neurophysiology: An Approach to Human Communication," *Approaches to Human Communication,* Rochelle Park, N.J.: Hayden Book Co., 1972.

63. J. Z. Young, *Doubt and Certainty in Science,* Oxford University, 1970, and "Biology: An Approach to Human Communication," *Approaches to Human Communication,* Rochelle Park, N.J.: Hayden Book Co., 1972.

64. Particularly relevant contributions of Ervin Laszlo include *System, Structure and Experience,* New York: Gordon and Breach, 1969, *The World System,* New York: Braziller, 1972, and "Basic Concepts of Systems Philosophy" in this volume.

65. Of the numerous contributions of Alfred G. Smith, *Communication and Culture,* New York: Holt, Rinehart, and Winston, 1966, "Anthropology: An Approach to Human Communication," *Approaches to Human Communication,* Rochelle Park, N.J.: Hayden Book Co. and "Change, Channels and Trust," *Communication and Social Change,* Rochelle Park, N.J.: Hayden Book Co. (in preparation) are especially relevant.

66. James G. Miller, "Living Systems," *Behavioral Science,* Vol. 10, 1965, p. 338.

67. *Cf.* Lee Thayer, *Communication and Communication Systems,* Homewood, Ill.: Irwin, 1968, p. 17.

68. *Cf.* Kenneth Boulding, "General System Theory—Skeleton of Science," *Management Science,* Vol. 2, 1956, edited and included as Chapter 2 of this volume.

69. Additional discussion of the concepts of individual and multi-person systems is provided on pp. 137–140 "General System Theory: An Approach to Human Communication," *Approaches to Human Communication,* Rochelle Park, N.J.: Hayden Book Co., 1972.

70. Gordon W. Allport, *Becoming,* New Haven: Yale University, 1955.

71. Alfred Korzybski, *Science and Sanity,* Lakeville, Conn.: International Non-Aristotelian Library, 1933, 1948; Wendell Johnson, *People in Quandaries,* New York: Harper, 1946 and Richard W. Budd, "General Semantics: An Approach to Human Communication," *Approaches to Human Communication,* Rochelle Park, N.J.: Hayden Book Co., 1972.

72. Lee Thayer, "On Human Communication and Social Development," a paper presented at the first World Conference on Social Communication for Development, Mexico City, March, 1970.

73. Jose M. R. Delgado, *Physical Control of the Mind,* New York: Harper and Row, 1969 especially Ch. 5–7. See "Neurophysiology: An Approach to Human Communication," *Approaches to Human Communication,* Rochelle Park, N.J.: Hayden Book Co., 1972.

74. Peter Berger and Thomas Luckman, *The Social Construction of Reality,* Garden City: Doubleday, 1966; and Peter Berger, *The Sacred Canopy,* Garden City, Doubleday 1969, Ch. 1.

75. *Cf.* Anatol Rapoport, "Man—The Symbol-User," *Communication: Ethical and Moral Issues,* Lee Thayer, ed., New York: Gordon and Breach, 1973.

76. *Cf.* Erving Goffman, *Relations in Public,* New York: Basic Books, 1971. Ch. 1.

77. A phrase for which I am indebted to David Davidson.

78. *Cf.* Hugh D. Duncan, *Symbols in Society,* London: Oxford University, 1968. *Communication and Social Order,* Oxford University, 1962, and *Symbols and Social Theory,* New York: Oxford University, 1969.

79. *Cf.* Anatol Rapoport, "Man, The Symbol-User," *Communication: Ethical and Moral Issues,* New York: Gordon and Breach, 1973.

80. Lower-order animals function in some rather sophisticated multi-individual collectivities, but the nature of those organizations and the requisite individual roles are usually genetically predetermined and highly predictable. In contradistinction, human communication makes possible—in fact requires—active participation in these processes.

81. *Cf.* Herbert Blumer, *Symbolic Interactionism,* Englewood Cliffs: Prentice-Hall, 1969 and "Symbolic Interaction: An Approach to Human Communication," *Approaches to Human Communication,* Rochelle Park, N.J.: Hayden Book Co.

82. *Cf.* Paul Watzlawick et al., *Pragmatics of Human Communication,* New York: Norton, 1967; R. D. Laing, *The Politics of Experience,* London: Penguin, and Thomas Szasz, *The Manufacture of Madness,* New York: Harper and Row, 1970. An interesting example of the point was provided at an annual conference of the American Psychological Association, held in April 1974, where by a majority vote, it was determined that homosexuality is no longer an illness.

83. *Cf.* Erving Goffman, *Relations in Public,* New York: Basic Books, 1971, Ch. 2.

84. *Cf.* Christian Norberg-Schulz, *Existence, Space and Architecture,* New York: Praeger, 1971 and *Shelter: The Cave Re-examined,* Don Fabun, Beverly Hills: Glencoe Press, 1971.

85. *Cf.* Albert Upton, *Design for Thinking,* Stanford: Stanford University Press, 1961 and *Creative Analysis* (with Richard W. Samson), New York: E. P. Dutton, 1961.

86. *Cf.* Alfred G. Smith, in "Anthropology: An Approach to Human Communication," and Bent Stidsen, "Economics: An Approach to Human Communication," *Approaches to Human Communication,* Rochelle Park, N.J.: Hayden Book Co., 1972.

87. *Cf.* Magorah Maruyama, "Metaorganization of Information," *General Systems Yearbook,* Society for General Systems Research, Vol. XI, 1966.

88. *Cf.* Wendell Johnson and Dorothy Moeller, *Coping With Change,* New York: Harper and Row, 1972, pp. 3–55, a discussion of "scientific" versus "magic" explanation. For an exploration of religious explanations, see Peter Berger, *The Sacred Canopy,* Garden City: Doubleday, 1969.

89. *Cf.* Richard W. Budd, "General Semantics: An Approach to Human Communication," *Approaches to Human Communication,* Rochelle Park, N.J.: Hayden Book Co., 1972.

2

Media, Intimacy,
and Interpersonal Networks

In "The Veldt," a short story by Ray Bradbury, the Nursery is a room in the future in which dreams and fantasies become reality. In this room the children are transported to any place in any time. Of late the children have been spending more and more time on the African veldt with its herds of wild beasts. The parents are anxious because the children are spending all their time in the Nursery. The father is discussing the effects of the Nursery on his children with a friend. The friend advises him,

> where before they had a Santa Claus [for a father] now they have a Scrooge. Children prefer Santa. You've let this room and this house replace you and your wife in your children's affections. This room is their mother and father, far more important in their lives than their real parents. And now you come along and want to shut it off. No wonder there's hatred here. You can feel it coming out of the sky. Like too many others, you've built it around creature comforts. Why, you'd starve tomorrow if something went wrong in your kitchen. You wouldn't know how to tap an egg. Nevertheless, turn everything off. Start new. It'll take time. But we'll make good children out of bad in a year, wait and see.[1]

This story of the future is interesting for what it reveals about media and interpersonal relationships. We find "The Veldt" intriguing because it implicitly relates the sophisticated media environment of the future with our private fears and dreams. The Nursery can turn our deepest fantasy into reality—a reality that leaves nothing to the imagination. "The Veldt" is interesting also because of what it implies about travel, space and privacy. Toward the end of the story the friend, Mr. Mclean, sees the two children seated in the Nursery having a picnic. He asks for their parents. The children answer, "They'll be here directly." "Good, we must get along," replied Mr. Mclean. In the distance he sees the lions fighting and clawing and then quieting down to feed in silence under shady trees. The story ends a paragraph or so later and we are left thinking about our own nurseries and the shocking possibilities.

FEIFFER

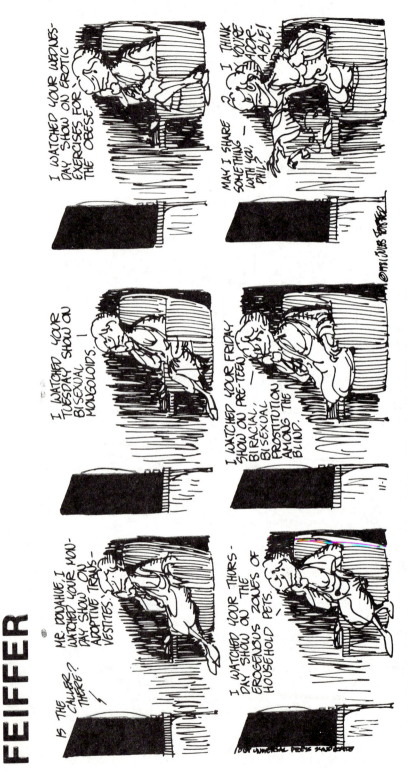

Media Transcend Time and Space

One of the implications of Bradbury's short story is that media are doing terrible things to us. This is a misconception, but one that is quite common among media critics. It is the thing to be said: the media are doing bad things, good things, things, but certainly things are being done to us. It is an error to blame the media for everything we dislike, but it is not wrong to recognize our own confusion about the media, because media themselves create ambivalent and often contradictory relationships.

To exist in a media world requires an understanding of a number of contradictions which confound our concepts of time and space. For example, how can you be in two places at the same time? A simple answer is, give your friends a photograph of yourself. In the process by which media connect and transcend time and space our sense of personal space is altered and our spacial relationships are modified. In this section we explore the consequences of the changes in our concept of geographical and personal space resulting from the use of media to connect us with almost anyone, any place on the globe, and even on the moon.

We began this section with a fictional encounter of the future. Let us contrast that with a realistic encounter which occurred several years ago, but which then seemed like science fiction. On May 31, 1965, one of the editors of this book participated in the first intercontinental TV classroom exchange.[2] It took place between the United States and France. A French class at the West Bend High School, Wisconsin, assembled with its teacher at the unusual hour of 7:00 A.M. on the Memorial Day holiday. It is probable that only an international "incident" would entice students into school during a holiday.

On that particular morning, the class was to be combined for one hour with its counterpart at the Lycée Henri IV of Paris. The interconnection was accomplished by means of the Early Bird Satellite, with the TV unit of the University of Wisconsin handling the video and audio pick-up in the West Bend classroom. The signals from cameras and microphones were sent across the country by microwave to Andover, Maine (the North America ground station of the Communications Satellite Corporation).

At Andover, the picture and sound signals were transmitted 22,300 miles out into space to the Early Bird Communications Satellite which is a synchronous (stationary) orbiting instrument located above the Equator between Africa and South America. The signals were received by Early Bird and retransmitted 22,300 miles back to earth to be received at a European ground station located at Plemeur-Bodou, France. It was here that the American television picture consisting of 525 scan lines was translated to a French television picture consisting of 819 scan lines. The picture was then transmitted to the classroom of the Lycée Henri IV.

The French Broadcasting System had their cameras and microphones located in the classroom. The sound pictures originating there followed in reverse the same 47,000 mile route just described. Remember that this is almost twice the distance around the earth. When the hour-long class began it was

7:30 A.M. in West Bend and 1:30 P.M. in Paris. The American students spoke in French, the French students in English.

While such TV classrooms have not become commonplace, we have become accustomed to daily satellite communication. Print, radio, telephone, television and photography are transmitted via satellite without concern for geographic boundaries. The students in West Bend, Wisconsin and Paris, France spoke to each other only vaguely aware that they were separated by 3000 miles. The matter of 47,000 miles was never a consideration. The miles dissolved into mediated interpersonal relationships and the students' lives were changed by their participation in an event which altered their view of world geography. Think of that American student at home after this Trans-Atlantic experience, "I spoke to Jean in Paris today. He was wearing a Beatles button." "But you weren't in Paris, you never left Wisconsin." The argument is soon resolved, but the implications for interpersonal relationships are startling.

The Paradox of Communication

We became space travelers with Samuel Morse's invention of the telegraph. It allowed the sender/receiver to transcend space technically and symbolically. All subsequent inventions of media facilitated instantaneous transmission over time and space. (The word "television" is a derivation of the Greek word "tele," meaning at a distance, and the Latin verb "video," meaning "I see.")

Whether we are talking about sounds conveyed over a great distance or seeing and hearing over great distances, the model is always two individuals attempting to communicate with each other. There is no medium that cannot be used for interpersonal communication. There is no medium that cannot be used for mass communication. The telephone can be used to broadcast to many people. The television can unite two people in a dyadic relationship. It all depends on the intent of the sender and the choice of the receiver. In either case the function is to eliminate space and alter time.

Media affects how we relate to others and the circumstances in which those relationships exist. Is it necessary to visit a relative when a telephone call will do just as well? Why go to the trouble of going to a concert, or a drama or sports event? Space can be transcended by media and we can participate in relative comfort. Richard Sennett in *The Fall of Public Man* points out that electronic communication is one means by which the very idea of the "public" man has been put to an end. It is wrong though to believe that media alone are responsible for our loss of contact and intimacy. Sennett states the case clearly:

> the impulses to withdraw from public life began long before the advent of these machines; they are not infernal devices, according to the usual scenario of technological monster; they are tools invented by men to fulfill human needs. The needs which the electronic media are fulfilling are those cultural

impulses that formed over the whole of the last century and a half to withdraw from social interaction in order to know and feel more as a person.
These machines are part of the arsenal between social interaction and personal
experience.[3]

We can see the formation of a strange paradox suggested by Sennett and intrinsic to media—the paradox of isolation and visibility. The potential for interpersonal networks has been extended beyond the barriers of space and
time. An environment in which we talk to each other and see each other while
we are actually in the presence of the other is no longer necessary to interpersonal communication. This has produced a confusing paradox. Interpersonal intimacy has traditionally entailed physical nad psychological closeness.
We could be intimate only with those that we could be close to, physically
and emotionally. As Edward T. Hall has pointed out in his works on nonverbal
communication,[4] we actually divide personal space into intimate and social
distance depending on how close we allow others to come.

The media, however, have made it necessary to rethink what we mean by
space and environment. Space, defined as distance, is not relevant to a telephone call (until we receive the bill from the telephone company). There was
a time not so long ago when a long distance call was accompanied by a lot of
transmission noise. But every now and then the call would come through
with such clarity that one would say, "It sounds like you're in the next room."
It is now commonplace to extend our psychological, intimate selves as the
physical space between ourselves and others has become irrelevant. If you
live in an urban community, the chances are that you know very little about
your neighbors, but are "intimate" with persons who live far from your
neighborhood. It is likely that you have not visited a relative who lives in the
same city in the recent past, but that you have seen Johnny Carson, Merv
Griffin, and Dick Cavett, among others, on a regular basis. This is not meant
to chastise, but to point out the paradoxical effects that media have on all our
close relationships. Now, we are all space travelers.

It is difficult to resist the temptation to pass judgment on the effects of
media on our relationships. It takes a bit of a struggle to stay away from the
"technology as monster" type of analysis. We must recognize that there is a
mixture of positive and negative elements influencing our interpersonal communication when it is mediated communication; that is, dependent upon
media for completion.

Think of a very intimate relationship: the one with your doctor.

In the near future automated histories may be taken with the patient being
present before a computer. A patient can press the appropriate pushbutton
on a Touch-Tone telephone in response to questions generated orally from
a central computer console. The verbal questions emanating from the machine
are prerecorded, and they, like the visual displays on the cathode ray tube,
branch, depending upon the patient's answers. In the more distant future computers will be able to participate in a verbal dialogue with the patient.[5]

Which is more important to you: an intimate give-and-take relationship between yourself and the family doctor, or an efficient, accurate encounter with a talking computer? Be careful with your answer. A doctor can make a mistake or be influenced by his emotions, but the computer does not make errors. What will you risk?

The Expansion of Space and Nonphysical Intimacy

Each of us has a common set of expectations regarding interpersonal relationships. That is, we share a model of behavior in which participants expect to process the actions and reactions of other persons using the full complement of senses. It is also obvious that face-to-face interaction occurs only where the participants physically inhabit contiguous space.

The media relationships made possible by the interposition of typographical, iconic, and electronic media are distinctly different from the face-to-face relationship in several ways: by the elimination of the need for contiguity, by the shifting emphasis of sensory modes, and by the development of unique relationships that are media based—that is, without the medium the relationship would not exist. Thus, the telephone represents a relationship based solely upon the use of the auditory sense with the other senses—touch, sight, smell, and taste temporarily placed in reserve.

Obviously it is possible for relationships to be established with individuals who have never shared a contiguous place. We accept, sometimes even prefer, intimate relationships facilitated by media in which physical presence is not only absent, but is a prerequisite. It is probably true that at one time the motivation for all mediated communication was the transcendence of time and space to accommodate the limitations of place. The evolution of media technology has brought about the extraordinary separation of place from communication. Whereas formerly communication could occur only within the context of a place, place has become irrelevant as space has been bridged by the media. Each of us participates in media relationships in which we do not know where the other person is, nor does it matter. The telephone company provides the 800 number in order to facilitate transactions that do not require a place for completion. At one time we thought of radio and television in terms of the places from which the signals emanated. Satellite communication and cable connection have antiquated that notion. Now there is no space on earth far enough away to be insulated from the media of communication. The unusual has become the normal. The irony is that what counts is connection, not the places connected. We have made possible nonphysical intimacy, an intimacy that requires no face-to-face contact.

When you become aware of your place in a media-dependent world, the confusion between negative and positive effects of media appears. It is marvelous that our interpersonal networks are not limited by distance. But does intimacy over distance suggest any negative features? That is not easy to answer. Let's look at a letter from the poet Dylan Thomas to his mother and father:

Dear Mother and Dad,

How are you both? It's a long, long time since a letter came from you; or is it that time moves so slowly here and one looks forward so much to the postman? Or, postwoman, rather, a little woman too, who walks about twenty miles a day, up & down these steep Florentine hills, in the baking sun. Whatever it is, we do want to hear from you soon. Letters from England seem to take, on the average, five days to get here.[6]

Is a Dylan Thomas letter different, aside from style and orality, from a telephone call, a home movie of the family, or a video cassette made from light portable equipment? Dylan Thomas writes his mother and father using a form of communication which is less than ideal. The ideal is for Thomas to be together with his parents, but because this is not possible he uses the postal letter. We have come to respect the letter form of interpersonal communication, but we are not as sure of ourselves when intimate communication involves the newer technological forms of communication. Doubts can arise when we see persons using the more sophisticated forms of communication to avoid the risk of direct interaction. "I'll talk to him/her on the phone because I can hang up when I want to." "I'd rather watch TV in my room than try to talk with my mother or father." "I just love Barry Manilow. He really understands me!" What does it mean when we are more "intimate" with media personalities than we are with people who are physically close to us?

Every medium of communication changes us. Every technological innovation has positive as well as negative potential. Holography will arrive in the not so distant future. Imagine a medium which will allow us to see and talk to each other over great distances and to "walk around" each other in an illusory third dimension. We will be able to approximate the ideal interpersonal communication with one major exception; we will not be able to touch or feel the warmth of each other. Will this increased "closeness" without touch be positive or negative? Some possible answers can be found in the following readings.

Notes

1. Ray Bradbury, "The Veldt," *The Illustrated Man.* (New York: Bantam Books, 1951).
2. Dreyfus, Lee S. and Gary Gumpert, "Students Visit Via Satellite," *The NAEB Journal,* Vol. 25, (May–June 1966), pp. 6–7.
3. Sennett, Richard, *The Fall of Public Man,* (New York: Alfred A. Knopf, 1977), pp. 282–83.
4. Hall, Edward T., *The Hidden Dimension,* (New York: Doubleday, 1969), and *The Silent Language,* (New York: Doubleday, 1959).
5. Maxmen, Jerrold S., *The Post-Physician Era: Medicine in the Twenty-First Century,* (New York: John Wiley & Sons, 1976), p. 18.
6. *Selected Letters from Dylan Thomas,* edited with commentary by Constantine Fizgibbon, (New York: New Directions Books, 1966), p. 310.

JAMES A. DANOWSKI

Interpersonal Network Structure and Media Use: A Focus on Radiality and Non–Mass Media Use

Who do you talk with the most? Who do each of these persons talk to? If you plotted all the dyadic communications involved in these exchanges you would have a diagram of your interpersonal communication network. Danowski explores the ways in which interpersonal communication networks are structured, the psychological orientations of persons to networks, and the ways media exposure become part of networks. His analysis helps us understand how interpersonal communication networks account for people's use of media and vice versa.

Most treatments of interpersonal communication and media are concerned with mass media. Yet, non-mass media—what we may call, "micro media"—are pervasive. This reading focuses on these different media communication channels. I will examine the structure of individuals' personal networks and their mass-micro media use. My research has found that people with a particular type of network use micro media more and use mass media less. Before I describe these types of networks and the related patterns of media use, I will take a closer look at different kinds of micro media.

Cathcart and Gumpert (1983) have defined four types of non-mass media: interpersonal mediated communication, media simulated interpersonal communication, person-computer interpersonal communication, and unicommunication. Two of these are directly relevant to this reading:

1. Interpersonal mediated communication. This type of communication occurs between two persons or among group members. Rather than occurring face to face, however, interaction is mediated by some form of communication technology, including telephone conversations, letters, electronic mail, computer bulletin boards, group computer conferencing, and audio and video teleconferencing.
2. Unicommunication. This communication is mediated by objects of clothing, adornment, and personal possessions which indicate status and role. It also includes more explicit messages—like those imprinted on T-shirts, jackets, caps, bumper stickers, armbangs, and buttons—that are used for self-expression.
3. Informational display media. These are media designed and used to

communicate instrumental (rather than expressive) information, and are placed in space such that individuals may see them in the course of other activities, like shopping, walking, riding, driving, etc. Examples include signs, posters, banners, flyers, bulletin boards, displays, billboards, and electronic message boards.

Having defined several types of micro media of interest, let us now consier some characteristics of interpersonal communication. Some of the basics include the raw amount of communication and the number of friends or contacts, but these do not usually explain much of human behavior. A particular variable that is powerful is the structure of the person's interpersonal network. Rather than just counting the number of contacts, or the amount of communication, structural variables measure the *pattern* of linkage among individuals. A way to think of these linkage patterns is to consider the extent to which the individuals with whom a person talks talk with one another. The more they do, the more "interlocking" the network (Rogers and Argawala-Rogers, 1976). Conversely, the less they do, the more radial is the network. In other words, a person with a radial network talks with people who do not talk much with one another. The people in such an individual's network are more diverse in characteristics than those in more interlocking networks (Laumann, 1976). In interlocking networks, the members are more like one another and they behave more uniformly. Group norms operate more strongly on them.

Mapping Your Network

Before I profile the characteristics of individuals varying in radiality, take a few moments and map your own network structure. This will show you how the variable is operationalized. Figure 1 shows the basic instrument used.

In studies we use statistical analysis based on a sample of people to precisely compute the network index. Because we cannot do this with your data, we will simplify the procedures.

Think of the three people you talk with most on a social basis. Jot their names down in the triangle, square, and diamond. (If you cannot think of any, or just one, you are a "relative isolate." (The concepts of radiality do not apply.) Next estimate how often each of the others talk with one another. Answer the last three questions on Figure 1.

Normally, with a sample we would use median-splits on communication frequencies for each pair of nodes. Because that will not be possible for you, we will use an approximation. If a pair of your contacts talks less than once per week on average, give that pair a score of zero. If they talk

FIGURE 1. Personal Network Instrument

Think of the three people you talk with most. Write their first names or initials in the square, diamond, and triangle below. Then answer questions A through F below.

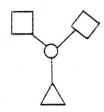

A. On the average, how often do you talk with the person in the <u>square</u>? (Check one.)

☐ several times a day or more ☐ about once or twice a month
☐ once or twice a day ☐ less than once or twice a month
☐ about once or twice a week ☐ never

B. On the average, how often do you talk with the person in the <u>triangle</u>? (Check one.)

☐ several times a day or more ☐ about once or twice a month
☐ once or twice a day ☐ less than once or twice a month
☐ about once or twice a week ☐ never

C. On the average, how often do you talk with the person in the <u>diamond</u>? (Check one.)

☐ several times a day or more ☐ about once or twice a month
☐ once or twice a day ☐ less than once or twice a month
☐ about once or twice a week ☐ never

D. On the average, how often does the person in the <u>square</u> talk with the person in the <u>triangle</u>? (Check one.)

☐ several times a day or more ☐ about once or twice a month
☐ once or twice a day ☐ less than once or twice a month
☐ about once or twice a week ☐ never

E. On the average, how often does the person in the square talk with the person in the diamond? (Check one.)

☐ several times a day or more ☐ about once or twice a month
☐ once or twice a day ☐ less than once or twice a month
☐ about once or twice a week ☐ never

F. On the average, how often does the person in the triangle talk with the person in the diamond? (Check one.)

☐ several times a day or more ☐ about once or twice a month
☐ once or twice a day ☐ less than once or twice a month
☐ about once or twice a week ☐ never

weekly or more often, then give the pair a score of 1. Do this for each of the three pairs. Then, add up the values. If all three are 1's, then you have a highly interlocking network. You are low in radiality. If all are zero, you are highly radial. If you are in between, note whether you are closer to the radial or interlocking end. Let us now turn to the media use profiles associated with this aspect of interpersonal network structure.

Mass Media Use

Do individuals with more radial networks expose more or less to mass media? One might expect that because they talk to more diverse people, radial network individuals would expose more to mass media for its conversational utility. Several studies, however, show the opposite pattern. Actually, radial network individuals expose less to the mass media of television, radio, and newspapers (Danowski, 1975; Danowski and Adler, 1983a; 1983b). And, their exposure to different media is less equal; they have lower channel "entropy," in other words more structure in their media use profile (Danowski, 1974). Radial network individuals also read employee publications less (Danowski and Van Engen, 1983). Conversely, the individuals with more interlocking networks are the ones who expose more to mass media. Does the lower mass media exposure profile of more radial network people extend to non-mass media as well? Evidence suggests not.

Informational Display Media

In two studies so far we have found that radial network individuals expose more to some informational display media. In an investigation of the statewide donors to a Wisconsin charitable health organization, we discovered that more radial network individuals report getting more information about such organizations from billboards and posters (Danowski and Adler, 1983a). They even reported getting information on billboards from one of the six organizations studied that did not use that medium.

In another study we examined the entertainment and media behaviors of a random sample of university undergraduates. We found that more radial network students reported getting more entertainment information from posters and banners around campus (Danowski and Adler, 1983b). They also reported gaining more information from direct observation of entertainment facilities. These results from two diverse samples lead us to hypothesize that more radial network individuals expose more to various informational display media. Future research can investigate uses of more of these media in relation to network structure. Our hunch is that more radial network individuals have a generalized preference for informational display media.

Unicommunication

Because we have recently discovered the possible higher informational display media preference associated with network radiality, we have yet to investigate a related micro medium, what Gumpert (1975) first labeled "unicommunication." We hypothesize that more radial network individuals pay more attention to the messages that others display on their T-shirts, hats, jackets, coffee cups, pens, novelty items, stickers, buttons, bumper stickers, etc. Given the definition of unicommunication, more radial network individuals may also notice more about the clothing people wear and the kinds of possessions they display, and attribute more meanings to them. Although more radial network individuals may observe more unicommunication messages, do they also display more unicommunication messages themselves? This is an interesting question for further research.

Interpersonal Mediated Communication

Network structure is also associated with uses of interpersonal mediated communication. Cook (1982) found with a sample of Chicago area public relations practitioners that those with more radial work-communication networks used telephones more for organizational communication. Looking at other interpersonal media, a study of state extension professionals revealed that more network radiality was associated with greater use of (1) dyadic electronic mail, (2) a large group form of electronic mail—"broadcasting," and (3) audio teleconferencing (Danowski, 1982). A study concerned with residential telephone use among a random sample of Dane County, Wisconsin, residents yielded evidence that individuals with more radial networks made more long-distance calls (Danowski, 1985).

Possible Explanations for Radiality's Relation to Non-Mass Media Use

First, consider the findings about mediated interpersonal communication. What are some possible theoretical explanations that might be tested in future research? One study has found that individuals who prefer computer-mediated dyadic communication over face-to-face interaction had higher empathy—the ability to understand thoughts and feelings from another's point of view (Hughey, 1985). Interpersonal mediated communication takes place with restricted sensory channels. Less "social presence" (Short, Williams, and Christie, 1976) is communicated compared to unmediated face-to-face interaction. Successful use of these media, therefore, requires participants to interpret restricted information from the others' perspectives, to fill in the sensory, cognitive, and emotional gaps in information that these media create. Perhaps individuals who are more empathically skilled are more comfortable with media use for interpersonal communication; they make fewer errors in interpreting what others are trying to communicate, experience less frustration, and use the media more efficiently. Thus, they may be less reluctant to use these media.

There is an interesting causality issue. Are those preferring computer-mediated communication doing so because they are challenged by the opportunity to exercise empathy, or did they develop greater empathy as a result of using various forms of mediated interpersonal communication?

Another explanatory factor to consider is the personality orientation of "locus of control." An internal locus of control exists if someone feels that he or she can control his or her own life. While feeling that environmental factors or fate controls them more is an external locus of control. Research has found that persons with more radial networks have higher internal locus of control (Danowski, 1975). They place higher value on personal autonomy (Danowski, 1981). They are more negative toward their organizational leaders, and want to have more decision-making power themselves (Danowski, 1976) But, if they perceive decision-making involvement to be more formal than real—a kind of "rubber stamping" participation—they are less likely to get involved (Schomish, 1983).

This control orientation of individuals with more radial networks may account for their greater use of mediated interpersonal communication. These forms of communication allow participants greater control over the interaction than is usual in face-to-face communication (Johansen, 1979). Because radials are attracted to the control opportunities these media provide, they may use these opportunities.

Another consideration is that perhaps radial network individuals have needs to communicate more with individuals who are geographically dispered. Mediated interpersonal communication enables this. The telecommunction-transportation tradeoff may be significant.

Informational Display Media

Let us turn now to consider the findings about radial network individuals' informational display media uses. Why would this kind of network structure be associated with such media orientations? Mass media provide coarse-grained descriptions of the environment. Could these individuals have a high need to survey their environment in a fine-grained way? A high surveillance need would require greater contact with diverse others who are geographically scattered to provide fine-grained information about what is happening in a range of environments.

Another possible clue to explaining the informational display media use

comes from Cathcart and Gumpert (1983). They suggest that unicommunication, closely related to informational display media, enable individuals
to attach a wide range of possible meanings to the brief messages displayed. These messages are also usually quite highly symbolic. Brief slogans, names, logos, or pictures often appear that are intended to communicate large domains of meaning. In other words, the messages are quite
abstract in terms of their meaning category width, the scope of referents
for the textual or graphic symbols used.

What if we assume that information display media are more abstract than
other media? Meyer (1985) found that individuals who had more abstract
cognitive functioning in general stored more abstract traits about other
people, organized this information more abstractly and retrieved it more
quickly. Such person-perception skills may be linked to empathic skills. We
can form a chain of reasoning. More radial network individuals use more
empathic skill. These are associated with abstract thinking. Information
display media and unicommunication contain more abstract information
than do other media. Therefore, radial network individuals find these
abstraction-oriented media to be compatible with their cognitive styles.

Direct evidence of the possibility that individuals with radial networks
have more abstract cognitive systems comes from another radiality study.
I found that more radial network individuals had a cognitive space about
energy topics that had more non-linear dimensions (Danowski, 1981). In
nontechnical tems, radials had more abstract mental functioning.

Given my discussion of radial network individuals, it is surprising that
they are opinion leaders. This finding may offer other explanatory routes,
which I consider after discussing the nature of this opinion leadership. Radial network individual's opinion leadership is "polymorphic"; that is, they
are asked about such multiple topics as politics, interpersonal relationships, and entertainment activities. Two studies using the radiality index
have confirmed this (Danowski and Adler, 1983a; 1983b).

Why do people seek out radial network individuals for opinions about
a wide range of topics? Perhaps the seekers realize that radial network individuals are positioned to know a lot about what is going on in different
network regions. Maybe people seek out radial network individuals to discuss interpersonal problems, rather than talking about this with their close,
interlocking friends. This may be particularly the case if the relational
problems are with someone in the interlocking network. The individual may
not want the tightly linked others to know that he or she feels out of step
with someone else in the group. The radial network individual may be perceived as a safe sounding-board, worldly, and knowledgeable.

Consider how the higher opinion leadership of individual networks may
provide another route to theoretically explaining the micro media use pro-

file. Being asked for opinions requires having something worthwhile to say to the asker is less likely to return. Askers probably have more interlocking, networks, thus sharing common mass media information sources. The unique information with which radial network individuals can provide them may have been gleaned from non-mass sources. These media may fuel radial network individuals' opinion leadership. Non-mass media may have even higher conversational utility than found for newspapers (Atkin, 1972).

Other Areas for Future Research

In addition to investigating the theoretical explanations for the current findings about radiality and media use, researchers may fruitfully consider whether radiality is also associated with the other non-mass media suggested by Cathcart and Gumpert (1983): media simulated interpersonal communication, and person-computer communication. Are radial network individuals more or less likely to use person-computer media? One such type of medium is constituted by databases containing environmental surveillance information such as abstracts of news stories, periodical articles, newsletter content, bibliographic references, and various primary information. On the other hand, are radial network individuals more or less likely to participate in simulated interpersonal media like radio talk shows, telethons, and so forth? Perhaps some of the findings and possible explanations discussed in this reading can lead to hypotheses about these other forms of non-mass media.

Conclusion

In summary, there are several avenues with apparent promise for developing theoretical explanations for the findings about interpersonal network structure and micro media use. More empirical work on these explanations can help us make sense of the intriguing media use profiles of radial network individuals: lower mass media use and higher use of informational display media and interpersonal mediated communication. Such research can further integrate rather disparate areas of communication research: mass media, micro media, interpersonal networks, psychological orientations, and cognitive functioning.

KARL ERIK ROSENGREN and SWEN WINDAHL

Mass Media Consumption as a Functional Alternative

Professors Rosengren and Windahl have been studying groups in Sweden to determine under what circumstances people prefer media interaction over face-to-face interaction and what form this preference takes. They describe alternate ways available for gratifying our need for social interaction, i.e., parasocial interaction and character identification. What results is a typology of media consumption based on social needs.

Read the essay by Horton and Wohl for a more elaborate description of how and why we form para-social relationships with radio and television personalities.

. . . Our aim in this paper is to investigate a special family of media functions for the individual. We are trying to relate a certain type of gratification to a certain type of audience characteristic. Underlying this attempt is the conviction that sooner or later mass media research must cease using raw demographic variables for its independent variables, and simple amount of consumption for its dependent variable. Instead, various sociological and social psychological variables should be introduced as independent or intervening variables, while the dependent variable, the mass media consumption, should be qualitatively differentiated into various types of consumption. Before presenting our version of this programme, we must first discuss some relations between the individual, his needs and his possibilities to satisfy these needs in various ways.

We all have the most various types of needs. Suppose that we are interested in the study of one special, fairly well defined need.[1] Suppose there is more than one way of satisfying this need, ways numbering 1, 2, 3, . . . n. These are functional alternatives, one of which may, but not necessarily must, stand out as the natural one—for biological, psychological or cultural reasons.[2] Let us call this alternative "way 1." The possibilities to use way 1 of need satisfaction are supposed to vary on the individual and environmental levels. (Environment is here taken to include all extra-individual variables: social-psychological, social and societal.) When his individual and/or environmental possibilities to use this way of need satisfaction are small or even non-existent, the individual tends to satisfy the

From *Sociology of Mass Communications,* edited by Denis McQuail (Penguin Education, 1972), pp. 166–194. This selection copyright © Denis McQuail, 1972. Reprinted by permission of the publisher, Penguin Books Ltd.

same need by means of one or more of the functional alternatives offered by society and its culture, ways 2, 3, . . . *n*.

Given these assumptions, a typology of possibilities for need satisfaction may be established. Individual and environmental possibilities for need satisfaction in way 1 may each be divided into satisfactory and non-satisfactory, which gives us a typology of four cases.

Once the possibilities are organized in this way the four cells of the typology may be seen as the values of a new variable, *degree of dependence on the functional alternatives*. When an individual has satisfactory individual and environmental possibilities to satisfy the need in way 1, he is only to a small degree dependent on the functional alternatives. When he has non-satisfactory possibilities to satisfy the need in this way, he is very dependent on the alternatives. Cells 2 and 3 may be seen as intermediary cases, possibly resulting in the same intermediary degree of dependence on functional alternatives for need satisfaction.

As an example, let us take the need for social interaction, which we trust to be fairly general, demanding some capacities of the individual (e.g. a certain degree of extroversion, empathy and socialization) and of his environment (e.g. someone to interact with). Also, there is a "natural" way of satisfying the need: face-to-face interaction with real, living human beings; and there are functional alternatives for the satisfaction of the same need, for instance, writing letters, reading books, attending to such mass media as radio, television, newspapers, magazines.[3]

A well socialized person, high on extroversion and empathy, has satisfactory individual possibilities to satisfy his need for social interaction in the natural way, way 1, i.e. by means of interaction with real human beings. If he also has partners and other prerequisites (time, for instance), his environmental possibilities may also be said to be satisfactory, and, by definition, his dependence on such functional alternatives as reading books or listening in will be low (cell 1).

The highly introverted person, on the other hand, low on empathy, whose socialization leaves much to be desired, may be said to have non-satisfactory possibilities on the individual level to satisfy his need for social interaction in way 1. If his environment is equally lacking in this respect, he will be very dependent on such functional alternatives as may be offered, for instance, by the mass media (cell 4). And now let us continue our theoretical argument.

When we considered the suggested typology from the point of view of the individual and his relations to the functional alternatives, we arrived at the variable "degree of dependence." But one might equally well look at the typology from the angle of the functional alternatives and their relations to way 1. These relations may be seen as defined by the possibilities

		Environmental possibilities to find satisfaction in a given way:	
		Satisfactory	Non-satisfactory
Individual possibilities to find satisfaction in a given way:	Satisfactory	1	2
	Non-satisfactory	3	4

Figure 1. Typology of possibilities to satisfy a given need in a given way

to satisfy the given need in way 1. That is, for each of the four cells of the typology of possibilities presented in Figure 1, we will get a special relationship of the functional alternatives to way 1. In this way some of the terms used in the debate may be given a somewhat more precise meaning.[4] This is done in Figure 2.

Figure 2, then, implies a suggestion for a more precise terminology. The terms themselves, of course, are mere labels, and could be changed without much ado. Nevertheless, it seems to us that when there are satisfactory individual and environmental possibilities to use way 1, a functional alternative is precisely a supplement. (See Webster's *Dictionary of Synonyms:* "*Supplemental* implies an addition to something relatively complete.") When neither of these possibilities is satisfactory or even existent, the functional alternative may with some justification be called a substitute for way 1. (See Webster's *Dictionary of Synonyms:* "Substitute: . . . surrogate, makeshift, stopgap.") A complement is what functional alternative is when there are individual but not environmental (or environmental but not individual) possibilities of satisfying the need in way 1. (See Webster's *Dictionary of Synonyms:* "Complement , , implies a completing.") It should be pointed out that the labels are by no means intended to be evaluative, although, because of the paucity of the language, we have had to choose labels some of which sound nicer than others. This is in spite of the fact that all functional alternatives may serve in each of the four cells; that is,

| 1 Supplement | 2 Complement |
| 3 Complement | 4 Substitute |

Figure 2. Relations of functional alternatives to way 1, as defined by possibilities of satisfying the given need in way 1 (see Figure 1)

1 Change	2 Compensation
3 Escape	4 Vicarious experience

Figure 3. Motives for seeking functional alternatives, as defined by possibilities of satisfying the given need in way 1 (see Figure 1)

one man's substitute may very well be another man's supplement. Thus, the same functional alternative to actual social interaction—say, a TV play—may be either a supplement, a complement, or a substitute, depending on the circumstances.

The functional alternative may be sought by the individual for various reasons or motives. We believe that these motives should also preferably be defined in terms of the individual's possibilities to use way 1 for need satisfaction. So again we use the four cells of the typology of Figure 1, this time to distinguish between four types of motives (that is, here we find it meaningful to differentiate between the two intermediary cases). This is done in Figure 3.

Like Figure 2, Figure 3 implies a suggestion for a more precise terminology. Again the terms are but labels and could be changed without much consequence to our argument. But all the same we find them meaningful, at least to a degree. It is meaningful, we think, to assume that the man who has large individual and environmental possibilities to satisfy a given need in a given way is motivated by a wish for change when seeking functional alternatives to the first way of satisfaction. A man, on the other hand, who as an individual perfectly well could avail himself of the given way of finding satisfaction but whose environment offers no possibility to do so, such a man may with some justification be said to seek compensation in a functional alternative for what society denies him. The less talented or gifted, without individual possibilities for need satisfaction in the given way, but living—as far as our way 1 of satisfaction is concerned—in a world of plenty, may be seen as seeking escape from his frustrating situation. And the individual, finally, who has no possibilities of his own and is offered none from his environment either, his experience in this respect obviously will be vicarious. (To stick to our interaction example: this is the poorly socialized youngster without friends, who turns to the mass media, seeking a substitute—vicarious experience—for what his individual and environmental situation denies him.)

Starting from a typology of possibilities for need satisfaction (large and small individual and environmental possibilities for satisfaction in a given way), continuing by way of a new variable with three or four values (degree of dependence on functional alternatives) and a typology of functional alternatives (supplement, complement, substitute), we ended up with a typology of motives for seeking functional alternatives (change, compensation, escape, vicarious experience). How do we use all these concepts, the reader may rightly ask.

In principle they could be used whenever a social scientist is investigating individuals with needs that may be satisfied in a way that demands individual and social or societal resources of some kind, at the same time as there are other ways of finding satisfaction—the functional alternatives. In this paper we will apply the argument to the need for social interaction, which we have already used a couple of times for illustrative purposes.

This is hardly the first paper that has been devoted to the problem of mass media and the need for interaction. What one experiences, approaching the subject, is rather a feeling of *embarras de richesses,* and the embarrassment is caused not least by the richness of the terminological florilegium of the subject. There is hardly a dearth of terms like escape, substitute, compensation, fantasy, vicarious experience, etc. Before trying to express some of the thoughts hidden behind the terms, let us, however, introduce still another typology, pertaining to the special need on which we have now focused our attention: the need for interaction.

Interaction is a special type of relation between individuals. Another one is identification. If the first may be roughly determined as mutual stimulation and response, the other may be equalled for our purposes with the act of imagining oneself to be in the place of another person.[5] Stretching these somewhat elastic definitions, both relations may be said to exist also between a real human being and an individual—an "actor"—of the mass media world: the hero or anti-hero of the TV play or the magazine story, the well-known columnist of the newspaper, the disc-jockey of the radio programme. At least this is what has been contended in more than one investigation about uses and gratifications of the mass media. Identification, of course, in these cases may be highly temporary and shallow, existing, perhaps, only during the fleeting moments of a mass media scene of heightened tension of relief. Interaction must be imaginary (the audience partaking only imaginarily in the action), one-sided or mutual only in a very special way (for instance, an entertainer tells a joke and then pauses, to let the far-off audience laugh).

The two kinds of relations—identification and interaction—may be used to construct a typology of relations between a real individual and one or more "actors" of the mass media (Figure 4).

This fourfold table gives us four types of relation. We label them from the point of view of the public and call the relation contained within cell

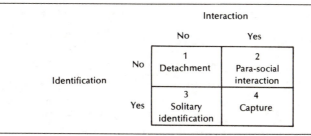

		Interaction	
		No	Yes
Identification	No	1 Detachment	2 Para-social interaction
	Yes	3 Solitary identification	4 Capture

Figure 4. Typology of relations between audience and actors of mass media

1 *detachment.* (From the point of view of the "actor" we might have called it "lack of rapport," for instance.) This is the case when the individual neither identifies nor interacts with any actor of the mass media content he is consuming.[6]

The relation of cell 2 we call *para-social interaction,* borrowing the term from an imaginative and insightful paper by Horton and Wohl (1956). . . . In short it denotes the interaction with somebody of the mass media world more or less as if he were present in person, without losing even momentarily one's identity. The mutuality of this type of interaction is of a very special sort.

The relation of cell 3 we believe is very rare or virtually nonexistent in reality. We feel it is rather difficult to identify with somebody of the mass media content consumed, without at the seme time interacting with the rest of the cast. But especially in the case of a one-man show, or when one person or role is very dominating, identification without interaction may, of course, occur. We have named this type of relationship *solitary identification.*

The relation of cell 4 we call *capture.* This is the opposite of the relation of cell 1: the individual both identifies with one or more of the "actors" and also interacts with one or more other actors of the mass medium he is attending to. The interaction, of course, is imaginary.

The four types of relationship may be seen as forming the values of a new variable, which we prefer to call *degree of involvement.* The variable may be seen as having three values, that is, we prefer to collapse as before the two intermediate cases into one. We suggest the possibility of a positive correlation between degree of dependence as defined above and degree of involvement. The more dependent one is on one or more of the mass media as purveyors of functional alternatives to real interaction, the higher one's degree of involvement would tend to be (see Turner, 1958). We also hypothesize a positive correlation between degree of involvement and amount of consumption: the higher the degree of involvement, the larger

		Content supplies explicit and concrete information	
		Yes	No
Content is fictional	No	1 News, current affairs, educational content, etc.	2 Entertainment, music, etc.
	Yes	3 Instructional plays, certain features, etc.	4 Drama, plays, novels, short stories, etc.

Figure 5. Typology of media content

the mass media consumption. In both cases the relationship probably is mutual or interdependent (see Zetterberg, 1965, pp. 72 ff.).

We believe that irrespective of degree of dependence on the mass media, irrespective of motives and degree of involvement, the need for interaction (and, indeed, all needs that may be satisfied, in one way or another, by the mass media) may be satisfied by almost any type of media content. But this does not mean that we must expect no correlation at all between preference for, and consumption of, certain types of media content on the one hand, and degree of dependence, motives for seeking the functional alternative of the news media, or degree of involvement, on the other. Therefore, our argument should be connected with a typology of content.

Again, we resort to a fourfold typology, obtained this time by cross-tabulating the two concepts of fictitiousness and informativeness (Figure 5). We take it for granted that it is possible to distinguish between fictional and non-fictional media content, although we are of course aware of the fact that there must be borderline cases. Informative media content to us means such media content that by the communicator (yet another tricky concept!) is intended to convey explicit and concrete information of some sort.

The figure shows what types of content items we feel should be placed in the various cells, and we do not have to enlarge upon that any more, although we freely admit that the typology is primitive indeed and needs elaboration. We think that a better version of a media content typology of this kind (i.e. content seen from the point of view of the medium or the communicator) should ultimately be correlated with a typology of the kind suggested by Emmett (content seen from the point of view of the consumer) (1968). However, in this paper we will have to let suffice with the typology just offered.

In analogy with our previous strategy we may now see our four types of media content as values of a new variable, *degree of reality proximity of media content*. Content in cell 1, being nonfictional and supplying explicit and concrete information, is closer to reality, we feel, than content in cell 4, being fictional and non-informative, the contents of cells 3 and 4 coming in between these two extremes.

Let us remark here, parenthetically, that we are not unaware of the fact that we have not defined "reality" at all. Starting from another set of explicit or implicit evaluations than those that form the implicit platform of this paper, it is very easy to arrive at a different conception of reality and consequently at a different ordering of the cells on the variable "degree of reality proximity." Thus we would not quarrel if anybody suggested that at least some dramas and novels are very close to reality indeed— "reality" in a certain sense of the word, and "close" in a certain sense of the word, that is.

Accepting our definition of the variable "degree of reality proximity" we could correlate it with the variable "degree of dependence" and "degree of involvement" as earlier defined, and our hypothesis would be that high degree of dependence and involvement would tend to go together with preference for and consumption of media content with a low degree of reality proximity, both identification and interaction being easier to establish with this type of content. As before, we believe that the hypothesized correlations probably represent a mutual or interdependent relationship.

Finally, a word or two should be said about the effects of mass media consumption. As a rule, effect studies and functional studies are seen as belonging to two different approaches. The catchword "what do the media do to people, and what do people do with the media" is sometimes used to characterize the two different approaches. But according to Merton, functions are a certain type of effect (1963, p. 51), and even if in this case one takes functions to mean uses, types of gratification, etc., it is quite possible to ask what effect a given use made of the mass media, or a given gratification obtained from them, may have. Thus we are convinced that sooner or later the two traditions must merge.

Waiting for such a merger it is urgent that effect arguments be as sophisticated as possible. However, it seems that it is not possible to be very sophisticated at the present stage of mass communication research. A minimum requirement would be to distinguish between long-term and short-term effects, and between effects on the individual and on society or parts of society. It is to be expected that effects of mass media consumption should vary not only with amount of consumption, but also with degree of dependence, motives for seeking the functional alternatives offered by the mass media, degree of involvement and degree of reality proximity of the content consumed. Consequently, one should try to heed variables such as these. Also, evaluations should be kept out of the argument as much and for as long as possible, so that they may be made with greater precision, and perhaps, greater weight, when at last they really are made. . . .

Notes

1. We loosely equate need with drive. In many or most cases we are probably thinking of acquired drive: "a motive, need, or source of motivation (rarely defined) that is a product of learning" (Brown, 1968, p. 280).

2. Merton (1963, p. 34 *passim*). The arguments of the rest of this paper hold true even if the functional alternatives are equivalent, so there is no more or less self-evident 'way 1' among them.

3. "There is good reason to consider this *basic drive for contact* the most important factor in keeping all communication in operation" (Nordenstreng, 1969, p. 254).

4. An excellent overview of the literature on mass media as substitute, supplement, escape, etc., may be found in Lundberg and Hultén, 1968, ch. 9. Lundberg and Hultén refer to well-known works by, for instance, Bailyn, Berelson, Hemmelweit, Riley and Riley, Schramm, Steiner, and also to some less-known pieces of research.

5. See Theodorson and Theodorson (1970) and also, among others, Emery (1959), Kelman (1961) and the literature cited by these authors.

6. Note the related concept of "adult discount," introduced in Dysinger and Rucknick (1933) and Blumler, Brown and McQuail (1970, p. 31).

DONALD HORTON and R. RICHARD WOHL

Mass Communication and Para-Social Interaction: Observation on Intimacy at a Distance

This article first appeared in 1956 in the *Journal of Psychiatry*. It was one of the early explorations of the way media and media performers create the illusion of an interpersonal relationship. The authors call this a "para-social relationship" because it is based upon an implicit agreement between the performer and viewer that they will pretend the relationship is not mediated— that it will be carried on as though it were a face-to face-encounter. An example of this para-social relationship can be found among the viewers of the Johnny Carson show. Carson performs as though he were speaking directly to the viewer. They become a "team," where the viewer is privy to Carson's thoughts and feelings and Carson acts in a reciprocal manner. All other persons on the show are merely props used to enhance this "intimate" relationship between Carson and the viewer. As a consequence many viewers report that they "know" Johnny better than they do their next-door neighbor.

Notice how many television and radio shows utilize the "para-social" technique; *Eye Witness News,* for example, where the reporter-analyst-commentator is speaking directly to you, letting you in on feelings, jokes, and personal references. Does the radio DJ carry on a conversation with you as you drive along in your car? Think about how many of these surrogate interpersonal relationships you have with media performers.

One of the striking characteristics of the new mass media—radio, television, and the movies—is that they give the illusion of face-to-face relationship with the performer. The conditions of response to the performer are analogous to those in a primary group. The most remote and illustrious men are met as if they were in the circle of one's peers; the same is true of a character in a story who comes to life in these media in an especially vivid and arresting way. We propose to call this seeming face-to-face relationship between spectator and performer a *para-social relationship*.

In television, especially, the image which is presented makes available nuances of appearance and gesture to which ordinary social perception is attentive and to which interaction is cued. Sometimes the "actor"— whether he is playing himself or performing in a fictional role—is seen engaged with others; but often he faces the spectator, uses the mode of direct address, talks as if he were conversing personally and privately. The audience, for its part, responds with something more than mere running observation; it is, as it were, subtly insinuated into the program's action and internal social relationships and, by dint of this kind of staging, is ambiguously transformed into a group which observes and participates in the show by turns. The more the performer seems to adjust his performance to the supposed response of the audience, the more the audience tends to make the response anticipated. This simulacrum of conversational give and take may be called *para-social interaction.*

Para-social relations may be governed by little or no sense of obligation, effort, or responsibility on the part of the spectator. He is free to withdraw at any moment. If he remains involved, these para-social relations provide a framework within which much may be added by fantasy. But these are differences of degree, not of kind, from what may be termed the ortho-social. The crucial difference in experience obviously lies in the lack of effective reciprocity, and this the audience cannot normally conceal from itself. To be sure, the audience is free to choose among the relationships offered, but it cannot create new ones. The interaction, characteristically, is one-sided, nondialectical, controlled by the performer, and not susceptible of mutual development. There are, of course, ways in which the spectators can make their feelings known to the performers and the technicians who design the programs, but these lie outside the para-social interaction itself. Whoever finds the experience unsatisfying has only the option to withdraw.

What we have said so far forcibly recalls the theatre as an ambiguous meeting ground on which real people play out the roles of fictional characters. For a brief interval, the fictional takes precedence over the actual, as the actor becomes identified with the fictional role in the magic of the theatre. This glamorous confusion of identities is temporary: the worlds of fact and fiction meet only for the moment. And the actor, when he takes his bows at the end of the performance, crosses back over the threshold into the matter-of-fact world.

Radio and television, however—and in what follows we shall speak primarily of television—are hospitable to both these worlds in continuous interplay. They are alternately public platforms and theatres, extending the para-social relationship now to leading people of the world of affairs, now to fictional characters, sometimes even to puppets anthropomorphically transformed into "personalities," and, finally, to theatrical stars who appear in their capacities as real celebrities. But of particular interest is the creation by these media of a new type of performer: quiz-masters, announcers, "interviewers" in a new "show-business" world—in brief, a special category of "personalities" whose existence is a function of the media themselves. These "personalities" usually, are not prominent in any of the social spheres beyond the media.[1] They exist for their audiences only in the para-social relation. Lacking an appropriate name for these performers, we shall call them *personae*.

The Role of the Persona

The persona is the typical and indigenous figure of the social scene presented by radio and television. To say that he is familiar and intimate is to use pale and feeble language for the pervasiveness and closeness with which multitudes feel his presence. The spectacular fact about such personae is that they can claim and achieve an intimacy with what are literally crowds of strangers, and this intimacy, even if it is an imitation and a shadow of what is ordinarily meant by that word, is extremely influential with, and satisfying for, the great numbers who willingly receive it and share in it. They "know" such a persona in somewhat the same way they know their chosen friends: through direct observation and interpretation of his appearance, his gestures and voice, his conversation and conduct in a variety of situations. Indeed, those who make up his audience are invited, by designed informality, to make precisely these evaluations—to consider that they are involved in a face-to-face exchange rather than in passive observation. When the television camera pans down on a performer, the illusion is strong that he is enhancing the presumed intimacy by literally coming closer. But the persona's image, while partial, contrived, and penetrated by illusion, is no fantasy or dream; his performance is an objectively perceptible action in which the viewer is implicated imaginatively, but which he does not imagine.

The persona offers, above all, a continuing relationship. His appearance is a regular and dependable event, to be counted on, planned for, and integrated into the routines of daily life. His devotees live with him and share the small episodes of his public life—and to some extent even of his private life away from the show. Indeed, their continued association with him acquires a history, and the accumulation of shared past experiences gives additional meaning to the present performance. This bond is symbolized by allusions that lack meaning for the casual observer and appear occult to the outsider. In time, the devotee—the "fan"—comes to believe that he "knows" the persona more intimately and profoundly than others do; that he "understands" his character and appreciates his values and motives.[2] Such an accumulation of knowledge and intensification of loyalty, however, appears to be a kind of growth without development, for the one-sided nature of the connection precludes a progressive and mutual reformulation of its value and aims.[3]

The persona may be considered by his audience as a friend, counselor, comforter, and model; but, unlike real associates, he has the peculiar virtue of being standardized according to the "formula" for his character and performance which he and his managers have worked out and embodied in an appropriate "production format." Thus his character and pattern of action remain basically unchanged in a world of otherwise disturbing change. The persona is ordinarily predictable, and gives his adherents no unpleasant surprises. In their association with him there are no problems of understanding or empathy too great to be solved. Typically, there are no challenges to a spectator's self—to his ability to take the reciprocal part in the performance that is assigned to him—that cannot be met comfortably. This reliable sameness is only approximated, and then only in the short run, by the figures of fiction. On television, Groucho is always sharp; Godfrey is always warm-hearted.

The Bond of Intimacy

It is an unvarying characteristic of these "personality" programs that the greatest pains are taken by the persona to create an illusion of intimacy. We call it an illusion because the relationship between the persona and any member of his audience is inevitably one-sided, and reciprocity between the two can only be suggested. There are several principal strategies for achieving this illusion of intimacy.

Most characteristic is the attempt of the persona to duplicate the gestures, conversational style, and milieu of an informal face-to-face gathering. This accounts, in great measure, for the casualness with which even the formalities of program scheduling are treated. The spectator is encouraged to gain the impression that what is taking place on the program gains a momentum of its own in the very process of being enacted. Thus Steve Allen is always pointing out to his audience that "we never know what is going to happen on this show." In addition, the persona tries to maintain a flow of small talk which gives the impression that he is responding to and sustaining the contributions of an invisible interlocutor. Dave Garroway, who has mastered this style to perfection, has described how he stumbled on the device in his early days in radio.

> Most talk on the radio in those days was formal and usually a little stiff. But I just rambled along, saying whatever came into my mind. I was introspective. I tried to pretend that I was chatting with a friend over a highball late in the evening. . . . Then—and later—I consciously tried to talk to the listener as an individual, to make each listener feel that he knew me and I knew him. It seemed to work pretty well then and later. I know that strangers often stop me on the street today, call me Dave and seem to feel that we are old friends who know all about each other.[4]

In addition to creating an appropriate tone and patter, the persona tries as far as possible to eradicate, or at least to blur, the line which divides him and his show, as a formal performance, from the audience both in the studio and at home. The most usual way of achieving this ambiguity is for the persona to treat his supporting cast as a group of close intimates. Thus all the members of the cast will be addressed by their first names, or by special nicknames, to emphasize intimacy. They very quickly develop, or have imputed to them, stylized character traits which, as members of the supporting cast, they will indulge in and exploit regularly in program after program. The member of the audience, therefore, not only accumulates an historical picture of "the kinds of people they really are," but tends to believe that this fellowship includes him by extension. As a matter of fact, all members of the program who are visible to the audience will be drawn into this by-play to suggest this ramification of intimacy.

Furthermore, the persona may try to step out of the particular format of his show and literally blend with the audience. Most usually, the persona leaves the stage and mingles with the studio audience in a question-and-answer exchange. In some few cases, and particularly on the Steve Allen show, this device has been carried a step further. Thus Allen has managed to blend even with the home audience by the maneuver of training a television camera on the street outside the studio and, in effect, suspending his own show and converting all the world outside into a stage. Allen, his supporting cast, and the audience, both at home and in the studio, watch together what transpires on the street—the persona and his spectators symbolically united as one big audience. In this way, Allen erases for the moment the line which separates persona and spectator.

In addition to the management of relationships between the persona and performers, and between him and his audience, the technical devices of the media themselves are exploited to create illusions of intimacy.

> For example [Dave Garroway explains in this connection], we developed the "subjective-camera" idea, which was simply making the camera be the eyes of the audience. In one scene the camera—that's you, the viewer—approached the door of a dentist's office, saw a sign that the dentist was out to lunch, sat down nervously in the waiting room. The dentist returned and beckoned to the camera, which went in and sat in the big chair. "Open wide," the dentist said, poking a huge, wicked-looking drill at the camera. There was a roar as the drill was turned on, sparks flew and the camera vibrated and the viewers got a magnified version of sitting in the dentist's chair—except that it didn't hurt.[5]

All these devices are indulged in not only to lure the attention of the audience, and to create the easy impression that there is a kind of participation open to them in the program itself, but also to highlight the chief values stressed in such "personality" shows. These are sociability, easy affability, friendship, and close contact—briefly, all the values associated with free access to and easy participation in pleasant social interaction in primary groups. Because the relationship between persona and audience is one-sided and cannot be developed mutually, very nearly the whole burden of creating a plausible imitation of intimacy is thrown on the persona and on the show of which he is the pivot. If he is successful in initiating an intimacy which his audience can believe in, then the audience may help him maintain it by fan mail and by the various other kinds of support which can be provided indirectly to buttress his actions.

The Role of the Audience

At one extreme, the "personality" program is like a drama in having a cast of characters, which includes the persona, his professional supporting cast, nonprofessional contestants and interviewees, and the studio audience. At the other extreme, the persona addresses his entire performance to the home audience with undisturbed intimacy. In the dramatic type of program, the participation of the spectator involves, we presume, the same taking of successive roles and deeper empathic involvements in the leading roles which occurs in any observed social interaction.[6] It is possible that the spectator's "collaborative expectancy"[7] may assume the more profound form of identification with one or more of the performers. But such identification can hardly be more than intermittent. The "personality" program, unlike the theatrical drama, does not demand or even permit the esthetic illusion—that loss of situational reference and self-consciousness in which the audience not only accepts the symbol as reality, but fully assimilates the symbolic role. The persona and his staff maintain the parasocial relationship, continually referring to and addressing the home audience as a third party to the program; and such references remind the spectator of his own independent identity. The only illusion maintained is that of directness and immediacy of participation.

When the persona appears alone, in apparent face-to-face interaction with the home viewer, the latter is still more likely to maintain his own identity without interruption, for he is called upon to make appropriate responses which are complementary to those of the persona. This 'answering' role is, to a degree, voluntary and independent. In it, the spectator retains control over the content of his participation rather than surrendering control through identification with others, as he does when absorbed in watching a drama or movie.

This independence is relative, however, in a twofold sense: First, it is relative in the profound sense that the very act of entering into any interaction with another involves *some* adaptation to the other's perspectives, if communication is to be achieved at all. And, second, in the present case, it is relative because the role of the persona is enacted in such a way, or is of such a character, that an *appropriate* answering role is specified by implication and suggestion. The persona's performance, therefore, is open-ended, calling for a rather specific answering role to give it closure.[8]

The general outlines of the appropriate audience role are perceived intuitively from familiarity with the common cultural patterns on which the role of the persona is constructed. These roles are chiefly derived from the primary relations of friendship and the family, characterized by intimacy, sympathy, and sociability. The audience is expected to accept the situation defined by the program format as credible, and to concede as "natural" the rules and conventions governing the actions performed and the values realized. It should play the role of the loved one to the persona's lover; the admiring dependent to his father-surrogate; the earnest citizen to his fearless opponent of political evils. It is expected to benefit by his wisdom, reflect on his advice, sympathize with him in his difficulties, forgive his mistakes, buy the products that he recommends, and keep his sponsor informed of the esteem in which he is held.

Other attitudes than compliance in the assigned role are, of course, possible. One may reject, take an analytical stance, perhaps even find a cynical amusement in refusing the offered gambit and playing some other role not implied in the script, or view the proceedings with detached curiosity or hostility. But such attitudes as these **are**, usually, for the one-time viewer. The faithful audience is one that can accept the gambit offered; and the functions of the program for this audience are served not by the mere perception of it, but by the role-enactment that completes it.

The Coaching of Audience Attitudes

Just how the situation should be defined by the audience, what to expect of the persona, what attitudes to take toward him, what to "do" as a participant in the program, is not left entirely to the common experience and intuitions of the audience. Numerous devices are used in a deliberate "coaching of attitudes," to use Kenneth Burke's phrase.[9] The typical program format calls for a studio audience to provide a situation of face-to-face interaction for the persona, and exemplifies to the home audience an enthusiastic and "correct" response. The more interaction occurs, the more clearly is demonstrated the kind of man the persona is, the values to be shared in association with him, and the kind of support to give him. A similar model of appropriate response may be supplied by the professional assistants who, though technically performers, act in a subordinate and deferential reciprocal relation toward the persona. The audience is schooled in correct responses to the persona by a variety of other means as well. Other personae may be invited as guests, for example, who play up to the host in exemplary fashion; or persons drawn from the audience may be maneuvered into fulfilling this function. And, in a more direct and literal fashion, reading excerpts from fan mail may serve the purpose.

Beyond the coaching of specific attitudes toward personae, a general propaganda on their behalf flows from the performers themselves, their press agents, and the mass communication industry. Its major theme is that the performer should be loved and admired. Every attempt possible is made to strengthen the illusion of reciprocity and rapport in order to offset the inherent impersonality of the media themselves. The jargon of show business teems with special terms for the mysterious ingredients of such rapport: ideally, a performer should have "heart," should be "sincere"; [10] his performance should be "real" and "warm." [11] The publicity campaigns built around successful performers continually emphasize the sympathetic image which, it is hoped, the audience is perceiving and developing. [12]

The audience, in its turn, is expected to contribute to the illusion by believing in it, and by rewarding the persona's "sincerity" with "loyalty." The audience is entreated to assume a sense of personal obligation to the performer, to help him in his struggle for "success" if he is "on the way up," or to maintain his success if he has already won it. "Success" in show business is itself a theme which is prominently exploited in this kind of propaganda. It forms the basis of many movies; it appears often in the patter of the leading comedians and in the exhortations of MC's; it dominates the so-called amateur hours and talent shows; and it is subject to frequent comment in interviews with "show people." [13]

Conditions of Acceptance of the Para-Social Role by the Audience

The acceptance by the audience of the role offered by the program involves acceptance of the explicit and implicit terms which define the situation and the action to be carried out in the program. Unless the spectator understands these terms, the role performances of the participants are meaningless to him; and unless he accepts them, he cannot "enter into" the performance himself. But beyond this, the spectator must be able to play the part demanded of him; and this raises the question of the compatibility between his normal self—as a system of role-patterns and self-conceptions with their implicated norms and values—and the kind of self postulated by the program schema and the actions of the persona. In short, one may conjecture that the probability of rejection of the proffered role will be greater the less closely the spectator "fits" the role prescription.

To accept the gambit without the necessary personality qualifications is to invite increasing dissatisfaction and alienation—which the student of the media can overcome only by a deliberate, imaginative effort to take the postulated role. The persona himself takes the role of his projected audience in the interpretation of his own actions, often with the aid of cues provided by a studio audience. He builds his performance on a cumulative structure of assumptions about their response, and so postulates—more or less consciously—the complex of attitudes to which his own actions are adapted. A spectator who fails to make the anticipated responses will find himself further and further removed from the base-line of common understanding.[14] One would expect the "error" to be cumulative, and eventually to be carried, perhaps, to the point at which the spectator is forced to resign in confusion, disgust, anger, or boredom. If a significant portion of the audience fails in this way, the persona's "error in role-taking"[15] has to be corrected with the aid of audience research, "program doctors," and other aids. But, obviously, the intended adjustment is to some average or typical spectator, and cannot take too much account of deviants.

The simplest example of such a failure to fulfill the role prescription would be the case of an intellectual discussion in which the audience is presumed to have certain basic knowledge and the ability to follow the development of the argument. Those who cannot meet these requirements find the discussion progressively less comprehensible. A similar progressive alienation probably occurs when children attempt to follow an adult program or movie. One observes them absorbed in the opening scenes, but gradually losing interest as the developing action leaves them behind. Another such situation might be found in the growing confusion and restiveness of some audiences watching foreign movies or "high-brow" drama. Such resistance is also manifested when some members of an audience are asked to take the opposite-sex role—the woman's perspective is rejected more commonly by men than vice versa—or when audiences refuse to accept empathically the roles of outcasts or those of racial or cultural minorities whom they consider inferior.[16]

It should be observed that merely witnessing a program is not evidence that a spectator has played the required part. Having made the initial commitment, he may "string along" with it at a low level of empathy but reject it retrospectively. The experience does not end with the program itself. On the contrary, it may be only after it has ended that it is submitted to intellectual analysis and integrated into, or rejected by, the self; this occurs especially in those discussions which the spectator may undertake with other people in which favorable or unfavorable consensual interpretations and judgments are arrived at. It is important to enter a qualification at this point. The suspension of immediate judgment is probably more complete in the viewing of the dramatic program, where there is an esthetic illusion to be accepted, than in the more self-conscious viewing of "personality" programs.

Values of the Para-Social Role
for the Audience

What para-social roles are acceptable to the spectator and what benefits their enactment has for him would seem to be related to the systems of patterned roles and social situations in which he is involved in his everyday life. The values of a para-social role may be related, for example, to the demands being made upon the spectator for achievement in certain statuses. Such demands, to pursue this instance further, may be manifested in the expectations of others, or they may be self-demands, with the concomitant emergence of more or less satisfactory self-conceptions. The enactment of a para-social role may therefore constitute an exploration and development of new role possibilities, as in the experimental phases of actual, or aspired to, social mobility.[17] It may offer a recapitulation of roles no longer played—roles which, perhaps, are no longer possible. The audience is diversified in terms of life-stages, as well as by other social and cultural characteristics; thus, what for youth may be the anticipatory enactment of roles to be assumed in the future may be, for older persons, a reliving and reevaluation of the actual or imagined past.

The enacted role may be an idealized version of an everyday performance—a successful para-social approximation of an ideal pattern, not often, perhaps never, achieved in real life. Here the contribution of the persona may be to hold up a magic mirror to his followers, playing his reciprocal part more skillfully and ideally than do the partners of the real world. So Liberace, for example, outdoes the ordinary husband in gentle understanding, or Nancy Berg outdoes the ordinary wife in amorous complaisance. Thus, the spectator may be enabled to play his part suavely and completely in imagination as he is unable to do in actuality.

If we have emphasized the opportunities offered for playing a vicarious or actual role, it is because we regard this as the key operation in the spectator's activity, and the chief avenue of the program's meaning for him. This is not to overlook the fact that every social role is reciprocal to the social roles of others, and that it is as important to learn to understand, to decipher, and to anticipate their conduct as it is to manage one's own. The function of the mass media, and of the programs we have been discussing, is also the exemplification of the patterns of conduct one needs to understand and cope with in others as well as of those patterns which one must apply to one's self. Thus the spectator is instructed variously in the behaviors of the opposite sex, of people of higher and lower status, of people in particular occupations and professions. In a quantitative sense, by reason of the sheer volume of such instruction, this may be the most important aspect of the para-social experience, if only because each person's roles are relatively few, while those of the others in his social worlds are very numerous. In this culture, it is evident that to be prepared to meet all the exigencies of a changing social situation, no matter how limited it may be, could—and often does—require a great stream of plays and stories, advice columns and social how-to-do-it books. What, after all, is soap opera but an interminable exploration of the contingencies to be met with in "home life?" [18]

In addition to the possibilities we have already mentioned, the media present opportunities for the playing of roles to which the spectator has—or feels he has—a legitimate claim, but for which he finds no opportunity in his social environment. This function of the para-social then can properly be called compensatory, inasmuch as it provides the socially and psychologically isolated with a chance to enjoy the elixir of sociability. The "personality" program—in contrast to the drama—is especially designed to provide occasion for good-natured joking and teasing, praising and admiring, gossiping and telling anecdotes, in which the values of friendship and intimacy are stressed.

It is typical of the "personality" programs that ordinary people are shown being treated, for the moment, as persons of consequence. In the interviews of nonprofessional contestants, the subject may be praised for having children—whether few or many does not matter; he may be flattered on his youthful appearance; and he is likely to be honored the more—with applause from the studio audience—the longer he has been "successfully" married. There is even applause, and a consequent heightening of ceremony and importance for the person being interviewed, at mention of the town he lives in. In all this, the values realized for the subject are those of a harmonious, successful participation in one's appointed place in the social order. The subject is represented as someone secure in the affections and respect of others, and he probably senses the experience as a gratifying reassurance of social solidarity and self-confidence. For the audience, in the studio and at home, it is a model of appropriate role performance—as husband, wife, mother, as "attractive" middle age, "remarkably youthful" old age, and the like. It is, furthermore, a demonstration of the fundamental generosity and good will of all concerned, including, of course, the commercial sponsor. [19] But unlike a similar exemplification of happy sociability in a play or a novel, the television or radio program is real; that is to say, it is enveloped in the continuing reassurances and gratifications of objective responses. For instance there may be telephone calls to "outside" contestants, the receipt and acknowledgement of requests from the home audience, and so on. Almost every member of the home audience is left with the comfortable feeling that he too, if he wished, could appropriately take part in this healing ceremony.

Extreme Para-Sociability

For the great majority of the audience, the para-social is complementary to normal social life. It provides a social milieu in which the everyday assumptions and understandings of primary group interaction and sociability are demonstrated and reaffirmed. The "personality" program, however, is peculiarly favorable to the formation of compensatory attachments by the socially isolated, the socially inept, the aged and invalid, the timid and rejected. The persona himself is readily available as an object of love—especially when he succeeds in cultivating the recommended quality of "heart." Nothing could be more reasonable or natural than that people who are isolated and lonely should seek sociability and love wherever they think they can find it. It is only when the para-social relationship becomes a substitute for autonomous social participation, when it proceeds in absolute defiance of objective reality, that it can be regarded as pathological.[20]

The existence of a marginal segment of the lonely in American society has been recognized by the mass media themselves, and from time to time specially designed offerings have been addressed to this minority.[21] In these programs, the maximum illusion of a personal, intimate relationship has been attempted. They represent the extreme development of the para-social, appealing to the most isolated, and illustrate, in an exaggerated way, the principles we believe to apply through the whole range of "personality" programs. The programs which fall in this extreme category promise not only escape from an unsatisfactory and drab reality, but try to prop up the sagging self-esteem of their unhappy audience by the most blatant reassurances. Evidently on the presumption that the maximum of loneliness is the lack of a sexual partner, these programs tend to be addressed to one sex or the other, and to endow the persona with an erotic suggestiveness.[22]

Such seems to have been the purpose and import of *The Lonesome Gal,* a short radio program which achieved such popularity in 1951 that it was broadcast in ninety different cities. Within a relatively short time, the program spread from Hollywood, where it had originated, across the country to New York, where it was heard each evening at 11:15.[23]

The outline of the program was simplicity itself. After a preliminary flourish of music, and an identifying announcement, the main and only character was ushered into the presence of the audience. She was exactly as represented, apparently a lonesome girl, but without a name or a history. Her entire performance consisted of an unbroken monologue unembarrassed by plot, climax, or denouement. On the continuum of para-social action, this is the very opposite of self-contained drama; it is, in fact, nothing but the reciprocal of the spectator's own para-social role. The Lonesome Gal simply spoke in a throaty, unctuous voice whose suggestive sexiness belied the seeming modesty of her words.[24]

From the first, the Lonesome Gal took a strongly intimate line, almost as if she were addressing a lover in the utter privacy of some hidden rendez-vous:

> Darling, you look so tired, and a little put out about something this evening. . . . You are worried, I feel it. Lover, you need rest . . . rest and someone who understands you. Come, lie down on the couch, relax, I want to stroke your hair gently . . . I am with you now, always with you. You are never alone, you must never forget that you mean everything to me, that I live only for you, your Lonesome Gal.

At some time in the course of each program, the Lonesome Gal specifically assured her listeners that these endearments were not being addressed to the hale and handsome, the clever and the well-poised, but to the shy, the withdrawn—the lonely men who had always dreamed, in their inmost reveries, of finding a lonesome girl to comfort them.

The world is literally full of such lonesome girls, she urged; like herself, they were all seeking love and companionship. Fate was unkind, however, and they were disappointed and left in unrequited loneliness, with no one to console them. On the radio, the voice was everybody's Lonesome Gal:

> Don't you see, darling, that I am only one of millions of lonely girls. I belong to him who spends his Sundays in museums, who strolls in Central Park looking sadly at the lovers there. But I am more fortunate than any of these lovers, because I have you. Do you know that I am always thinking about you? . . . You need someone to worry about you, who will look after your health, you need me. I share your hopes and your disappointments. I, your Lonesome Gal, your girl, to whom you so often feel drawn in the big city where so many are lonely. . . .

The Lonesome Gal was inundated with thousands of letters tendering proposals of marriage, the writers respectfully assuring her that she was indeed the woman for whom they had been vainly searching all their lives.

As a character in a radio program, the Lonesome Gal had certain advantages in the cultivation of para-social attachments over television offerings of a similar tenor. She was literally an unseen presence, and each of her listeners could, in his mind's eye, picture her as his fancy dictated. She could, by an act of the imagination, be almost any age or any size, have any background.

Not so Miss Nancy Berg, who began to appear last year in a five-minute television spot called *Count Sheep*.[25] She is seen at 1 A.M. each weekday. After an announcement card has flashed to warn the audience that she is about to appear, and a commercial has been read, the stage is entirely given over to Miss Berg. She emerges in a lavishly decorated bedroom clad in a peignoir, or negligee, minces around the room stretches, yawns, jumps into bed, and then wriggles out again for a final romp with her French poodle. Then she crawls under the covers, cuddles up for the night, and composes herself for sleep. The camera pans down for an enormous close-up, and the microphones catch Miss Berg whispering a sleepy "Good-night." From out of the distance soft music fades in, and the last thing the viewers see is a cartoon of sheep jumping over a fence. The program is over.

There is a little more to the program than this. Each early morning, Miss Berg is provided with a special bit of dialogue or business which, brief though it is, delights her audience afresh:

> Once, she put her finger through a pizza pie, put the pie on a record player and what came out was Dean Martin singing "That's Amore." She has read, with expression, from "Romeo and Juliet," "Of Time and the River," and her fan mail. She has eaten grapes off a toy ferris-wheel and held an imaginary telephone conversation with someone who, she revealed when it was all over, had the wrong number.[26]

Sometimes she regales her viewers with a personal detail. For instance, she has explained that the dog which appears on the show is her own. Its name is "Phaedeaux," she disclosed coyly, pronounced "Fido."

It takes between twenty and twenty-six people, aside from Miss Berg herself, to put this show on the air; and all of them seem to be rather bemused by the success she is enjoying. Her manager, who professes himself happily baffled by the whole thing, tried to discover some of the reasons for this success in a recent interview when he was questioned about the purpose of the show:

> Purpose? The purpose was, Number 1, to get a sponsor; Number 2, to give people a chance to look at a beautiful girl at 1 o'clock in the morning; Number 3, to do some off-beat stuff. I think this girl's going to be a big star, and this was a way to get attention for her. We sure got it. She's a showman, being slightly on the screwball side, but there's a hell of a brain there. She just doesn't touch things—she caresses things. Sometimes, she doesn't say anything out loud, maybe she's thinking what you're thinking.[27]

The central fact in this explanation seems to be the one which touches on Miss Berg's ability to suggest to her audience that she is privy to, and might share, their inmost thoughts. This is precisely the impression that the Lonesome Gal attempted to create, more directly and more conversationally, in her monologue. Both programs were geared to fostering and maintaining the illusion of intimacy which we mentioned earlier in our discussion. The sexiness of both these programs must, we think, be read in this light. They are seductive in more than the ordinary sense. Sexual suggestiveness is used probably because it is one of the most obvious cues to a supposed intimacy—a catalytic for prompt sociability.

Such roles as Miss Berg and the Lonesome Gal portray require a strict adherence to a standardized portrayal of their "personalities." Their actual personalities, and the details of their backgrounds, are not allowed to become sharply focused and differentiated, for each specification of particular detail might alienate some part of the audience, or might interfere with rapport. Thus, Miss Berg, despite the apparent intimacy of her show—the audience is invited into her bedroom—refuses to disclose her "dimensions," although this is a piece of standard information freely available about movie beauties.

The Lonesome Gal was even more strict regarding personal details. Only once did she appear in a public performance away from her radio show. On that occasion she wore a black mask over her face, and was introduced to her "live" audience on the same mysteriously anonymous terms as she met her radio audience. Rumor, however, was not idle, and one may safely presume that these rumors ran current to provide her with a diffuse glamour of a kind which her audience would think appropriate. It was said that she lived in Hollywood, but that she originally came from Texas, a state which, in popular folklore, enjoys a lively reputation for improbabilities and extravagances. Whispers also had it that French and Indian blood coursed in her veins, a combination all too likely to suggest wildness and passion to the stereotypes of her listeners. For the rest, nothing was known of her, and no further details were apparently ever permitted.

The Image as Artifact

The encouragement of, not to say demand for, a sense of intimacy with the persona and an appreciation of him as a "real" person is in contradiction to the fact that the image he presents is to some extent a construct—a facade—which bears little resemblance to his private character. The puritanical conventions of the contemporary media make this facade a decidedly namby-pamby one. With few exceptions, the popular figures of radio and television are, or give the appearance of being, paragons of middle-class virtue with decently modest intellectual capacities. Since some of them are really very intelligent and all of them are, like the rest of us, strong and weak, good and bad, the facade is maintained only by concealing discrepancies between the public image and the private life.

The standard technique is not to make the private life an absolute secret—for the interest of the audience cannot be ignored—but to create an acceptable facade of private life as well, a more or less contrived private image of the life behind the contrived public image. This is the work of the press agent, the publicity man, and the fan magazine. How successfully they have done their work is perhaps indicated by the current vogue of magazines devoted to the "dirt" behind the facade.[28]

Public preoccupation with the private lives of stars and personae is not self-explanatory. Sheer appreciation and understanding of their performances as actors, singers, or entertainers does not depend upon information about them as persons. And undoubtedly many members of the audience do enjoy them without knowing or caring to know about their homes, children, sports cars, or favorite foods, or keeping track of the ins and outs of their marriages and divorces. It has often been said that the Hollywood stars—and their slightly less glamorous colleagues of radio and television—are modern "heroes" in whom are embodied popular cultural values, and that the interest in them is a form of hero-worship and vicarious experience through identification. Both of these interpretations may be true; we would emphasize, however, a third motive—the confirmation and enrichment of the para-social relation with them. It may be precisely because this is basically an illusion that such an effort is required to confirm it. It seems likely that those to whom para-social relationships are important must constantly strive to overcome the inherent limitations of these relationships, either by elaborating the image of the other, or by attempting to transcend the illusion by making some kind of actual contact with him.

Given the prolonged intimacy of para-social relations with the persona, accompanied by the assurance that beyond the illusion there is a real person, it is not surprising that many members of the audience become dissatisfied and attempt to establish actual contact with him. Under exactly what conditions people are motivated to write to the performer, or to go further and attempt to meet him—to draw from him a personal response—we do not know. The fan phenomenon has been studied to some extent,[29] but fan clubs and fan demonstrations are likely to be group affairs, motivated as much by the values of collective participation with others as by devotion to the persona himself. There are obvious social rewards for the trophies of contact with the famous or notorious—from autographs to handkerchiefs dipped in the dead bandit's blood—which invite toward their possessor some shadow of the attitudes of awe or admiration originally directed to their source. One would suppose that contact with, and recogniton by, the persona transfers some of his prestige and influence to the active fan. And most often such attempts to reach closer to the persona are limited to letters and to visits. But in the extreme case, the social rewards of mingling with the mighty are foregone for the satisfaction of some deeply private purpose. The follower is actually "in love" with the persona, and demands real reciprocity which the para-social relation cannot provide.

A case in point is provided in the "advice" column of a newspaper.[30] The writer, Miss A, has "fallen in love" with a television star, and has begun to rearrange and reorder her life to conform to her devotion to this man whom she has never actually met. It is significant, incidentally, that the man is a local performer—the probability of actually meeting him must seem greater than would be the case if he were a New York or Hollywood figure. The border between Miss A's fantasies and reality is being steadily encroached upon by the important affective investment she has made in this relationship. Her letter speaks for itself:

> It has taken me two weeks to get the nerve to write this letter. I have fallen head over heels in love with a local television star. We've never met and I've seen him only on the TV screen and in a play. This is not a 16-year-old infatuation, for I am 23, a college graduate and I know the score. For the last two months I have stopped dating because all men seem childish by comparison. Nothing interests me. I can't sleep and my modeling job bores me. Please give me some advice.

The writer of this letter would seem to be not one of the lonely ones, but rather a victim of the "magic mirror" in which she sees a man who plays the role reciprocal to hers so ideally that all the men she actually knows "seem childish by comparison." Yet this is not the image of a fictional hero; it is a "real" man. It is interesting that the newspaper columnist, in replying, chooses to attack on this point—not ridiculing the possibility of a meeting with the star, but denying the reality of the image:

> I don't know what you learned in college, but you are flunking the course of common sense. You have fallen for a piece of celluloid as unreal as a picture on the wall. The personality you are goofy about on the TV screen is a hoked-up character, and any similarity between him and the real man is purely miraculous.

This case is revealing, however, not only because it attests to the vigor with which a para-social relationship may become endowed, but also because it demonstrates how narrow the line often is between the more ordinary forms of social interaction and those which characterize relations with the persona. In an extreme case, such as that of Miss A, her attachment to the persona has greatly invaded her everyday life—so much so that, without control, it will warp or destroy her relations with the opposite sex. But the extreme character of this response should not obscure the fact that ordinarily para-social relations do "play back," as it were, into the daily lives of many. The man who reports to his friend the wise thing that Godfrey said, who carefully plans not to make another engagement at the time his favorite is on, is responding similarly, albeit to a different and milder degree. Para-social interaction, as we have said, is analogous to and in many ways resembles social interaction in ordinary primary groups.

The new mass media are obviously distinguished by their ability to confront a member of the audience with an apparently intimate, face-to-face association with a performer. Nowhere does this feature of their technological resources seem more forcefully or more directly displayed than in the "personality" program. In these programs a new kind of performer, the persona, is featured whose main attribute seems to be his ability to cultivate and maintain this suggested intimacy. As he appears before his audience, in program after program, he carries on recurrent social transactions with his adherents; he sustains what we have called para-social interaction. These adherents, as members of his audience, play a psychologically active role which, under some conditions, but by no means invariably, passes over into the more formal, overt, and expressive activities of fan behavior.

As an implicit response to the performance of the persona, this para-social interaction is guided and to some extent controlled by him. The chief basis of this guidance and control, however, lies in the imputation to the spectator of a kind of role complementary to that of the persona himself. This imputed complementary role is social in character, and is some variant of the role or roles normally played in the spectator's primary social groups. It is defined, demonstrated, and inculcated by numerous devices of radio and television showmanship. When it has been learned, the persona is assured that the entire transaction between himself and the audience—of which his performance is only one phase—is being properly completed by the unseen audience.

Seen from this standpoint, it seems to follow that there is no such discontinuity between everyday and para-social experience as is suggested by the common practice, among observers of these media, of using the analogy of fantasy or dream in the interpretation of programs which are essentially dramatic in character. The relationship of the devotee to the persona is, we suggest, experienced as of the same order as, and related to, the network of actual social relations. This, we believe, is even more the case when the persona becomes a common object to the members of the primary groups in which the spectator carries on his everyday life. As a matter of fact, it seems profitable to consider the interaction with the persona as a phase of the role-enactments of the spectator's daily life.

Our observations in this paper, however, are intended to be no more than suggestions for further work. It seems to us that it would be a most rewarding approach to such phenomena if one could, from the viewpoint of an interactional social psychology, learn in detail how these para-social interactions are integrated into the matrix of usual social activity.

In this connection, it is relevant to remark that there is a tradition—now of relatively long standing—that spectators, whether at sports events or television programs, are relatively passive. This assertion enjoys the status of an accredited hypothesis, but it is, after all, no more than a hypothesis. If it is taken literally and uncritically, it may divert the student's attention from what is actually transpiring in the audience. We believe that some such mode of analysis as we suggest here attunes the student of the mass media to hints *within the program itself* of cues to, and demands being made on, the audience for particular responses. From such an analytical vantage point the field of observation, so to speak, is widened and the observer is able to see more that is relevant to the exchange between performer and audience.

In essence, therefore, we would like to expand and capitalize on the truism that the persona and the "personality" programs are part of the lives of millions of people, by asking how both are assimilated, and by trying to discover what effects these responses have on the attitudes and actions of the audiences who are so devoted to and absorbed in this side of American culture.

Notes

1. They may move out into positions of leadership in the world at large as they become famous and influential. Frank Sinatra, for example, has become known as a "youth leader." Conversely, figures from the political world, to choose another example, may become media "personalities" when they appear regularly. Fiorello LaGuardia, the late Mayor of New York, is one such case.
2. Merton's discussion of the attitude toward Kate Smith of her adherents exemplifies, with much circumstantial detail, what we have said above. See Robert K. Merton, Marjorie Fiske, and Alberta Curtis, *Mass Persuasion: The Social Psychology of a War Bond Drive;* New York, Harper, 1946; especially Chapter 6.
3. There does remain the possibility that over the course of his professional life the persona, responding to influences from his audience, may develop new conceptions of himself and his role.
4. Dave Garroway as told to Joe Alex Morris, "I Lead a Goofy Life," *The Saturday Evening Post,* February 11, 1956; p. 62.

5. Garroway, *Saturday Evening Post*, p. 64.

6. See, for instance: George H. Mead, *Mind, Self and Society*; Chicago, Univ. of Chicago Press, 1934. Walter Coutu, *Emergent Human Nature*; New York, Knopf, 1949. Rosalind Dymond, "Personality and Empathy," *J. Consulting Psychol.* (1950) 14:343–350.

7. Burke uses this expression to describe an attitude evoked by formal rhetorical devices, but it seems equally appropriate here. See Kenneth Burke, *A Rhetoric of Motives*; New York, Prentice-Hall, 1950; p. 58.

8. This is in contrast to the closed system of the drama, in which all the roles are predetermined in their mutual relations.

9. Kenneth Burke, *Attitudes Toward History, Vol. 1;* New York, New Republic Publishing Co., 1937; see, for instance, p. 104.

10. See Merton's acute analysis of the audience's demand for "sincerity" as a reassurance against manipulation. *Mass Persuasion*, pp. 142–146.

11. These attributes have been strikingly discussed by Mervyn LeRoy, a Hollywood director, in a recent book. Although he refers specifically to the motion-picture star, similar notions are common in other branches of show business. "What draws you to certain people?" he asks. "I have said before that you can't be a really fine actress or actor without heart. You also have to possess the ability to project that heart, that feeling and emotion. The sympathy in your eyes will show. The audience has to feel sorry for the person on the screen. If there aren't moments when, rightly or wrongly, he moves the audience to sympathy, there's an actor who will never be big box-office." Mervyn LeRoy and Alyce Canfield, *It Takes More Than Talent*; New York, Knopf, 1953; p. 114.

12. Once an actor has succeeded in establishing a good relationship with his audience in a particular kind of dramatic role, he may be "typed" in that role. Stereotyping in the motion-picture industry is often rooted in the belief that sustained rapport with the audience can be achieved by repeating past success. (This principle is usually criticized as detrimental to the talent of the actor, but it is a *sine qua non* for the persona whose professional success depends upon creating and sustaining a plausible and unchanging identity.) Sometimes, indeed, the Hollywood performer will actually take his name from a successful role; this is one of the principles on which Warner Brothers Studios selects the names of some of its actors. For instance, Donna Lee Hickey was renamed Mae Wynn after a character she portrayed, with great distinction, in *The Caine Mutiny*. See "Names of Hollywood Actors," *Names* (1955) 3:116.

13. The "loyalty" which is demanded of the audience is not necessarily passive or confined only to patronizing the persona's performance. Its active demonstration is called for in charity appeals, "marathons," and "telethons"; and, of course, it is expected to be freely transferable to the products advertised by the performer. Its most active form is represented by the organization of fan clubs with programs of activities and membership obligations, which give a continuing testimony of loyalty.

14. Comedians on radio and television frequently chide their audience if they do not laugh at the appropriate places, or if their response is held to be inadequate. The comedian tells the audience that if they don't respond promptly, he won't wait, whereupon the audience usually provides the demanded laugh. Sometimes the chiding is more oblique, as when the comedian interrupts his performance to announce that he will fire the writer of the unsuccessful joke.

Again, the admonition to respond correctly is itself treated as a joke and is followed by a laugh.

15. Coutu, *Emergent Human Nature,* p. 294.

16. See, for example, W. Lloyd Warner and William E. Henry, "The Radio Day Time Serial: A Symbolic Analysis," *Genetic Psychol. Monographs* (1948) 37:3–71, the study of a daytime radio serial program in which it is shown that upper-middle-class women tend to reject identification with lower-middle-class women represented in the drama. Yet some people are willing to take unfamiliar roles. This appears to be especially characteristic of the intellectual whose distinction is not so much that he has cosmopolitan tastes and knowledge, but that he has the capacity to transcend the limits of his own culture in his identifications. Remarkably little is known about how this ability is developed.

17. Most students of the mass media occupy a cultural level somewhat above that of the most popular programs and personalities of the media, and necessarily look down upon them. But it should not be forgotten that for many millions indulgence in these media is a matter of looking up. Is it not also possible that some of the media permit a welcome regression, for some, from the higher cultural standards of their present status? This may be one explanation of the vogue of detective stories and science fiction among intellectuals, and might also explain the escape downward from middle-class standards in the literature of "low life" generally.

18. It is frequently charged that the media's description of this side of life is partial, shallow, and often false. It would be easier and more profitable to evaluate these criticisms if they were formulated in terms of role-theory. From the viewpoint of any given role it would be interesting to know how well the media take account of the values and expectations of the role-reciprocators. What range of legitimate variations in role performance is acknowledged? How much attention is given to the problems arising from changing roles, and how creatively are these problems handled? These are only a few of the many similar questions which at once come to mind.

19. There is a close analogy here with one type of newspaper human-interest story which records extreme instances of role-achievement and their rewards. Such stories detail cases of extreme longevity, marriages of especially long duration, large numbers of children; deeds of heroism—role performance under "impossible" conditions; extraordinary luck, prizes, and so on.

20. Dave Garroway, after making the point that he has many "devout" admirers, goes on to say that "some of them . . . were a bit too devout." He tells the story of one lady "from a Western state" who "arrived in Chicago [where he was then broadcasting], registered at a big hotel as Mrs. Dave Garroway, opened several charge accounts in my name and established a joint bank account in which she deposited a large sum of money. Some months later she took a taxi to my hotel and informed the desk clerk she was moving in. He called a detective agency that we had engaged to check up on her, and they persuaded her to return home. Since then there have been others, but none so persistent." *Saturday Evening Post,* p. 62.

21. This group presumably includes those for whom "Lonely Hearts" and "Pen Pal" clubs operate.

22. While the examples which follow are of female personae addressing themselves to male audiences, it should be noted that for a time there was also a

program on television featuring *The Continental,* who acted the part of a debonair foreigner and whose performance consisted of murmuring endearing remarks to an invisible female audience. He wore evening clothes and cut a figure in full conformity with the American stereotype of a suave European lover.

23. This program apparently evoked no very great amount of comment or criticism in the American press, and we are indebted to an article in a German illustrated weekly for details about the show, and for the verbatim quotations from the Lonesome Gal's monologue which we have retranslated into English. See "Ich bin bei dir, Liebling . . . ," *Weltbild* (Munich), March 1, 1952; p. 12.

24. This is in piquant contrast to the popular singers, the modesty of whose voice and mien is often belied by the sexiness of the words in the songs they sing.

25. The details relating to this show are based on Gilbert Millstein, "Tired of it All?" *The New York Times Magazine,* September 18, 1955; p. 44. See also "Beddy-Bye," *Time,* August 15, 1955; p. 45.

26. *The New York Times Magazine,* p. 44.

27. *The New York Times Magazine,* p. 44.

28. Such magazines as *Uncensored* and *Confidential* (which bears the subtitle, "Tells the Facts and Names the Names") enjoy enormous circulations, and may be thought of as the very opposite of the fan magazine. They claim to "expose" the person behind the persona.

29. M. F. Thorp, *America at the Movies;* New Haven, Yale Univ. Press, 1939. S. Stansfeld Sargent, *Social Psychology;* New York, Ronald Press, 1950. K. P. Berliant, "The Nature and Emergence of Fan Behavior" (unpublished M.A. Thesis, Univ. of Chicago).

30. Ann Landers, "Your Problems," *Chicago Sun-Times,* October 25, 1955, p. 36.

ROBERT CATHCART

Our Soap Opera Friends

Are you part of the growing number of persons addicted to the "soaps"? After a half century of broadcasting, soap operas have become a staple of American life and they draw an audience far more extensive that the mythical "house-wife" soap opera fanatic. In an essay devoted to the traditional daytime soap opera Cathcart examines it as surrogate interpersonal communication. He explains the conventions of plot, structure, and production which make it possible for the viewer to be drawn into intimate emotional involvement with the characters. He describes the needs of viewers and the social conditions that create an environment where soap opera viewing can be a satisfying substitute or surrogate for interpersonal emotional expression.

"It's just like soap opera," is a phrase so common we cannot doubt the important place of "the soaps" in American life. Since its inception in the 1930s as the staple of daytime radio, soap opera has provided listeners/viewers with surrogate families, relatives, and neighbors exploring intimate interpersonal relationships against a backdrop of the pressing social issues of the day. In the 1930s radio soap opera characters spent days—even months—talking about the attractive young widow who had moved into the neighborhood, posing a threat to existing family relationships. Or, they heatedly discussed what to do with the knowledge that Martha had had an illegitimate child 15 years earlier. In the 1940s and 1950s the same sets of characters, now on both radio and television, faced the spectre of divorce, anguishing over its impact on family and friends, or they worked out their mixed feelings about Josh's affair with his secretary. In the 1960s and 1970s television soap opera talk centered around the birth of a deformed baby, or a rebellious wife or daughter who ran off to the big city. In the 1980s . . . well, we all know that Luke began his relationship with Laura by raping her.

No matter how the social issues have changed, the cast of characters has not. There is always a family with many kin, some grown children, a mother-in-law, a domineering father or boss, at least one set of sibling rivals, a woman who is compassionate and understanding, another who is a bitch goddess, and at least one troubled male who is trying to make things work out. House and office settings predominate, along with "intimate" public settings like a bar or tavern where intense talk can take place. The important thing in soap opera is not the social issues, the settings, or the cast of characters per se, but an intricate plot which allows for *communication about interpersonal relationships*. You don't have to be a soap opera addict to know that it provides Americans with a daily ongoing, unending emotional look at themselves. The emotional dimension of interpersonal communication is the substance of soap opera.

Soap opera is a form of *mediated interpersonal communication*. Interacting with soap opera is a way of expanding interpersonal relationships. By accepting the persona of one or more soap opera characters we can extend and/or substitute for our emotional involvement with others. Soap opera interaction places us in a special community, with much more intense interpersonal networks than we can actually attain in everyday life. In soap opera land we might have an absolutely hateful mother or mother-in-law, a dishonest business partner, a mentally ill brother or sister, a mysterious uncle, a famous but alcoholic doctor, a beautiful but troubled lover, etc., all interconnected and interacting in ways which we seldom experience in our personal lives. Becoming hooked on soap opera plugs us into interpersonal networks where for an hour or more each day we can lipsynch our own actual and fantasized emotional involvements. Every possible nuance of human relationship is explored and reexplored without end. Every conceivable personal tragedy which could befall family or friends is set before us. We are invited to probe our emotions through a soap opera persona.

The dramatism of soap opera offers no solutions to life's problems, no happy endings, no catharsis, and no guide to the transcendent meaning of life (Porter, 1979). Human activity in soap opera unfolds without any grand plan. Tragedy befalls the innocent as well as the guilty. Ethics and morality are strictly situational. Although there are moments of high climax and heroic action, these do not bring insight or release, for the next episode returns to the same old problems, the nagging doubts, the selfish concerns, the ongoing emotional tension. Although somewhat glamorized and certainly intensified, soap opera lives, like our own, merely go on without teaching us any great lessons. Soap opera confirms what we know from our experience; it is not events and action that really matter, *but how we talk about them*. It is both reassuring and satisfying to know that our own daily talk has been made into a video art form.

If soap opera is such a satisfying surrogate interpersonal activity, why, then, do many nonviewers and critics regard it with contempt? Many claim there is little morally or educationally uplifting about soap opera; soaps do not inspire us the way a good dramatic work should. It is true that soap opera is easy to attack as a dramatic art because it seems to offer nothing except emotional self-indulgence. Little or no imagination is required.

Viewers are free to bring to the involvement whatever they wish. Interpretations made by viewers of a character's motives and meanings are just as valid as those of the writers. Unlike traditional drama, the viewer does not have to worry about what the writer intended, about missing some important symbolism or failing to appreciate superb acting. All the viewer has to do is become involved, join in and accept the premise that soap opera is like real life. Unlike elite cultural art forms, anyone can partake of soap opera. It requires no special effort, no special knowledge or preparation. It tells us that life is just like we experience it on televsion—or would experience it if we could.

Its easy availability to the mass audience makes it suspect and its enshrinement of the ordinary makes it unworthy because the traditional art forms are designed to tell us that life can and should be *more* than ordinary experience. Many of us feel that television viewing time should be productive and uplifting even when used for entertainment. No wonder many viewers deny their enthrallment with soap opera or put down those who admit attachment, for the soaps mire us ever deeper in our daily emotional experiences. In the American value hierarchy, speaking to the point, sticking to the issue, being objective, and not getting involved in personalities stands far above chewing the fat, shooting the bull, letting down your hair, and being emotional. Yet, all of us spend hours, days, even years in "pointless" discussion of the meaning of ordinary interactions with others and how we feel about ourselves. A mother and father can spend hours talking about the "real" reason their son's girl friend called them on the phone. A husband and wife may spend days discussing that casual remark of a neighborhood couple that they used to be "swingers." A mother and daughter can converse for months about the dinner given by the daughter for her in-laws; who said what to whom, how many times, why, who said what in return, etc. A young, romantically involved couple can spend endless hours discussing how "she" really feels about "his" best friend. To admit to such "unproductive talk" would make us appear self-indulgent and small minded. We prefer to think, or have others think, that we spend the bulk of our interpersonal time profitably solving problems enlightening others as well as ourselves. To admit to heavy soap opera involvement is to accept that we not only participate in unending interpersonal emotional talk but that we want to extend and expand that kind of involvement.

Despite disclaimers, survey data reveal that 50 to 70 million Americans watch soap operas, and that 20 million or more watch it on a daily basis. The myth that only frustrated housewives with nothing else to do are soap opera addicts has been exploded by research revealing that millions of males, from parking lot attendants to physicians to at least one Supreme Court justice, are equally involved in soap opera interaction. On campuses across the nation, students and professors arrange their schedules to allow time for their favorite soap. The presence of a dozen or more soap opera magazines like *Daily TV Serials, Day Time Television,* summaries, and previews in local newspapers and TV news shows, as well as interviews with soap opera characters, attest the legitimization and institutionalization of soap opera in American life. For over five decades (and even longer if one counts Victorian era magazine and newspaper serials and American comic strips like "Mary Worth" and "Brenda Starr") soap opera has carved a special niche for itself in postindustrial society. It is neither traditional drama nor the framed narrative of the "sit com" or the prime-time dramatic serial. Instead, it is, like para-social interaction, a form of pseudo-interpersonal communication. It allows viewers to engage in a type of mediated interpersonal communication if they will accept certain constraints on their involvement while at the same time tacitly agreeing to play an answering role.

Let us explore what it is that makes soap opera interaction an extension of, and substitute for, face-to-face interpersonal communication. First, we should note that soap opera and major broadcast networks were partners in an ideal marriage. In the early days of TV, broadcast stations, to maintain their FCC licenses, had to agree to broadcast in daytime hours, i.e., during the time when most children were in school and a large part of the population was at work. For this they needed low-cost programming because they could not attract advertising revenue for the small daytime audience. Soap operas, like game shows and talk shows, can be produced at a fraction of the cost of a prime-time show. Soap operas, unlike game shows, do not require advertisers to give away products. There is a "natural link" between advertisers, viewers, and consumers. The name "soap opera" replaced "daytime drama" because producers of soap became the main sponsors of daytime serials which attracted a large following of housewives who were the main purchasers of soap. The manufacturers of housekeeping products and cosmetics are still the primary sponsors of daytime soap opera. Their continued commitment to soap opera constitutes part of the loyalty which binds the sponsor, the network, the directors, the actors, and the viewers to the soap opera community. This arrangement is highly profitable to all concerned. The networks recoup the costs of a week's programming in one day. Advertisers have direct access on a daily basis to their most potent customers at rates much less than prime time. Producers, directors, writers, actors, and crews have regular 9 to 5 jobs (something very rare in the entertainment business). Viewers can "examine" the latest commercial products in the comfort of their homes, learning what's new, where it is available, and how it compares, secure in the knowledge that they are not missing out on what their neighbors have access to. This symbiotic relationship has made soap opera a staple of the broadcast industry. Changing work habits, flextime jobs, new roles for women, and alternate family arrangements are altering and will continue to alter this complementary mix. However, our need for fulfilling emotional interpersonal interaction ensures the longevity of soap opera.

Para-social interaction—interpersonal involvement with a television show personality—e.g. Johnny Carson, Phil Donahue—depends on an unspoken agreement that the personality will perform as though conversing face to face with the viewer and the viewer will take on an answering role which compensates for the distance inherent in mass mediated communication. Each is rewarded for maintaining this implicit agreement. The personality is supported and kept in a celebrity position and the viewer can reap the benefits of interpersonal intimacy without risk. The implicit arrangement between soap opera and the viewer is similar but not exactly the same. In the first place, soap opera characters do not speak directly through the lens to viewers and TV production techniques do not coach viewers to respond as though it were face-to-face communication. Rather, soap opera characters are "on stage" performing acting roles, playing out a script as though there were no audience present. It is this, more or less, traditional dramatic form that disguises the fact that soap opera is pseudo-interpersonal communication (Rosengren and Windahl, 1972).

If we look carefully at how soap opera differs from stage or movie drama and prime-time framed narrative drama, we will see that it is more akin to a stylized replay of daily life. First, and foremost, dramatic time is slowed down to fit the cycle of real time. If a character is sick or hospitalized, it takes several weeks of soap opera episodes for that person to recover. A soap opera pregnancy lasts nine months, a divorce may take six months or a year to complete, a secret affair may go on for years in actual time. In all traditional drama, time is compressed. On the stage, Henry VIII can be born, live through five marriages, conquer all his enemies, and die within the space of three hours of actual time. In a movie, Henry Fonda and Katharine Hepburn can live out the final two years of their relationship in one hour and 45 minutes. Even Archie Bunker can make several trips to the dentist within the space of a 24-minute episode. The reason for this is, of course, that a drama is not portraying life as it actually is but is trying to have us gain insight into the reasons behind human behavior, to understand some moral, or to feel release and escape from ordinary events by compressing and distorting the time involved. Soap opera is markedly different. It does not hold up a mirror to life, it is life. We are invited to spend some time (actual time) with our soap opera friends just as we are invited to spend some time with our school friends, our work friends, our neighbors, and our family. When we interact with soap opera, we do not expect events to be speeded up, repetitive talk to be dispensed with, motives to be openly revealed. We expect to be involved in the ordinary stuff (which can include broken romances, untrustworthy friends, hateful parents, loss of a job, even illness and death) that people in real time talk about and feel about. Talking about our dates, our jobs, our suspicions, our doubts, and our feelings is what we do over and over, day in and day out. Soap opera instutionalizes the pace and feel of daily talk. It doesn't rush us, it doesn't force us to accept a writer's philosophy. It doesn't present us with a conclusion.

The lack of conclusions or failure to wrap up the drama into a final climax is another way that soaps differ significantly from more usual dramatizations. No one lives happily ever after in soap opera. Persons with greedy, grasping personalities are not suddenly transformed by some climactic event. There are no superhero detectives or cowboys to ensure that evil is punished and good rewarded just before the final fadeout. And there is no internal or external narrator to explain to us what it all means. Soap operas, like life, simply go on. To be sure, they involve us in many more human dilemmas, tragedies, illnesses, and catastrophies than anyone of us could experience in several lifetimes, but they do not preach at us (at least not directly) by bringing every event and human relationship to some significant conclusion. Nor do they try to transform all human frailty into comedy. What they give us is a chance to talk out, to express how we feel about, all the emotional problems humans could possibly face in the here and now. Soap opera says to us that there are no solutions, just human relationships. It says, come join with us and we will give you an unending panoply of human involvements in which you can explore your own feelings (Adler, 1979).

Soap opera drama, unlike other dramatic forms, never strays from the contemporary. No soap opera is ever set in pre-Civil War times or on the starship Galactica. Soap opera does not invite us to stand outside of time in order to learn some lesson about life or to fulfill some imaginary yearning. Instead, it firmly anchors us to the time in which we live. The settings are contemporary, dress and language are of the moment. And, as we mentioned earlier, human predicaments are framed by contemporary social issues. It is no accident that soaps are ahead of prime-time TV—even Hollywood movies—in exploring rape, abortion, child abuse, and drug addiction.

In order to keep us involved on an interpersonal level, soap opera relationships must reproduce the same emotional tensions that exist in our everyday lives. (Davis and Baron, 1981). Even those who object to talking about controversial subjects in public are invited to join in through character personae who reflect their feelings. By never straying from the contemporary, by relating characters to the pressing emotional issues of the moment, by substituting talk for action, soap opera invites the viewer into the scene on his or her own terms. Whereas traditional drama requires the observer to maintain a certain distance and objectivity, soap opera drama uses every device to destroy dramatic distance, to make it easy for the viewer to accept that he or she is part of the soap opera community.

The camera work and the formulaic production of soap opera effectively destroy dramatic distance. What appears to some critics as dramatic weakness—the repetitive monotony of camera angles, lighting, setting, camera movement, and editing—works to establish a simple, clear code making it easy for viewers to follow the story line and to identify with the characters. There are no unexpected or unusual camera shots. The settings are familiar and unchanging. The overworked dramatic chords of music are fixed signals of suspense and emotion. The very obviousness and repetitiveness of soap opera production grammar works to make the viewer forget about the camera and production techniques. "Realistic illusion" is the goal of soap opera filmic technique. When done skillfully, it lulls the viewer into a state of obliviousness to the art and craft of production. One imagines the camera as simply a peephole into reality. The importance of this for soap opera is that it gives the viewer the sense of being there—being in on the conversation, the emotional tension, the gestural nuance—without having to work intellectually to transcend either the dramatic or mediated distance.

It is true, of course, that all producers and directors of staged drama strive to minimize art and craft thereby making possible the willing suspension of disbelief. But, unlike the soap opera producer, the dramatist utilizes deviations from the dramatic routine to heighten tension, to create anticipation, and to achieve dramatic impact. Unusual and unexpected movements and forms are purposefully employed requiring the audience to go along with the dramatist's interpretation of reality (Meyrowitz, 1978). For example, in a motion picture film, the camera might pan to the ceiling and linger there, ignoring the characters conversing below. Or, the camera might shift back and forth rapidly from a closeup of a galloping horse and sweaty rider to maximum distance shots where both appear as a tiny blur on a vast desert. In a stage production, the lights might suddenly dim, the actors frozen in a tableau while a ghostly lit figure appears high up in the proscenium. Such production tricks require the audience to accept the play on the dramatist's terms. For a staged drama to work, there must be a dramatic distance for the audience to transcend—a transcendency that moves audience members outside themselves and into the dramatic world of the play.

Soap opera effects are achieved in a quite opposite manner. There are no tricks or "violations" of the soap opera filming code. The production format remains what it has been for over 30 years. The idea is to not provoke the viewer with unusual techniques. New camera techniques, like the halo frame in dream sequences, are introduced slowly over long periods of time. In soap opera everything works to maintain the realistic illusion of viewer participation *within* the group. For this reason, commercials are clearly separate from the soap opera story. When the commercial appears, the soap opera performance stops abruptly. Then the commercial disappears and the story resumes as though the characters and the viewers had only blinked their eyes. Each new soap opera episode begins with the camera picking up the action where it left off in the last one. At the start, the program logo is superimposed over the action, assuring the viewer that he or she is in the right place. It is like seeing the familiar street sign as you turn into your neighborhood street. There are no narrators or announcers to set the scene or incidentally remind us that it is happening in some other time and place. As the camera moves in on the characters and the action begins, the camera eye becomes our eye and we step into the setting, ready to partake of the interaction.

In many ways, the camera is the key to understanding soap opera as a surrogate form of interpersonal communication (Meyrowitz, 1978). Over the years a distinctive type of camera movement and framing has created the audiovisual codes which are the language of soap opera. There exists an intense, intimate camera style suited to the concentrated emotions that make up the content of soap opera (Timberg, 1982). It is the closeup and extreme closeup shot, combined with slow truck-ins and outs, a circling camera, and rapid reaction shots which distinguishes soap opera from other dramatic programming. Prime-time narrative drama keep us at a spectators distance through the use of medium and long shots and fixed camera angles and distances. Just as the canned laughter of the sitcom reminds us that we are an audience and not directly involved with the characters. Soap opera camera style works constantly to bring us "physically" and emotionally closer to its characters. As the camera moves right up to their eyes and mouths we see, hear, and feel every emotional nuance. Nothing about the person escapes our view. The camera even enters into the mind of the character in dream and memory sequences. At such intimate camera distance we cannot remain apart from the story and its characters any more than we can remain aloof from the conspirator who whispers in our ear. We can, when the camera lets us, step back and view the two or three characters as they speak their lines, but soon the camera is circling or trucking slowly drawing us up to the characters and into their intense emotions. The ritual over-the-shoulder shot, along with the reaction shot, makes us a participant in the ongoing dialogue. The closeup, subjective shot makes us a party to the emotional expressions of anger, jealousy, sorrow, rage, pity, and self-doubt.

It is not just repetitive camera shots and angles that make soap opera so emotionally involving. There are a whole host of conventions which make it easy for the viewer to "read" the emotional story line and follow the intricate and intertwined plots. For example, the ritual opening of a scene with a closeup of a face, the eyes looking not into, but just past the camera, is accompanied by a dramatic chord of music and a long silence. This adjusts us to the scene and prepares us for the troubling confrontation which is about to unfold. Not a word is spoken, but the music helps us anticipate the interaction which will follow. The long pause signals us to recall what happened in the last scene with this person and to ready ourselves for the lines about to be spoken.

The lighting for soap opera, as well as the music, is so stylized that anyone flipping the TV channel selector would immediately recognize a soap opera even if the characters and the setting were unfamiliar (Timberg, 1982). Soap opera lighting, like the camera, brings us into close involvement with the performers. As a rule, there is little back lighting and rarely is the whole set illuminated evenly—conventions which are hallmarks of sitcoms and prime-time narrative drama. Lighting is always foreground in a soap opera with characters or other significant objects spotlighted. The lighting keeps us focused on the performers, enabling us to concentrate on the nonverbal nuances—tight jaw, the flicker of anger in the eyes, the trembling lip—which are so vital to emotional communication. The surrounding darkness or semidarkness characteristic of many soap operas may also contribute to the sense of personal isolation and loneliness which is the unspoken theme of soap opera.

To end a scene, the ritual is reversed. The camera moves in close, the troubled eyes look obliquely past it, and the dramatic chord of music freezes the scene into a tableau. The pause allows us to fully absorb the emotional meaning of the scene, to fix it in mind and hold it until we return to that character and his or her problem. Holding that final shot just as the door closes or the phone is hung up gives us a chance also to glimpse "true feelings" and to look as deeply into the character as our imaginations will let us.

There are, also, devices to help us keep track of the five or six simultaneously unfolding plots. One of them is "parallelism." If one scene ends in a confrontation over a third person in a love affair, the next scene will also involve a triangular relationship. Or, if a scene ends with a charater finally placing the phone call that has been avoided, the next scene will begin with someone just having concluded a telephone call. In this way the viewer is not called on to make too great an emotional and intellectual transition. The level of intensity of involvement and the type of interaction is carried over from one scene to another making it easy for the viewer to maintain the same feelings in each scene.

Telephones, doorbells, and doors also work to make possible the connections among the diverse couples and triples of soap opera. A soap opera could hardly proceed without the telephone which intervenes to end a scene, or to bring news we already know but the characters do not, or to move us to another place where an overwrought couple are awaiting a call which will bring the fateful news. The telephone is one of the most important symbols in soap opera. Often shown in close up, it symbolizes talk, which is the action of soap opera. It can also symbolize apartness—the waiting for a call or the connection with another that never comes. Or, it can symbolize the missing other whose call or potential call interjects into the conversation of the couple on camera. Or, it can symbolize being left behind or left out as when the phone rings and rings in an empty room and we fully comprehend what missing that call will mean in the life of one of the characters.

Doors and doorbells serve a similar symbolic function in soap opera. The ringing of the doorbell can signal the arrival of another character with all that portends for emotional confrontation (Porter, 1979). Or, it can signal a mysterious arrival, one not counted on, arousing fear of the unknown. Doors, of course, are symbols of separateness wherever they appear. We speak of closing the door on an episode in our own lives or slamming the door in the face of reality. In soap opera a door can close us in with a character while shutting out others. Or, it can effectively close one scene and open another. Doors are always being closed in soap operas—slowly, tentatively, firmly, with a bang—symbolizing that separateness which is so often the driving force behind soap opera involvement.

Taken together, all these production elements work, not only to move us into the intimate, intense, emotional world of soap opera, but also to give particular soap operas their own visual style (Timberg, 1982). Some, like *General Hospital* and *All My Children,* strive for realistic portrayals and a quickened pace. They rely on bright and harsh lighting, few dissolves, many quick cuts, and closeups of settings and equipment along with sounds of "the real world" filtered into the music and dialogue. Others, like *The Young and The Restless,* rely on chiaroscuro lighting, slow dissolves, gauzy dream sequences, muted background sounds, and strong dramatic musical chords to establish a more fantasylike setting.

What is it that makes soap opera so attractive to so many? Certainly it is not their refined dramatic interpretations nor their ability to provide lighthearted emotional release or adventurous escape. Instead, it is their use as a surrogate to interpersonal communication. Like para-social interaction, soap opera can be used to expand, or substitute for, face-to-face interaction, to compensate for the lack of enough emotional involvement with others, and to coach us in the appropriate responses to be made when we become involved in personal, emotional relationships. In more traditional societies where people are highly involved in family and neighborhood relationships, where complex personal involvements are part of daily activities, and where birth, courtship, marriage, illness, and death are the constant concern of everyone in the community, there is little need for surrogate interpersonal acts, or mediated fictional dramas to teach people how to be involved with others and how to satisfy their emotional hunger.

The high mobility and intense individualism of contemporary American society has broken down the small town and neighborhood networks which in the past provided us with ongoing emotional involvement in the affairs of family, friends, and neighbors (Adler, 1979). Today, there are no community wells, communal laundries, general stores, courthouse steps, or coffeeshops where people gather to discuss who dies, who's ill, who's about to deliver a baby, be wed, be divorced, or leave home. Even bars and taverns are replacing such gossip with large-screen football and hockey displays and talk-drowning video games. Such matters have become privatized and we have fewer and fewer opportunities to involve ourselves fully in the personal problems of others or to give vent to our emotions when we feel frustrated, fearful, betrayed, or simply in need of emotional stroking. What can be more satisfying than a continuing, predictable, dependable soap opera which helps meet our needs to know about and talk about life's large and small crisis as well as the ongoing human dilemma. If soap operas are mainly talk, so are our daily lives. If soap opera deals repetitively with love affairs, personal hurts, nagging spouses, domineering bosses, rivalrous siblings and friends, and frustrating turns of events, so does our daily talk. If soap opera provides no final answers to human problems and no transcendent meaning to human events, neither do the circumstances in which most of live. It is no wonder that the initial audience for soap opera was the 1930s housewife. Confined to a house, faced with daily drudgery of house care and child care, cut off from neighbors and kin by suburban sprawl, but afforded some personal time by modern gadgetry, she found in soap opera a way to partake of the emotional involvement which had been traditionally part of family and community life.

Today, soap operas are drawing increasing numbers of college students and young workers to their audience. This increase reflects continuing changing family and community social patterns (Davis and Baran, 1981). Young people who seek and find independence at earlier and earlier ages are increasingly removed from family and neighbor involvements. Two-career parents and dispersed families reduce emotional involvement with parents, grandparents, and other relatives. Urban-suburban life styles make intimate community ties difficult and force young persons to have close involvements only with their peers and favorite media personalities, neither of which provide a full range of emotional experience or the role models for appropriate responses to such ongoing problems as physical and emotional illness, divorce, death, and the more ordinary crisis of daily life. Soap opera can and does provide a surrogate means of meeting these emotional interpersonal needs. For college students and others schedules can be arranged to provide time for afternoon viewing. For the young person merging into adulthood, soap opera can offer involvement with a substitute family and a community, complete with a variety of characters and events affording an opportunity to try out a wide range of responses and emotions. What would life be like if they or their fiances were suddenly to contract cancer? How would they feel if they were to learn that their parents were about to divorce, or if one of them had been carrying on an illicit affair? What if they came to have a domineering, demanding mother-in-law or had to work for a boss who was dishonest and immoral? Answers and answering roles can be found in soap operas. You can get close to the characters, study their reactions, and imagine yourself in their position without embarrassment or fear of disapproval. You can become the "missing other" inherent in all soap opera plots, inserting yourself into the highly intense and extremely involving interpersonal relationships. This is what soap opera is all about. It meets the need, for an hour or two each day, for the emotional interpersonal intimacy which is difficult to come by and much too time consuming in actuality in our fast-paced, go-it-alone, do-your-own-thing society.

John L. Caughey

Social Relations with Media Figures

How many media figures can you name? You may be surprised at the number there are and you may be even more surprised to realize how much you know about each and how much time you spend thinking and talking about them. In the following essay, Caughey claims that Americans pass much of their lives in the "other worlds" of the media and explains how these other worlds become part of our *social* world. He delineates the ways in which we learn to participate in these mediated social worlds, the artificial roles and relationships which are formed and how media production techniques induce pseudo-involvement with media figures. His conclusion is that if we are to understand our society we must be aware of these mediated social relationships.

In order to act acceptably, or pass as a member of society, an individual is required to know about particular people.[1] On the Pacific island of Fáánakkar, a person unable to tell the names, salient characteristics, and personal histories of members of his or her own matrilineage would immediately be unmasked as an outsider. A member of Fáánakkar is also expected to know the names, characteristics, and personal histories of Fáánakkar spirits.[2] In any given society it may not be enough to have information about those one "knows"; one may also be required to possess information about beings one has never actually met. In American society it is not spirits that one is required to know about—it is media figures.

There are several classic tests of whether or not a person is truly "American." In Europe during World War II, strangers dressed in American uniforms and speaking fluent English might be Americans lost from their own units or German spies. Standard interrogation questions designed to test American affiliations included inquiries about persons the individual could not be expected actually to know—for example, "Who plays first base for the Philadelphia Phillies?" Answering such questions successfully was literally of life or death significance. A similar situation occurs during psychiatric interviews in American mental hospitals. Here failure to answer questions about American media figures—"Name the last four presidents"—is taken as a serious symptom of mental abnormality.[3]

The true American knows about more than a handful of baseball players and politicians; he knows about hundreds of different examples from many

different fields. It is simply taken for granted that an American will know
about a huge swarming throng of unmet figures through his consumption
of the various media—through television, movies, radio, books, magazines, and newspapers. Within this group will be many sports figures, politicians, historical personages, actors, musicians, authors, columnists, announcers, disc jockeys, talk show hosts, and other celebrities, as well as all
the fictional characters in the novels, plays, movies, television shows, and
comic strips that are familiar to him.[4] The enormous number of beings in
this artificial social world—commonly numbering well over 1,000—includes several times as many "persons" as those in his real social world.
As one informant noted, "When I sat down and started to list media figures that were significant to me, my mind was overwhelmed by the volumes of names and faces. . . . We are bombarded by thousands of media
figures."

And it is not enough merely to know who these beings are. An American
is expected to possess extensive information about them. Even an average
fan knows more than a baseball player's name. He also knows his team,
uniform number, position, batting average, salary, and something about
his appearance, personality, medical history, and off-the-field conduct. In
the fall of 1980 millions of Americans knew about George Brett's hemor-
rhoids and Terry Bradshaw's marital difficulties. Would Terry's problems
with JoJo Starbuck affect his quarterbacking? The *Washington Post's* sports
columnists presented not only Terry's views of the situation, but also his
coaches' views, his teammates' views, and even JoJo's views.

Extensive information of this sort is absolutely essential for adequate
participation in many standard American activities. It is necessary for adequate media comprehension, since media productions of all kinds are
sprinkled with allusions to the characteristics of media figures who are
identified by name alone. Sometimes only first names (Jackie," "Reggie,"
"Bo," "Elvis," "Goldie," "Liz") or even initials ("JR," "RMN," "MM")
are offered. Such knowledge is also socially necessary, since many American conversations revolve around the activities of media figures.

For example, *all* members of a minor league baseball team, the Alexandria Dukes, faithfully watch the soap opera *General Hospital*. Partly they
do so for aesthetic reasons ("It's one of the most exciting sopa operas
around"), but partly they watch out of social necessity. As a pitcher says,
"Can't miss GH. You have to keep up. We talk about it everywhere, on
the field, in the batting cage. . . ." What they talk about is the social entanglements of the fictional characters such as "vulnerable" Laura, "clever,"
Luke, "stoic" Jessie, and "conniving" Heather. Pseudo mutual acquaintances of this kind often provide American strangers in airplanes, taxicabs,
or bars with the primary basis for socializing. Of *General Hospital* the

baseball player adds, "Besides, when we go out to the bars and talk to girls, they all know about *General Hospital*. It's something we can talk about. . . ."[5] In other social situations, analogous information is de rigueur.[6] Information about media figures is a core aspect of American cultural knowledge.

But Americans not only know about media figures. Despite the complete lack of real face-to-face contact, they also feel strongly about them. They are indifferent to a few, but they like or dislike others, and toward some they feel truly powerful emotions. In discussing their feelings informants sometimes use terminology associated with the evaluation of performers ("talented," "entertaining"); more commonly they evaluate media beings personally. For example, those they dislike are characterized as "shallow," "phony," "manipulative," "dishonest," "mean," "pompous," "crude," and "snobbish." People characterize unmet media figures as if they were intimately involved with them, and in a sense they are—they engage in pseudo-social interactions with them. Just as the people of Fánakkar engage in social relations with spirits, Americans involve themselves with their particular "gods." A major form of artificial social involvement is through media consumption.

As Peter Berger and Thomas Luckmann observe, the theater illustrates our participation in "multiple realities" outside ordinary social life. In attending the theater a person is psychologically drawn out of his objective social world into the realm of the play. At one moment he is talking with his companion in the next seat. At the next moment both are absorbed in the fictional doings of an eighteenth-centruy drama.

> The transition between realities is marked by the rising and falling of the curtain. As the curtain rises, the spectator is "transported to another world," with its own meanings and an order that may or may not have much to do with the order of everyday life. As the curtain falls, the spectator "returns to reality," that is, to the paramount reality of everyday life by comparison with which the reality presented on the stage now appears tenuous and ephemeral. . . .[7]

Such vivid "transporting" experiences characterize *all* forms of media consumption. Every time an American enters a movie theater, turns on a media machine, or opens a book, newspaper, or magazine, he or she slips mentally out of the real social world and enters an artificial world of vicarious social experience.

Americans pass much of their lives in the "other worlds" of the media. By age sixteen, a contemporary child has spent more time watching TV than attending school. The average adult watches more than three hours of TV per day. Mass media consumption in general occupies 50 percent of all leisure time.[8] Take an American adult's evening of leisure. Picking up the evening newspaper, unmet reporters take the reader into a parade of national and international situations, from a mass murder in New York, through a Middle Eastern coup, to a strike in Japan. For relief the individual turns to the comic page. As he reads down the page from strip to strip, he shifts from the realm of fifteenth-century English knights ("Prince Valiant"), through French Foreign Legionnaires ("Crock"), to futuristic outer space "(Star Wars")", and back home to the realm of middle-class American suburbanites ("Hi and Lois"). And this is just the first ten minutes. He picks up a popular novel and enters the "romantic" world of the antebellum South. After an hour, he turns to TV, and spinning the dial, he flips from reality to reality, from *The Waltons* to *Dallas* before settling on *Buck Rogers*. Even here commercials interrupt this reality and transport him back and forth from outer space to twentieth-century supermarkets, bathrooms, and bars.

The cultural variability of these multiple realities is less than might be expected. Comic strips, popular novels, television programs, and commercials present outer space monsters, Nazi Germans, fifteenth-century knights, and nineteenth-century Southern plantation owners who not only speak late twentieth-century American English, but who operate with values, motives, and roles firmly locked to the assumptions of the contemporary American middle class. But the lack of cultural variability does not contradict the important fact that the average American's media experience takes him daily through a large number of complex "scenes" beyond those of his actual experience.

It is essential to recognize that these other worlds are *social* worlds. In each form of media consumption, the individual is not transported to deserted landscapes or empty rooms, but into crowded social scenes peopled by hundreds of different human or humanlike media creatures. He is tangled temporarily in elaborate systems of *social interaction*. How does an individual connect to such artificial social worlds?

First, an individual connects to a media world because it *seems* vividly real. Our familiarity with the media tends to obscure this point, but it is evident in the rections of people exposed for the first time to movies or television. On Fáánakkar many of my informants were just beginning to see movies. While visiting the nearby district administrative island, they would sometimes go to a rusty old Quonset hut where American musical, cowboy, and war movies were occasionally shown. Typically, the islanders assumed that the moviemakers had somehow recorded ongoing events in the lives of real soldiers and cowboys; they took these vivid images as real records of actual behavior. An even more striking example is provided by the reactions of early American movie audiences. "They accepted the flat flickering images as reality. When locomotives thundered down the track, when waves rolled towards the camera, people in the front rows ran screaming for the exits."[9]

Contemporary American children, attracted early by the seemingly real quality of television, have to learn to make reality distinctions between different kinds of programs. A five-year-old who was already familiar with the distinction between "live" sportscasts and staged fictional productions misinterpreted his first view of professional TV wrestling: Bill Blackthorn was set upon by the huge villain who, despite the referee's frantic efforts, resorted to the most vicious tactics. Grabbing Bill by the shoulders, he repeatedly smashed his head—battering ram style—into the ring corner post. Picking up Bill, he spun him around over his head and hurled him down on the floor of the ring. Bill lay motionless on the floor of the ring. "Bill Blackthorn is down. . . ," the announcer intoned. The five-year-old interrupted and said with horror, "Bill Blackthorn is dead!" Whether the person thinks that what seems to be happening is fictional or "live," that which absorbs him in the production is its seeming "reality." To an important extent the flickering images are apprehended as *people*.

An individual connects to media experience through learned systems of knowledge for processing perceptions about human social conduct. To understand the contents of any media production, the individual must use culturally encoded cues to recognize social situations, personality types, and social roles. One must be capable of determining each character's intended place in the situation—broadly speaking, that so-and-so is the "villain" or the "hero" or, more narrowly, that so-and-so is having certain feelings about what is happening but is disguising these to fool some other character.[10] All this involves wielding an enormous amount of complex information about symbolic social relations. The cultural structuring of this process is clearly revealed when people misconceptualize foreign media productions. South Sea islanders, for example, may construe information in American cowboy movies intended to show friendship between the hero and his side-kick as indicating that the two are members of the same matrilineal kin group.

The individual also connects to a media production by assuming a social role that links him structurally to the social drama he consumes. In the least intricate form, the individual watches (or listens to, or reads about) the social interactions of media figures in the passive role of "observer." He watches the action in much the same way he watches his neighbors arguing through a lighted window. Although behaviorally passive, the individual must be emotionally interested in what he beholds, or he will shift his attention to other matters. Media productions, of course, are deliberately structured to engage the "human interest" of the audience; they focus relentlessly on what are culturally considered the "highlights," such as violent moments, of the social situations and relationships they portray. This is so effectively accomplished that a child watching a boisterous cartoon or even an adult reading a suspense novel typically becomes so fascinated that it may be difficult to catch his attention. The intensity of this absorbed state leads some researchers to compare media consumption to the trance-like altered states of consciousness induced by drug consumption.[11] Manipulated by a steady stream of dramatic dialogue and tense or amusing interaction, the individual becomes so absorbed that the proper label for this role is not "observer" but "voyeur."

Often the individual is drawn more directly into the media drama. He or she shifts from the role of observer to that of participant and "enters" the other world. Sometimes the individual remains himself but is drawn into a pseudo relationship with the media being. Thus the individual may find himself "interacting" with media beings when literature takes a conversational tone ("Dear Reader . . .") or when a TV figure such as an announcer, politician, or comedian speaks directly out of the television and addresses the audience personally. Here media consumption directly parallels actual social interaction. D. Horton and Richard Wohl have analyzed this artificial or "seeming face-to-face relationship between spectator and performer" and demonstrated that it is "closely analogous to and in many ways resembles social interaction in ordinary primary groups." In order to engage the audience, the "greatest pains are taken by the persona to create an illusion of intimacy," as by facing the camera and imitating the conversational style, tone, and mannerisms of personal relationships. Watching such a performer's image, the spectator does not remain "passive." His or her "psychological response is closely analogous to that in an actual social relationship." In apprehending the total communication and in decoding gestural, situational, and linguistic cues, the spectator is compelled to select some role complementary to that assumed by the performer. This may involve psychologically playing "the admiring dependent to his father-surrogate" or "the earnest citizen to his fearless opponent of political evils" or even "the loved one to the person's lover."[12]

A vivid example was the popular 1951 radio program *The Lonesome Gal*. This program consisted entirely of a female voice engaged in a conversational monologue. "Darling, you look so tired and a little put out about something this evening . . . you are worried, I feel it. . . . Come, lie down on the couch, relax, I want to stroke your hair gently. . . ." She spoke to the individuals in her audience "as if she was addressing a lover in the utter privacy of some hidden rendezvous."[13]

Of course, the spectator may reject the performer's gambit and react with antagonism; in doing so he is still engaged in pseudo interaction with the media image. As Alan Blum has shown, lower-class blacks commonly engage in hostile joking relationships with white TV performers. Sometimes this role playing is overt, as when "the spectator would chide the performer, cajole him, answer his questions directly, warn him of impending dangers, compliment him, and so on."[14] The strategies employed by an audience usually represent "some variant of the role or roles normally played in the spectator's primary social groups."[15]

Such role playing sometimes transcends psychological reactions and linguistic responses and extends to physical action—as when the viewer kisses the TV, makes a rude gesture at the TV image, or even hurls objects at the screen. Seizing on the commercial possiblities of this pseudo interaction, an American firm markets styrofoam "TV Bricks" which can be safely hurled at offending media beings.

A third form of artificial role playing involves the complex processes of "identification."[16] Here people temporarily abandon their own identities and social roles and, by imaginatively projecting their consciousness onto the media image, take on alternate personal and social identities. Sometimes media identification involves living celebrities. Frederick Exley offers an example from American sports.

> I spent . . . Sundays with a few bottles of beer at the Parrot, eyes fixed on the television screen, cheering for my team. *Cheering* is a paltry description. The Giants were my delight, my folly, my anodyne, my intellectual stimulation. With Huff I "stunted" up and down the room among the bar stools, preparing to "shoot the gap"; with Shofner I faked two defenders "out of their cleats," took high, swimming passes over my right shoulder and trotted, dipsy-doodle-like, into the end zone; with Robustelli I swept into backfields and with cruel disdain flung flatfooted, helpless quarterbacks to the turf.[17]

In a similar way, people may also vicariously live out the experiences of totally fictional characters. Through identification they may feel the hero's or heroine's emotions, endure the character's personal tragedies, and achieve his or her social triumphs. The constructors of media worlds lavish considerable effort on techniques that not only invite but virtually force this kind of identification. A telling example is their success in inducing identification not only with imaginary humans but also with imaginary dogs, rabbits, and pigs.

Most media productions employ a variety of techniques to induce pseudo involvement. A cowboy drama may employ camera work that switches the audience back and forth between the roles of voyeur and identified participant—as in the following hypothetical movie script.

1. Shot from across the room of the hero picking up a pair of binoculars. We can see him standing at the window looking out.

2. Shot through the binoculars of distant Indian warriors riding toward us across the plain. Here we are the hero; we see what he sees.
3. Shot of the heroine in a low-cut dress walking over and looking tenderly at the hero. We see them both from the middle distance facing each other. They think they are alone but we are watching.
4. Close-up shot of the heroine's face and upper trunk, full face, as she stares lovingly up at the hero. Here we become the hero again and get fully the look she is sending at him.

In practice the techniques are often more subtle, but the effect is the same. The individual is pulled out of the objective social world and transported into the midst of an imaginary social world in which he or she participates in the most intense and initmate fashion. In a single week an average American plays roles in hundreds of social situations beyond those of actual social experience.

Social involvement with media figures is not confined to periods of actual media consumption. Even when the TV is turned off, the book closed, or the newspaper thrown away, people continue to engage in artificial social relationships with the figures they have "met" in the media. Our fuzzy thinking about media beings is reflected in the lack of a precise vocabulary with which to specify the kinds of relations hips that actually exist between media figures and media consumers. Virtually everyone with any interest in a media being is classifed simply as a "fan." The derivation of this term is significant. The word "fan" comes from the term "fanatic," which is derived from the Latin *fanaticus*, "someone inspired to frenzy by devotion to a deity," a person "possessed."[18] However, as as ordinarily used, both in common parlance and in social analysis, the term "fan" is inadequate. It does not begin to do justice to the variety of attachments to media figures that exist in American society—and it does not do justice to the real structure of these attachments. Psychiatrist Lawrence Freedman suggests that "most fans are normal individuals who become involved in a continuing esthetic appreciation of a star."[19] In fact, the basis of most fan attachments is something much more than this.

Interviewed about their interest in a given figure, many fans attempt to explain their attachment by specifying an actual social relationship whose emotional quality is similar to that which they feel to the star—one celebrity will be seen as a "father figure," another as a "sister type" or a "friend." This leads us in the right direction. The basis of most fan relationships is not an esthetic appreciation but a social relationship. Fans have attachments to unmet media figures that are analogous to and in many ways directly parallel to actual social relationships with real "fathers," "sisters," "friends," and "lovers." I will consider two other major varieties below, but I will begin with the most dramatic example, "artificial romance." Here the fan casts the media figure in the role of imaginary lover.

Ruth Steinhagen had a romantic attachment to baseball player Eddie Waitkus. She was not engaged in an "esthetic appreciation" of Waitkus; she was in love with him. The psychiatric report argues that her relationship was abnormal from the start, but this is not the case. All the patterns of behavior that Steinhagen engaged in prior to the time she decided to murder her imaginary lover are standard among those many—probably millions—of normal Americans who have love relationships with unmet media figures. The data for the analysis that follows come partly from published sources, but most of the detailed information comes from my own research with seventy-two Americans who are or have been engaged in such artificial love relationships. Fifty-one of these relationships involved females (ranging in age from eight to sixty-two), all of whom had intense romantic attachments to male celebrities they had not actually met. The objects of their affections included Paul McCartney, John Lennon, John Travolta, Donny Osmond, Elton John, Roger Daltrey, Gary Cooper, Frank Sinatra, O. J. Simpson, Bill Bradley, Marlon Brando, Rudolf Nureyev, Richard Chamberlain, Dick Cavett, James Dean, Charlton Heston, Rhett Butler, Bobby Sherman, Jonathan Hart, Clint Eastwood, Robby Benson, Richard Dreyfuss, Cat Stevens, Burt Reynolds, and Robert Redford.

Like Steinhagen, most of my informants explicitly described their relationships in romantic terms. They were "infatuated with," "fixated on," "obsessed with," "crazy about," or (most commonly) "in love with" the favored media figure. Erotic attraction is a basic part of the appeal. "At this time I did not have a boyfriend, so Elton John filled that role. . . . I was in love with him. Even though he was far from what people would view as sexually appealing, I was highly attracted to him." For one seventeen-year-old, it was the eyes. "I fell in love with him [John Travolta] when he appeared in *The Boy in the Plastic Bubble*. I liked his beautiful blue eyes. . . . Although I have somewhat outgrown my teenage fetish, I can't help but think of him from time to time. When I see those blue eyes, I still melt." Another informant, age twenty-one, is even more explicit.

It almost takes my breath away to look at him or even think about him, and seeing him magnified on the movie screen makes him look even more like a Greek God. . . . He's elegantly dark, with short, thickly waving hair pushed hurriedly away from his face. . . . His nose is precisely formed, his lips thin but soft and sensitive. Coarse, dark, curling hair covers his chest, arms and legs, and this masculine look is heightened by the contrasting softness of his back and his fingers. . . .

The intensity of these love relationships is often as strong as that of a "real" love affair. As an Elvis Presley admirer put it, "No one will ever understand how I feel. I love him! He has given me happiness and excitement in my life that will never die."[20]

But aside from these intense feelings, what do such relationships involve? First, they involve regular, intense, romantically structured media consumption. "I saw the film [Saturday Night Fever] not only once, twice, but six times." In viewing a dramatic production, the individual sometimes projects herself into the female lead and plays out romantic interactions with her media lover. "I put myself in the wife's role; my personality took over her part." In other cases, the individual personally responds in the role of romantic partner.

> I lust for him in a daydreamy way when I watch him in the show.
> He sang a song he wrote with such feeling and conviction that I was enchanted. The fact that he wrote it indicated to me that those were powerful emotions he personally felt. I wanted to climb right through the screen.
> From the moment he first walked on stage, I was completely enchanted. His movements and speech were spellbinding, and I found that I couldn't take my eyes off him.

One twenty-year-old with a crush on Roger Daltrey of The Who describes her first concert as follows:

> As I sat in my seat waiting for the concert to begin, my heart was pounding with the excitement. Then the lights went out and The Who appeared on stage. From that point on, I was totally absorbed in the concert. I didn't speak to my friend, who was sitting next to me, nor did I move my eyes away from the stage. I felt as though The Who were playing their songs just for me. I was surrounded by their music. When I left the concert, I felt exhilarated, as though I had actually met The Who in person.

This reaction is described again and again. The individual feels that the TV singer is singing directly to her. Mass media productions—including those in magazines and posters—are taken as *personal* communications.

> I would go grocery shopping with my mother just so I could leaf through the various teen magazines that contained heartthrob stories about Donny, who at twelve years old was made out to be a loving, sensitive and caring young man. I, too, covered my walls with posters of Donny, which were inscribed with personal statements such as, "To you, from Donny" or "I love you, Donny." I secretly thought that the messages on his posters and on his records were directed towards me, and often I would become openly emotional over them. For instance, in one of his records he cried out, "Help me, help me please," and I played it repeatedly while crying for poor Donny.

Such relationships are not confined to media consumption. Typically they develop into elaborate patterned forms of behavior that constitute sym-

bolic substitutes for actual interaction. Several parallel the behavior of separated real lovers. We have noted that Ruth Steinhagen collected and treasured all sorts of mementoes and media information about Eddie Waitkus,
including photographs and press clippings, and that at night she spread these
out in a kind of shrine. Such collecting behavior is standard.

> At this time, I decided that I was going to live and die for my man Elton John.
> I started collecting every album he made and memorized every word of every
> song. Whenever I found an article in a newspaper or magazine, I cut it out
> and placed it in a scrapbook. Of course, this was the scrapbook that I would
> present to him once he met me and fell in love with me. My world became
> Elton John. I had four huge posters of him in my bedroom.

Steinhagen was preoccupied with Eddie's uniform number and, because
of his background, she developed a special interest in Lithuania and Boston. My informants report the same kind of interest seemingly insignificant
details. A Beatles fan put it this way:

> I relished every little detail I could find out about Paul. If I read that he ate
> scrambled eggs and bacon for breakfast, I developed a sudden love for scram-
> bled eggs—one food I had always hated. Details of his life became extremely
> important to me. I wanted to know when he woke up, when he went to bed,
> what color socks he wore, and if he like french fried or mashed potatoes.

More important aspects of the beloved's life assume critical significance.
The figure's career successes and setbacks are taken seriously and emotionally, as are personal events such as a sickness in the celebrity's family. Of
particular concern are events that affect the individual's role orientation to
the beloved. Several informants were distraught by media reports that Elton John was bisexual.

> Since I was emotionally involved with Elton John, his announcement of his
> bisexuality was devastating to me. I no longer could view him as a suitable
> boy friend, lover, or marriage partner.
> While reading the newspaper I came upon an article stating that he was gay.
> No way, I thought. Not my Elton. He just hasn't met me yet. If he knew me,
> he would become "normal." But then the articles and stories started pouring
> in from every source about him. Could it be true? The love of my life, gay? I
> took down all but one poster of him in my room. . . . He had let me down.
> . . . How could he do this to me!

A similar, if slightly less distressing, problem occurs when the media figure
marries someone else. "I still remember the hurt and loss I felt in my senior
year of high school when I was told by a friend that Donny Osmond was
going to get married. . . . No, he's a Mormon. He'll *never* get divorced.
It really dashed my hopes."

People are not only interested in the beloved's life events; they typically take up parallel activities. A 1974 letter to "Dear Abby" offers an illustrative, if extreme, example.

> DEAR ABBY: How can I meet Prince Charles? I have always admired him, and it has been my dream to meet him one day, but I'm not having any luck. I've written him several letters, and each time his secretary has answered saying: "The Prince of Wales regrets that he is unable to meet you."
>
> I am a normal, intelligent 20-year old college girl. I'm told I am pretty and have a pleasant personality. I've read everything I could find about the royal family in general and Prince Charles in particular. I'll bet I know more about the royal family than most people living in England and the rest of the United Kingdom.
>
> I hope you won't think I'm crazy, but I have been taking horseback riding lessons, and I plan to take flying lessons when I can afford it because I know those are Prince Charles' favorite sports. Also, if we ever meet I will have something to talk to him about.
>
> Abby, you're supposed to have all the answers. Can you help my dream come true?[21]

Such activity is often keyed to hopes of an actual meeting. Indirect communications are also often attempted. Many celebrities receive thousands of fan letters from their adoring lovers, but these letter writers probably constitute only a fraction of the star's actual romantic following. While several of my informants thought about writing to their imaginary lovers ("I wanted to write to him to ask him to wait for me until I got older"), few actually did so.

However, *pseudo communications* were standard. Ruth Steinhagen talked out loud to pictures of Eddie Waitkus. Such behavior is typical

> This poster [of Bobby Sherman] soon reigned alone on my closet door. I played the album constantly, singing along while staring into Bobby's eyes. Sometimes I would take to the poster as if it was Bobby Sherman alive in my room. He [Donny Osmond] had this song about pulling a string and kissing you. Everytime I'd hear this song, I'd pull a purple thread and kiss his poster.

Such external symbolic interactions are paralleled by something even more significant. Steinhagen had fantasies about meeting, dating, and marrying Eddie Waitkus. Far from being extraordinary, such fantasy interactions are *characteristic* of this kind of social relationship.

Certain fantasies occur again and again. One involves "the meeting," an imagined social situation in which the beloved first interacts with his fan.

> I began to fantasize about meeting Roger Daltrey. I'd imagine myself sitting in a bar or at a pool and seeing Roger Daltrey walk over and sit next to me. We would start small talking and I would casually mention that he was one of the members of The Who. He'd smile shyly and say, "Yes."

Of course, the celebrity does not just notice the fan. He is smitten. One girl imagined how her beloved would spot her in a restaurant and, struck by love at first sight, would "send me a single rose with a note."

Another young woman, a law student, regularly conjures up a series of alternative meetings with O. J. Simpson.

> Prince Charming crashes into the back of my brand new silver sports Mercedes with his sleek, red Jag. He races to the front of my car with every intent to curse me out, but once he notices the twinkle in my eyes, he asks me out for dinner instead.
>
> This time O. J. Simpson is still active in the NFL. As he runs a fly pattern and makes the game-winning touchdown, he crashes into me and my cameras in the end zone. As he helps me up, he notices the twinkle in my eyes and I notice his twinkle. We fall in love and live happily after.
>
> We sometimes meet because he needs help. On these occasions, I am the best lawyer in town. . . . a willing soul ready to do battle.

A fourth scenario involves an even more dramatic rescue. Ironically, this fantasy was related to me less than two weeks before John Lennon's death:

> As a bystander in a crowd listening to O. J. Simpson give his farewell football speech, I notice a suspicious-looking man. He is about to shoot Simpson. Just in the nick of time I leap between Simpson and the bullet, saving his life but critically wounding my own. As I fall to the ground the six-foot-two-inch former running back catches me in his arms and gently places his coat under my head as he rests me on the ground. As a tear runs down his lean, smooth face, he says nothing and kisses me just as I close my eyes. Now I turn into the suffering heroine. Others realize the bravery and courage it took for me to risk my life. People from all over the world visit me in the hospital, and of course, immediately after a full recovery, O. J. Simpson and I get married and live happily ever after.

While many fantasies focus on the meeting and courtship aspects of the relationship, others picture the marriage that follows.

> At that time I imagined I could communicate with Paul. I had long conversations with him. I imagined meeting him and having him fall in love with me. Of course, he begged me to marry him and we lived happily ever after. . . . He had to go away for concerts abut he was always true-blue and loyal to me, of course. . . . He always came home from trips and told me how much he missed me.

Sometimes people seek to translate such fantasies into real meetings. Several of my informants not only hoped but expected to meet their lovers. Occasionally people actually succeed. "Groupies" represent a culturally recognized category of successful celebrity seekers who have managed to turn a fantasy attraction into a "real" relationship. Several of my informants made token efforts to meet their lovers by attending a "personal appearance." One of my Elton John fans gives a characteristic example.

> Somehow time flew, and the night of the concert was here. I looked beautiful as I left the house, smiling from ear to ear, knowing that somehow this would be the night. Maybe he would see me in the audience and fall magically in love and invite me on stage to do a song with him. Or maybe he would spot me and send one of his guards for me. It didn't matter how, it just had to happen!

Relatively few people seriously attempt a meeting. Tacitly, at least, they often seem to realize not only that an actual meeting is virtually impossible, but that the fantasy is better than an actual encounter.

> Although I dream of Prince Charming falling in love with me, I know in my heart that he never will, that I will never meet him and much less hold him. All this doesn't matter. What does matter is the creations of my imagination.

Most, while recognizing the unlikelihood of an actual meeting, retain a ray of hope. Recalling her adolescent crush, one young woman said, "I'd still like to meet him; I'd be perfect for him."

Romantic fan relationships are common among adolescent girls. An informant who grew up with the Beatles noted that in her day it was considered odd *not* to have a crush on one of the Beatles. Tacit cultural rules make it more acceptable for young females overtly to express such relationships than for people of other age or sex categories to do so. Nevertheless, such relationships are not confined to adolescent girls. A letter to a TV "answer man" makes this point forcefully: "I'm an adult so don't treat this question lightly, please. I am absolutely in love with Richard Thomas. . . . I don't mean a crush; I mean love. I think about him every waking moment of every day and I must write and tell him. Please, his private address so I can tell him how serious I am."[22] This letter is not unique. Many of my informants were well out of their adolescence, and one of my John Travolta fans was in her fifties. The following enjoyed by aging celebrities such as Frank Sinatra and Liberace demonstrates that such fantasy love relationships can extend far beyond adolescence. An elderly suburban matron with grown children still has a "special thing" for Frank Sinatra. When depressed, she pours herself a drink and listens to his romantic songs. Her attraction began some forty years ago. Like many of her age mates, she has had, in effect, a lifelong affair with Sinatra.

Men also have such relationships. John Hinckley is not an adolescent girl, nor was his relationship to Foster unusual. Although they tend to be more secretive about them, few of my male informants completely denied ever having had such relationships. Some of them described such attractions in detail. Among the female stars they have "loved" are Bonnie Raitt, Jane Fonda, Donna Summer, Princess Caroline of Monaco, Brooke Shields, Diane Keaton, Ann-Margret, Cheryl Tiegs, Joan Baez, and Yvette Mimieux. One man reported a series of such relationships extending through much of his adolescence. As this example suggests, most of the patterns described for female love relationships are paralleled among males.

> I would read all I could about the actresses I had crushes on in *TV Guide*, *Life*, *Look* and, whenever I visited my grandmother, in *TV Screen* and *Movie Mirror*. Yet all these crushes pale in comparison to my love for Yvette Mim-

ieux. I had a crush on YM for a long time—at least four or five years. It all stated with an episode of Dr. Kildare called"Tyger, Tyger," in which YM played a devil-may-care Southern California surfer girl. From that time on, I watched every show that YM was in that I possibly could. I would imagine meeting her in one way or another. I imagined her coming to a basketball game in which I played really well, or would imagine heroically saving her life, sometimes sacrificing my own in the process—but never before she had a chance to kiss me and thank me.

Again, such relationships regularly extend beyond adolescence. Another Yvette Mimieux fan was only "turned off" in his mid-thirties, when he was disappointed by her "cruelty" in the movie *Three in the Attic*.

Homosexuals, too, engage in artificial love relationships, such as the TV newswriter who had a long-term crush on a black ballad singer. He found the singer "physically attractive and appealing," followed his career with interest, and kept several scrapbooks on him. He bought all the singer's records and collected information from friends who knew him personally. He was "overjoyed" to learn that the singer was gay, and then began "to fantasize in earnest."[23]

Ethnographic investigation shows that elaborate love realtionships with unmet media figures are not characteristic just of American schizophrenics. On the contrary, such relationships represent a significant, and pervasive, culture pattern in modern American society. But *why* are Americans given to these relationsips?

Both the forms and the contents of the contemporary American media are conducive to the development of such relationsips. Especially through the vehicle of the electronic media, the individual is regularly transported into the midst of dramatic social situations involving intimate face-to-face contact with the most glamorous people of his time. The seeming reality of this experience naturally engenders emotional reactions—especially since these figures are deliberately and manipulatively presented in the roles of sexual objects and lovers. Given their intimate, seductive appearance, it would be peculiar if the audience did *not* respond in kind.

But in addition, these relationships often fill gaps in the individual's actual social world. As Elihu Katz and Paul Lazarsfeld observe, escapist media often serves as a direct substitute for socializing activity.[24] If the social situation is dissatisfying, an individual may compensate with artificial companions. When a person accustomed to company at dinner must dine alone, he or she typically substitutes artificial beings by way of a book, newspaper, or TV program. This suggests that an individual would be most likely to engage in a media love relationship when he or she is without a real or satisfying actual lover. While sometimes valid, such an interpretation does not fully suffice. It does not explain the suburban grandmother who had a lifelong "affair" with Frank Sinatra despite forty years of marriage. It does not explain why, in adolescence and in later years, artificial love relationships often persist after an actual lover is found. Take one of the fans introduced earlier. This young women, like several other informants, explicitly offered the "substitute lover" interpretation herself:

> Donny Osmond served to replace a missing element in my life. At this time I had little relationships with other boys. My sister and many of my friends did have these relationships. Donny and I had such a relationship, and I had yearned for one. . . . My feeling eventually began to fade as I did begin to have crushes on real boys in sixth and seventh grade.

However, as she herself remarked, the relationship with Osmond "faded" but did not end. It persisted through her senior year in high school and even now, at age twenty-two, she still buys Donny Osmond magazines and retains her fan club card. While she is now engaged in serious relationships with real lovers, she still has various artificial love relationships. "Now I have the same kind of relationship with Buck Williams [basketball star]. He's sooooo great, wow!"

In its simplistic form, the "substitute lover" theory assumes that the imaginary lover will disappear when the real lover appears. Tacitly it assumes that real love relationships are better than imaginary love relationships. The first assumption is often untrue, and the second may also be unwarranted. In some ways fantasy relations are often *better* than real love relationships. Media figures are more attractive then ordinary mortals, and they are carefully packaged—through makeup, costuming, camera angles, and film editing—to appear even better. Even when portrayed in a tired or disheveled condition, they seem cute, humorous, and "sexy." The media figure's prowess is typically almost supernatural. The hero is so strong and brave that the villains are always overcome ("His shoulders and arms are massive—secure comforters that are capable of doing away with any problem . . ."). The media figure's personality is also carefully sanitized, glamorized, and perfected. The continually brave, kind, interested, patient, and passionately devoted lovers of many media worlds are not to be found in reality. Celebrities are also more "successful" than ordinary people. This connects to a powerful American value. Extreme material wealth taps yet another basic American interest. Finally, since the figure is worshipped by millions of others, the star has a legitimacy and appeal lacking in a person who is not "somebody."

But it is fantasy that helps to make these relations superior to actual social interactions. To love a glamorous rock star through the media is to make a kind of initmate contact with a powerfully appealing figure—but you remain, in this dimension, only one of millions of other fans. However, through fantasy, the rock star moves from the public realm and picks you out of the crowd to be his special friend, lover, and wife. Landing such a widely adored figure confirms your self worth; it makes *you* somebody. It is analogous to landing the most popular boy or girl in high school, only better. One Donny Osmond fan put it this way:

> I fantasized and dreamed aobut him constantly, thinking that if Donny ever bumped into me somewhere or met me, he would immediately fall in love with me and whisk me away. I wasn't really jealous of the other girls who liked him because I knew that if he met me he would forget about them.

One of her rivals had similar plans.

> I felt we were meant for each other, and if only we could meet, all my dreams would come true. Since Donny was a famous superstar, this gave me a feeling of superstar worth also.

Sometimes this gratifying elevation of the self is based solely on becoming the beloved figure's chosen lover or spouse. In other cases the individual's fantasy includes stardom for himself or herself as well. Like several other informants, an Elton John fan pictured herself literally sharing the stage with her idol:

> I saw Elton as the necessary contact I needed to break into the music business. I would frequently fantasize that Elton would hear me play the piano, fall in love with me, then take me on tour with him as an opening act. These fantasies were always very elaborate and intense and provided me with a way to fulfill all my dreams and desires.

Through fantasy, a media love relationship is exquisitely tuned not to the needs of the celebrity, but to the needs of the self. Imaginary lovers unfailingly do what you want with grace, enthusiasm, and total admiration. The whole course of the relationship is under your control. The relationship runs—and reruns—its perfectly gratifying course from dramatic and glamorous first meetings, through courtship and consummation, to happily-ever-after marital bliss. And through it all a fantasy lover smiles fondly, never complaining, never burping, never getting a headache, never wrecking the car or making you do the dishes. You owe her no obligations. He is there when you want him and gone when you do not. Real love relationships include all sorts of unfortunate realities: fantasy love relationships do not. It is not surprising that Americans sometimes prefer fantasy lovers to ordinary mortals.

A second media figure relationship, which also directly parallels an actual social relationship, is based on antagonism. Most informants can readily list media figures they despise. Controversial public figures like Howard Cosell, Jane Fonda, William Buckley, George Steinbrenner, Richard Nixon and villainous fictional characters like Alan Spaulding *(Guiding Light)*, or JR *(Dallas)* are commonly mentioned examples. Considering that the individual has never met these people, and that many of them are fictional beings, the level of hostility is often astonishing. Sometimes these negative feelings lead the individual to elaborate an artificial social relationship that is the inverse of the sterotypic fan relationship. Here the basis of the relationship is not esthetic appreciation, admiration, or love, but hatred, anger, and disgust.

As with love relationships, media consumption is often intense. Several informants have developed antagonisms to local talk show hosts, and sometimes they watch such shows for the pleasure of hating the celebrity. Soap opera fans are often as interested in characters they dislike as those they admire. "He is one of the most self-centered, arrogant, selfish, uncaring persons I have ever come across," said one informant. "His main purpose is to have power at the cost of others. . . . I watch him with feelings of hatred. . . . I am overjoyed to see other characters beat him at his own game." One set of three young men used to come together out of their mutual dislike of a TV evangelist. Their mutual relationships, both with each other and with this media figure, suggested the opposite of a fan club. They used to watch this evangelist's television show regularly because they thought he was an amusing "farce." When he apperared on the screen they would laugh and ridicule him.

Such relationships often have an important fantasy dimension. Serious participants conjure up fantasy meetings with their enemies and carry out imaginary arguments with them. Sometimes these pseudo interactions become violent. An otherwise peaceful informant described fantasies about torturing and killing "evil" politicians. These pseudo interactions, both in media consumtpion and fantasy, allow the expression of a hatred that is more extreme and presumably more satisfying than that which can safely bo expressed in real social relations. The media figure's humanity can be denied in a way that a real person's physical presence makes difficult. One runs no risks of legal punishment or retaliation since the hated figure cannot fight back.

These relationships sometimes goad people to attempts at actual consummation. It may seem amusing that an actor who plays a villainous soap opera husband is regularly stopped on the street and berated for treating his "wife" so badly. Unfortunately, serious attacks sometimes result from such imaginary relationships.

A far more common and significant group of relationships are those in which the media figure becomes the object of intense admiration. Such relationships approximate the general stereotypic conceptualization of the fan, but much more is involved than esthetic appreciation. Characteristically, the admired figure comes to represent some combination of idol, hero, alter ego, mentor, and role model.

The media figures around whom informants have built intense admiration relationships are surprisingly diverse. Consider the following examples: John Wayne, Judy Garland, Loren Eiseley, Steve Carlton, Betty Ford, Neil Young, Ralph Ellison, Charles Manson, Frank Zappa, Jane Fonda, Arnold Palmer, Hawkeye Pierce, Jack Kerouac, Barbra Streisand, Woody Allen, Anne Frank, Bruce Springsteen, James Dean, Olivia Newton-John, James Bond, Diana Rigg, Tony Baretta, Isak Dinesen, Clint Eastwood, and Mary Tyler Moore. People express strong emotional orientations to such figures, speaking not only of "admiration" and "sympathy," but also of "worship" and (platonic) "love." Again people frequently characterize the attraction by comparing it to a real social relationship. They speak of their hero as a "friend," "older sister," "father figure," "guide" or "mentor."[25] As with the love relationships, the general source of the appeal is clear. Media figures are better than ordinary people. They have godlike qualities that are impossible for mortals to sustain. Furthermore, the emotional attachment is not complicated by the ambivalence that characterizes actual relationships; admiration is unchecked by the recognition of faults and limitations.

One man pointed out that the "father figure" he admired—a fictional John Wayne-type TV cowboy—outshone his real father in every respect. His father has several admirable qualities and he "loves him very much." But as a child he "needed someone to identify with," and his father did not measure up. A young woman described the perfection of her "TV mother," Mary Tyler Moore, and showed how Moore shifted from parent figure to role model.

> It all began when I used to watch *The Dick Van Dyke Show* about eleven years ago, so I was ten years old at that time. The first thing I can remember from that time is how much I admired Mary; after all, she was slender, feminine, funny, talented, intelligent, cute, attractive, a kind mother, a loving wife, a caring friend, a good cook, a clean housekeeper, and more. . . . Mary became the person that I wanted my mother to be. . . . I would watch my mother cooking, for example, and I would imagine that my mother was just like Mary.
>
> Things really took a turn when I got into junior high school about eight years ago. *The Mary Tyler Moore Show* had been on TV for about three years by that time, but I didn't pay much attention until I realized that I wanted to learn how to become a woman for myself . . . and I had the perfect person to model myself after: Mary. On her show she was a career woman and still as perfect as before; she dressed well, she was slender, she knew how to cook, she was independent, she had a nice car, she had a beautiful apartment, she never seemed lonely, she had a good job, she was intelligent, she had friends, etc. There was *still* nothing wrong with her.

From out of thousands of glamorous alternatives, why does the fan seize on one particular figure rather than another? The appeal is often complex, but the admired figure is typically felt to have qualities that the person senses in himself but desires to develop further. The admired figure represents an ideal self-image. Of course, it is sometimes difficult to establish whether the similarity existed prior to the "meeting" or whether it developed after the media relationship flowered. Sometimes, as in the following account, both factors are involved. As a high school student at an overseas international school, this informant did not have access to the most current American television fare.

> I became familiar with the character Tony Baretta of the TV police series when newly arrived friends from the United States started to call me "Baretta." I learned that I looked a good deal like him—short, stocky, and black hair. The fact that I was from New York and had a tough guy reputation also helped.
>
> Eventually the series came to Belgium and I saw who this character was. I was not displeased at our apparent similarity. He portrayed a hard but sensitive character, a heavily muscled tough guy who at the same time could be counted on to help people through thick and thin. I also enjoyed his speech, attitudes towards smoking, and life in general.
>
> Once I started looking at the series, my behavior, largely because of peer expectation, started to resemble that of Baretta's more closely. . . . The next day after the series had been on friends and fellow students would say things like, "Man, I caught you on TV last night." Soon most people called me "Baretta" or "Tony" and I was sort of expected to play this character. . . . Often I would dress like him. Tight, dark blue T-shirts were a favorite during the warmer months. Naturally I was soon anxiously awaiting the weekly airing of the series and soon had assimilated many of his mannerisms. Although I never sounded like him, I do say many of his phrases: "You can take that to the bank," "Don't roll the dice if you can't pay the price," etc. . . . The TV character probably helped cement my character into the mold that is now me.

As this case also suggests, the media figure's appeal may be linked to the individual's actual social relationships. Here others made and supported the initial identification ("You are Tony Baretta"). One young woman's fifteen-year fixation on a soap opera character began with her social situation as a first grader. Arriving home from school she wanted to be with her mother, so she would sit down with her and watch *Guiding Light*. A young golfer's attraction to Arnold Palmer developed in part because Palmer came from a neighboring town and because his father, also an avid golfer, deeply admired Palmer. Many people have been turned on to a given novelist or musician by a friend who admired the figure and gave the person his first book or record as a present. In some cases the initial interest may be insincere. One young man, charmed by a female Bob Dylan fan, feigned appreciation of this musician in order to ingratiate himself with the woman. In the process he gradually developed a genuine interest in Dylan that continues up to the present—long after the woman has gone.

Once the initial identification has been made, patterned forms of behavior typically develop. As with artificial love relationships, the individual typically collects totemlike jewelry, T-shirts, locks of hair, photographs, posters, first editions, records, tapes, newsclippings, and concert programs. Media consumption is also likely to be intense. The individual reads the author's work repeatedly ("I read the novel five times"), or travels long distances to attend a concert. During media consumption, personal involvements tends to be sympathetic and emotional. "From the minute she stepped on stage I was in a trance. I was mesmerized by everything she did and I could actually see myself doing the same singing. . . . It actually gave me the chills." As this passage implies, identification is usually significant. Sometimes it is partial ("When I watch the show I think to myself how much I would like to be like her"); sometimes it is complete ("When I see her I don't see a TV character, I see myself").

Admiration relationships with media figures also have an important fantasy dimension.[26] As with love relations, fantasies link the individual *socially* with the admired figure. Three types of fantasies are especially common. In the first the individual meets the idol, in the second the person becomes someone like the idol, and in the third he or she becomes the idol.

Fantasy encounters are not mere meetings. One does not just shake the celebrity's hand and move on. A close and intimate social relationship is established. Several informants played out elaborate scenarios with writers whose work they admired. One man imagined journeying to the reclusive writer's home, becoming fast friends, and going out on drinking bouts full of brotherly adventure. A young woman liked to imagine herself visiting Loren Eiseley. "I visualized the two of us drinking coffee while sitting at a comfortable old kitchen table in his house. We would talk about philosophy, time, exploring damp caves, and reactions to nights in the country."

A standard variant of this fantasy involves establishing a professional role relationship with the admired figure.

> Steve Carlton is a six-foot five-inch 220-lb. pitcher for the Philadelphia Phillies. Since I myself am a frustrated athlete, I admire Carlton. He was given a great body and he has made the best possible use of it. Carlton possesses all the physical attributes I wish I had. . . . Carlton is also an expert in martial arts and is intellectual, having studied psychology and Eastern philosophy. I admire the man because he is the type to accomplish tasks and achieve goals.

This fan has several fantasies about establishing a social relationship with his idol.

> One has me in the big leagues pitching for the Phils and Carlton becomes my friend, takes me under his wing, and I become his protégé. I have also imagined that one day I will become Carlton's manager and that we have a great relationship. He admires me for my managing and coaching ability.

Another variant involves becoming, imaginatively, a close relative of the admired figure. One middle-aged woman, now herself a professional writer, described her attachment to Isak Dinesen. As a child she read and reread Dinesen and sought out all the biographical information she could find. She not only spent much time "reliving" scenes from the writer's adventurous life—"art school in Paris, her marriage to a Swedish count, the beginning of her African adventure . . ."—but she also constructed fantasies about growing up in Africa as Isak Dinesen's daughter. The dynamics of such fantasy interactions involve several different components but, again, a crucial dimension is the elevation of the self. Acceptance by the admired figure is the vehicle for indirect self-acceptance. (I admire them—I am like them—they accept me—I am a good person.)

In the second type of fantasy, the individual becomes someone like the admired figure and lives out experiences similar to those of the idol. An admirer of Jack Kerouac frequently imagined himself hitchhiking across the United States and Europe. Often a curious new self emerges, an imaginative combination of the fan and the admired figure. The following description comes from an admirer of *Gone with the Wind*.

> In my fantasies I see myself dressed in one of those beautiful hoop skirt dresses complete with parasol, hat, and fan—making me your typical Southern belle. I would speak in a sweet Southern accent. I would belong to a very wealthy Southern family with a large plantation stretching out for miles. My family would entertain frequently and I would grow up becoming very well raised in the social graces. As a woman, I would be very at ease with others, hospitable, and charming in my relationships with men. In my fantasies I look like myself, and I still have some of my own peculiar habits and personality traits, but I do take on most of Scarlett's charming attributes—her vivaciousness and way of dealing with people, the way she carries herself, etc.

One step further, in the third type of fantasy, the fan abandons his or her self and *becomes* the media figure. This is a common desire ("I would change places with him in a moment," "If I could be anyone else it would be her"). In fantasy the desire is realized. A young man studying to be a doctor reported a special relationship with James Bond, agent 007. In reality he sees himself as very different from Bond. The young man is "afraid of decisive action," Bond is cool and calculating; he "thrives on security," Bond gambles; he "feels compelled to ask for advice and permission," Bond is independent; he is "sexually naive," Bond is a Don Juan. However, through his artificial relationship a transformation of self occurs. In his media consumption and fantasy he sloughs off his own "inadequate" personality and turns into James Bond. Here, in fantasy, the individual's consciousness is "possessed" by the media self; it colors perception, patterns decision making, and structures social behavior.

Such an influence is not confined to fantasy. In the actual world as well, the admired figure sometimes guides actual behavior. First, the fan may adopt the idol's appearance.[27] One teenage fan went to the barbershop with a picture of his hero and asked the barber to "cut my hair just like Fabian's." Writer Caryl Rivers describes a series of imitative identifications: "I had a Marilyn Monroe outfit—off-the-shoulder peasant blouse, black tight skirt and hoop earrings . . . When Grace Kelly came along, I swept my hair back and wore long white gloves to dances and practiced looking glacial. I got my hair cut in an Italian boy style like Audrey Hepburn. For a while I was fixated on lavender because I read that Kim Novak wore only lavender."[28] She goes on to describe how facial expressions were also borrowed and incorporated.

> I wanted the kind that I saw in movie magazines or [on] billboards, the kind that featured THE LOOK. THE LOOK was standard for movie star pictures, although the art reached its zenith wth Marilyn Monroe. Head raised above a daring décolletage, eyes vacant, lips moist and parted slightly—that was generally agreed to be looking sexy. I practiced THE LOOK sometimes, making sure the bathroom door was locked before I did.[29]

Such relatively superficial influences are often part of a deeper identification in which the media figure's values and plans are incorporated into the fan's social behavior. This is menatlly accomplished in ways that directly parallel fantasy interactions. Operating in his or her own identity as someone who wants to act like the ideal figure, the individual may employ the media figure as a mentor or guide. Probably this is often unconscious. But sometimes the individual deliberately turns to the guide for help.

> Especially when I am upset, I think about her [Anne Frank's] outlook. I look to her as a reference. Then I try to act like she did.
> Woody Allen plays the role of amy pseudo conscience. He discriminates what is silly and irrelevant from what is worthwhile. . . . In awkward situations, I tend to rely on what I've seen him do or say.

A Mary Tyler Moore admirer shows how such a process can move beyond advice to deeper forms of self-transformation.

> I used her personality in my . . . anticipations about myself, especially when I had a problem. I would find myself thinking "What would Mary do?" . . . I would imagine myself in the situation that I wanted to be in . . . and also that I was exactly like Mary, that I had her sense of humor, her easygoing manner, etc. . . . This was a daily occurrence for me until about five years ago. . . . It was a way to solve my problems or to guide my behavior according to a model of perfection; a natural result was that I was pleased about how I conducted myself, especially with other people. I ended up regretting my behavior a lot less when I behaved as I thought Mary would behave. As a teenager I was very concerned about meeting role expectations, but with Mary inside my mind, it was much easier to meet those expectations.

As in certain fantasies, the fan here *becomes* the idol. Occasionally the fan consciously seeks to induce this self-transformation. "Sometimes I find myself saying, 'You are Carlton. Believe you are and so will everyone else.' " Here the fan overtly acts according to the hero's values, goals, and plans.

Because of such identification, media figures exert pervasive effects on many different areas of actual social life. Sports provide a good example. Many—probably most—American athletes are affected by media exemplars. Even the most successful professional athletes regularly report such role modeling. O. J. Simpson, for example, deliberately patterned himself after Jim Brown. This kind of imitation is so common that sports interviewers regularly ask their subjects about this aspect of their sports development. Many of my own informants reported on this process. The young golfer whose hero is Arnold Palmer reads all the Arnold Palmer how-to-do-it books, studies his games on television, practices his style of shots, and pretends to be Arnold Palmer while actually playing golf.

A successful college basketball player described her close relationship to a favorite professional player.

> Many times I sit and stare at a basketball court and imagine Bill down there warming up with a series of left- and right-handed hook shots . . . and still there are other times when after seeing him play on TV I imagine myself repeating all his moves. . . . On the court I pattern many of my offensive moves from Bill Walton.

As is typical with such artificial relationships, the imitation of sports behavior is part of a more profound influence. A young tennis star shows vividly how his pattern of play is but one manifestation of a larger imitation of values and lifestyle.

> I'm extremely aggressive on the court, I guess. I really like Jimmy Connors's game. I model myself after him. I read somewhere that he said he wants to play every point like it's match point at Wimbledon. . . . I like the individualism of tennis. It's not a team sport; it's an ego trip. You get all the glory yourself. That's what I thrive on, ego. . . . I want to become No. 1 in the world and become a millionaire. . . . I want to become like Vitas Gerulaitis, with the cars, the shopping in Paris, and the girls.[30]

As American idols, media figures do not influence merely one narrow aspect of life. They influence values, goals and attitudes, and through this they exert a pervasive influence on social conduct.

Given such evidence, it may seem odd that the existence of imitative media effects is still debated. The focal area of research here had been antisocial conduct in general and violence in particular. While most researchers now conclude that violent media promotes imitative actual aggression, a few deny this.[31] They argue that violent TV fare "evaporates" or that it has a "cathartic," pacifying effect on the audience. One problem involves the behavioristic methods by which much of the research has been carried out. Many researchers seek only to assess the immediate observable effects of media consumption, as by experiments in which test children are shown a film of violence and then observed and rated as to level of aggressive action afterwards. Some such studies reveal imitative effects, others do not. However, this approach ignores a crucial intervening variable, the individual's consciousness and mind set.[32] How a viewer reacts to a given media figure's example may critically depend on the kind of artificial-imaginary social relationship he or she has established with the figure. A closely related variable is the effect the communications have not on immediate overt behavior but on the individual's consciousness and knowledge. Just because the individual does not immediately engage in imitative violence does not mean that he or she has not been affected. When the media figure is a personal hero, the individual's tendency toward violence may have been confirmed or increased. The individual may also have learned new ways of attacking, fighting, shooting, stabbing, or torturing other people.

People vividly remember the aggressive techniques of their heroes and they see an astonishing number of examples of aggression. One estimate suggests that between the ages of five and fourteen the average American child has witnessed the violent destruction of 13,000 human beings on television alone.[33] Furthermore, Americans often rehearse what they have witnessed in the media. American children regularly imitate the violent antics of their media heroes in play, sometimes immediately after media consumption, sometimes days, weeks, or even months after the original exposure. Playing *Star Wars,* playing "guns," playing "Cowboys"—these media-derived games are among their most common pastimes. Children and adults also "practice" violent routines by adopting the hero's persona and playing out scenes of violence in their fantasies. The violence of American inner experiences can often be directly linked to particular media productions. Media violence does not evaporate. It affects attitudes, enters the stock of knowledge, and is acted upon in fantasy. It is thus readily available—in practiced form—for use in actual conduct as well. One American criminal who has spent fifteen years in jail spoke as follows:.

> TV has taught me how to steal cars, how to break into establishments, how to go about robbing people, even how to roll a drunk. Once, after watching a *Hawaii Five-O,* I robbed a gas station. The show showed me how to do it. Nowadays [he is serving a term for attempted rape] I watch TV in my house [cell] from 4 P.M. until midnight. I just sit back and take notes. I see 'em doing it this way or that way, you know, and I tell myself that I'll do it the same way when I get out. You could probably pick any ten guys in here and ask 'em and they'd tell you the same thing. Everybody's picking up on what's on TV.[34]

The following case shows how an antisocial media figure may guide an unmet fan. At the time, the informant, then thirty, was teaching at a California college. His mentor was Charles Manson.

> At the time Manson was busted for the Tate-LaBianca murders, I was very much interested in his group and especially the power control he exerted over the women. At the time Manson was being tried in the Hall of Justice in Los Angeles, several of his followers were holding a vigil on the streets outside the courthouse. They had shaven their heads and carved swastikas on their foreheads. I had seen them on TV and wanted to talk with them. So I drove to L.A. and did just that.
>
> I was very curious as to how such an insignificant person could garner such devotion from the women in his clan. Through brief talks with the willing group on the sidewalk, I soon got an inkling. The girls loved Charles because he was a forceful, dominant man whom they thought was godlike and was the savior for their kind: middle-class, confused, drugged, unstable, etc. youths. . . . Charles used biblical quotes, song lyrics, and drugs to partially control his flock; the real element of power, according to the girls, was the hypnotic spell his eyes could achieve in any face-to-face experience. . . . At the time I had been teaching a course in folklore and mythology and been caught up in the occult, mind games, mysticism, sexual myths, therapeutic processes, etc. Also at this time I was doing drugs heavily. . . . I was also experiencing a breakdown in my marriage. The point is that I was on the edge and very impressionistic. When I talked to the Manson girls who were convinced of the power of Charles's eyes, I acknowledged that sense of power in myself.
>
> I began to experiment with "eye psychology" in my social relationships. I used it on colleagues, strangers, and especially on young . . . women in my classes. For the most part it worked. In my sensitive state, I saw positive control of others result through my hypnotic gaze. To wit: one young woman I concentrated on fell under my spell. She confessed her love for me and was convinced that my eyes, etc., brought her under my control. She would do anything for me. At this point I pulled a Charles Manson. I gave her drugs, told her what was good and what was bad, completely controlled her social behavior. She was obligated to me and I was in no way obligated to her. I was on a power trip; she was on a slave trip. I, the manipulator, was in control. . . . After I got off heavy drugs, and after my marriage broke up, I was guilt-ridden. In my drugged-out state I probably had had the same perverted dreams as Charles.

But it is not just relations with the antisocial types, the real or imaginary media villains, that promote antisocial conduct; it is relations with heroes as well. And not just the James Bonds and Barettas, but the all-American good guys, the Gary Coopers and the John Waynes. Their teachings on violence are clear. Violence may be regrettable, but it is often justified and required (only a coward would back down). Violence is the proper solution for difficult and threatening social situations. Vengeful violence is satisfying, and successful violence will be admired and rewarded (after the killing you get the girl). The mass media did not create these values. They have their roots deep in the American value system. But our mass media promotes these teachings in a more pervasive, glamorized, insistent, and unrealistic way than does any other social world the individual is likely to visit. Like Ruth Steinhagen, Mark Chapman, and John Hinckley, we are the children of this world.

Role modeling is one way in which media figures affect actual behavior. Throughout this chapter we have touched on many other ways as well. Because they invade the individual's fantasies, media figures also affect economic and political behavior and structure all kinds of decision making. I noted earlier that media figures as pseudo mutual acquaintances often provide the basis for socializing. The ultimate example here is fan clubs, organizations of real people who come together and interact out of their mutual attraction to a celebrity none of them may have actually met face to face.[35]

There are many other occasions when actual social interactions are affected because the people involved are simultaneously interacting imaginatively with media beings. Two people may "visit" while watching a TV program. In some cases, they switch their attention back and forth between the two worlds; at other times, they attend to both.[36] The typical American date often follows such a pattern. A young man and woman, attending a movie together, may be separately involved in the same public fantasy (the movie) while still retaining some minimal "real" contact, perhaps by holding hands. This kind of date, common in early stages of courtship, permits the couple to be together but removes the strain of confronting each other directly. After leaving the movie, people can simultaneously recall and comment on their personal reactions to the artificial social events they have just independently experienced together. A more dramatic example occurs when a man and a woman engaged in sexual intercourse are also each "away," experiencing separate sexual fantasies with media beings.

Definite rules govern the ways in which an individual who is physically present in a social situation may simultaneously involve himself with media figures. These tacit rules often specify the attention an individual owes to real relationships as distinct from that which he may legitimately devote to artificial interactions. A person is usually expected to abandon or lower his participation in the artificial world whenever a pressing claim is advanced by present real others ("It's time for supper," or "Someone is knocking on the door"). Tardiness in "coming back" usually calls for apologies. The presence of these rules is often revealed by their transgression, and people may become seriously annoyed when they receive less attention than media others. In many households, it is offensive for an individual to read at the dinner table. The seasonal laments of "football widows" constitute another case in point. Professional advice-givers like "Dear Abby" sometimes describe other examples. One woman worried about the time and attention her husband lavished on "girlie magazines." Another complained that her husband was angry when she revealed her fantasies. Here media figures are perceived as rivals.

Such social patterns, like other aspects of media relationships, typically strike people as amusing. Those who have been through intense media relationships often recall them with embarrassment, and those outside them often respond with derision. This reaction—so predictable as to have the status of a culture pattern—is worthy of analysis in its own right. Imitative role modeling in general tends to evoke amusement. There seems to be something funny about a person imitating someone else. But as Phillip Slater has pointed out, imitation is basic to our enculturation.[37] We are not born with social plans and identities. We have to develop these through cultural learning in social situations. We become our "selves" to a large extent through positive and negative role modeling on figures in our social environments. It is just that we like to pretend otherwise. Perhaps the humor of imitation involves a dimly felt sense of its unstated power, the incongruity between our pretended independence and our actual derivative dependence. Our amusement also comes from the sense of incongruity involved in choosing as hero or lover not a real person but an unmet image who appears only on the page of a book or the screen of a television—perhaps a totally fictional character as well, the figment of someone *else's* fantasy.

From one perspective this does seem strange—with so many real people to choose from, why pick a phantom? But from another perspective it makes perfectly good sense, because media figures are "better" than ordinary people. Another factor is the nature of the particular figure chosen. Older Americans often sneer at the idols of the young. They seem so one-dimensional, so discreditable, so unrealistic. An early Beatles fan had to "combat" her father over her infatuation with Paul McCartney since her father viewed him as "a long-haired bum." Here again, however, the problem is in the perspective. Like others of her time, this adolescent was not looking for a conventional establishment model but for an idol who expressed her own rebelliousness and her longing for romantic extremes beyond the boundaries of adult compromise.

Finally, the sense of ridicule merges with media criticism. Attachments to media figures seem undesirable because the media are seen as promoting antisocial, false, unrealistic, and shallow value orientations.[38] Few Americans would deny this, but it is also far from the whole story. As recent survey research suggests, even the popular mass media can be shown to have many "prosocial" effects.[39] My own ethnographic investigation also indicates that imaginary relationships with media figures can have many beneficial effects.

Artificial contact with an admired figure—whether through books, television, records, or imagination—is often felt to be subjectively beneficial. Like a meeting with a good friend, the artificial communication may lift the person out of a bad mood. Often the contact is sought for just this reason. The following informant speaks for the fans of many other musicians. "When I hear their music, I always feel good, even if I was feeling lousy. . . . I know every word and nuance of their songs. Their spirit lifts me up and makes me feel pleased with life. Their music helps my world to continue properly." Often, as with this informant, it is not only that the music is cheering but that the message is felt to be "inspirational," because it helps people develop and affirm strongly felt values. A twenty-seven-year-old nurse offered the following account:

> When the antiwar protests of 1968 made headlines by attracting hundreds of thousands of demonstrators to Washington, Peter, Paul, and Mary performed at the monument grounds. . . . I remember hearing those folk heroes speak and sing, and I remember distinctly the feeling of camaraderie which they instilled in the crowd. Unlike other performers, they were able to inspire me toward ideals of the brotherhood of man. Through my contacts with the performances and appearance of this folk trio, I met other like-minded people.
>
> Peter Paul, and Mary were the embodiment of the sixties in their concerns for social justice and peace, and in their idealism, optimism, and enthusiasm. I identified with their values as did many of my peers. I admired their ideals and shared their concerns. After the Vietnam War ended, Peter, Paul, and Mary espoused new causes, including conservation. I continued to embrace the values they represented.

Gratitude for help of this kind is expressed toward many popular musicians, including John Lennon and the Beatles. If the figure dies, the person feels the loss of both friend and mentor.

Other kinds of media figures are similarly important. Like other autobiographies, *The Diary of Anne Frank* has been of enormous personal significance to several of my informants. "I admired her courage and strength and I tried to incorporate that aspect of her personality into my own." Fictional characters may have the same effect:

> True, this novel is a work of art, is fiction, but in some ways it is more than that to me. It is a piece of art that contains knowledge on how to live. This novel is a how-to-do-it book containing countless mental recipes for a healthy existence, all of which comes from Ellison's head and is passed on through the persona of the "invisible man."

Often the individual credits a media figure with having helped him or her to reach traditional kinds of American values and ideals. Sometimes the model is a political figure—a notable example would be John F. Kennedy—but often it is a celebrity far outside the conventional political field.

> Arnold Palmer played the role model to me. He taught me several things which I still hold today. One thing Arnold taught me was competitiveness. He taught me to enjoy and to thrive on being a good, clean competitor. Arnie's determination not to give up and to keep on trying showed me the way to succeed in anything is never to give in. Secondly, Arnold Palmer illustrated to me how to be a good sportsman. He never once shouted out to an opponent, judge, or spectator. He demonstrated to me how to "keep my cool" under pressure and to be a gentleman on and off the golf course. Thirdly, Arnie showed to me that he never forgot about his "roots." In other words, Arnold Palmer was proud of where he came from.

Even conversions to traditional religious orientations have been directly attributed to relationships with media figures, as with a previously depressed woman for whom "God became real" through the autobiographical works of a religious writer whom she first encountered on a televised version of the Billy Graham Crusade.

As these examples indicate, a media relationship may influence the individual in the development of a variety of very different value orientations. Whether or not one personally agrees with a given orientation, we are talking here about positive media effects. Even the most silly and superficial of fictional mass communication figures can sometimes lead to something significant. One informant described his relationship with a character on the 1959–63 family situation comedy, *The Many Loves of Dobie Gillis*. The show concerned the antics of a middle-class grocer's family and assorted friends and customers. For my informant, the significant figure was the "beatnik" character Maynard G. Krebs.

> Maynard was clad in a sweatshirt with holes, chinos, and sneakers. His hair was longer than Dobie's crew cut and he sported a goatee. He had dropped out of school and the creators of the series made a point of having Maynard hiccup everytime he mentioned the word "work." Most of the time Maynard just hung around doing nothing. Maynard G. Krebs was the media's version of the "beatnik." Maynard had and has continued to have a profound effect on my personal development.
>
> In order to understand Maynard's lasting influence, it is necessary to understand a little about me as an eight- or nine-year-old child. I was the classic 50-lb. weakling . . . someone who was bad at sports. I was so bad that not only was I always the last one chosen in team sports, but the team captains would argue over who would get stuck with me. At eight or nine sports were important, the rites of passage for one's boyhood. Since I was a failure at this test, I was ostracized, made to feel different from the other boys.
>
> Maynard, although a friend of Dobie's, was clearly different from the other characters on the TV show. Hence the reason for the identification with the "beatnik." The identification lasted. . . . between 1964 and 1965 my hair got longer and from the beginning I identified with the counterculture. People would

say things about the length of my hair and make fun of the way I looked. Again I was the different one, an outsider, a deviant.

In 1967 I read Ginsberg's *Howl* for the first time. Now, six or seven years after Maynard's caricature, I had "real" contact, through literature, with the Beats. Ginsberg, Kerouac, Snyder and the others were major forces in the counterculture and the fascination, influence, and sometimes imitation grew. . . . Later, in my twenties, I would occasionally grow a goatee, something I had wanted to do from the day I saw Maynard's.

From the late 1960s through today I spend much of my spare time reading the Beats—works about them and their literature. Through their writings I was introduced to the San Francisco poets, Black Mountain poets, as well as those who had influenced their writings from the past—Blake, Whitman, Thoreau, Miller and others. Many of my friends became musicians, poets, photographers, political activists, and other social misfits. . . . Twenty years later my emphasis in graduate school is bohemianism, the artist-intellectual and nonconformist, and his or her role in American cultural history. A lasting effect indeed.

The positive influence of media figures can extend throughout adult life. Sometimes these adult relationships involve less imitation and more in the way of a critical appreciation of the figure's life and philosophy. However, as in other media relationships, the individual often seeks regular forms of "contact" with the admired figure through personal fantasy, through the electronic media, and through repeated readings of an author's work. Sometimes the individual resorts to other devices as well. Robert Coles, often hailed as "a major social critic," and even a "saint," has been deeply affected by the life work of a variety of unmet beings. He feels that his own work has been helped by these figures and to heighten this influence he has hung their photographs in the study where he writes.

> Here he has chosen to be scrutinized by pictures of people who, by their life and work, openly challenge him. Among them, Simone Weil, a tortured, frail French writer who literally starved herself to death when the Resistance wouldn't send her on a dangerous mission; George Orwell ("People think of '1984' and forget his exposes of capitalism, of the coal mines"); the Catholic Worker's Dorothy Day; Walker Percy ("Ten pages of 'The Moviegoer' are worth all the words I've written"); and George S. Bernanos, whose "The Diary of a Country Priest" is Coles's favorite book ("He fought the temptation to ignore life's uncertainties and ambiguities"). . . .[40]

Attachments to media figures do not have a simple, one-sided effect on American life. They have complex positive and negative consequences. But taken together it is clear that such pseudosocial relationships constitute a pervasive and powerfully significant influence. Any approach to American society that ignores these social relationships is seriously incomplete.

Notes

1. Cf. Ward H. Goodenough, *Cultural Anthropology and Linguistics,* Georgetown University Monograph Series on Language and Linguistics, no. i (Washington, D.C., 1957), 167.
2. John L. Caughey, *Fáánakkar: Cultural Values in a Micronesian Society,* University of Pennsylvania Publications in Anthropology, no. 2 (Philadelphia, 1977), 17–23.
3. Cf. John L. Caughey, "Identity Struggles in the Mental Status Examination," paper presented at the seventy-seventh annual meeting of the American Anthropological Association (Los Angeles, 1978).
4. The large set of beings I refer to here as "media figures" could be subdivided by many different criteria. In certain ways historical figures and live celebrities *are* different from fictional characters. For my purposes, however, they may all be usefully classified together. All three groups represent unmet figures beyond the circle of our actual social acquaintances. Historical persons like living authors or politicians are "media figures" because we know about them largely through biographies, essays, autobiographies, and documentaries. Even if an actual social acquaintance should tell us something about a media figure, he is likely to have obtained this information through the media.
5. Gary Pomerantz, "On the Road with the Dukes," *Washington Post,* 7 July 1981.
6. One study of blue collar workers showed that a large majority (85 percent) regularly read newspaper comic strips and that most of them habitually discussed them with each other. See Leo Bogart, "Adult Talk About Newspaper Comics," *American Journal of Sociology* 61 (1955), 26–30. Cf. Irving L. Allen, "Talking About Media Experiences," *Journal of Popular Culture* 16 (1982), 106–15, and Garth Jowett and James Linton, *Movies as Mass Communication,* (Beverly Hills: Sage, 1980), 83, on media as social integrators; James Lull, "The Social Uses of Television," *Human Communication Research* 6 (1980), 197–209, on the social uses of television in family interactions; and John M. Roberts, Chien Chiao, and Triloki N. Pandey, "Meaningful God Sets From a Chinese Personal Pantheon and a Hindu Personal Pantheon," *Ethnology* 14 (1975), 121–48, on "significant figure sets."
7. Peter Berger and Thomas Luckmann, *The Social Construction of Reality* (New York: Anchor, 1966), 25. Cf. Peter H. Wood, "Television as Dream," in Horace Newcomb, ed., *Television: The Critical View* (New York: Oxford, 1979), 517–35.
8. John L. Caughey, "Artificial Social Relations in Modern America," *American Quarterly* 39 (1978), 73. Cf. Donald F. Roberts and Christine M. Bachen, "Mass Communication Effects," in Mark Rosenzweig and Lyman Porter, eds., *Annual Review of Psychology* (Palo Alto, 1981), 310–17. For other reviews of the mass media, see Michael R. Real, "Media Theory: Contributions to an Understanding of American Mass Communications," in *American Quarterly* 32 (1980), 238–58; and Lawrence E. Mintz, "Recent Trends in the Study of Popular Culture," in Robert Walker, ed., *American Studies* (Westport, Conn.: Greenwood, 1983).
9. Arthur Knight, *The Liveliest Art* (New York: Mentor, 1957), 8.
10. Cf. Orinn Klapp, *Heroes, Villains and Fools* (Englewood Cliffs: Prentice-Hall, 1962).

11. Cf. Marie Winn, *The Plug-In Drug* (New York: Bantam, 1977).

12. D. Horton and R. Richard Wohl, "Mass Communications and Para-Social Interaction," *Psychiatry* 19 (1956), 215–28. For an elaboration on this classic essay, see Jan-Erik Nordlund, "Media Interaction," *Communication Research* 5 (1978) 150–75.

13. Ibid., 217. On newscasting as parasocial interaction, see Mark Levy, "Watching TV News as Para-Social Interaction," *Journal of Broadcasting* 23 (1979), 69–80.

14. Alan Blum, "Lower Class Negro Television Spectators: The Concept of Pseudo Jovial Skepticism," in Arthur Shostak and William Gomberg, eds., *Blue Collar World* (Englewood Cliffs: Prentice-Hall, 1964), 432.

15. Horton and Wohl, "Mass Communications and Para-Social Interaction," 228.

16. On media identification, see Jowett and Linton, *Movies as Mass Communication*, 91–92.

17. Frederick Exley, *A Fan's Notes* (New York: Ballantine, 1968), 2.

18. *Webster's Third New International Dictionary* (1966).

19. Linda Witt interview with Lawrence Freedman, "Up Front," *People* 15 April 1981.

20. Jerry Hopkins, "The Fans," in Harry Hubel, ed., *Things in the Driver's Seat: Readings in Popular Culture* (Chicago: Rand McNally, 1972), 166.

21. "Dear Abby," *Philadelphia Evening Bulletin*, 1 April 1974.

22. "T.V. Time," *Philadelphia Evening Bulletin*, 17 November 1973.

23. John L. Caughey, "Media Mentors: Adults' Fantasy Transactions with Celebrities," *Psychology Today* 12 (1978), 47.

24. Elihu Katz and Paul Lazarsfeld, *Personal Influence* (Glencoe: Free Press, 1955).

25. These data are patterned along a number of different social dimensions. For example, admired figures tend to be both older than the fan and of the same sex. If the admired figure is of the opposite sex, the fan is more likely to be female.

26. Seymour Fesbach, "The Role of Fantasy in the Response to Television," *Journal of Social Issues* 32 (1976), 71–85, makes a strong case for the importance of fantasy in analysing mass communications effects. However, he takes the argument in a very different direction from that developed here. He argues that it is important to distinguish "fantasy" programs (such as fictional movies) from realistic programs (such as news broadcasts) in assessing media effects. My concern here is with the fantasies induced by media consumption. While I agree that it is sometimes important to assess the viewers' definition of the reality of media productions, I regard all media consumption as similar to fantasizing. For a supporting argument, see Thomas R. Lindlof, "Fantasy Activity and the Television Event: Considerations for an Information Processing Construct of Involvement," *Communication Year Book* 4 (1980), 277–91. As is usual with such work, neither of these researchers is concerned with the pseudosocial relationships that dominate such processes.

27. The extreme case here is plastic surgery designed to make the fan resemble his or her idol. According to the president of the American Nasal and Facial Surgery Institute, "Many people have been requesting surgery to make them look like celebrities." Among the most requested features are Brooke Shields's lower lip, Bo Derek's ears, and John Travolta's cheekbones. "People," *Washington Post*, 25 August 1981.

28. Caryl Rivers, "I Fell in Love With Montgomery Clift," *New York Times*, 2

August 1973. Cf. her *Aphrodite at Mid-Century* (New York: Doubleday, 1973).

29. Ibid.

30. Ted Rodgers, "Groetsch Isn't Hazy About Tennis Goals," *Philadelphia Evening Bulletin,* 26 April 1978.

31. For a recent review of the research, see Roberts and Bachen, "Mass Communication Effects," 340–42.

32. Cf. Donald Roberts, "The Nature of Communications Effects," in Wilber Schramm and Donald Roberts, eds., *The Processes and Effects of Mass Communications* (Urbana: University of Illinois, 1971), 363.

33. Otto Larsen, quoted by Melvyn DeFleur, *Theories of Mass Communications* (New York: McKay, 1970), 136.

34. From *TV Guide,* as quoted by Action for Children's Television in an untitled, undated pamphlet distributed by ACT, 46 Austin St., Newtonville, Mass. 02160.

35. Similar gatherings include Star Trek, Beatles, and science fiction conventions. Again there are parallels with religious groups.

36. Caughey, "Artificial Social Relations," 66. Cf. Timothy Meyer et al., "Non-Traditional Mass Communication Methods: An Overview of Observational Case Studies of Media Use in Natural Social Settings," *Communication Yearbook* 4 (1980), 261–75.

37. Phillip Slater, *The Pursuit of Loneliness,* second ed. (Boston: Beacon Press, 1976), 26.

38. For a recent critical view, see Jerry Mander, *Four Arguments for the Elimination of Television* (New York: Morrow, 1978).

39. On "prosocial effects," see Roberts and Bachen, "Mass Communication Effects," 342–44.

40. Paul Wilkes, "Robert Coles: Doctor of Crisis," *New York Times Magazine,* 26 March 1978.

JOSHUA MEYROWITZ

Television and Interpersonal Behavior: Codes of Perception and Response

This essay is a unique analysis of the relationship of space as portrayed through the television camera, and space experienced interpersonally. Very few studies have analyzed the photographic "grammar" of the televised image. Combining Horton and Wohl's concept of the "para-social relationship," in which the television performance is experienced like a live interaction, with the interpersonal theories of Edward Hall (The Silent Language) and Erving Goffman (The Presentation of Self in Everyday Life), Meyrowitz develops the concepts of "para-proxemics" and "para-social impressions." His point is that television shots (close-up, medium, and wide shots) and camera locations (behind the head, over the shoulder) are related to the way in which we perceive and react to interpersonal distances and face-to-face relationships.

After reading this essay you will better understand how the television medium itself, quite apart from the content of the program, works to involve you with the image and to make you feel as though it were an interpersonal encounter. Read the essay by Horton and Wohl on para-social relationships to better understand Meyrowitz. Also, if you are not already familiar with the works of Hall and Goffman, two noted social anthropologists, you may want to acquaint yourself with their ideas about how we use space to communicate and how we develop personal relationships.

In 1956, Donald Horton and R. Richard Wohl wrote of the television viewer's "illusion of face-to-face relationship with the performer."[1] They called this phenomenon a *para-social relationship*. Horton and Wohl claimed that the "conditions of response to the performer are analogous to those in a primary group,"[2] and they described the ways in which the mediated relationship psychologically resembled real-life encounters.

Horton and Wohl's description of "para-social" interaction might logically have led other theorists to use the structure and characteristics of face-to-face interaction to explore response to television. But what are the "characteristics" of face-to-face interaction? When Horton and Wohl wrote their article, there were few, if any, theories of interpersonal behavior which could be "borrowed" and used to study the structure of television. As a result, researchers have generally looked elsewhere for sources of theories and methodologies. And yet over the same period of time in which television research has grown and multiplied, an increasing amount of important work has been done in describing the structure of interpersonal behavior and in identifying interpersonal behavior "codes." It may now be possible, therefore, to test, or at least further explore, Horton and Wohl's contention that television is experienced in a manner resembling live interaction.

Two significant researchers of interpersonal behavior are anthropologist Edward T. Hall and sociologist Erving Goffman. Hall has studied, among other things, the ways in which people use space and adjust interaction distances to suit different types of relationships. He has analyzed the "meaning" of different interpersonal distances. A significant part of Goffman's work deals with the ways in which people—both alone and in "teams"—constantly structure their appearance and behavior to convey socially meaningful messages and impressions.

Hall and Goffman present the kind of ethnographic data normally found in the work of anthropologists studying strange or primitive societies. Their observations, however, illuminate our own culture and behavior. Hall and Goffman try to make us aware of perceptions and actions which are normally intuitive and unconscious. Their work, therefore, does not tell us about behavior patterns which are foreign to us, but about patterns we know but do not usually know we know.

The work of Hall and Goffman suggests that there is an observable structure to interpersonal behavior—a structure that encompasses "elements" or "variables" which are commonly manipulated by people to create specific meanings and effects. It is possible that variables inherent in interpersonal behavior correlate in some way to variables used in television production. The "meaning" of a close-up or a long shot, for example, may have something to do with the meaning of different interpersonal distances. And the ways in which scenes and people are revealed to the viewer in television's para-social relationship may have something to do with the ways in which live impressions are given and received. This essay will explore the relevance to television of two interpersonal behavior codes: *proxemics* and *impression management*.

Proxemics

In the 1950s Edward T. Hall served as director of the State Department's Point Four Training Program for foreign-bound administrators and technicians. In the training process, Hall found that language was a surprisingly small problem. The disappearance or muting of the language barrier did not, in itself, open up communication between Americans and foreigners. Americans abroad still ran into tremendous difficulties accomplishing their goals. In fact, language gave them only a few clues to the general organization of behavior and lifestyle in other cultures. Many intercultural encounters ended badly, often with lingering mutual disrespect, and sometimes, more distressingly, with violence.

Hall contends that many such intercultural difficulties stem from Americans' ignorance of the structure of their own behavior and their belief that American behavior patterns are "natural" and "correct" while all other patterns are crazy or stupid. Often, claims Hall, we tend to see all foreigners as "underdeveloped Americans."[3]

Hall argues that nonverbal behavior varies as often and as consistently as linguistic behavior. He also believes that there are many unspoken, but very real patterns of behavior—what he calls *silent languages*—which serve to organize action and thought in any given culture. In the past, "culture" has often been dealt with as a single mass of undifferentiated behavior which must be understood through "empathy." Hall feels, however, that if there is any hope of establishing real channels of intercultural communication, *elements* of culture must be identified. If elements or "isolates" of culture can be found, then comparison and "translation" of some sort would be possible. With this in mind, Hall set out to identify and describe patterns of behavior which vary culturally.

Hall is best known for his work in *proxemics,* a term he coined to describe man's spatial behavior patterns. Man's perception and use of space are apparently biologically based, but they are modified by culture. Thus while people everywhere respond to spatial cues, each culture tends to organize space in its own specific way.

One aspect of proxemics which has been explored by Hall is the amount of distance established between two people when they interact. Hall has described the existence of four discrete and measurable *spatial zones: intimate, personal, social* and *public* (each with a near and far phase). Each zone represents a range of interpersonal distance and each tends to be used for a different type of interaction. People tend to select a given zone on the basis of their relationship and the given topic of conversation. A man and his wife, for example, tend to stand at a different distance from each other than a man and his secretary. (Indeed, a wife may become angry with her husband for simply exhibiting "inappropriate" spatial behavior with other women.) Gestures, voice volume, even choice of language, vary with distance.

Hall claims that the existence and use of these spatial zones is universal, but that the range of distance associated with each zone varies with culture. For similar types of interactions, for example, Latin Americans will likely choose an interpersonal distance different from that chosen by North Americans. Such variations in spatial behavior may cause misunderstandings in intercultural encounters. Members of other cultures, for example, may be perceived as "aggressive" or "cold" simply because they seem to stand "too close" or "too far away."

Hall's theory of proxemics has received support from many sources. Research has shown that a decrease in interpersonal distance causes an increase in galvanic skin response (GSR), a measure of stress and emotion.[4] Distance also affects the selective perception of available information; verbal messages, for example, are more easily attended to at a greater distance.[5] Further, the selection of a proxemic zone is apparently so consistent that distance has been suggested as one way of operationally defining interpersonal relationships.[6]

Hall's theory can also be "tested" informally. You may want to start paying attention to the amount of distance which you establish between yourself and others when you speak. Does it vary with relationships? Try to consciously change the distance during a conversation. Move closer, move farther away. What does the other person do? Do you feel uncomfortable moving during an interaction? If so, why? Perhaps you are changing the "meaning" of the interaction. See how close you can come to a stranger in an open space without feeling uncomfortable or obligated to speak to him. (You will probably find that this distance varies depending upon whether you approach face-to-face, back-to-back, and so forth.) Try to talk to a close friend about intimate personal matters while standing fifteen, or more, feet apart. Try to speak to someone about grand schemes and great expectations while standing nose-to-nose. While in an airport, or train station, or a large party, see how your involvement and response to conversations among other people varies with your distance from them. If you interact with a member of another culture or subculture, try to become aware of differences in the use of space. If you try any of these proxemic tests, you will probably become very much aware of the fact that "space speaks."

Para-Proxemics

What relevance might our perception and use of space have to the structure and "meaning" of televised sequences? An obvious point of departure is the "framing variable": the choice of close-ups, medium shots, or long shots to frame the portrayed scene. The very language of television and film shots suggests that distance is a factor in choosing them—*close*-up and *long* shot, for example. Oddly enough, however, shot selection is only rarely discussed in terms of distance. More often shots are analyzed in terms of image size or abstract concepts of "adjustment." Film scholar Lewis Jacobs, for example, notes that:

The size of an object affects our feelings as well as our recognition and under-standing of it. "Big" and "little" particularize and generalize. The close-up focuses attention on what is important through magnification of relevant de-tails and exclusion of unwanted portions of a subject. The full shot encom-passes all of a subject and facilitates recognition.[7]

And film theorist André Bazin explained the prevalence of the medium shot by suggesting that

the director returns as often as he can to a shot of the characters from the knees up, which is said to be best suited to catch the spontaneous attention of the viewer—the natural point of balance of his mental adjustment.[8]

Hall's theory of proxemics, however, suggests a possible relationship be-tween perception of interpersonal distance and the "framing variable." Hall indicates that at any given interpersonal distance one sees a specific amount of the other person clearly. Such descriptions may be relevant to television shots. While a television lens distorts visual cues to some extent (no binocular vision, no peripheral vision, a specific depth of field over which the individual has no control, etc.), any given shot of a person frames the individual in a certain way. It may show only his head, or only his head and shoulders, or it may picture his whole body with varying amounts of space around it. In a particular shot, therefore, the way in which a person is framed may suggest an interpersonal distance between that person and the viewer.

Are there any other indications that a "framed picture" is perceived in terms of distance? Artist Maurice Grosser's analysis of the portrait suggests that distance is a significant factor in shaping viewer response. Grosser notes that the portrait is distinguished from other painting formats in that the closeness of artist and model yields "the peculiar sort of com-munication, almost a conversation, that the person who looks at the pic-ture is able to hold with the person painted there."[9] Indeed, Hall points out that Grosser's description of distance and communication in portraits coincides very closely with Hall's own description of spatial zones.

Implicit in Grosser's discussion of portraits is the fact that the absolute size of the figure is not the key variable determining response to a picture. What is important is the distance that is suggested by the *relative* size of the figure within the frame. Similarly, on television a close-up on a nine-inch screen may suggest the same interpersonal distance as a close-up on a twenty-one-inch screen.

The idea that *relative* size is more important than *absolute* size may seem unusual, but this is actually one of the ways in which we judge dis-tance in everyday life. Psychologists have discussed the "constancy of size" phenomenon, whereby people and familiar objects are perceived as remaining the same size, even though the size of the image that they cast on the retina changes markedly.[10] When our friends walk away from us there is a decrease in the size of the retinal image of them. And yet, we do not think of our friends as getting smaller; we think of them as going further away. Similarly, regardless of the size of the image of a person within the television frame, we might react to the picture in terms of distance, not size. In television, perhaps, the screen becomes a kind of "extended retina" for the viewer. The relative size of people or objects within the screen, therefore, would serve as a cue to the distance of people and objects from the viewer. Following Horton and Wohl's lead, I call this a *para-proxemic* relationship.

Para-Proxemic Model

Several perceptual phenomena in television viewing might be described in terms of proxemics. One is the visual "relationship" between the viewer and the image. This relationship exists at every moment that a person watches television. In any one shot the viewer is shown a specific amount of a scene, person, or object. The subject may be shot in close-up, medium shot, or long shot. This *framing variable* creates a *mediated distance* between the viewer and the content of the image. Shots of a football game, for example, can "place" the viewer directly outside of the huddle or in the last row of the stands. The distance is "mediated" and not "real" because the image is flat, conveys a limited amount of sensory information, and thus abstracts for the viewer only a fraction of the contingencies of actual physical presence. Response may be further affected by such *situational variables* as the nature of the televised event (documentary versus fiction, for example), viewer distance from the screen, screen size, viewing angle, and other aspects of the immediate environment (lighting, noise, architecture, number of other people present). Nevertheless, the television shot suggests an approximate distance from the televised subject. At any point, the image can be compared to something seen live at distance X.

A second type of distance—*portrayed distance*—is an extension of the viewer/image distance. Not only does the viewer experience the image at a *mediated distance,* but he also sees spatial relationships within the image. For example, in addition to seeing the huddle at a certain "distance," the television football spectator also sees distances among the players in the huddle. *Portrayed distances* apply to relationships among people and objects within the medium. At any point during televised sequences the apparent distance between characters and objects might be estimated.

Portrayed distances can be divided into two categories—*portrayed objective distance* and *portrayed subjective distance;* that is, a division may

be made on the basis of two types of shots—"objective" and "subjective."
An "objective" shot is one that "maintains the role of a detached observer" of the action, where the camera assumes "whatever angle will best
portray that action."[11] The point of view presented by the objective shot is
not that of any particular person within the scene. Instead it selects an observation point for the viewer. One way to represent an interaction between two people, for example, is to show them both at the same time by
using an objective shot. It is then possible to describe the physical distance
at which they appear to be standing from each other.

Much more significant, however, is an interaction between two characters that is portrayed through "subjective" shots. Here the viewer must
imagine the interpersonal distance because it is not shown directly. A subjective shot "assumes the point of view of one of the characters";[12] it shows
the viewer what one person within the action sees. A subjective shot of a
two-character interaction would show only one person, and the shot would
be taken from the angle and viewpoint of the second person. Subjective
shots are commonly used in television and film. In a conversation between
person A and person B, for example, first a subjective shot of person A
might be shown, then a subjective shot of person B, and then back to a
subjective shot of person A. Although only one person is shown in any one
such subjective shot, the manner in which the image is framed within the
screen may suggest a physical distance between the two characters.

There are thus at least three potential television "distances": (1)
mediated viewer/image distance, (2) *portrayed objective distance,* and (3)
portrayed subjective distance (Fig. 1).

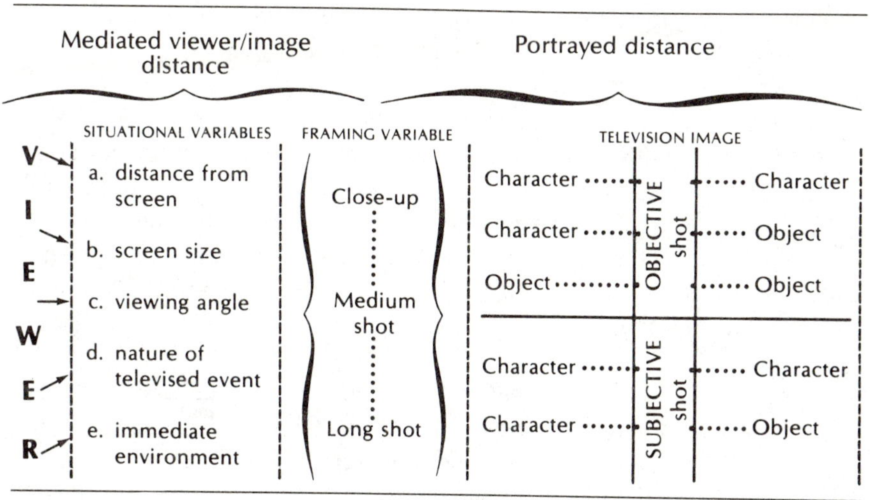

Figure 1.

A para-proxemic analysis of television shots has many significant implications for television theory. Proxemic conventions suggest both "appropriate" and "special effects" uses of media variables in relation to: (1) viewer orientation to a scene, (2) viewer perception and response to characters, and (3) viewer perception of relationships among characters.[13]

Viewer Orientation to a Scene. Live encounters do not begin suddenly. We approach buildings and rooms, see people first at a distance, and then come closer to begin interactions. At the end of interactions the process is generally reversed. On television as well, those scenes which seem to start and end "naturally" begin with long shots, progressively move in, and then end once again with long shots or a "fade-out." The fade-in and fade-out serve as a kind of shortcut "movement" into and out of scenes. Rarely do programs begin with a sudden cut from black, or a sudden cut to black.

The interpersonal experience of physical and perceptual transition can, however, be violated for special effects. Horror movies, for example, exploit sudden cuts into scenes and reorientations of the viewer without warning or transition. And a sudden cut to black can leave the viewer "hanging," still engrossed in the now unseen scene.

Once "brought into" a scene, the viewer must be gently moved around it, so as not to lose his bearing. Different shots may show him different parts of the scene—just as he would tend to look around a room—but if the shots alter the angle of viewing too drastically then the viewer may get lost. Shots, therefore, suggest visual behavior in live encounters. Indeed, although the "cutting" of shots is often thought of as a distortion of perception because we do not see the space in between (as we would in a "pan" shot), the cut actually closely resembles an individual's own scanning of a live scene. If I am watching two people talking in a live encounter, I will often look at one and then the other. I rarely attend to the space between them. In effect, I see in "cuts," not pans.

The interpersonal experience of orientation and vision can also be distorted for special effects. A director can purposely disorient the viewer by "moving" him around too violently. He can use "unnaturally" quick cutting or swift, long pans that give the viewer a swirling, spinning feeling. Such special effects give the viewer the sense of having "lost his ground." Both normal and special effects, therefore, can be related to live physical position and perception.

Viewer Perception of and Response to Characters. An understanding of proxemics is most helpful in analyzing our perception of and response to characters on television. Through para-proxemic variation, an actor in a television commercial, for example, may be presented to us either as an individual who makes a personal or intimate appeal (close-up) or as an authority whose approach is based on social role (medium or long shot).

Our response to what a character does or to what is done to him can also be interpreted in terms of proxemics. Actions in long shots, for example, tend to be viewed in terms of abstract "events," while close-ups focus attention on personal characteristics and response. If we see a policeman gunned-down in long shots, therefore, we tend to respond to the action: "shooting of a policeman." If, however, we come close enough to see tears running down the face of the wounded man, we have a very different response. Such variation in response is related to live experience.

The potential effect of para-proxemics on the perception of and identification with characters becomes clearer in a sequence involving more than one character. In a courtroom drama, for example, the director can juggle response to the judge and the defendant by simply varying the structure of the shots. If the judge is shown in long shots, the viewer's concern tends to be mainly with the judge's performance as a judge, while in close-ups the concern is with the judge's own feelings or his own response to his role. Alternating the types of shots presents a more complex response. The same manipulation is possible for the defendant. With shots that convey different distances, the director might be able to broadly recast the scenario: (1) judge vs. defendant (both seen in terms of "roles," in medium or long shot), (2) judge (medium shot) vs. man (close-up), (3) man vs. man (both close-ups), and so on. The notion that distance affects our response to characters can be further illustrated in a courtroom scene by the fact that many characters tend to serve only as "background." The court clerk, the stenographer, members of the jury, and others are not attended to very carefully *unless we see them close-up.*

It is important to note that many such changes in para-proxemic response are possible without any changes in dialogue or in much of what is often considered "content." Content variables, to be sure, interact with structural variables to mold the *exact* nature of our response, but the *intensity* of response is related to the distances established by shot structure. The content, therefore, may determine whether we feel sorry for a defendant or pray that he hangs; the content may determine whether we greatly admire the judge or are infuriated with his seeming bias. But the degree of response is related to para-proxemics. Similar content/structure interactions affect response in live encounters; distance determines intensity of relationships rather than specific behavior. Intimate space, for example, is the distance of both lovemaking *and* murder!

The ways in which we are para-proxemically oriented to characters in a scene may, at times, be a "distortion" of reality in that there could be no direct interpersonal analogue. We may, for example, see too much of too many people, too quickly from too many different perspectives to bear any direct relationship to actual physical presence. And yet the impact of such "distortion" may still be related to the types of feelings and response we experience in live encounters.

Viewer Perception of Relationships Among Characters. The framing variable in subjective shots also affects viewer understanding of the relationship among characters. Through subjective shots, the perceptions discussed in "response to characters" above are experienced through the eyes of a character within the drama. Para-proxemic variables in subjective shots indicate to the viewer the nature of a character's physical and psychological orientation to a scene. In a two-person interaction, for example, the framing variable will suggest distances between characters even though only one person is pictured in the shot. And the distances (as Hall suggests) indicate the intensity of the relationship among characters. Similarly, subjective shots portray general character orientation to actions and events.

Shots that portray the vision of a character can also distort "real" perception for special effects. If, for example, two people are shown in objective shots to be at opposite sides of a room, and yet in subjective shots they are shown to "see" each other in close-up, then psychological intimacy and emotional intensity is suggested. Conversely, if two people are shown in objective shots at "social" distance, and yet each views the other subjectively in long shots ("public" distance), then psychological isolation is suggested. Further, unmatched subjective shots may suggest nonreciprocal perception and response. A young man's sense of isolation from his parents, for example, might be portrayed through subjective shots. He may be "perceived" by his parents in medium shots, yet he "sees" them in long shots.

Hall's theory of proxemics, therefore, can be adapted to an analysis of television. The *framing variable* "places" the viewer within scenes or reveals spatial orientations of characters. Shots portray distances and therefore have a "meaning" which corresponds to the functioning of spatial cues in interpersonal interaction. My analysis of para-proxemics, however, suggests only a broad framework of viewer perception and response. Thus far, I have suggested how shots "position" the viewer, but I have not yet analyzed what the viewer sees from his position, how he makes any (social) sense of what he sees, and how and why he might choose to identify with some characters rather than others. Erving Goffman's theory of *impression management* suggests some preliminary answers to these questions.

Impression Management

In *The Presentation of Self in Everyday Life*,[14] Erving Goffman suggests that when a person enters a social situation he wants and needs to know something about the other participants and the given context. He may, for example, want to know the age, marital status, wealth, education, or intelligence of the other people. He may want to know the particular roles being played by others in the situation. He will need to know whether the situation is formal or informal, who is in charge, whom he must speak to first, and whether he is welcome or unwelcome. Conversely, people in the given setting will want to know something about the person who enters.

Goffman notes that much of this information is not "naturally" available. It may take years to fully know a person or understand how a group of people function in a given social establishment or institution. And yet, most social interaction requires instant judgments, alignments, and behavior. As a result, Goffman suggests, people are constantly mobilizing their energies to create socially meaningful "impressions."

Goffman argues that *impression management* has the character of "drama"; that is, all social roles are, in a sense, a performance where the individual actor highlights certain characteristics and conceals others. And just like any other drama, the stage must be properly set, the individual must often learn and rehearse his role, and he must coordinate his activities with fellow performers.

In most social encounters, Goffman argues, the individual tends to have a *front*: "that part of the individual's performance which regularly functions in a general and fixed fashion to define the situation for those who observe the performance."[15] Goffman discusses two aspects of *front*: the *setting*, and *personal front*.

The *setting* involves relatively fixed elements such as furniture, carpeting, statues, windows, and professional equipment. The setting itself establishes an expectation of roles and appropriate behavior. One of the differences between eating in Sardi's and eating in McDonald's is the distinctly different setting.

Variations in the *setting* influence the behavior of all involved. A scientist sitting in his laboratory both *feels* and *appears* more authoritative about his work than he does while playing golf. And a rock group leader may not feel he can give his "rap" to the audience unless he stands in front of his group with amplifiers and instruments at the ready. Similarly, the way in which a teenager arranges and decorates his room will suggest his attitude toward himself and his expectations in regard to formality and type of interaction with friends.

The *personal front* differs from the setting in that it is located within or on the performer himself. Personal front includes such features as age, height, sex, race, hair length, posture, style and quality of clothing, facial expression, and gesture.

Some aspects of personal front are fixed and do not change from situation to situation (unless one resorts to surgery or other drastic means). A good part of the personal front, however, can easily be changed or modified to suit the context and the role to be played in it.

In terms of a given interaction, Goffman divides personal front into *appearance* and *manner*. *Appearance* is that part of the personal front which includes such features as clothing, uniforms, and insignia, and which tells others the nature of the performer's social status in the given context. The same man will *appear* very different in a bathing suit than in a four-star general's uniform.

Manner is related to appearance, but it adds the dimension of the specific (and more variable) behavior which the individual exhibits in a given situation. Manner and appearance can be at odds. A person who appears to be of very high status, for example, may nevertheless behave toward others in a humble or egalitarian manner. A general, for example, may speak "man to man" to a private. Usually, however, we expect and experience some consistency between manner and appearance. We expect a man dressed in judge's robes (appearance) to behave sternly and judiciously (manner). And we expect a busboy (i.e., someone dressed as a busboy) to be humble and inconspicuous.

While we often believe that it is dishonest to "put on" a character or "play" a role, Goffman suggests that this is a foolish belief. Some people, it is true, may purposely give misleading impressions (con men, spies, undercover agents), but *all* individuals must give *some* impression. Thus, while a dishonest judge may pretend to be an honest judge, an honest judge must also play the role of "honest judge." He may, for example, have to avoid being seen in questionable places with questionable characters even if there is nothing "actually" inappropriate about his behavior. And even an honest judge must dress up properly, wearing black, not pink, robes. Impression management, therefore, serves as a kind of social "shorthand" through which people identify themselves and provide expectations about their behavior.

One of Goffman's most interesting observations about the management of impression is that any individual's behavior in a given setting can generally be broken down into two broad categories: what Goffman calls *back region* or backstage behavior, and *front region* or onstage behavior. In front regions, the individual is in the presence of his "audience" and he plays out a relatively ideal conception of the social role. A waiter is in a front region when he serves people in a restaurant. He is polite and respectful. He does not enter into the dinner conversations of his patrons. He does not comment on their eating habits or table manners. He rarely, if ever, eats while in their sight. In the dining hall, setting, appearance, and manner are carefully controlled. When the waiter steps from the dining room into the kitchen, however, he suddenly crosses the line between on-stage and backstage. He enters an area which is hidden from the audience and which he shares with others who perform the same or similar roles. Here, then, the waiter may make remarks about the "strange" people at table number seven, he may imitate patrons, he may give advice to a "rookie" waiter on methods of getting big tips, he may get out of role by sitting or standing in a sloppy manner. He may even get out of costume.

Goffman suggests that all people—from porters to presidents—share this distinction in behavior. All social roles depend upon selected behaviors. A doctor, for example, tends to hide his doubts, times of depression, sexual feelings, and personal likes and dislikes of patients. Similarly, virtually all role performers tend to have back regions where they and their "teammates" (those who share the same role or work to foster the same performance) relax, rehearse, make jokes about behavior in front regions, and sometimes work out strategies for future performances. When not in a courtroom, even a judge may joke about the physical appearance of a witness, he may ask a court clerk to speak more slowly when announcing the judge's entrance (a "stage direction") or he may telephone another judge to explore a legal technicality about which he is uncertain. All roles depend upon the performer having a back region. At the same time, all front region roles rely upon keeping the audience out of back regions. The social performer, like the stage actor, must have a private place to learn and rehearse his role. If he does not, he cannot build up to or maintain a performance which impresses his audience.

Teammates always have a different perception of the situation than do audience members. For the benefit of the audience, errors tend to be corrected before they can be seen, only end products are shown, and the dirty aspects of work are concealed. Many features of the performance, including the individual's perspective on his role, are saved for teammates. Even when an audience is present, teammates may furtively exchange glances, grimaces, or knowing winks.

Para-Social Impressions

The characteristics of live interaction which Goffman outlines may be related to perception of television drama in terms of (1) identifying situations and characters, (2) aligning (or teaming) the viewer with selected characters, and (3) revealing relationships among characters.

Identifying Situations and Characters. As Goffman describes it, *front* plays a very significant, though often unnoticed role in the perception of television scenes. Opening shots of sequences generally reveal the *setting* and then the *appearance* of characters. Indeed, when a single shot of a setting or of a character is not sufficient for identification, there may be a slow scan of the scene or of the individual. To set the scene for "the eccentric millionaire," for example, there may be an opening shot of a mansion followed by a pan of a collection of strange and extravagant art works. The "highly decorated general" may himself be slowly scanned to reveal his medals and stern demeanor. In virtually all television drama such "establishing" shots begin sequences and set expectations for the type of interaction that is to come.

Further, shots throughout a sequence allow the viewer to monitor variations in the *manner* of characters. They reveal the character's changing orientation to ongoing events. Such shots combined with information about the setting help to flesh-out the fine points of character and behavior.

Television shots, therefore, especially "establishing shots," reveal to us what we would normally look for upon entering a live encounter. If impression management is a kind of social shorthand, then television shots are a shorthand of a shorthand. Shots quickly display those aspects of setting and personal front which "performers" in live interactions purposely highlight and express.

Aligning (or Teaming) the Viewer with Selected Characters. In many social situations we find ourselves in one of two positions in relation to each other person: we are either an audience to their front region role, or we are a teammate concerned to some extent with their "carrying off" their performance before others. Our perception and orientation to situations varies tremendously depending upon those in the situation whom we see as teammates. There is, for example, a great difference between visiting a classroom, where one of our friends is a student, and visiting a classroom where one of our friends is the teacher. We tend to view the "action" from the perspective of our "team." We are generally concerned that our teammates perform their roles well and make good impressions. And as teammates, we are usually given access to back region rehearsals, relaxations, comments about the "audience," and teammates' perceptions of their own roles.

In television drama as well, the structure and arrangement of shots can establish a "character" for the viewer; that is, the camera can make the viewer a teammate of selected characters.

Sometimes the camera makes the viewer a teammate by simply "placing" him in a back region or giving him the back region view of the front region performance. If we see a judge from *behind* his bench, and we see him scratch his legs or twiddle his thumbs, we have a significantly different relationship with him than if we view him from the front and at a low angle. Such variables combine with para-proxemic effects to align the viewer with characters. And again, dialogue and abstract descriptions of actions will tell us only a small fraction of the "meaning" of televised sequences.

A key to the structure of many detective dramas rests in the timing and extent of the revelation to the viewer of the criminals' back region behavior. Do we have the same information as the detective? Less or more? Are we teamed with the detective or with the criminals? The order in which we get to "know" characters (as is often the case in real-life) can also affect our alignment. If we get to know the detective first, we may become aligned with him. Even if we later see the criminals in their back regions, we may view ourselves as spies, not teammates. On the other hand, if we get to know the criminals very well and see law enforcement personnel in their front region roles only, we may align with the criminals. Such variables can account, in part, for the markedly different viewer attitude toward the criminals in *The Untouchables* and *The Godfather*.

Alignments and teaming are used most unabashedly in war and cowboy dramas. Here, the perspective established by chosen shots clearly distinguishes "them" from "us." The enemy is generally seen in front region roles only. But "our boys" are seen in both back and front regions. Further, we tend to be shown situations from the position of "our side." Indeed, we literally see scenes primarily from one *side*. Often we are "placed" right behind our men, as if we stand with them. When the enemy fires, he fires on us. When one of our boys is wounded, we are upset; but a hundred Indians, outlaws, or Germans can be blown to bits, and we cheer. That such response has more to do with structure than ideology is demonstrated by some antiwar films which show both sides alternately and equally (giving us the perspective of God?). Here the futility and stupidity of war seems apparent.

Even "objective" shots, therefore, are rarely objective in the larger sense. When a character enters a room, for example, the side of the door from which the viewer watches the action is significant. The shot may not portray the vision of any specific character in the action, but the perspective established by it selects a position, and therefore a general response, for the viewer. At any given point in a television scene we may ask: Whose perspective do I have? What do I know about these characters? Who are my "teammates"? Who do I see only in their front region roles? Who do I like and why?

Revealing Relationships Among Characters. Through subjective shots the viewer sees those aspects of setting and personal front which a character observes. A common technique in detective dramas, for example, is to show the viewer features of the setting or personal front which the detective finds odd or suspicious. Subjective shots can also reveal to the viewer the nature of alignments among characters. Subjective shots may reveal collusive looks between characters suggesting a teammate relationship. In a murder drama, for example, a gun may be found behind a bush, and the viewer may see a collusive look between the widow of the murdered man and the next-door neighbor. Through subjective shots, therefore, the viewer learns whether characters view themselves as teammates or as audience members for each other's roles.

In summary, Goffman's theory of impression management is of relevance here because it suggests a number of similarities between interpersonal interaction and the structure of television sequences. Both are dramatic in nature, highly structured, rehearsed, and planned. Both involve highlighting socially significant cues. Both involve the perception of action and character in terms of social context and personal alignments.[16]

Conclusion

Proxemics and impression management are only two of many interpersonal behavior codes which have been outlined by researchers in recent years. They alone, however, provide a rich source of insight into the nature of viewer response to television.

Content/Structure Interaction. Television research has generally focused on content *or* on structure. The analysis presented here, however, suggests that televised sequences are understood through a structure/content interaction. The key to the "meaning" of such an interaction lies in the content/structure interface of live perception and response. A shout in real experience has one meaning at 25 feet and quite another at 25 inches; a "member of the opposite sex" has one meaning at 5 feet and another at 5 inches. Moreover, a person's response to a given person or event depends upon his perception of the social context and his knowledge of, and identification with others in the situation.

In the same way, a piece of television content—such as an act of violence—has no meaning in and of itself. The intensity of response is affected by the "distance" from the action. And the nature of the response will vary with the viewer's relative relationship with characters. A violent attack, for example, may be committed (1) on a teammate by a stranger, (2) on a stranger by a teammate, (3) by one teammate on another teammate, or (4) by one stranger on another stranger. In each case the viewer's response would be different.

Furthermore, just as a unit of television content has no meaning apart from the way in which it is presented, so does a production variable have no inherent meaning apart from the portrayed content and relevant social context. A low angle shot, for example, might be understood in one way when picturing a judge or a politician (people who are "looked up to" in real life) and another way when picturing a young boy or a waiter. A low angle shot may in one case enhance credibility and in another cause uneasiness, mistrust, or fear. Again, the real-life matrix of meaning provides the framework for perception and response.[17]

Implications for Directors. Many of the television "grammar" studies are designed to systematically investigate the validity of production guidelines that have developed through intuition and trial-and-error. The analysis presented here suggests a source of the director's intuition: the unconscious behavior codes of interpersonal behavior. Production guidelines, therefore, may need less experimental investigation than is often assumed. In television, as in interpersonal behavior, if it "feels" right, it probably is right.

A major exception to the "feeling right" rule, however, is intercultural communication. If television cues are "equivalent" to interpersonal cues, then perception of a given television sequence will vary culturally. All cultures, for example, may be able to "understand" paraproxemics (just as all cultures "understand" proxemics). Yet, response to a given shot may be quite different in different cultures. A Latin American, for example, may perceive people on North American television as being cold and unfriendly, even to each other; North Americans may find people on Latin American television pushy and aggressive.[18] While intercultural communication through distribution of film is often thought of as a means of enhancing understanding and good-will, visual media may actually reinforce stereotypes and prejudices. Some cross-cultural translation of visual material may be necessary.

Impact of Media on Interpersonal Behavior. Interpersonal behavior preceded television. To describe a structural similarity between television and live encounters, therefore, is to demonstrate the ways in which interpersonal behavior affects media. And yet, if there is a strong common denominator between television "relationships" and face-to-face interaction, then the widespread use of television may also have an impact on interpersonal behavior. Television may, for example, teach or reinforce proxemic behavior patterns for children. Television may sensitize individuals to significant aspects of *setting* and *personal front* in given contexts. Indeed, worldwide distribution of television programs may create a trend toward homogenization of previously variant proxemic patterns and characteristics of impression management.

Furthermore, if Goffman is correct in assuming that interpersonal behavior is a kind of drama where the "scripts" depend upon controlling performances carefully and *restricting* access to performers, then electronic media may be restaging the social drama as a whole. Electronic media may change the arenas in which many people play their roles and alter the identity and size of their audiences. As a result, electronic media may change the type and amount of access that people have to each other and thereby affect the nature of the roles that can be successfully played. I have explored some of these possibilities elsewhere.[19]

A Symbolic Link. Even when the content of television programs is nonfictional, there is a limit to the extent to which the analogue between live and para-social interaction can be taken. After all, television images are only images. They convey a limited amount of sensory data, they give the viewer little choice over field of view and focus, and they therefore present only a small range of the perceptual and psychological phenomena associated with physical presence. There can, for example, be no real threat or seduction in television—even when a shot is para-proxemically "equivalent" to intimate distance. And rarely could a viewer be expected to actually foster the performance of a televised "teammate." We are, therefore, left with the question: What is the nature of the connection between interpersonal codes and our understanding of televised sequences of action?

I suggest that the link is a symbolic one. Television images are symbolic of live experience. That is, we do not respond to the televised situation as we would to a real situation, but we respond to the *concept* of the real situation.[20]

This symbolic link is similar to "suspension of disbelief" in drama. When we watch someone being attacked on the stage we do not yell "Police!" but we do feel pity; that is, we respond to the *idea* of attack. Similarly, the meaning of many television cues may rest in unconscious interpersonal codes such as proxemics and impression management. When we see a performer in a close-up, therefore, we do not get directly sexually aroused or frightened, but we respond to the idea of intimacy or aggression. Similarly, when we are set up as the teammate of an outlaw we respond to the concept of being a criminal.

This symbolic link explains why distortion in the image or in the combination of images does not negate the relationship between television and interpersonal reality. Distortion must be distortion of something. The basis of comparison remains the nature of perception and response in real-life social encounters.

Notes

The author wishes to acknowledge the helpful criticisms and suggestions of Joseph Dominick and Paul Levinson.

The ideas presented in this article were first explored in the author's unpublished master's thesis, "The Relationship of Interpersonal Speaking Distances to Television Shot Selection," Queens College, CUNY, 1974.

1. "Mass Communication and Para-Social Interaction," *Psychiatry*, 19 (1956), p. 215.
2. Ibid., p. 215.
3. The discussion of Hall's work is based on two of his books: *The Silent Language* (Greenwich, Conn.: Fawcett, 1959) and *The Hidden Dimension* (Garden City, N.Y., Anchor, 1966).
4. G. McBride, M. G. King, and J. W. James, "Social Proximity Effects on Galvanic Skin Responses in Adult Humans," *Journal of Psychology*, 61 (1965), 153–157.
5. Bernard Steinzor, "The Spatial Factor in Face to Face Discussion Groups," *Journal of Abnormal and Social Psychology*, 45 (1950), 552–555.
6. Frank N. Willis, Jr., "Initial Speaking Distance as a Function of the Speakers' Relationship," *Psychonomic Science*, 5 (1966), 221–222.
7. Lewis Jacobs, "The Meaningful Image," in *The Movies as Medium*, ed., Lewis Jacobs (New York: Farrar, Straus and Giroux, 1970), p. 25.
8. André Bazin, "The Evolution of the Language of Cinema," in *What is Cinema?* by André Bazin, ed. and trans. Hugh Gray (Berkeley: University of California Press, 1967), p. 32.
9. *The Painter's Eye* (New York: Rinehart, 1951), p. 9.
10. See, for example, William H. Ittelson, *Visual Space Perception*, (New York: Springfield, 1960), pp. 169–188.
11. Herbert A. Lightman, "The Subjective Camera," in *The Movies as Medium*, ed. Lewis Jacobs (New York: Farrar, Straus and Giroux, 1970), p. 61.
12. Lightman, p. 62.
13. While the focus in this discussion is on television drama, much of the analysis is relevant to nonfiction television programs (documentaries, televised trials, videotaped court testimony, Congressional hearings and debates, etc.) and even to perception of other visual media such as cinema and still photography.
14. (New York: Anchor, 1959).
15. Goffman, p. 22.
16. Some social critics have argued that America is losing a grip on "reality" as an outcome of high media use. In *The Image* (Atheneum, 1961), for example, Daniel Boorstin describes the great outbreak of "pseudo-events." Yet Goffman's model of face-to-face encounters suggests that *all* social interaction is staged. Indeed the significance of our new forms of communication may be that the planning and staging of media events cannot be hidden as simply as can the planning of simpler face-to-face encounters. A President, for example, cannot hide his media advisors as easily as the average businessman can hide the suggestions of his wife and his tailor. Media, therefore, do not present events which are inherently "false"; they do, however, present events that are *seemingly* less "real." Media do not *create* pseudo-events, but they do make the falseness of events visible.

17. The social context variable explains some of the seemingly contradictory findings of television "grammar" studies. The difference in results in camera angle investigations can be explained in terms of a shot/context interaction.
18. Other interpersonal codes which vary with culture and which may affect perception of television include: rules of eye behavior, pace of interactions, and value orientations. See, for example, Edward T. Hall, *The Silent Language* and Edward C. Stewart, *American Cultural Patterns: A Cross Cultural Perspective* (Pittsburgh: Regional Council for International Education, 1972).
19. For a general theory on the impact of television on the performance of social roles, see Joshua Meyrowitz, *No Sense of Place: A Theory on the Impact of Electronic Media on Social Structure and Behavior,* Doctoral Dissertation, New York University, 1978. For a specific application of the theory to political communication, see Meyrowitz, "The Rise of 'Middle Region' Politics," *Et cetera,* 34 (1977), 133–144.
20. The ability to maintain distance from an event and yet respond to it *as if* it were real was described in 1912 by Edward Bullough in " 'Psychical Distance' as a Factor in Art and an Esthetic Principle," reprinted in *A Modern Book of Esthetics,* ed. Melvin Rader (New York: Henry Holt and Co., 1952). The application of "psychical distance" to television has been suggested by Gary Gumpert in "Psychical Distance and Television Theatre," unpublished paper, University of Wisconsin, 1963.

DAVID L. ALTHEIDE and ROBERT P. SNOW

The Grammar of Radio

Radio has been with us much longer than television, but it has never evoked the intense study and interest in its effects that TV has. Still, it is an extremely important medium, one that has changed dramatically in its form and function during the past several decades and that touches on the lives of all of us. David L. Altheide and Robert P. Snow describe the ways in which radio interacts with our daily existence, how it structures time, sets the tempo for our day, connects us with the community, caters to our moods, and provides us with dee-jay role models.

Is radio your first media contact of the day? Would you ever drive an automobile without the radio on? Could this medium be one of your closest and most important companions? Read "Mass Media and Face-to-Face Communication: Bridging the Gap," by Robert Avery and Thomas McCain in Section 1 for an analysis of people's use of "talk" radio.

Radio's appeal is that it serves both utilitarian or practical tasks and playful moods without immobilizing the listener. In describing the functions of radio, Harold Mendelsohn argued that, in addition to simply transmitting news, time, and temperature, radio brings the outside world into the home or car; provides an organization for the routines of the day; and serves as a social lubricant. As an organizer of daily routine, radio wakes us in the morning, gets us to work, and provides a variety of moods for evening and late-night activity. As a social lubricant, radio provides content to talk about with others, we may interact vicariously with the radio personality, or we may play and sing along with the program. To understand the media culture of radio, we will examine radio format in terms of the grammar of radio; factors that influence radio content; the radio personality; and, finally, speculate on some hypothetical consequences of radio format.

The grammar of radio consists of ways in which the use of time, the organization of content, and conversation make this a very personalized medium. In brief: time follows the listener's pace through daily routine; content is organized into segments that meet music subculture requirements as well as daily routine activities; and radio talk augments the time and organizational factors of grammar. In making sense of radio grammar it also must be remembered that entertainment is the basic underlying form for this grammar.

Reprinted from David L. Altheide and Robert P. Snow, *Media Logic*, pp. 24–34, © 1979 Sage Publications, Inc., with permission.

Uses of Time

Unlike television, radio presents time according to "normal" everyday routine. Whereas television alters time in drama, news, and comedy programs, radio follows an exact linear progression of time, keeping pace with the listener's sense of real time throughout the day. This enables the listener to use the radio as a clock and a metronome; during the hurried pace of the morning and afternoon rush-hour periods, radio constantly reports the time to the listener, and maintains a tempo that keeps pace with the listener's use of time. For example, the morning drive-time is a hurried pace of getting dressed, fed, and off to work. The midday period is a relaxed moderate pace, with things picking up again during the afternoon rush-hour period. Early evening is usually a time to wind down, and the late-night hours can range from slow romance to the funky beat of nighthawks. The type of tempo variation not only caters to listener routines, it helps establish these routines.

The most important element of time and tempo is the music presented by radio stations. Since each musical piece has a particular tempo, a record can sustain an intended pace and flow of time. Rock stations are almost frantic, while "beautiful music" stations maintain a slow, soothing tempo. In addition, a particular rhythm is established by alternating slow, moderate, and up-tempo records. This rhythmic variation provides a sense of balance within the general tempo of a time segment. Developing this rhythmic balance has become such a sophisticated operation that many stations now employ computer technology to insure appropriate music scheduling.

To augment and support music tempo, disc jockeys establish an appropriate conversational tone and pace. During drive-time periods, they project calm sympathy for the rush-hour-bound commuter. At midday periods, their tone and pace is relaxed and comforting. With changes occurring throughout the day, the conversational tone and pace of the "deejay" corresponds to the music tempo and, consequently, the routines of the listener. For example, rock stations use a ten-to-twenty second interval between records with a voice-over the end of one record, a short quip, and a voice-over the beginning of the next record. In this fashion, conversation is integrated into the music tempo without mood interuption. Easy-listening stations string three or four records together without interruption and then identify the artists. In this case, talk is a momentary pause that prevents the tempo from becoming too monotonous. Jazz station deejays often use their knowledge of music to "back" one record over another with no change in the beat. Following this feat of skill, the jazz jock may give a lengthy reporting of the individual artists, tell when the recording was made, and make some comment about its quality. Here, the conversation is used partially to legitimize the particular musical selection.

To summarize, radio time corresponds to how listeners carry out their daily routines. In this sense, radio time is subordinate to listener time, with radio facilitating and helping to establish the sense of time a listener wants to achieve. For many listeners, using radio to establish and sustain their uses of time has become a routine in itself.

Organization and Scheduling

The organization of content in radio programs has become a sophisticated procedure in the past twenty years. During the mass-audience period of the 1930s and early '40s, radio used block programming much as television uses today. In radio, block programs were homogeneous segments of quarter-, half-, or hour-long periods in which the music of a band or artist was supported by one or two advertisers. As the record industry expanded (with nonbreakable 45s and LPs) the hit parade was born, and radio scheduled music according to its popularity. With the baby boom and the advent of youth-oriented rock 'n' roll, the record industry boomed and began pressuring radio stations to create and play hits. Radio was now in a position to exercise greater control over music entertainment through new formats.

The most successful new format, sometimes called the Drake Format after its originator, developed in rock music and gradually spread to middle-of-the-road popular music stations. In this format the radio hour is broken into three or four separate segments, with each segment further organized into specific categories of record popularity, such as a hit, an "up-and-comer," a "golden oldie," and so on. With this format a station could use as few as 30 records for an entire broadcast day. One consequence of this format was a high degree of standardization for a particular station and similar stations throughout a music subculture. Program directors now had absolute control over what records were played and when they were scheduled.

Given the apparent success of what is now called "formated" radio, it is difficult to find a so-called "free form" station—one in which the disc jockey selects the records and determines when they are played. Today, music is scripted according to a grammar that in part programs the listening audience.

Special Features of Vocal Communication

Radio achieves an intimate interpersonal character referred to earlier by serving specialized audiences and subcultures. To reach these specialized audiences, the station must speak the appropriate subculture language; bubblegum rock, jazz, country, soul, and the rest are uniquely different in jargon, rhythm, pitch, and other speech characteristics. On bubblegum stations the deejay speaks fast, using teenage slang. In contrast, jazz audiences require a slow, cool style. On news, talk radio, and background music stations, the communicators follow a "middle-of-the-road" policy that some listeners describe as middle-class anonymity. Given the unique language character of a subculture, radio stations follow the language of their audience, rather than forcing listeners to accept something that is dissonant.

Radio communication is also clear, crisp, pleasing to the ear, and devoid of long (dead air) pauses. The talk of radio professionals appears articulate and polished, although on occasion we hear glaring bloopers and inane comments. But in major radio markets mistakes are rare, and so, for the average listener, the radio personality represents an ideal model of communication within a specialized subculture. In some cases, such as large urban MOR stations, the talk may even be described as "slick." To be slick is to flaunt a skill or talent beyond what is necessary for the situation—extraordinary behavior that is a vital element of entertainment.

Finally, radio grammar has a low degree of ambiguity. A radio may be switched on at any time and a listener will immediately understand what is happening. Several factors contribute to low ambiguity. Each music type is very distinctive, and after hearing only a few bars, almost anyone can identify the type of content that will follow. Voice rhythm is also an indication of content—compare religious radio to news, rock, or classics and the rhythm is readily apparent. Voice types are also standardized according to a station's content so that, even if you tune in during a break in the music, the station is identifiable. Content is instantly intelligible in radio and other "live" electronic media—there is no opportunity for an instant replay.

Definition of Content

In addition to the content of radio discussed in the preceding section, there are nongrammatical factors that influence radio format. One of these factors is the limitations of Federal Communications Commission regulations and the self-imposed broadcasting code. Since the airwaves are defined as public domain, radio stations are required to be licensed by the federal government. Regulated by the FCC, these licenses stipulate the frequency band and broadcasting power limitations of a station. In addition, the FCC requires a specific amount of broadcast time be devoted to public service announcements. Beyond these technical restrictions, the FCC supports the self-imposed code of ethics developed by the National Association of

Broadcasters. In addition to such guidelines as the amount of advertising that is suggested in a given period of time, the code serves as a framework for upholding community values and norms to the extent that a lack of proper public spirit and decorum could actually result in the loss of a station's license. But on an informal level, media tend to regard themselves as guardians of community well-being. This ethical gatekeeping responsibility function is a well-established tradition and, as such, it is part of the overall media logic. Of course, what constitutes the media's sense of guardianship and what actually happens through media action may be quite different. At any rate, radio defines its content in terms of ideals and ethics designed to serve the station's definition of community well-being.

In addition to the formal and informal aspects of broadcasting codes, radio stations establish program content according to specific audience requests. These requests may range from the familiar music request line to demands by irate listeners offended by apparent attacks on what they hold sacred. With respect to music requests, large urban stations seldom play specific requests, although they do use this audience contact as an indicator of music and program popularity. Regarding irate listeners, stations distinguish between the common "crank call" and those influentials who represent potential bad public relations for the station. Radio is thus highly sensitive to audience response as advertising rates rise and fall according to audience size.

The final, and perhaps most important, factor in defining radio content is the entertainment perspective. As entertainment, radio meets all the criteria of entertainment previously discussed. Music is extraordinary in the talent and skill of the performer, in the moods and enjoyment that emerge while listening, and in the star character that musical groups provide to the members of various music subcultures. Talent and skill are judged differently by different listeners, but every music aficionado can recognize the presence or absence of those qualities. Radio stations occasionally try to "hype" a performer of dubious talent, but this is rarely successful. Even established stars who sluff-off or "lose it" are quickly dropped by a listening audience. Music stars who maintain their status represent what is extraordinary about the entertainment part of a subculture. The group "Kiss" is outrageous, Dolly Parton is country innocence with pizzazz, Herbie Hancock is a jazz genius, and Elvis is immortal.

Music is also a critical part of the vicarious character of entertainment. Music makes the mood that is important in achieving vicarious involvement as well as overt commitments. To this end, radio supplies the music that listeners need to facilitate various behaviors, both entertaining and nonentertaining. Since a radio can be carried anywhere, the variety of music available on radio makes it possible to dial in and out of various moods at will. A listener may tune in MOR for getting to and from work, listen to mellow mood music for lounging or romance, get hard rock or disco for Friday night, dial in country for long night drives, and listen to classics on Sunday morning. Every mood is formated by specialized ratio. Above all else, radio is enjoyable as a background or foreground activity.

The Radio Personality

The "personality" has been a fixture in radio for some time. Arthur Godfrey was king in this category, establishing the criteria by which radio communicators are still judged today. Although the format has changed considerably over the past two decades, the "personality" is still the factor that makes entertainment radio work. Throughout the broadcast day, the "air" personality develops a personal relationship with listeners. At one time or another we have had our favorites: Imus in New York, Bill Haywood in Phoenix, Steve Cannon in Minneapolis, and the likes of Cousin Brucie, the Real Don Steele, Jazzbo Collins, Daddy O'Dailey—the list seems endless. These personalities seem to accomplish two things: first, they talk to us personally and we feel part of an exclusive club, and second, they entertain, using every feature of the entertainment format.

The radio personality usually employs comedy; with well-planned "ad lib," a successful deejay enlivens the mundane and eases the listener's tensions. For most listeners, the drive-time hour of the day are difficult periods. Getting out of bed to face another routine day, fighting traffic to and from work, going home to perhaps more routine, the listener may be in a fairly anxious and negative mood. During these periods, the radio comedians usually have a funny story, a few wry quips, or perhaps a comedy routine. Even the practical information that listeners need, such as time, temperature, and road information, is spiced with comedy—a joke about the weather, a satirical comment on city hall, a jibe at traffic engineers or auto mechanics, and the inevitable reference to sex are all part of the comedy routine. Life during this drive-time period is serious business, but it is a relief to "take it on the lighter side."

When radio personalities develop the skills and talent to attract large audiences, they may become role models in specific music subcultures and for middle-of-the-road audiences. The role model of a music subculture involves both verbal behavior and a physical appearance image. The rock-jock is a young, hip, zany male with lots of hair and the clothes of a well-heeled teenager. Talk on the air must be spiced with plenty of teenage jargon. Never mind that some rock-jocks are bald and over forty—it's the image that counts. Jazz-jocks must demonstrate knowledge about the music and artists, be "up" on the latest sounds, and preferably have a very "cool" style. Middle-of-the-road personalities may run a wide range of verbal behavior and appearance, but they must be respectable. While these descriptions are overgeneralizations, the point is that part of the media culture of radio is an on-the-air personality who typifies the music.

Radio stations realized the power of the disc jockey in the early 1960s when they initiated disco concerts at which the deejay would play records at the local armory or high school gym. Soon the stations were doing weekend remotes and finally promoting big name concerts—SEE THE BEATLES with Murray the K (often called the Fifth Beatle). The same phenomena occurred for country music, middle-of-the-road, jazz, and, of course, soul. Listeners reasoned that if the radio personality was at the concert, then the music must be good. Soon deejays were selling products on television, appearing at charity affairs, and even conducting workshops at local schools on everything from the problems of communicating in today's world to drugs and dating. Radio personalities have become influential. As a part of media culture, the radio personality is a focal point and semi-leader of the music subcultures. How the radio personality behaves represents that music subculture both to those in the subculture and to outside observers. The radio personality is part of the music itself—as much a star as the recording artists.

In the 1960s, rock deejays became so powerful that a few developed cult followings. Record companies treated these personalities royally—the money was big and the prestige high. While it is doubtful these radio stars could "break" a musical group, they could be very helpful in promoting a newcomer or assisting a rise on the sales charts. A good word from Wolfman Jack and who knows what heights could be reached. But radio personality influence is not limited to rock music. Late night talk show hosts are currently the giants of the industry. Appearing knowledgeable on every subject, they are highly influential with their listeners.

The radio personality's influence is vast: we may emulate the role modeling behavior of the radio personalities; we may buy products they personally endorse. When they talk about a subject, it may legitimize that subject for us—we may even pay more attention to them than to the experts. Radio personalities form an inextricable part of the culture in which they participate. They don't simply transmit culture, they *are* media culture.

Hypothetical Consequences

One of our primary concerns in this book is to identify the extent to which people tend to adopt the logic of media, which in turn affects their definitions of reality. With radio, this is a difficult task. People use radio for purposes that are extraneous to the medium. With television, the captive viewer becomes immersed in whatever is being presented on the screen and often, for the moment, accepts what the medium offers. In contrast, people use radio to facilitate other activities, such as getting to work, eating, reading, making love, and so on. Even when radio is being listened to attentively, the listener is often engaged in some other activity. Consequently, listeners employ radio to stay in touch with realities that are formed in other contexts. This is not to say that radio is without influence, for it serves as a guideline, reference point, and legitimizer for those realities established in other contexts.

Listeners basically trust their radio stations to play quality music that is current. In this sense, radio serves as guiding framework and reference point for maintaining contact with a particular music subculture. The listener can be informed and at the same time feel in touch with like-minded people. However, this is a vicarious involvement, and over a long period of time the listener may feel estranged and require face-to-face contact with others in this subculture. To meet this need, radio promotes live concerts. Therefore, radio can mediate contact among members of a subculture and also stimulate or perpetuate a particular type of music.

Radio is also a legitimizing agent. As mentioned previously, radio personalities discussing a subject or playing a song demonstrate the legitimacy of that content. Given trust in a station by its listeners, the content of that station represents knowledge and evidence in a practical sense. Just as the content of a news program is accepted as "news," so too are the music and talk of a favorite radio station accepted as truth. The danger here is that "hype" can become a powerful media tool—listeners may be unaware they are being "hyped" to buy a particular record or attend a particular concert but influenced just the same. Radio may create a feeling that if you do not follow the subculture's lead, you will be "out of it."

Radio format also has a major influence on the recording industry. While the record companies are constantly looking for that new sensation, they must make hits to stay in business. For a record to get air play it must fit a station's format. It is one thing to make albums that sell, but quite another to make a record fit the time requirements and the tempo of the radio format. Given these requirements, record companies often make single copies that are shorter in length than the same piece on an album. They may also arrange music for each instrument and have artists record each arrangement separate from the others. The final product is then mixed according to the formula dictated by the record company. Thus, radio format has a definite influence on what is recorded and how it is recorded.

Another consequence of radio is the rapid consumption of talent. With our capability of instant dissemination of information and the apparent desire for instant knowledge, a situation exists in which a musical hit is established everywhere at the same time. Consequently, hits rise and fall at a rapid pace. If a song writer and musician wish to stay atop the charts, they must constantly create new material and maintain contact with the public. The schedule and pressure is so intense that few artists last more than several years at the hit level. This talent consumption is part of the larger issue David Riesman et al. discussed in *The Lonely Crowd*—we live in a consumption society. Radio and other media simply increase the pace of consumption, especially for musical entertainment.

There are other problem areas that deserve elaboration, but brief mention must suffice. One is the socializing impact of radio. Such stars as David Cassidy, Shaun Cassidy, Donny Osmond, and Andy Gibb are recent examples of the "boy next door" who provides a wholesome come-on or vicarious education and seduction prior to real dating. Later on, hard rock, country, and MOR tell the listener about the real problems of love, family, work, and so on. As with the case of preadolescent girls, radio also serves as a facilitator for adjusting to various turning points in one's life. Radio may be a companion for those with the "blues," such as the recently separated or divorced, or those who have lost a job or a loved one. As a facilitator, radio also helps recapture the "good old days," as evidenced by the current rash of nostalgia radio programs.

In summary, the consequences of an entertainment perspective worked through radio format are varied. Through radio, music entertainment is changed, talent is consumed, radio personalities may become influential role models, and listeners may become dependent on radio for seeking what they feel is legitimate information. While radio is a culture of its own, it also serves as the unique character of various subcultures. To this extent, radio, as a specialized medium, may serve as a model for what television could become.

PETER MOSS and CHRISTINE HIGGINS

Radio Voices

Radio, in this age of television predominance, has taken on the role of a familiar family member—accepted, unquestioned and treated as part of the scene. Popular commentators and researchers alike have focused our attention on the electronic tube, to the neglect of radio. Radio, however, continues to outdraw audiences in both time and number. It is, in the words of Moss and Higgins, "an important part in the 'cultural day.' " They claim that one of the things that makes radio important as a medium is that it is the one place where the human voice comes into its own as meaning making. In this essay they analyze three cases of discourse on Australian talk radio revealing the complex range of conversation broadcast daily. They chart the kinds and levels of radio discourse and suggest that such analysis can reveal a great deal about our political, social, and cultural values.

We recommend that you also read the essays by Robert Avery and Thomas McCain and by David Altheide and Robert Snow to further understand the many uses we make of radio.

The general educational, social, and cultural preoccupations with television over the past two decades have masked the discrete functions of radio (Mendelsohn, 1964; Troldahl and Skolnik, 1968; Smith, 1972; Ebbesen 1975; Avery, 1980). Radio still functions in the way that a senior member of the American industry claimed it did 25 years ago (Macdonald, 1980, p. 88):

> The public didn't stop loving radio despite T.V. It just started liking it in a different way—and radio went to the beach, to the park, the patio and the automobile. . . . Radio has become a companion to the individual instead of remaining a focal point of all family entertainment. An intimacy has developed between radio and the individual.

Modern urban societies contribute to personal alienation and breakdown of face-to-face communication. Radio, in the past, was seen as a potential force in the amelioration of that condition. Brecht, for example, developed a theory of radio as two-way communication (Hood, 1979):

> [The] Radio must be transformed from a mechanism of distribution into one of communication. The Radio would be the most fantastic mechanism of communication imaginable in public life, a tremendous channel system. That is, it would be that if it realized the capacity not only to broadcast, but also to re-

This article originally appeared in *Media, Culture and Society*, vol. 6, no. 4, 1984. It has been revised for this volume. Reprinted by permission of Academic Press, Inc., London.

ceive; not only to make the listeners hear, but also to make them speak: not to isolate them, but to put them into contact with each other.

Since the 1930s, "talk radio" or "access radio" has grown, largely ignored by researchers, and in the United States, at least, it has attained prominent status as an informal social and cultural feedback device. Turow (1979) found that the main reason for participating was a need for interpersonal communication. In Europe, Losito (1978) using Italian data, showed that of three groups of callers two groups conformed to what he termed the *Confession Call*—the need to share a personal crisis or a traumatic experience—and the Exhibitionist Call—to present oneself publicly, to hear one's voice in public. And Ray Brown (1978, p. 125) in England, in his research into local radio, claimed:

phone-ins really do allow the community to hear itself and . . . it offers opportunities for identification or social interaction with a wide range of "ordinary" people.

Recently, in Australia, two industry-sponsored reports have suggested further and greater complexity. One survey claimed that for the past four consecutive years those people who tune in to commercial radio spent more time listening than they spent watching commercial television. On average, radio is listened to for two hours per week more than TV is watched (Radio Marketing Bureau, 1983).

More interestingly, a recent report suggests that radio is not used merely for background noise (or as "wallpaper" as the industry terms it) without much attention being devoted to it. Stations which concentrate on music output probably still provide background, but there appears to be a different situation for the talk and news formats—specifically, that talk stations "out-perform music stations in attention levels" of audiences. According to the report over 50 percent of the audience to two Sydney talk stations listen "very carefully" to programs and news bulletins (Radio 2GB, 1983). Commercially inspired research may or may not be the most reliable of sources but these two pieces of audience material indicate, if nothing else, that radio, in some contexts, and for some audiences, plays an important part in the "cultural" day.

Recently, Higgins and Moss (1981, 1982), in recognition of the plurality and ubiquity of usage, have attempted detailed analyses of varieties of radio texts and have directed attention at a missing element in research: the place and function of voice and how it is used separately as mediator, controller, activator, of dialogue and interaction in talk and phone-in shows. This work opens up new possibilities for research because it refocuses the critical gaze, sharply contrasting the language of the medium and of human conversations. Higgins and Moss' work has isolated a factor heretofore ignored in media criticism and in doing so questions the widely held view that much in radio is banal and irrelevant to serious human concerns. This "factor" is a subtle and, at times, unpredictable complexity. The complexity arises from the nature of radio's dramatic reflexivity—the demands made on members of the audience and on the medium itself by the range and variety of human voice. The variety of language and the notes, and tunes, of the human voice come into their own in meaning making in this medium. The listener (and performer, especially in open-line and talk formats) has to interpret nuance, must learn to read between the differing pitches of words, must be able to assess the meanings which may be attached to silence, and generally be able to explore with some confidence the possibilities of language in the construction of radio messages. Allowing for the absence of a face-to-face-partner, the skills involved in radio talk are akin to those which we painfully learn in day-to-day conversations.

John Gumperz calls these skills "verbal repertoire," where speakers continually select the appropriate code and interaction process for specific contexts. In radio conversations, for the regular audience attuned to familiar formats and host/performer manner, interaction is wholly in accord with these known (and learned) selection procedures and filters.

The absence of a tangible audience or interactant obviously makes radio talk a very different process from ordinary conversation, but in some important respects it makes dialogue easier, certain styles and conventions have evolved which allow and encourage conversation.

Goffman (1972, p. 34) has argued that many conversational acts are intrinsically face threatening:

> When a person volunteers a statement of message . . . he commits himself and those he addresses, and in a sense places everyone in jeopardy. By saying something, the speaker opens himself up to the possibility that the intended recipients will affront him by not listening or will think him forward or offensive in what he has said.[1]

The potential hazards of interaction necessitate what Goffman calls "face-work"—ways of mitigating possible threats to the "faces" involved so that interaction may continue smoothly. Goffman's work indicates in a general way how conversational roles are established and modified in process but his examples are largely concerned with ritual exchanges and he rarely deals with more subtle factors which may be involved in any given, natural speech situation. His recent work on radio speech illustrates this weakness very well for he uses "texts" taken from published examples of howlers made by radio announcers and disk jockeys (Goffmann, 1981). His analyses are playful and clever but they do not advance our understanding of radio conversations nor do they attempt to grapple with the complex business of how members of an audience use the medium to create both dialogue with a host/station and to create small moments of culture in the struggle to make meanings.

Radio dialogues are easier than face-to-face interaction for members of the audience, conversing with familiar hosts in recognizable formats, because the hosts are restricted in the range of speech strategies they can adopt. Radio hosts, in fact, are prisoners of the personae which they and their stations have manufactured. Horton and Wohl (1956) have argued that the persona of the host or star, while contrived in actuality, takes on imagined densities of reality over time. The host's radio existence "is a regular and dependable event, to be counted on, planned for, and integrated into the routines of daily life." The "personality" offers values such as "sociability, easy affability, friendship, and close contact—briefly, all the values associated with free access to and easy participation in pleasant social interaction in primary groups" (pp. 213, 215).

However, radio services audiences in far more various ways than as intimate friend and has created more styles than those connected only with persona-theory (see Avery, 1978). Stations throughout the world offer many responses to local cultural conditions or to conditions assumed by particular stations and announcer-hosts. There are major city stations in Australia whose well-paid hosts are deliberately abrasive and offensive; others serve as a kind of social service of the air, giving advice and specific agency referrals for particular social and personal problems; in Atlanta, Georgia, there is a late show on a black-American station, hosted by "Alley Pat," whose pattern can only be described as a relentless rapping irony. His mockery of his race serves to hide a more serious intent of establishing claims to an exclusive urban dignity. In Italy, radio seems to be in a permanent state of chaos, or, at best, precarious equilibrium where "communist radio," "freak" radio, and "personal advertisement" radio, among others, vie with the predictable commercial fare. The situation is akin to the non-news section of big daily newspapers, especially in the advertisement sections.

Radio seems to have developed, therefore, into a reflection of shifting cultural and group interests—a presenter of both majority and minority commitments and a channel for relaying to "the audience out there" the varieties of subcultural urgencies and conditions of life. Radio has potential as a powerful demoncratic tool. To some extent it has become that; the "radio map" of a nation offers audiences the chance to both share and to contribute to culture.

Discourse Properties

The task for radio researchers is to begin to chart the kinds and levels of radio's discourses. The rest of this reading describes a number of functions and types of radio talk, and we argue that, because of the variety of function and the variousness of expression which the medium both offers and generates, it possesses the potential to develop into a powerful oppositional force to mainstream, mass technological culture.

Given space limitations, we are able to indicate only the broad configurations of radio talk within the subgenres of talk-back and "access" radio. These seem, however, to be generalizable categories related to a number of programs offering different kinds of conversational opportunities.

The crucial factor for interactants, be they host, caller, or studio guest, is the extent to which combinations of discourse elements aid or inhibit text realization. We have identified five general discourse properties which contribute to the creation of radio on-air texts:

1. *Text-making intention* which might be suggested by
2. *Rhetorical levels* aided by
3. *Interactants' complicity or noncomplicity* in text making, which could be underpinned by
4. *The persona* of the host which is sustained by[2]
5. *The audience's* perception and acceptance of that persona.

Michael Halliday's work (1978, pp. 136–137) in sociolinguistic analysis offers some useful ideas in relation to the concept of text:

> A text is the product of its environment and its function in that environment . . . in the normal course of events is not something that has a beginning and an ending. The exchange of meanings is a continuous process that is involved in all human interactions; it is not unstructured but it is seamless, and all that one can observe is a kind of periodicity in which peaks . . . alternate with troughs—highly cohesive moments with moments of relatively little continuity.

Talk-back and phone-in programs demonstrate this seamlessness in vivid ways when our "reflexive" schematization is employed in the analysis of texts. The implication is that the text conversations must be "read" as wholes where each reflexive component is simultaneously being negotiated with all the other components. Analysts of media texts who concentrate on one or more components only develop skewed readings. For example, researchers whose interests are in ideological and hegemonic aspects of discourse tend to look at messages, especially the text-making intent and the rhetorical level. But, by ignoring the other elements, analytic models are produced which suggests that media messages are *only* instrumental, that is, designed to bring about action of some kind in terms say of ideological agreements. Our examples demonstrate a more varied set of purposes for this radio genre and also indicate the complexity of discourse. The reader should be aware that our examples are taken from Australian radio but this source in no way invalidates our arguments. In its essentials, Australian radio could be transposed to any developed Western country without the listener feeling any sense of disjunction or confusion.

INTERVIEW WITH DAME NANCY BUTTFIELD *

HOST†   Hello, Dame Nancy. Nancy Buttfield, author of *The Great Challenge.*

DAME NANCY: Hello, and it's not *The Great Challenge,* although it *is* one, it's called *So Great a Change.*

HOST   How long did it take you to write the book?

DAME NANCY: Oh, a couple of years, there was a great deal of research in it; I've really tried to tie it to the developing history of South Australia; it's really, you know, the Holden family are really a South Australian family, and as each member, as the generation goes on, I've also documented the historical development as well.

HOST: What sort of a beginning did it have, I've seen a copy of the share issue, and the check General Motors . . . ?

DAME NANCY: . . . yes, when they merged with Holden.

HOST   What was that, $500,000 or something?

DAME NANCY: Oh no, it was a bit more than that, it was a million, a bit over a million pounds.

HOST: I bet that was quite a song, I mean . . . ?

DAME NANCY: . . . Oh, it was, there was a lot of criticism at the time that General Motors had bought it too cheap.

HOST: What year was that?

DAME NANCY: 1931.

HOST: How long had Holden been going as a motor car manufacturer before that?

(1)   DAME NANCY: Well, my father started, actually started the motor body building, he went right from the start when motor cars first came into the country, which is about 1900. At that time there were about a million and three quarters horses which in other words there was one horse to every two people, now there is one motor car to every two people, because he started then and it has sort of gone on from that time. They didn't become Holden's Motor Body Buildings until a few years later, it had to sort of grow.

HOST: Why the title *So Great a Change?*

(2)   DAME NANCY: Well, because my great-grandfather who as a young man came to South Australia, he was about 17, was writing in his diary, a copy of which I have, and he was talking about a tremendous dust storm in April. He said this huge dust storm came up, and he said, "it is incredible that so great a change could happen in such a short time." But I thought that it is a very

* Daughter of the founder of the first and only indigenous Australian car manufacturer.

† A very popular South Australian radio personality.

good title because when you go back and see the change so quickly from horses and horse-drawn vehicles to the sort of motor cars you can buy today in about 50 years, it is a remarkable story.

(3)   HOST: All the anecdotes, I guess, that are in the book, do you have any favorites?

DAME NANCY: Oh, I think probably the ones about my grandfather; he was a tremendous prankster, a bit erratic, he used to always think up things to impress people. I can remember him, he told a young University student that had come to join the firm, that he was being a bit obnoxious and he better go home and he would ring him when he wanted to see him. So this young man got a bit sick of sitting at home and not being called, so he came back to the office without being told. My grandfather put him in the car, drove him around to the cemetery, and said, "see all those gravestones there," he said, "all those people thought they were indispensable, like you."

(4)   HOST: I like that. What about the story that turned up in the review in the paper, I think it was yesterday, about Sir Edward being not allowed to join the Club, what was that all about?

DAME NANCY: Oh, yes, that was in the days of the Establishment; they thought that trade was absolutely non-U, it all had to be professions, and anybody who joined the Adelaide Club had to be a professional. But after all, professionals haven't done as much for their country as some of the people in trade.

HOST: What do you think we can do for the country at the moment, I'm talking about the sort of enterprise that started the car industry which supports millions of people in employment directly or indirectly?

DAME NANCY: What can we do today?

HOST: Let's say we make you Prime Minister for a week.

DAME NANCY: I'd hate to be Prime Minister for a week because I think whatever the Prime Minister does it will always be wrong whatever party it is, he is just built up in order to throw bricks at. I do think that the Australian workman, good as he is, and I don't think there is a better workman throughout the world, is badly led and if only he could be persuaded to knuckle down and get on with the job instead of always going on strike, I think they would all be more secure in their jobs and there would be better production and the whole country would benefit.

HOST: Yes, you have really got to look without being political, not so much at the Australian worker and whether he wants to go on strike.

DAME NANCY: . . . at the leadership of the workers.

HOST: Well, it is rather difficult to get to the worker and say is this your strike? Do you really believe democratically that this is the thing to be doing?

DAME NANCY: Oh, that's right, the poor things are terrified, there are so many recriminations come through if they do happen to stand up

	against the desire to strike. I don't think the average work-man wants to, certainly his wife doesn't.
HOST:	Let's talk about the State, let's talk about the things we have initiated in this State and the fact it really doesn't seem to be the most go-ahead State at the moment. After all, it gave birth to the car industry, this State. What would you like to see done to revitalize this State?
DAME NANCY:	I'd like to see us go back to what happened, now you are really touching again on a good part of this book. My father knew in his years of work that this state had to be a manufacturing state, we haven't got the resources to be what the other states are, we haven't got oil, not much anyway, haven't got all those things, we haven't got the people. He knew it had to be man-ufacturing. He set out to attract industry here and he did, and I mention many of them that were brought here, but he had a Premier, he would only have to send a cable from London saying, look I've got an industry that is interested in coming, such as the Australian Cotton Textile Industry that came, what can you do as an incentive to come here rather than go to any other state, and immediately Sir Thomas would cable back, oh, we would give them this, that and the other in tax concessions or other things; now that's all gone. The incen-tive for people to come here because it was a better state to produce in is now absolutely gone because we are the worst state to produce in, all these incentives have gone, we are now saddled with long service leave, workers' compensation, you know all these things, which people just say well, if we haven't got the advantages of the mass of people to sell to, why would we go there.
HOST:	Well Dame Nancy, I thank you for your time and good luck with the book.

Dame Nancy Buttfield, without prompting in the first instance, pro-claims the state of her book *So Great a Change* in her first major utter-ance: "I've really tried to tie it to the developing history of South Aus-tralia." She also points up the fact here that her family have been closely linked to, and been influential in, the development of the state through a major commercial enterprise. The host, apparently interested in the way the topic is developing, encourages his guest to develop her text through his questions, encouraging tone and general air of complicity, which pro-vides interpersonal support for the speaker and affirms the significance of the unfolding theme for the audience.

Meaning is constantly shaped by the expressive conventions of the dis-course. Words resonate, emitting potential significance for listeners. The way the language slants the presentation of content in this transcript makes an interesting study. In exchange (1), words denoting growth predominate: "Started," "right from the start," "first came," "gone on," "become," "grow." These connote the dynamic nature of the car industry's development, due to Dame Nancy's family's efforts and ingenuity. This is further highlighted by the "then and now" contrasts: "At that time there were a million and three quarters horses . . . now there is one motor car to every two people because he started then . . ." Similarly, in her next exchange (2), the images relate to movement, size, intensity: "tremendous," "huge," "great a change," "short time." In explaining the title of the book using the analogy of the speed and intensity of the "tremendous dust storm," Dame Nancy is again able to emphasize the apt nature of such a title and to relate it to her family's pioneering spirit and business acumen. Contrast is a rhetorical device employed here in similar fashion to that of the preceding exchange. Thus these exchanges or utterances are closely integrated into her developing theme.

This interviewee has strong text-making intent and she is articulate and confident enough to voice her text with great clarity. However, it is also evident that it is the host's complicity that considerably assists in the realization of that text. The host's role throughout the interaction is mainly interpersonal; that is, he facilitates the making of meaning by his guest by means of the question he asks, but he does not actually contribute *content* to the text. What is most interesting is the way the discourse is shaped and directed by the host. His is an enabling function.

The next two questions he asks (host utterances 3 and 4) are particularly happy choices, showing his skill in such interactive situations, particularly in assessing and anticipating the likely direction of the discourse from this point on.

The host is thus instrumental in introducing the anecdote about the young university student and the second one about Dame Nancy's grandfather, Sir Edward, both of which are able to be easily integrated into the text at this point. In the first, there is the implied contrast between "the professions" and "trade"; in the second the disparaging nature of the comparison becomes explicit and the exchange ends with a firm evaluating comment: "After all, professionals haven't done as much for their country as some of the people in trade."

The host's *persona* also requires comment at this point. From regular listening to this host's programs, it is clear that he is a "small l" liberal, a keen supporter of free enterprise, antistrike and rather skeptical about "experts" or professionals (Higgins and Moss, 1982, p. 28). Thus, because he supports the sorts of views Dame Nancy is expressing, he is able to exhibit such a high degree of complicity in the text-making process. Elizabeth Burns defines role play as "composed behaviour devised to transmit beliefs, attitudes and feelings of the kind the composer wants us to have" (Burns, 1972,

p. 124). It is through skillful and supportive role play of this kind that the host makes his contributions to the interaction.

Going back to the transcript, the host then asks a far more leading question about the present: "What do you think we can do for the country at the moment?" thus signaling the introduction of a state-of-the-nation discussion. Key words here are "enterprise," "supports," "millions of people," "employment." The lady responds by moving, at the host's clear direction, onto a related topic and one dear to the host's own heart—the intransigence of the Australian worker, his excessive desire to strike, the irresponsible leadership by union officials and the resultant low levels of economic growth and uncertain employment prospects in Australia at present (Higgins and Moss, 1982, pp. 114–118).

From this point on the host ceases simply to carry out a facilitating role in the text making. He enters it in his own right. Strong, reciprocal rhythms develop from now on as each speaker supports the other. While the host is speaking of "the Australian worker and whether he wants to go on strike" and asks the rhetorical question "Do you really believe democratically that this is the thing to be doing?"—thus signaling the undemocratic, un-Australian practice of striking—Dame Nancy is replying in tandem and with words like "terrified" and "recriminations," suggesting the intimidatory power of union bosses. In the last long statement from Dame Nancy, another undercurrent emerges—the myth of the leader's power, but even that power has died, she suggests, because "we are now saddled with long service leave, workers' compensation. . . ." Once leaders like Sir Thomas Playford and her father had the world at their fingertips, now they have lost their bargaining power—apparently because of the intransigence of the workers. The host, a skilful message maker, realizes that he has no need to comment further, so he lets the interview end with Dame Nancy's lament for the passing of the "good old days," of untrammeled free enterprise. The reasons for the State's lack of progress have been identified to the host's satisfaction and there is no need for him to question further or to sum up the theme directly for the audience.

Although it may seem to the listener that the audience for this dialogue is principally the two participants in the interaction, there are clear signals to the wider audience (who seem almost to be eavesdroppers overhearing a cozy chat) of the ideological significance of the text that has been made. Both have been complicit in the realization of a culture text about the causes of the present economic doldrums affecting South Australia and, specifically, the car industry—excessive strikes and the unreasonable demands and expectations of the worker. Dame Nancy has been the major overt text maker while the host's role has been mainly responsible for shaping, "editing," and directing the discourse and "staging" the performance. The finished product—the text—emerges as more than the sum of its parts; it becomes, on completion, a separate entity, liberated from belonging to either participant. It becomes public, transcends its creators and, by the nature of its creation in language, is imprinted with cultural meaning. It is then the audience's task to extract the approved meanings from the text. Because of our shared general culture, listeners are equipped to make such discoveries. (However, as is the case with any text, there is not likely to be a complete matching of meanings when any *individual* audience member decodes a text.)

Our next example shows the extent to which radio discourse can be used by members of audience to present meanings which border on the subversive and which effecitvely prevent any *active* dispersal of conventional dominant ideology.

ESSENTIAL SERVICES LEGISLATION*

CALLER *(Female):* I want to refer to that lady two calls back. I am utterly amazed that nobody else has rung up and complained at the Essential Services Bill.

HOST 1: Yes.

CALLER: The last two days you have hinted strongly to people that if it goes through their freedom of speech would be taken away. But where are they now with their voices all silent?

HOST 2: Well, I guess it's the age-old problem that people don't really know what's in the legislation including the State members of parliament who were supposed to discuss it yesterday. All they were discussing was a summary.

CALLER: I think everyone should be ringing their State M.P.'s and saying we don't want this thing. It's a bad thing and what's wrong with Queenslanders? Are they all a bit trop | from having their brains addled by the sun or what?

HOST 3: Well, I hope not. (laughs) I've never heard it put quite like that before.

CALLER: That's what's wrong with them. They're such a lethargic mob! They deserve all they get. This is the time they should be out in the streets, saying, "No, we don't want this thing!" Next we'll be told what church we can go to, won't we?

HOST 4: Well, let's hope that never happens. But at the same time I talked to Dr. Edwards was it Tuesday morning?—and as I said to Dr. Edwards the end of legislation—you know—the end of the Essential Services Act is after they have been out on strike for 48 hours that they're dismissed. Then what? And Dr. Edwards had to admit that they didn't have "a then what." They didn't know what happens next.

---

* From a Queensland radio station morning show.
† Trop—colloquial Queenslandese, meaning, affected by tropical climate to the extent of irrationality, a mild insanity.

> Now, if you're setting up legislation to try to create industrial stability and at the end of the legislation is a big stick and the big stick doesn't work, then the whole exercise is a waste of time.

CALLER: That's quite right. But the way things are going now, it's going from bad to worse. And I've rung you before and said it's time Queenslanders pulled the wool off their eyes and just had a look at what was going on and stopped this creeping cancer of the dictatorship that is coming out of our State Parliament.

HOST 5: (pause) Alright, thanks (pause). I presume that was your punch line? (pause) Ah, yes—I'll leave it at that. It's 8½ to 10.

The lady caller, who is outraged, begins on a challenging note: "I am utterly amazed . . ."—the host replies only: "Yes"—a simple acknowledgment and no more. He doesn't take up the invitation to confirm or deny her amazement, in fact he doesn't offer to interact with her in any way. However, the caller is motivated enough to continue, despite the lack of a prompt or any sign of enthusiasm from the host.

The woman continues to speak emotively and rhetorically on her subject and the host's next point (host exchange 2), is almost tangential to the caller's point. It seems as if he is trying to deflect or deflate her. He acts similarly in the next exchange (host 3) with the added attempt to trivialize the caller's argument by laughing and commenting only on the caller's rhetorical question rather than on the substance of her previous evaluation. He sidesteps the caller's questions so that her remaining utterances are really examples of monologue. There is no attempt made by the host to make meaning or even to entertain. However, he is not merely neutral, he is obstructive. Either the host cannot handle the controversy, or he prefers to deflate a caller who is genuinely angry over a serious political issue. Certainly the end of the call seems to indicate the latter. After the caller's inflammatory mention of the "cancer of the dictatorship . . . of our State Parliament," the host virtually disallows further communication and terminates the call in a most uncharacteristic way. As well as being unable to handle this caller, the host is also unwilling to *use* her! It is clear that the caller makes the text unaided by the host. All her contributions are strong and dramatic whereas most of his (few) statements are basic interpersonal ones. His role here is to suppress controversy and to avoid conflict. Although the caller is eventually shuffled off the air, her meaning and powerful judgments are not controlled by the host and she has gotten her viewpoint across. Her polemic appears to catch the host off balance and she is able to withstand his classic avoidance ploys. In fact, it may be that as a reaction to his obstructive approach the caller redoubles her efforts to force her message through to the audience. Certainly she becomes more heated and speaks more forcefully as the interaction proceeds.

The caller makes this text completely for there is no complicity from the host; he merely dismisses her at the first opportunity. It is true that he *has* regulated the impact of the text by foreshortening the exchange and by attempting to trivialize it but the assertiveness and rapid realizations in the discourse of the caller's cultural meanings are clear indications of a potential for the transmission of meanings other than the preferred or dominant ones in this type of exchange.

Although the host is not aggressive in turning the interaction towards dominant meanings, indirectly he indicates the strength of the "preferred" reading of the situation by closing the conversation immediately after the caller's provocative comments about the State government. By closing in this way and also by classifying her closing statement as a "punch line," a term associated with comedy routines, the host also makes a deeper kind of structuring for the audience. In effect, he signals the illegitimacy of the caller's messages. This is quite in line with standard hegemonic theory. But even in acknowledging this, an important point is missed: that the medium has not been able to prevent an alternative set of meanings being broadcast.

Although the role play structured by the host (persona) may appear open-ended and flexible, appropriate audience roles are perceived by listeners from familiarity with the persona and the conventions for interaction already established in earlier performances. The host must always take into consideration the projected role of the assumed audience when he adopts his persona. Thus he builds his performance on a cumulative structure of assumptions about their response. Therefore, in the majority of talk-back exchanges there is complicity between the host and caller or interviewee in their common acceptance of the conventions which have created and sustained the host's persona. Burke refers to the "coaching of attitudes" (Burke, 1945, p. 79), which seems an apt phrase to refer to the cues and clues given to the audience over a period of time to guide them in developing an appropriate response to a particular (created) radio personality. Thus the audience is geared to anticipating a particular style of performance. This caller, well aware of host persona, has chosen to refuse the host-created role in order to establish, powerfully and rapidly, *her* text. This has been realized by stress being placed upon some of our categories (rhetorical level, text-making intent, awareness of the host persona, and consciousness of the audience at large).

As we mentioned earlier, the host person's style or role is constructed and maintained by reason of its constant, familiar nature and because audience members respond to it in what become familiar, predictable ways. However, not all audience members are prepared to accept this. Individual members of the audience may adopt "impromptu" roles of their own, quite outside the usual format, and thus provide interesting variants of the host-caller interaction pattern.

The following example is one where the host persona is quite unable to assert itself sufficiently to control, contain or deflect an importunate caller. Indeed, he is virtually put off the air, reduced to silence by the caller's vehemence and determination to speak.

*The Refusal of Medical Treatments Act**

	HOST:	Hello, there?
(1)	CALLER:	Is that you, Alex?
	HOST:	Yes, go ahead.
(2)	CALLER:	That man that was just on—
	HOST:	Yes.
(3)	CALLER:	I wouldn't call him a man (um) I think he's of a very poor type and if he's the type of a person that wants to start and govern the elderly people's lives, he wants cutting up. He's a perfect Hitler.
	HOST:	What do you mean, wants to govern people's lives?
(4)	CALLER:	I lost my man, he was riddled with cancer.
	HOST:	Yes.
(5)	CALLER:	First of all, it was an eye—
	HOST:	Yes.
(6)	CALLER:	Then it was his arm, then it went down to his legs, then it was his bowels.
	HOST:	Yes.
(7)	CALLER:	Then it was his penis.
	HOST:	Yes.
(8)	CALLER:	There wasn't a part of him that wasn't riddled with it and that man fought and fought for his life.
	HOST:	Yes.
(9)	CALLER:	Because he didn't want to leave me.
	HOST:	Well?
(10)	CALLER:	And as for that man wanting to decide for people, they want to sew his mouth up.
	HOST:	Yes. You see I think—
(11)	CALLER:	A very vicious thing for a man to say.
	HOST:	Well, I think you've missed the point entirely. That's not what—
(12)	CALLER:	I didn't miss the point. I heard it all. And as for him wanting—
	HOST:	No, just a moment, that's the very opposite—
(13)	CALLER:	(Two words not distinguishable)
	HOST:	No, just a moment—
(14)	CALLER:	God help them!
	HOST:	Just—
(15)	CALLER:	(Three words not clear)
	HOST:	Just aah . . .
(16)	CALLER:	(Two words not clear) . . . looking for a rise
	HOST:	I'm sorry that—

* A Melbourne open-line program.

(17)   CALLER: So am I.

     HOST: That you view it that way. I think in fact—aah—that to suggest he's wanting to remove the right from the person is the very opposite to what is saying but I'm not—aah—seeking to—aah—defend—um—Mr. McKenzie's Bill, after all that's going to be aired. I'm sure quite a deal. Well, I think that you've missed the point when you suggest that he's seeking in any way to take away the right from anyone. I'm sorry you've had such a loss and are so—vehement as to—um—use such descriptions and terms. *Nightline*, coming up to the news . . .

The call is generated by an earlier interview with Mr. McKenzie, a state legislator who initiated "The Refusal of Medical Treatments Act," which attempts to give the terminally ill the right in law to refuse further treatment if they so desire. It is clear from the outset that the caller has no wish to interact with her host, indeed, refuses to do so at several points. Nor does she wish to address a wider audience. This is a case of publicly rehearsing private grief and bitterness over the death of her husband. Her comments have nothing to do with the topic—the right of refusal of medical treatment by the terminally ill—indeed, she has entirely missed the point as the host realizes, probably as early as exchange 3 and certainly by 11. The topic is simply the trigger for a self-generating monologue.

The first set of judgments (caller exchange 3)—"very poor type," "wants cutting up," "a perfect Hitler"—alert the audience to the possibility of a controversial and thus entertaining dialogue between host and caller. The host is quick enough to realize that the lady has probably misinterpreted the substance of the bill (host exchange 3). However, the caller totally ignores his question and compulsively continues with her own personal narrative. This builds up a powerful rhythm as she speaks of the inexorable spread of cancer, from one part of her husband's body to the next, ending climactically and pridefully on the note, "That man fought and fought for his life because he didn't want to leave me."

It becomes increasingly difficult to contain this caller as host exchanges 11 and 12 indicate. The lady, sustained by the momentum of her own anger, wants no intervention let alone contradiction from the host. The final section of the transcript (exchanges 13 to 17) shows the host totally helpless, unable to force his way into the caller's persistent flow of words. He vainly tries on several occasions (13, 14, 15, 16) to interact with her but is reduced, in the end, to taking the only possible way out to end her monologue and get rid of the caller (exchange 17). It is clear that he has been quite overwhelmed by the emotionalism of the call, which transgresses all the conventions of on-air civility and the conventions governing the anticipated audience response to the host's persona as well. The usual host role—

the cheery, chatty, confident, and controlling personality—has proved quite inadequate to cope with such a vehement caller. Indeed, he seems relieved to be able to leave the "stage" at this point and retreat into the wings to recover his equanimity—"coming up to the news."

There is no attempt at performance on the host's part, or opportunity for it, as he struggles to exist linguistically—to remain "on stage," as it were. Thus, he is not in any way complicit in text making.

Interestingly enough, while the text-making intent of the caller is strong and the language recklessly emotive, there is no adequate realization of the text, because the audience for the outburst seems only to be the self. The caller does not dramatize herself or her topic, nor does she present herself in performance. Indeed, she appears to lose all consciousness of the fact that she is giving a public performance of a kind. Just as there is no play without an audience; on radio, there is no text realization without an awareness of audience and a certain presentation of self appropriate to the context of situation. These, plus the lack of any interaction, let alone complicity, negate the possibility of text being realized.

The Complexity of Radio Talk

We have attempted to demonstrate that an important element in speech situations is negotiation for control. Our examples indicate that the host in the role of interviewer of studio guests and as a participant in phone-in conversations ultimately has the power. He is in control of the mechanics of the radio program. It is the host who admits the guest or caller to the airwaves, he begins the conversation, and he decides on the airtime the interviewee or caller will receive.

However, the host is clearly more in control in the studio interview situation where he or his producer has invited the guest, a known public figure, well in advance of the show. This being so, the host can prepare himself for the interview. This means that he can contain the discourse within predetermined boundaries and he can also structure his questions to elicit the kind of response he wants—in line with station policy and/or his own views.

In addition, the face-to-face situation of the interview which permits eye contact, the use of nonverbal cues to meaning such as gesture, facial expression, and so on, make for a more intimate, more relaxed style of presentation where the host knows he is in control. In such situations, both participants are usually seasoned public performers; and although a certain show of deference may be necessary if the guest has significant status, there is less competition for control in the interview of this kind. What results from the listener's situation is an exchange which makes up in polish and assurance what it lacks in spontaneity—a consciously "staged" performance where meaning making can proceed with ease.

However, the host is in a very different situation with anonymous callers. Certainly, there is no need for a show of deference, because the person, as an unknown, has no status. But here the host, despite his ultimate authority, is in a situation of threat. He cannot anticipate the caller's subject, the reason for calling, commitment to the topic, emotional state, and so on. As an experienced performer, of course, most radio hosts are adept in detecting very early in the exchange the clues they require to manage the discourse, and indeed, in some cases, to manipulate their caller so as to make certain host-preferred meanings are "created" for the the audience.

In many cases, callers make this easy for their host, who has, as was said above, a familiar, often respected, or admired persona. Callers thus tend to unconsciously acknowledge the host's superior status and their own position of relative powerlessness by their frequent appeals to the host for confirmation or approval of the views they express, their deferential tone, and the fact that rarely do they contradict or question the host or challenge his evaluations. Clearly such discourse has a different shape and style from the studio interview and the different power relationships are in no small way responsible for these differences. (That hosts can be vulnerable however, and indeed may lose control of the situation, is illustrated in *The Refusal of Medical Treatments Act*. All the host has left, there, is the power to terminate.)

Speech situations are thus a potent means of imposing our version of the world on others as well as our view of ourselves and where we stand relative to others in the social structure. That this is so should provide callers who are strongly motivated and well prepared with an opportunity to dominate the air waves, albeit briefly, and it illustrates that radio has the potential to act as an antihegemonic force and therefore as a medium capable of fostering democratic participation in general culture.

In this discussion we showed that radio talk in this particular genre is more complex than is normally recognized and corresponds closely to the nature of conversations in everyday life. The latter point is seen in the close connection between "facework" theory in life and the recognition and utilization of "persona" in radio. But the other elements in our model are also significant in the overall production of meanings because they are part of the seamlessness inherent in spontaneous human interaction.

This kind of radio talk is not mere squirrel chatter: the conversations exhibit more or less high levels of organization and have far less redundancy than face-to-face talk. We would argue that the basic reason for this is that participants have recognizable and specific intent in meaning making. Callers, in general, make their "texts" in full knowledge of their hosts' styles or personas; hosts usually determinedly maintain this persona, thus aiding interaction. Perhaps the most interesting observation is that the element which creates most impact in life talk (strong or weak language style or rhetoric) does not necessarily do so in radio talk unless supported by the other aspects previously explained.

The examples of radio talk used in this reading are not offered as representative types but as varied examples of the complex range of conversations broadcast daily from different types of radio stations. There are two features which the dialogues have in common: first, they exhibit different kinds of intimacy; second, they function as either social cement (keeping together the day-to-day, taken-for-grantedness of life) or as attempts to develop personal coherence in the face of the unexpectedness of life (the Medical Treatment Bill, for example). These functions of media have long been recognized and they have been widely used for the dispersal of conventional political, social and cultural values. However, with the rapid increase in the numbers of radio stations (virtually radio subcultures in some countries), the possibilities for discussion of new, even subversive, meanings are increased. Given the apparent (intuitive?) recognition by members of audiences of the significant elements in radio talk and the confidence with which many people use them, there is room for optimism for a redrawing of some of our culture maps within this particular mass medium.

Notes

1. It is worth considering the possibility that Goffman's conversational commitments are not inevitable nor are they natural outcomes of the effort to make human contacts. The threats may be culturally created or socially manipulated by educational institutions, for example.
2. See Horton and Wohl, *op. cit.*

SIDNEY H. ARONSON

The Sociology of the Telephone

Telephoning has been described as "interposed" private communication. While it is not strictly speaking a mass medium, it is a type of mediated communication that exists on a massive scale: a potent instrument of social change, as sociologist Sidney Aronson points out. Like other media of communication, it has significant effects on our interpersonal lives. Aronson describes the effects of the telephone on social institutions.

Can you conceive of carrying on your interpersonal relationships without the aid of the telephone? Do you feel cut off from your friends when you can't be reached by phone? Does the telephone ever permit more intimacy than face-to-face communication?

Amid the welter of recent writing on the phenomena of "modernization" and social change, scant attention has been granted to technological innovations themselves as direct sources of new human needs and behavior patterns. Yet it seems apparent that the kind of modernization experienced by the Western world, and more specifically the United States, over the past century is intimately tied, both as cause and effect, to the availability of the telephone as an easy, efficient and relatively inexpensive means of communication. This may seem only to restate the obvious, yet how rarely is the telephone so much as mentioned in contemporary discussions of social change or modernization?[1] This is the more remarkable as the process of communication, generically considered, has come to be recognized as *the* "fundamental social process" without which society and the individual self could not exist. Communication-in-general (if such a thing can be imagined) has been much studied, but the meaning and the consequence for individuals of being able to pick up something called a telephone and rapidly transmit or receive messages have been all but ignored. As with so many other aspects of social life, that which we take most for granted usually needs to be most closely examined.

This inattention to the social consequences of the telephone is the more surprising still in light of the importance usually attached to the presence or absence of mass media of written communication in explaining differences among societies. It has become usual to distinguish between pre-industrial and industrial societies, each type manifesting distinctive characteristics partly attributable to the widespread dissemination and accessi-

From the *International Journal of Comparative Sociology*, vol. 12, no. 3 (September 1971). Reprinted by permission of the publisher.

bility (by way of general literacy) of the printed word. It is surely conceivable that the presence or absence of a system of two-way oral-aural communication may account for equally important differences between types of societies, that the distinction between a society with and one without a developed telephone system may be as great as that between one with and one without a developed system of printed media or even as great as that between a literate and a nonliterate society. A necessarily brief examination of the history of the telephone in the United States will support these assertions.

Whether a matter of social structure or of "national character," American society not only fosters technological innovation but typically embraces it with alacrity once it occurs. The introduction and almost immediate acceptance of the telephone in the United States after 1876 is characteristic. That Americans at that particular moment in history wanted to or "needed" to communicate in new and faster ways facilitated the transformation of their behavior and the structure and character of their society.[2] The remainder of this article will present a brief survey of some of the areas of American life where the "modernizing" impact of the telephone has been most pervasive and obvious. If the discussion that follows may seem, by implication at least, to give to the telephone an unwarranted primacy as an agent of modernization, such an overstatement of the case can be justified as an understandable reaction to ninety-odd years of scholarly neglect, not to say disdain. The telephone, like modernization itself, has insinuated itself into even the most remote crevices of American life; the ubiquity of its ringing as an accompaniment to our daily lives can perhaps best be compared to the ever present tolling of church bells in a Medieval village or *bourg*. The railroad, the electric light, the automobile, even the bathroom—not to speak of the more dramatic radio and television—have all been granted their moment on the scholarly stage, to be examined more or less intensively, more or less dispassionately. The time seems overripe for a comprehensive examination of the slighted telephone. Nor is the story by any means all told. The recent development of a "picturephone," which adds the visual capability of television to the traditional telephone, promises to make a new chapter in the history of Bell's creation as well as a new dimension to human communication.

The Telephone and the Economy

What can be said regarding the most pervasive effects of the telephone on the organization and conduct of American economic life, aside from the obvious rise of the American Telephone and Telegraph Company itself as an economic monolith?

Perhaps the most conspicuous of these effects has been the dramatic contraction in the time needed to establish communication, transmit orders and consummate business transactions, what for the sake of brevity, may be called "transaction time." By bringing two or more persons, often separated by long distances, into direct and immediate communication, the telephone eliminated much of the time which otherwise would have been spent in writing letters or traveling to meetings. Telephoning did not, of course, replace written communication and face-to-face meetings; it rather supplemented them and altered somewhat their character. The telephone greatly speeded the pace and the responsiveness of business at the same time that it tended to change the relations among businessmen from those between whole personalities to those between differentiated, functionally specific "roles," a fact which may help to explain the almost compulsive informality and conviviality that obtains when businessmen finally do come together face-to-face. This suggests that the increased efficiency of doing business may have been paid for, in part, by a decrease in the personal and emotional satisfactions of business activity. We are, for example, all aware that the insistent ringing of the telephone usually takes priority even over an ongoing face-to-face business conversation. The significance of this ordering of priorities needs to be examined as does the actual extent to which various kinds of businesses are dependent for their conduct on telephonic conversation.[3]

● ● ●

The Telephone, the Community and Social Relationships

The transformation of many aspects of urban life can be traced to the influence of the telephone either directly or in combination with other aspects of modernization. For the sake of convenience one can divide these effects into three classes: effects on the physical appearance of the community; effects on social interaction, and effects on patterns and models of communication among people.

The influence of the telephone on the design of urban and suburban areas has probably been minor compared to that of innovations in the realm of transportation (including the elevator) and the effects of building and zoning codes. But the telephone probably facilitated the separation of workplace from residence so characteristic of the American economy.

Far more important have been the effects of the telephone on the patterns and the quality of social relationships in urban areas. Those sociologists and social cirtics who studied the urban environment during the first thirty years of this century almost universally lamented the waning role in society played by primary groups and the declining solidarity of the neighborhood itself. They contrasted the impersonal, fragmented quality of contemporary urban life with an image of warm personal relationships believed to have characterized small towns and urban neighborhoods of an earlier age. (The degree to which this image corresponded to reality is not significant in this connection.) Earlier communities were thought of essentially as interacting groups of kinsmen and neighbors (who were also one's friends). In such communities all but the very wealthy were likely to confine their social contacts to members of their extended families and those living in close physical proximity; it was difficult and costly (of time if not always of money) to get to know others and it was not considered necessary. People's horizons were limited, in large part by the difficulties of other than purely local transportation and communication. The invention of the telephone, among other developments, helped to extend those horizons.

The breakdown of the earlier style of community life is regarded by most sociologists as the consequence chiefly of large scale industrialization and urbanization, of all that is connoted by the development of a "mass society." The extended family, the most important primary group, often disintegrated and dispersed as its consistuent units, responding to expanding economic opportunities, scattered over an ever widening geographical area. Although later studies have shown that the conjugal family is less isolated than once thought and although sociologists have discovered new types of primary groups in American life they have tended to see the latter as shifting friendship groups and cliques grounded either in the formal work situation or in informal associational activities rather than as stable groups on the model of the family. Completely overlooked has been the changing nature of the "neighborhood," made possible by the almost universal availability of the telephone.

With the spread of the telephone, a person's network of social relationships was no longer confined to his physical area of residence (his neighborhood, in its original meaning); one could develop intimate social networks based on personal attraction and shared interests that transcended the boundaries of residence areas. It is customary to speak of "dispersed" social networks to denote that many urban dwellers form primary groups with others who live physically scattered throughout a metropolitan area, groups which interact as much via the telephone as in face-to-face meetings.[4] Such primary groups constitute a person's "psychological neighborhood." Modern transportation, of course, makes it possible for such groups to forgather in person, but it is highly doubtful that they could long sustain their existence without the cohesion made possible by the telephone.

The nature, the structure and the functions of such psychological neighborhoods and telephone networks, whether or not they are considered to be "primary" groups, are very obscure. The author has discovered one such network consisting of a group of elderly widows living alone who maintain scheduled daily telephone contacts as a means of insuring the safety, health, and emotional security of the group's members. The questions yet to be answered are, in brief, who talks to whom, for how long, for what reasons and with what results?

By this circuitous route we return to the question raised earlier, that of what functions the use of the telephone serves for individuals rather than for the structure of the society as a whole or its constituent institutions. This question requires detailed investigation but it may be suggested that among the most likely functions are the reduction of loneliness and anxiety, an increased feeling of psychological and even physical security and the already mentioned ability to maintain the cohesion of family and friendship groups in the face of residential and even geographic dispersion. Recent sociological inquiries have illuminated somewhat the role of the telephone in maintaining the cohesion of families in the face of pressures of industrialization, but little is known about the variables (e.g., distance, degree of kinship, stage of the family cycle) associated with variations in these patterns.

Finally, it may not be amiss to suggest that, at least in the early years of its existence, the possession of a telephone may have served both to define and to enhance the social status of individuals, a function which, for a time, probably every consumer-oriented technological innovation has served.

While the various questions and hypotheses we have examined above have been raised in relation to urban life, they are no less valid when applied, *mutatis mutandis*, to the conditions of rural life. The rural, relatively isolated "folk" society (gemeinschaft) has frequently been idealized by nostalgic critics of contemporary "mass society" (gesellschaft) because such writers deplore the loss of those warm, primary-group relations and that sense of belonging to an organic, solidary community which they believe—or imagine—to have characterized earlier rural and small town life. The type case of such a social order—as the origin of the idea in late nineteenth century German sociological romanticism immediately suggests—was rather the European peasant village or castle town of the High Middle Ages than the American farming community of the 1880s or 1890s. The typical American rural family of that period lived on its own farm, separated from any neighbors by distances ranging from a quarter mile to five miles or more. In consequence, the local town, which had to be within a few hours ride by horse and wagon, served chiefly as a trading center rather than as the scene of a richly textured organic community life.

This is not to deny, however, that such towns served important socializing functions, especially on those occasions—weekends and holidays—when all the families from the hinterland gathered there to renew acquaintanceships, buy provisions, compare experiences and entertain themselves and each other. The persistent theme of loneliness in accounts of nineteenth century American farm life suggests, however, that the "official" model of rural American society is closer to ideological fiction than to historical fact.[5] For these reasons it may be suggested that the increasing modernization of rural America, far from eroding primary group ties, actually strengthened them by expanding the area from which primary (and secondary) group members could be selected while simultaneously freeing people from social and psychological dependence on what may at times have been uncongenial neighbors. The telephone broke through the isolation of the rural family.

Moreover, the very construction of telephone lines in rural areas often gave impetus to social solidarity, as farmers frequently organized informal groups to string wires.[6] That these early farmers' mutual societies were organized so that all the farms in a given locality were on the same telephone line probably contributed further to the sense of shared communal identity. The whole area served by a telephone cooperative could intercommunicate simultaneously and, apparently, it was not unusual for all the families served by a single line to get on the phone at the same time to hear the latest news and discuss common problems. Since farmers' wives were especially susceptible to feelings of loneliness and isolation, the telephone here too helped to allay personal anxiety.[7]

The following statistic may illuminate both the importance of the telephone on the farm and its rapid acceptance by the rural population (which is typically thought to be more tradition bound than urban dwellers): according to the special telephone census of 1907, 160,000 (73 percent) of Iowa's approximately 220,000 farms were already supplied with telephone service.[8] The major share in this development was the work of farmers' cooperatives. Assuredly, other factors such as the need for mutual aid and the economic advantages of being able to obtain up-to-date information on market conditions in the cities and towns played their part in the rapid spread of rural telephone service, but the importance of more strictly sociological and psychological factors must not be underestimated.[9]

If the suggestions thus far advanced are ultimately confirmed by additional research it may turn out that the extent to which rural life in America actually does or ever did exhibit the characteristics of a solidary, organic community so often imputed to it is primarily the result of modernization and specifically of the introduction and spread of the telephone.

This would also help to explain the greater uniformity of values and attitudes among the rural population; for people who share common problems and interact frequently with one another tend to develop similar values and attitudes and to inhibit the expression of deviant sentiments. That rural areas have typically been served by party rather than individual lines has tended to make rural telephone conversations relatively public, thus facilitating both the reinforcement of dominant attitudes and the suppresion of deviant ones.[10] This situation stands in sharp contrast to that prevailing in the heterogeneous urban residential neighborhood with its mixing of people from many "psychological neighborhoods," within which no single set of attitudes or behaviors could easily be imposed. In urban areas telephone messages tended to be transmitted on one- or two-party lines and even if one's physical neighbors took exception to one's expressed values or behavior a person could usually find support for his "deviance" within his psychological neighborhood. Urban "deviance" is thus but the Janus face of privacy.

A discussion of the social effects of the telephone would, however, be incomplete were reference to its relationship to other modes of communication omitted. In the absence of research one can only suggest these relationships through a series of questions. Does telephone communication lessen or increase total face-to-face communication? Does it supplement or replace the letter? How does telephone communication change the character of face-to-face and of written communications? What effects has use of the telephone had on the rate of use of the telegraph and on the letter writing habits of Americans? Has there occurred specialization within the media of communication wherein certain kinds of messages are considered appropriate for transmission by telephone while other kinds are transmitted by telegraph (e.g., the congratulatory message) or by letters? And if so, why? What is the effect—in political campaigns and direct selling—of a telephone message directed to a particular person as against a newspaper, radio, or telephone message addressed to a mass, anonymous audience?[11]

Although these questions have not as yet been subjected to systematic research, some of them have been the subject of discussion and study.

Among the first generation of Americans to use the telephone were those who were concerned about the ways in which people behaved while talking on the phone and the rules evolving to govern that behavior. Some objected to Bell's invention precisely because it seemed to generate new codes of conduct which were at variance with those governing face-to-face relationships. One can easily imagine the responses of men and women of social standing at discovering a social climber at the other end of the line. Other critics were shocked by the apparent absence of inhibitions when people spoke on the phone. One wrote of impulsive women who "say things to men and to each other over the telephone that they would never say face to face." Others complained about people who made calls at inappropriate times, or who phoned last minute invitations, or about the obligation to return a call if one was missed.[12]

An early, more scientific approach to the question of how people behave on the telephone consisted of a study of the words spoken. The study, conducted in New York City in 1931, analyzed 1000 telephone conversations. Eighty-thousand words were spoken in that sample of calls. Only 2240 (3 percent) different words were employed and 819 of these were used only once. Thus 1421 of the total number were words used over and over again. The study demonstrated not only the diminutive character of the vocabulary of the average American telephoner but suggested, at least, the general contents of the conversations: the most frequently used words were "I" and "me."[13]

In recent years, it has been observed that for some time the telephone has come to be used as an instrument of aggression and hostility. Such uses for the phone can probably be traced back to its earliest days, but the additional anonymity provided by automatic dialing no doubt greatly encouraged the use of the telephone for such purposes. The behavior ranges from the standard April Fool joke (i.e., calling the zoo and asking for Mr. Wolf) to the sex deviants who call women unknown to them personally and whose conversational style varies from the use of seductive language to enormous obscenity. There is also a kind of "persecution" apt to occur between acquaintances and friends which consists of calling at intervals, letting the phone ring until it is answered and then hanging up. "Crankcalls" probably are akin to poison pen letters.

The opportunity to talk on the phone may also function to limit and to deflect the expression of hostility. Loud haranguing on the wire can mitigate situations that might otherwise lead to blows if the antagonists were face-to-face. The practice of screaming at the operator may serve as a safety-valve. Whether she is employed by the telephone company or handles the switchboard for a large firm, the operator can be a built-in victim or target for the caller.

Over the past century the telephone has been diffused throughout America. As it has done so, it has helped to transfor life in cities and on farms and to change the conduct of American business, both legitimate and illegitimate; it imparted an impetus toward the development of "mass culture" and "mass society" at the same time it affected particular institutional patterns in education and medicine, in law and warfare, in manners and morals, in crime and police work, in the handling of crises and the ordinary routines of life. It markedly affected the gathering and reporting reporting news and patterns of leisure activity; it changed the context and even the meaning of the neighborhood and of friendship; it gave the traditional family an important means to adapt itself to the demands of modernization and it paved the way both technologically and psychologically, for the thematically twentieth century media of communication: radio and television.[14]

The Comparative Perspective

While this discussion has concentrated on the cumulative impact of the telephone on American society over the past century, there are obvious advantages to examining its effects both in other industralized societies of differing cultural traditions and in newly industrializing areas. The consequences of the telephone in other industrial societies have not necessarily been identical to those in American society and may, in fact, have been quite different, for any number of reasons. Only a comparative historical approach can distinguish recurrent structural and psychological effects of the telephone (or any other technological innovation) from idiosyncratic ones, can delineate the range of varying cultural contacts in channeling the effects of technological innovation. Studying the consequences of the telephone as it is being introduced in developing nations is, on the other hand, analogous to observing an experiment, with history as the laboratory.

Furthermore, there are theoretical issues at stake which perhaps can only be resolved through comparative study. What degree of modernization in the American or Western sense is, for example, possible in the absence of a well-articulated telephone system? A reflection on Daniel Lerner's *The Passing of Traditional Society* (New York, 1958) may be pertinent here. Either there were no developed telephone systems in the Middle East in the mid-1950s (almost certainly not true in the case of Turkey) or the author overlooked their significance for, despite an incisive analysis of the role of mass communications in the modernization of such societies, he nowhere mentions the telephone in that connection. It may be that essential social communication in such societies emanates from a few strategic elite groups and is disseminated among the largely illiterate masses primarily by way of radio and television. Is an elaborate widely-dispersed telephone system necessary to successful modernization given the existence of the latter? The role of the transistor radio in the modernization of underdeveloped nations certainly cries out for analysis. These are more than idle questions for postprandial senior common room debate: governments for developing societies require a rational basis for assigning priorities and allocating resources for the development of communications systems.

Notes

1. The number of telephones present in a country is frequently used as an indicator of "modernization" by sociologists, but the process by which telephone communications contributed to the changes implied by that term are not considered.

2. This statement should not be taken as advancing a monocausal theory of social change predicated on the idea of direct technological determinism. Far from it. Mutual independence has always characterized technicological and social change.

3. On the extent to which American businessmen hastened to take advantage of the telephone, see American Telephone and Telegraph Company, *National Telephone Directory* (New York, October, 1894), (New York, October, 1897); Department of Commerce and Labor, United States Bureau of the Census, *Special Reports Telephones: 1907* (Washington, 1910), 74–75; Herbert N. Casson, *The History of the Telephone* (Chicago, 1910), 204–211.

4. On the notion of "social networks" see Elizabeth Bott, *Family and Social Network* (London, 1957).

5. Pound, *The Telephone Idea,* 32; *Special Reports: Telephones 1907,* 75.

6. United States Department of Agriculture, Farmers' Bulletin No. 1245, *Farmers' Telephone Companies* (Washington, 1930), 5–6; Frank Gordon, "To Teach Farmers Telephone Repairing," *World Repairing," Word,* XXII (January, 1915), 722.

7. H. P. Spofford, "Rural Telephone: Story," *Harper's Monthly Magazine,* Vol. 118 (May, 1909), 830–837; H. R. Mosnot, "Telephone's New Uses in Farm Life," *World's Work,* IX (April, 1905), 6103–4; "Spread of the Rural Telephone Movement," *Scientific American,* Vol. 104 (February 18, 1911), 162; Frederick Rice, Jr., "Urbanized Rural New England," XXXIII (January, 1906), 528–548.

8. *Special Reports: Telephones* 1907, 18, 23.

9. *Ibid.,* 74–75. Access to the Telephone was regarded as being so essential to life on the farm that the United States Department of Agriculture issued a bulletin in 1922 designed to assist farmers in establishing and improving telephone service. See *Farmers' Telephone Companies.*

10. Spofford, "Rural Telephone: Story," 830–837; Mosnot, "Telephone's New Uses in Farm Life," 6103–4.

11. For a discussion of some of these questions see G. S. Street, "While I Wait," *Living Age,* Vol. 276 (March 15, 1913), 696–7; Antrim, "Outrages of the Telephone," 125; Andrew Lang, "Telephone + Letter-Writing," *The Critic* XLVIII (May, 1906), 507–508; "Telephone and Telegraph Prospects," *The Journal of Political Economy,* XXII (April, 1914), 392–394.

12. Antrim, "Outrages of the Telephone," *Lippincotts' Monthly Magazine,* Vol. 84 (July 1890), 125–126.

13. "The Frequency of Words Used Over the Telephone," *Science,* Vol. 74 (August 14, 1931) supplement, 11–13. Everyday conversations have more recently been studied by a number of ethnomethodologists. See Emanuel A. Schegloff, "Sequencing in Conversational Openings," *American Anthropologist,* Vol. 70 (December, 1968), 1075–1095; *The First Five Seconds: The Order of Conversational Openings,* Unpublished Ph.D. dissertation, Depart-

ment of Sociology, University of California, Berkeley, 1967; Emanuel A. Schegloff and Harvey Sacks, "Opening Up Closings" unpublished manuscript; Donald W. Ball, "Toward a Sociology of Telephones and Telephoners," in Marcello Truzzi, ed., *Sociology and Everyday Life* (Englewood Cliffs, N.J., 1968), 59–74.

14. Virtually each topic deserves at least a chapter of its own. The following references are intended as a guide to subjects not discussed elsewhere in this paper. "Improvements in the Telephone," *Literary Digest,* Vol. 92, (January 1, 1927), 42–49; "Few Telephones Mean High Death Rate," *Ibid.,* Vol. 105 (May 24, 1930), 105; H. T. Wade, "Telephones Throughout the Fleet," *World's Work,* XV (March, 1908), 9991–2; "Battles by Telephone," *Literary Digest,* Vol. 50 (June 19, 1915), 1464; "Directing An Attack," *Scientific American,* Vol. 83 (March 17, 1917), Supplement, 166; M. B. Mullett, "How We Behave When We Telephone," *American Magazine,* Vol. 86 (November, 1918), 44–45; Dr. Alfred Gradenwitz, "A German Police Telephone: Scientific Aids for Patrol Service," *Scientific American,* Vol. 75 (January 25, 1913), Supplement, 61; "A Pocket Telephone," *Literary Digest,* Vol. 44 (March 30 1912), 639; "Private Telephone System in School," *Journal of Education,* (March 31, 1910), 355; William F. McDermott, "Emergency Calls," *Today's Health,* XXIX (November, 1951), 38; "Mine Rescue Telephone Equipment," *Scientific American,* Vol. 109 (November 1, 1913), 340; "Telephone in the Mississippi Flood," *Literary Digest,* Vol. 99 (August 20, 1927), 21; Alfred M. Lee, *The Daily Newspaper in America* (New York, 1937); A. H. Griswold, "The Radio Telephone Situation," *Bell Telephone Quarterly,* I (April, 1922), 2–12; S. C. Gilfillan, "The Future Home Theatre," *The Independent,* LXXIII (October 10, 1912), 886–891; W. Rupert Maclaurin, *Invention and Innovation in the Radio Industry* (New York, 1949).

LINDA COSTIGAN LEDERMAN

Communication in the Workplace: The Impact of the Information Age and High Technology on Interpersonal Communication in Organizations

A great deal has been written about the potential effects on individuals of the new computer technologies. But what about the effects on us as part of commercial and governmental organizations—the places where we work and earn a living? Lederman addresses the question of what will happen to our ideas about work, about bosses, and about company organizations as "high tech" moves into the organizational world. She begins with a brief overview of existing theories of organizations and then considers how the coming "information revolution" will force us to alter these theories. She follows with an extensive analysis of what changes to expect in all types of organizations as they apply high-tech media designed to cope with the new age of information. The issues she raises are relevant not only to organizations but to you as future employees in a high-tech world.

Communication in organizations takes many forms. It is spoken and written. It is direct and mediated. It is formal and informal. It flows in many directions: up, down, across. In a word, it is part and parcel of what the organization runs on. "Communication is as necessary to an organization as the blood stream is to a person. Just as a person gets arteriosclerosis, a hardening of the arteries which impairs efficiency, so may an organization get infosclerosis, a hardening of the communication arteries, which produces similar impaired efficiency."[1]

Viewed this way, communication is the process of transmitting information within the organization about all aspects of that organization: its people, its products/services, its planning/designing, its reason for being. It is the flow of information through the various channels among the various people within the organization at the various levels of responsibility.[2]

A Brief History of Schools of Thought on Organizations

Organizations have long been a subject of study and concern for theorists attempting to understand them. It was the Industrial Revolution which gave the initial impetus for the first systematic study of organizations. Prior to that time, work-related organizations were small. They were often family

This article was written expressly for the present volume. Copyright © 1986 by Linda Lederman.

enterprises based on time-honored traditions, peculiar to the families which founded and continued to operate them from generation to generation. Because these businesses were essentially family operations, the relationships among those who worked in them were usually based on the traditional lines of authority which exist within families. The Industrial Revolution with its emerging factories and large company organizations changed that.

Theories of Organization

The first theory of organizations—the classical or scientific school—viewed organizations as machines and concerned itself with theories for the efficient operation of those machinelike organizations.[3] A division of labor, task-related, and often redundant jobs, bureaucratic hierarchial structure designed to produce products and services efficiently regardless of the cost in human experience are indicative of the classic theory of organizations. "Organization" in classical terms meant specialization and division of labor and authority. Good management and effective leadership within this frame of reference centered on productivity. The classical or scientific school revolved around the notion of designing organizations as efficient machines. People within the organizations were seen as cogs within those machines.

The classical school was replaced in the late 1930s by what has come to be referred to as the human relations school. As opposed to the classical school's viewing organizations as machines, the human relations school saw organizations as consisting of people. Good organizations were seen as working entities in which people were motivated to do their work. Impetus for this change in thinking is attributed to the work of Elton Mayo and his studies at the Hawthorne Works of the Western Electric Corporation.[4] Initially the research was undertaken within the classical framework with an attempt to determine factors which might make workers do their jobs more efficiently. It was with these studies, however, that the human element was first identified as a significant factor in the operation of organizations. Whereas the classical theorists spent little time with the reasons behind what people do at work, human relations theorists concentrated on the "whys" of human work behavior, or the motivations for it.

By the late 1940s and early 1950s, the human relations school was popular and had, for the most part, replaced the earlier classical school. But just as the Industrial Revolution had provided the initial impetus for the emergence of the factory and large corporate-structure organization, World War II provided the impetus behind what was to emerge as the next school of thought about organizations—the sociotechnical systems school.[5] The name most usually used to describe this school is the systems school. In it, the organization is conceived as a system or complex entity comprised of interrelated parts which function as a whole. Just as workers in the classical school were seen as cogs in a machine or in the human relations school as individuals with unique and idiosyncratic motives for doing good work, the systems school viewed workers as components of systems. Viewed this way workers perform a function and are like other functioning units within the system.

The fourth and last of the recognized schools of thought about organizations grew out of the systems way of thinking. Known as the contingency school and based in the sociotechnical systems approach, its contribution to thinking about organizations is the notion that no single theory of organizational design is superior or sufficient to predict organizational effectiveness.[6] Effective organizations are seen as contingent on a number of factors which need to be dealt with situationally.

From this brief synopsis of theories of organizations, two things should become clear. First, despite differences in conceptions about how organizations function, they are entities in which people interact with one another and thus provide a context in which interpersonal communication is central. Second, theories about organizations and how they function have emerged in part as the consequence of major societal influences, such as the Industrial Revolution and World War II and the modern scientific revolution.

Given this history, it becomes easier to understand that organizations as they exist today and as they are likely to be conceptualized will be dramatically affected by the revolution of our time—the information revolution.

The Information Revolution and the Contemporary Organization

The revolutionary nature of the information explosion of contemporary times was first noted by information scientists in 1972 in the proceedings of the Conference Board.[7] These scientists identified the trends and the coming of an age in which information more than products or services was becoming the basis of the economy. They pointed out a new differentiation between society's "haves" and "have nots": information access and acquisition rather than material acquisition.

Any number of writers since then have identified different criteria indicating changes in the quantities of information being produced and consumed by contemporary Americans. Chesebro and Bonsall note that in a given year, the average American will read or complete 3000 notices and forms, read 100 newspapers and 36 magazines, watch 2463 hours of television, listen to 730 hours of radio, read 3 books, buy 20 records, talk on the telephone almost 61 hours, and encounter 21,170 advertisements.[8] If other people with whom we talk are also viewed as sources of information, and we add in the time spent in an average year talking with others, the picture which emerges is the average person swimming in a daily stream of information.

Thus, the primary characteristic of the times, is that there is so much information being produced and consumed by so many of us that it is easy to characterize the age as a time of an information explosion.

A second and related characteristic is that the media which predominate as sources of information are primarily electronic.[9] Electricity is a central component in their design and because of this common base, many of the new technologies can be integrated with one another. Moreover, given the interactive nature of many of the new media, they provide new channels for interpersonal communication. Telephones, citizen-band radios, and, most recently, personal computers with their capacity for electronic bulletin boards and electronic mail, are instances in which interpersonal communication is facilitated and altered by the electronic nature and availability of the new media.

One of the most dramatic arenas in which information technology and the information explosion is changing the face of contemporary life is the workplace. The impact of rapidly changing technology on the workplace of the present and future has become a serious concern and subject of debate. On one side of the debate are innovators and advocates of technological change who paint a utopian picture of a future society, envisioning offices in which technological innovations remove the drudgery from routine tasks. They see machines liberating people from work as it is now known. Others, less enchanted by the technologies, afraid of their potential impact on the fabric of society, present a very different view. They envision the advent of an Orwellian society in which electronic surveillance and the invasion of personal privacy are commonplace.[10]

This debate underscores the extent to which our culture is becoming increasingly based on the creation, distribution, and use of information rather than products or services. Moreover, the information technologies are here, usable now, and generally economical enough to be widespread.[11] Even the words appearing on the page you now read have traveled through several contemporary technologies from the time they were first encoded by the author and entered into her personal computer.

The Organization in the Information Age

There are two ways to look at the business organization in the information age. First, on a macroscopic level, as information-related enterprises. Second, on a microscopic level, in terms of the effects of the age of information and information technology on organizational communication within it.

On a macroscopic level, the economy of contemporary times is largely based on the production and distribution of information and of information-related products and services. Thus, more and more organizations are in the business of creating, supplying, storing, disseminating, packaging, distributing, or mediating information and/or of producing, selling, and/or distributing technologies related to any of the aforementioned information transactions. On this level of analysis the information age has affected the organization in the very nature of the business in which it is engaged and the product/service with which it is dealing. The creation of information has increased in such geometric proportions that information today is often stockpiled as an entity generally in the form of databases. Many of the society's business organizations can be classified as information-related industries.

Obviously, not all organizations are information or information-related industries, any more than all organizations in the industrial society were industrial in nature. The point is that the information-related organization has now emerged, accounts for at least 25 percent of the country's economy, and is rapidly on the rise.[12] On the macroscopic level, then, organizations of today reflect the information age.

On a microscopic level, the information age has effected the functions of most contemporary organizations regardless of the nature of their business. Consequently, organizational theorists are beginning to examine the impact of the current information age. Because the most obvious source of impact are the new technologies, especially the computer, many organizational theorists are addressing themselves to a wide range of questions concerning the effects of emerging technology on the workplace as we now know it.

Their are two focal points of scrutiny. First, there are those technologies which are designed to facilitate and/or supplement face-to-face, written, or telephonic communication within the organization. These are referred to as "interactive technologies." Interactive technologies provide for potential changes in organizations via computer-mediated communication. These technologies are and can be used to assist, facilitate, and/or make possible better communication between people. Time and space as variables affecting communication are eliminated by these technologies. A memo written in New York can travel via satellite and computer technology to London to be read almost immediately. Two businesspeople who need to interact do not have to travel to the same city or location: they can speak with one another via telecommunications technologies without leaving the workplace in which each is located.

Second, there are technologies which involve humans interfacing with computers, the "computer-human technologies." Computer-human communications provide for potential changes in replacing human-human interfaces with human-computer interfaces. For example, an executive who wants to update correspondence with a client over a long time does not have to ask a secretary to dig out files and review them. The executive can pull them up from a personal computer, located at the fingertip. The executive does not have to have a secretary to answer all correspondence. Form letters can be stored in computer files and sent out without secretarial assistance. In both instances, technology replaces the human being with whom the executive would have once interfaced to get the needed information.

Thus, the advent of the information age and its technologies result in a number of changes in organizations. The office as a place in which workers congregate was an indirect outgrowth of the Industrial Revolution with emphasis on its automation and centralization. Industrialization changed the production process from one which was basically a home-based artisan production to one in which the factory system prevailed. When the Industrial Revolution took people away from the farms and out of the small family businesses and transplanted them into factories, the location and nature of the workplace changed. The workplace was no longer rooted in nature or at home. Although the products and/or services were still tangible, the environment in which they were produced and the demands of that environment on the individual were different.

Just as many of the things produced in the Industrial Society were tangible items, much of the work also remained physical. In the shift to the information-related organization, however, this is changing. More people are working with ideas or information technology and the outcomes of their work are often less tangible (more effective storage and retrieval of information, for example) than the outcomes of the industrial organization (better mousetraps). As a result, changes in the workplace, as we know it, have begun to appear.

Emergent Issues in Organizational Communication

There are many issues which arise as a result of these changes, the most important of which are discussed as follows.

Blurring of Lines Between Office and Home

One of the already observable effects of technology on the organization in the information age is the blurring of the lines between office and home. Technology makes it possible for more and more work to be done at home both during and after work hours. Telecommunications and interactive personal computers make it possible for workers to remain home and complete much of the specific work tasks once done in offices. In fact, work at times can be completed more efficiently in the home where the worker is free from the distractions of the office—unexpected callers, short-notice meetings, co-workers with interruptions.

As more and more of the work once reserved for the office can be done from home, lines of differentiation between home and office become fuzzier. "Work," which was once seen as a place to which the worker traveled, a place away from home, becomes an activity which can be engaged in regardless of the place. The idea of the "office" as a place filled with individuals conversing with one another in fact-to-face activities (work related or not) is potentially replaceable by an image of the "office" as a place in which the individual alone, in front of a computer terminal, has mediated access to the people and data that he or she needs.

The change in the notion of "work" from a place to an activity has implications for distinctions between work and leisure activities, too. When "work" was what one did at the office, there was a clear distinction between work and leisure. When "work" can be done at office or at home, and when one's computer can be used for a range of activities, the distinction between which is work and which is leisure is more difficult to make. These become questions for the individual as well as those people with whom the individual lives.

The blurring of lines between office and home is changing much of the socialization inherent in office routine. When workers work together in the office, the presence of co-workers is a key element for observing and modeling office behavior. The new clerical employee, for example, in the traditional office, has been able to learn office procedures for typing, filing, and copying materials by watching others or asking questions. This obviously changes when work is done away from the office.

The structure placed on the worker's use of time is lost when the work is done at home within a personal time frame. In the conventional office, the worker is accountable both for the use of time and for the amounts of time spent in completing the work assignments. When work is done away from the office, this is no longer true.

Finally, the blurring of lines between the home and office result in the loss of one of the defining components of the traditional office: the presence of co-workers for substantial parts of the workday. Co-workers account for one of the major job satisfactions: social interaction with others. These interactions may be totally work related, or primarily social (coffee breaks or lunch times) but in either case they provide the individual with contact for significant portions of the work day with other human beings. When one works primarily at home, this satisfaction is lost.

How much impact new technology will have on changing the nature and structure of the organization both as the place in which work is done and in which one is socialized as a worker depends on whether work at home is supplemental to work at the office or a substitution for it. Clearly, the potential exists for technology to allow work at home to substitute for work at the office. At present, however, it functions primarily to supplement office work.

Centralization in Organizational Communication

A second issue in organizational communication is the potential change in the structure of the organization resulting from the new technologies within the context of the office itself: centralization. In organizational communication, centralization is defined as the control of information flow, resources, and decision making by higher management. The question is whether the introduction and use of new technologies, especially computers, will cause organizational centralization or decentralization. Decentralization is defined in organization communication as more democratization of decision making and information flow.

The solution lies in the recognition that humans use technology, not vice-versa. Most recent research indicates that computers do not cause centralization or decentralization but tend to support or enhance established trends that already exist within given organizations.[13]

The Nature of Work in the Organization

The third area in which the new technologies are changing the organization is in the nature of work itself. Computer-based technologies free human beings from a number of tasks which once they alone could perform. This is particularly true of routine, mechanical tasks which were once performed by the unskilled laborer or the laborer skilled in the performance of the mechanized task. A case in point is the impact on employment of the introduction of word processing. Although some people have argued that word processing makes some positions in the organization vulnerable, in general what has happened is that some kinds of white-collar positions have become more available. In a 1980 study, it was found that although there has been a decrease in stenographic positions, there has been a dramatic increase in the number of file clerks and secretarial positions available in the same period.[14] Many positions held by secretaries were found to require less typing, incorporating tasks once held by middle-level managers.[15] Instead of eliminating jobs, these data suggest that positions are upgraded when humans are freed from tasks machines can perform.

Another change in the nature of work is reliance on new technologies to supplement or supplant communication which until now has been conducted in face-to-face contexts, by telephone, or by hard-copy (written) interaction. An old bromide in organizations is that organizations run on paper. This alludes to the overuse of written communication in the organization as it has existed until now. Technology today replaces the need for hard-copy communication in most instances.

Organizations conduct much of their internal business in meetings. When computer conferencing replaces face-to-face meetings, it drastically affects group process and gives rise to questions regarding the appropriate uses of the computer, and its suitability for conferencing.[16]

Although the new technology makes for more immediate contact across great distances, there are aspects of communication which it does not allow. Compared with face-to-face communication, computer conferencing does not allow for nonverbal communication nor for the social presence of others. It does not allow cues for sequencing of the interaction (turn taking), nonverbal feelings (affects), or intentions. Communicating via the computer is thus a different experience communicationally. To the extent that communication is a major part of the work that is done in the office, communicating differently means that this aspect of work is different from what it was without the computer. The communication skills for dealing with others in meetings, for knowing how to take turns, to read nonverbal behaviors, to assess the feelings (affects) of others, and to determine their intentions become less relevant. Instead, other skills, such as the use of explicit language, immediate reaction and sensitivities to the linear and demanding nature of this kind of communication, and ability to adapt to technology, are required.

Although some people fear that the introduction of technology will displace humans from the workplace, the evidence indicates otherwise. Routine and unskilled kinds of jobs are the most likely to be subjected to the automation which the new technologies make possible. Jobs which require more discretion, judgment, and higher-level abilities are less apt to be relegated to technology.[17] Some organizational theorists argue that the long-range implications of these changes in the nature of work are that the entire work force itself must be upgraded. This upgrading, they assert, must be at a pace that exceeds that of the rate of the introduction of new technologies able to do more and more in the workplace.[18]

The introduction of new technologies provides new areas of work and different ways in which work is done in the workplace. To the extent that work is what the organization is about, changes in the nature of work in the organization are changes in the institution itself.

The Work Force

The fourth area in which organizational theorists are concerned with changes in the organization is in the work force. As mentioned before, as the nature of work changes, so too, do the demands on workers. As the intelligence of computer software increases to include the ability to encode ambiguous human knowledge and decision rules, the demand for skilled professionals changes. This allows paraprofessionals (e.g., in medicine, law, and accounting) to perform some of the tasks once relegated to the trained professional alone.[19] Thus, although the professionals are freed from tasks which are routine, they need deal with more high level interpretatiave and judgmental levels, and the paraprofessionals replacing them are people who once might have had less demanding jobs in organizations.

Technology provides another possibility in terms of the labor force. Employers faced with the problem of insufficient labor supply may no longer need to relocate businesses in order to find enough skilled and affordable workers. Instead, new technologies may be used to replace workers rather than trying to attract new workers.

Masters or Slaves: Workers Feelings in the Information Age
The last important issue emerging in relation to the introduction of new technologies into the contemporary organization to be discussed here, is the feelings of workers. Because contemporary Americans spend more than one half of their waking hours in adult life at work (or coming or going to and from it), feelings about work and job satisfaction are critical. Hmiestra in studying four organizations found that in talking about their experience with information technology, workers began to associate technology with a speeding up of their organizational life.[20] They seemed to experience the information technology as a kind of powerful agent for change and the speed with which that change is occurring was perceived more as a revolution than an evolution.

The more central question, however, is whether workers feel that the technologies which replace or supplement their work tasks are their tools or their masters; whether they are liberated by them or enslaved. Initially, researchers in organizations addressed this question by looking for data to suggest feelings of alienation. These feelings to date have not been found to exist. But organizational theorists are concerned with the potential for such a sense of isolation and loss of human contact, as organizations are influenced by the advent of the new technologies. The issue of workers' feelings is one of real concern as the office in the information age emerges.

Future

It is a certainty that change is occurring and that the workplace is being effected by new technology and the information explosion. The organization is changing in terms of where work is done (home or office), how decisions are made and who in the organization participates in those decisions, and who the workers are and where they come from. These changes will create institutions which are different from organizations as that have existed since the Industrial Revolution. Just what those new institutions will be like can only be speculated about at present.

Notes

1. Keith Davis, *Human Behavior at Work,* New York: McGraw-Hill, 1972 p. 379.
2. Davis, p. 379.
3. For discussion of the classical school, see G. March and H. Simon, *Organizations,* New York: Wiley, 1958.
4. These studies have become landmark work. For discussion, see, for example, Alex Carey, "The Hawthorne Studies: A Radical Criticism," *American Sociological Review,* 32, 1967, pp. 403–416.
5. C. Churchman, R. Ackoff, and R. Arnoff, *Introduction to Operations Research,* New York: Wiley, 1957.
6. R. Lawrence and J. Lorsch, *Organization and Environment Managing Differentiation and Integration,* Boston: Harvard University Press, 1967.
7. Conference Board. *Information Technology: Some Critical Implications for Decision Makers,* New York: Conference Board, 1972.
8. J. Chesebro and D. Bonsall, *Computer-Mediated Communication: Human Relationships in A Computerized World,* unpublished manuscript.
9. J. Chesebro and D. Bonsall, Computer-mediated communication. A paper presented at the Eastern Communication Association convention, Philadelphia, PA, 1984.
10. R. Rice, "The Impacts of Computer-Mediated Organizational and Interpersonal Communication," in *Annual Review of Information Science and Technology,* M. Williams, ed., (White Plains, N.Y.: Knowledge Industry Publications, 1980, pp. 221–249.
11. G. Hmiestra, "Teleconferencing, Conference for Face and Organizational Culture," in *Communication Yearbook 6,* M. Burgoon, ed., Beverly Hills, Cal.: Sage, 1982, p. 5.
12. Peter Drucker, *Technology, Management and Society,* New York: Harper & Row, 1976, 18.
13. R. Tricker, "The Impact of Information Systems on Organizational Thinking," in *Information Processing 1977: Proceedings of the 1977 International Federation of Information Processing Congress,* B. Gilchrist, ed., New York: North-Holland, 1977, pp. 213–221.
14. R. B. White, "A Prototype of the Automated Office," *Datamation,* 23 (4), 1977, pp. 83–90.
15. White, "Automated Office," p. 287.
16. Rice, "Computer-Mediated Communication," p. 277.
17. M. Kochen, "Information and Society," in *Annual Review of Information Science,* M. Williams, ed., White Plains, N.Y.: Knowledge Industry Publications, 1983, p. 287.

18. Kochen, "Information," p. 289.
19. These are trends which are beginning to be seen in many work areas—those cited here are only a few drawn from various reports.
20. G. Hmiestra, "You Say You Want a Revolution? Information Technology in Organizations," in *Communication Yearbook 7*, B. Bostrom, ed., Beverly Hills, Cal.: Sage, 1983, pp. 802–829.

ROBERT CATHCART and GARY GUMPERT

The Person-Computer Interaction: A Unique Source

This essay explores the person-computer relationship. It uses the accepted interpersonal communication model as the basis for determining the psychological parameters of person-computer transactions. It is proposed that the computer functions as a proxy in the interpersonal communication dyad and that this, in turn, creates source ambiguity resulting in dissonance. The essay examines the means of resolving this state of dissonance and suggests that the traditional dyadic model is being modified by the person-computer paradigm.

Ithiel del Sola Pool in the forward to *The Coming Information Age* states that prior to the introduction of the computer, every communication device "took a message that had been composed by a human being and (with some occasional loss) delivered it unchanged to another human being. The computer for the first time provides a communication device by which a person may receive a message quite different from what any human sent. Indeed, machines may talk to each other" (Dizard, 1982, xi–xii). With the rapid introduction of computers, both personal and institutional, into everyday life we are witness to one of the most profound changes in communication since the invention of cuneiform and the clay tablet—the technology which first made it possible to imprint symbols of human vocal messages and to transport them physically from sender to receiver.

Each new technological communication innovation has its effect on information transfer and processing. Each new technology has expanded human communication capabilities over time and space, and has resulted in altered interpersonal relationships (Cathcart and Gumpert, 1983). Communication technologies themselves have been altered in usage through various combinations of media: for instance, the telephone with radio, the photograph with motion pictures and television, and so on. Today, another radical shift in communication is occurring through the combining of the computer with electronic and telephonic communication technologies.

Types of Computer-Human Functions

Computers, in conjunction with other media, have already made remarkable inroads into our daily activities and have altered certain interpersonal

From *Information and Behavior,* vol. 1, edited by Brent D. Ruben. New Brunswick, N.J.: Transaction, 1985.

relationships. At present, human-computer interaction takes place in the following three ways:

1. Unobtrusive functions—those in which the utilization of the computer is not evident to the user, for instance, digital recordings and telephone connections (Covvey and McAlister, 1982).

2. Computer-facilitated functions—where persons use a computer for the purpose of expediting communication. This function refers to communication *through* a computer rather than *with* a computer. Electronic mail, for example, represents a change of medium (paper to display screen) in which the computer is interposed between sender and receiver. In this case, the computer is a high speed transmitter of what is essentially a written message. The same holds true for computer bulletin boards and other computer networks which allow messages to be stored and retrieved at the convenience of senders and receivers without reliance on intermediaries such as printers, librarians, postal clerks, telephone operators, and so on (Levy, 1983).

3. Person-computer interpersonal functions—situations where one party activates a computer which in turn responds appropriately in graphic, alphanumeric, or vocal modes establishing an ongoing sender/receiver relationship (Cathcart and Gumpert, 1983). Two basic types of computers are utilized in this activity: the dedicated computer which is fundamentally unifunctional, and where the interaction generally requires no training of the operator; and the multifunctional computer where training is required and the person must accommodate himself or herself to particular forms of computer language such as BASIC, Pascal, LOGO, and so on (Papert, 1980).

   Today we have no choice but to interact with a computer rather than with another human being when we wish to locate information stored in data banks, pay monthly bills via telephone connection with a bank's computer, or withdraw or deposit money from a twenty-four hour bank teller machine. In these cases, there is no way to process the transaction other than by "talking to" or having "dialogue" with a computer. For these transactions, the computer is programmed to interact in a manner replicating face-to-face interpersonal communication (Vail, 1980).

It is our intention to discuss the phenomenon of communicating *with* a computer rather than *through* a computer. We will argue that in this situation the computer serves as a proxy for another person, thus establishing an interpersonal communication dyad. For there to be interpersonal dialogue, there must be an exchange of messages. The interpersonal reciprocal act implies the existence of both a sender and a receiver, as well as mutually understood linguistic codes.

Characteristics of Dyadic Communication

The accepted dyadic model of interpersonal communication posits interchangeable sender-receiver roles in situations where immediate and continuous feedback produces communication which is symbolic, non-repeatable, and nonpredictive. That is to say, the message is created through symbolic processing, the meaning of which in turn is determined by the relationship of sender and receiver. In addition, such messages, at least in face-to-face dyads, are evanescent and therefore nonrepeatable. Such interpersonal dialogue is characterized by maximum sender-receiver control of the exchange and equal responsibility for the outcomes.

Person-Person Communication

It is the dynamic relational quality among sender, receiver, and symbols which makes interpersonal exchanges creative and nonrepeatable (Millar and Rogers, 1976). Each interpersonal exchange is situation specific—created on the spot, the outcome not known in advance. There is always a creative element in human communication because of the symbolic nature of language and the fact that meaning is produced through the symbolic process, not by the symbols themselves.

Though there are grammatical rules and norms which govern the use of language, these do not limit the outcomes of communicative exchanges, i.e., the meanings and motives which are the result of the exchange of messages. Because of the creative and nonpredictive qualities of interpersonal communication we are always "at risk" in such situations, in that misunderstanding, rejection, and loss of self-esteem are always possible (Miller and Steinberg, 1975).

This is not to say that face-to-face interpersonal communication is the only or even preferred way to have dialogue. Rather, it is to point out how important sender and receiver relationships and symbolic functions are in all human communication.

Mediated Interpersonal/Communication

We have suggested elsewhere that when a technological medium in interposed in the interpersonal dialogue, there are produced significant differences in the content of the exchange and the relationship of sender and receiver. We have referred to this activity as mediated interpersonal communication (Cathcart and Gumpert, 1983). For the mediated exchange to work as interpersonal communication, there must be tacit agreement that the participants will proceed as though they are communicating face to face.

For example, when a television personality communicates directly to an audience *through* a television camera, interpersonal norms are used to simulate face-to-face interaction, and the viewer tacitly agrees to respond as though face to face with the television personality. This "intimacy at a distance" is the basis of parasocial interaction (Horton and Wohl, 1956). A telephone conversation is another example of a mediated interaction which proceeds as if it were a face-to-face encounter (Aronson, 1971).

It is apparent in these two cases that the interpersonal sender-receiver relationship is maintained even though there is limited feedback and some restrictions on the possible outcomes. We maintain that for dialogue to take place it is important that an interpersonal sender/receiver relationship be established and that the symbolic process maintained.

Person-Computer Communication

The interaction of person and computer, on the other hand, creates a unique mediated sender-receiver relationship. This idiosyncratic relationship happens because computers, unlike other machines, can as Ithiel de Sola Pool suggests, "respond" and produce messages, apart from any human source. For the first time a technology can not only speed and expand message exchange, but it can also respond with its own message to a human partner. The computer in this mode becomes a proxy for a sender-receiver in the communication dyad.

In this situation we tacitly accept the computer as a substitute for some person with whom we would interact were the computer not available. We give the computer commands, we ask it questions, and it responds. It gives us commands, asks us questions, and we respond. We appear to be reproducing dyadic communication based upon an immediate sender-receiver relationship. But, this dialogue is a strange one in which the human, capable of speech, responds through tactile means of keyboard, touch-tone or touch-screen as the computer, a machine, responds with visual displays and sound reproductions/imitations of the human voice. The computer user agrees to communicate as though the computer were a message source, simulating interpersonal exchanges even though in reality there can be no duplication of the creative, nonpredictive human interpersonal dialogue.

The computer is programmed to respond in certain ways depending on the input it receives from the human user. There appears to be a dyadic exchange which develops according to message input and feedback, but in actuality the exchange is always limited and predictive because of the binary nature of information processing within the computer. This makes the relational and control aspects of the dyadic exchange quite different from that of the human interpersonal dialogue, even where the person-computer interaction has been programmed to replicate person-to-person communication.

The key to the difference between person-to-person communication and person-to-computer communication is the "program." Because computers must be programmed, the outcome of the "dialogue" is predictable, even though the computer branches its responses based on the unprogrammed inputs of the user. What happens, of course, is that the user becomes "programmed" to provide the kinds of input that are compatible with the computer. Thus the relationship shifts to one where the computer is in control and is responsible for the outcome of the communicative exchange.

Impact of Person-Computer Communication

It may seem strange to speak of control and relationship when examining human-computer interaction, but this tact is worth exploring if we are to understand computer effects on intrapersonal and interpersonal communication. In the person-to-person dyadic model, sender-receiver roles are interchangeable, just as message and feedback are reciprocal and creative. A relationship exists based upon the perceptions of sender or receiver and the symbolic content of messages exchanged. This relationship is furthered or altered depending on what is disclosed, what needs are satisfied, and what social and cultural norms prevail. The content of the message and feedback is shaped at the outset and throughout by the relational aspect of sender and receiver interaction. Examples abound and are obvious. The way a parent and child communicate is shaped in part by the familial relationship and evolves depending on what each discloses and what each perceives the relationship to be at any given time. The unique relationship and the limitless possibility of producing meaning symbolically implies that the outcome cannot be predicted—only indicated.

When the human dyadic exchange is *mediated*, the sender-receiver relationship is altered. If we cannot see, but only hear the source, less information is processed and our perception of source is altered. We necessarily compensate for this loss and in so doing the relational quality of the interchange is modified. When the only way we can reach out and touch someone is through the exchange of oral-aural signals, we cannot have the same relationship as when we can physically touch, smell, taste, and visually see the other person. When feedback is delayed as in letter writing or attenuated as it is in radio and television interactions, there is a marked difference in the alliance of sender and receiver. Still, in every mediated communication there is a relationship based on the perception that each person has of the other, and the fact that whatever messages are produced are the result of symbolic processing between two or more individuals.

The Problem of the Source

What is our perception of, and relationship to, the source when we interact with a computer? Here we face a dilemma. The source of the message/feedback produced is not the hardware, even though we are "talking to" the machine. We might consider that the programmer who creates the software is the source. But, then we are confronted with even more ambiguity. A programmer produces software for a particular computer in suitable computer language. That program can be used in millions of computers. But, when one of us is "talking" with the computer, we are not interacting with the programmer. We have no idea who that person is, nor did the programmer have in mind trying to reach us with a message. The programmer's interaction is with the computer, not with the user.

Conceivably the program itself could be the source of the message and feedback. The user activates the program and once initiated the program begins to guide and direct the form and content of the dialogue. The program, however, provides only a framework or a context in which the exchange takes place. Only certain kinds of inputs and responses will be accepted. The program cannot decide to pursue a new line of inquiry—create new meanings or symbols—nor can it change its role in relationship to the user as the dialogue proceeds.

Computer as Human-Like

The ambiguity regarding the source in the person-computer dialogue necessitates resolution of a dissonant situation. If the user is to accept that communication *with* a machine rather than *through* a machine is possible, then it follows that some adaptation or tacit agreement must occur if that state of ambiguity is to be resolved. One common solution has been to anthropomorphize the computer—to attribute human characteristics to the machine. Examples abound, like "I usually get my way, but it makes me do tricks first." The relationship appears to vary, depending on the program utilized. A number of relational possibilities exist: tutor, coworker, competitor, student, and master. It is interesting to note that much of "computerphobia" is to be found in the potential master-slave relationship (Turkle, 1982). For example, one can buy a software program called ABUSE in which the computer will insult you, make fun of your inputs, or shame you by solving problems that you can't solve. In any case, anthropomorphizing the computer is required in order to establish the relationship necessary to make dialogue possible. We supply the computer—the machine—with human attributes. Thus, we can react as though it were a proxy—human—source and a receiver.

The desire on the part of the user to reduce ambiguity and dissonance is but one of several factors that result in the anthropomorphizing of the computer. Humanizing the computer is also prompted by the physical and electronic properties of the computer and by the nature of programming which uses the interpersonal dyad as an operational model. Interpersonal cues are provided by the programs, and the user agrees to participate in a simulated interpersonal relationship. Such reciprocity makes anthropomorphizing the computer different from that with other machines such as automobiles, airplanes, and boats.

Human-like symbolic responses are programmed into the computer. Complicated and subtle relationships are created where a computer user chooses to allow his or her reaction to be manipulated and controlled in order to fulfill the ideal of interpersonal dialogue. For example, the user relinquishes control of the dialogue to a "humanness" which is programmed into the machine. The result is a symbiotic relationship that permits the user to experience an ongoing dialogue. Instead of viewing himself or herself as a machine which has been programmed to provide the "correct" responses—which is, after all, what interaction with a computer is all about—the user imputes human qualities to the machine in order to make possible the semblance of interpersonal communication.

Additional user accommodations are dictated by the anthropomorphized computer relationship. For example, most computer programs require the fabrication of spontaneity—the impression that what is occurring has not been programmed. Unlike high risk/low predictability face-to-face relationships, person-computer relationships are predetermined, and articulated spontaniety is built in. This pretense of uniqueness is, of course, the basis of any interactive program in which branched responses and combinations are possible. Theoretically, the computer has a response or alternative for every one of our idiosyncratic inputs. It is, however, the spontaneity or nonrepeatability of the person-to-person dialogue that cannot be fulfilled.

Interpersonal communication is creative—unpredictable—precisely because of the symbolic potential of human language. The ambiguity of human language and the relational and situational attributes of the human dialogue allow unique and unpredictable outcomes. That is, human communication is a process of continual creation and re-creation of reality. In short, anthropomorphizing the computer is required because the user agrees to interact as though the dialogue were spontaneous and unique, thus producing the necessary person-to-person relationships so essential to interpersonal communication.

Computer as a Tool

Computer anthropomorphizing, though widespread, is not the only means of reducing the dissonance faced in communicating with a computer. An alternative is to take the position that the computer is "just a machine"

(Turkle, 1982). In this case the relationship appears to be that of a human being to a tool which extends human capabilities; the computer is an extension of the human brain and a high speed calculator.

If one views the computer as a machine that does nothing but what it is told to do, then the user must think of computer responses as messages to himself or herself from himself or herself. The user must accept the position, tacitly or directly, that he or she is both source and receiver of the produced dialogue. This appears to alter the sender-receiver relationship to one where the user is master of the machine. It does not, in reality, alter computer control of the dialogue. To interact with a computer the user must accept the computer on its own terms. That is, the user must use the computer's language and believe in its computations.

When people insist that their relationship with the computer is that of person-to-machine, it suggests that they are willing to accept what we call "inanimate dialogue." The tacit agreement in this case is that the user knows best and is always in control of the machine, but will go along with computer commands and responses in order to get what he or she wants. There still must be established a satisfactory sender-receiver rationale in the person-computer interaction in order to overcome the dissonance created when a person receives machine made messages, that is, interacts with a machine which produces messages apart from any other human.

Control and Predictability

Whether one anthropomorphizes the computer or insists that it is only a machine, the computer exercises significant control over the dialogue and its outcomes. This is true because the human is forced to use the computer's language and the language of the computer insists on unambiguous information and predictable outcomes (Phillips, 1983).

Despite continued progress in developing computers which can respond to human language in human-like language, and which have artificial intelligence that resembles human intelligence, computers do not engage in symbolic processing. Computers exist because they circumvent the unpredictableness of human symbolization. They reduce all information to on-off signals. They cannot be sidetracked. Once the inputs are received and transformed into binary signals, the outcomes are inevitable. Anything which does not fit is rejected. Anything which is accepted is made to fit into the binary mode. Thus, there can be no new meanings generated, no creative outcomes as the result of chance encounters. The whole purpose of computers is to eliminate such "human error"—creativity—and to speed the process of counting and calculating by eliminating those aspects of human communication which get in the way of reaching predictable conclusions.

Uniqueness of Human Communication

It is the ambiguity of human language and its metaphorical function which make it possible for humans to act together in unique ways. It is also the ambiguity of language and the randomness of symbolizing which allows for emotional, even capricious and unpredictable interaction. A computer, on the other hand, is never capricious. Its language is digital—intelligible to computer circuitry. Computers reject the disorderly and the ambiguous. Computing is a process of regularization. If the computer is not able to respond to the question asked, the question must be changed. The computer is entirely logical. Even when computers randomly program, their randomness is perfectly random.

When the human chooses to, or is forced to, interact with a computer, the control of the dialogue shifts to the computer even though the human must turn on the machine and give it commands to make it function. The control shifts because the computer demands that the dialogue be carried on with its language and within its programmed parameters. As put by Professors Ducey and Yadon (1983) in describing the need for computer courses in the curriculum:

> Once students have accepted and become familiar with the need to state a problem and its solution in concrete, precise and unambiguous terms, the true creativity of computing is more easily appreciated.

Even though humans program computers, it is not possible to program a computer to be reciprocal and spontaneous with its human counterpart. The human, on the other hand, is more adaptable and can learn to function digitally, can learn to be more like a computer. The implication is that as we continue to computerize facets of our soceity, interpersonal skills will shift from the management of human relationships and the formulation of intersubjective truth to the management of information and the arriving at of mathematical certainty (Carey, 1982).

The person-computer dyad resembles the interpersonal communication model, first because it is designed to emulate it by producing a responding mechanism which interacts with the user as a proxy for another human; and second, because it requires the user to implicitly agree that there is an interpersonal sender-receiver relationship functioning. It differs from the two-person dyadic model in that it cannot produce spontaneous and unpredictable outcomes.

The binary nature of the computer and its processing is the antithesis of human symbolic processing where senders and receivers produce meanings and solve problems based on the ambiguities of human language and the evolving dynamic interpersonal relationship. The fact that computers can perform extremely complex operations at high speed and have almost limitless memory makes them very potent tools in the extension of human power. They are, however, of a different order than past machines that have also extended that power. Computers force humans into relationships which have serious implications for the future. Armelle Gauffenic (1983), a specialist in systems analysis at the Ecole Superieure de Commerce in Paris, has put it very well:

> As systems develop they gradually deprive the individual of interpersonal contact and communication, thus altering his affective psychological and emotional balance and isolating him in a relationship with the machine. While the nature of that relationship depends on the interface potential, the general rules obtaining are those of computer science; efficiency, rationality, the utmost simplification, etc. This new form of communication, this language of modern times, in which any concession to the superfluous—to mere form—is out of the question forces the mind and the intellect to conform to its mould if they are not to become impotent and maladjusted (p. 137).

Conclusion

The person-computer interaction is a reality. Dialogue with computers will increase as millions of personal computers are purchased and interface with mainframes and databanks. The implications of this mediated inter-personal connection are already altering our society—even before the effects have been realized. The computer brings with it extraordinary benefits: relieving people of tedious tasks, making possible massive storage of information and instant retrieval, solving medical and scientific problems in minutes which before would have taken a lifetime. But at the same time, disquieting consequences also loom on the horizon: speed and efficiency become the norm, mathematical processing replaces human symbolizing, individual isolation is increased, the frailities of human behavior become exaggerated.

Every technological innovation in communication alters the status quo and every such development results in the reallocation of communication priorities and values. This paper is not intended to denigrate or disparage the computer and its uses, but rather to stimulate research into the functions and uses of computers as human proxies. It is not the technology of the computer which is in question, but rather the process which occurs when the human and the computer interact, as they must. Social scientists have long been aware of, and have studied, the effects of the human-machine interaction in our postindustrial society. The need now is to study the consequences of a system in which machines and humans converse with each other.

3
Mediated Reality

Flip the switch and the world is yours. There is no need to pretend. Space is irrelevant—it dissolves with electronics. Time is altered. The past can be preserved. The present frozen. You can be assured that the future will be stored and saved, in case you missed it. What was it like to hear music only when musicians were present? What was it like to depend on travelers for news about relatives who lived a hundred miles away? There was a time when our contact with the world was pretty much limited to what we could see, hear, touch, feel and smell. There was no doubt when we said "I know it! I can see it, touch it, feel it!" That was direct sensory experience. But what does it mean today when we say "I can see it" or "I can hear it!"? It has become increasingly difficult to distinguish between that which is real—directly sensed first hand, and that which is "real"—indirectly sensed through media.

Time and Space Binding

In our interaction with the environment we are, by definition, selective. Through our selective perception we transform disorder into order. To that task we bring our past experiences, our past relationships, and our unique personalities. Each of us perceives the environment through idiosyncratic filters. We each create a reality from the world "out there."

The process of selecting and abstracting is, at times, quite direct. We feel the heat, we smell the aroma. But an existence limited to direct sensory experience would be so primitive it would prevent human development. Ultimately, we require some form of media to extend our abstracting capabilities. Psychologist James J. Gibson, in his study of human perception, made the following pertinent observation:

> In speaking, painting, sculpting, and writing, the human animal learns to *make* sources of stimulation for his fellows, and to stimulate himself in doing so. These sources, admittedly, are of a special sort, unlike the sources in the "natural" environment. They are "artificial" sources. They generate a new kind of perception in man, which might be called knowledge, or perception at second hand. The so-called accumulation of knowledge in a society of men, however, depends wholly on communication, on ways of getting stimuli to the sense organs of individuals.[1]

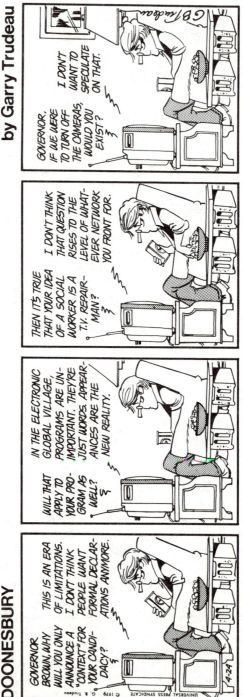

Essential to communication is the dissemination of knowledge over time and space. Essential to the dissemination of knowledge over time and space are media. Media has time and space binding capability.

Media are the means for the present to understand the past. Media function throughout time to generate and preserve knowledge. Cave drawings, gravestones, footprints in cement, graffiti on public walls, and even libraries are ways of the past to communicate with the future. It is this process of time and space binding, more than anything else, that shapes our perception of reality.

Reality Confirmation

The essence of living is "now" and experientially our concern is with the moment. Once the moment occurs, however, it is gone. The present melts into memory. Media, however, intercede between the moment and the memory. They capture and freeze the moment, preserving it in its "real" form. The memory as well as the moment are altered by the presence of media artifacts. The fleeting moment of "now" is de-emphasized. It need not be experienced firsthand. It is replaced by the artifact of "now"—the media-constructed reality.

Is the essence of experience the moment or the photograph of the moment? The still photograph illustrates how a medium can alter the relationship between the individual and the dimension of time that surrounds events. It is interesting to see how the photograph has more and more become a form of reality confirmation rather than merely a record of the past or an individual artistic expression. Have you "experienced" the Spanish Steps in Rome, the Eiffel Tower in Paris, or Westminster Abbey in London unless you have a record of the visit—a photograph? Without the photographic record what would be the proof that you had been there—proof to others and proof to yourself?

If you want instant proof you can use a Polaroid camera or a Sony portable TV camera and cassette recorder. The advantages are obvious. The long time delay in processing is eliminated. If you "missed" the first time, there is always a second chance. Proof of one's presence at a site or event is provided while still on the spot. Confirmation of reality need not wait.

Audio tape-recordings are another example of media altering the moment and memory. Everything is placed on tape: baby's first words, the wedding ceremony, the funeral ceremony, telephone conversations, interviews. Increasing numbers of students attend classes armed with tape recorders. While most see this as an aid to note taking, the presence of the tape recorder alters the event. A classroom lecture is a participatory activity involving both the teacher and the student at the moment of delivery. The tape recording, though faithfully preserving the professor's comments, alters the event. The professor becomes performer while the student becomes spectator.

An intriguing use of audio tape-recording is revealed in the Watergate Hearings. President Nixon recorded conferences and meetings involving himself and aides—without the participants' awareness. Why? One possible answer is that a recorded conversation is more "official" than a nonrecorded one. "On the record" is a frequently used phrase in Washington to identify official statements. Consider the implications of that phrase. Conversations actually occur which do not officially exist. These are "off the record." So the President of the United States is involved in "off the record" conversations which he secretly knows are "on the record." It is assumed that the presence of the tape recorder did alter the President's conversations and actions. The President was seemingly more concerned with future judgment than with present interaction. Conversations become objects or artifacts when preserved on tape. In this case, the Presidential tapes were the "real" objects that determined Nixon's future.

The addition of the "instant replay" to the technical repertory of television is another example of reality confirmation and reality selection. Not only can any play in a game be shown immediately after the event occurred, but it can be frozen, played backwards, and several versions from various cameras can be shown, sometimes simultaneously. To what extent are we developing a dependency on instant replay to confirm reality? The answer is evident when we see the latest use of instant replay. Now videotape playback is shown not only to the home viewer, but shown also on a giant screen to the audience at the arena or stadium. Both the home viewer and the stadium spectator can concentrate less on the execution of an intricate play because, if it is important, the replay will be available. Instant replay tells us what is important and confirms the reality of what is before our eyes.

The Media Jet

The issues examined here reveal that subtle shifts in our perception of reality have occurred and are occurring. Yet, we often are unaware of these changes and the role of media in bringing them about. For example, we all know how important it is to be in the proper location for seeing an event as it happens. We usually report exactly where we were standing when we witnessed an accident, or how far away we are from an object being described. But where are we when we watch a televised event? This is difficult to answer. The obvious response is that we are sitting in the living room, or family room, or bathroom—wherever the ubiquitous television set is located. But beyond our physical presence in front of the set, where are we? Where are our senses in relationship to the event being televised?

The phrase "I'm looking at the television set" is not an adequate description of perceiving events on the screen. Individuals neither watch a TV set nor look at the screen. The viewer may be physically outside the screen, but is psychologically beyond the screen. An explanation of this can be found by examining the television process itself. Let's look at a hypothetical but common television presentation. A visiting dignitary comes to visit the United

States and is greeted, not only by the necessary officials, but also by a host of TV cameras and personnel. The plane taxis down the runway, the dignitary comes down the steps, proceeds along the red carpet with the hosts and is introduced to the American people. The visitor delivers a short speech, gets into a car and leaves the airport in a motorcade. You can imagine the television coverage. A number of cameras have been placed strategically to achieve adequate vantage points. The television director switches from one camera to another, from a view of the celebrity to the sight of visitors standing in the background. As the coverage unfolds, the director chooses the wide shot being transmitted from the left of the dignitary and then switches to a close-up from the right side. And so it goes from camera to camera, from shot to shot. Do you assume that each camera represents a different personality viewing the event? No! You view the event through a single proxy—the television eye. The person at home, while sitting in a stationary position, is not static psychologically. The viewers accept psychological multiplicity. Multiple cameras do not suggest or represent various personalities, rather they constitute one personality capable of radical shifts in time and space. If the individual viewer were outside the screen psychologically, he or she could never accept this extraordinary manipulation of presence through time and space. That is, one would have to articulate that each camera represented a view of separate individuals and not that of oneself. That is not what happens when we participate in a television event.

Just as we do not assume several personalities while watching a televised event, we are not "at home" while watching the event. That is, we are not seeing the event from our home. The "media jet" teleports us, at least psychologically, to the event. To what degree do we distinguish between "the" event and a mediated event? How dependent are we on being at media events? To what extent have media events become substitutions for our participation in "real" events?

If the "media jet" did *not* teleport us, at least psychologically, through time and space, we could readily distinguish between experiencing firsthand events and secondhand events. But as urban society continues to extinguish agrarian existence, human beings become increasingly sedentary and more dependent upon mediated contact with the environment. The paradox for twentieth-century urban citizens is that while we have gained a tremendous number of mediated contacts with a world far beyond, we have lost some of the relationship with immediate community and present environment: a relationship achievable primarily through primary sensory contact. The importance of immediate local environment has been negated or de-emphasized in the creation of a global community not based upon the usual limitations of time and space.

Media Semantics

Some clarification may be needed at this point to escape a potential semantic morass. Central to this discussion of reality and perception is a distinction between the nature of mediated and nonmediated experience. Obviously, it would be foolish to claim that media relationships with reality are nonexperiences, just as it would not be helpful to place a value judgment on media experience in relation to nonmedia experience. Ideally we want to heighten experiential awareness and develop experiential differentiation, not do away with any sensory experiences.

To watch a play on television and to see a play in the theater are two distinct experiences, even though the same play and cast are involved. A wildlife TV program about the prairie dog is not the same as an actual encounter with a prairie dog. At some point the omnipresence of media does begin to negate sensory differentiation. "I talked to her yesterday," is quite different from "I talked to her on the telephone yesterday." "I saw the game" and "I saw the game on television" are phrases referring to totally different experiences. And, as the videophone becomes commonplace, what does "I talked to her yesterday" really signify? One does not have to be an alarmist to see an increasing degree of experiential ambiguity resulting from the increasing amount of technogically mediated communication. The woman who phones her grocer and has the order sent out says, "I did my shopping." At what point do people who watch the telecast of the arriving dignitary say, "I was there"? Who can deny that, to a certain extent, the statement is true?

The probability seems high that in an urban society the vicarious media experience might push the firsthand encounter into the background. And why not? The nature of urban contact can be unpleasant, uncertain, and often confusing. The safety of a mediated environment in which the human being is enclosed and protected, but not isolated, is very appealing. To go to the ballgame means a chance encounter with inclement weather, discomfort with crowds of strangers, and contact with smells that might be offensive. It's easier to watch a show on the Florida Everglades than to venture into an area which can be dangerous and where insect life would certainly make its presence known. Some might argue that the tremendous growth of tourism has placed an increased importance on firsthand experience with the world. But is that really the case? Upon examination, we find that tourism is as mediated as that magic seat in front of the TV set. The shift from the living room environment to the encapsulated world of the jumbo jet, to the uniform boxes of hotels and motels, is not a radical change in sensory experience but merely an amplification of the media jet. It is virtually impossible to exist in contemporary society without developing a dependency on or addiction to media.

Media Distinctions

The intersection of reality and media perception occurs in three major ways. (1) All mediated representations are circumscribed by the defining properties of a specific medium. That means that each medium's treatment of the same event would differ in terms of what would be transmitted and received. Therefore, the televised political convention is not the political gathering that would have been observed within the confines of the arena and is distinct from a newspaper account of the proceedings. (2) We process media information by learning and internalizing a receptive mode for each medium, i.e., we learn and accept the conventions for watching a film, which contrast with the convention and techniques required for reading a newspaper or a book (even in the latter case there are differences; one cannot read a newspaper with the mind set required for a book). The creation of a narrative by an author assumes certain abilities on the part of the consumer, particularly the ability to read. The reconstruction of a film involves a decoding ability which necessitates the transformation of two dimensional images into three dimensional imagined images. (3) The internalization of processing requirements for each medium is absorbed into the cognitive options we have in communication processing. The prevalence of different media with their own depictions require multiple perspectives of reality. Each one of us is capable of looking at a non-mediated situation with a media filter. We are able to experience directly sensed situations as if a medium had been interposed between the event and our perceptions of that event. For example, many of us look at the world as if we were a camera. One indication that this phenomenon actually occurs is the prevalence in our language of media metaphors. A "close-up" experience, a "frame" of reality, "focusing" in on a problem—all suggesting media perspectives that accompany our daily encounters. What is being examined in this section is our media interaction and its influence upon our perceptions of reality.

Note

1. James J. Gibson, *The Senses Considered as Perceptual Systems* (Boston: Houghton Mifflin Co., 1966), pp. 26–27.

GARY GUMPERT

The Ambiguity of Perception

"It's a poor sort of memory that only works backwards."

LEWIS CARROLL
Through The Looking Glass

This article was written for an issue of *Et cetera* devoted to "Media and Culture." In it, Gumpert examines a new, and as yet relatively unexamined, aspect of the electronic media—the widespread use of videotaping. He describes the situation where the majority of everything we see on TV is videotaped. (The same is true for radio shows where audiotaping is widespread and where all "live talk" shows are delayed seven seconds before being transmitted.) This time-freezing process makes it possible to alter, edit, reshoot, etc., while allowing the source to present the material as though it were "live."

Gumpert asks us to consider the psychological ramifications of a situation where we can no longer depend on our senses to perceive what is "live" and what has been "recorded." Consider how we decide when something presented on the electronic media is "live" and what difference that makes in our judgment. What distinguishes listening to a rock group on a recording that has been contrived by putting together dozens of tracks from various taping sessions, and seeing and hearing a "real live" performance? Which do you prefer, "electronic perfection," or face-to-face interaction with all its possible slip-ups and errors?

We depend upon concepts of time and space in order to function in and interpret reality. Here and there, now and then, what was and what will be—all are percepts which guide us through the world. Without these operational frames life would be absolutely chaotic. Fantasy could not be distinguished from reality, tomorrow would be today, and history would never have occurred. We assume that all "normal" individuals operate in a universe essentially agreeing on basic definitions of time and space; for all, there is a yesterday and a tomorrow. But the world is changing and today is repeatable, yesterday can be preserved, and we can be here and there simultaneously. The development of modern media technology is altering the perceptual frames through which individuals operate in their daily lives.

In most circumstances the frame of reality is quite evident. We believe

From *Et cetera*, vol. 34, no. 2 (June 1977). Reprinted by permission of the International Society for General Semantics.

we are aware of where and when we are. The writer is aware of words being typed. Fingers are in contact with typewriter keys in an attempt to convey thoughts through individual signs and symbols. Through auditory, tactile, and visual senses the writer knows and is aware of what is happening "now." "Now" is momentary, fleeting, a transition between past and future, defined by what has happened and what will occur. We are bound to the present because of a belief that it is controllable, that the manipulable "now" determines the undetermined future. The author's "now" is transformed into the reader's "now" as these past thoughts are read.

An awareness of time and space is taken for granted in the process of communication. We know where we are when we communicate. The conventions are not generally articulated. On a simplistic level, if in the course of this essay the author addresses you in the present tense, you play a game with him: you pretend that the author is uttering the words as you are reading them, although you know that this is certainly not the case. This process involves both a physical and psychological dimension, but the awareness of process and convention is central to the manipulation of time and space in communication. As the technology of communications media grows more complex, as we absorb that technology into our lives, we become less aware of process and this signals the potential alteration or perhaps obliteration of time and space conventions. This in turn determines our perception of reality. Two facets of our changing perceptions of reality will be examined in this essay: What is "now," and what is "perfection"?

The Perception of Now

The increasing use of videotape recording provides an intriguing example of technological effect upon psychological process. The President of the United States addresses the American people through the means of a live, televised broadcast. Time has not been altered, while space is bridged by the medium of television. Distance is dissolved through electronic connection. The viewer can be several hundred or several thousand miles away from the White House. The event is concurrent with its perception. The President is speaking at the very moment that individuals are watching and listening to him. The speech exists in time. Ideas through words, tone, and gesture have been developed, are developing, and will develop. Theoretically, no linguistic or environmental possibilities are locked out from potential occurrence. The viewer does not know what will happen as the President speaks to the nation. Indeed, the President himself, while having developed a plan or strategy, can never be totally sure of what will happen during the next few minutes. He might make a mistake, a stranger conceivably might wander in front of the cameras thereby distracting him. An illness might suddenly surface. Perhaps a new idea may suddenly occur which the President might insert into his prepared text. The possibilities are infinite. The tension of unpredictability always hovers over the moment.

This dramatic aspect of viewer-speaker confrontation is quite different when a newsclip portion of the speech is included in the late evening television news coverage. The viewer knows (is conditioned to a convention) that the news includes the coverage of past events.

Because of the existence of videotape recording, the President, for a number of reasons, may decide to prerecord his speech. He can achieve a greater degree of perfection by using tape. The danger of mistakes in an important address can be totally avoided. A nervous mannerism or some faltering in delivery can be eliminated. Whatever the reason, the videotaped speech is substituted for the live broadcast. Is there a difference between watching an unedited recording of the address and a live broadcast of the same event? Most people are not able to distinguish a difference. (The author has not conducted formal research on this question. It is certainly an area that should be carefully examined.) If both events are hypothetically identical, do psychological differences exist between those two situations because one is recorded and one is live?

Let us assume that the viewer at home cannot detect a difference between the live and the taped speech, and that the latter is being transmitted, but *is not identified as a videotaped event.* No problem exists if the viewer does not know of the possibility of videotape recording. Obviously he must assume that the broadcast is live. But if the viewer has an awareness of the possible use of the technology of videotape, psychological differences can become rather important.

An immediate sense of ambiguity is introduced, since an either/or situation exists. Is the speech live or taped? Is it happening now? If it is taped, it is not happening now. If it is taped, where is the President of the United States while he is appearing on television? When was the speech recorded? If the speech is (was) taped, even though the content has not yet been revealed, what will happen has already occurred. The content of the videotape is predetermined. Therefore the relationship between subject and speech is altered by an awareness of technological means. The viewer is no longer a participant in an actual event, since participation is never predetermined. The viewer of the videotaped speech does not participate, but reacts to an orchestrated event.

Participant versus viewer is a contrast of activity versus relative passivity. In that regard, the nature of the medium is relevant. In the case of film projected in a theater, in those days when news was an integral part of the movie theater experience, there was never a confusion in regard to the "nowness" of the depicted event. People knew that they were watching something that had been filmed at a prior time. Film has to be developed, shipped to a location, projected upon a screen via a mechanical device. People are aware of this process. Film is not confused with the reality of liveness. When President Roosevelt appeared on film in the motion picture theater, it was not assumed that he was sitting in the White House at the same time that the viewer was observing him in the theater. The genre of drama is being excluded from this discussion since it involves a special set of conventions based upon an act of self-deception which allows the fictional to assume the cloak of reality. Nevertheless, general technical observations can be made comparing television and film which transcend genre, and the effect of which is intuited on a perceptual level.

> In film, the time continuum is broken down into a series of separate, discrete, frozen nows. Each frame represents an arrested now, *a state of being.* We have an accurate record of this now—as it was. In reality, the film is a selection of *past* moments. *The film is a record of the past.*[1]
>
> In live television, the time continuum is represented by an integrated continuously moving image. The now cannot be pinpointed; it is in a *state of becoming.* While each film frame is a record of the past, the *television frame is a reflection of the living present.*[2]

The nondramatic cinematic event is not confused with the object. The screen is not the event. The screen reflects the event. In television the event exists through the screen. While film involves a separation in time and space (by mere definition of process), television potentially dismisses time and emphasizes space.

In television the live event invites participation because the lack of predestination places a degree of potency in the hands of the individual. If the future is not determined ahead of time, perhaps the individual can hope, wish, charm, or even cast a spell which will affect that which has not yet happened. It is the case of the sports fan *involved* in a tense moment during the baseball game. He yells, perhaps pounds the table, or strokes his lucky charm, in an effort to will circumstances in the favor of his team. He believes that his will can determine the future. Of course, this fantasy represents an impossibility. The cold hand of logic is clear. An individual separated by miles from the contest cannot affect the outcome of the contest, but nevertheless, the rituals are enacted. There is an implicit belief that the participant can determine the future. *We all play the game.* The same belief applies to the situation of the broadcast of a presidential address. To some degree the individual viewer believes in his potential power over the event. The viewer seeks the aura of uncertainty in which he can cast his evil spell, dispense a blessing, or merely hope.

A further example of the effect of videotape upon the nature of viewer experience, related to the example of the presidential address, can be demonstrated through the analysis of the telecasting of a sports event. The spectator at a football game is caught up in the atmosphere surrounding him and probably identifies with one of the teams. It has been the author's experience that even if he is unfamiliar with the teams, he nevertheless quickly identifies with one of them. To some extent, the athletic event is the modern version of a morality play, inviting identification with the "good guys" who hopefully will win over the "forces of evil." On a second level, we have the situation in which the same event is seen live on television. Certainly the force of atmosphere disappears, but the tension of unpredictability remains, along with the "morality" aspect of the contest. Probably the spectator now has a "better seat" through the magnification and editing process of live television. On a third level, we have the same event, but the entire game has been videotaped. If the viewer is unaware of the technology of videotape or actually believes that what he is seeing is live, there is no change in his relationship to the game. The degree of tension has not been defused. On a fourth level, the individual watches a videotaped game, knows that it has been videotaped, but does not know the outcome. Now a subtle change occurs, because of the awareness that the outcome is predetermined, since all the forces in action were resolved and completed at a prior time. The edge of excitement has been blunted. The viewer in this situation is forced to assume the dramatic convention of the "willing suspension of disbelief" in order to recapture the keen excitement of the game: "I'll pretend that it hasn't happened yet." (This author has even gone to the trouble of hiding the newspaper and avoiding any newscasts so that he would be unaware of the outcome in order to preserve the suspense of "not knowing.") On the last level, the viewer is involved with a videotape of a game which has already occurred, and he is aware of the outcome. At this point, the total relationship of the individual to the game changes radically. The excitement of conflict, of the unpredictable morality play, vanishes and gives way to an analytical mode of viewing. It is not who won or lost the game that matters so much; *how* the game was won or lost is of primary importance. The morality play has given way to a display of skill. Clearly, it is the presence of videotape that has affected the psychological relationship between viewer and event.

In the case of the President addressing the nation, the frame of reality, or the degree of "nowness," is clear when the videotape process is identified. When it is unidentified and a realization of process (an awareness of the technology) is present, a state of dissonance is introduced. Note that a non-videotaped program must also be identified, since the potential presence of videotape suggests that *all* programs may be videotaped. In short, if viewers are aware of the existence of videotape technology and its uses in television, but are *not* clearly informed about which broadcasts are taped and which are not, they must always experience some ambiguity about the time frame in which the events they are seeing actually occur.

Because a state of ambiguity is generated by the introduction into television of the videotaping process, an atmosphere of cynicism and doubt surrounds viewer responses to televised events. Perhaps the President does not really exist. The videotape could have been produced several months or several years ago. The giant conspiracy syndrome can make sense, if time and process are not labeled accurately. If videotapes are not identified or authenticated for date, the conclusion can be reached that *all* programs are completed and taped before transmission. Since the seeds of scepticism have been planted . . . When *did* the President actually make the speech? Hours, days, or weeks ago? If he isn't talking to us now, where is he? Could he be ill? Perhaps the country is run by a group of powerful individuals who control a file of prepared videotaped Presidential addresses. How many people have seen the President, without benefit of television, within the past year? How many persons have ever seen him at all? Perhaps . . .

But back to reality and a very real example of the problem. It is assumed that television newscasts are live broadcasts with filmed and videotaped news inserts. Authenticity is a basic value inherent in the transmission of the newscast. The concept of the newscast suggests that the format is flexible enough to allow for the inclusion of late developments which occur during the course of the broadcast. The latest news will be presented to the public. Indeed, the "on the spot reporter" capability distinguishes the electronic news services from newspapers and periodicals, which can cover events in greater depth and perspective. Several years ago the formats and presentational style of television newscasts were altered in order to present to the public an atmosphere of a *real* working newsroom. The trend has been away from a formalized, artificial, presentational style. Often, in the background, one can see busy editors in their shirtsleeves while the news is being presented. It is therefore surprising to discover that the CBS television newscast is taped at 6:30 p.m. (Eastern Standard Time) and, while it is broadcast live to a limited number of stations on the East coast, most of the East coast receives the broadcast at 7:00 p.m. via tape. The rest of the nation receives a taped version later, depending upon the time zone involved. If late items do develop, the video tape is interrupted with a live insert. It is possible, of course, to broadcast live if necessitated by a major late-breaking news event. To some extent, the aura of "immediacy" which pervades the newscast is a facade which is manufactured for authenticity.

The relationship of the videotaping process to our perception of reality has been discussed so far in rather absolute terms, but there are additional factors which complicate the issue. Let us examine a relatively simple interview between two people which has been videotaped. A number of assumptions are made by the viewer about such a situation: the tape which is broadcast is a faithful copy of the original event; that event was an ongoing interaction between two people which began at one point in time and ended at a later point in time. These assumptions are quite tenuous, since videotape editing can alter and rearrange events. The question is not whether programs should be recorded, but rather, to what extent should tape be *edited* when a program is recorded? At the root of the problem is the audience's perception of the event before editing and the degree of manipulation involved as editing is introduced. Any edited event has an idealized basis existing in the world of real time and space. Even the simple concept of a close-up assumes an understanding that the head has not been severed from the body and in "real" time and space a totally connected individual exists safe and sound.

The purist's position would be to object to any editing of videotape. That is not the position being taken here. Editing can be a useful and creative tool. When is it objectionable? To answer that question, let us return to that hypothetical interview. Scene one takes place in the garden. The interviewee is wearing a yellow dress. The interviewer says, "Let's go into the house now." Scene two is juxtaposed to the previous one, and the interviewee is now wearing a brown dress. The edit is obvious. There was no time (on the tape) for the pair to walk into the house. It is taken for granted that cameras and recorders stopped to allow for a change in location and dress. The viewer does not object, because the convention is understood and the viewer was not deceived. Now the circumstances are altered slightly. Instead of recording the interview for the purpose of broadcast, the producer has recorded it for the purpose of editing for broadcast. Instead of recording the amount required for the broadcast, he has recorded double that amount, with the understanding that the material will be reduced by half through editing. A sentence or two is eliminated. Several large sections are rather dull and are dropped. Comments made late in the interview are shifted to the beginning. Eventually the interview will be broadcast, but it has assumed the character of a pseudo-event (fabricated, manufactured, rearranged for presentation), although it is presented as if the interaction now being witnessed has actually once existed in real time. The audience is not supposed to know about the procedures utilized to create the event. For lack of a more descriptive phrase, this type of manipulation of the perception of reality can be called "hidden tampering." The product is objectionable, because it has no relationship to what it pretends to be—a real interview. It is a created situation delivered as an authentic event.

It seems puzzling that most people are not concerned with the matter of accurate labeling in the case of television recording. Perhaps the reasoning runs this way: "What does it matter? So what if the videotape is substituted for the live broadcast? The content has not changed! The speaker intended to communicate a specific series of points to the public and has used the latest technology in order to assure himself that the message is conveyed as he intended." Or, "What does it matter if sections were shifted around or perhaps eliminated? I'm only going to judge what I see on the tube." How does one reply to such hypothetical reactions? The matter goes beyond that of content; it involves authenticity of experience with content. We discern a difference between a roaring fire and a photograph of a roaring fire. If these differences were not apparent, potential calamity would await the individual so confused. But even minor or insignificant confusion of authenticity should be important. There is a need to be able to tell the difference between real and artificial, between a creation of nature and an artifact of man, between fantasy and reality, between what was, what is, and what will be. Just as we are impelled to classify and label objects in our environment in order to achieve structure and order, we should be driven to authenticate mediated events in time and space. The lack of apparent concern with this specific question suggests the degree to which our sensory awareness or acuity has been narcotized, the degree to which we have abdicated sensory responsibility. Sensory responsibility requires a degree of accuracy in recognizing the nature and magnitude of sensory impression.

There is also an ethical dimension to the problem. Does the producer of a nondramatic, unedited videotape substituted for a live broadcast have a responsibility for identifying that act? Should deceptive types of editing be identified? The answer to both questions is, Yes! Anything short of that action is manipulation. Duplicity is discernable, manipulation is not. Individuals have the ability to discern truth and falsehood. However, there is no way to distinguish an unedited videotape from a live broadcast—if minimal technical standards are maintained. If the individual cannot discern "then" from "now" or the "real" from the "specious," manipulation is a distinct possibility. It seems quite clear that the individual has the right not to be deceived, that he or she should have the tool to avoid manipulation—the proper labeling of a videotaped production.

The Perception of Perfection

Human beings have always had the desire to record and to preserve events. It is a long way from prehistoric cave paintings to electronic and filmic recording, although the motivation for such acts is probably quite similar. In the previous section of this essay we explored the confusion which can result when time and space distinctions are altered through the nonlabeling of recordings. The issue to be examined now is how the presence of recordings has altered, or can alter, our perception of a live event.

One source of the appeal of a live event is its fallibility. Something can go wrong. A mistake or error always lurks in the wings of the performance. Indeed, the extraordinary performance rests on a precarious tightrope where a slight error in judgment results in failure. The abysmal performer does not take a chance; neither does the dull, prosaic display of talent ever approach the daring of the extraordinary. One index of a great performance is the degree to which the ordinary, the mundane, is transcended. Greatness is the transcendence of failure.

Why are we so fascinated by the tightrope act, the lion tamer, or the flying trapeze artists? Is it the beauty and grace of movement? Perhaps, but it seems that, in addition, the danger involved in each of these acts is a predominating attraction for the spectator. A strange contradiction in emotion is inherent in the appreciation of an act surrounded by risk or danger. We require that the potential for calamity be present, to a frightening, imaginary degree, although the fruition of that calamity is not desired—or is it? The threat cannot merely remain a threat. The frightful moment must occur to someone in order to underscore the fact that "the daring young man on the flying trapeze" is truly "daring." The potentiality for tragedy, for disaster, for failure, underscores and defines success. This observation is not limited to spectacular performances which involve physical danger. The principle applies to all arts. The rendering of one composition is exceptional, the other merely adequate. Why? The audience sits quietly bored at one performance and is electrified at the next. "There's magic in the air!" An actor knows when a fellow thespian goes beyond the normal enactment of a role and wanders into the shadowy domain where greatness and failure are almost fraternal.

But the technology of recording has altered the relationship between spectator and event. The audience has been so indoctrinated in the cult of perfectability that the concept of the "perfect" has become almost meaningless. The nature of the altered relationship between spectator and event can be demonstrated by examining any number of areas in the performing arts. In this case, the focus will be on music.

Certainly, the technology of recording has affected both the audience and artists of music. The late piano virtuoso Artur Schnabel articulated his concern in regard to recordings:

> In 1929 I was asked once again whether I would not agree to make records. Until then I had consistently refused to do so. One of the chief reasons for my refusal was that I did not like the idea of having no control over the behavior of the people who listen to music which I performed—not knowing how they

would be dressed, what else they would be doing at the same time, how much they would listen. Also I felt that recordings are against the very nature of performance, for the nature of performance is to happen but once, to be absolutely ephemeral and unrepeatable. I do not think there could ever have been two performances of the same piece by the same person which were absolutely alike. That is inconceivable.[3]

It is fortunate that Schnabel agreed to record, because a record of his artistry has been preserved for today's listeners. At the same time, his hesitancy can be respected and his premise that the same artist could not duplicate two identical performances is significant because replication is the major motive for purchasing a record. The record performance never changes until the disc is worn out, at which point it is repurchased. Today the medium of music is the recording. "Where music was once propagated locally by the individual, it is now propagated generally by the phonograph record, the radio and the motion picture sound track. . . ."[4] Today, the greatest proportion of musical contact is not with the performer, but with sound.

The art of audio technology has progressed to a point where a performance is no longer merely recorded. A recording can be produced with the aid of twelve or sixteen separate tracks and a host of electronic effects. The results are often highly inventive and brilliant. But in what way has this development altered our perception of musical perfection? Before its impact can be appreciated, some distinction should be made between types of recordings in relation to performance.

1. A *"live" recording* is the record of a performance. It is essentially unedited and can be considered a faithful facsimile of a prior event.

2. The *"live augmented" recording* uses studio facilities to enhance a basically live performance. The artist or producer seeks the best possible recording, in terms of quality of performance and audio fidelity. This is achieved through the use of multiple tracks, countless takes, and electronic enhancement, but the purpose is to refine the original rendering of the artist. This type of recording can, through the aid of electronic technology, provide the perfectability which is the goal of any artist. It should be pointed out that it is possible, and it is a frequent occurrence, to achieve a perfect recording of an artistically inferior performance, and generally critics will evaluate recording and performance separately.

3. The *"studio" recording* is not restricted by what might or might not happen in a live performance, but uses audio technology as an additional musical instrument. The result is a performance *not possible* under normal live conditions. The technology is integral to the ultimate recording. This category of recording does not pretend to be anything other than what it is—a studio-produced work of art. The source of the problem is in the

confusion which arises between the "live" recording and the "live augmented" recording.

Formerly, the live concert was the stimulus for record sales. "That was great. Has it been recorded? Let's buy it." The live concert was the criterion upon which a recording was judged. "It's almost as if I were there. I can remember the moment." Today, the live concert is judged by the standard of the recording, which may provide the motivation to attend the concert. "The record was fantastic. Let's go see him in person." This is a reversal in motivation, and the problem arises when the audience is disappointed by the performance. The audience is unhappy because the performer has not lived up to the virtuosity displayed on the recording. In all probability the recording has been artificially enhanced, and the audience, unaware of the fact (confusion of recording categories one and two), evaluates the live performance (nonrecorded) against standards that truly reside only in the realm of the ideal. Note that there is probably little confusion between the "studio" recording the "live" recording.

If a performer is talented, and on a given day plays with talent, and is inspired by the gods, he or she might almost reach the level of performance which is achieved every day in the recording studio—a level of performance which need not tolerate mistakes. There is no room for a mistake in a world when perfection can be manufactured—why should there be? If that note slightly off pitch can be fixed, why allow it into the home, where it reflects upon both artist and producer? The struggle of an artist to enter the realm of perfectability is awesome compared to the ease with which the studio technician can change, substitute, alter, or manufacture notes, passages, and sections. Yet the two processes compete for critical and commercial acceptance. Obviously, a recording studio can take a performance and perfect it, as long as the artist provides a basic level of competence in the rendering of the composition. But a great live performance cannot be manufactured; furthermore, it requires a milieu in which the nonperfect and potential failure exist side by side. An audience accustomed to the perfect has no patience for the fallible performer who walks an artistic tightrope—not when the perfect is so easily obtained by turning on the stereo. The perfect is accessible and repeatable. The struggle for perfection and its relationship to the human spirit is submerged and lost.

There is another dimension to the cult of perfectability, and that is centered in the nature of the experience and its environment. Greater and greater stress has been placed on the quality of musical sound. The automobile, that home away from home, is equipped with stereophonic tape decks. Sound in the home itself has progressed from high fidelity to stereophonic and to quadrophonic sound. The room has "living presence." The wired room is not a substitute for attending the concert; rather, electronics have transformed the living room into the concert hall—even though the room is comparatively miniscule when compared to the hall. The dimensions of the environment become even less important with the addition of earphones which allow for unadulterated, ear-to-ear sound. Now the concert hall is in your head. If the concert is literally shifted into the living room, is the aesthetic ambience of the concert hall also moved into the environment of the home? The two experiences are quite dissimilar, although the lines which distinguish between them have become increasingly blurred. Paradoxically, as multichannel sound streams into modern, boxlike living rooms, the live concert hall experience becomes increasingly more alien. The stress is placed on perfecting the auditory sense, to the degree that the total sensory involvement found in the live situation is absent. Lost is the dynamic involvement of individual and performer in which the auditory, visual, and tactile senses all play an important role. Parenthetically, living room habits have invaded many public events such as concerts and films, as extraneous conversations increasingly compete for attention.

Undoubtedly audio technology has altered our standards of excellence because of the ambiguity involved in the perception of medicated events. Concert hall is confused with living room. Mechanical and electronic perfection are jumbled with artistic quality. Part of the problem could be solved by identifying recordings which are "electronically enhanced." The solution of greater import is the education of the public to distinguish between modes of performance and the performance itself. In addition, it is necessary to articulate criteria in judging each form.

The perception of reality is increasingly dependent upon media technology, but our vision of the world, while increased in scope, is also distorted by the very media which serve us. *The perception of now* indicates that mediation can deemphasize authenticity while stressing availability of experience. *The perception of perfection* reveals how the struggle for purity of expression has been placed in the background as multiplicity of the unflawed is accentuated. The impact of media might be self-evident, but the effects upon our perception of reality are hidden behind the seductive rewards of media technology. Are the issues discussed in this essay important ones which require discussion and resolution, or is the *ambiguity of perception* merely an exercise in philosophical inquiry? The very fact that this question is asked in proxy for the reader suggests the degree to which the problems discussed have been lost in the exhilaration of technological progress.

"Portions of this program
were pre-recorded."
Which portions?

Notes

1. Herbert Zettl, *Sight, Sound, Motion: Applied Media Aesthetics* (Belmont, California: Wadsworth Publishing Company, 1973), p. 254.
2. *Ibid.*, p. 255.
3. Artur Schnabel, *My Life and Music* (New York: St. Martin's Press, 1961), p. 96.
4. Henry Pleasants, *Serious Music—And All That Jazz!* (New York: Simon and Schuster, 1969), p. 91.

EDMUND CARPENTER

The New Languages

Brain of the New World,
What a task is thine,
To formulate the modern
. . . to recast poems, churches, art
WHITMAN

Anthropologist Edmund Carpenter takes issue with those who hold that one medium, such as the printed word, is more accurate or factual than another. It is his position that each medium has its own language and bias; therefore ideas or events are best communicated through the medium which has the most appropriate "language" or "bias" for that idea or event. The important concept is that "each medium, if its bias is properly exploited, reveals and communicates a unique aspect of reality, of truth."

When reading in Carpenter you may have to withhold your usual notions about language—that is, if you think of language mainly as the words, sentences and grammatical rules that you were taught in connection with learning to read and write. Think of language as the camera lens, the close-up, the montage, the split screen, the quick cut, the voice-over, sounds unconnected with objects. How does the medium put things together? What about the spaces and time units that are part of its grammar? if you begin to think of language in this way you will understand what Carpenter means by the "new" languages.

English is a mass medium. All languages are mass media. The new mass media—film, radio, TV—are new languages, their grammars as yet unknown. Each codifies reality differently; each conceals a unique metaphysics. Linguists tell us it's possible to say anything in any language if you use enough words or images, but there's rarely time; the natural course is for a culture to exploit its media biases.

Writing, for example, didn't record oral language; it was a new language, which the spoken word came to imitate. Writing encouraged an analytical mode of thinking with emphasis upon lineality. Oral languages tended to be polysynthetic, composed of great, tight conglomerates, like twisted knots, within which images were juxtaposed, inseparably fused; written communications consisted of little words chronologically ordered.

From *Explorations in Communication,* edited by Edmund Carpenter and Marshall McLuhan. Copyright © by Beacon Press. Reprinted by permission of Beacon Press and Jonathan Cape Ltd.

Subject became distinct from verb, adjective from noun, thus separating actor from action, essence from form. Where preliterate man imposed form diffidently, temporarily—for such transitory forms lived but temporarily on the tip of his tongue, in the living situation—the printed word was inflexible, permanent in touch with eternity: it embalmed truth for posterity.

This embalming process froze language, eliminated the art of ambiguity, made puns "the lowest form of wit," destroyed word linkages. The word became a static symbol, applicable to and separate from that which it symbolized. It now belonged to the objective world; it could be seen. Now came the distinction between being and meaning, the dispute as to whether the Eucharist *was* or only *signified* the body of the Sacrifice. The word became a neutral symbol, no longer an inextricable part of a creative process.

Gutenberg completed the process. The manuscript page with pictures, colors, correlation between symbol and space, gave way to uniform type, the black and white page, read silently, alone. The format of the book favored lineal expression, for the argument ran like a thread from cover to cover, subject to verb to object, sentence to sentence, paragraph to paragraph, chapter to chapter, carefully structured from beginning to end, with value embedded in the climax. This was not true of great poetry and drama, which retained multi-perspective, but it was true of most books, particularly texts, histories, autobiographies, novels. Events were arranged chronologically and hence, it was assumed, causally; relationship, not being, was valued. The author became an *authority;* his data were serious, that is, *serially* organized. Such data, if sequentially ordered and printed, conveyed value and truth; arranged any other way, they were suspect.

The newspaper format brought an end to book culture. It offers short, discrete articles that give important facts first and than taper off to incidental details, which may be, and often are, eliminated by the make-up man. The fact that reporters cannot control the length of their articles means that, in writing them, emphasis can't be placed on structure, at least in the traditional linear sense, with climax or conclusion at the end. Everything has to be captured in the headline; from there it goes down the pyramid to incidentals. In fact there is often more in the headline than in the article; occasionally, no article at all accompanies the banner headline.

The position and size of articles on the front page are determined by interest and importance, not content. Unrelated reports from Moscow, Sarawak, London, and Ittipik are juxtaposed; time and space, as separate concepts, are destroyed and the *here* and *now* presented as a single Gestalt. Subway readers consume everything on the front page, then turn to page 2 to read, in incidental order, continuations. A Toronto banner headline ran: TOWNSEND TO MARRY PRINCESS; directly beneath this was a second headline:

Fabian Says This May Not Be Sex Crime. This went unnoticed by eyes and minds conditioned to consider each newspaper item in isolation.

Such a format lends itself to simultaneity, not chronology or lineality. Items abstracted from a total situation aren't arranged in casual sequence, but presented holistically, as raw experience. The front page is a cosmic *Finnegans Wake.*

The disorder of the newspaper throws the reader into a producer role. The reader has to process the news himself; he has to co-create, to cooperate in the creation of the work. The newspaper format calls for the direct participation of the consumer.

In magazines, where a writer more frequently controls the length of his article, he can, if he wishes, organize it in traditional style, but the majority don't. An increasingly popular presentation is the printed symposium, which is little more than collected opinions, pro and con. The magazine format as a whole opposes lineality; its pictures lack tenses. In *Life*, extremes are juxtaposed: space ships and prehistoric monsters, Flemish monasteries and dope addicts. It creates a sense of urgency and uncertainty: the next page is unpredictable. One encounters rapidly a riot in Teheran, a Hollywood marriage, the wonders of the Eisenhower administration, a two-headed calf, a party on Jones beach, all sandwiched between ads. The eye takes in the page as a whole (readers may pretend this isn't so, but the success of advertising suggests it is), and the page—indeed, the whole magazine—becomes a single Gestalt where association, though not causal, is often lifelike.

The same is true of the other new languages. Both radio and TV offer short, unrelated programs, interrupted between and within by commercials. I say "interrupted," being myself an anachronism of book culture, but my children don't regard them as interruptions, as breaking continuity. Rather, they regard them as part of a whole, and their reaction is neither one of annoyance nor one of indifference. The ideal news broadcast has half a dozen speakers from as many parts of the world on as many subjects. The London correspondent doesn't comment on what the Washington correspondent has just said; he hasn't even heard him.

The child is right in not regarding commercials as interruptions. For the only time anyone smiles on TV is in commercials. The rest of life, in news broadcasts and soap operas, is presented as so horrible that the only way to get through life is to buy this product: then you'll smile. Aesop never wrote a clearer fable. It's heaven and hell brought up to date: Hell in the headline, Heaven in the ad. Without the other, neither has meaning.

There's pattern in these new media—not line, but knot; not lineality or causality or chronology, nothing that leads to a desired climax; but a Gordian knot without antecedents or results, containing within itself carefully selected elements, juxtaposed, inseparably fused; a knot that can't be untied to give the long, thin cord of lineality.

This is especially true of ads that never present an ordered, sequential, rational argument but simply present the product associated with desirable things or attitudes. Thus Coca-Cola is shown held by a beautiful blonde, who sits in a Cadillac, surrounded by bronze, muscular admirers, with the sun shining overhead. By repetition these elements become associated, in our minds, into a pattern of sufficient cohesion so that one element can magically evoke the others. If we think of ads as designed solely to sell products, we miss their main effect: to increase pleasure in the consumption of the product. Coca-Cola is far more than a cooling drink; the consumer participates, vicariously, in a much larger experience. In Africa, in Melanesia, to drink a Coke is to participate in the American way of life.

Of the new languages, TV comes closest to drama and ritual. It combines music and art, language and gesture, rhetoric and color. It favors simultaneity of visual and auditory images. Cameras focus not on speakers but on persons spoken to or about; the audience *hears* the accuser but *watches* the accused. In a single impression it hears the prosecutor, watches the trembling hands of the big-town crook, and sees the look of moral indignation on Senator Tobey's face. This is real drama, in process, with the outcome uncertain. Print can't do this; it has a different bias.

Books and movies only pretend uncertainty, but live TV retains this vital aspect of life. Seen on TV, the fire in the 1952 Democratic Convention threatened briefly to become a conflagration; seen on newsreel, it was history, without potentiality.

The absence of uncertainty is no handicap to other media, if they are properly used, for their biases are different. Thus it's clear from the beginning that Hamlet is a doomed man, but, far from detracting in interest, this heightens the sense of tragedy.

Now, one of the results of the time-space duality that developed in Western culture, principally from the Renaissance on, was a separation within the arts. Music, which created symbols in time, and graphic art, which created symbols in space, became separate pursuits, and men gifted in one rarely pursued the other. Dance and ritual, which inherently combined them, fell in popularity. Only in drama did they remain united.

It is significant that of the four new media, the three most recent are dramatic media, particularly TV, which combines language, music, art, dance. They don't, however, exercise the same freedom with time that the stage dares practice. An intricate plot, employing flash backs, multiple time perspectives and overlays, intelligible on the stage, would mystify on the screen. The audience has no time to think back, to establish relations between early hints and subsequent discoveries. The picture passes before the eyes too quickly; there are no intervals in which to take stock of what has happened and make conjectures of what is going to happen. The observer is in a more passive state, less interested in subtleties. Both TV and film are nearer to narrative and depend much more upon the episodic. An intricate time construction can be done in film, but in fact rarely is. The soliloquies of *Richard III* belong on the stage; the film audience was unprepared for them. On stage Ophelia's death was described by three separate groups: one hears the announcement and watches the reactions simultaneously. On film the camera flatly shows her drowned where "a willow lies aslant a brook."

Media differences such as these mean that it's not simply a question of communicating a single idea in different ways but that a given idea or insight belongs primarily, though not exclusively, to one medium, and can be gained or communicated best through that medium.

Thus the book was ideally suited for discussing evolution and progress. Both belonged, almost exclusively, to book culture. Like a book, the idea of progress was an abstracting, organizing principle for the interpretation and comprehension of the incredibly complicated record of human experience. The sequence of events was believed to have a direction, to follow a given course along an axis of time; it was held that civilization, like the reader's eye (in J. B. Bury's words), "has moved, is moving, and will move in a desirable direction. Knowledge will advance, and with that advance, reason and decency must increasingly prevail among men." Here we see the three main elements of book lineality: the line, the point moving along that line, and its movement toward a desirable goal.

The Western conception of a definite moment in the present, of the present as a definite moment or a definite point, so important in book-dominated languages, is absent, to my knowledge, in oral languages. Absent as well, in oral societies, are such animating and controlling ideas as Western individualism and three-dimensional perspective, both related to this conception of the definite moment, and both nourished, probably bred, by book culture.

Each medium selects its ideas. TV is a tiny box into which people are crowded and must live; film gives us the wide world. With its huge screen, film is perfectly suited for social drama, Civil War panoramas, the sea, land erosion, Cecil B. DeMille spectaculars. In contrast, the TV screen has room for two, at the most three, faces, comfortably. TV is closer to stage, yet different. Paddy Chayefsky writes:

> The theatre audience is far away from the actual action of the drama. They cannot see the silent reactions of the players. They must be told in a loud voice what is going on. The plot movement from one scene to another must be marked, rather than gently shaded as is required in television. In television,

however, you can dig into the most humble, ordinary relationships; the relationship of bourgeois children to their mother, of middle-class husband to his wife, of white-collar father to his secretary—in short, the relationships of the people. We relate to each other in an incredibly complicated manner. There is far more exciting drama in the reasons why a man gets married than in why he murders someone. The man who is unhappy in his job, the wife who thinks of a lover, the girl who wants to get into television, your father, your mother, sister, brothers, cousins, friends—all these are better subjects for drama than Iago. What makes a man ambitious? Why does a girl always try to steal her kid sister's boy friends? Why does your uncle attend his annual class reunion faithfully every year? Why do you always find it depressing to visit your father? These are the substances of good television drama; and the deeper you probe into and examine the twisted, semi-formed complexes of emotional entanglements, the more exciting your writing becomes.[1]

This is the primary reason, I believe, why Greek drama is more readily adapted to TV than to film. The boxed-in quality of live TV lends itself to static literary tragedy with greater ease than does the elastic, energetic, expandable movie. Guthrie's recent movie of *Oedipus* favored the panoramic shot rather than the selective eye. It consisted of a succession of tableaux, a series of elaborate, unnatural poses. The effect was of congested groups of people moving in tight formation as though they had trained for it by living for days together in a self-service elevator. With the lines, "I grieve for the City, and for myself and you . . . and walk through endless ways of thought," the inexorable tragedy moved to its horrible "come to realize" climax as though everyone were stepping on everyone else's feet.

The tight, necessary conventions of live TV were more sympathetic to Sophocles in the Aluminium Hour's *Antigone*. Restrictions of space are imposed on TV as on the Greek stage by the size and inflexibility of the studio. Squeezed by physical limitations, the producer was forced to expand the viewer's imagination with ingenious devices.

When T. S. Eliot adapted *Murder in the Cathedral* for film, he noted a difference in realism between cinema and stage:

> Cinema, even where fantasy is introduced, is much more realistic than the stage. Especially in an historical picture, the setting, the costume, and the way of life represented have to be accurate. Even a minor anachronism is intolerable. On the stage much more can be overlooked or forgiven; and indeed, an excessive care for accuracy of historical detail can become burdensome and distracting. In watching a stage performance, the member of the audience is in direct contact with the actor playing a part. In looking at a film, we are much more passive; as audience, we contribute less. We are seized with the illusion that we are observing an actual event, or at least a series of photographs of the actual event; and nothing must be allowed to break this illusion. Hence the precise attention to detail.[2]

If two men are on a stage in a theater, the dramatist is obliged to motivate their presence; he has to account for their existing on the stage at all.

Whereas if a camera is following a figure down a street or is turned to any object whatever, there is no need for a reason to be provided. Its grammar contains that power of statement of motivation, no matter what it looks at.

In the theater, the spectator sees the enacted scene as a whole in space, always seeing the whole of the space. The stage may present only one corner of a large hall, but that corner is always totally visible all through the scene. And the spectator always sees that scene from a fixed, unchanging distance and from an angle of vision that doesn't change. Perspective may change from scene to scene, but within it remains constant. Distance never varies.

But in film and TV, distance and angle constantly shift. The same scene is shown in multiple perspective and focus. The viewer sees it from here, there, then over here; finally he is drawn inexorably into it, becomes part of it. He ceases to be a spectator. Balázs writes:

> Although we sit in our seats, we do not see Romeo and Juliet from there. We look up into Juliet's balcony with Romeo's eyes and look down on Romeo with Juliet's. Our eye and with it our consciousness is identified with the characters in the film, we look at the world out of their eyes and have no angle of vision of our own. We walk amid crowds, ride, fly or fall with the hero and if one character looks into the other's eyes, he looks into our eyes from the screen, for, our eyes are in the camera and become identical with the gaze of the characters. They see with our eyes. Herein lies the psychological act of identification. Nothing like this "identification" has ever occurred as the effect of any other system of art and it is here that the film manifests its absolute artistic novelty.
>
> . . . Not only can we see, in the isolated "shots" of a scene, the very atoms of life and their innermost secrets revealed at close quarters, but we can do so without any of the intimate secrecy being lost, as always happens in the exposure of a stage performance or of a painting. The new theme which the new means of expression of film art revealed was not a hurricane at sea or the eruption of a volcano: it was perhaps a solitary tear slowly welling up in the corner of a human eye.
>
> . . . Not to speak does not mean that one has nothing to say. Those who do not speak may be brimming over with emotions which can be expressed only in forms and pictures, in gesture and play of feature. The man of visual culture uses these not as substitutes for words, as a deaf-mute uses his fingers.[3]

The gestures of visual man are not intended to convey concepts that can be expressed in words, but inner experiences, nonrational emotions, which would still remain unexpressed when everything that can be told has been told. Such emotions lie in the deepest levels. They cannot be approached by words that are mere reflections of concepts, any more than musical experiences can be expressed in rational concepts. Facial expression is a human experience rendered immediately visible without the intermediary of word. It is Turgenev's "living truth of the human face."

Printing rendered illegible the faces of men. So much could be read from paper that the method of conveying meaning by facial expression fell into desuetude. The press grew to be the main bridge over which the more remote interhuman spiritual exhanges took place; the immediate, the personal, the inner, died. There was no longer need for the subtler means of expression provided by the body. The face became immobile; the inner life, still. Wells that dry up are wells from which no water is dipped.

Just as radio helped bring back inflection in speech, so film and TV are aiding us in the recovery of gesture and facial awareness—a rich, colorful language, conveying moods and emotions, happenings and characters, even thoughts, none of which could be properly packaged in words. If film had remained silent for another decade, how much faster this change might have been!

Feeding the product of one medium through another medium creates a new product. When Hollywood buys a novel, it buys a title and the publicity associated with it: nothing more. Nor should it.

Each of the four versions of the *Caine Mutiny*—book, play, movie, TV—had a different hero: Willie Keith, the lawyer Greenwald, the United States Navy, and Captain Queeg, respectively. Media and audience biases were clear. Thus the book told, in lengthy detail, of the growth and making of Ensign William Keith, American man, while the movie camera with its colorful shots of ships and sea, unconsciously favored the Navy as hero, a bias supported by the fact the Navy cooperated with the movie makers. Because of stage limitations, the play was confined, except for the last scene, to the courtroom, and favored the defense counsel as hero. The TV show, aimed at a mass audience, emphasized patriotism, authority, allegiance. More important, the cast was reduced to the principals and the plot to its principles; the real moral problem—the refusal of subordinates to assist an incompetent, unpopular superior—was clear, whereas in the book it was lost under detail, in the film under scenery. Finally, the New York play, with its audience slanted toward Expense Account patronage— Mr. Sampson, Western Sales Manager for the Cavity Drill Company— became a morality play with Willie Keith, innocent American youth, torn between two influences: Keefer, clever author but moral cripple, and Greenwald, equally brilliant but reliable, a businessman's intellectual. Greenwald saves Willie's soul.

The film *Moby Dick* was in many ways an improvement on the book, primarily because of its explicitness. For *Moby Dick* is one of those admittedly great classics, like *Robinson Crusoe* or Kafka's *Trial,* whose plot and situation, as distilled apart from the book by time and familiarity, are actually much more imposing than the written book itself. It's the drama of Ahab's defiance rather than Melville's uncharted leviathan meanderings that is the greatness of *Moby Dick*. On film, instead of laborious tacks through leagues of discursive interruptions, the most vivid descriptions of whales and whaling become part of the action. On film, the viewer was constantly aboard ship: each scene an instantaneous shot of whaling life, an effect achieved in the book only by illusion, by constant, detailed reference. From start to finish, all the action of the film served to develop what was most central to the theme—a man's magnificent and blasphemous pride in attempting to destroy the brutal, unreasoning force that maims him and turns man-made order into chaos. Unlike the book, the film gave a spare, hard, compelling dramatization, free of self-conscious symbolism.

Current confusion over the respective roles of the new media comes largely from a misconception of their function. They are art forms, not substitutes for human contact. Insofar as they attempt to usurp speech and personal, living relations, they harm. This, of course, has long been one of the problems of book culture, at least during the time of its monopoly of Western middle-class thought. But this was never a legitimate function of books, nor of any other medium. Whenever a medium goes claim jumping, trying to work areas where it is ill-suited, conflicts occur with other media, or, more accurately, between the vested interests controlling each. But, when media simply exploit their own formats, they become complementary and cross-fertile.

Some people who have no one around talk to cats, and you can hear their voices in the next room, and they sound silly, because the cat won't answer, but that suffices to maintain the illusion that their world is made up of living people, while it is not. Mechanized mass media reverse this: now mechanical cats talk to humans. There is no genuine feedback.

This charge is often leveled by academicians at the new media, but it holds equally for print. The open-mouthed, glaze-eyed TV spectator is merely the successor of the passive, silent, lonely reader whose head moved back and forth like a shuttlecock.

When we read, another person thinks for us: we merely repeat his mental process. The greater part of the work of thought is done for us. This is why it relieves us to take up a book after being occupied by our own thoughts. In reading, the mind is only the playground for another's ideas. People who spend most of their lives in reading often lose the capacity for thinking, just as those who always ride forget how to walk. Some people read themselves stupid. Chaplin did a wonderful take-off of this in *City Lights,* when he stood up on a chair to eat the endless confetti that he mistook for spaghetti.

Eliot remarks: "It is often those writers whom we are lucky enough to know whose books we can ignore; and the better we know them personally, the less need we may feel to read what they write."

Frank O'Connor highlights a basic distinction between oral and written traditions: " 'By the hokies, there was a man in this place one time by name of Ned Sullivan, and he had a queer thing happen to him late one night and he coming up the Valley Road from Durlas.' This is how a folk story begins, or should begin. . . . Yet that is how no printed short story should begin, because such a story seems tame when you remove it from its warm nest by the cottage fire, from the sense of an audience with its interjections, and the feeling of terror at what may lurk in the darkness outside."

Face-to-face discourse is not as selective, abstract, nor explicit as any mechanical medium; it probably comes closer to communicating an unabridged situation than any of them, and, insofar as it exploits the give-take of dynamic relationship, it's clearly the most indispensably human one.

Of course, there can be personal involvement in the other media. When Richardson's *Pamela* was serialized in 1741, it aroused such interest that in one English town, upon receipt of the last installment, the church bell announced that virtue had been rewarded. Radio stations have reported receiving quantities of baby clothes and bassinets when, in a soap opera, a heroine had a baby. One of the commonest phrases used by devoted listeners to daytime serials is that they "visited with" Aunt Jenny or Big Sister. BBC and *News Chronicle* report cases of women viewers who kneel before TV sets to kiss male announcers good night.

Each medium, if its bias is properly exploited, reveals and communicates a unique aspect of reality, of truth. Each offers a different perspective, a way of seeing an otherwise hidden dimension of reality. It's not a question of one reality being true, the others distortions. One allows us to see from here, another from there, a third from still another perspective; taken together they give us a more complete whole, a greater truth. New essentials are brought to the fore, including those made invisible by the "blinders" of old languages.

This is why the preservation of book culture is as important as the development of TV. This is why new languages, instead of destroying old ones, serve as a stimulant to them. Only monopoly is destroyed. When actor-collector Edward G. Robinson was battling actor-collector Vincent Price on art on TV's *$64,000 Challenge,* he was asked how the quiz had affected his life; he answered petulantly, "Instead of looking at the pictures in my art books, I now have to read them." Print, along with all old languages, including speech, has profited enormously from the development of the new media. "The more the arts develop," writes E. M. Foster, "the more they depend on each other for definition. We will borrow from painting first and call it pattern. Later we will borrow from music and call it rhythm."

The appearance of a new medium often frees older media for creative effort. They no longer have to serve the interests of power and profit. Elia Kazan, discussing the American theater, says:

> Take 1900–1920. The theatre flourished all over the country. It had no competition. The box office boomed. The top original fare it had to offer was *The Girl of the Golden West.* Its bow to culture was fusty productions of Shakespeare. . . . Came the moving pictures. The theatre had to be better or go under. It got better. It got so spectacularly better so fast that in 1920–1930 you wouldn't have recognized it. Perhaps it was an accident that Eugene O'Neill appeared at that moment—but it was no accident that in that moment of strange competition, the theatre had room for him. Because it was disrupted and hard pressed, it made room for his experiments, his unheard-of subjects, his passion, his power. There was room for him to grow to his full stature. And there was freedom for the talents that came after his.[4]

Yet a new language is rarely welcomed by the old. The oral tradition distrusted writing, manuscript culture was contemptuous of printing, book culture hated the press, that "slag-heap of hellish passions," as one nineteenth century scholar called it. A father, protesting to a Boston newspaper about crime and scandal, said he would rather see his children "in their graves while pure in innocence, than dwelling with pleasure upon these reports, which have grown so bold."

What really disturbed book-oriented people wasn't the sensationalism of the newspaper, but its nonlineal format, its nonlineal codifications of experience. The motto of conservative academicians became: *Hold that line!*

A new language lets us see with the fresh, sharp eyes of the child; it offers the pure joy of discovery. I was recently told a story about a Polish couple who, though long resident in Toronto, retained many of the customs of their homeland. Their son despaired of ever getting his father to buy a suit cut in style or getting his mother to take an interest in Canadian life. Then he bought them a TV set, and in a matter of months a major change took place. One evening the mother remarked that "Edith Piaf is the latest thing on Broadway," and the father appeared in "the kind of suit executives wear on TV." For years the father had passed this same suit in store windows and seen it both in advertisements and on living men, but not until he saw it on TV did it become meaningful. This same statement goes for all media: each offers a unique presentation of reality, which when new has a freshness and clarity that is extraordinarily powerful.

This is especially true of TV. We say, "We have a radio" but "We have television"—as if something had happened to us. It's no longer "The skin you love to touch" but "The Nylon that loves to touch you." We don't watch TV; it watches us: it guides us. Magazines and newspapers no longer convey "information" but offer ways of seeing things. They have abandoned realism as too easy: they substitute themselves for realism. *Life* is totally advertisements: its articles package and sell emotions and ideas just as its paid ads sell commodities.

Several years ago, a group of us at the University of Toronto undertook the following experiment: 136 students were divided, on the basis of their over-all academic standing of the previous year, into four equal groups who either (1) heard and saw a lecture delivered in a TV studio, (2) heard and saw this same lecture on a TV screen, (3) heard it over the radio, or (4) read it in manuscript. Thus there were, in the CBC studios, four controlled groups who simultaneously received a single lecture and then immediately wrote an identical examination to test both understanding and retention of content. Later the experiment was repeated, using three similar groups; this time the same lecture was (1) delivered in a classroom, (2) presented as a film (using the kinescope) in a small theatre, and (3) again read in print. The actual mechanics of the experiment were relatively simple, but the problem of writing the script for the lecture led to a consideration of the resources and limitations of the dramatic forms involved.

It immediately became apparent that no matter how the script was written and the show produced, it would be slanted in various ways for and against each of the media involved; no show could be produced that did not contain these biases, and the only real common denominator was the simultaneity of presentation. For each communication channel codifies reality differently and thus influences, to a surprising degree, the content of the message communicated. A medium is not simply an envelope that carries any letter; it is itself a major part of that message. We therefore decided not to exploit the full resources of any one medium, but to try to chart a middle-of-the-road course between all of them.

The lecture that was finally produced dealt with linguistic codifications of reality and metaphysical concepts underlying grammatical systems. It was chosen because it concerned a field in which few students could be expected to have prior knowledge; moreover, it offered opportunities for the use of gesture. The cameras moved throughout the lecture, and took close-ups where relevant. No other visual aids were used, nor were shots taken of the audience while the lecture was in progress. Instead, the cameras simply focused on the speaker for twenty-seven minutes.

The first difference we found between a classroom and a TV lecture was the brevity of the latter. The classroom lecture, if not ideally, at least in practice, sets a slower pace. It's verbose, repetitive. It allows for greater elaboration and permits the lecturer to take up several *related* points. TV, however, is stripped right down; there's less time for qualifications or alternative interpretations and only time enough for *one* point. (Into twenty-seven minutes we put the meat of a two-hour classroom lecture.) The ideal

TV speaker states his point and then brings out different facets of it by a variety of illustrations. But the classroom lecturer is less subtle and, to the agony of the better students, repeats and repeats his identical points in the hope, perhaps, that ultimately no student will miss them, or perhaps simply because he is dull. Teachers have had captive audiences for so long that few are equipped to compete for attention via the new media.

The next major difference noted was the abstracting role of each medium, beginning with print. Edmund M. Morgan, Harvard Law Professor, writes:

> One who forms his opinion from the reading of any record alone is prone to err, because the printed page fails to produce the impression or convey the idea which the spoken word produced or conveyed. The writer has read charges to the jury which he had previously heard delivered, and has been amazed to see an oral deliverance which indicated a strong bias appear on the printed page as an ideally impartial exposition. He has seen an appellate court solemnly declare the testimony of a witness to be especially clear and convincing which the trial judge had orally characterized as the most abject perjury.[5]

Selectivity of print and radio are perhaps obvious enough, but we are less conscious of it in TV, partly because we have already been conditioned to it by the shorthand of film. Balázs writes:

> A man hurries to a railway station to take leave of his beloved. We see him on the platform. We cannot see the train, but the questing eyes of the man show us that his beloved is already seated in the train. We see only a close-up of the man's face, we see it twitch as if startled and then strips of light and shadow, light and shadow flit across it in quickening rhythm. Then tears gather in the eyes and that ends the scene. We are expected to know what happened and today we do know, but when I first saw this film in Berlin, I did not at once understand the end of this scene. Soon, however, everyone knew what had happened: the train had started and it was the lamps in its compartment which had thrown their light on the man's face as they glided past ever faster and faster.[6]

As in a movie theater, only the screen is illuminated, and, on it, only points of immediate relevance are portrayed; everything else is eliminated. This explicitness makes TV not only personal but forceful. That's why stage hands in a TV studio watch the show over floor monitors, rather than watch the actual performance before their eyes.

The script of the lecture, timed for radio, proved too long for TV. Visual aids and gestures on TV not only allow the elimination of certain words, but require a unique script. The ideal radio delivery stresses pitch and intonation to make up for the absence of the visual. That flat, broken speech in "sidewalk interviews" is the speech of a person untrained in radio delivery.

The results of the examination showed that TV had won, followed by lecture, film, radio, and finally print. Eight months later the test was read-ministered to the bulk of the students who had taken it the first time. Again it was found that there were significant differences between the groups exposed to different media, and these differences were the same as those on the first test, save for the studio group, an uncertain group be-cause of the chaos of the lecture conditions, which had moved from last to second place. Finally, two years later, the experiment was repeated, with major modifications, using students at Ryerson Institute. Marshall McLu-han reports:

> In this repeat performance, pains were taken to allow each medium full play of its possibilities with reference to the subject, just as in the earlier experiment each medium was neutralized as much as possible. Only the mimeograph form remained the same in each experiment. Here we added a printed form in which an imaginative typographical layout was followed. The lecturer used the blackboard and permitted discussion. Radio and TV employed dramatiza-tion, sound effects and graphics. In the examination, radio easily topped TV. Yet, as in the first experiment, both radio and TV manifested a decisive advan-tage over the lecture and written forms. As a conveyor both of ideas and infor-mation, TV was, in this second experiment, apparently enfeebled by the de-ployment of its dramatic resources, whereas radio benefited from such lavishness. "Technology is explicitness," writes Lyman Bryson. Are both radio and TV more explicit than writing or lecture? Would a greater explicitness, if inherent in these media, account for the ease with which they top other modes of performance? [7]

Announcement of the results of the first experiment evoked considerable interest. Advertising agencies circulated the results with the comment that here, at last, was scientific proof of the superiority of TV. This was unfor-tunate and missed the main point, for the results didn't indicate the superi-ority of one medium over others. They merely directed attention toward differences between them, differences so great as to be of kind rather than degree. Some CBC officials were furious, not because TV won, but because print lost.

The problem has been falsely seen as democracy *vs.* the mass media. But the mass media *are* democracy. The book itself was the first mechanical mass medium. What is really being asked, of course, is: can books' mo-nopoly of knowledge survive the challenge of the new languages? The an-swer is: no. What should be asked is: what can print do better than any other medium and is that worth doing?

Notes

1. *Television Plays,* New York, Simmon and Schuster, 1955, pp. 176–78.
2. George Hoellering and T. S. Eliot, *Film of Murder in the Cathedral,* New York, Harcourt, Brace & Co., 1952, p. vi; London, Faber & Faber, 1952.

3. Béla Balázs, *Theory of Film,* New York, Roy Publishers, 1953, pp. 48, 31, 40; London, Denis Dobson, 1952.

4. "Writers and Motion Pictures," *The Atlantic Monthly,* 199, 1957, p. 69.

5. G. Louis Joughin and Edmund M. Morgan, *The Legacy of Sacco and Vanzetti,* New York, Harcourt, Brace & Co., 1948, p. 34.

6. Béla Balázs, *op. cit.,* pp. 35–36.

7. From a personal communication to the author.

The Electric Revolution

Are you aware of the development of "schizophonia?" Do you partake of "audio analgesia?" These are terms coined by R. Murray Schafer. He refers to our sonic environment and implies the psychological changes resulting from the acoustical revolution. Schafer claims that the telephone, phonograph, and radio have produced portable acoustic space; this in turn has changed our definition of what is signal and what is noise. Human beings have always been surrounded by sound, but now we can and do create our own sonic environments and take them with us wherever we go.

The Electric Revolution extended many of the themes of the Industrial Revolution and added some new effects of its own. Owing to the increased transmission speed of electricity, the flat-line effect was extended to give the pitched tone, thus harmonizing the world on center frequencies of 25 and 40, then 50 and 60 cycles per second. Other extensions of trends already noted were the multiplication of sound producers and their imperialistic outsweep by means of amplification.

Two new techniques were introduced: the discovery of packaging and storing techniques for sound and the splitting of sounds from their original contexts—which I call schizophonia. The benefits of the electroacoustic transmission and reproduction of sound are well enough celebrated, but they should not obscure the fact that precisely at the time hi-fi was being engineered, the world soundscape was slipping into an all-time lo-fi condition.

A good many of the fundamental discoveries of the Electric Revolution had already been made by 1850: the electric cell, the storage cell, the dynamo, the electric arc light. The detailed application of these inventions occupied the remainder of the nineteenth century. It was during this period that the electric power station, the telephone, the radio telegraph, the phonograph and the moving picture came into existence. At first their commercial applications were limited. It was not until the improvement of the dynamo by Werner Siemens (1856) and the alternator by Nikola Tesla (1887) that electrical power could become the generating force for the practical development of the discoveries.

One of the first products of the Electric Revolution, Morse's telegraph (1838), unintentionally dramatized the contradiction between discrete and contoured sound which, as I have said, separates slow from fast-paced societies. Morse used the long line of the telegraph wire to transmit messages broken in binary code, which still relied on digital adroitness, thus maintaining in the telegrapher's trained finger a skill that related him to the pianist and the scribe. Because the finger cannot be wiggled fast enough to produce the fused contour of sound, the telegraph ticks and stutters in the same way as its two contemporary inventions, Thurber's typewriter and Gatling's machine gun. As increased mobility and speed in communication continued to be desired, it was inevitable that, together with the act of letter-scratching, the telegraph should give way to the telephone.

The three most revolutionary sound mechanisms of the Electric Revolution were the telephone, the phonograph and the radio. With the telephone and the radio, sound was no longer tied to its original point in space; with the phonograph it was released from its original point in time. The dazzling removal of these restrictions has given modern man an exciting new power which modern technology has continually sought to render more effective.

The soundscape researcher is concerned with changes in perception and behavior. Let us, for instance, point up a couple of observable changes effected by the telephone, the first of the new instruments to be extensively marketed.

The telephone extended intimate listening across wide distances. As it is basically unnatural to be intimate at a distance, it has taken some time for humans to accustom themselves to the idea. Today North Americans raise their voices only on transcontinental or transoceanic calls; Europeans, however, still raise their voices to talk to the next town, and Asians shout at the telephone when talking to someone in the next street.

The capacity of the telephone to interrupt thought is more important, for it has undoubtedly contributed a good share to the abbreviation of written prose and the choppy speech of modern times. For instance, when Schopenhauer writes at the beginning of *The World as Will and Idea* that he wishes us to consider his entire book as one thought, we realize that he is about to make severe demands on himself and his readers. The real depreciation of concentration began after the advent of the telephone. Had Schopenhauer written his book in my office, he would have completed the first sentence and the telephone would have rung. Two thoughts.

The telephone had already been dreamed of when Moses and Zoroaster conversed with God, and the radio as an instrument for the transmission of divine messages was well imagined before that. The phonograph, too, has a long history in the imagination of man, for to catch and preserve the tissue of living sound was an ancient ambition. In Babylonian mythology there are hints of a specially constructed room in one of the ziggurats where whispers stayed forever. There is a similar room (still in existence) in the Ali Qapu in Isfahan, though in its present derelict state it is difficult to know how it was supposed to have worked. Presumably its highly polished walls and floor gave sounds an abnormal reverberation time. In an ancient Chinese legend a king has a secret black box into which he speaks his orders, then sends them around his kingdom for his subjects to carry out, which I gloss to mean that there is *authority* in the magic of captured sound. With the invention of the telephone by Bell in 1876 and the phonograph by Charles Cros and Thomas Edison in 1877 the era of schizophonia was introduced.

Schizophonia

The Greek prefix *schizo* means split, separated; and *phone* is Greek for voice. *Schizophonia* refers to the split between an original sound and its electroacoustical transmission or reproduction. It is another twentieth-century development.

Originally all sounds were originals. They occurred at one time in one place only. Sounds were then indissolubly tied to the mechanisms that produced them. The human voice traveled only as far as one could shout. Every sound was uncounterfeitable, unique. Sounds bore resemblances to one another, such as the phonemes which go to make up the repetition of a word, but they were not identical. Tests have shown that it is physically impossible for nature's most rational and calculating being to reproduce a single phoneme in his own name twice in exactly the same manner.

Since the invention of electroacoustical equipment for the transmission and storage of sound, any sound, no matter how tiny, can be blown up and shot around the world, or packaged on tape or record for the generations of the future. We have split the sound from the maker of the sound. Sounds have been torn from their natural sockets and given an amplified and independent existence. Vocal sound, for instance, is no longer tied to a hole in the head but is free to issue from anywhere in the landscape. In the same instant it may issue from millions of holes in millions of public and private places around the world, or it may be stored to be reproduced at a later date, perhaps eventually hundreds of years after it was originally uttered. A record or tape collection may contain items from widely diverse cultures and historical periods in what would seem, to a person from any century but our own, a meaningless and surrealistic juxtaposition.

The desire to dislocate sounds in time and space had been evident for some time in the history of Western music, so that the recent technological developments were merely the consequences of aspirations that had already been effectively imagined. The secret *quomodo omnis generis instrumentorum Musica in remotissima spacia propagari possit* (whereby all forms of instrumental music could be transmitted to remote places) was a special preoccupation of the musician-inventor Athanasius Kircher, who discussed the matter in detail in his *Phonurgia Nova* of 1673. In the practical sphere, the introduction of dynamics, echo effects, the splitting of resources, the separation of soloist from the ensemble and the incorporation of instruments with specific referential qualities (horn, anvil, bells, etc.) were all attempts to create virtual spaces which were larger or different from natural room acoustics; just as the search for exotic folk music and the breaking forward and backward to find new or renew old musical resources represents a desire to transcend the present tense.

When, following the Second World War, the tape recorder made incisions into recorded material possible, any sound object could be cut out and inserted into any new context desired. Most recently, the quadraphonic sound system has made possible a 360-degree soundscape of moving and stationary sound events which allows any sound environment to be simulated in time and space. This provides for the complete portability of acoustic space. Any sonic environment can now become any other sonic environment.

We know that the territorial expansion of post-industrial sounds complemented the imperialistic ambitions of the Western nations. The loudspeaker was also invented by an imperialist, for it responded to the desire to dominate others with one's own sound. As the cry broadcasts distress, the loudspeaker communicates anxiety. "We should not have conquered Germany without . . . the loudspeaker," wrote Hitler in 1938.

I coined the term schizophonia in *The New Soundscape* intending it to be a nervous word. Related to schizophrenia, I wanted it to convey the same sense of aberration and drama. Indeed, the overkill of hi-fi gadgetry not only contributes generously to the lo-fi problem, but it creates a synthetic soundscape in which natural sounds are becoming increasingly unnatural while machine-made substitutes are providing the operative signals directing modern life.

Radio: Extended Acoustic Space

A character in one of Jorge Luis Borges's stories dreads mirrors because they multiply men. The same might be said of radios. By 1969, Americans were listening to 268,000,000 radios, that is, about one per citizen. Modern life has been ventriloquized. The domination of modern life by the radio did not take place unnoticed; but whereas opposition to the Industrial Revolution had come from the working classes, who feared the loss of their jobs, the principal opponents of the radio and the phonograph were the intellectuals. Emily Carr, who wrote and painted in the British Columbia wilderness, hated the radio when she first heard it in 1936.

> When I go to houses where they are turned on full blast I feel as if I'd go mad. Inexplicable torment all over. I thought I ought to get used to them and one was put in my house on trial this morning. I feel as if bees had swarmed in my nervous system. Nerves all jangling. Such a feeling of angry resentment at that horrid metallic voice. After a second I have to clap it off. Can't stand it. Maybe it's my imperfect hearing? It's one of the wonders of the age, simply marvelous. I know that but I *hate* it.

Hermann Hesse, in *Der Steppenwolf* (1927), was disturbed by the poor fidelity of the new electroacoustical devices for the reproduction of music.

> At once, to my indescribable astonishment and horror, the devilish metal funnel spat out, without more ado, its mixture of bronchial slime and chewed rubber; that noise that possessors of gramophones and radio sets are prevailed upon to call music. And behind the slime and the croaking there was, sure enough, like an old master beneath a layer of dirt, the noble outline of that divine music. I could distinguish the majestic structure and the deep wide breath and the full broad bowing of the strings.

But more than this, Hesse was revolted by the schizophonic incongruities of broadcasting.

> It takes hold of some music played where you please, without distinction or discretion, lamentably distorted, to boot, and chucks it into space to land where it has no business to be. . . . When you listen to radio you are a witness of the everlasting war between idea and appearance, between time and eternity, between the human and the divine . . . radio . . . projects the most lovely music without regard into the most impossible places, into snug drawing-rooms and attics and into the midst of chattering, guzzling, yawning and sleeping listeners, and exactly as it strips this music of its sensuous beauty, spoils and scratches and beslimes it and yet cannot altogether destroy its spirit.

Radio extended the outreach of sound to produce greatly expanded profiles, which were remarkable also because they formed interrupted acoustic spaces. Never before had sound disappeared across space to reappear again at a distance. The community, which had previously been defined by its bell or temple gong, was now defined by its local transmitter.

The Nazis were the first to use radio in the interests of totalitarianism, but they have not been the last; and little by little, in both East and West, radio has been employed more ruthlessly in culture-molding. Readers of Solzhenitsyn's novel *Cancer Ward* will recall the "constant yawping" of the radio which greeted Vadim when he went to the hospital and the way he detested it. I recall, twenty years ago, hearing the same loudspeakers blaring out their cacophonies of patriotism and spleen on station platforms and in public squares throughout Eastern Europe. But broadcasting has now gone public in the West as well. It may be hard for younger readers to appreciate what has happened but, up until about a decade ago, one of the most salient differences between cities like London or Paris and Bucharest or Mexico City was that in the former there were no radios or music in public places, restaurants or shops. In those days, particularly during the summer months, BBC announcers would regularly request listeners to keep their radios at a low volume in order not to disturb the neighborhood. In a dramatic reversal of style, British Railways recently began beaming the BBC regional service throughout railway stations (I have heard it over loudspeakers in Brighton Railway Station, 1975). But they still have a long way to go to catch Australian Railways, which plays the ABC light program on trains from 7 a.m. to 11 p.m. during the three-day run from Sydney to Perth. In my compartment in 1973 it was impossible to shut it off.

In the early days one listened to the radio selectively by studying the program schedule, but today programs are overlooked and are merely overheard. This change of habit prepared modern society to tolerate the walls of sound with which human engineering now orchestrates the modern environment.

The radio was the first sound wall, enclosing the individual with the familiar and excluding the enemy. In this sense it is related to the castle garden of the Middle Ages which, with its birds and fountains, contradicted the hostile environment of forest and wilderness. The radio has actually become the bird-song of modern life, the "natural" soundscape, excluding the inimical forces from outside. To serve this function sound need not be elaborately presented, any more than wallpaper has to be painted by Michelangelo to render the drawing room attractive. Thus, the development of greater fidelity in sound reproduction, which occupied the first half of the present century—and in a way may be thought of as analogous to the development of oil paints, which also rendered possible greater veracity in art—is now canceled by a tendency to return to simpler forms of expression. For instance, while the transition from mechanical to electrical recording (Harrison and Maxfield) extended the available band width from three to seven octaves, the transistor radio reduced it again to something like its former state. The habit of listening to transistor radios outdoors in the presence of additional ambient noise, often in circumstances which reduce the signal-to-noise ratio to approximately one to one, has in turn suggested the inclusion of additional noise which, in some popular music, is now engineered right onto the disc, often in the form of electroacoustical feedback. This, in turn, leads to new evaluations of what is signal and what is noise in the whole constantly changing field of aural perception.

The Shapes of Broadcasting

Radio programing needs to be analyzed in as much detail as an epic poem or musical composition, for in its themes and rhythms will be found the pulse of life. But detailed studies of this kind appear never to have been undertaken. . . . [I]t will not be out of place here to make a few general comments.

At first radio broadcasts were isolated presentations, surrounded by extended (silent) station breaks. This occasional approach to broadcasting, now absent from domestic radio, can still to some extent be experienced with shortwave broadcasts, where station breaks are often several minutes long and are accompanied by short musical phrases or signature tunes. (This attractive practice is only slightly spoiled by the unlikely choice of instruments used on some stations: thus, the calls of Jordan and Kuwait are played on the clarinet, those of Jamaica and Iran on the vibraphone—that is, they are played on instruments so distinctly non-indigenous that one might suppose they were originally recorded in New York.)

During the 1930s and 1940s schedules were filled out until the whole day was looped together in unsettled connectivity. The modern radio schedule, a confection of material from various sources, joined in thoughtful, funny, ironic, absurd or provocative juxtapositions, has introduced many contradictions into modern life and has perhaps contributed more than anything else to the breakup of unified culture systems and values. It is for this reason that the study of joins in broadcasting is of great importance. The montage was first employed in film because it was the first art form to be cut and spliced; but since the invention of magnetic tape and the compression of the schedule, the shapes of broadcasting have followed the editor's scissors also.

The function of the montage is to make one plus one equal three. The film producer Eisenstein—one of the first to experiment with montage—defines the effect as consisting "in the fact that two film pieces of any kind, placed together, inevitably combine into a new concept, a new quality, arising out of that juxtaposition." The *non sequiturs* of the montage may be incomprehensible to the innocent though they are easily accommodated by the initiated. I recall one night in Chicago, at the height of the Vietnam War, listening to an on-the-spot report of the grisly affair, sponsored by Wrigley's Chewing Gum, whose jingle at the time was "Chew your little cares away!" I mentioned the experience to a class of students at Northwestern University the next day. They were interested in my opposition to the war, but failed to see my point about the gum. For them the elements had been montaged as part of a way of life.

Since the advent of the singing commercial on North American radio, popular music and advertising have formed the main material of the radio montage, so that today, by means of quick cross-fades, direct cuts or "music under" techniques, songs and commercials follow one another in quick and smooth succession, producing a commercial life style that is entertaining ("buy baubles for your bippy") and musical entertainment that is profitable ("five million sold").

Radio introduced the surrealistic soundscape, but other electroacoustical devices have had an influence in rendering it acceptable. The record collection, which one may observe in almost every house of the civilized world, is often equally eclectic and bizarre, containing stray items from different periods or countries, all of which may nevertheless be stacked on the same phonograph for successive replay.

I am trying to illustrate the irrationality of electroacoustic juxtapositioning in order that it might cease to be taken for granted. One last story. A friend was once on an aircraft that supplies a selection of recorded programs of different types for earphone listening. Choosing the program of classical music he settled back in his seat to listen to Wagner's *Meistersinger*. As the overture soared to a climax, the disturbed voice of the stewardess suddenly interrupted the music to announce: "Ladies and gentlemen, the toilets are plugged up and must be flushed with a glass of water."

As the format of radio tightened, its tempo increased, substituting superficiality for prolonged acts of concentration. Heavyweight fare like the famous BBC Third Programme was dismissed to be replaced by material with more twist and appeal. Each station and each country has its own tempo of broadcasting, but in general it has been speeded up over the years, and its tone is moving from the sedate toward the slaphappy. (I am speaking here only of Western-style broadcasting; I am not sufficiently familiar with the monolithic cultures of Russia or China.) In the West, material is being increasingly pushed together, overlapped. In a World Soundscape Project in 1973 we counted the number of separate items on four Vancouver radio stations over a typical eighteen-hour day. Each item (announcement, commercial, weather report, etc.) represented a change of focus. The results ran as follows:

Station	Total Number of Items	Hourly Average
CBU	635	35.5
CHQM	745	41.0
CJOR	996	55.5
CKLG	1097	61.0

Stations broadcasting popular music are the fastest-paced. The duration of individual items of any kind rarely exceeds three minutes on North American pop stations. Here the recording industry discloses a secret. On the old ten-inch shellac disc, the recording duration was limited to slightly over three minutes. As this was the first vehicle for popular music, all pop songs were abbreviated to meet this technical limitation. But curiously, when the long-play disc was introduced in 1948, the length of the average pop song did not increase in proportion. This suggests that some mysterious law concerning average attention span may have been inadvertently discovered by the older technology.

One acoustic effect is rarely heard on North American radios: silence. Only occasionally, during broadcasts of theater or classical music, do quiet and silence achieve their full potentiality. A graphic level recording of a popular station will show how the program material is made to ride at the maximum permissible level, a technique known as compression because the available dynamic range is compressed into very narrow limits. Such broadcasting shows no dynamic shadings or phrasing. It does not rest. It does not breathe. It has become a sound wall.

Sound Walls

Walls used to exist to delimit physical and acoustic space, to isolate private areas visually and to screen out acoustic interferences. Often this second function is unstressed, particularly in modern buildings. Confronted with this situation modern man has discovered what might be called *audioanalgesia,* that is, the use of sound as a painkiller, a distraction to dispel distractions. The use of audioanalgesia extends in modern life from its original use in the dental chair to wired background music in hotels, offices, restaurants and many other public and private places. Air-conditioners, which produce a continuous band of pink noise, are also instruments of audioanalgesia. It is important in this respect to realize that such masking sounds are not intended to be listened to consciously. Thus, the Moozak industry deliberately chooses music that is nobody's favorite and subjects it to unvenomed and innocuous orchestrations in order to produce a wraparound of "pretty," designed to mask unpleasant distractions in a manner that corresponds to the attractive packages of modern merchandising to disguise frequently cheesy contents.

Walls used to exist to isolate sounds. Today sound walls exist to isolate. In the same way the intense amplification of popular music does not stimulate sociability so much as it expresses the desire to experience individuation . . . aloneness . . . disengagement. For modern man, the sound wall has become as much a fact as the wall in space. The teenager lives in the continual presence of his radio, the housewife in the presence of her television set, the worker in the presence of engineered music systems designed to increase production. From Nova Scotia comes word of the continuous use of background music in school classrooms. The principal is pleased with the results and pronounces the experiment a success. From Sacramento, California, comes news of another unusual development: a library wired for rock music in which patrons are encouraged to talk. On the walls are signs stating NO SILENCE. The result: circulation, especially among the young, is up.

> They never sup without music; and there is always fruit served up after the meat; while they are at table, some burn perfumes and sprinkle about fragrant ointments and sweet waters: in short, they want nothing that may cheer their spirits.
>
> Sir Thomas More, *Utopia*

Moozak

If the Christmas card angels offer any proof, utopian creatures are forever smiling. Thus Moozak, the sound wall of paradise, never weeps. It is the honeyed antidote to hell on earth. Moozak starts out with the high motive of orchestrating paradise (it is often present in writings about utopias) but it always ends up as the embalming fluid of earthly boredom. It is natural then that the testing-ground for the Moozak industry should have been the U.S.A., with its highly idealistic Constitution and the cruddy realities of its modern life styles. The service pages of the telephone directories beam out its advertisements to clients in every North American city.

> MUZAK IS MORE THAN MUSIC—PSYCHOLOGICALLY PLANNED—FOR THE TIME AND PLACE—JUST FLIP THE SWITCH—NO MACHINES TO ATTEND / FRESH PROGRAMS EACH DAY—NO REPETITION—ADVISED BY BOARD OF SCIENTIFIC advisors—OVER 30 YEARS OF RESEARCH—PAGING AND SOUND SERVICE—FAST ROUND-THE-CLOCK SERVICE—MUZAK BRAND EQUIPMENT—OFFICES—INDUSTRIAL PLANTS—BANKS—HOSPITALS—RETAIL STORES—HOTELS AND MOTELS— RESTAURANTS—PROFESSIONAL OFFICES—*SPECIALISTS IN THE PSYCHOLOGICAL AND PHYSIOLOGICAL APPLICATIONS OF MUSIC.*

Facts on Moozak program design are elementary. The programs are selected and put together in several American cities for mass distribution. ". . . program specialists . . . assign values to the elements in a musical recording; i.e., tempo (number of beats per minute); rhythm (waltz, fox trot, march); instrumentation (brass, woodwinds, strings), and orchestra size (5 piece combo, 30 piece symphony, etc.)." There are few solo vocalists or instrumentalists to distract the listener. The same programs are played to both people and cows, but despite the happy claim that production has in both cases been increased, neither animal seems yet to have been elevated into the Elysian Fields. While the programs are constructed to give what the advertising calls "a progression of time"—that is, the illusion that time is dynamically and significantly passing—the implicit malaise behind the claim is that for most people time continues to hang heavily. "Each 15-minute segment of MUZAK contains a rising stimulus which provides a logical sense of forward movement. This affects boredom or monotony and fatigue."

Although no precise growth statistics have ever been published, there can be no doubt that these bovine sound slicks are spreading. This does not perhaps so much indicate a lack of public interest in silence as it demonstrates that there is more profit to be made out of sound, for another claim of the Mooze industry is that it provides a "relaxed background to profit." When we interviewed 108 consumers and 25 employees in a Vancouver shopping mall, we discovered that while only 25 percent of the shoppers thought they spent more as a result of the background music, 60 percent of the employees thought they did.

Against the slop and spawn of Moozak and broadcast music in public places a wave of protest is now clearly discernible. Most notable is a resolution unanimously passed by the General Assembly of the International Music Council of UNESCO in Paris in October, 1969.

> We denounce unanimously the intolerable infringement of individual freedom and of the right of everyone to silence, because of the abusive use, in private and public places, of recorded or broadcast music. We ask the Executive Committee of the International Music Council to initiate a study from all angles—medical, scientific and juridical—without overlooking its artistic and educational aspects, and with a view to proposing to UNESCO, and to the proper authorities everywhere, measures calculated to put an end to this abuse.

There is a parallel to this resolution: when, in 1864, Michael Bass proposed his Bill to prohibit the sounds of street singing in the city of London, he drew substantial support from the musical profession itself. With the 1969 UNESCO resolution sonic overkill was apprehended by the musicians of the world as a serious problem. For the first time in history an international organization involved primarily with the *production* of sounds suddenly turned its attention to their *reduction*. In *The New Soundscape* I had already warned music educators that they would now have to be as concerned about the prevention of sounds as about their creation, and I suggested that they should join noise abatement societies to familiarize themselves with this new theme for the music room.

In any historical study of the soundscape, the researcher will repeatedly be struck by shifts in the perceptual habits of a society, instances where the figure and the ground exchange roles. The case of Moozak is one such instance. Throughout history music has existed as figure—a desirable collection of sounds to which the listener gives special attention. Moozak reduces music to ground. It is a deliberate concession to lo-fi-ism. It multiplies sounds. It reduces a sacred art to a slobber. Moozak is music that is not to be listened to.

By creating a fuss about sounds we snap them back into focus as figures. The way to defeat Moozak is, therefore, quite simple: listen to it.

Moozak resulted from the abuse of the radio. The abuse of Moozak has suggested another type of sound wall which is now rapidly becoming a fixture in all modern buildings: the screen of white noise, or as its proponents prefer to call it "acoustic perfume." The hiss of the air-conditioner and the roar of the furnace have been exploited by the acoustical engineering profession to mask distracting sound, and where they are in themselves not sufficiently loud, they have been augmented by the installation of white noise generators. A desideratum from America's most prominent firm of acoustical engineers to the head of a music department shows us that if music can be used to mask noise, noise can also be used to mask music. It ran: "Music Library: There should be enough mechanical noise to mask page turning and foot movement sounds." The mask hides the face. Sound walls hide characteristic soundscapes under fictions.

Prime Unity or Tonal Center

In the Indian *anāhata* and in the Western Music of the Spheres man has constantly sought some prime unity, some central sound against which all other vibrations may be measured. In diatonic or modal music it is the fundamental or tonic of the mode of scale that binds all other sounds into relationship. In China an artificial center of gravity was created in 239 B.C. when the Bureau of Weights and Measures established the Yellow Bell or Huang Chung as the tone from which all others were measured.

It is, however, only in the electronic age that international tonal centers have been achieved; in countries operating on an alternating current of 60 cycles, it is this sound which now provides the resonant frequency for it will be heard (together with its harmonics) in the operation of all electrical devices from lights and amplifiers to generators. Where C is tuned to 256 cycles, this resonant frequency is B natural. In ear training exercises I have discovered that students find B natural much the easiest pitch to retain and to recall spontaneously. Also during meditation exercises, after the whole body has been relaxed and students are asked to sing the tone of "prime unity"—the tone which seems to arise naturally from the center of their being—B natural is more frequent than any other. I have also experimented with this in Europe where the resonant electrical frequency of 50 cycles is approximately G sharp. At the Stuttgart Music High School I led a group of students in a series of relaxation exercises and then asked them to hum the tone of "prime unity." They centered on G sharp.

Electrical equipment will often produce resonant harmonics and in a quiet city at night a whole series of steady pitches may be heard from street lighting, signs or generators. When we were studying the soundscape of the Swedish village of Skruv in 1975, we encountered a large number of these and plotted their profiles and pitches on a map. We were surprised to find that together they produced a G-sharp major triad, which the F-sharp whistles of passing trains turned into a dominant seventh chord. As we moved about the streets on quiet evenings, the town played melodies.

The Electric Revolution has thus given us new tonal centers of prime unity against which all other sounds are now balanced. Like mobiles, whose movements may be measured from the string on which they are suspended, the sound mobiles of the modern world are now interpretable by means of the thin line fixture of the operating electrical current.

CHARLES TURNER

Music Videos and the Iconic Data Base

Music videos or MTV's are a recent phenomenon which have swept like a whirlwind into our media world. Turner sees MTV not as a passing fad but as a logical step in the process of creating a "new perceptual agenda." His insightful analysis reveals the significance of MTV as another imaging technology drawing upon that collective iconic database which has been building since the invention of photography and is continually fed by motion pictures and television. The result, claims Turner, is the "Myth of Digitalis"—the belief that one's world, one's past, one's body, one's very self are composed of discrete, separable, sortable bits of data.

A conjunction of commercial necessity, perceptual conditioning and the image retrieval capacity of contemporary telecommunications have converted the visual record of our culture into an *iconic data base*. We should have seen it coming.

Historical Rewind

By the end of the 1970s, certain forces in the marketplace of visual experience were reaching a critical mass. As cable channels joined traditional broadcast outlets to give us more to look at, the nature of what we saw was changing. News stories and commercials grew shorter and more frequent; hit series were rerun at all hours; the instant replay became the *sine qua non* of TV sports. Our pictorial entertainment was coming in briefer, recycled segments, and we were learning—albeit unconsciously at first—to choose among and return to favored images. Pictures didn't just fade away anymore; they were *out there* somewhere; they could come back.

The new consumer hardware was instilling a similar, though more participatory lesson. A home with a video cassette recorder became a place for practicing visual selection, storage, and recall. A family room with a video game was suddenly an arena for exploring image manipulation and the impulse to control "the tube." A den with a personal computer turned a desk into a lab where the glowing contents of a 3 x 4 screen could be rearranged and combined at will. It didn't matter whether we all actually

had a "PC" or a "VCR." We watched the commercials, we read the magazines, we got the idea. The idea was:

> Play/record/pause/erase,
> load/save/edit/delete—
> pictures are like words;
> they're not *real,*
> they're *information.*

As this shared, if tacit, acceptance of pictures-as-data spread through the
society at large, the current generation of popular musicians was discovering that the same consumer technologies reshaping America's "blip culture" (Toffler, 1980, p. 181) were also diverting teen dollars away from
the Top 40. A dip in the birth rate and two OPEC-bred recessions didn't
help. There were fewer adolescents out there, and most had less disposal
income to spend on the escalating price of petro-based discs and cassettes.
To make matters worse, radio programmers were chasing aging baby
boomers with "adult contempo" formats that screened out the glandular
thump of teenage rock'n roll. No access, no hits.

Cable television, however, had access to spare. Caught out by their medium's overexpansion, nervous programmers were looking for fresh and
inexpensive content. Enter an army of music merchandisers dispensing free
"product" for "promotional consideration," and the success of MTV and
its spinoffs is explained. Almost. The cumulative effect of all those quickie
news clips and zoomy ads, those thousands of replays and video games,
provides the rest of the story. Conditioned by a lifetime of packaged vi-
suality, bred to the manipulation of high-tech paraphernalia, pop musicians and their fans entered the 1980s with a *new perceptual agenda,* a
joint readiness for watching instead of listening, for sharing the music in
pictorial bits and bytes.

Accessing the Invisible Data Base

For example, take the sequence from Adam Ant's "Strip" in which a scene
from a well-known film is recreated. Adam and his lacy love are camping
it up in an old Victorian bed chamber, when she suddenly darts into a
modern shower stall. The color footage turns to black & white, the camera
peers in on the girl from a high angle, and the editing accelerates to approximate (you guessed it) Hitchcock's notorious cinematography from
Psycho. A moment later we see her typing unharmed in an office.

Music videos are full of such casual *allusions.* References to famous movies
and television shows, popular film genres and graphic styles, even other
videos, come and go with noticeable regularity. Often the pirated sources

are hardly memorable, just *rememberable*. In "Girls," by Dwight Twilly, for instance, athletes and cheerleaders spy on one another in a lumpish recreation of the heavily promoted peekaboo scene from *Porky's*.

A certain playfulness seems to be at work; the video maker accesses a communal pool of mnemonic images; the viewer dips into the pool, recalling each source and enriching the communication with a musical rendition of Tony Schwartz's "resonance principle" (1974, p. 25). Remembering becomes a part of the pleasure, as if in watching Weird Al Yankovic (in "Eat It") mimicking Michael Jackson (in "Beat It") recycling the Hollywood adaptation of a stage play *(West Side Story)*, we were each involved in some collective, flash-card version of that other popular database activity, "Trivial Pursuit."

What to make, then, of the many allusions in music videos obviously not geared to delivering a blip of immediate recognition? Only a film buff, for example, might be expected to spot the visual paraphrases of Cocteau's *Beauty and the Beast* in the empty hallways and living statuary of K.C.'s "Give It Up," or the replication of *The Cabinet of Dr. Caligari* in the tilt shots, iris transitions, and expressionistic settings of Rainbow's "Can't Let You Go." Specific attribution does not appear to be the payoff.

As a communicative technique, allusion, although ancient in origin, is quite contemporary in the way it triggers the "closure response" so endemic to mediated experience (Becker, 1983). Although most younger viewers might fail to recognize the replication of Magritte and Dali paintings in the surreal desert imagery of "Hold Me" by Fleetwood Mac, they might very well sense the video's associative strategy.

"These fragments have I shored against my ruin," wrote T. S. Eliot to close his evocative assemblage of headline poetics and cinematic symbols (1934, p. 46). For an audience since weaned not only on the discontinuities of newspapers and film but the elliptic montage of innumerable commercial breaks, connection may be its own reward. And if Eliot's "heap of broken images" has now become critic George W. S. Trow's "context of no context" (1981, p. 51), that mediated wasteland where *linkage is all* and meaning follows after, no matter; for there may be something going on out there on Trow's great "grid of the two hundred million," something more useful, perhaps, than "Trivial Pursuit."

The clue may lie in another pictorial strategy to be found in music videos, a straightforward acquisitive technique which goes beyond allusion to the literal insertion of earlier iconic data. In "The Curley Shuffle," for example, highlights from various Three Stooges films are edited to the beat of the song. Larry, Moe, and Curley slap and gouge and punch each other with perfect musical timing. In comparable videos, actuality footage and clips from fiction films are employed.

The connective pleasure of this *quotation* technique emerges when watching a presentation like Jules Shear's "When Love Surges." In sequence after sequence dancers from the 1920s and 1930s hoof across the screen. Some of the footage seems to come from a newsreel of an artist and model's ball, some from early Hollywood musicals, some from the comedies of the silent era. The montage is a whirl of movement in which viewer knowledge of faces, dates, and titles, although peaked and teased, does not really seem to matter. Instead, the eye is fascinated by something else, held by the way successive comedians and dancers each seems to move so flawlessly, so lightly to the urgent drive of the contemporary song. Is that Chaplin break dancing? A tiny kinesthetic implosion occurs within.

A few years back, around the time the group Blondie was enjoying a hit album called "Eat to the Beat," systems theorists Budd and Ruben (1979, p. 106) were framing a cognitive phenomenon they dubbed "information metabolism." For mental stability and growth, they asserted, people have always been compelled to assimilate the cultural disorder around them into nurturing worldviews of negantropic change. Circuitously, through our eyes and responding muscles, this is what the beat of a video like Shear's may be encouraging us to do. It seems to invite us subliminally to counterprogram the ambient disorganization of our iconic era into synchronized, nostalgic visions. The past is drawn rhythmically into the present, imposing a transient coherence where before there may have been none.

In a sequence with bemusing signal value in this regard, Cyndi Lauper, in the opening moments of her video, "Time After Time," sits on the cluttered bed of an Airflow trailer watching television next to her sleeping boyfriend. Clutching a large statuette of the RCA dog against herself (!), she mouths with mournful precision a dialogue between Marlene Dietrich and Charles Boyer droning out of the TV. After the film actors have talked melodramatically of parting, with Lauper lip synching their exchange throughout, the singer switches off the movie and herself departs in clownish angst. Without overloading the analogies, the sequence portrays both the form and function of its own acquisitive technique. Explicitly, the video exemplifies a pictorial structure in which an appropriation from our mediated storehouse is retrieved to fashion meaning in a current communication. Implicitly, it dramatizes, if satirically, a need to bring continuity out of disarray by linking the new life to the old images.

Videos of similar impulse use techniques of traditional montage with increasing sophistication to integrate new footage with appropriated materials. In "The Heart of Rock'N Roll," Huey Lewis edits himself into the royal line of his profession by inserting his own black-and-white visage between performance clips of Chuck Berry, Bill Haley, and the young Elvis. In "501 AM," reaction shots from the film, *Shane,* are intercut so subtly with the video's ongoing antics that when a smile from Alan Ladd in buckskin follows precisely on the image of a western blond in hot pants, our recall of the old movie is forever reprogrammed.

Music videos of this kind are doing more than just drawing on the Great Intersubjectivized American Image-Bank. Their visualizations are, additionally, a step more self-aware, as if to suggest, "The image-bank is *there* and we, the video makers, are a part of it." Nowhere is this up-tick in iconic consciousness more vividly realized than in "Radio Ga-Ga" by Queen. The futuristic panoramas of Fritz Lang's *Metropolis* are not simply intercut with suitable shots of the band. Through electronic matting techniques, the performers are almost seamlessly inserted into the daunting cityscapes of that future past, thus pulling it—reconstituting that past—into an imagined visual present. For the viewer, such music videos may offer an even more insistent prompt to "metabolize"—an invitation to impress an image of ourselves on our disordered cultural memory. Iconic past pours into present like the unleashed waters at the climax of *Metropolis,* flooding the "context of no context" with a linkage outside of time.

Dramatizing the New Perceptual Agenda

The tendency of music videos to allude to and quote pictorial information points to our internal iconic data base without actually envisioning its invisible presence. In an analogous manner, a second set of indicators dramatizes the impact of our imaging tools on the new perceptual agenda without really spelling out their influential role. For example:

> A young man sits at a drafting table, filling in the frames of a story board with magic markers. As he draws, the events he sketches come to life, halting the departure of a girl who wants to leave him. (Nick Hayward, "On a Sunday")
> The affair between an upwardly mobile inner city girl and a fashion photographer is enacted in a series of photo sessions in which the viewer, by means of subjective camerawork, is permitted to see her as the photographer himself perceives her through his lens. (Madonna, "Borderline")
> A young artist at his easel flashes back to an incident from his childhood in which his unsympathetic father so harrasses him for painting that he, the child, spills paint—in colorful slow motion—across the floor. (The Fixx, "Saved by Zero")
> Yet another man at a drawing table pauses contemplatively at his work as the camera pulls back to reveal, in a frame-like portal behind him, a little boy with a teddy bear departing from his mother down a winding empty highway. A moment later the child is at the table and he, the young man, is poised on the highway, alone within the frame. (Kenny Loggins, "Heart to Heart")

These scenarios may be doing no more than substituting the visual media as private symbols for their performer's own struggles to communicate and develop musically. Yet, considering the centrality of representational technologies in our lives, the choices they portray may also reflect a more widely held orientation to the way we have come to "envision" ourselves communicating.

TV critics have long been fond of noting that television has become only "about television." That observation, cast in behavioral terms, finds verification here: visual tools increasingly turn up as favored props in the dramatization of those human travails recurrent in popular song. No doubt the interpersonal woes of American boy meets girl, the intrapersonal trials of being born in the U.S.A., are still played out on MTV behind the wheels of bright red cars. An automobile, however, can only get you there, not preserve for you your reaction to the ride. As indicators of our expanded reflexive awareness (Budd and Ruben, p. 108), visual media seem to be the vehicles of choice. They can transmit an interaction literally, interpret it technically, and now it seems, by virtue of their very presence within the frame, let us know that we know what's going on. Instant replay: the tool becomes the sign of its effect.

Interestingly, what may be the most recurrent motif in the short history of music videos—the face in the mirror—turns up here as a link to the central function of this second set of indicators. In a strange sequence from "Here Comes the Rain Again," Annie Lennox of the Eurythmics studies herself in a three-mirror vanity while, behind her, her musical partner records pictures of her with a movie camera:

> We watch her watching herself,
> as he records her watching herself,
> so that immediately, in reverse angle,
> we may watch how he watches her watching herself.

This time it is their own image which the performers appropriate and multiply, as if in mediated self-acquisition there were a need to go beyond merely linking oneself temporarily to the unseen data base. The adaptive clue, in other words, the hint which links the earlier strategies of allusion and quotation to these recurrent scenarios of media-framed experience is that, for performer and viewer alike, the technologies of visualization appear to signify not only an amplified self-awareness, but a wishful means to assimulating the teeming image bank.

Perceiving the Iconic Data Base

This wish evokes an almost mythic adaptive risk: a third group of indicators suggests that to control the image bank one must become *like* the image bank; to master the new perceptual agenda one must first accept its analogy that self and world are nothing less—or nothing more—than the sum of the information they possess. That analogy begins with the act of seeing:

A young boy with luminescent eyes stares up at Bonnie Tyler. . . ("Total Eclipse of the Sun")

Political violence on a TV screen is shown reflected in the pupil of a teenage girl. . . ("Under Cover of the Night")

A blindfolded man, bound to a phonograph spindle, is shot through the eye with an electric bolt that courses through his nervous system. (The title sequence from "Friday Night Videos")

The camera zooms in on the face of Matthew Wilder, dissolves to a closeup of his eye, then moves through the pupil to find the performer inside playing electric pianos and operating tape recorders among retinal nerves and electric wires. A moment later he is playing an acoustic piano in an empty room where gravity is reversed and things fall upward to the ceiling. ("Bouncing Off the Wall")

The earlier preoccupation with visual *tools* devolves in these sequences into attention paid to visual *perception* per se. If extensions of sight, like canvas and storyboard, camera, and mirror can lead to an amplification of self-awareness, then to look into the eye itself may lead to "the heart of light" (Eliot, p. 30). We *become* what we behold wrote media theorist Edmund Carpenter (1970) to explain why we create information in the form of the way we receive it. Perhaps the high incidence of ocular imagery in music videos serves to direct us back through the eye, to *behold* what we have become. It should be remembered that Louis Buñuel, in one of cinema's most decried and celebrated images, began his corrective assault on another generation's misperceptions by slicing an eye in half for the opening sequence of his film *Le Chien Andalou.*

Once the means to sight are revalued as just another imaging technology, the world thus seen is no longer a natural place, becoming, instead, a totally mediated environment in which the forms and contents of visual communication coexist with or displace the normally tangible habitat. In "New Frontier," for example, Donald Fagen encounters an unexpected kind of fallout on a date in a backyard bomb shelter. He has no sooner lost his glasses when Picasso's "Three Musicians" and lots of little squigglies by Miro begin to perform before his eyes. A figure in another abstract painting puts on the singer's glasses while U.S. government animations from the salad days of atomic paranoia fill the air around him. Magazine advertisements, Soviet propaganda, and Michelangelo's famous handshake cross the screen.

In Culture Club's "Miss Me Blind," strips of film roll down the edge of the frame, multiplying its central image. A window shade turns into a screen for a closeup of Boy George. The film strip returns to run through an alley, and the group begins to climb across a limbo of Japanese printing, kicking the characters around in inky silhouette. Images of the eyes recur throughout. As in "New Frontier," media forms and content are no longer retrievable referents from an image bank offscreen; they mingle in and become objects of the material world. The performers do more than simply place themselves against or within the old clips and footage; they *play* amid pictorial data as if to do so were the "natural" state of affairs. In a pivotal image from Duran Duran's "The Reflex," a wall of water breaks unexpectedly from a huge video concert screen, pouring down its contents on the audience. It is as if the invisible data base had finally broken into view.

In similar videos, this perception of the environment as data form combines with the earlier dramatization of mediated experience to produce the now explicit suggestion that we are filled with—are ourselves screens and containers for—representational information:

> Images of the group Platinum Blond are projected on the faces and bodies of the band members as they sit and stand in front of a flashing television set. ("It Really Doesn't Matter")
> In a burst of light, the body of Nik Kershaw becomes an image portal in which we see occurring the things which have happened to him and the things about to happen. ("Wouldn't It Be Good")
> A nerdish Billy Rankin, tracking down a hipper image of himself he has seen on TV, encounters his twin as a towering guitar player whose body outline is filled with video static. ("Baby Come Back")

Images such as these are still one step on the perceptual agenda away from viewing ourselves as atomized blips of data. Nevertheless, their contents begin to suggest the unraveled end of that same adaptive function which, at its other pole, portrays our shattered cultural mirror as a chance for image building and reflective play. On the one hand, a presentation like "Baby Come Back" uses video static to connote an emptiness within; a counter-self of meaningless visual noise, whereas, on the other hand, a video such as "Mind My Have Still I" by the group What Is It juggles the same motif between so many Xeroxed, crayoned, and pixillated images of the band that the rolling, flashing static comes to stand for—not an emptiness to be feared—but an energy to be tapped and shaped.

"Everything we do is music," John Cage once quipped (in McLuhan, 1967) in arguing that active perception invests any noise with meaning. One might recast that line today to read:

> Everything we do,
> everything we see,
> everything we *are*
> is information.

This double-edged perspective, which might be labeled, "digitalis," is, at once, both a dangerous and a curative view. We are what we eat what we are. . . .

The Myth of "Digitalis"

"Digitalis" is the bottom line of the new perceptual agenda, the neoprimitive belief that one's world, one's past, one's body, and one's very self are composed of discrete, separable, sortable bits of data. It's an ambivalent mythology. Once you've learned to play with your society's pictorial history, once you've begun framing your everyday existence with tools of image retrieval and creation, once you've vacated nature and taken up residence among the visual forms of mass-mediated communication, once you've admitted to seeing—within yourself, and around yourself—the iconic data base, then you begin to worry. And what you worry about is a primordial form of entropy and change:

> Sitting on the edge of a sink, like little puppets, Ric Ocasek and his girlfriend are wearing each other's heads. As they sing, the heads detach and sail into the air, returning to their rightful owners, who are now floating in a rowboat in the sink. As the rowboat goes under, the camera pulls back to show the couple in the lens of a pair of sunglasses on Ocasek's face. The singer reaches up to take off the glasses, but his whole face comes with them. Water streams out of his open head, washing prior images from the video along with it. ("You Might Think")
>
> Thomas Dolby, dressed as a little boy, sits on a psychiatrist's couch. Both he and the doctor sport large cubes where their heads should be. The sides of the cubes show pictures of their heads. As the "treatment" procedes, they both tear images off the front of their cubes, one image for each emotion or reaction they express. At one point, a giant eye replaces Dolby's face; a moment later, he opens a door on the side of his cube. Inside are blinking lights. ("Hyperactive")
>
> Members of the group Yes, as flat as paper dolls strung upside down in white, empty space, begin to swing from left to right in unison. Together they bend, they fold, they spindle; their bodies rotate like the hands of a clock around their heads. Then suddenly they flip apart, sailing off across the screen in all directions. ("Leave It")

The dark side of these amusing displays is a manic anxiety about "The Third Wave," about the psychic strain of having to work too hard to "synch" an inner worldview to a shifting outer world. Among the archetypal "symbols of transformation," that universal code of identities in transition—cultures under adaptive stress—the motif of decapitation has typically signified a fear of cognitive dismemberment and dispersion (Neumann, 1954, pp. 141–143). "How can my head hold all the images I've seen?" Ocasek seems to ask. "If your brain were a digital computer," Dolby's video replies, "then you could eyeball life one picture at a time." But

"Leave It" suggests that the option is mute; you either string along adaptively—even if it twists your head off—or you "lose synch" and go to pieces. They are in a bind: once the world is held to be a mass of interchangeable data, and the mind is seen as no more than the sum of the pictures it contains, then the head, awash in imagery, is viewed as interchangeable, too. In clever dissolution they become what they behold.

But is this real, or is it Memorex?

Well, as any good Structuralist will remind you, there are two sides to every story, two poles to any mythology. If the flip side here is fear of fragmentation, then the hit side becomes a celebration of synthesis, recombination—"getting it all together." Videos like John Couger's "Jack and Diane," Paul Simon's "Renee & Georgette Magritte," and "No Tengo Dinero" by Righeria demonstrate how the same imaging tools that have inadvertantly created the iconic data base can also shape its autobiographic snapshots and cultural scrapbooks into scenarios of comforting visual order. This, in adaptive terms, may be what the myth of "digitalis" is all about. Music videos which embody a two-way vision of the new perceptual agenda are showing us both how to acknowledge the burdens and reconstitute the pieces of the information explosion.

In "Diana D," a perky dancer in leotards works tirelessly in accelerated motion at trying to assemble the visage of Chuck Mangione, split up before her on six large television monitors. She hauls and stacks, lifts and piles the heavy sets, but each time she succeeds in composing a picture of the trumpeter on the monitors, he changes his position and she has to begin all over. But she does begin all over. And over. And over.

He says: "These fragments have I shored against my ruin . . ."

We say: "Eat to the beat!"

SUSAN SONTAG

The Imprisoning of Reality

Does the camera "see" things better than you do? Are photos more "real" than what you saw or can remember? These and other related questions are explored by Susan Sontag in this excerpt from her provocative book, *On Photography*.

Although most of us do not think of photography as a mass medium in the usual sense, Sontag describes how it is a mediated experience which is carried out on a massive scale; one which has become institutionalized in our society. What is more important, she explains, is that reality is defined by photography.

Reality has always been interpreted through the reports given by images; and philosophers since Plato have tried to loosen our dependence on images by evoking the standard of an image-free way of apprehending the real. But when, in the mid-nineteenth century, the standard finally seemed attainable, the retreat of old religious and political illusions before the advance of humanistic and scientific thinking did not—as anticipated—create mass defections to the real. On the contrary, the new age of unbelief strengthened the allegiance to images. The credence that could no longer be given to realities understood *in the form of* images was now being given to realities understood *to be* images, illusions. In the preface to the second edition (1843) of *The Essence of Christianity*, Feuerbach observes about "our era" that it "prefers the image to the thing, the copy to the original, the representation to the reality, appearance to being"—while being aware of doing just that. And his premonitory complaint has been transformed in the twentieth century into a widely agreed-on diagnosis: that a society becomes "modern" when one of its chief activities is producing and consuming images, when images that have extraordinary powers to determine our demands upon reality and are themselves coveted substitutes for first-hand experience become indispensable to the health of the economy, the stability of the polity, and the pursuit of private happiness.

Feuerbach's words—he is writing a few years after the invention of the camera—seem, more specifically, a presentiment of the impact of photography. For the images that have virtually unlimited authority in a modern society are mainly photographic images; and the scope of that authority stems from the properties peculiar to images taken by cameras.

Such images are indeed able to usurp reality because first of all a photograph is not only an image (as a painting is an image), an interpretation of the real; it is also a trace, something directly stenciled off the real, like a footprint or a death mask. While a painting, even one that meets photographic standards of resemblance, is never more than the stating of an interpretation, a photograph is never less than the registering of an emanation (light waves reflected by objects)—a material vestige of its subject in a way that no painting can be. Between two fantasy alternatives, that Holbein the Younger had lived long enough to have painted Shakespeare or that a prototype of the camera had been invented early enough to have photographed him, most Bardolators would choose the photograph. This is not just because it would presumably show what Shakespeare really looked like, for even if the hypothetical photograph were faded, barely legible, a brownish shadow, we would probably still prefer it to another glorious Holbein. Having a photograph of Shakespeare would be like having a nail from the True Cross.

Most contemporary expressions of concern that an image-world is replacing the real one continue to echo, as Feuerbach did, the Platonic depreciation of the image: true insofar as it resembles something real, sham because it is no more than a resemblance. But this venerable naïve realism is somewhat beside the point in the era of photographic images, for its blunt contrast between the image ("copy") and the thing depicted (the "original")—which Plato repeatedly illustrates with the example of a painting—does not fit a photograph in so simple a way. Neither does the contrast help in understanding image-making at its origins, when it was a practical, magical activity, a means of appropriating or gaining power over something. The further back we go in history, as E. H. Gombrich has observed, the less sharp is the distinction between images and real things; in primitive societies, the thing and its image were simply two different, that is, physically distinct, manifestations of the same energy or spirit. Hence, the supposed efficacy of images in propitiating and gaining control over powerful presences. Those powers, those presences were present in *them*.

For defenders of the real from Plato to Feuerbach to equate image with mere appearance—that is, to presume that the image is absolutely distinct from the object depicted—is part of that process of desacralization which separates us irrevocably from the world of sacred times and places in which an image was taken to participate in the reality of the object depicted. What defines the originality of photography is that, at the very moment in the long, increasingly secular history of painting when secularism is entirely triumphant, it revives—in wholly secular terms—something like the primitive status of images. Our irrepressible feeling that the photographic process is something magical has a genuine basis. No one takes an easel painting to be in any sense co-substantial with its subject; it only represents or refers. But a photograph is not only like its subject, a homage to the subject. It is part of, an extension of that subject; and a potent means of acquiring it, of gaining control over it.

Photography is acquisition in several forms. In its simplest form, we have in a photograph surrogate possession of a cherished person or thing, a possession which gives photographs some of the character of unique objects. Through photographs, we also have a consumer's relation to events, both to events which are part of our experience and to those which are not—a distinction between types of experience that such habit-forming consumership blurs. A third form of acquisition is that, through image-making and image-duplicating machines, we can acquire something as information (rather than experience). Indeed, the importance of photographic images as the medium through which more and more events enter our experience is, finally, only a byproduct of their effectiveness in furnishing knowledge dissociated from and independent of experience.

This is the most inclusive form of photographic acquisition. Through being photographed, something becomes part of a system of information, fitted into schemes of classification and storage which range from the crudely chronological order of snapshot sequences pasted in family albums to the dogged accumulations and meticulous filing needed for photography's uses in weather forecasting, astronomy, microbiology, geology, police work, medical training and diagnosis, military reconnaissance, and art history. Photographs do more than redefine the stuff of ordinary experience (people, things, events, whatever we see—albeit differently, often inattentively—with natural vision) and add vast amounts of material that we never see at all. Reality as such is redefined—as an item for exhibition, as a record for scrutiny, as a target for surveillance. The photographic exploration and duplication of the world fragments continuities and feeds the pieces into an interminable dossier, thereby providing possibilities of control that could not even be dreamed of under the earlier system of recording information:writing.

That photographic recording is always, potentially, a means of control was already recognized when such powers were in their infancy. In 1850, Delacroix noted in his *Journal* the success of some "experiments in photography" being made at Cambridge, where astronomers were photographing the sun and the moon and had managed to obtain a pinhead-size impression of the star Vega. He added the following "curious" observation:

> Since the light of the star which was daguerreotyped took twenty years to traverse the space separating it from the earth, the ray which was fixed on the plate had consequently left the celestial sphere a long time before Daguerre

had discovered the process by means of which we have just gained control of this light.

Leaving behind such puny notions of control as Delacroix's, photography's progress has made ever more literal the senses in which a photograph gives control over the thing photographed. The technology that has already minimized the extent to which the distance separating photographer from subject affects the precision and magnitude of the image; provided ways to photograph things which are unimaginably small as well as those, like stars, which are unimaginably far; rendered picture-taking independent of light itself (infrared photography) and freed the picture-object from its confinement to two dimensions (holography); shrunk the interval between sighting the picture and holding it in one's hands (from the first Kodak, when it took weeks for a developed roll of film to be returned to the amateur photographer, to the Polaroid, which ejects the image in a few seconds); not only got images to move (cinema) but achieved their simultaneous recording and transmission (video)—this technology has made photography an incomparable tool for deciphering behavior, predicting it, and interfering with it.

Photography has powers that no other image-system has ever enjoyed because, unlike the earlier ones, it is *not* dependent on an image maker. However, carefully the photographer intervenes in setting up and guiding the image-making process, the process itself remains an optical-chemical (or electronic) one, the workings of which are automatic, the machinery for which will inevitably be modified to provide still more detailed and, therefore, more useful maps of the real. The mechanical genesis of these images, and the literalness of the powers they confer, amounts to a new relationship between image and reality. And if photography could also be said to restore the most primitive relationship—the partial identity of image and object—the potency of the image is now experienced in a very different way. The primitive notion of the efficacy of images presumes that images possess the qualities of real things, but our inclination is to attribute to real things the qualities of an image.

As everyone knows, primitive people fear that the camera will rob them of some part of their being. In the memoir he published in 1900, at the end of a very long life, Nadar reports that Balzac had a similar "vague dread" of being photographed. His explanation, according to Nadar, was that

> every body in its natural state was made up of a series of ghostly images superimposed in layers to infinity, wrapped in infinitesimal films. . . . Man never having been able to create, that is to make something material from an apparition, from something impalpable, or to make from nothing, an object—each

Daguerreian operation was therefore going to lay hold of, detach, and use up
one of the layers of the body on which it focused.

It seems fitting for Balzac to have had this particular brand of trep-
idation—"Was Balzac's fear of the Daguerreotype real or feigned?" Nadar
asks. "It was real . . ."—since the procedure of photography is a materi-
alizing, so to speak, of what is most original in his procedure as a novelist.
The Balzacian operation was to magnify tiny details, as in a photographic
enlargement, to juxtapose incongruous traits or items, as in a photographic layout: made expressive in this way, any one thing can be connected with everything else. For Balzac, the spirit of an entire milieu could
be disclosed by a single material detail, however paltry or arbitrary-seem-
ing. The whole of a life may be summed up in a momentary appearance.[1]
And a change in appearances is a change in the person, for he refused to
posit any "real" person ensconced behind these appearances. Balzac's fan-
ciful theory, expressed to Nadar, that a body is composed of an infinite
series of "ghostly images," eerily parallels the supposedly realistic theory
expressed in his novels, that a person is an aggregate of appearances, appearances which can be made to yield, by proper focusing, infinite layers
of significance. To view reality as an endless set of situations which mirror
each other, to extract analogies from the most dissimilar things, is to anticipate the characteristic form of perception stimulated by photographic
images. Reality itself has started to be understood as a kind of writing,
which has to be decoded—even as photographed images were themselves
first compared to writing. (Niepce's name for the process whereby the
image appears on the plate was heliography, sun-writing; Fox Talbot
called the camera "the pencil of nature.")

The problem with Feuerbach's contrast of "original" with "copy" is its
static definitions of reality and image. It assumes that what is real persists,
unchanged and intact, while only images have changed: shored up by the
most tenuous claims to credibility, they have somehow become more seductive. But the notions of image and reality are complementary. When
the notion of reality changes, so does that of the image, and vice versa.
"Our era" does not prefer images to real things out of perversity but partly
in response to the ways in which the notion of what is real has been progressively complicated and weakened, one of the early ways being the criticism of reality as façade which arose among the enlightened middle classes
in the last century. (This was of course the very opposite of the effect intended.) To reduce large parts of what has hitherto been regarded as real
to mere fantasy, as Feuerbach did when he called religion "the dream of
the human mind" and dismissed theological ideas as psychological projections; or to inflate the random and trivial details of everyday life into

ciphers of hidden historical and psychological forces, as Balzac did in his encyclopedia of social reality in novel form—these are themselves ways of experiencing reality as a set of appearances, an image.

Few people in this society share the primitive dread of cameras that comes from thinking of the photograph as a material part of themselves. But some trace of the magic remains: for example, in our reluctance to tear up or throw away the photograph of a loved one, especially of someone dead or far away. To do so is a ruthless gesture of rejection. In *Jude the Obscure* it is Jude's discovery that Arabella has sold the maple frame with the photograph of himself in it which he gave her on their wedding day that signifies to Jude "the utter death of every sentiment in his wife" and is "the conclusive little stroke to demolish all sentiment in him." But the true modern primitivism is not to regard the image as a real thing; photographic images are hardly that real. Instead, reality has come to seem more and more like what we are shown by cameras. It is common now for people to insist about their experience of a violent event in which they were caught up—a plane crash, a shoot-out, a terrorist bombing—that "it seemed like a movie." This is said, other descriptions seeming insufficient, in order to explain how real it was. While many people in non-industrialized countries still feel apprehensive when being photographed, divining it to be some kind of trespass, an act of disrespect, a sublimated looting of the personality or the culture, people in industrialized countries seek to have their photographs taken—feel that they are images, and are made real by photographs.

A steadily more complex sense of the real creates its own compensatory fervors and simplifications, the most addictive of which is picture-taking. It is as if photographers, responding to an increasingly depleted sense of reality, were looking for a transfusion—traveling to new experiences, refreshing the old ones. Their ubiquitous activities amount to the most radical, and the safest, version of mobility. The urge to have new experiences is translated into the urge to take photographs: experience seeking a crisis-proof form.

As the taking of photographs seems almost obligatory to those who travel about, the passionate collecting of them has special appeal for those confined—either by choice, incapacity, or coercion—to indoor space. Photograph collections can be used to make a substitute world, keyed to exalting or consoling or tantalizing images. A photograph can be the starting point of a romance (Hardy's Jude had already fallen in love with Sue Bridehead's photograph before he met her), but it is more common for the erotic relation to be not only created by but understood as limited to the photographs. In Cocteau's *Les Enfants Terribles,* the narcissistic brother and sister share their bedroom, their "secret room," with images of boxers, movie stars, and murderers. Isolating themselves in their lair to live out their private legend, the two adolescents put up these photographs, a private pantheon. On one wall of cell No. 426 in Fresnes Prison in the early 1940s Jean Genet pasted the photographs of twenty criminals he had clipped from newspapers, twenty faces in which he discerned "the sacred sign of the monster," and in their honor wrote *Our Lady of the Flowers;* they served as his muses, his models, his erotic talismans. They watch over my little routines," writes Genet—conflating reverie, masturbation, and writing—and "are all the family I have and my only friends." For stay-at-homes, prisoners, and the self-imprisoned, to live among the photographs of glamorous strangers is a sentimental response to isolation and an insolent challenge to it.

J. G. Ballard's novel *Crash* (1973) describes a more specialized collecting of photographs in the service of sexual obsession: photographs of car accidents which the narrator's friend Vaughan collects while preparing to stage his own death in a car crash. The acting out of his erotic vision of car death is anticipated and the fantasy itself further eroticized by the repeated perusal of these photographs. At one end of the spectrum, photographs are objective data; at the other end, they are items of psychological science fiction. And as in even the most dreadful, or neutral-seeming, reality a sexual imperative can be found, so even the most banal photograph-document can mutate into an emblem of desire. The mug shot is a clue to a detective, an erotic fetish to a fellow thief. To Hofrat Behrens, in *The Magic Mountain,* the pulmonary x rays of his patients are diagnostic tools. To Hans Castorp, serving an indefinite sentence in Behrens's TB sanatorium, and made lovesick by the enigmatic, unattainable Clavdia Chauchat, "Clavdia's X-ray portrait, showing not her face, but the delicate bony structure of the upper half of her body, and the organs of the thoracic cavity, surrounded by the pale, ghostlike envelope of flesh," is the most precious of trophies. The "transparent portrait" is a far more intimate vestige of his beloved than the Hofrat's painting of Clavdia, that "exterior portrait," which Hans had once gazed at with such longing.

Photographs are a way of imprisoning reality, understood as recalcitrant, inaccessible; of making it stand still. Or they enlarge a reality that is felt to be shrunk, hollowed out, perishable, remote. One can't possess reality, one can possess (and be possessed by) images—as, according to Proust, most ambitious of voluntary prisoners, one can't possess the present but one can possess the past. Nothing could be more unlike the self-sacrificial travail of an artist like Proust than the effortlessness of picture-taking, which must be the sole activity resulting in accredited works of art in which a single movement, a touch of the finger, produces a complete work. While the Proustian labors presuppose that reality is distant, photography implies instant access to the real. But the results of this practice of instant access are another way of creating distance. To possess the world in the form of images is, precisely, to reexperience the unreality and remoteness of the real.

The strategy of Proust's realism presumes distance from what is normally experienced as real, the present, in order to reanimate' what is usually available only in a remote and shadowy form, the past—which is where the present becomes in his sense real, that is, something that can be possessed. In this effort photographs were of no help. Whenever Proust mentions photographs, he does so disparagingly: as a synonym for a shallow, too exclusively visual, merely voluntary relation to the past, whose yield is insignificant compared with the deep discoveries to be made by responding to cues given by all the senses—the technique he called "involuntary memory." One can't imagine the Overture to *Swann's Way* ending with the narrator's coming across a snapshot of the parish church at Combray and the savoring of *that* visual crumb, instead of the taste of the humble madeleine dipped in tea, making an entire part of his past spring into view. But this is not because a photograph cannot evoke memories (it can, depending on the quality of the viewer rather than of the photograph) but because of what Proust makes clear about his own demands upon imaginative recall, that it be not just extensive and accurate but give the texture and essence of things. And by considering photographs only so far as he could use them, as an instrument of memory, Proust somewhat misconstrues what photographs are: not so much an instrument of memory as an invention of it or a replacement.

It is not reality that photographs make immediately accessible, but images. For example, now all adults can know exactly how they and their parents and grandparents looked as children—a knowledge not available to anyone before the invention of cameras, not even to that tiny minority among whom it was customary to commission paintings of their children. Most of these portraits were less informative than any snapshot. And even the very wealthy usually owned just one portrait of themselves or any of their forebears as children, that is, an image of one moment of childhood, whereas it is common to have many photographs of oneself, the camera offering the possibility of possessing a complete record, at all ages. The point of the standard portraits in the bourgeois household of the eighteenth and nineteenth centuries was to confirm an ideal of the sitter (proclaiming social standing, embellishing personal appearance); given this purpose, it is clear why their owners did not feel the need to have more than one. What the photograph-record confirms is, more modestly, simply that the subject exists; therefore, one can never have too many.

The fear that a subject's uniqueness was leveled by being photographed was never so frequently expressed as in the 1850s, the years when portrait photography gave the first example of how cameras could create instant fashions and durable industries. In Melville's *Pierre,* published at the start of the decade, the hero, another fevered champion of voluntary isolation,

> considered with what infinite readiness now, the most faithful portrait of any one could be taken by the Daguerreotype, whereas in former times a faithful portrait was only within the power of the moneyed, or mental aristocrats of the earth. How natural then the inference, that instead of; as in old times, immortalizing a genius, a portrait now only *dayalized* a dunce. Besides, when every body has his portrait published, true distinction lies in not having yours published at all.

But if photographs demean, paintings distort in the opposite way: they make grandiose. Melville's intuition is that all forms of portraiture in the business civilization are compromised; at least, so it appears to Pierre, a paragon of alienated sensibility. Just as a photograph is too little in a mass society, a painting is too much. The nature of a painting, Pierre observes, makes it

> better entitled to reverence than the man; inasmuch as nothing belittling can be imagined concerning the portrait, whereas many unavoidably belittling things can be fancied as touching the man.

Even if such ironies can be considered to have been dissolved by the completeness of photography's triumph, the main difference between a painting and a photograph in the matter of portraiture still holds. Paintings invariably sum up; photographs usually do not. Photographic images are pieces of evidence in an ongoing biography or history. And one photograph, unlike one painting, implies that there will be others.

"Ever—the Human Document to keep the present and the future in touch with the past," said Lewis Hine. But what photography supplies is not only a record of the past but a new way of dealing with the present, as the effects of the countless billions of contemporary photograph-documents attest. While old photographs fill out our mental image of the past, the photographs being taken now transform what is present into a mental image, like the past. Cameras establish an inferential relation to the present (reality is known by its traces), provide an instantly retroactive view of experience. Photographs give mock forms of possession: of the past, the present, even the future. In Nabokov's *Invitation to a Beheading* (1938), the prisoner Cincinnatus is shown the "photohoroscope" of a child cast by the sinister M'sieur Pierre: an album of photographs of little Emmie as an infant, then a small child, then pre-pubescent, as she is now, then—by retouching and using photographs of her mother—of Emmie the adolescent, the bride, the thirty-year old, concluding with a photograph at age forty, Emmie on her deathbed. A "parody of the work of time" is what Nabokov calls this exemplary artifact; it is also a parody of the work of photography.

Photography, which has so many narcissistic uses, is also a powerful instrument for depersonalizing our relation to the world; and the two uses are complementary. Like a pair of binoculars with no right or wrong end, the camera makes exotic things near, intimate; and familiar things small, abstract, strange, much farther away. It offers, in one easy, habit-forming activity, both participation and alienation in our own lives and those of others—allowing us to participate, while confirming alienation.

Note

1. I am drawing on the account of Balzac's realism in Erich Auerbach's *Mimesis*. The passage that Auerbach describes from the beginning of *Le Père Goriot* (1834)—Balzac is describing the dining room of the Vauquer pension at seven in the morning and the entry of Madame Vauquer—could hardly be more explicit (or proto-Proustian). "Her whole person," Balzac writes, "explains the pension, as the pension implies her person. . . . The short-statured woman's blowsy *embonpoint* is the product of the life here, as typhoid is the consequence of the exhalations of a hospital. Her knitted wool petticoat, which is longer than her outer skirt (made of an old dress), and whose wadding is escaping by the gaps in the splitting material, sums up the drawing-room, the dining room, the little garden, announces the cooking and gives an inkling of the boarders. When she is there, the spectacle is complete."

DAVID L. JACOBS

Domestic Snapshots: Toward a Grammar of Motives

While Susan Sontag explores the mediated experience of "photography," Jacobs focuses on a unique form of that medium—the "snapshot." The snapshot requires relationships and a context in order to be understood. How aware are you when posing before your relative's camera that your "iconic self" is being preserved for the future? To what extent do you change your personality in the presence of the "instamatic"? The snapshot, unlike the photograph, creates interpersonal relationships when viewed in conjunction with the rest of the family snapshots.

Photography is unique among the visual arts in that virtually anyone can make satisfactory images. With Instamatics and Polaroids even young children can make adequately exposed and focused pictures. Simple, inexpensive equipment has made amateur photography an incalculably popular pastime. Helmut Gernsheim estimated in 1963 that 100 million people around the world take billions of snapshots every year.[1] In 1964 12 million British amateur photographers took 600 million photographs, and in the process spent some 69 million pounds.[2] A mere thirty years after the invention of the polaroid process an estimated 50 million Americans own polaroid equipment.[3] Whatever the precise figures, the popularity of the medium is seen everywhere in our society. An overwhelming majority of American households are equipped with at least one camera with which the family creates a storehouse of images about itself. Photography is fully democratic: its popularity is shared by people representing virtually all social, economic and racial groups.

The snapshots produced in such prodigious numbers by untrained, amateur photographers are the subject of this reading. The popularity of photography seems to have its sources in something other than fashion or faddishness. Too many people for too many years have been attracted to the medium for such glib answers to be taken seriously. Photography, clearly, is a *bona fide* phenomenon, and it should be regarded as such. Photography, because of its great popularity, obviously satisfies certain individual and social needs. In order to account for the popularity of photography,

From *Journal of American Culture*, vol. 4, no. 1 (Spring 1981), pp. 93–105. Reprinted by permission of the publisher.

then, we must speculate on the nature of these needs, and try to determine how photography, and specifically snapshooting, helps to satisfy them.

Unfortunately there is little substantive literature, and thus no established methodology that equips us for this kind of endeavor. Magazines like *Popular Photography, Camera 35,* and *Modern Photography* serve basically to disseminate technical information. They are filled with chatty columns that inform their readers how to make "better" pictures. Though they appeal to amateur photographers, they seldom if ever raise serious critical questions about their readers' work. Less mass-oriented writers are usually concerned with either the history of the medium or the photographs of "art photographers" or other professionals, most of whom work in quite different modes. Snapshots, and their makers, receive very little attention.

The few references we do find to snapshots often have the effect of discouraging further thought on the matter. Most writers have treated the snapshot with considerable disdain. Alfred Stieglitz regarded with contempt "every Tom, Dick and Harry who . . . learn how to get something or other on a sensitive plate,"[4] Stieglitz's well-known dictum that "art is for the few and by the few," furthermore, hardly served to encourage critical attention to popular photography.[5] Helmut Gernsheim, in his massive but flawed *History of Photography,* devotes one four-page chapter to "push-button photography." He claims that the simplicity of the "Brownie" cameras in the 1880s "did much for the popularization—and subsequent decadence—of photography."[6] He adds that, the "new camera enthusiasts were entirely devoid of artistic training and feeling," and that simplified equipment replaced the "ardent amateur" with "the new machine man."[7]

Beaumont Newhall, in his influential history of the medium, displays none of Gernsheim's hauteur, perhaps because he never really deals with the subject. He discusses small camera work (e.g., 35 mm) in terms of photographers like Erich Salomon and Cartier-Bresson, and in his two pages on the polaroid process he emphasizes its technical aspects.[8]

It is worth noting that those writers who pose the most interesting questions about snapshots do so from sociological and psychological perspectives. Marie Czach, writing in a recent *Afterimage,* reviews an exhibit of 300 photographs (and another 300 artifacts) entitled, "At Home, Domestic Life in the Post Centennial Era, 1876–1920." Particularly interesting are her insights about the role snapshots play in establishing identity. She argues that the pictures of A. H. Dahl comprised

> part of a system which bound the Norwegian community together and enhanced its sense of achievement by the visible documentation of economic success, as well as the more subtle satisfaction of participation in the developing of American national taste.[9]

In claiming that the pictures "show what people were proud of, thought interesting, and what they wanted to show others," Czach suggests that some snapshots represent self-made signs of class identity, and, more specifically, material acquisition and upward mobility.

Stanley Milgram and Paul Byers also write provocatively on the imaging qualities of snapshots, though they emphasize individuals within a family rather than more extended groups or communities. Milgram, a professor of psychology at the City University of New York, argues that "photographic portraits are best seen as the product of a social relationship," and he is especially interested in the "self-presentational energy" that some subjects manifest as they are photographed.[10] Byers, an anthropologist at Columbia University, sees photographs "as objects with which people arrange and rearrange relations among themselves," and he adds that

> the photographer is *always* a part of the context of events he is photographing; he can never photograph human behavior without being part of it, and his photographs are necessarily a product of his interaction and selectivity.[11]

Byers suggests that this idea can provide interesting insights into how we experience and judge certain kinds of snapshots.

> . . . when a mother looks at a photograph of her child and does or does not like it, she is comparing the photograph with her own image of the child. If the photograph matches her image with satisfactory congruence, the picture is good. If it does not, the photograph is unsuitable.[12]

Both Byers and Milgram ground their ideas in what I would call a relational model. We will return to this idea later.

Interesting as the ideas advanced by Czach, Milgram and Byers may be, all three writers are limited by the lack of solid, verifiable research on the subject of popular photography. I share their difficulties, and, like them, am forced to speculate. There has been no carefully conducted research concerned with how people regard photographs of themselves, or snapshots that they themselves made. And no one has studied how families relate to the historical archives that family albums and collections represent. Accordingly I am forced to posit a rather vague and amorphous "most people," and then speculate about how they may be regarding their creations. The one demonstrable fact is the omnipresent evidence that snapshooting is a tremendously popular activity.

According to the *Oxford English Dictionary*, "snapshot" was originally a hunting term, a "quick shot taken without deliberate aim, especially one of a rising bird or quickly moving animal." The word was first applied to photography by Sir John Herschel, who, in 1860, imagined a photographer taking a "snapshot" in a fraction of a second. Herschel's use of the word singles out a characteristic of snapshots that is still pertinent: the fact that they are quickly made images. Kodaks and polaroids are small, light and take "fast" films that allow their users to hand hold the camera in virtually any situation. The snapshooter, with such equipment at his disposal, can react quickly to a scene and still emerge with satisfactorily exposed and focussed prints.

Such equipment is perfectly suited for the snapshooter's objectives. Wilson Hicks argues that in snapshots the subject matter is much more important than technical proficiency:

> Even though little Alice's face is chalked out by the sun, or half lost in a shadow, it is still little Alice. The viewer, knowing her so well, by a trick of the imagination sees the real little Alice whenever he looks at her image, which he deludes himself into believing is much better than it actually is.[13]

The snapshooter is primarily interested in whether the subject is recognizable. Issues like composition, uniform sharpness throughout the picture plane, or rich tones are subordinate. Snapshooters do not often employ unusual camera angles. Typically, the subjects stare directly into the camera, and the photographer takes the picture at eye level. The equipment simplifies the technical variables so that the photographer can direct most of his attention toward his subject.

The straightforward presentation of the subject, then, is an important characteristic of snapshots. Furthermore, these subjects are usually people who are known to the photographer, and, in the case of group portraits, people who are known to one another. The subject, most of the time, is family or close friends who are situated among familiar surroundings, like the home itself.[14] The setting is often an important consideration for analyzing snapshots. As Milgram suggests, "the meaning of a photograph emerges not only from the people in it, but in their linkage to the objects that surround them."[15]

Snapshots are remarkably domestic. Not only do they usually treat the family within domestic contexts but often several members of the family share in their making. The camera changes hands, and so the snapshooter of one moment will soon be the subject. The snapshooter's role is temporary, and affected by the act that another family member will soon be taking the pictures. Furthermore, while there are often differences in class, race and economic status between professional photographers and their subjects, the snapshooter and his subjects are peers. Domestic snapshots are images in which members of the family have taken turns as imagers and those imaged, and in which the members of a set—the family—have envisoned, photographically, other members of the same set.

Domestic snapshots do not typically document such mundane events as the family watching television, or working in the kitchen, or mowing the lawn. Rather, snapshots are usually made when the family is engaged in extraordinary experiences. Whether it is the excitement of a child opening packages under a Christmas tree or first seeing her birthday cake, or the marriage of a relative, or the family at the beach, the snapshot documents moments that are easily distinguishable from the everyday experiences of the family. They depict times of special or heightened activity, and, at times, significance. The participants in such an event realize that the occasion is special, and they realize that they are photographed precisely because of this specialness. As participants, they are conscious both of the meaning of the event, and their roles within it.

Such consciousness has several implications for the often-heard claims that snapshots are *informal* images. As we have seen, snapshots are usually made during special days that have particular significance, and often a formally established network of symbolism. These events are often accompanied by a set of private symbolic behaviors (who packs the car; stopping at certain restaurants *en route;* a particular kind of birthday cake) that are based upon a family's unique experiences. Other occasions are significant by virtue of the culture at large. Holidays like Christmas, Thanksgiving and Independence Day incorporate symbolism that is intrinsic to the events themselves. Most often there is a combination of private and public symbols. In weddings, for example, the exchange of rings is a public symbol, while the rings themselves often embody a couple's private symbolism. It is generally true that the occasions which evoke snapshooting are accompanied by a set of established, semantically fixed symbols that define and contribute to the uniqueness of the day.

These symbols often determine how the snapshooter selects his materials. The snapshooter takes pictures of his daughter blowing out birthday candles or opening presents, or of a relative with knife poised over a browned bird. In instructing the children to hold balloons, Willie Johnson includes in his image symbols that typify his daughter's birthday (Fig. 1). At times the continuity of the action becomes less important than seizing the symbolic moment, and thus the snapshooter's commands to wait until all is in readiness, or until the subjects are properly arranged. The snapshooter, in such cases, consciously poses his subjects rather than responding to events, symbolic or otherwise, as they naturally unfold. He situates the family within a preconceived symbolic matrix.

The subjects, of course, are also cognizant of such matrices, and they often are self-directorial. In the above examples the subjects, unless they are very young, willingly delay candle-blowing, present-opening or turkey-carving until the requisite image is made. This is even more the case when adults are posing in symbolically rich situations. In short, the subjects wholly participate in the image-making process. They, too, are consciously en-

Willie Johnson

Figure 1.

gaged in making images that incorporate the symbols or symbolic actions that are part of the occasion.

As the events that snapshooters usually record are exceptional, so too is the behavior of the participants. Holidays can evoke in us culturally prescribed and sanctioned kinds of behavior. A family on Christmas morning is interested in projecting a positive image of itself in part because of the ambience that surrounds the day itself. This can have a countervailing effect upon the depressed moods that often accompany the December holidays. We have all witnessed a would-be festive table populated by hostile, argumentative and apparently unhappy relatives. Yet when the camera appears all are smiling. Most of us, long before we reach adolescence, have been taught to smile—to "say cheese"—for the camera. But beyond this, we can explain this kind of transformation in terms of our wanting to portray ourselves in a positive fashion. We image ourselves with the full knowledge that we will subsequently "re-experience" the moment by looking at the snapshot. Such projection, or, in Stanley Milgram's term, "self-presentational energy," is derived from the nature of the event depicted (holidays like Christmas are times of joy); or from a sense of family ("we are close knit, and happy in one another's company"); or from a sense of self ("I am happy"; or when looking back at the image, "I was happy then"). We are not wholly "natural" at such moments; rather, we project images of ourselves, poses that sometimes harden into postures.

The mere presence of a camera can evoke a certain amount of posing.

Familiar as we may be with having our pictures taken, few of us could say that our behavior remains identical regardless of the presence or absence of a photographer. Even if the snapshooter is a trusted member of the family our behavior changes. All parties are conscious that pictures are to be taken. This mutually shared awareness translates into certain conventional snapshot grammars that can readily be seen in Willie Johnson's picture (Fig. 1). The children and mother look directly and unabashedly into the camera. There is not even a pretense of casualness. Obviously, these people were not arranged in a pyramid in the middle of a birthday party. The picture, rather, is carefully posed, with the shorter, young children in front. And Johnson, no doubt, told all parties to smile, though with only partial success. We can think of this picture as typical of many shapshots insofar as the subjects are conscious that their picture is being taken, and do not pretend otherwise. While "props" like Christmas trees, living room furniture, or, for that matter, other people, might abound, the subjects do not, typically, relate to them in the picture. Rather, they present themselves to the camera, or more accurately, to the person behind the camera. The subjects communicate their awareness that this situation, this pose, this arrangement, exists only for the sake of making pictures.

I have argued that many, if not most snapshots can usefully be thought of as domestic images. Their domesticity is reflected in the kinds of situations and attitudes that snapshots customarily depict, and in their iconic conventions. It is important to add that the snapshooter and his subjects later become the principal audience of the pictures. Unlike photographs that appear in the media, which are directed toward a vast, heterogeneous audience, snapshots are made of, by, and for a small, mutually known group. The snapshooter and his subject can dwell quite successfully within a realm of privately symbolic poses and expressions, whose importance can only be recognized by a handful of initiates. In short, snapshots often reflect a specific and exclusive iconography. Their meaning is often specific to the snapshooter, his subject and the audience.

In this respect snapshots can be contrasted to the kinds of images included in Edward Steinchen's landmark exhibition, *The Family of Man*. Carl Sandburg, who was Steichen's brother-in-law, writes in the Prologue to the book that stemmed from the exhibition:

> The first cry of a newborn baby in Chicago or Zamboango, in Amsterdam or Rangoon, has the same pitch and key, each saying, 'I am! I have come through! I belong! I am a member of the Family." [16]

Throughout the Prologue, Sandburg, with more than a little sentimentalism, emphasizes the archetypal, universal message of the images. The audience is not given, and is not dependent upon specific information about these subjects in order to apprehend the meaning of the photographs. Indeed, Steinchen might well have argued that the specific identities of the subjects of these images, and even their class and nationality, are irrelevant. The images included in *Family of Man* are generalized by virtue of their lack of specificity and context.

With a snapshot, however, familiarity with its contexts greatly assists us in appreciating and understanding its meaning. If we are unfamiliar with the subject and setting of a given snapshot, then for us the picture is semantically limited. To be sure, we can look at such images with pleasure, and in some cases can gain considerable information from them. When we look, for example, at a thirty year old snapshot of strangers, we can learn much about how people lived in that period. But, at the same time, if I look at a snapshot taken of me, thirty years ago, in my living room, I bring to that image a wealth of information and memories. I animate that image in ways that no one else, excepting other members of my family, can approximate.

We can make the same kind of distinction with Frank Allison's untitled snapshot (Fig. 2). In this snapshot the fountain and its graffiti may have a special, shared significance for the snapshooter, subject and audience. The fountain may have been the site of countless family picnics in the past. Or perhaps the graffiti were the aftermath of some infamous, drunken spree. Such prior, extra-photographic knowledge would be essential in reconstructing the context and meaning of this image. If we are unaware of the symbolic context, then we view the snapshot with vastly impoverished eyes. Snapshots are often ciphers that mystify, that defy reconstruction. But if, on the other hand, we know or are a part of its contexts, then the snapshot becomes a rich source of associations and meanings.

The relationships involved in snapshot photography are virtually unique in that the photographer, his subjects and the audience for the image usually derive from the same social unit: the nuclear family. This remarkably enclosed and discrete set of interrelationships is, I would argue, the major defining characteristic of most snapshots. Unlike many forms of photography, snapshots are usually made with the full awareness by all parties that pictures are being made. And, unlike most forms of professional photography, snapshots are made with the understanding that the primary audience for the images is the snapshooter and the subjects themselves. In snapshots, all of the participants—the imager, those imaged and the audience for the images—are known to one another, and usually intimately. Accordingly, snapshots reflect the social relationships and interactions of a given family. They are signs for how members of the family simultaneously image themselves and are imaged by other family members. It is with this in mind that I will suggest some of the sources of the vast popularity of snapshot imagery.

Frank Allison

Figure 2.

So far we have looked at the kinds of subjects and events which the snapshooter typically concerns himself with, how snapshots incorporate a mixture of public and private symbolism, and, perhaps more important, the fact that snapshots are usually made by, of, and for the nuclear family. Some of these characteristics are themselves partial explanations for the popularity of snapshots within our society. The fact that cameras are both affordable and easy to use is, if not exactly a cause, then at least a condition for this popularity. If, for example, video tapes shared these qualities, the snapshot might well be obsolete.

But beyond this practical level there are more subtle issues at work. Man, to alter the well-known phrase, is the image-making animal. And, we might add, his favorite image is usually himself. It has only been within the last 125 years, however, that most people have had the opportunity to be part of a visual image. Our distant ancestors, unless they were monied or artistically inclined, have not left us the legacy of their countenances. In the past portraits have been a function of wealth. People of the lower classes, when they were included in paintings at all, were usually placed in genre pictures which they probably never saw; these paintings, like most art, were the exclusive domain and property of the landed classes.

Those wealthy or titled people who sat for portraits knew that the results would be displayed publicly, whether in a castle or in the galleries that adorned many manors. As E. H. Gombrich has written, the portrait was

> . . . an image commissioned and made to sum up the sitter's social status and career, and to hand down his features as a memorial to his descendants and as a monument to later ages.[17]

A portrait was immortality constructed in oils, and accordingly the sitter often devoted considerable time and money to it. He was interested, not surprisingly, in emerging with a positive, self-aggrandizing image.

With the invention of photography portraits were no longer an exclusive privilege of wealth. The daguerreotype was inexpensive, and within the reach of millions of pocketbooks. The historian Robert Taft estimates that by the mid-1850s some three million daguerreotypes were made every year in America alone.[18] The majority were portraits made in studios. The invention of simple hand cameras by Eastman in the 1880s allowed people to make their own pictures instead of having to rely upon the skills of the professional. Some 100 years later all of us, by virtue of improved photographic technology, are photographed with unprecedented frequency. We are, if nothing else, the most imaged society in history.

While the invention of photography broadened the scope of portraiture, I would argue that the psychology of those portrayed basically remained the same. After all, the snapshot, like the oil painting, is also destined for a family gallery, though it is most often in the form of a scrapbook. The snapshot is still an image, even if humbler in origins and design, which attests to the sitter's existence, and which will outlast him as well. I do not believe that there is a fundamental difference, psychologically, between Henry VIII posing for Holbein the Younger, and Mr. Jones posing for Mrs. Jones on the front stoop. Both subjects project what they hope to be positive qualities, and in both cases the images become a part of history, even if with Henry VIII it is a national, public history, while with Mr. Jones it is the history of a family.

The popularity of snapshooting stems in large part from the fact that it provides us with a readily accessible means by which we can image and be imaged. The snapshooter and his subject are *both* engaged in imaging processes, and both, albeit in different ways, expend what we earlier termed self-presentational energy. This energy is at the heart of the snapshot, and thus we should examine it in more detail.

Sam Jones poses for a picture to be taken by his father, Walter. Sam addresses, or "presents" himself to a variety of audiences. On the most immediate level, he images himself for family and friends. Such an audience, while it obviously knows the "real" Sam, is not necessarily a supportive audience for the snapshot itself. Indeed, many snapshot subjects have found

that families and friends can be a most critical audience. This could well
be true for another primary audience of the snapshot, Sam himself. The
snapshot becomes a means by which Sam views himself, and he may well
be disappointed in the result insofar as his mental self-image may not conform with the specific, frozen image that the camera affords him. Beyond
this, it is also possible that his self-image is not wholly positive, which will
affect how Sam presents himself, and how he relates to the subsequent image. Many portrait photographers have discussed the problems of satisying
a client in similar terms. The late Imogen Cunningham, whose career in
photography spanned 75 years, said that she often felt "despondent" after
a session with a sitter because of

> . . . people's lack of acceptance of anything I did. Very often people can't
> face themselves. They can't live with the faces they were born with. It's not a
> nice occupation to try to please people with their own faces.[19]

Sam is also projecting himself into time. He knows that at some future
date he will use this snapshot and others as mnemonics for earlier periods
of his life. If Sam is over, say, ten years old, he has probably seen his parents use snapshots or home movies in this way, and it is likely that he has
done the same with old pictures of himself. Sam, as he poses for his father,
makes a partial history of himself; he projects an image into a known format, the snapshot, that he will later use as a means of re-experiencing his
past. Similarly, he knows that this same image may be used by his children
in order to "know" their father at an earlier age, and by their children,
who may know his bodily self exclusively from the snapshots they inherit.
Indeed, for that great majority of us who will not be remembered for heroic acts or immortal creations, snapshots may well be the main items that
survive us. Sam, then, is not only making a history for himself, but he also
is projecting himself to an audience for whom the images will be a major
historical source for their deceased ancestor. The snapshot, seen from this
perspective, represents a kind of immortality, a fact that significantly affects how Sam presents himself.

Father and son are equally concerned with viewers who will, at a later
date, view the snapshot mnemonically. An awareness of the audience affects both snapshooter and subject in similar, if not identical psychological
ways, although their means of enactment differ significantly. While Sam
presents himself to a variety of audiences, his father Walter enacts this
"presentation" through the powers of the camera. Photographs are man-
made, despite the presence of what many have viewed as an autonomous
image-making machine, the camera. While the snapshooter has fewer options than the photographer who works with a Leica or Hasselblad, the
most important option of all is fully operative: Walter Jones selects. He

positions himself in relationship to his subject; or he may tell Sam to stand in a certain way, or hold his hands behind his back, or put his hat on. And then Walter peers through the viewfinder, watching his son, waiting for the right moment. The decisive moment for Walter Jones is a function of his relationship with his son; it is born out of the totality of his experiences with and feelings about Sam. Walter waits until what he sees in the viewfinder approximates his *mental* image of Sam. Walter's selections and Sam's self-presentation are both, in their different ways, efforts to make a snapshot that conforms to their respective mental images. In both cases, as Kenneth E. Boulding writes in a different yet appropriate context, it is "this subjective knowledge . . . this Image that largely governs [their] behavior."[20]

While Sam's primary interest lies in imaging himself, Walter's intentions are somewhat more complex. He may, on one level, try to image his son in a way that is compatible with Sam's self-image. It is not unusual for snapshot subjects to give instructions to the snapshooter, much as wealthy patrons told painters how they wish to be portrayed. But Walter is also imaging his son in terms of how he sees him. His "subjective knowledge," his mental image of Sam, in part determines how Walter fills the picture frame, and when he snaps the shutter. Moreover, Walter is also, on a more subtle level, imaging himself as Sam's father. Walter wants to make a positive, idealized portrait, for if Sam is portrayed positively, then it speaks well for the father. Imagine, for a moment, the familiar tableau of a proud parent showing snapshots of their children. Walter takes his snapshot to work, and his co-workers see a seemingly well-adjusted, content, smiling young man. Walter beams with pride for his upstanding son, and for himself insofar as the snapshot reflects his tutelage. The snapshot is a symbol for Walter's fatherhood, and Sam's smiling countenance is an index for his father's adeptness at his task.

The model suggested above may be faulted for taking the snapshot too seriously. We know from experience that not all snapshots involve such complex patterns of psychological projections, or such ponderous existential underpinnings. We do not, after all, experience our driver's license picture as a sign for our immortality. And we do not invariably wax narcissistic whenever a camera appears on the scene. My account of Walter and Sam Jones is proposed as a paradigm of the levels of imaging that *can* operate in snapshots. It is unlikely that any one snapshot would incorporate all, or perhaps even most of these levels of imaging. But, at the same time, it is difficult to imagine a snapshot situation that does not involve at least some of these factors. As Thomas Szasz says, "the self is not something one finds; it is something one creates";[21] the Joneses create iconic selves, although they may not be fully aware that such a creative process is at hand. I believe that in virtually any snapshot the photographer and his subject are involved in self-imaging processes.

These processes, for all of their complexity born of motives, audiences and definitions of self, result in snapshots that are almost always idealized. We all know, both from those social scientists who have predicted, described and analyzed the demise of the nuclear family, and from our own experiences, that a family's intricate network of inter-relationships is never wholly positive. But snapshots, though they usually treat domestic situations, seldom reflect negative experiences or emotional states. They do not depict a very wide range of moods, emotions or attitudes. We seldom see Sam as contemplative, hostile, doubting or confused, even though these moods, need it be said, are with all of us on occasion. Rather, the smile— the presentation of a positive self—is virtually omnipresent in snapshot imagery. We have seen that the photographer and his subject have considerable control over the final picture. If Sam resolutely smiles, then we have a picture of a smiling man; and Walter, because of the selections he can make with the camera, possesses substantial powers in rendering his subject as he sees fit. Snapshooter and subject are, in a sense, making propositions to themselves and their audiences. These propositions are directed to themselves ("this is my real self") and to others ("this is how I would be seen and remembered"). Thus we emerge with idealized, self-aggrandizing images that can be thought of as mythic projections of ourselves and our views of others. There is, in other words, a self-created and self-directed rhetoric at work in snapshot imagery.

These idealized and highly conventional images are gathered into family albums, which are in turn rhetorical histories insofar as they render the past in laudatory or self-serving terms. Suzanne K. Langer has suggested that

> Memory is the great organizer of consciousness. It simplifies and composes our perceptions into units of personal knowledge.[22]

Family albums, in turn, condition memories. Like any history, family albums are born of selections. As we have seen, important choices are made during snapshooting, and this is also the case when some snapshots are selected for family albums, and others discarded. Family albums, then, are not particularly reliable indices for our actual histories. Rather, they are constructs that *propose* positive histories. They attest to the fact that we are part of a legacy, a bloodline, a way of ascribing meaning and value. In them we are imaged as significant participants in the family's history. Family albums, in short, reflect the same kinds of biases, motives and historiographical difficulties that any historical work manifests. Their relationship to actual history is properly thought of as metaphorical.

Snapshooting in modern America represents much more than a popular recreational activity. It is part of a long, if not always glorious, tradition in Western society. We share with our forebears the sometimes narcissistic desire to be imaged for posterity. Snapshooting allows us to reify mental images that might otherwise remain unexpressed. We use snapshots to communicate to ourselves, and those around us, and those who will succeed us, that we in fact exist. With snapshots we become our own historians, and through them we proclaim and affirm our existence.

Notes

1. Helmut and Alison Gernsheim, *Creative Photography* (Detroit: Wayne State University Press, 1963), p. 13.
2. Helmut and Alison Gernsheim, *The History of Photography* (New York: McGraw-Hill, 1969), p. 134.
3. *The Editors of Time-Life Books, Light and Film* (Alexandria, VA.: Time-Life Books, 1977), p. 134.
4. Alfred Stieglitz, "The Hand Camera—Its Present Importance," *The American Annual of Photography* (1897); reprinted in *Photographers on Photography,* ed. Nathan Lyons (Englewood Cliffs, N.J.: Prentice-Hall, 1966), p. 108.
5. Mary Ann Tighe, review of *Alfred Stieglitz and the American Avant-Garde,* by William Innes Homer, in *New York Times Book Review,* 8 May 1977, p. 9.
6. Helmut and Alison Gernsheim, *The History of Photography,* p. 422.
7. Ibid.
8. Beaumont Newhall, *The History of Photography* (New York: The Museum of Modern Art, 1964), pp. 152–159, 195–196.
9. Marie Czach, " 'At Home': Reconstructing Everyday Life Through Photographs and Artifacts," *Afterimage* 5 (Sept., 1977), p. 11.
10. Stanley Milgram, "City Families," *Psychology Today* (Jan., 1977), pp. 59.
11. Paul Byers, "Cameras Don't Take Pictures," *Columbia University Forum* (Winter, 1966); reprinted in *Afterimage* (April 1977), pp. 8–9.
12. Byers, p. 9.
13. Wilson Hicks, "Photographs and Public," *Aperture* 2 (1953), p. 4.
14. While vacation snapshots would at first appear to be significant exceptions to these generalizations, I would argue that they, too, are essentially domestic. Obviously, a snapshot of the Grand Canyon does not treat a known or domestic setting. But while the scene itself is alien, the family, or at least some of its members, are usually prominently included in the picture. Such images are not, predominantly, documents of the place; rather they announce: "The Franklins were here." They represent, in this way, the family's assertion of its existence in foreign climes.
15. Stanley Milgram, "City Families," *Psychology Today* (Jan. 1977), p. 62.
16. Carl Sandburg, "Prologue" to *The Family of Man,* created by Edward Steichen (New York: Museum of Modern Art, 1955), p. 2.
17. E.H. Gombrich, "The Mask and the Face: The Perception of Physiognomic Likeness in Life and Art," in *Art, Perception, and Reality* (Baltimore: Johns Hopkins University Press, 1972), p. 16.

18. Robert Taft, *Photography and the American Scene* (New York: Macmillan Co., 1938; reprint ed., New York: Dover Publications, 1963), p. 76.

19. Interview with Barnaby Conrad III, in *Interview with Master Photographers* (New York: Paddington Press, Ltd., 1977), p. 49.

20. Kenneth E. Boulding, *The Image* (Ann Arbor: University of Michigan Press, 1956), p. 6.

21. Thomas Szasz, *The Second Sin* (Garden City: Anchor Press/Doubleday, 1973), p. 55.

22. Suzanne K. Langer, *Feeling and Form* (New York: Scribner's Sons, 1953), p. 263.

GEORGE LELLIS

Perception in the Cinema: A Fourfold Confusion

This essay presents a unique view of cinema form and function. It describes the four fundamental perceptual contradictions which define the film experience. It is this confounding of perception, according to Lellis, that makes motion pictures interesting and exciting. We all know that movies are not "real," yet filmic technique presents actions and locations so realistically that we are transported to another time and place where objects and events have their own reality. If, as the author contends, films produce their own reality, do other media also have a unique reality?

Movies mix perception with deception. Film is a medium which helps us to see the world as we might not otherwise. Our perception of the world through film is based on four fundamental areas of perceptual confusion:

1. the technical area, whereby most movies seek to hide the methods by which they produce their illusions
2. the boundary between theatrical presentation and what we customarily call "real life"
3. the contradictory nature of cinema as both public entertainment and a replication of subjective, individual, and often dreamlike experience
4. our tendency to experience a film as spontaneous, uninterpreted reality, even while the very nature of the medium tends to invest a movie's imagery with symbolic force and significance.

The pleasure of watching a film comes from the constant interplay and dialectic between these contradictory tendencies.

The Confusion of Continuity

Film historians often trace the birth of the storytelling film to Georges Méliès, who performed trick photography to dazzle his audiences with fantastic, unreal images. Méliès had originally been a magician, a conjurer, and he found in the film medium an extension of a whole tradition of magical illusion making.

All movies are a kind of magical conjuring of images. Moving pictures are not really pictures that move, but rather a succession of still images projected so quickly that they appear to move. Cinema is, in the words of theorist Pascal Bonitzer, "interested in what it cannot be." That is, it is built on two other fundamental illusions: the illusion of off-screen space and the illusion of continuity between shots.[1]

The traditional movie seeks always to imply a world larger than what is in a particular frame at the moment. (In reality what is usually beyond the frame are a cameraman, a director, lighting and sound equipment, visitors to the set, and a host of other people and objects which would destroy the illusion the film is creating.) We are encouraged to think of what is in the frame as part of a larger whole.

Filmmakers use editing to create a sense of both spatial continuity (by showing what is implied beyond the edges of the frame of a previous shot) and temporal continuity. Although movies are usually photographed out of sequence and in bits and pieces, these pieces are assembled in such a way as to minimize audience consciousness of that process. Filmmakers attempt to create the illusion of a smooth, uninterrupted continuity between shots in a given scene while they hide the process whereby they create this convincing illusion.[2] The standard Hollywood rules of filmmaking are that the best creative decisions in terms of framing, cutting, camera angles and movement are those that do not call attention to themselves but allow the viewer to become involved in the plot, characters and action. They are a form of magic and deception that we take for granted.

Film magic differs from the kind that can be achieved in a live performance. Theorists of the medium such as Hugo Münsterberg and Jean Mitry have observed how every technique of all but the most primitive filmmaking is an analogue to some type of physiological human perception.[3] The close-up simulates actual physical intimacy by narrowing the field of what one can see. Camera movement approximates the sensations of human movement through space (to a point where some viewers may get nauseous when a camera is placed on a moving roller coaster). Mitry considers the use of the zoom displeasing precisely because there is no physiological analogue to it in human perception.

Thus the film medium becomes a form of participatory magic. In the traditional theater, one can never be more than just an extremely involved observer to the action. In film, however, a subjective camera shot can show the viewer exactly what a character sees; a tracking shot allows him to move exactly as the character is moving; a pan allows him to "turn his head." In the theater, the willing suspension of disbelief on which drama is based is primarily an intellectual exercise. At the movies, one submits to an experiential contradiction whereby one has physiological sensations of what one knows to be false.

Film is a medium in which inanimate, discreet, two-dimensional pictures are made to simulate subjective human experience. Our pleasure at watching a film is based on the essential contradiction between what is real and what is illusory, between what we believe and what we pretend to believe.

In this respect, the kind of recording of an actor's performance that goes on in a film is very different from that of a musical performer on a phonograph record. Although there are some noteworthy exceptions, in most cases even the best stereophonic, high fidelity phonograph equipment is still viewed as a substitute for a live performance. The attraction of seeing, let us say, Liza Minnelli or Richard Burton on the screen is very different from the satisfaction we get from a live stage performance. With the latter, one can only observe from a distance. On screen, one can approach them without fear, get closer to them by means of the close-up than would otherwise be socially acceptable, invade what anthropologists would call their "personal space."[4] Movie stars are literally larger than life when projected on the screen and part of the magic of film is to give us the feeling of relating intimately to them.

Most of the so-called techniques of the narrative film are deceptions. They create a sense of spatial and temporal continuity where none may previously have existed. They create the false sense of a complete world within the film.

The Confusion of Reality

In any film we are aware of two levels of reality. One is the movie's natural reality; the second its theatrical reality. On the natural level, a film documents the reality that is put in front of it. We see what certain locations look like and the physical qualities of certain actors. In some instances we may see real people doing activities which they would still be doing even if the camera were not there. On the theatrical level, we realize that some things may have been staged for the camera. Actors may be reciting lines that were written for them. There may be artificial sets or lighting effects. And if nothing has been staged or arranged for the camera, certain things may still be dramatized or emphasized through effects of composition, camera movement and editing.

Few films can escape combining these levels. Scientific documents recording natural phenomena probably seek to avoid the theatrical level. A totally animated film may have no natural level. But theatrical or fiction films combine these two to an extent. A film may emphasize one level or another, but even some films we label "documentary" have a highly developed theatrical side.

The result of this mixture is that filmmakers and audiences alike often confuse the two levels of reality. Sometimes the confusion is intentional, sometimes it is not. Films tend either to dramatize the natural reality they record, or naturalize the dramatic substance of what they present. In the first case, the film medium changes our perception of the real world. In the second, the filmmaker uses the real world to make a fictional story more credible. Let us consider each case.

Films May Dramatize the Natural

The very act of making a film often encourages a filmmaker to bring out what is inherently theatrical in his subject. The simple need to edit material forces him to pick out what may be most unusual or dramatic. The very insertion of a close-up privileges one object or face over another, and suggests the reshaping of materials from reality into some sort of familiar structure.

It is standard practice to praise a documentary filmmaker for his sense of dramatic structure. That is, documentary material becomes most effective, most watchable, most appreciated by an audience when it is manipulated to give shots a sense of progression and point. Critics consider Robert Flaherty to be the father of the documentary film, yet what Flaherty did in *Nanook of the North* and other works was not simply to show exotic and far away places; countless newsreels had done that from almost the very beginning of the medium. Rather, Flaherty's contribution was in his use of dramatic structure and filmmaking technique. Flaherty was, not surprisingly, also accused of falsifying Eskimo life. The world's first great documentary filmmaker achieved his status precisely by injecting elements of theatricality into his work.

All of those elements that give a documentary a look of professionalism, such as smooth continuity, music or the use of commentary, are elements that impose something of an artificial structure on the materials being shaped. The more control a filmmaker exercises over his materials, the more risk there is of falsifying them. Yet attempts to avoid the falsification that comes with slickness do not necessarily avoid the confusion of reality with fiction. Filmmakers in the *cinéma vérité* movement, where cameramen with lightweight equipment follow people around at their everyday business with relative spontaneity, have observed that the process of photographing people brings out a certain latent exhibitionism. Critics often accuse the subjects of these films of overprojecting their feelings, of dramatizing themselves—in short, of acting. Even if filmmakers are simply more inclined to turn their cameras on people with a flair for self-disclosure, the subject is rendered theatrical in either case.

One approach of the modern cinema has been to use a natural setting as the starting point for a film and to let a story seem to grow out of that setting.[5] The Italian cinema from Rossellini through Antonioni has produced numerous films which emphasize a natural, untheatrical sense of place (through location shooting) and people (often through nonprofessional actors) onto which is grafted a story which is purposely episodic and understated. Often the acting in such films is improvised, which further blurs the line between theatricality and reality.

Critics often praise such works for their truthfulness, minimizing the essential contradictions of them as staged works about reality. For these critics the process of finding drama in real life is more honest than its opposite, adding the impression of real life to the dramatic.

Films May Naturalize the Dramatic

The introduction of elements of natural reality or documentary into a fictional film increases its credibility. One can more easily suspend one's disbelief when the place where the action is occurring looks real and when the actors do not look like actors. The lesson which Hollywood learned from Italian neo-realism was not so much to look to the common people for stories from everyday life, but that even the most ridiculous story appears a little more reasonable if shot on a real street instead of in a studio.

The shooting of a fiction film in the style of a documentary is a common technique of the modern cinema. A film like Gillo Pontecorvo's *The Battle of Algiers* is a textbook example of the fiction film that aspires to a documentary style. It uses grainy, newsreel style photography to restage events from the Algerian war, and has been widely praised for its honest sense of reality. This use of high speed, grainy film is a direct example of exploiting an audience's associations to create an impression of reality. That is, the film's graininess does not show us more of the natural setting or of the physical qualities of its North African nonprofessional actors. Rather, Pontecorvo uses it because the audience is accustomed to graininess in newsreels. It becomes easier to believe that the director's restaging is authentic because of it, even though he has carefully constructed it for dramatic impact.

We find also in cinema a tendency toward what some critics call a dedramatization of theatrical situations, particularly with regard to acting. Writers have long commented on how subtle (restrained) acting is far more effective in a medium which traditionally relies heavily on the close-up to communicate the feelings of dramatic characters. Critics commonly cite such acting as realistic, and certainly it is compared to the stylization prevalent in the theater in the early part of the century. But writer Jean Cayrol has suggested that film encourages conventionalized acting and gestures precisely because if we were to see extremes of real emotion expressed under the scrutiny of the camera's lens, in close-up, the result would be too disturbing, unsettling or even unbelievable.[6] We prefer the comfortable alternative of understatement and supposed subtlety.

We see here a kind of compensatory mechanism. The close-up makes the scene more intense, so the actor underplays it to bring it down to an acceptable level. Indeed, the objection made earlier to the way in which *cinéma vérité* causes people in real life to dramatize themselves may in this light be an oversimplification. What may cause the objection is the refusal by the audience to accept what real expression of emotion looks like. Psychologists note the relative taboo in our culture against looking at people at those times when they express intense, intimate emotion. Yet that is exactly what film invites us to do.

While film can give the ordinary places, objects and events of everyday life a dramatic dimension, it can also make the dramatic or theatrical seem ordinary and everyday. Several years ago I visited the city of Lyon a few months after having seen the film *The Clockmaker,* which takes place in that city. Much of the action of the film—clearly shot on real locations—takes place in and around the clockmaker's store. In walking through the old quarter of the city, I ran across the very shop used in the film, but was amazed to find that it was hardly a typical shop, but rather one of the most picturesque storefronts in the whole city. A Frenchman might have recognized the poetic license involved, but my assumption in watching the film—supposedly about an ordinary clockmaker—was that the location was also typical and unexceptional.

In every case, this naturalization of the dramatic comes in part from the way we put the film we are watching into a context built up by other movies we have seen. We judge the realism of photography from other films which emphasize natural lighting and spontaneous shooting, the realism of a performance from other performances as much as from watching behavior in life, the realism of a location from both its context in the film and the way locations are usually used in films.

The Confusion of the Collective Dream

Critics and psychologists have long commented on the superficial similarities between moviegoing and the dreaming state.[7] One attends a film in a darkened room, in a state of physical immobility (usually at night), frequently to see fantasylike stories acted out. Even more striking is the way movies resemble dreams by creating a sense of experiencing events physically as well as mentally (as opposed simply to watching them, as one would do with a stage production). People go to the movies for many of the same reasons that they dream—to fantasize their desires, to put certain disturbing elements of the world around them into a context whereby they make poetic (if not always logical) sense, to escape from the pressure of the real world and regain a certain psychological equilibrium with regard to it.

Yet moviegoing is also dreaming made social. Most people prefer not to go to the movies alone, and many films, particularly comedies, play much better to a full auditorium than to an empty one. Roland Barthes has commented on the almost orgylike quality of the usual moviegoing experience: one has an intimate, often erotic and dreamlike experience with a crowd of strangers. This is quite the opposite, Barthes points out, of television viewing, the physical circumstances of which are both familiar and familial.[8]

This leads to a third confusion inherent in film. We are alone with the film (since it reproduces subjective experience), yet we are not alone (there is the audience around us). This presence of the audience adds to our simultaneous sense of belief and disbelief. Hardly anyone thinks twice about watching a film on television alone. The small screen, the lights on in the room, the commercial interruptions all establish a contact with the real world that renders the experience nonthreatening and often rather shallow. It is much harder to imagine sitting alone in a large theater to watch a Cinerama or widescreen 70 mm production without the comfort of a surrounding audience. Moviegoing involves making oneself physically immobile and submitting to a passive experience very much akin to a dream during sleep. The larger the screen, the more complete one's immersion in the image. And the more one needs the assurance that there are other spectators. Only the real movie buffs sit in the front row.

This blend in moviegoing between a communal experience and one that is physiologically and subjectively involving has been the film medium's most vital response to the challenge of television. The *Ben Hur* style spectacle films of the 1950s, the "head films" of the 1960s, the *Star Wars* and *Close Encounters* of the 1970s all offer this alternative. In watching them, the audience wants to stretch itself in both directions—toward surrender to magical illusion or trance on the one hand, without sacrificing the security of the group on the other.

Ideal movie going conditions involve a delicate balance. We are annoyed when the person behind us talks or the person in front of us is wearing a wide brimmed hat, yet we like to be able to turn to a companion during a particularly frightening episode. We like to reserve the right to believe or disbelieve what we see on the screen.

The Confusion of the Symbolic[9]

The nature of moviegoing as a social, public activity has yet another purpose. We use our companions in the audience to *make sense* of what we have seen. The discussion that may follow a film becomes one reason for going: there is a common experience to talk about to a date, a spouse or a visiting uncle. This collective making sense of a film becomes an equivalent to the secondary elaboration process described by Freud with regard to dreams. When awake, the dreamer adds information to his dreams to give them sense and coherence.

For the moviegoer, simple value judgments of "good" or "bad" may sometimes suffice, whereas this process of making sense may become more complicated if the film is confusing, disturbing or challenging. The conclusions drawn need not coincide with those intended by the filmmaker, as evidenced by the rednecks who cheered *Easy Rider* when the hippies were massacred. Each person makes sense according to his own experience.

To the extent that a film exploits what I have called our theatrical awareness, we feel a need to make sense of it as a film. When we sense the filmmaker as a manipulator or a magician, we try to determine what he is saying. If we believe a documentary completely, as a totally honest representation of the world, we don't attempt to make sense of the documentary, but of the world itself. Let us put it differently: to the extent that a film makes us aware of a theatrical level, it creates for itself a symbolic level. A character is no longer a specific individual, but representative of a kind of person. The milieu in which a film takes place is no longer just a place, but representative of a country, a region or a culture.

Here the analogy to dreaming becomes particularly interesting. The dreamer takes pieces of his experience and re-experiences them while dreaming in a form that gives them symbolic meaning. The filmmaker does something very similar. He takes pieces of the real world he records, reshapes them through editing and other means, and gives them meaning. For the viewer, the material is experienced first as an imitation of immediate, direct, subjective consciousness. On reflection (which may be almost immediate), he gives this meaning. The illusion of physiological involvement that the film medium provides makes it very much a form of *human consciousness made symbolic*. This confusion between the film experience as a form of raw, uninterpreted, immediate experience and reflective, symbolic experience is the fourth area of confusion in the medium.

Film theories that see motion pictures simply as recorders of reality ignore the way in which the context of putting something into a film always makes the image mean more than what it simply is. (We dream in images of specific people, but that does not prevent these mental images from frequently having the most general and unspecific meanings.) In rare instances film material may be virtually nonsymbolic. A doctor may use a movie camera with x-ray equipment to record a patient's breathing or swallowing patterns. For that doctor, it would be simply a way of seeing that patient's abnormality—like a mirror. When that footage is put into a medical training film, however, it becomes symbolic or a whole pattern of medical aberration. Theatricalized even further in a fiction film, this image could gain further meanings, depending on its context.

Film is not merely a transmitter of images from the real world. Rather, it is a medium which comes to invest those images with meanings derived from the contexts under which they are sent and received.

The Pleasure of the Confusion

The attraction of the film medium lies in the enjoyment we get from these varied confusions. Critics have long been aware of the ambiguities between natural and theatrical levels of reality. As George Amberg has written:

> The elaborate strategy of realism, developed and perfected in the film studios over the years, is more than a bagful of technical tricks: it is a cunning device *to make facts sell fiction.* The encounter with the unfamiliar, the illicit, the daring, the impossible, or the improbable within a verifiable frame of reference allows the audience to enjoy the experience as though it were authentic. This compromise between the quest for truth and the quest for wonder, a compromise that is uniquely cinematic, provides a neat solution for the average spectator's ambivalent attitude toward vicarious gratification. For, on the one hand, he craves to be carried away into experiences transcending his own limitations; on the other, he is haunted by the fear of becoming the victim of a fraud.[10]

What Amberg ignores is that the reverse is also true: that films also use many structures of fiction to sell facts. The favorite structure of the effective propaganda film is to organize facts and events from the real world into effective drama. By dramatizing reality, the medium is often used for educational and persuasive purposes. We admire an effective piece of socially conscious filmmaking for its ability to sell ideas without making its manipulations falsify the truth.

The classic cinema seeks to minimize or ignore any explicit contradiction between the magical and material, the natural and theatrical, the specific and symbolic levels of a film. The modern cinema—the works of Godard, Fassbinder, the *cinéma vérité* movement or John Cassavetes—often underlines and emphasizes the ways in which one level may influence another. Modern films may use editing which calls attention to itself, emphasize improvised acting whereby the spontaneous emotions or thoughts of the actor mix with the character he is portraying, or even show the process whereby the film is being photographed. Even when the contradictions are made explicit, they are still a source of fascination.

If we look at the confusions inherent in the medium we can understand why the portrayal of certain subjects, such as sex and violence, are among the most popular and controversial uses to which film is put. Our reaction to the realistic portrayal of violent actions is all the stronger because of the medium's ability to make us feel like participants rather than spectators. We react in part physiologically. Our instincts of self-preservation cause us to. This physiological reaction may range from fainting at the sight of blood on the screen to a slight shudder at the same stimulus. In either case our physical reaction (be it mild fear or intense revulsion) is a step ahead of our mental processes (which tell us it isn't real). When it *is* real, as in newsreel footage of war, violence on the screen can be justly disturbing. When it is faked, it is one of the strongest magic tricks the medium can effect. Unlike on the stage, where we have the security of seeing actors take curtain calls, we may even be uncertain whether to believe or not.

Some people thus react to violence on the screen on the aesthetic grounds that it makes them respond physically to images they do not wish to respond to. Yet it is presumably the charge of this physiological response that also makes violence so popular. It is such an intense illusion. Others object to graphic violence on the screen on the grounds that it naturalizes the dramatic. With repetition, the extraordinary, dramatic depiction of violence becomes ordinary because the other contexts of the film are ordinary and believable. A murder becomes like the clockmaker's storefront—extraordinary to experience in real life, taken for granted on the screen.

A similar process holds true for the portrayal of sex. Watching real or simulated sexual activity on the screen seems to produce actual physiological arousal even more strongly than similar portrayals in print or still photography. This physiological arousal is one of the most extreme forms of confusion between the dramatic and the natural. Pornographic films are used as a direct substitute for voyeurism and often make little use of the technical developments of the medium. The precious distinction between hard and soft core is a distinction between direct recording of reality and theatrical fakery.

As with the violent film, the objections to pornography come from people who wish to maintain a rational control over their bodies. And again the pornographic genre is accused of trivializing something which should not be treated casually. Pornography particularly begs the issue of whether film is a private or public experience. Because of the taboos in our culture against the public experience of sexuality, people who are comfortable banishing eroticism to the ghetto of the skin flick house, where it is the private experience of solitary, middle-aged males, may be uncomfortable with a change in mores that makes it acceptable as public entertainment for mixed company.

Even those who object strongly to portrayals of violence or sex in film still seek physiological involvement in what they see. Those who avoid erotic or violent cinema often seem to prefer comedies, which provide for a physical surrender to laughter. It takes a real puritan (be he a Pentacostal or a post-Brechtian theorist) to object to all theatrical situations in which the mind does not completely dominate one's physiological reactions.

The pleasure that we get from technological innovation in the cinema comes from the way in which new techniques create their own confusions and unique perceptual situations. Color, for example, at once makes images more lifelike and prettier, so that it intensifies both sides of the natural/theatrical confusion. Sound completes a film's illusion of reality, but also provides for commentative effects. The failure of 3-D movies to take significant hold may be attributed to the way in which they stylize the film image in an unrealistic way.[11] Each technology provides for a new kind of magical illusion.

Conclusion

Because it involves a dialectic among four essential confusions of perception, the film medium has grown to become a potent, entertaining and controversial form of expression. As a type of magic, it presents fragments of film as a continuity existing in space and time. Through its relatively accurate recording of the surface qualities of reality, it blurs the audience's awareness of what is real and what is theatricalized. Through the similarities between standard film exhibition and the dreaming state, we experience a film both individually and as an audience. Finally, most films achieve a balance between simulating unstructured, immediate experience and allowing for reflection and conceptualization about that experience.

Notes

1. Pascal Bonitzer, "Hors-champ (un espace en défaut)" *Cahiers du Cinéma,* No. 234–35 (December 1971–January 1972), pp. 16–18.
2. We refer here to the rule (the Hollywood cinema) rather than the exceptions (filmmakers like Eisenstein, Godard or Duras).
3. Hugo Munsterberg, *Film: A Psychological Study* (New York: Dover Publications, 1969); Jean Mitry, *Esthétique et psychologie du cinéma,* two volumes (Paris: Editions universitaires, 1963).
4. Edward T. Hall, *The Hidden Dimension* (Garden City, N.Y.: Doubleday & Company, Inc., 1966).
5. In his *Theory of Film,* Siegfried Kracauer discusses a similar idea which he calls the "found story" (New York: Oxford University Press, 1960), pp. 245–51.
6. Jean Cayrol and Claude Durand, *Le droit de regard* (Paris: Editions du Seuil, 1963), pp. 61–65.

7. See especially Christian Metz, "Le film de fiction et son spectateur (Etude me-tapsychologique)," *Communications,* No. 23 (1975), pp. 108–35, and Su-sanne K. Langer, *Feeling and Form: A Theory of Art* (New York: Charles Scribner's Sons, 1953), pp. 411–15.

8. Roland Barthes, "En sortant du cinéma," *Communications,* No. 23 (1975), pp. 104–107.

9. We use the term "symbolic" in the broad sense, to refer to all forms of com-munication which establish meaning by convention.

10. George Amberg, "The Ambivalence of Realism: Fragment of an Essay," in *The Art of Cinema: Selected Essays,* edited by George Amberg (New York: The Arno Press and The New York Times, 1972), pp. 151–52.

11. "One mistake of early 3-D movies was the advertising. It was claimed 3-D made movies more realistic when in fact 3-D is about as realistic as Orphan Annie. It was the heightened, surreal, distorted sensation that made it fun." (Tom Shales, "If You Can't Take It, Remove Your Glasses," *The Washington Post,* September 2, 1977, p. B–3).

LANCE STRATE

Media and the Sense of Smell

Even though we are aware of the odors around us, we seldom think of our sense of smell as important to communication. Even more rarely do we associate our olfactory sense with modern technology. This is not surprising inasmuch as telephone, TV, radio, and film do not utilize an olfactory channel. Aside from a few unusual excursions into "smellovision" and "odorama," smell has not been used in a technological medium of communication. This unusual essay by Lance Strate explores the nuances of olfactory communication, revealing it as a dynamic phenomenon interacting with our social, cultural, and technological environment. He points out that the function of and our reliance on the olfactory sense are being changed by our dependence on the new technology of communication. Will the sense of smell be incorporated into future media and be used to persuade and entertain us?

During one episode of *Monty Python*[1] we were given a rare glimpse of an outsider's view of America. As a scene shifts to the Pentagon, the music swells, and there, sitting behind an immense desk, is a five-star general. Acting as if he were unaware of the camera, he sniffs each of his armpits. Apparently, our British cousins find our concern over body odor odd and amusing. They seem to be saying that we are overly anxious about the scent of our armpits. The question behind *Monty Python*'s observation is why is it that when we say that something smells, we mean that it smells *bad*?

To answer this question, the olfactory component of the act of communication need be examined. That is one of the purposes of this article; to explain the nature and function of olfactory communication. The other purpose is to explore the relationship among olfactory media, mass media, and interpersonal intimacy. The act of communication is a multisensory, multichannel transaction. Olfaction is a significant, albeit often overlooked, factor in communication, and thus an analysis of olfactory communication and media should further our understanding of the act of communication.

The Characteristics of Olfactory Communication

We can begin by listing several basic characteristics of olfactory communication. The first is that olfactory communication, like any other com-

This article was written expressly for *Inter/Media*. Copyright © 1982 by Lance Strate.

munication, is a transaction; the individual is both perceiver and producer of odor (and anyone who has ridden a rush-hour subway during the summer months can attest to this fact). Furthermore, the effects of olfactory communication are difficult to gauge, and are relative to individual and cultural characteristics. Finally, olfactory communication aids in the individual's boundary maintenance; it is a factor in the individual's perception of personal distance and personal space. Thus, olfactory communication is modified by the individual's perception of olfactory space.

If our understanding of olfactory communication is based on a transactional process, then the individual can be examined as a producer of odors as well as a perceiver of odors. Individual body odors vary according to age, sex, complexion, and diet. One aspect of human odor production presently being studied is the likelihood of human pheromones. Pheromones are a group of biologically active substances, similar to hormones. There are two types of pheromones: primer pheromones, which trigger permanent physiological changes in the receiver, and releaser pheromones, which evoke immediate and reversible change in behavior. Among mammals, pheromones are involved in the formation of social hierarchies, territorial behavior, individual imprinting, and primary reproductive effects. Alex Comfort cites several factors that support the hypothesis that pheromones exist in humans. The first factor is that pheromone interaction is present in social mammals, including primates. Moreover, human beings have organs whose equivalents among lower animals serve a pheromone-producing function. There is also some evidence of cross-specific reactions (i.e., humans react to musk; bulls, goats, and monkeys react to the odor of women). Finally, Comfort notes the following:

> Humans have a complete set of organs which are traditionally described as non-functional, but which, if seen in any other mammal, would be recognized as part of a pheromone system. These include apocrine glands associated with conspicuous hair tufts, some of which do not produce sweat and most presumably produce some other functioning secretion; a developed prepuce and labia, and the production of smegma (the sebaceous secretion that collects beneath the prepuce or around the clitoris). This system in adults seems over-elaborate for the relatively small releaser role of odor in most cultures. The amputatory assault on these recognizable pheromone-mediating structures in many human societies implies an intuitive awareness that their sexual function goes beyond the decorative. A conspicuous and apparently unused antenna array presupposes an unsuspected communications system.[2]

Carl Sagan makes a similar observation:

> Other methods of finding a mate have been developed in reptiles, birds, and mammals. But the connection of sex with smell is still apparent neuroanatomically in higher animals as well as anecdotally in human experience. I some-

times wonder if deodorants, particularly "feminine" deodorants, are an attempt to disguise sexual stimuli and keep our minds on something else.[3]

According to Comfort, the production of odors by humans probably has subliminal effect on other humans. However, the effects are confounded by other stimuli transmitted over other channels. Thus, the effects are difficult to measure. Part of the problem is that humans are the least distinguished of all the animal species as olfactory perceivers. The evolutionary process that brought humans to their present erect, upright position also brought their nose away from the ground, thus reducing the effectiveness and importance of olfactory perception (while simultaneously increasing the effectiveness and importance of visual and auditory perception). Also, it is difficult to gauge the effects of olfactory sensations on the human psyche. Havelock Ellis discusses this point:

> The sense of smell still remains close to touch in the vagueness of its messages though its associations are often highly emotional. It is the existence of these characteristics—at once so vague and so specific, so useless and so intimate—which has led various writers to describe the sense of smell as, above all others, the sense of imagination. No sense has so strong a power of suggestion, the power of calling up ancient memories with a wide and deep emotional reverberation, while at the same time no sense furnishes impressions which so easily change emotional color and tone, in harmony with the recipient's general attitude. Odors are thus specially apt both to control the emotional life and to become its slaves. Under the conditions of civilization the primitive emotional associations of odor tend to be dispersed, but, on the other hand, the imaginative side of the olfactory sense becomes accentuated, and personal idiosyncrasies tend to manifest themselves in this sphere.[4]

Odors, in a general, nonspecific manner, affect our emotions, trigger memories, and affect our interpersonal communication (especially in regard to courtship and sexual relations). Specific effects of olfactory substances are difficult to measure; scientists have so far been unable to generate a system of primary units of olfactory information. R. H. Wright states that the *minimum* channel capacity of the nose is twenty-eight bits per second.[5] R. W. Moncrieff[6] could isolate olfactory effects only in terms of a hedonic (pleasure-giving) classification system. He found that age, sex, and, to a lesser degree, temperament (extrovert/introvert) all are determinants in the perception of relative pleasantness or unpleasantness of odors. He also found that there was greater consensus among his subjects in the perception of relative unpleasantness of odors than in relative pleasantness. Among the substances perceived as unpleasant were products with a "fecal note in their odor." Moncrieff also noted that children were more tolerant toward this type of substance. Circumstantial evidence can be found to support the association of fecal odor with unpleasantness as either inherent biologically or as derived through socialization. Obviously, there is a need for cross-cultural studies of odor preferences. Edward T. Hall has noted cultural differences in olfactory communicative behavior:

> Arabs apparently recognize a relationship between disposition and smell. The intermediaries who arrange an Arab marriage usually take great precautions to insure a good match. They may even on occasion ask to smell the girl and will reject her if she "Does not smell nice," not so much on esthetic grounds but possibly because of a residual smell of anger or discontent. Bathing the other person in one's breath is a common practice in Arab countries. The American is taught not to breathe on people. He experiences difficulty when he is within olfactory range of another person with whom he is not on close terms, particularly in public settings. He finds the intensity and sensuality overwhelming and has trouble paying attention to what is being said and at the same time coping with his feelings. In brief he has been placed in a double bind and is pushed in two directions at once. The lack of congruence between U.S. and Arab olfactory systems affects both parties and has repercussions which extend beyond mere discomfort or annoyance.[7]

Hall states that olfaction plays a role in the individual's boundary maintenance and his concept of personal distance and personal space. Olfactory space is thus a component of personal space. As previously noted, Comfort states that among mammals pheromones are involved in the formation of social hierarchies and territorial behavior. Therefore, the phenomenon of olfactory space has a biological basis. However, both Comfort and Sagan try to explain the use of deodorants through the likelihood of human pheromones; in this endeavor they commit the error of ethnocentricity. Hall and *Monty Python* demonstrate that Americans have a relatively exaggerated sense of olfactory space. Moreover, deodorants are as much a technology as a cultural artifact.

The Functions of Olfactory Media

Throughout history, the human race has attempted to modify and control its environment. Olfactory space and olfactory communication are modified and controlled by olfactory technology, that is, olfactory media. Our contemporary olfactory media include perfumes, incense, cologne, dental preparations such as toothpaste and mouthwash, shaving preparations such as shaving cream and aftershave, deodorants, tobacco, and the list goes on. The use of incense, which is often associated with religion, mysticism, and meditation, is probably related to the ability of olfactory sensations to affect emotional states and invoke memory. Perfume has been used for hierarchical purposes. In Exodus 30:1–38 we find the first recorded recipe for perfume, along with instructions for its use. The holy perfume was only to be used by the priests. The anointing of the kings of the Israel was a symbolic act, allowing the fledgling royalty into the olfactory environment of the priests. However, the most celebrated function of perfume is that of increasing interpersonal attractiveness. Ellis speculates on the origin of this function:

> Since there are chemical resemblances and identities even of odors from widely remote sources, perfumes may have the same sexual effects as are more primitively possessed by the body odors. It seems probable that . . . perfumes were primitively used by women, not as is sometimes in civilization, with the idea of disguising any possible natural odor, but with the object of heightening and fortifying the natural odor. If the primitive man was inclined to disparage a woman whose odor was slight or imperceptible—turning away from her with contempt as the Polynesian turned away from the ladies of Sydney: "They have no smell!"—women would inevitably seek to supplement any natural defects in the same way as, even in civilization, they have sought to accentuate the sexual prominences of their bodies.[8]

According to Ellis, perfume was first used as an olfactory form of falsies. Similarly, Marshall McLuhan defines media as extensions of human faculties. In this sense, perfume is an extension of the individual's ability to produce odors. Respect for and fear of this extension is revealed in an act of the English Parliament in 1770:

> That all women, of whatever age, rank, profession, or degree, whether virgins, maids, or widows, that shall, from and after such Act, impose upon, seduce, and betray into matrimony, any of his Majesty's subjects, by the scents, paints, cosmetic washes, artificial teeth, false hair, Spanish wool, iron stays, hoops, high-heeled shoes, bolstered hips, shall incur the penalty of the law in force against witchcraft and like misdemeanours and that the marriage, upon conviction, shall stand null and void.[9]

It is not until the twentieth century that we encounter a whole new array of olfactory media whose primary function is not to enhance body odors, but to mask them (i.e., deodorants, feminine hygiene spray, mouthwash, air freshener, etc.). The cultural attitude that has developed along with the new olfactory media is best exemplified by the following passage from *The Mala Rubinstein Book of Beauty,* under the heading of "The All-Importants":

> There's a part of your body that is invisible—but can make or break the impression you create; can make you nice to be near—or decidedly *not.* That, of course, is body odor. Regardless of how often you bathe, use of a deodorant daily is a "must." The type you use depends upon individual need and preference. Best for most women is an anti-perspirant deodorant, which serves the dual purpose of eliminating unpleasant odor and keeping the underarms dry.
> Fastidious care must, of course, extend to the vaginal area. The frequency and type of douche you use depends on you and your doctor's recommenda-

tion. A reliable vaginal deodorant used after the bath or morning shower should be part of your daily routine. It surprises me that Americans, who often make a cult of cleanliness, have never adopted the European bidet. For freshness throughout the day—where the bidet doesn't exist—there are pre-moistened paper towelettes that also deodorize.[10]

Not only does our friend Mala provide us with a strong and zealous view of our present cultural attitudes toward odor, but she also gives us a clue to its development. Odorlessness is associated with cleanliness. Odor and dirt are associated with disease. The association between odor and disease is not recent, however. The ancient Babylonians and Assyrians used fumigations and incense as medical treatment; perfume was an ingredient in the embalming oil of the ancient Egyptians. Incense and perfumes remained popular as remedies for diseases during the Middle Ages. When the scientific paradigm about the causes of disease changed, public belief did not. Beginning in 1860, Louis Pasteur, Joseph Lister, and Robert Koch contributed to the development of the antiseptic. Inherent in the idea of the antiseptic is that invisible disease can be eliminated. If disease is still associated with odor in the public mind, doesn't the antiseptic suggest the elimination of invisible odor through a deodorant? Theodor Rosebury[11] criticizes the common misconception in our culture that the cleaner we and our environment are, the healthier we are. While this may have been true once, we have carried the concept to such extremes as to make it dysfunctional. The use of deodorants, feminine hygiene sprays, etc., have no health value and can even create health problems. Our cult of cleanliness includes the worship of the mystical properties of soap, a situation Roland Barthes is highly critical of:

L'important, c'est d'avoir su masquer la fonction abrasive du détergent sous l'image délicieuse d'une substance à la fois profonde et aérienne qui peut régir l'ordre moléculaire du tissu sans l'attaquer.[12]

Ivan Illich[13] criticizes our attitudes toward pharmaceuticals, toward the ability of medicine, of the pill, to cure disease. Given our association of odor and disease, our mystification and overuse of soap and deodorants is consubstantial with our attitudes toward pharmaceuticals. We deify the cure-all product, and it is not coincidental that this attitude fits in nicely with our consumerism-based economy. Mass production techniques also had a significant influence. The 1870s saw the rise of mass production in the soap industry as well as the introduction of perfumed soap. Also, synthetic perfumes were accidentally discovered by organic chemists in the late nineteenth century. This discovery led to increased production of perfumery materials at a much lower cost, and consequently, increased consumption of these materials, promulgated by the mass media. The use of "scare techniques" became popular in the twentieth century, leading to advertising copy such as "My first date with *HIM* tonight! So I'm bathing with fragrant cashmere bouquet soap . . . it's the *lovelier way* to avoid offending!" and "Are you as dainty at night as you are by day? Charming wives *never* risk offending. . . ."[14] The purpose of olfactory media is no longer to increase relative pleasantness in the individual, but to avoid unpleasantness. While the mass media are often accused of the creation of needs where there are none, it seems that in this instance the mass media were merely playing upon pre-existing cultural values toward odor, cleanliness, and disease. To avoid offending, one must be clean in the antiseptic sense, free of odor and disease. The invasion of olfactory space becomes a signal of contagion.

Mass Media and Olfactory Space

The exaggerated sense of olfactory space was probably further influenced by what Richard Sennett refers to as "the fall of public man."[15] Sennett's thesis is that over the past three centuries people in Western societies have shifted from playing socially accepted public roles to viewing social relations as self-disclosure. The nineteenth century was particularly characterized by a profound fear of involuntary personal disclosure. This was the Victorian era. The fear of involuntary self-disclosure also extended to the olfactory realm. Sennett cites a physician on the faculty of the University of Marburg, Carl Ludwig. Ludwig felt that the origin of the "green sickness," a euphemism for chronic constipation in women, lay in "the fear women have had of accidentally farting after eating, leading to a constant tensing of the buttocks."[16] Sennett states that our present era is a product of a flip-flop from fear of involuntary disclosure to emphasis on self-disclosure and the desire to indiscriminately place all social relations on an intimate basis. However, our sense of olfactory space has not made the transition. We have remained Victorian in our management of our olfactory space. Perhaps our attitudes toward odor, cleanliness, and disease have prevented the changeover.

It is interesting to note that, in contemporary society, perfume advertisements are usually markedly different from deodorant advertising. While the latter is often based on the aforementioned scare techniques, the former does not seem to be. Perfume advertising seems to appeal to a sense of identity, to the type of person who would wear the particular perfume. Perfume ads also usually contain abstract visual imagery, perhaps in an attempt to visualize the emotional and memory-inducing effects of scent. When perfume advertisements are related to social interaction, it is generally from a positive perspective. Instead of the subtle threat of social unacceptability, perfume ads tend to emphasize increased success in social interactions. What is consistently deemphasized in advertisements is perfume's characteristic of being an odorous substance. A study comparing perfume and deodorant advertising would be very enlightening.

The mass media also affect our attitudes toward odor in a less blatant manner. Marshall McLuhan[17] has noted that the transition from print media to electronic media has ended the monopoly of the visual, and reintegrated our senses. Foremost among the electronic media is television, which appeals to us on a visual, auditory, and (according to McLuhan) tactile level. Notably absent from these elements of the sensorium is the olfactory component. Susan Sontag[18] states implicitly, and Gary Gumpert[19] explicitly, that our mass media have altered our standards of perfection. Through photographic and recording media we are presented with a standard of perfection unrealizable in the non-mediated world. Photographic techniques such as retouching allow women of almost mythic quality to grace the centerfold of *Playboy* and, amazingly enough, this perfect beauty is also free of any offending odors.

The media also affect our sense of olfactory space through personal distance cues. Hall states that a culture's personal distance cues are implicit within a culture's art forms. The artist works from the existing personal distance cues of the culture that produced him. The relationship of the viewer to the work of art is determined by the personal distance cues transmitted by the work of art. The intimate personal distance cues given by television and other electronic media parallel the emphasis on intimacy and self-disclosure associated, in the twentieth century, with the fall of the public man. However, the intimate personal space is odorless; the news anchorman never has perspiration odor, the disc jockey never has bad breath. We are given an exaggerated perception of our own olfactory space, or at least reinforced in our desire to keep our olfactory space free of invasion (or infection) of outside odors. Edward Bullough recognized the dual-edged sword of cultural art forms:

> The working of distance is, accordingly, not simple, but highly complex. It has a *negative*, inhibitory aspect—the cutting-out of the practical sides of things and of our practical attitude to them—and a *positive* side—the elaboration of the experience on the new basis created by the inhibitory action of Distance.[20]

Our mass media present us with an odor-free world, which reinforces our over-exaggerated sense of olfactory space. With this in mind, is it any wonder that so many people can accept (and even prefer) the display of plastic flowers and plastic fruit? Another technological innovation that has reinforced this situation is the development and widespread use of ventilation systems and air conditioning during the 1940's. William N. McCord and William N. Witheridge[21] state that the foremost function of these inventions is to rid the air of offensive odors, thus protecting and expanding the individual's olfactory space. Recent attempts at antismoking regulation are an assertion of the olfactory space of the nonsmoker. It is significant that this issue manifests itself after widespread acceptance of the idea that smoking is injurious to health, in light of our association of odor and disease.

Our deodorizing imperative seems to indicate that olfactory stimulation is perceived as noise. When competing stimuli create noise, channel inhibition constitutes noise reduction. While we have traditionally studied the media of communication, it seems that we also must study the media of inhibition—blindfolds, sunglasses, earplugs, and sound-proofing.

The function of olfactory media has not been limited to the inhibition of odors. T-shirts and women's underwear with fragrances are now available (good for up to fifteen washings) in such scents as orange, fish odor, diesel fuel, marijuana, whiskey, and pizza. Ruth Winter states that scented ink with a bacon aroma was once used in a newspaper ad, but problems arose when neighborhood dogs began taking the papers from the porches where they were delivered and chewing them up.[22] Future technological developments may provide us with the ability to implant odor on a long term basis, and perhaps we will be able to obtain an olfactory version of a tatoo.

The Future of Olfactory Media

The subtler effects of odors are also being exploited. In the 1970s, twenty percent of all fragrance manufactured was used in perfume and toiletries. The rest was used to scent a variety of products including detergents, furniture polish, tobacco, tea, medicine, window cleaners, stationery, paints, pens, nail polish, greeting cards, stockings, used cars, and glue factories. The addition of a lemon scent to Joy detergent in 1966 proved successful, and since that time marketing experts have been using fragrance not just to cover bad odors, but to increase the attractiveness of the product. Future technologies may bring us an olfactory form of muzak (aimed at behavior modification).

It is likely that most developments in olfactory technologies will be used in conjunction with other technologies in a multi-channel presentation. Microfragrances, commonly known as scratch-and-sniff, are particularly suited for print media. By scratching, the receiver breaks millions of miniscule plastic bubbles, releasing fragrances. While mostly used for advertising, microfragrances have also been used in educational material, especially for the blind. The use of scratch-and-sniff cards as an integral part of the movie *Polyester* failed precisely because microfragrances are print-biased. The one-at-a-time scratching of microfragrance areas is not suited to the continuous flow of the motion picture; the connections between the visual image and the fragrance become strained and caricature-like. Aldous Huxley conceived of a much more elegant multichannel presentation almost fifty years ago. The following passage is a description of the olfactory medium used in Huxley's "feelies":

> The scent organ was playing a delightfully refreshing Herbal Capriccio—rippling arpeggios of thyme and lavender, of rosemary, basil, myrtle, tarragon; a series of daring modulations through the spice keys into ambergris; and a slow return through sandalwood, camphor, cedar, and newmown hay (with occasional subtle touches of discord—a whiff of kidney pudding, the faintest suspicion of pig's dung) back to the simple aromatics with which the piece began. The final blast of thyme died away; there was a round of applause; the lights went up.[23]

Technological innovation, such as Huxley describes, can modify our olfactory communication and our sense of olfactory space. Still, change in our sense of olfactory space will probably be predicated on change in our attitudes towards cleanliness and disease. In the future, we may be able to tolerate an olfactory environment with more than just a faint trace of ozone. We may no longer feel compelled to sniff our armpits or to think that everything that smells, smells bad. But then again, who nose?

Notes

1. Monty Python is a comic / satiric television series produced by the BBC and often aired in the USA on PBS stations.
2. Alex Comfort, "The Likelihoood of Human Pheromones," in Martin C. Birch, *Pheromones* (New York: North-Holland Pub., 1974), p. 388.
3. Carl Sagan, *The Dragons of Eden* (New York: Random House, 1974), p. 69.
4. Havelock Ellis, *Psychology of Sex* (New York: Mento Books, 1963), p. 46.
5. R. H. Wright, *The Science of Smell* (New York: Basic Books, 1964), p. 82.
6. As described in *Odour Preferences* (New York: John Wiley, 1966).
7. Edward T. Hall, *The Hidden Dimension* (Garden City: Doubleday & Co., 1969), p. 49.
8. Ellis, *op. cit.,* pp. 49–50.
9. William A. Poucher, *Perfumes, Cosmetics, and Soaps, Vol. II* (New York: D. Van Nostrand Co. Inc., 1936), pp. 16–17.
10. Mala Rubinstein, *The Mala Rubinstein Book of Beauty* (Garden City: Doubleday & Co., 1973), pp. 159–160.
11. Theodore Rosebury, *Life on Man* (New York: Viking Press, 1969).
12. Roland Barthes, *Mythologies* (Paris: Éditions du Seuil, 1957), p. 40.
13. Ivan Illich, *Medical Nemesis, the Expropriation of Health* (New York: Pantheon Books, 1976).
14. Ann Bramson, *Soap, Making It, Enjoying It* (New York: Workman Publishing, 1975), pp. 78; 80.

15. Richard Sennett, *The Fall of Public Man* (New York: Vintage Books, 1978).
16. *Ibid*, p. 182.
17. Marshall McLuhan, *Understanding Media, The Extensions of Man* (New York: New American Library, 1964).
18. Susan Sontag, *On Photography* (New York: Farrar, Straus, Giroux, 1978).
19. Gary Gumpert, "The Ambiguity of Perception," *Et Cetera* Vol. 34, no. 2 (June 1977).
20. Edward Bullough, " 'Psychical Distance' As A Factor in Art and An Esthetic Principle," in Melvin Rader, ed., *A Modern Book of Esthetics* (New York: Holt, Rinehart and Winston, 1960), p. 396.
21. William N. McCord and William N. Witheridge, *Odors, Physiology and Control* (New York: McGraw-Hill Books, 1949).
22. Ruth Winter, *The Smell Book* (New York: J. B. Lippincott & Co., 1976), p. 123.
23. Aldous Huxley, *Brave New World* (New York: Harper & Row, 1946), pp. 198–201.

SHERRY TURKLE

Computer as Rorschach

The computer is being introduced rapidly into our office and homes as another component in a huge media system. A new relationship is being formed,
one in which we will no longer be passive receivers of electronic fare, but
will interact directly with media sources and channels.

According to Sherry Turkle of the Massachusetts Institute of Technology,
some of us suffer from "computerphobia," others from "computer addiction." Almost all of us are in awe of this powerful new "machine" but perhaps only a few of us realize how many computer-human interactions are
being imposed upon us without choice. Turkle examines our subjective reactions to a medium that is altering our concepts of self.

There is an extraordinary range of textures, tones, and emotional intensity
in the way people relate to computers—from seeming computer addiction
to confessed computerphobia. I have recently been conducting an ethnographic investigation of the relationships that people form with computers
and with each other in the social worlds that grow up around the machines. In my interviews with people in very different computing environments, I have been impressed by the fact that when people talk about
computers they are often using them to talk about other things as well. In
the general public, a discourse about computers can carry feelings about
public life—anxieties about not feeling safe in a society that is perceived
as too complex, a sense of alienation from politics and public institutions.
Ideas about computers can also express feelings about more private matters, even reflecting concerns about which the individual does not seem
fully aware. When we turn from the general public to the computer experts, we find similar phenomena in more developed forms. There, too,
ideas about computers carry feelings about political and personal issues.
But in addition, the expert enters into relationships with computers which
can give concreteness and coherence to political and private concerns far
removed from the world of computation. In particular, the act of programming can be an expressive activity for working through personal issues
relating to control and mastery.

Of course, among technologies, the computer is not alone in its ability
to evoke strong feelings, carry personal meaning, and create a rich expres-

Published by permission of Transaction, Inc. from *Society*, Vol. 17, No. 2, Copyright © 1980
by Transaction, Inc.

sive environment for the individual. People develop intense and complex relationships with cars, motorbikes, pinball machines, stereos, and ham radios. If computers are an exception to the general rule that there is a subjective side to people's relationships with technology, it is insofar as they raise this commonly known phenomenon to a higher power, and give it new form as well as new degree.

Other technologies, knives for example, can serve as projective screens: do we associate them with butter or with blood? But we can come close to having people agree that before it is a part of eating or killing, a knife is a physical object with a sharp edge. We shall see that the elusiveness of computational process and of simple descriptions of the computer's essential nature undermine such consensus and make the computer an exemplary "constructed object," a cultural object which different people and groups of people can apprehend with very different descriptions and invest with very different attributes. Ideas about computers become easily charged with multiple meanings. In sum people often have stronger feelings about computers than they know.

The Subjective Computer

A ticket agent who uses computers to make airline reservations begins a conversation about the computer by presenting it as a totally neutral object—programmed, passive, completely under the control of its operators and their input, threatening only in its impersonality—and then moves on in the same conversation to descriptions of the machine as a presence in which the line between person and thing seems nearly to dissolve. When confronted in a conversation by the possibility of computers which might serve as psychotherapists, judges, or physicians—that is, whose functions would be ones which are now seen as quintessentially "human"—many people react with a force of feeling by which they themselves are surprised. Some people try to neutralize feelings of discomfort by denying that such things as intelligent computers could exist outside of science fiction, but then try to buttress their arguments by adding in unabashed self-contradiction that while such things may be possible, they "ought not be allowed to happen." In talking about computers, people often make implicit reference to two scenarios that have long been explicit in science fiction plots: computers might change something about the way people think, and computers might develop minds of their own. In the complexity of our responses to the idea of machine intelligence, we see an expression of our stake in maintaining a clear line between the human and the artificial, between what has consciousness and autonomy and what does not, between a notion of "mechanical" calculation and of "human" judgment and emotion. The fact that the computer touches on a sphere—intelligence—that man has long thought to be uniquely his, means that even popular discourse about computers can raise tense questions about what is man and what is machine.

Questions like this are posed, if only implicitly, by our everyday use of language; that is, by our use of computational metaphors. In our culture, the fact that there is talk about such things as repression, the unconscious, and the superego, influences the way in which people think about their problems, their pasts, and their possibilities, even for people who do not "believe in" psychoanalysis. In the case of psychoanalysis, technical ideas were taken up as powerful metaphors by a nontechnical public and used as building blocks in a discourse about politics, education, and the self; that is, as building blocks in the development of a psychoanalytic culture. These ideas took many shapes and turned up in many different places as they became integrated into advice to the lovelorn as well as into theories of psychology. Computers, too, introduce a world of new language to those who work with and around them. And since this language is about cognitive processes that often seem at least superficially analogous to those which go on in people, this language is brought into everyday vocabulary.

Students speak of "dumping core" when they are asked to spill back course contents during an exam. Engineers complain of being "stuck in a loop" when problem solving is difficult and all paths lead to dead ends. A travel brochure for a condominium village in Hawaii assures the reader that a stay in Wailea means a sure addition to his "fond memory bank." Today's language for thinking about thinking is growing richer in computational metaphors. When we say that we have an idea that needs to be "debugged," we are referring to a computational model of dealing with global complexity through local intervention. When a computer scientist refuses to be interrupted during an excited after-dinner conversation and explains that he needs to "clear his buffer," he is using an image of his mental terrain in which access to interactive processing capacity can be blocked by a buffer zone that must be empty before it can be crossed.

We do not yet know whether these metaphors, commonly dismissed as "manners of speaking," are having an effect on the way we think about ourselves, perhaps by effecting an unconscious transfer between our ideas about machines and our ideas about people. In academic psychology, however, such transfer has become explicit: in the mid-1950s, the presence of the computer, a complex material embodiment of cognitive functions, gave American psychologists a new model for thinking about cognition, one which stressed the need to posit complex internal processes in order to understand even simple behavior (something that traditional behaviorism, in its attempts to avoid theorizing about internal states and processes, had declared outside the realm of good science). For example, behaviorists had spoken of the behavior of "remembering," but computational models reintroduced the notion of "a memory" into general psychology. Today, computational and information-processing models seem on their way to becoming the new dominant paradigm in psychology and have made serious inroads in other behavioral and social sciences. It is a plausible conjecture that, as in the case of psychoanalysis, today's technical computational language will filter into tomorrow's popular language.

Some might imagine that such subjective aspects of the computer presence and the use of computation for model building are either a private matter, of concern to the individual involved, or of interest to the theoretical psychologist, but without any bearing on issues of public concern except insofar as *misinformation* about computers can obscure discussion of public problems. In fact, the situation is more complex. We can observe the "subjective computer" in the language and the projections of individuals, but it does impact on the collectivity. There are several ways in which it can influence our approach to issues concerning computers in public life. First, when the computer acts as a projective screen for other social and political concerns, it can act as a smokescreen as well, drawing attention away from the underlying issues and onto debate "for or against computers." Second, feelings about computers (often largely projective in origin) can become formalized into "ideologies" of computer use, that is, into beliefs about what the computer can, will, and should do. These powerful computer ideologies can decrease our sensitivity to the technology's limitations and dangers as well as blind us to some of its positive social possibilities. And finally, along with the "constructed computer" comes the social construction of computer expertise.

When a school wishes to purchase a computer system, whom shall they consult? There are at least a hundred thousand Americans who have bought small, personal computers for their homes. Many are parents—it is natural that the school and the PTA should look to them as experts. And from a purely technical point of view, many of them are. But we shall see that the relationship of many computer hobbyists to the computer carries a vision of what is important in computation that systematically leaves some things out. Other "expert" groups introduce different biases.

The general public tends to think of a computer expert as defined by purely technical criteria but, in fact, computer experts are often distinguished from each other by subjective stances (such as an emotional feeling about what is important about computation) as well as by their technical capabilities. Even people who are extremely sensitive to the way in which personal preoccupations and political preferences can masquerade as "neutral" expertise in other technical fields often think that in computer science, things are different. One popular image is that computer expertise is a neutral quantity that can be acquired like a piece of hardware and be relied upon to perform in a steady and reliable way. It is as though people tend to see computer experts (often referred to as "computer people") as being "like computers." But different relationships with computers, different aesthetics of how to use them and what they are good for, structure computational value systems whose implications extend far beyond the technical. Even preferences among styles of programming can have a politics. One programming aesthetic puts a premium on having all elements of the program "on the table" and available to the programmer as "primitives." With so many little pieces, each one has to be made as small as possible to get them to all fit into the workspace, and so the criteria of elegance for this "flat" style of work are associated with highly condensed programming at the bottom level. Before the recent plummeting in the cost of memory, this ground floor condensation allowed economies of memory space that made its elegance highly cost effective. But because the structural building blocks are small, condensed, and numerous, modifications are virtually impossible without changing the whole system. An alternative aesthetic (top down, structured programming) builds up hierarchical programs using large, internally unmodifiable modular blocks. This often uses more memory but allows easy modifications with less reliance on a master programmer. The system is socially desirable, but some programmers find it constraining, unaesthetic, "good for organization, but bad for the artist." We shall return to the question of computational values and politics. Here I want only to suggest that understanding different subjective relationships with computation may be necessary to understanding and evaluating the views of computer experts on issues of public policy such as what kind of computer system needs to be built in a given situation. Indeed, such understanding may be a necessary step towards a kind of computer literacy that prepares the citizen to make responsible political judgments.

Computer as Smokescreen

Computational metaphors are only one element in the construction of a new, highly charged, and often highly self-contradictory popular discourse about computers. There is the everyday reality: the average American meets computer power when he makes a telephone call, uses a credit card, books a motel room, goes to the bank, borrows a library book, or passes through the checkout counter of the local supermarket. There is the science-fiction surrealism: the computer of the future is presented as threatening (HAL in *2001*), all-knowing (the "Star Trek" computers), and all-powerful (in the movie *Demon Seed,* a computer succeeds in impregnating a woman, resulting in a computer-human baby). And there is media image making, as television, popular journalism, advertisements, even games and toys, bombard us with an extraordinary range of images about what the computer really is and what it might be. The computer is portrayed as supercalculator, superenemy, superfriend, supertoy, supersecretary, and in the case of the bionic people who populate television serials and children's imaginations, computer as a path into a future of supermen and women.

Computers are portrayed as good and bad, as agents of change and of stagnation. Talking about computers and money, computers and education, computers and the home, evokes tension, irritation, anticipation, excitement. Some of the intensity reflects the schizophrenic splittings in the images of computers in our culture. But some of it comes from the use of the computer as a projective screen for other concerns. And although we do not yet know if computational metaphors and ideas about computers are changing the way we think, it is already clear that our popular and highly projective discourse about computers can discourage us from thinking things through.

Consider, for example, the problem of how computers make it easier to violate the privacy of the individual through the automatic accumulation of data about him. Traditional notions of the right to privacy are challenged when most social transactions leave an electronic trace. The computer presence has made the problem of privacy more urgent and visible. More attention is being devoted to it because decisions about its protection can no longer be postponed when there is the prospect of their being "hardwired" into national information systems. But all too often, discussions of computers and privacy focus on the computer. This draws attention off the fact that organizations violated citizen privacy long before there were computers to help them do the job. And attention is drawn off the fact that the root of this serious problem lies not in our computer systems but in our social organization and political commitments and that its solution must be searched for in the realm of political choice, not of fancier technology. On the issue of privacy, the computer presence could serve to underscore an underlying problem; instead, talk about the computer serves as its smokescreen.

A similar smokescreen effect is present in the following images of the computer, all of them comments made by computer science professionals at a recent symposium on computers and society.

The Computer that Constrains:

> You get on an elevator and you're wearing a badge in a particular office building and you try to go to the fifth floor. The computer in the elevator says, "No, that's not your floor."

The Computer that Encourages Violence:

> A group of students were standing around a console playing Space War and I heard one student say to the other: "Don't you think we should get more points for killing than for merely surviving?" It was a perfectly reasonable statement in that context, and I'm afraid it may turn out unhappily to become a slogan for the era of the home computer.

The Computer that Atrophies the Mind:

> Now that we're using calculators and no longer multiply in our heads, we may find an almost epidemic rise in things like dyslexia, learning disabilities, inability to work, a propensity to industrial accidents and auto accidents.

Let us consider the third image: the computer that atrophies the mind. Later discussion made it clear that the speaker who prophesied that the calculator age meant an increase in learning disabilities was deeply concerned about the contemporary crisis in education, where functional illiteracy after a high-school career has become commonplace. But our understanding of that crisis is not advanced if concern about a falling educational standard is expressed as complaints about calculators that may disenable multiplication neurons. The other images carry similar dangers. The fact that computer games are violent, like the fact that television programs are violent, makes a statement not about technology but about our society. The most disturbing thing about the student's comment about the game of Space War has nothing to do with computers. Its language is not very different than that which was used while our government was fighting and justifying the war in Vietnam, to take only one example. That we now see it reflected back to us on television and CRT screens is a comment not on the computer presence but on the internalized violence of our society.

Sophisticated information systems do facilitate increased surveillance of individuals, and shoot 'em down video games on personal computers can multiply the images of violence that enter our livingrooms. This tendency of computers to increase the urgency of many problems could in principle give rise to sharper social criticism. But in practice this seldom happens. Complaints about *computers* invading privacy and about *computer* games being violent are daily used to short-circuit discussion of political responsibility and the banalization of violence. Behind our conversations about the computer that constrains us (the computer that "won't let you off on the fifth floor," or, as in another common example, "won't let you change your airline reservation") is often our sense of having limited access to what we want to see and understand. There are people and large organizations behind the "computer" that constrains. When people's sense of political limitation is translated into statements about technology, about computers "hiding things from us," political discussion has been neutralized and the possibility for appropriate action has been subverted.

It is easy to catalogue the interests (industrial, governmental) that tend to be served when political choices are represented as technical problems. These interests exert forces from without. But other forces, harder to catalogue, also encourage this same kind of obfuscation. In a certain sense, these come from within. If a memory or a dream disturbs our sense of who we are as individuals, we "forget" it—we make it unconscious. As a society, we also find ways to "forget" the collectively unacceptable. Comfortable and habitual inactions are threatened by serious talk about such matters as how the decisions of large corporations affect our political and biological environment or about the consequences of gross inequalities of resources and power. We develop a paradoxical language for talking about such matters that allows us to forget the real issues. And one of the most powerful of these languages is technical. The strategy is not new, and insofar as the computer has a role here, it is to provide new means towards already familiar ends. But the new means make a difference.

People are particularly willing to embrace the computer as a technical explanation for things that might otherwise raise disturbing questions. Consider the situation of the airline clerk we met earlier. She frequently finds herself confronted by the anger of clients whose reservations cannot be honored. Her standard excuse is "Our computer fouled up." Like workers in a thousand other bureaucracies all over the world, the airline clerk need never call the organizational policies of her company into question. She need never call her employer into question because the computer is there to blame. It is felt by her to be an autonomous entity (it can act with agency) and so it is *blamable*, yet it is not a fellow worker to whom she would feel bonds of loyalty. This permits her a conscience-calming collusion with the client without jeopardizing her security as a "company person." What is it about the computer that makes it such an effective actor in situations like this? In order to answer this question we need to step back and try to understand people's tendency to anthropomorphize computers. Most particularly, we need to appreciate that it is deeply rooted in the nature of the computer itself. It does not necessarily reflect a lack of information or naive beliefs in the "intelligence of machines," either present or future. Many who find the anthropomorphization of computers offensive would like to make it go away by educating the public to understand "what computers really are." But they miss an epistemological issue: computation is irreducible. We can know more and more about it, but we never come to a point where we can completely define it in terms of more familiar things.

The computer theorist, like other scientists, sets up a conceptual frame of reference within which he works, and defines the computable within this framework. But even then, what he has isolated as the computable, the "essential computer," presents no easy analogies with other objects in the world (as the airplane does the bird)—except, of course, and this is a point to which we shall return, for its analogies with people. To explore this further requires that we proceed by a kind of paradox. We try to understand the epistemological isolation of the computer by looking at some of the many ways in which people try to projectively relate it to other things, each valid within a particular horizon, although many are inconsistent with each other.

Computer as Rorschach

The computer's capacity as a projective device resembles that of the Rorschach, perhaps the best known and most powerful of psychology's projective measures. In the Rorschach, the individual is presented with an ambiguous stimulus, a set of inkblots. How he responds to them is a window onto his deeper concerns. And so it is with the computer. First, as in the case of the Rorschach, whose blots suggest many shapes but commit themselves to none, we have noted that the computer is difficult to capture by simple description. We can say that it is made of electrical circuits, but it does not have to be. A computer can be made (and several—for fun— have been) of tinkertoys, and quite serious computers have been made using fluidic rather than electrical circuits. Although airplanes can come in all shapes and can be described in all sorts of ways, there is no conceptual problem in stating their essential function: they fly. There is no equally elegant, compelling, or satisfying way of defining the computer. Of course, one could say that it computes, that it executes programs. But the execution of a program can be described on many levels: in terms of electronic events, machine language instructions, high-level language instructions, or through a structured diagram which represents the functioning of the program as a flow through a complex information system. There are no necessary one-to-one relationships between the elements on these levels of description, a feature of computation which has led philosophers of mind to see the computer's hardware-software interplay as highly evocative of the irreducible relationship between brain and mind. The irreducibility of the computer to other things encourages, indeed it even seems to coerce, its anthropomorphization. This is further reinforced by the computer's interactive properties (you type to it and it types back to you) and by the unpredictability of programs (although the programmer inputs all instructions, their interaction soon becomes sufficiently complex that one can seldom foresee the results of their operation).

Computers are certainly not the only machines that evoke anthropomorphization. We often talk about machines as though they were people: we complain that a car "wants to veer left." We even talk to machines as though they were people: we park a car on a slope and warn it to stay put. But usually, when we "talk to technology," we have a clear path in mind for transforming any voluntary actions we may have ascribed to a machine into unambiguously mechanical events. We know that friction on the wheels caused by the emergency brake will prevent gravity from pulling the car down the hill. But when we play chess with a computer and say that the computer "decided" to move the queen, it is much harder to translate this decision into physical terms. Of course, an engineer might well reply that "all the computer really does is add numbers." And indeed, in a certain sense, he is right. But thinking of the computer as adding does not get us very far towards understanding why the computer moved the queen. Saying that the computer decided to move the queen by adding is a little like saying Picasso created *Guernica* by painting. And there is more than a touch of irony in the engineer's trying to undermine the anthropomorphization of the computer by using what is ultimately an anthropomorphic imagine of adding.

The reaction to ELIZA, a conversational natural language program that simulated the responses of a Rogerian psychotherapist, threw people's tendency to attribute human characteristics to computers into sharp relief. By picking up on key words and phrases it had been programmed to recognize, the program was able to ask questions and make responses ("I AM SORRY TO HEAR YOU ARE DEPRESSED," "WHAT ELSE COMES TO MIND WHEN YOU THINK OF YOUR FATHER?") that made "sense" in its conversational context (a therapy session).

Most of those who originally had access to ELIZA knew and understood the limitations on the program's ability to know and understand. The program could recognize character strings, but it could not attribute meaning to its communications or those it received. And yet, according to its creator, Joseph Weizenbaum, and much to his consternation, the program seemed to draw some of them into closer relationships with it. People confided in the program, wanted to be alone with it, seemed to attribute empathy and understanding to it. In my conversations with students about their experiences with ELIZA, the personalization of the involvement with the program often seemed tied to the issue of predictability. Many referred to the feeling of being "let down" when the program became predictable. When they had cracked the code, when they knew which inputs would provoke which responses, when they knew which inputs would cause the program to become "confused," then "computer confidences" became boring.

People tend not to experience themselves or other people as completely predictable. When asked what it means to be a person and not a machine, most people use plain talk to describe what the more philosophically minded might call the "ineffable." Machines are most people's everyday metaphor for invoking predictability and, insofar as the computer is able to simulate the kind of unpredictability we associate with people, it threatens our concept of machine. Here is a machine that is not "mechanistic." Locally, it has mechanistic components, but seen globally, these disappear and you are dealing with a system that surprises.

Something else that makes analogies between the computer and mechanical antecedents (like adding machines) unsatisfactory is that computers can be programmed into autonomy from their human users. On the simplest level, after a few sessions of an introductory computer science course, the novice programmer knows how to write programs that would, in principle, go on forever, let us say, because step three is an instruction that says return to step one. Such programs will never stop; that is, until somebody "kills" them by pulling out the plug, turning off the machine, or pressing a special control key on the computer terminal which is designed for just such moments. I interviewed a group of college students as they went through an introductory programming course and most could remember strong feelings about what one referred to as his first "forever program."

"Forever" is overwhelming because we can't know it or our place in it. Perhaps a "forever program" gives a glimpse, however ephemeral, of what it might mean. Such glimpses are rare, sometimes occasioned by looking at a mountain, or at a sunset, and are almost always accompanied by strong emotions. In the case of the iterative program, the image of "forever" is created by the programmer himself, perhaps intensifying its evocative power, its fascination.

The computer demonstration called the GAME OF LIFE has this evocative quality. The game begins with a checkerboard of dark and light cells in a given state; cells turn from dark to light and light to dark depending on the state (dark or light) of their immediate neighbors. Such local instructions produce a changing, evolving global pattern. Like a biological system, this computer program can generate global complexity out of local simplicity. The game fascinates, touching on our fascination with self-perpetuating systems, with generativity, and "forever." It also brings into focus a compelling tension between local simplicity and global complexity in the working of the computer. Locally, each step can be predicted from the step before. But the evolution of the global pattern is not graspable. This play between simplicity and complexity is among those things that makes computation a powerful medium for the expression of issues related to control. And perhaps it is in the range of programming relationships that this projective potential is maximally realized.

Programming as Projective

Depending on how the programmer brings the computer's local simplicity and global complexity into focus, he will have a particular experience of the machine as controlled or controlling. Both levels are there; people display different patterns of selective attention to each of them and end up with different relationships to control and power in their programming work. Out of this range of relationships we will look at two very different ones. We see a first style in X, an ex-programmer, now a university professor who describes himself as "having been a computer hacker." X experiences his computer power as a kind of wizardry. Wizards use spells, a powerful local magic. X's magic was local too. He described his "hacker's" approach to any problem as a search for the "quick and dirty fix" and described his longterm fantasy that he could walk up to any program, however complex, and "fix it, bend it to my will." As he described his intervention, he imitated the kind of hand gestures that a stage magician makes towards the hat before he pulls out the rabbit.

X's involvement was in a struggle with the program's complexity—what was most gripping for him was being on the edge between winning and losing. He described his hacking as walking a narrow line: make a local fix, stay aware of its potential to provoke unpredicted change or crash the system, test each system's flexibility to the limit. For X, the narrow line has "holding power." Stories of weekends at the terminal with little to eat and little or no rest were common, as were reflections on not being able to leave the terminal when debugging a program clearly required getting some sleep and looking at the whole in the morning instead of trying to "fix it" by looking at it line by line all night. For X it was his style of programming that led him to identify with what was for him a computer "subculture," that of the hacker. His process of identification seemed analogous to that of a creative independent virtuoso who recognizes his peers not by the "job" they have nor by their academic credentials, but because they share his sense of the personal importance, the urgency of creating in the medium in which they work.

Many hackers have dropped out of academic programs in computer science in order to devote themselves exclusively to computers. Based neither on a formal job nor on a research agenda, the coherency of the hacker subculture follows from a relationship with the "subjective computer": that is, with a set of values, a computational aesthetic, and from a relationship with programming that may be characterized as devotion to it as a thing in itself. In university settings all over the country, where hackers are often "the master programmers" of large computer operating systems, academic computer scientists complain that the hackers are always "improving the system," making it more elegant according to their aesthetic, but also more difficult to use.

Some have characterized the hacker's relationship with computation as "compulsive," but its urgency can be otherwise described. The hacker grapples with a computational essence—the issue of how to exert control over global complexity by mastery of local simplicity. The mechanism embodied in the lines of code under his immediate scrutiny is always simple, determined, certain—but the whole constantly strains to escape the limit of his ability to "think of it all at once," to see the implications of his actions on the larger system. And this is precisely what he finds so exciting.

A second programmer, Y, is also a computer professional, a microprocessor engineer who works all day on the development of hardware for a large industrial data system. He has recently built a small computer system for his home and devotes much of his leisure time to programming it. Whereas for hacker X, the excitement of programming is that of a high-risk venture, Y likes it as a chance to be in complete control. Although Y works all days with computers, his building and programming them at home is not "more of the same." He experiences his relationship to the computer as completely different in the two settings. At work he describes himself as part of a whole that he cannot see and over which he feels no mastery or ownership: "At work what I do is part of a big system; like they say, I'm a cog." At home he works on well-defined projects of his own choosing, projects whose beginning, middle, and end are all under his control. To him, the home projects seem a kind of compensation for the alienation of his job. He observes that he works most intensively on his home system when his tasks at work seem mostly a project of "somebody else having parceled things out . . ." and furthest away from any understanding of "how the whole thing fits together."

X and Y have very different senses about what is most satisfying about programming. These translate into different choices of projects, into different computational values, and ultimately into what we might call different computational aesthetics. X likes to work on large, "almost out of control" projects; Y likes to work on very precisely defined ones. X finds documentation a burdensome and unwelcome constraint. Y enjoys documentation; he likes to have a clear, unambiguous record of what he has mastered. Much of his sense of power over the program derives from its precise specifications and from his attempts to continually enlarge the sphere of the program's local simplicity. There is certainly no agreement between X and Y about what constitutes a "good" program or a "good" computer application.

X, like many other people I have spoken to who identify with the hacker subculture, sees business systems and IBM and its products (FORTRAN, COBOL, IBM timesharing, and IBM computers themselves) as particularly "ugly." A company like IBM is interested in system reliability, and this means trade-offs in the system's "plasticity." A hacker may complain that such systems hold back both the computer and the programmer. He is often more sympathetic to computer applications which touch on the area of Artificial Intelligence, the enterprise of programming computers to do things (like having vision, speech, and chess-playing ability) that are usually considered intelligent when done by people. His sympathy is not surprising. In Artificial Intelligence projects, the hacker can see an embodiment of his sense of what is most exciting about the computer—the way unpredictable and surprising complexity can emerge from clever local ideas. At the other extreme, programmer Y's commitment to computers is to what is most precise, predictable, and controllable. For Y, what is powerful about the computer is definitionally in a different realm than the human mind with its vagueness and unpredictability. He may rule Artificial Intelligence out of court because there is as yet no agreed upon specification of what it is to be "intelligent." ("How can you build something which has not been reduced to 'specs'?") For the hacker, this usually poses no problem. In fact, his sense of computational power is incompatible with "specs."

People bring computers into their homes for many different reasons, but questionnaire data on over a hundred computer "hobbyists" (here defined as people who have had a computer in their home for several years—that is, before the advent of mass marketed "turnkey" systems) and nearly 150 hours of follow-up interviews with 30 of them suggested that Y's style of dealing with the computer, his computational values and aesthetics, are widely shared in this group. Like Y, other hobbyists have built their computers from kits, and many continue to work as close to the machine as possible, preferring assembly language to higher level languages, and preferring to write their own assemblers even when commercial ones are easily available. The hobbyist's relationship with the computer he has worked on, often built "from scratch," and nearly always carefully documented, can be heavily invested with a desire for a kind of personal control that can be passed on to his children.

Although advertisements for personal computers have stressed that they are an investment in your child's education—that computers have programs that can teach algebra, physics, the conjugation of French verbs—

hobbyists don't speak about the importance of giving their children a competitive advantage in French, but of a competitive advantage in "the computer." Most hobbyists feel that the stakes are high. They believe that computers will change politics, economics, and everyday life in the twenty-first century. Owning a piece of it, and having complete technical mastery over a piece of it, is owning a little bit of control over the future.

For many hobbyists with whom I spoke, the relationship with their home computer carries longings for a better and simpler life in a more transparent society. *CoEvolution Quarterly, Mother Earth News, Runner's World,* and *Byte* magazine lie together on hobbyists' coffee tables. Small computers become the focus of hopes of building cottage industries that will allow the hobbyist to work out of his home, have more personal autonomy, not have to punch a time card, and be able to spend more time with his family and out-of-doors.

Some see personal computers as a next step in the ecology movement: decentralized technology will mean less waste. Some see personal computers as a way for individuals to assert greater control over their children's educations, believing that computerized curricula will soon offer children better educations at home than can be offered in today's schools. Some see personal computers as a path to a new populism: personal computer networks will allow citizens to band together to run decentralized schools, information resources, and local governments.

Many of the computer hobbyists I have interviewed talk about the computers in their livingrooms as windows onto a future where relationships with technology will be more direct, where people will understand how things work, and where dependence on big government, big corporations, and big machines will end. They represent the politics of this computer-rich future by generalizing from their special relationship to the technology, a relationship characterized by simplicity and a sense of control. In this tendency to generalization, they are not alone. People often take a particular way of relating to the computer; that is, they take their personal sense of what is important, interesting, and valuable about computers, and generalize it into beliefs about "computers in general." This process of generalization and ideology formation can be rapid. I saw it begin with a group of 25 college students, computer "newcomers," whom I followed through their first computer science course. I spoke to them several times during the course about their reactions to learning about computers and programming: how did they see the computer, how did they feel about what they were learning.

Many of the students began the course with an image of the computer as a complex and powerful entity. But for some, with an elementary knowledge of the machine and of programming came a way of thinking

about the computer that began to approach the view we have characterized as common to many hobbyists, a view of the computer as simple and
controllable. ("The machine is dumb; just a giant calculator.") And for
about half of the students, an image of a primitive computer whose power
was based on the ability to perform arithmetic functions became their image for all of computation. In the process, their attention turned away
from questions relating to the complexity of computation. They showed
little interest in highly speculative issues about the future of Artificial Intelligence or in such down-to-earth problems of sloppily written complex
systems that have gotten out of hand. Such systems (written, rewritten,
and locally revised by different programmers, indeed by different teams of
programmers through the years) can become a patchwork of local fixes,
each with an inevitable, but often unknown, impact on the working of the
whole. If you need to change such programs, the change can only take the
form of yet another local fix, and the results of doing so are unpredictable.
When we refer to such systems as incomprehensible, this does not mean
that we cannot understand their local workings. It means that we cannot
act on the program as though we understood it as a whole. We cannot
know the consequences of our actions. The programs become autonomous
in the sense that making changes to them becomes too "dangerous" to try.
But because the students saw the programs they were writing in their course
as easily modifiable, they could not really see how such problems could
arise. Several dismissed the very possibility with the phrase "Garbage in—
Garbage Out" (GIGO).

One might think that the problem here is in the nature of "introductory" material. In the teaching of chemistry, for example, we usually find
that it makes most sense to begin with the simplest stuff, with the material
that will give students the most confidence that they can make the subject
"their own." And then when they move on from their high-school to their
college chemistry classes, they are shown how to cast aside their high-
school models of atoms as "wrong." Images of electron shells and precise
orbits are replaced by models of orbitals, suborbitals, and probability
densities. But in the case of the computer, things are different. The kind of
programming that typically goes on in an introductory course encourages
an emphasis on the "local simplicity" view of the computer. But at every
level of expertise you can have a choice of focusing on simplicity or on
complexity. There is no "truth" in the Rorschach inkblots that you finally
see if you examine them long enough, and a particular set towards computation can be maintained at very different levels of expertise.

By the end of their one semester course, most students in my study had
averaged seventy-five hours at the computer terminal. Many of the hobbyists I interviewed who had logged many thousands of hours and had

completed some very complex projects were as solidly committed as the students to a view of the computer that focused on its local simplicity. And like the students, they, too, used their experience with the computer as a basis for dismissing issues that might emerge from computational complexity. It may well be that for some of them, their use of the computer as enblematic of the personally and politically controllable gave them strong reasons to want to hold on to this view. But that they were *able* to do so reflects something about the nature of computation. The view of computation as locally simple can be shared by programmers at very different levels of expertise because it is not technically wrong: all programs can be described locally, and *at least in principle* all programming goals can be achieved while retaining complete control over the system. *In practice,* many hobbyists are led by their passion for documentation to become masters of the art of local (most often line-by-line) description of programs and are led by the individualism of their computer culture into habits of work and choices of programming projects that reinforce a style of highly controlled programming. Thus a tradition, an aesthetic, and relationships both with people and machines maintain a sense of computation similar to that which tends to be encouraged by working with the small, tightly controlled programming projects typical of first courses.

The "blind spots" of those who invoked formulas like GIGO to dismiss the problem of incomprehensible programs went beyond the inability to see the consequences of computational complexity. The remark reflects a vision of programming as a technical act and as an individual act: if a program is incomprehensible, it is because someone wrote bad code. For an individual working alone that might be true, but it is a mistake to think about computation in other settings as an extension of the computation that one does in one's home or for a problem set.

Computation is a social act, the sum total of everything it takes to make a particular computational event occur: the hardware, the teams of people creating the necessary software, the organizations of people, bureaucracies, and industries in which it happens. The incomprehensibility of the large programs used by such organizations as the Internal Revenue Service can have a great deal to do with such social factors as the uncommitted relationship between the programmers and the organization, the structure and the instability of the programming teams, the way in which authority is delegated. Even the programming environment in which the work is done (what languages are used, what debugging systems are available, etc.) can depend on political choices within the organization. None of these factors is intrinsic to computation. None of these factors is made apparent by extrapolating from most experiences of recreational or classroom computation.

Our discussion of "blind spots" and of programming experience helps us to bridge our earlier distinction between social problems that follow from what computers do and those that follow from how people think about computers. The social problems that arise from the presence of cumbersome, effectively unmodifiable programs in large organizations are in the class of problems raised by "what computers do." These problems may be compounded by difficulties in understanding their nature that are rooted in more subjective perceptions. The way in which we, as a society, deal with problems posed by what computers do is influenced by our ways of thinking about computers. The subjective side of computation is not without its objective consequences. The blind spots that I noticed among my sample of beginning students and hobbyists are only one example. We spoke about the computer "as Rorschach." But of course there is a difference. Unlike Rorschach blots, computers are also powerful social actors, and what people project onto them—these "socially constructed computers"—can themselves become social presences that influence policy makers, educators, engineers and the general public. In the last analysis, how people think about computers *is* "something that computers do."

Computer Literacy

The observation that the way people think about computers can exacerbate problems caused by what computers do leads easily to a standard response: educate them. There is an active movement of advocates and activists of "computer literacy," the minimum that everyone needs to know about computers in order to function effectively as a citizen. Schools and federal agencies, magazines and clubs, the computer industry, even the manufacturers of children's games are all entering the business of educating the public. There is no doubt that people are learning more about computers. But our glimpse of the subjective side of computation alerts us to some potential problems about what they may be learning. In most cases, and certainly in computer literacy courses that use curricula designed for grade school and adult education classes, people are learning simple programming skills and a set of "facts" about the computer. But we have seen that "facts" about the computer do not come in neutral information packets. Computer literacy is usually defined as knowledge about the computer. If we accept the idea of computation as a social act, it would be more appropriate to define it as knowledge about computers and people. In this essay, we have raised several issues that need to be taken into account by this kind of humanistic computer literacy movement.

We have seen that what seems like the obvious first step in computer education, learning to write small programs, can lead to a paradox. The computer educator hopes to give the student a more objective understanding, but the result can be to bias the student's perception of computation against recognizing phenomena associated with complexity. Several possible strategies have been suggested for dealing with this paradox. The student's model of computation might develop differently if his first computer experience was to modify a large pre-existing program rather than to create his own tiny ones. Explicit discussion of issues related to system complexity could be introduced into elementary computer education.

A second issue relates to selection. There clearly are different styles of relating to computers. The styles are so distinct that those who practice one are prone to see those who practice another as wrong, fuzzy headed, even bizarre. When speaking about programmers and their styles, we used the metaphor of subcultures. A standard computer literacy curriculum easily could become the vehicle which defines the "normal" and the "deviant" among these cultures. Any educationally "official" computer culture will encourage only some people to think of working with computation as being a good "fit" with who they are. When we think about computer education in the next decade, we are no longer talking about the education of a small group of people who will become computer specialists, computer experts. We are talking about computer literacy for the masses of people who will need to feel comfortable with computers in order to feel comfortable and unintimidated by daily life. The goal should be to give as many of them as possible the sense of belonging in a computer-rich society.

A third issue has to do with an unknown: how different styles of relating to computers may transfer to other things. We have noted that choosing a programming language and a programming style implies a cluster of cultural characteristics, values, ways of thinking, X's and Y's programming styles suggest strategies for dealing with problems that have nothing to do with the computer. There may be a transfer of some of these ways of thinking from computation to other things. If we acknowledge that a computer literacy program may be training in habits of thought, then it must be evaluated in these larger terms.

There is the fourth issue of anthropomorphization. The phenomenon makes many people uneasy. Some hope that objective knowledge about how computers "really" work will make it go away. But anthropomorphic imagery, supported by the computer's projective capacities, seems deeply embedded in the nature of computation. A responsible approach to computer education must take it more seriously, must understand its genesis and multiple functions, whether in the end it decides to oppose, exploit, or ignore it.

A fifth and final issue touches on the way in which the computer—as it becomes implicated in ways of thinking about politics, religion, psychology, and education—can raise challenging, even disturbing, questions for individuals. For example, in an introductory programming course, a college sophomore saw how seemingly intelligent and seemingly autonomous systems can run on programs. This led him to his first brush with the idea (which others have first encountered via philosophy or psycholoanalytic thought) that there might be something illusory in people's subjective sense of autonomy and conscious self-determination. Having seen this idea, he rejected it, with arguments about the irreducibility of man's conscious sense of himself that paralleled those of Freud's more hostile contemporaries both in their substance and in the emotion behind them. In doing so, he made explicit a commitment to a concept of man to which he had never before felt the need to pay conscious attention.

The reference to psychoanalysis brings us full circle to an analogy I made at the beginning of this article. There, I noted that twentieth-century popular culture has appropriated psychoanalytic ideas that were first developed in a technical context, and I conjectured that computational models for thinking about the mind might undergo a similar fate. Here I consider a very different aspect of the analogous relationship between computation and psycholanalysis—not how they can be similarly *accepted* but how they both carry messages which are likely to be resisted and *rejected*. Psychoanalytic notions of the unconscious, of infantile sexuality, and of Oedipal relationships provoked strong resistance before being accepted into either academic or popular cultures. Psychoanalysis is a framework for thinking—we might call it a "subversive science"—that challenges humanistic and "common sense" models of man as an autonomous agent. In doing so, it calls into question some of our taken-for-granted ways of thinking about ourselves. Computational frameworks share some of this "subversive" quality. They, too, provoke strong feeling. Opinions are divided: some people welcome computational analogies with people as the basis for a new kind of scientific humanism, while others warn that such models deny us that which is specifically human in our nature. Some embrace the prospect of Artificial Intelligence as an adventure for the human spirit, while others see much about the enterprise as obscene.

Although the phenomena around the "subjective computer" we have dealt with in this essay are highly visible in our culture, the groups that are most involved in computer education and the computer literacy movements tend to ignore them. Each has a different reason for doing so. The computer industry is committed to presenting computers as neutral technical objects that can enter daily life in a non-disruptive way. The personal computer magazines and hobbyist movement have a different motive for "normalization." Their effort is to assimilate everything to activities within the technical reach and the intellectual style of the owner of a very small system. Schools are intent on avoiding the controversial. They have had enough trouble with sharp debates over sex education and such experiments as the Man as a Course of Study program. They are willing to "take on" computation as a cost-effective adjunct to their standard curricula. It is not in their immediate interest to "see" other aspects of the computers they have taken on.

The leadership of industrial, recreational, and educational computing share a language for talking about computer education and computer literacy that is technical and instrumental and selectively ignores the more highly charged aspects of the computer presence. When these do come up, they tend to be denied as nonexistent, viewed as transitional phenomena that people need to be educated out of so that computers may more appropriately be seen as "just a tool." Of course the computer is a tool, but man has always been shaped by his artifacts. Man makes them but they in turn make him. In the case of the computer, we may confront a tool that can catalyze a change in how we think about ourselves; for example, by making us aware on a daily basis of being only one among many other possible forms of "rule driven" intelligence.

We spoke of the emergence in the mid-twentieth century of a psychoanalytic culture, a culture that had an influence on how people thought about their lives, about raising their children, and about the stability and instability of political systems. It is too soon to tell whether we are entering a computer culture that will have anything near this level of impact on us. But in our discussion of the subjective computer we began to see traces of such a culture in formation. There is the rapid spread of computional ideas into everyday language, there is the appropriation of information-processing models in psychology as well as in other behavioral and social sciences. If psychoanalytic ideas became culturally embedded through their embodiment in therapeutic practice, computational ideas are growing their own roots in education. There are cultures growing up around the computer that use the machines as metaphors for thinking about people and social organization. We wear a dangerous set of blinders if we do not appreciate and further explore how computers can become the carriers of culture and of a challenge to our way of thinking about ourselves. If nothing else, a fuller appreciation of this subjective side of the technology should lead us to a critical reexamination of what each of us takes for granted about "the computer" and to an attitude of healthy skepticism towards any who propose simple scenarios about the "impact of the computer on society."

ANTHONY SMITH

The Self and Postindustrial Society

In this essay, Anthony Smith, Director of the British Film Institute in London, explores the psychological context of technological transformation and the resultant new priorities which develop in conjunction with the cultural assimilation of new media of communication. To what extent will the perceptual bias of the computer influence the way we perceive ourselves? To what degree is the concept of "self" evolving and being redefined in our post-industrial society? Compare the positions taken by Susan Sontag, George Lellis, and Sherry Turkle with the ideas expressed by Anthony Smith.

Among students of aesthetics and culture an attempt is today being made to reopen a number of questions which have preoccupied theology and philosophy for millenia, questions concerning our fundamental nature as the subjects of experience—questions which have become important again because of the changing ways in which our culture now seems to be operating. It is difficult to make the intellectual leap from electronics to psychology, particularly when one is simultaneously interrogating the basic notions of psychology itself, but it is nonetheless important today to ask ourselves basic cultural questions about our new electronic world.

When we watch a movie on a television screen what process of cultural work are we actually carrying out? To what extent do we face the screen as individuals? What kinds of moving image narrative can we take, and what do we reject, and in what circumstances? A movie culture is essentially collective in a civilization: everyone has to make the decision to accept a certain sequence of images and read them in the same way if the communication is to work at all, but how do we come to make those transsociety agreements to read a sequence in a given way? And since we do make such collective compacts to what extent are all the elements of a culture—newspapers, broadcasting, education, fashion, contemporary idioms—indispensable parts of a whole? And if they are, then where are we? Individuals or collaborators in the experience of a society, mediators or operators of our culture, atoms within a mass or manipulated accomplices? Above all, what kinds of *self* are we acquiring in this stage of civilization?

Each social or economic system has bred or has been bred within its own

This article originally appeared in *Intermedia*, vol. 12, no. 6, November 1984. It has been rewritten for this volume.

system for training perception, as well as within its own technology. It is notoriously impossible to separate out causality between these: did the invention of writing transform the nature of human memory or did the historical process of transformation operate in the reverse direction? Did the ideas of the Renaissance precede its crucial advances in technique (perspective) or technology (printing) or did these inventions occur autonomously and in turn change the way in which Italians and other Europeans saw the world? We can never clarify these conundrums: rather, the answers we supply to them are themselves determined by the preceptual and intellectual operations of our own time.

But we can begin now to think about the whole psychological context of technological transformation, particularly about the one in the midst of which we live today. It must by its nature be closely tied to a wider transformation of our ideas about psychology, about national cultures, about relations between the individual and society, for the present transformation entails two very basic shifts in new concepts of work and new ways of registering and transmitting images and records of the world. Naturally, one must at the outset of any such speculation abandon any rigid notion of causality. The development of the computer through its various stages and onwards to its fifth stage may itself be the result of previous shifts in our consciousness, newly established biases, as it were, among the senses, which are now working themselves out in terms of a new industry and a new technology.

The changing fields of perception are difficult to describe, for in language the meaning of words changes to make them appropriate to the ways in which we perceive. If one traces the evolution of the word "sense" itself, together with all its present day derivatives, one can gain an appreciation of what I mean. The notions of pain and of emotion have altered very greatly in the era of mechanized medicine and psychological treatment; historians of medicine sometimes question whether pain itself constituted quite the same problems for individuals two centuries and more ago. Certainly, emotion occupied a totally different cultural and social function before the word itself existed that we use today. The "passions" of earlier eras were very different in their social resonances and functions from our "emotions."

The various processes of intellect were recategorized with the coming of the industrial era and may be reconceptualized once more in the postindustrial era. Consider how, for example, the idea of labor came to separate itself from the idea of work in the industrial era; labor came to be a separable, quantifiable entity, spread across society, abstracted from the individuals who provided it, but work is a process which connects the doer with the product or service provided. Industry also changed our notions of time from the seasonal or cyclical to the cumulative or developmental. The very notion of development, as we use the term today, was impossible before time came to be treated, like labor, as a quantity, a separable substance, capable of being measured, exchanged, valued. History came to be seen differently, as a developmental process, and things or people outside the acknowledged fields of perception as primitive or exotic. As religious explanations for human behaviour came to appear supernatural and receded, other explanations had to be found for hysteria and the idea of the unconscious. Later the subconscious evolved to remove the element of mystery from the new objectified perceptual world. These were all the counterparts of the Gutenbergian, typographic, information systems: information itself, through print, became both detachable from the holder of knowledge, and transferable and reproducible, an object of exchange.

In the industrial age the chief intellectual quality has been rationality, the principal sense has been vision and the main moral quality has been individualism. These interdependent biases constitute a whole system of perception, a framework through which we have come to see the world. Within this framework the individual self is trained to respond to a culture and contribute to a culture in which the apparatus of emotion is pressed back into the individual. Where Rensaissance passion was a visible operation of the personality, influenced by the forces of nature and society, the emotions are essentially disturbances or aberrations of the mind to which individuals are prone. Each person came to be seen to have an "inside" and an "outside"; the novel came in the eighteenth and nineteenth centuries to act as the main interpretative genre of literature, analyzing, explaining, contextualising the new "self" in the new society. The work of the novelist has been to locate the individual, reconcile the invisible feelings of each subject of social experience to that experience.

Typographic society placed an extreme emphasis upon sight. The new priorities of society and of thought came to depend far more upon the eye than upon the memory or the ear or the sense of touch. As knowledge came to be augmentative rather than recollective in the new era of Galilean research, the whole apparatus of society came to depend more and more upon calculations, notions, theories which could be expressed only through writing and shared only through printing. Within the function of sight, an extreme division took place between text and image, a division which can be partly grasped by looking at Renaissance and pre-Renaissance images with the help of some of the work of the new school of art historians.

Gesture of Venus

In Botticelli's famous painting at the Uffizi, the Primavera, there is a central figure, Venus, who looks out of the painting directly at the spectator.

On either side of her is a group of mythological dancing figures and behind her is a carefully worked forest or orchard; above her a figure of Cupid. Venus's left hand rests in front of her, to the left of her girdle, and her right hand is raised, apparently conducting the music. But in fact her right hand is raised, the palm facing outwards and the fingers loosened, falling almost, to the shape of a fan. She is in fact inviting us, employing the formal medieval religious gesture of invitation, into her kingdom, and, as we enter, we look to the right and to the left at the groups of figures, each one of whom and each group of whom are elaborately and quite precisely attempting to indicate through symbolic poses and gestures various layers of meaning. The gesture and movement of each one, the arrangement of the dance all have precise meanings, much of which is lost to us today. Much of the meaning is doubtless contained in a wealth of contemporary allusion, or comment upon the formal meanings of the gestures, the steps of the dance, the symbolic significance of every flower, of every eye contact between the figures. But the arrangement of the painting actually helps us, for if we follow the gesture of Venus, we go inside the world of the painting and start to work with the complex symbolic material from there. Even if we read every surviving piece of contemporary work on manners, on dance, painting, our task will still not be done, for we cannot possess the ability to decode the theology, cosmogony and simple social allusion which Botticelli has packed into his work. Probably much of the meaning which the painting is or was capable of generating was subconscious, in the sense of being based upon an interconnected set of beliefs and assumptions which were automatic in contemporary spectators. But the process of discerning the meaning was dynamic, more than a mere reading-off of signification against motif. The meaning of the painting is not closed off. It tails off into the consciousness of the spectator whose own reading of the work helps to finalize the experience of the art of looking, to make the appreciation. In other words, the painting contains an argument; it is a text which has to be read, from and with an imagination.

What we do when we try to look at all thoroughly at such a work is to read it. "Read" is the nearest verb we have to describe the process. It involves a special kind of looking. A film director of the present day performs a comparable task to that of the Renaissance painter in a way, but the director does most of the looking work in advance, on the spectator's behalf. We are shown the scene from different angles. We are positioned within the work by the artist. We no longer read visual images because that part of the function of looking has been industrialized, as it were, away from us. The mechanics of cinematic image-making extracts much of the signifying material and sets it out so that it can be quickly absorbed or consumed by the spectator. Much iconographic material remains for us to decode, but we are so thoroughly trained as audiences in industrialized societies, so suffused with the culture of the images of fiction, news, entertainment, so quick to take every allusion, to place the genre within which we are working as spectators, that the work of looking takes but a moment. We do not have to read our images, although when we do try to apply the processes of reading to pictures in an educated way, we find, today, that we can look *though* film and television somehow into the secret inner workings of our own society, which in fact subtly frame the work and fuse our techniques for perceiving it into the techniques with which it has been constructed.

Advent of Moving Images

The creation of moving images and their arrival as the principal medium of culture, not as pervasive yet as printed text, but profoundly transforming of our ways of seeing the world, marks a new turning point in the evolution of the senses. Virginia Woolf wrote once that "in December 1910, human character changed." She was half consciously sensing the huge change in consciousness that was being registered in the works of Schoenberg, of Picasso, Russell and Whitehead, Einstein. It was the great change which we think of as the coming of the twentieth century, but it is a shift which is still in many ways working its way into our methods of apprehending the world. The culture of the moving image, when communicated across societies and between societies, is, as it were, deafening; it blots out other ways of experience and brings with it all the other languages and sign systems of which the dominant or providing culture is composed. Text has become subservient to image. Where language embodied in text transferred symbolically images and information about the world, the photographic image, as Susan Sontag puts it, is not so much a statement about the world as a piece of it. The image can communicate through dream and into dream. Moreover the image is never the emanation of an individual; it carries with it the basic patterns of perception of whole cultures. The image has become central to the economy of that consumer society which is dependent upon the constant acquisition and replacement of goods through their advertised images, to the point at which the cycle of purchase and obsolescence is dictated more by the wearing out of the advertising than of the product. The communicative skill of our society is thus concentrated in the task of making images perform great quantities of perceptual and cognitive work.

In a culture in which the computer acts increasingly as the chief form of memory there are already discernible new elements which one might treat as forms of perceptual bias. We can envisage within a decade (or less) the new medium of the interactive videodisc in which text and moving image are combined, a new kind of book in fact, portable, adaptable, perhaps not even fixed in content, but fusing in an artistic sense those two strands of our culture—text and moving image—which have hitherto been separated. Furthermore the computer breeds new habits of mind, new insistences upon the intellectual discipline of following procedures—the very heart of programming but utterly different from our inherited disciplines of the era of Gutenberg. The computer encourages a different kind of imagination—and that implies that quite major changes are in store for us as the subjects of cultural experience. The computer is today beginning to occupy the world of the senses. You feel it even when you begin to explore the potential of a word processor, when you search through a database, when you watch an organization involving a number of human beings transform itself with the advent of a new system. These are no longer simply new gadgets: they open up certain latencies of the mind, new preoccupations within the defining elements of our personalities.

Already one major cultural dispute exists around the computer, that of whether artificial intelligence (AI) is in fact a form of intelligence. John Searle argues that, in effect, a contrived facsimile of intelligence is not the same as a mind, while many proponents of AI claim that a machine which can do anything that one asks a human intellect to do must, by definition, be "intelligent." The controversy must intensify as the age of the fifth-generation computer arrives. It revolves around two quite arbitrary but necessary acts of language: first, the post-Renaissance emphasis on those capacities of the mind which we have selected to come under the label "intelligent," and second, the decision to mechanise those particular attributes through the procedures of programming.

One might ask whether a computer can sing: the answer must depend upon whether one is satisfied with one's original use of the word "sing" to include merely the external process of producing vocal music rather than the whole process of enjoyment and absorption of the emotion which precedes the acts of singing in humans. In other words, it is the attachment of the human being to the sense or faculty concerned which prevents the computer facsimile from being the "real" thing. We shall have to redefine many verbs. The human being, as subject, has a history and an intentionality. The subjectivity of the human is connected with that of all others and is grouped normally in nations, families and social classes. We approach the world through knowledge of it derived from the senses, whichever of our senses happens to function.

The advent of computer intelligence certainly drives us towards a new attempt to define ourselves as cultural beings operating in time and space. It obliges us to grasp some definition of human totality in order to locate the self. Every technological era since Descartes has redrawn the map of the human mind, analogically to coincide with the dominant technology of the day. But we have today to find a way to be defined as something other than particularly sensitive computers. It seems to me that this wholeness must lie somewhere in the historical sense, the sense of our own interconnections in time and space, in the shadow of which the computer's intelligence is but a copy, a representation, an intelligent picture, a piece of reality, but still object rather than subject. Like the Renaissance masterpiece it is a medium of communication, giving off meaning, rehearsing and reconstructing meaning in the process, but only in the course of the process, of being used. The difference between the hack and the computer is still that of subject and object.

This whole topic arises primarily because, in the wake of the so-called information revolution we are beginning to discover that the cultural industries are emerging as the commanding heights of the economy. The making of representations of the world in sound, text, and image is a major source of our very wealth as well as being the defining substance of our existence as subjects. There have always been profound political debates around the systems of information, but today it is in this cultural sector that ideology seems to be finding its fulcrum, rather than in the classical inherited industries. We can see the real ways in which our technology impacts upon us through our responses to the culture which we construct and consume. I am not arguing that we are simply the information which we use: rather that we exist in terms of a series of questions which are constantly rehearsed between ourselves and our cultures. We become the subjects rather than the objects of experience, the more we ponder the phenomena which compose a culture.

4
Media Values

Are you pleased when the hero in the movie or TV rides off alone to seek his destiny even though the grateful villagers have offered him wealth and security for having saved the village? Do you feel good when the woman in the soap opera gives up her job as a hospital administrator, as well as her intern lover, and returns to her husband, daughter, and home with a commitment to never stray again? Would you decide on a political career after you read and see in the news media that politicians are able to accept bribes and "feather their nests" at the taxpayer's expense? Do you expect medical doctors to be sacrificing of their personal lives and to take a deep and abiding interest in their patients? Do you try to act like Steve Martin or Carol Burnett when you are at a party? Have you ever quit listening to a radio DJ or stopped reading a magazine because you did not like the products advertised?

No matter how you answer these questions, your answers reflect in some way your values and your expectations about social and occupational roles. All of us carry around an organized set of attitudes and beliefs which constitute our value system. We apply our values (not always consciously) to persons, institutions, acts, behaviors and objects that confront us to determine how to feel, think and relate. If we see a fellow student cheating on an examination, our value system comes into play determining what we think, feel and do about the person and the act. At home our values affect how we act and react within the family setting. We might value pride or independence of thought much more highly than cooperativeness and compassion. As a consequence we react negatively to parental demands that we attend Uncle George's retirement party. If you have ever been "turned off" by a film, TV or radio program that used ethnic or racist humor, it was probably because of value conflict. If you were "turned on" by magazine ads showing a young virile man with clear blue eyes and a square jaw or a tall slender woman with long blonde hair and flawless skin, it was probably because of value congruence. In these and many other ways our value systems interact with the persons and events, including media persons and events, in our environment determining for us which feelings and responses are appropriate.

Individual and Societal Values

As individuals we use our values, not only to determine feelings, but to facilitate social relationships. Look around at your close friends and the groups

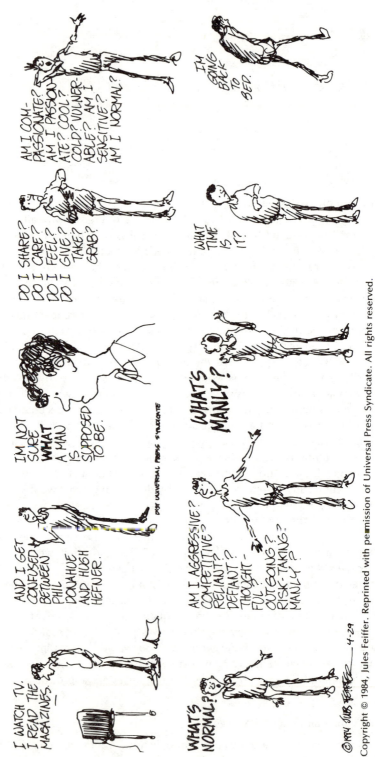

FEIFFER®

I WATCH TV. I READ THE MAGAZINES.

AND I GET CONFUSED BETWEEN PHIL DONAHUE AND HUGH HEFNER.

I'M NOT SURE **WHAT** A MAN IS SUPPOSED TO BE.

AM I COM-PASSIONATE? AM I PASSION-ATE? COOL? COLD? VULNER-ABLE? AM I SENSITIVE? AM I NORMAL?

DO I SHARE? DO I CARE? DO I FEEL? DO I GIVE? TAKE? GRAB?

I'M GOING BACK TO BED.

WHAT TIME IS IT?

WHAT'S NORMAL?

AM I AGGRESSIVE? COMPETITIVE? RELIANT? DEFIANT? THOUGHT-FUL? OUTGOING? RISK-TAKING? MANLY?

WHAT'S MANLY?

©1984 JULES FEIFFER 4-29

and organizations to which you belong. You will find great similarities in the types of persons and things you value and they value. When you reject persons or groups because of their behavior, you are rejecting their values as well. In a way, our values are continually being tested or compared to others' values in our interpersonal relationships.

When values are held in concert through strength of numbers, or tradition, they are said to be societal values. They govern individual behavior and set standards for that which is praised or rewarded in society. A society such as ours that values success pressures individuals to advance themselves and to seek the symbols of success. It also creates a structure that forces people to compete. It creates myths, dramas, literature and music extolling the virtues of success. Those who are successful are rewarded with praise, position, and influence; they become models for others to emulate. Some societal values become so entrenched that they are unquestioned, like individual freedom, or life, liberty and the pursuit of happiness.

Not all societal values are unquestioned nor are they all held in equal regard. As with individuals, societies have value hierarchies and sometimes the order of values change or move higher or lower on the scale. For example, many Americans are fond of saying that neighborliness or respect for others is not valued much anymore. Others claim that as technology has advanced, pride of workmanship has fallen on our scale of values while efficiency has risen. In societies where values are perpetuated primarily through the family, the school, the church and other local institutions, values tend to remain stable or to shift only slightly. Where societies are media dependent for information, socialization, and cultural projection, values systems tend to shift more rapidly. Furthermore, at any given moment, even in stable societies, values can be in conflict. For example, you may have long been taught that "honesty is the best policy" but find yourself working for a company that says loyalty to the company is more important than honesty with the customer. Or perhaps your parents place a high value on minding one's own business but your social club wants to help with a local youth rehabilitation program. How such value conflicts are resolved are a concern for both society and the individual. This concern is often reflected in battles over the content and control of the mass media.

In our nation we expect that the family and schools will not only dispense knowledge and skills, but will also inculcate the young with values. Schoolbooks like McGuffey's reader have always accompanied spelling lessons, grammar drills, history lessons, etc., with moral lessons which uphold the current value hierarchy. Where the values being perpetuated are unquestioned ones such as life and liberty, there is no problem. But when it comes to conflicting or shifting values, many people become concerned and want to control the means by which values are selected and projected. This is why community conflicts over electing schoolboard members and selecting school textbooks can arouse such bitter controversy. Those who determine school policies and the content of textbooks control the value hierarchy. Like school boards, those in control of the mass media directly influence the nation's value system. Some would want the Federal Communications Commission to act as "school board" for the electronic media. People who are concerned about television violence, about explicit sex in motion pictures, or about songs which promote drugs would have censors established to see that the public, and particularly the young, are exposed only to the correct values; or at least are not influenced by improper values. Others would have legislation passed to prevent the publication of the "wrong kinds" of literature or the showing of "improper" films. Still others would use boycotts and demonstrations to block the communication of undesirable values. In some societies, those in charge of the state take over direct control of mass media to insure that the public is exposed to only the official value hierarchy.

Mass Media Values

There is no doubt that the mass media have an important relationship to individual and societal values. We all learn values through experience and indoctrination. Beginning at about the age of two we are all continually exposed to the mass media. It follows that the media are an important source of value development. A cursory examination of media content would reveal that almost all media dramatizations are miniature morality plays in which individualism, freedom of choice, perserverance and faith in God triumphs. News presentations of foreign news are from the viewpoint of American rather than foreign values, and local news tends to stress the virtues of law and order and good citizenship. What makes the media so appealing is that they uphold our dominant value system. The mass media even go to some length to avoid taking positions where there is a strong value conflict.

The mass media are not simply mirrors reflecting societal values. They subtly, and sometimes not so subtly, shape our value hierarchy and even project values onto society. The media bring us into contact with a wide variety of people and events, providing us with the means to "cross-check" values upheld by our family, by our friends, and by our culture. This checking may reveal that values other than those we learned in our interpersonal relationships are important and we may be influenced to accept "external" values. Or we may reject them because they threaten our way of life. This is why some groups like the Amish so vigorously oppose any media inputs into their communities.

The very structure of the mass media can project values onto the whole society, values which otherwise may not have existed. For example, all the mass media are geared to presentation of material in short time segments. Television programs are generally limited to half-hour or hour-long lengths. Radio news items rarely exceed thirty seconds. Motion pictures hardly ever use more than two hours for a presentation. The time limit tends to place a great emphasis on action, movement and quick resolution. Things which are slow to evolve, which are not action oriented, and which tend to extend over a long period of time, do not get presented by the mass media. The media value action and quick resolution, and all of us are influenced. We may find that on an interpersonal basis we are looking for quick relationships, for fast resolution of interpersonal problems, and superficial encounters.

Perhaps, more subtly, the "grammars" of media (those elements and techniques which define a medium) have come to influence our values because the process of perception has been modified. For example, the use of the close-up lens in motion pictures, photography, and television has had a marked effect on our concepts of personal distance and social attractiveness. The close-up has made us more conscious of the human face. Faces with zits, dirty pores, or pockmarks are not appreciated by the close-up lens and therefore the visual media have sought out the flawless skin, bright teeth, and clear eyes. (Dental hygiene moved up the value scale with the development of the photographic camera and popular magazine advertising.) The media rejects facial imperfections or, when they are shown, they represent vulgarity or unhealthiness. All of us are taught to value a clear complexion. We have come to value it so highly that we are willing to pour billions of dollars into the cosmetic industry.

No doubt you can think of other ways that some values have been emphasized through the grammar of the media. Does radio sound place an emphasis on spoken fluency, on a voice that is deep, well modulated and male? Have we come to value "voices" like that? to trust them more than other kinds of voices? to think of them as more authoritative? Has the focus of the camera made the smiling face, the cheerful countenance, an important asset? Could George Washington or Abe Lincoln have made it in a mass media world? Is that the secret to Ronald Reagan's rise to the top? Another way to put the question might be, to what degree are all of us "on camera" or speaking through the microphone when we are communicating on an interpersonal basis?

Conflicting Values

It is important to recognize that the modern mass media have also contributed to the growing number of value conflicts in our society. As we mentioned earlier, there have always been value conflicts in our social system, but the modern media are projecting some values that may be threatening to long cherished traditional values. For instance, despite almost universal denunciation of commercials and other advertisements, the economic needs of the mass media have managed to create a new value for us—consumerism! The frequent trip to the supermarket or the shopping center has become an important part of the life of every American. The right to buy the newest nationally advertised product and to discard the old, out of date, out of style but still usable item has been firmly established. A whole way of life has grown up around the American shopping center. For very young children it has replaced the playground to become a training ground for a lifetime of consumerism. (Surveys indicate that two- and three-year-old children can distinguish among nationally advertised brands and can point them out on the store shelves). For teenage Americans, it has become the after-school place where all the latest products can be checked out so that one can be in style.

Media advertising has created a new value hierarchy: life, liberty and the pursuit of consumer products. Conflict arises with individuals and institutions who uphold "thrift" as an important value. It is hard to believe in saving one's money or saving energy or any of the other aspects of thrift when all the mass media make consuming not only exciting and attractive, but link it with "the American Way." The old tradition of thrift, the one that tells us to save our pennies for a rainy day, to never throw away something that could be mended or repaired, is dormant.

Another value conflict is created by our growing dependence on media to instruct us about what is important. This dependence conflicts with the more traditional value of self-reliance and independence of thought and action. In *The Lonely Crowd*, David Riesman claims that Americans have become "other directed" rather than "inner directed" or "tradition directed." Riesman suggests a connection between this shift and the mass media. Many other individuals are concerned that Americans are coming to value media experience more highly than firsthand experience, to value one-way communication more highly than two-way, interpersonal communication.

All of us have to learn which values are important, and we have to absorb them into our personalities. Parents, teachers, and peers have been the traditional source of such instruction. These sources of value instruction are now supported, and in some cases supplanted, by the mass media. The mass media have become our personal "educators." They instruct us about personal happiness and how to obtain it, success and how to achieve it, honesty and its rewards, greed and its punishment. Through advertising, dramatization, entertainment and news, we are all instructed, directly and indirectly, about the important values. The media provide us with interesting and exciting visual and auditory "lessons" about what happens when the "right" values are upheld. The media, more than interpersonal interaction, have become the testing grounds for our value systems. Is personal honesty something we value? We don't have to test it interpersonally to know where it stands in the value hierarchy. We can see and hear it tested every day through media "reality." This could be a valuable adjunct to the development of values, but as James Chesebro points out in his eleven year study of television, the television portrayals do not accurately reflect the diversity and complexity of the American value system. They disproportionately dramatize a very narrow set of roles and values.

It becomes exceedingly difficult to value the role of the aged in our society if the media continually portray old people as foolish and a bother to have around. It may be impossible for women to value independence when the media portrayal "rewards" those who become housekeepers and "punishes" the single independent woman by showing her to be lonely, neurotic, bitchy or secretly waiting for the right man to come along.

Roles and Values

The mass media do not always, or even usually, uphold values directly and explicitly, rather they are implicit in the situations and characters presented. It is mainly through media personalities and roles they enact that values are implied. The radio DJ is cool or hip; the news anchorperson is objective, not emotionally involved, serious but not overly concerned; the talk show host is convivial, nonthreatening, witty and caring; the cop-show hero is tough, independent, untrusting of others; the sit-com heroine is aggressive, talkative, easily diverted and warm-hearted. There tends to be a similarity among role types on the mass media and the values that go with each role. If the "let's not take all this too seriously" type newscaster becomes popular (i.e., attracts a large audience) then almost all the newscasters appear in this role, just as the popular sadistic cop-hero becomes the one for the other networks to imitate. In each case the role implies certain values and situations are manipulated in the media to make this type of role and its values appropriate.

Conflict exists in this situation because it reverses the fundamental relationship among role, value, and situation found in the usual interpersonal context. In face-to-face communication all of us must play a variety of roles. A student must not only fulfill the student role, but must balance the roles of son or daughter (mother or father), companion, lover, confidant, leader, follower, in all kinds of real world transactions. A teacher must be able to enact the roles of mother-father, husband-wife, disciplinarian, counselor, organizer, golfer. These roles are vital to human interaction because they represent the mutually agreed upon expectations that we hold for ourselves and for those with whom we interact. We learned from early childhood to observe role models—first parents and relatives, then teachers, and finally our peers—to learn which roles were appropriate to which situations. Through appropriate role taking we came to develop self-esteem and empathy (the ability to project oneself into the role of another). Values are inextricably bound with role modeling and role taking. The values we hold determine the appropriateness of the roles we assume and the roles we assume reenforce or negate values. Effective interpersonal communication is based on being able to enact roles which are appropriate to the situation. Our sense of self and other, our self-esteem and our ability to empathize is increased when the roles we take reflect values appropriate to the situation.

There are few problems when the media provide role models which reflect our social values and help us recognize the choices we have in selecting appropriate roles. Problems are created when media not only project role models but manufacture images which are mythic roles. When the media situation is manipulated to make it appropriate to the role, we have created for us an image of a role—a role that is always appropriate because the situation and the values have been manufactured for the role rather than vice versa. This is the difference between what Daniel J. Boorstin calls a celebrity and a hero. A hero is one who has appropriately reacted to the demands of the situation in a way that makes all of us feel that important values have been upheld. A celebrity is an image of a role and is dependent on the media to create situations and events appropriate to that role. In this case the values upheld are self-aggrandizement, popularity, and, frequently, monetary pay-off. It is Boorstin's belief, along with others, that the media have made us suspicious of role taking in our interpersonal relationships because of the confusion of image and role. There are those, also, who fear that when media images become the role models for young persons, we are bound to have an increase in alienation as more and more persons find out that these mythic roles are inappropriate for working out the day-to-day problems of interpersonal communication.

Communication, Values, and Popular Television Series—An Eleven-Year Assessment

This essay is based on a 1975 study published in the *Journal of Popular Culture*. In that essay Chesebro, along with Caroline Hamsher, set up a framework in which to categorize popular TV series and determine the values implicit. In this essay, Chesebro updates that earlier study and subsequent versions which appeared in the two previous editions of this volume. This essay extends his examination over an eleven-year period and demonstrates that his system of categories for analyzing the values implicit in TV series can be applied to constantly changing network schedules and programs. His method takes us past the usual comedic and dramatic qualities of these programs and into the underlying value systems which provide the foundations for the characterizations and plot lines. His examination clearly estblishes that popular entertainment forms are communicative acts that reflect, convey, and reinforce values.

The glowing images of the television screen now occupy an ever-present and central place within the typical American home. In 1984, the A. C. Nielsen Company reported that the average American household had its television set on for seven hours and two minutes a day, an increase of fourteen minutes from 1982 (Smith, 1984; Gardella, 1984). Although clearly functioning as a source of entertainment, television also serves multiple instrumental ends. Television is now the primary source of information about "what's going on in the world today"; it is also viewed as the most "believable" source of information (The Roper Organization, Inc., 1983, pp. 5, 6). Indeed, for children, television provides "the first introduction to events and people outside their daily experience" (Chira, 1983, p. C6). For many people, television is even assumed to directly cause many of the nation's problems. Two-thirds of the American population believe, for example, that there is a "relationship between violence on television and the rising crime rate in the United States" (The Gallup Report, 1982, p. 36). Others, such as the National Institute of Mental Health, argue that "there is overwhelming scientific evidence" that "excessive" violence on television is directly responsible for delinquent, agressive, and violent behavior among children (Schwartz, 1982; Collins, 1982).

Nonetheless, in terms of both behavior and preferences, television remains the central activity of Americans after sleep and work. Television "set owners spend less time attending social gatherings away from home, listening to the radio, reading books, engaging in miscellaneous leisure activities, attending the movies, conversing, watching television away from home, and doing household tasks" (Comstock, 1980, p. 500). Television set owners even sleep 13 percent less than nonset owners (Comstock, 1980, p. 500). They spend three-fourths of their total media time watching television and 40 percent of their total leisure time with television (Comstock, 1980, p. 500).

Moreover, viewers apparently prefer to watch television rather than be with other people or do anything else. Television is the most preferred leisure time activity in the United States (The Gallup Report, 1977, p. 14). Based upon a random sample of all Americans, the Gallup Organization (1977, p. 14) reports that "television watching" is now the "favorite way of spending an evening." Gallup specifically notes that television viewing is almost three times more popular than being "home with the family," four times more popular than being "with friends," and seven times more popular than "visiting friends and relatives" or engaging in social activities such as "participating in sports." Thus, whether measured by actual behavior or by stated preferences, television has emerged as the new "social companion" of the average American.

Although television viewing "increases throughout the day," it "peaks" and sustains its highest viewership "during prime-time" hours, between 8 and 11 P.M. everyday, with 40 to 70 percent of American households tuned in on any given evening (A. C. Nielsen Company, 1982, p. 5). The type of programs broadcast during prime time has certainly varied as popular tastes have changed. In November of 1981, for example, A. C. Nielsen reported that "situation comedies" were the "most popular program type" (1982, p. 11). By 1984, action-adventure, science fiction, and fantasy programs had displaced sitcoms in the rating (Gunther, 1984; Hinckley, 1984; Agena, 1983). Although prime-time television is extremely sensitive to dramatic changes in the popular culture, nonetheless between 1974 and 1984, prime-time, network-produced series—as opposed to prime-time soap operas, movies, variety shows, sports, and news and semidocumentaries—have constituted at least 58 percent to as high as 71 percent of all scheduled prime-time network programming.[1]

It would be a mistake to believe that these prime-time dramatic network productions function only as "pure escapist entertainment." Although these series are certainly designed to entertain, they are also constructed to convey "messages" to their viewers. Producers of these series freely admit that persuasive intents guide the development and execution of the series they provide. These producers intentionally formulate and portray certain values as more desirable than others. As Gerald M. Miller (1972, p. 10) has so aptly noted, "every communicative act involves, of necessity, a value judgement." In this sense, certain kinds of characters and plot developments are designed to foster and to reinforce certain value judgments but not others. Even in the more entertaining and simplistic of these series, the persuasive intent to alter the value orientations of others can be found. While noting that *Happy Days,* for example, "was a fantasy" and a "very soft, gentle show," its producers also sought "to teach" tolerance, the importance of being "nice to each other," and to reinforce the primacy of the "family unit" (Marshall, 1984). ABC perceived *Happy Days* as "presenting warm-hearted family humor and emphasizing sensible values" (O'Connor, 1984). In this case, the life-styles of those portrayed were designed to endorse a particular set of values at the expense of others. As *New York Times* television critic John J. O'Connor (1984) aptly summarized *Happy Days* when it completed its last show of its ten-year history: "Despite the attempts at keeping a slick veneer, everything is almost rigorously virtuous. The details may change but the patterns of living remain remarkably the same." Other producers have also been as direct about the values they seek to portray. Quinn Martin, producer of such series as *Streets of San Francisco, Cannon,* and *The FBI,* argues: "I am a patriot. In the police stories that I do, I show the police in an idealized way. Without respect for the police, I think we'd have a breakdown in our society. . . . So 90 percent of the time or more, we show the police as idealistic" (Efron, 1974, p. 3). The producer of *The Waltons,* Lee Rich, has reasoned that, "the success of this series is because of what is going on in the country today, the loss of values. Many people see ethical qualities of this family that they hope they can get back to" (Efron, 1974, p. 3). Similarly, Donald Wildmon protested the cancellation of *Little House: A New Beginning* because it would mean that the values promoted by the series might be lost: "*Little House* is the only program on television that consistently, week after week, comes out for the traditional value systems that have made this country great" (1983, p. A-2). Although the values being promoted differ, Davidson's (1974) and Murphy's (1983) surveys of the major television series suggest that virtually all producers use their series to secure specific persuasive objectives. In this context, Richard D. Heffner (1973, pp. 25–26) has argued that television series may appropriately be viewed as "subtle persuaders." As he put it, "Television, the newest and far more prevalent form of fiction, is even more profoundly influential in our lives—not in terms of the stories it tells, but more importantly, the values it portrays."

In the world of prime-time television, entertainment and persuasion can no longer be viewed as opposite ends of a continuum. Entertainment is often guided by explicitly persuasive objectives, while good persuasion is often extremely entertaining. Yet, viewers would prefer to believe that entertainment and persuasion are distinct and independent processes; they would prefer to believe that their favorite form of "escapism" is *not* directly shaping their value orientation. As I noted some eleven years ago when I first began to formally examine prime-time network television series: "viewers perceive the series predominantly as entertainment rather than persuasive acts. We may repeatedly observe that entertainment and persuasion are not exclusive dimensions: entertainment may be persuasive; persuasion may be entertaining. Yet, viewers act as if the series offered an opportunity 'to get away from all the pressures'" (Chesebro and Hamsher, 1975, p. 590). Rather than abandoning or softening this view, I now believe that entertainment is the dominant strategy or form used when persuasive endeavors are undertaken within the American culture. If this supposition is correct, we do have reason to examine popular prime-time network series to determine the degree to which they promote certain values rather than others and to explore the degree to which these television values are affecting our larger sociocultural system.

Objectives of This Study

The relationships among communication, values, and popular television series are complex; no single study is likely to reveal all of the dynamic intricacies among these three systems. In this reading, we can only begin the complex process of identifying the ways in which popular television series affect the values of viewers. This study is designed to identify the communication strategies employed on television series to convey and to reinforce selective values. Four questions mold the analysis offered here:

1. What patterns, types, or kinds of human relationships are portrayed in popular television series?
2. How are human problems and difficulties resolved in popular television series?
3. How have popular television series changed, particularly in the last eleven years?
4. What particular values are reinforced by popular television series and which of these values have been predominantly emphasized in the last eleven years?

In order to answer these questions, four lines of analysis are developed. First, a system is outlined for describing and interpreting popular television series. Some fifty-three different series were scheduled to appear regularly on the air during the 1984–1985 season, each with a host of different plot lines, minor characters, and ideas expressed each week. A classification system was needed to make some logical sense out of this barrage of messages. The formulation of such a system technically requires the presentation of a *theory of logical types,* which allows a critic to explain that symbol-using on popular television series in the context of a systematic framework. The theoretical system outlined here produces a framework that allows the critic to view a television series as essentially one of five communication strategies. This scheme is detailed shortly.

Second, these five types of communication are illustrated from television series in the 1984–1985 season.

Third, this framework is employed as a grid for classifying all television series in the 1984–1985 season and for identifying the long-term changes in the nature of communication patterns in these television series since the 1974–1975 season.

Fourth, the values promoted by these television series are explicitly identified as well as their relationship in the larger sociocultural system.

A Theory of Logical Types for Classifying Communicative Acts

In order to classify television series into a coherent yet sensitive and meaningful category system, the rules used for the formulation of the matrix itself should first be specified. Herbert W. Simons proposes that generic formulations should proceed along certain methodological lines:

> First, there must be a class of genres into which a particular genre can be put. . . . A second requirement for generic identification is that the categorizer must have clear rules or criteria for identifying distinguishing characteristics of a genre. . . . Third, the necessary and sufficient distinguishing features of a genre must not only be nameable but operationalizable; the categorizer must be able to tell the observer or critic how to know a distinguishing feature when he [or she] sees it. Finally, if items of discourse are to be consistently identified as fitting within one genre or another, it follows that these items should be internally homogeneous across salient characteristics and clearly distinguishable from items comprising an alternative genre. (Simons, 1975, p. 2)

These rules are used to formulate the communication matrix proposed here.

To generate a matrix, all communication acts must first be examined in the same way and on the same level of abstraction, or as Simons has put it, the items must be members of the same "class of genres." In this regard, other researchers have classified communicative acts based upon the type of manipulative *strategies* employed (Chesebro and Hamsher, 1974), the kind of *situations* in which communicative acts occurred (Bitzer, 1968), the apparent *purposes* of the sources of these communicative acts (e.g., Wilson and Arnold, 1976, pp. 132–147), or by the similarities or differences in the policies or *acts* recommended during communicative exchanges (Wrage, 1947). An *agent-centered* criterion is employed here to classify television series as communicative acts. Specifically, the kind of central character or central characters of the television series is the basis for distinguishing television series into different groups.

Having selected an agent-centered matrix, Simons' second methodological requirement becomes relevant: a set of "clear rules or criteria for identifying distinguishing characteristics of a genre" must be employed. Northrop Frye (1957, pp. 33–34) provides a convenient set of rules for distinguishing types of central characters in fiction. Because Frye's concern and the focal point of this analysis are similar, Frye's scheme is easily adapted as a mechanism for analyzing central characters on television series. In Frye's view, two variables generate and distinguish major kinds of communication systems: (1) the central character's apparent intelligence compared to that of the audience and (2) the central character's ability to control circumstances compared with that of the audience.

These two variables produce five kinds of communication systems.

In the *ironic communication system,* the central character is both intellectually inferior and less able to control circumstances than is the audience. In the ironic communication system, the person responsible for an act lacks both the scope and the appropriate kinds of interpretative concepts for assessing reality, as well as the skills necessary to mobilize or to generate the support required for concerted agreements and actions. All of us have faced this situation at one time or another. All of us have functioned ironically in the sense that we were less able than our immediate audience to understand what was occurring and how to handle the situation we had encountered. As a result, the act we carried out did not reflect or "say" what we meant. Whenever a disparity exists between what is said or done and what is meant, irony emerges. For the central characters placed within this category, this disparity is a central and constant feature of their behavior.

In the *mimetic communication system,* the central character is "one of us," cast as equally intelligent and equally able to control circumstances as those surrounding and viewing the central character. In mimetic communication systems, all are perceived, believed, or treated as equals: a common set of symbolic perceptions, descriptions, and interpretations of reality are shared by individuals if they are members of a mimetic system; moreover, members of such a system face and deal with similar problems and situations with equal skill. For all practical purposes, human interactions cast as mimetic appear to be "slices of everyday life."

In the *leader-centered communication system,* the central character is superior in intelligence to others but only in degree by virtue of special training, personality conditioning, and so forth. However, the central character in the leader-centered communication system confronts the same kind of circumstances as the audience and possesses no special skills in dealing with these circumstances. Thus, the leader generates a configuration of symbols for acting that others find compelling, and by virtue of the leader's ideas or conceptions, the leader and followers are able to act concertedly and thereby deal with their shared problems, situations, or questions.

In the *romantic communication system,* the central character is superior to members of the audience in degree, both in terms of intelligence and in terms of the ability to control circumstances. In romantic communication systems, the central character thus possesses a symbol system which allows her or him to account for more environmental variables in more incisive ways than others (intelligence) and to create more effective options and programs for acting on those environmental factors than others (control of the environment).

In the *mythical communication system,* the central character is superior in kind to others both in terms of intelligence and in terms of his or her ability to control circumstances. If we view Christianity as a communication system, for example, the "word of God" is presumed to stem from a kind of superior intelligence far beyond any kind of understanding humankind may ever possess as well as being capable of producing environmental changes which no mere mortal can ever achieve. Although "mystical" in nature, such symbol systems should *not* be viewed as somehow "less real" than any other mode of communication, for such systems have profoundly altered the attitudes, beliefs, and actions of massive groups of people.

These five communication systems constitute the basic distinguishing categories or framework for classifying television series. However, our ability to distinguish these communication systems remains incomplete, for the question emerges: "How does the critic determine the relationship between the central character and the audience?" Simons' third methodological rule for matrix formulation provides a response to this question, for it posits that systems must be *operationally discrete* as well as conceptually distinct: "the categorizer must be able to tell the observer or critic how to know a distinguishing feature when he [or she] sees it."

In order to identify operationally and systematically the unique pattern of dramatic action which characterizes each communication system, Kenneth Burke's (1961/1970, pp. 4–5) "dramatistic process' has been employed. As I have adapted Burke's notion of "dramatic process" for our purposes here, all human dramas are carried out in four discrete stages. These four stages and their concomitant critical questions are: (1) *Pollution*—"What norms are violated and cast as disruptive to the social system involved?" (2) *Guilt*—"Who or what is generally held responsible for the

Table 1. Types of communication dramas

Dramatistic Stages	Ironic	Mimetic	Leader-centered	Romantic	Mythical
Pollution	The central character violates major rules of the system.	Rules violated are minor and the result of accidents, the best of intentions, and/or circumstances.	Values of the central character are violated by others.	The central character identifies the significance and scope of the problem (a problem of mind, body, and spirit).	Universal problems beyond human control—unreasonable, overwhelming, and often religious/ideological—set off the drama.
Guilt	The central character is explicitly recognized as the cause of the pollution: scapegoating.	Guilt is easily admitted by agents because pollution is both insignificant and unintentional.	The central actor assumes responsibility for correcting the pollution: self-mortification.	The central character is the primary, if only, agent who identifies all of the dimensions of blame in a way that allows for correction.	Blame cannot be attached to any particular and individual agent—forces are to fault.
Purification	Characters beside the central character initiate acts to correct the pollution.	The accidents and/or circumstances are explicitly recognized; intentions are explained; forcing a reinterpretation and/or forgiveness for the pollution.	The leader mobilizes others to achieve the original ends through selective means chosen by the leader.	The more highly developed skills, intelligence, and sensitivity of the central character are combined in the unique fashion essential to produce the most desirable set of corrective acts.	Superhuman powers of the central character emerge during the corrective process.
Redemption	The central character is reestablished as the controlling force to reinitiate pollution.	The previous system can be reestablished with all characters "wiser" for the experience.	The leader's values are reestablished and explicitly recognized as controlling.	The central character is recognized overtly as the embodiment of all that's right.	A new social system is established due to unique powers of central character.

pollution?" (3) *Purification*—"What kinds of acts are generally initiated to eliminate the pollution and guilt?" and (4) *Redemption*—"What social system or order is created as a result of passing through the pollution, guilt, and purification stages?" This *pollution-guilt-purification-redemption* framework can be used to describe systematically behavioral differences among each of the five communication systems identified here. Thus, the dramatistic process allows us to detect operational differences among the five communication systems. Table 1 provides a complete conception of the behavioral matrix ultimately generated.

Surveys of popular television series carried out by this researcher for the last eleven years have led to several conclusions: (1) central characters in television series engage in explicit and varied behaviors when functioning in human relations or human dramas (conflict-resolution patterns); (2) the behaviors of central characters are repetitive or redundant, predominantly because of the requirements of the television series itself (see, e.g., Nord, 1983, pp. 295–298; and Snow, 1983, pp. 130–147); (3) these explicit behaviors can be classified into one of the five communication systems; and (4) the central characters in each category can be grouped together because they display shared, common, or redundant patterns of action at each stage of the dramatistic process in each type of communication drama. Thus, although Table 1 is presented here as a formal deductive system, it was derived inductively based on the actual behaviors of central characters on television series.

Symbolic and Dramatistic Progressions in Popular Television Series

The dramatic progressions that distinguish the ironic, mimetic, leader-centered, romantic, and mythical communication systems can be illustrated with specific television series from the 1984–1985 season. The ironic system is first examined and is appropriately revealed as a symbolic system by the character of Jack Tripper in *Three's a Crowd*.

The Ironic Communication System

An ironic character may assume several forms. The ironic character may *intentionally* assume a pretense of ignorance or pretend to learn from others in order to reveal the false conceptions of others. Such ironic characters purposely use words which convey the opposite meaning of their literal meaning, typically producing an incongruity between the normal or expected results and the actual results of a sequence of events. Thus, the notion of *Socratic irony* has come to identify the agent who intentionally pretends to be stupid in order to inconspicuously force an answerer to reveal false conceptions. On the other hand, *dramatic irony* exists when the audience understands the incongruity between what is said and what is known while the characters in the interaction are unaware of the incongruity. Or, *tragic irony* may exist when an attitude of detached awareness creates an incongruity between what is and what is known.

With Jack Tripper, dramatic irony dominates. In dramatic irony, the central character *unintentionally* articulates and defends positions which are inconsistent with known events. In such cases, the character may unknowingly become ironic; only the audience is aware of the incongruity. Unintended ironic behaviors may introduce a comic dimension. However, the sense of the ironic and the humorous posture of the character is a response of the audience in a dramatic irony. Ultimately, it is the intentions of the character, the environment in which the character exists, and the "universe of understanding" possessed by the audience which determine the degree to which a given set of behaviors is perceived as ironic.

In *Three's a Crowd,* Jack has left his roommates. Jack now owns his own restaurant and has found his true love, Vicky Bradford. An old-fashioned guy at heart, Jack wants to marry Vicky. Vicky does not; her parents were divorced and she didn't have the greatest childhood. As a result, Jack and Vicky are living together without the benefit of matrimony over Jack's restaurant, but in a building owned by Vicky's overbearing and directive father, who also owns 10 percent of Jack's restaurant. As a result, these three characters must continually interact, which creates in Jack's mind, an unnecessary crowd.

In one of the early shows of this series, the pollution and guilt or responsibility for the problem which Jack faces does not appear to be of his own creation. The fire inspector has determined that Jack must install an $8000 sprinkler system or be closed. Jack's apparent problem is to find the $8000. Hoping to preserve what independence he does have, Jack does not want to borrow more money from Vicky's father. Jack remains concerned, but he has no ready solution. Vicky seeks to offer advice and even to provide the needed financial assistance. Jack, however, notes that women simply "don't have the mind" for such matters. Whatever money Vicky does have, Jack reasons, should be spend on nail polish and eye makeup.

At this juncture, the real pollution and guilt governing this drama emerge. Without his fully recognizing it, a problem has been created by Jack, the "hero" of the series. Jack does not realize that Vicky has carefully and wisely managed and invested her money and does have some $10,000 at her disposal. Moreover, Jack does not realize that the problem he believes exists can be easily eliminated. Jack's error, of course, stems from his more serious tendency to stereotype women in general. Ultimately, then, without his knowledge, Jack has misinterpreted the situation on several grounds. First, the financial problem he is concerned about is immediately resolvable; Jack's concerns are misdirected. Second, Jack's stereotypical attitude regarding women creates a new problem Jack is unaware of, that he has offended Vicky by virtue of his condescending attitude. In all, then, the problem and responsibility for the problem defining the drama is ironic, for the hero of the drama has actually created the pollution.

Purification requires that Vicky resolve the issues governing the drama. She must explain to Jack that she does have the required money for the sprinkler system, that she is willing to share the money, and that Jack's attitude toward women in general created all of the worry and anxiety he has experienced as well as the irritation which Vicky has displayed. It is Vicky, then, and not the central hero of the drama, who has resolved both the financial and social problems which have governed the drama. As a final touch of purification, Jack does feel particularly foolish, if not stupid.

Yet, the final act of the drama is to perpetuate the ironic style of the series, for in the final few minutes of the show, Jack assumes the leadership position once again. The agent causing the problems is now back "in charge." We wait until next week so see what this ironic hero will then undertake. Whatever that action will be, we can feel confident that the hero of the series will cause the problem which others will resolve only to have him return, once again, to his leadership role.

The Mimetic Communication System

Marcel Marceau has frequently been identified as the outstanding mime of the twentieth century. On an empty stage, in whiteface and dressed in black, he silently copies and imitates scenes from everyday life. The acts he portrays are intended to reflect what all of us do—the common, the ordinary, or those "slices of life" all of us experience are revealed. Thus, Marceau portrays a "man walking in the rain against the wind," a "man walking upstairs," or a "man trapped in a box." His mimetic acts closely resemble real life, but the resemblance is superficial and therefore a form of what is technically identified as "comic ridicule." Although we may enjoy and laugh at the mime, the mimetic preformer also allows us to identify and therefore to prepare for those moments when others may find us in an embarrassing situation, and when we must admit the humor of our own everyday actions.

The mimetic form may also be employed to disarm us and make us view other persons or products as a normal part of our everyday lives when, in fact, such representations are persuasive efforts to make us endorse "foreign" agents or objects as part of us. Thus, the politician employs the mimetic form when he proclaims in the agricultural district: "I was once a farm boy myself" (see Burke, 1962, p. 522, also pp. 521–704). Or, the mimetic form is used to sell us paper towels or coffee: after being cast as "our next door neighbor" and therefore as a person to be trusted, Rosie then proceeds to reveal her overwhelming zeal and commitment to Bounty. Such bandwagon techniques are grounded in the mimetic form—a dramatic imitation of life, usually but not always in a slightly exaggerated manner, designed to reinforce or to alter perceptions, attitudes, beliefs, and actions.

Moreover, the mimetic forms can also be used to characterize entire patterns of human action. Such mimetic patterns attempt to cast both the "content" and the "manner" of dramas as everyday phenomena: the pattern thus minimizes the unusual and unique; it casts particular goals, values, beliefs, attitudes, concepts, actions, and manners as common or popular. Dramas operating within the constraints of this mimetic form typically portray incidents as common: problems are conceived as accidents, a product of misunderstood intentions, or the results of unavoidable circumstances, all of which ultimately creates the view that the problems involved are relatively insignificant and unpremediated. Once the accidental, unintentional, or circumstantial nature of the problem is confirmed, characters typically return to their previous and established modes of action, perhaps wiser for the experience.

The popular television series *Diff'rent Strokes* functions as an excellent example of the mimetic communication system, and it is used here to illustrate the pattern of interactions of a mimetic drama.

In one of the shows of the series, the problem or pollution, although not of societal importance, does affect Arnold's personal preferences. The issue is established in the playground at Arnold's school. Arnold and others are break dancing. Arnold is told by Lisa that he is a "rule breaker. Ya know, certain things aren't allowed in school. . . . You'll be sorry. School isn't the proper place for break dancing." To complicate matters, Arnold is then caught break dancing by Principal Stone: "Arnold, you know the rule against break dancing on school property. . . . When I make a rule, I expect it to be followed, that goes for dancing and the dress code." Never having heard of a dress code, Arnold asks, "What dress code?" "The one," announces Principal Stone, "that starts tomorrow. . . . There'll be no more spiked wristbands, sleeveless shirts, or sneaker with holes in them. Also, no bandanas, headbands, shorts, or jeans with knees ripped out. . . . And, as for the girls, there'll be no more off-the-shoulder tops." It is only at this last specification that Arnold protests: "But, sir, those shoulders keep a guy going." And the, upon thought, Arnold asks: "But, sir, what do clothes have to do with getting an education?" Arnold is informed: "It's a discipline, Arnold, and discipline is a big part of growing up."

Having established the "rules of the system" and therefore the potential conflict which sets off the drama, Arnold and the other children decide to violate the rules. Their decision to violate the dress code is explicit and ultimately rationalized as a "protest" and "strike." Among the children, the rationale develops: "Do you believe that guy? He's changing this place into a prison"; "Who does he think pays his salary?"; "He'd have no school to run without us, and I say we go on strike"; "We have to go on strike to protect our freedom—today it's headbands; tomorrow it's Trivial Pursuit." After some prodding by his "little love bug" and in order to impress her, Arnold decides to go on strike even though it "may be dangerous" and is "against the rules." In Arnold's view, "we're men of action. . . . We've been pushed around here long enough and we're not going to take it anymore. We demand our freedom." Yet, the issue is not of overwhelming societal importance. It is unclear that human rights are violated, and in the series itself, the strike is ultimately cast by Arnold as a way of satisfying personal preferences: "we're going on strike at school so we can wear things like wristbands, bandanas, and off-the-shoulder blouses." Yet, the strike itself does create the actual moment of conflict. The strike is "nonviolent," and so relatively unobtrusive that Lisa must even tell Principal Stone that "they're on strike." Nonetheless, Arnold is suspended from school for one week. Overall, then, a relative minor issue sets off the conflict, the conflict is a modest protest, and ultimately even the strike itself is grounded and cast as a matter of personal preference, with a comparatively minor punishment as the actual definition of the problem Arnold must deal with.

Although guilt would apparently be assumed by all of those involved in the decision to strike, Arnold ultimately becomes the scapegoat. He is appointed leader; he accepts this position to please his potential girlfriend rather than to function as the leader of a movement. Moreover, once Arnold is suspended, all of the other children abandon the strike effort, leaving Arnold to be the unfairly accused "leader" and "cause" of his suspension.

This problem (pollution) and responsibility (guilt) are resolved or purified when Arnold is able to explain his motives and intentions. At first, it appears that any resolution may be difficult to achieve. Arnold's father says that he is "disappointed" in him and notes that "a dress code is hardly sufficient reason for a five-day suspension." Arnolds asserts that "the issue is our personal freedom," but this explanation is initially dismissed as "silly." Yet, the matter is resolved the next day. Arnold father notes: "Arnold, I'm sorry that I wasn't more understanding. . . . When we talked yesterday, I'm afraid I wasn't really listening. . . . The idea of you doing something silly, getting suspended, that was disturbing. But, I don't feel that way now. . . . I think you should do what you feel is right." Thus, the resolution ultimately involves, and really only requires, that Arnold's father sanction Arnold's motives for protesting. Having secured such support, the conflict is effectively resolved.

We learn in the last few minutes of the show, however, that the social system will remain as it has and that Arnold may only be a bit wiser for the experience. Arnold's father notes that, "You know the dress code must be followed." Arnold agrees. His father further notes that the experience is not, however, without some redeeming value, for Arnold may "learn something" from the experience.

In essence, then, the mimetic drama places us inside the personal world of a single character. Although the problem this character faces may be personally important to the character, it is contained within the personal environment of the character. Accordingly, the degree of responsibility one must assume for such a personal problem is only a modest sense of guilt. Because both the problem and responsibilities assumed are so comparatively minor, the resolution or purification required in such a situation ultimately turns on an explanation of one's intentions and motives. Having explained one's self, and given the fact that the system has ultimately done no major damage to anyone, the system continues as it has, with the central character having perhaps learned a valuable lesson during the process. We have witnessed, then, a brief "slice" of someone else's life. While perhaps not earthshaking, certainly an interesting exploration has been revealed of the ways in which certain individuals may respond to particular situations.

The Leader-Centered Communication System

As a point of departure, a common-sense notion of a leader functions as an excellent description of the leader-centered communication system. Typically, leaders are believed to be those individuals who direct others, possess authority or influence, manage the affairs of a group, and possess some heroic characteristics. More particularly, from a communication perspective, leaders dominate others in the sense that they employ a set of symbols that mobilize the responses of others; they introduce and formulate goals; tasks, and procedures; they delegate or direct actions; they integrate or pull together the efforts of other individuals; they provide transitions or interconnections among events; and they appear confident of their values—others may, in fact, treat the value judgments of leaders as factual statements. Overall, then, leaders possess sets of conceptions which provide explanations for what is occurring even though they cannot avoid or handle these circumstances any better than others.

On the television series *Gimme a Break,* the character of Nell seems to satisfy the requirements of a leader. In the show examined here, Nell lets a friend of Samantha stay with the family until she learns he's not as charming as he appears.

The nature and essence of the pollution generating the drama is a direct result of Nell's definition of the situation. The violation of Nell's values as leader defines the pollution controlling this drama. Initially, Nell is "taken with" Jeff. He is tall, blond, good looking, complimentary, willing to work, and generally charming. His problem moves Nell: "His stepmother doesn't like him, and she turned his father against him. He's not going back home until he can prove to his father that he can make it on his own." As a result, it is Nell who decides that he can stay with the family. Yet, the audience knows before Nell that all cannot go well. While others in the home say nothing, 18-year-old Jeff is "moving too fast" romantically with 15-year-old Samantha, proposes that they take a trip to Acapulco, and begins to borrow money from all members of the family. After one week, when Nell discovers what has been happening, it is Nell who defines the problem and acts on this definition of the problem in two ways. First, Nell decides that Jeff's behavior has been excessive: "He's been trying to hustle us." Nell tells Jeff: "I want you packed and out of this house in five minutes, get it?" Second, Nell decides that Samantha and Jeff must end their relationship: "As far as you and Samantha are concerned, you are history."

Her standards having been violated, Nell assumes the responsibility for the conflict that has and will emerge. As she says to Samantha: "I told him to leave. I also told him that I didn't want him to speak to you any more. He was taking advantage of this whole family, especially you." Having defined the situation, Nell approriately assumes responsibility for the definition of the situation offered.

However, in the leader-centered drama, purification requires that Nell's values be confirmed. Yet, Samantha challenges Nell's definition of the problem: "That's not true." Nell holds her ground: "It is true Samantha. You don't know what you're talking about." Shifting ground, Samantha proclaims: "I love him. I hate you, Nell." Samantha runs from the room. Talking to herself, Nell resolves: "Stay calm, Nell. Kids are kids. She's going to be okay." One has the sense that Nell will let Samantha resolve this loss in her own way. However, Nell concludes: "Are you crazy? Talk to her." But, Samantha has left. Nell is "crazy" with concern until Samantha calls at five in the morning. Samantha's call removes any doubt about who functions as the leader in the family: "He took her money, and then he dropped her on the beach."

The final resolution or redemption places Nell squarely back in the leadership role; Nell has been right all along. As Samantha tells Nell:

> I don't understand, Nell. How could he just leave me like that. When he kissed me, I thought we had something special. . . . I'm never going to see him again.

He went to Tijuana. Then he said he was going to join the navy. I begged to go with him. But, you know what he said? He said I have it made. And, that I have a great family. I have someone to take care of me. And, he said he didn't have anything.

Thus, as leader, when her values had been denied, Nell posited the existence of a problem, assumed responsibility for how this problem was to be handled, fought for her own solution, and in the end, had her conception of reality, her values, and her role as leader confirmed.

The Romantic Communication System

In the romantic communication system, classical notions of romance are featured. The romantic hero or heroine possesses, or is treated or believed to possess, prodigious courage and endurance: the heroic are either believed to be or are cast as adventurous, idealized, and frequently mysterious; their tales are or are believed to be legendary, daring, and chivalrous. These classical conceptions of romance led us earlier to suggest that the central character in a romantic communication system would possess a symbol system which would allow the hero or heroine to account for more environmental variables in more incisive ways than others and to create more effective programs for acting on those environmental factors. Thus, while romantic agents are superior to others only in degree, the situations they face seem to contain almost overwhelming elements of unknown danger and risk as well as requiring remarkable levels of human power, intensity, dedication, and capacity. We almost expect that the ordinary laws of nature must be suspended if these dramas are to be successfully resolved. Clearly, romantic agents must be intellectually superior to others and be capable of exercising superior control of their environment.

On the television series *Scarecrow and Mrs. King,* we focus on Amanda King who only apparently lives the life of a typical housewife. She is divorced, with two children, and now lives with her mother in the suburbs. Although totally involved in this life-style, periodically Mrs. King passes through what is equivalent to the Cinderella transformation found in a traditional romance. Through a quirk of fate and unknown to her family or friends, she has become a part-time spy and government agent for a CIA-type bureau called the Agency. Although often a reluctant heroine until the action of the drama is on her, she is paired with a slick, smooth, and perhaps overly zealous agent. Her partner, code name Scarecrow, is Lee Stetson. He is an experienced, efficient, professional government agent. Although they are an unlikely team and certainly function in an unexpected relationship, this team combines the clever, concerned, innocent but common sense Mrs. King with the square-jawed, experienced, technologically wise, bronzed brawn of Scarecrow. Together this team defends nothing less than the nationals security of the country.

One show of this series, "Charity Begins at Home," aptly illustrates all of the key elements of the romantic communication system. As the show opens, we find ourselves within the office of the head of the Agency. Lee and other agents quickly detail both the nature of the pollution and the guilt to be resolved.

The issue in this particular case deals not only with national security but potentially with world-wide starvation and the collapse of the international world food supply. An international conspiracy sets off the particular drama, for a meeting is to occur between "three of the most dangerous and powerful men in this country." Jerry Perrine is calling this meeting. Although it was impossible to prove the case against him, Perrine has already blocked a wheat sale to the East which cost the Department of Agriculture some $200 million. The danger now, however, appears to be even greater, for these men "control billions of dollars worth of cash and credit." Thus, the opening scene reveals both the tremendous scope of the pollution as well as the guilt and power of the guilty party.

The resolution or purification of this problem requires that four steps be taken by Lee and Amanda.

First, the purification initially requires Amanda King's assistance. An unusually tight security system has been established by Perrine for his meeting. Perrine has agreed to hold an annual charity event on his ship; the event will function as the "cover" for his meeting. Through her normal community and charity connections, Amanda has annually been responsible for all refreshments at this charity event. In order for Scarecrow to infiltrate the group, then, Amanda must provide Lee with his cover as a bartender.

Second, once Amanda and Lee are on the ship, they uncover the full scope of the pollution. Employing the training he has acquired as a spy, Lee carefully follows the group and skillfully learns that Perrine and his colleagues have initially planned a $50 million swindle in the international futures market. Their plan is to purchase cheap commodities futures when excessive surpluses are predicted. They also possess the means to destroy agricultural commodities in certain countries and therefore to drive up the price of these commodities. Moreover, once the basis for the swindle is established, the $100 million worldwide rights to the fraud are to be sold. The impact of this swindle is even more powerful, for these cheap futures will mean that certain nations throughout the world will "never recover" from such losses. "Wall-to-wall famine" is predicted.

Although the scope of pollution is far greater than expected, Amanda must take the next step to resolve the drama, for Lee has been caught eavesdropping on Perrine and his colleagues. Lee is placed in a deep freeze. It is Amanda who sneaks up on his captives, knocks them out, and frees a semifrozen Lee. Without Amanda's intervention, we are left to believe that Lee would most certainly have died.

Finally, having uncovered the pollution, having identified the agents responsible as well as the means they intend to employ, Lee and Amanda are able to apprehend Perrine and his colleagues. In the final "fight scene," with the assistance of Lee's brawn and Amanda's clever common sense, all of these evil agents are apprehended.

In this drama, then, purification has required that the central characters—Scarecrow and Mrs. King—identify all dimensions of the pollution and all dimensions of blame. Moreover, they employ—not only more highly developed skills, intelligence, and sensitivity than most people possess—they utilize a unique and unexpected combination of these talents in order to produce the most desirable set of corrective acts. Thus, by virtue of their unique combination of skills, intelligence, and sensitivity, Scarecrow and Mrs. King function as a collective romantic hero.

The drama may thus pass onto its final stage, redemption. Nothing less than a major international disaster has been avoided as a result of the cleverness, skill, and spontaneous action of Scarecrow and Mrs. King. We are left with two major messages. First, that the highly technical and sophisticated skills of a government agency require the common sense and commitment of the ordinary citizen. Second, that the ordinary citizen will rise to the occasion, exceed the confines of the ordinary, and function as nothing less than a romantic heroine, if given the opportunity. A final redemptive scene emerges: America and its citizens can function as an agency for the good, foiling the plans of the evil, and moving a nation and the world towards a resolution of those problems which hamper international peace and harmony.

The Mythical Communication System

A myth is a fabricated, invented, or imagined story of historical events in which universal struggles concerning truth, beauty, and patriotism are depicted. In an almost sacred or timeless order (ritual or dream), a hero or heroine embarks on a long, unknown, and difficult journey in order to retrieve a "precious object" that is guarded by unusually powerful counteragents. In the process of completing the quest, the hero or heroine displays superhuman powers, thereby creating a myth, fantasy, illusion, or vision. Thus, Jason and Superman face universal problems beyond the responsibility of any particular human force. The resolution of these problems requires "superhuman" powers employed toward the formulation of a new social system.

On V, the problem or pollution generating the drama is global, if not interstellar. The survival of two different species of life are at stake. Specifically, the plot of the series turns on an invasion of Earth by a race of alien, human-size, and intelligent lizards who seek to gain control of the Earth. Initially, these "Visitors" arrive under friendly pretexts, disguised as human beings, offering a host of "rewards" such as complete cures for diseases such as cancer. However, their true purposes are quickly revealed. The objectives of these Visitors is to transport all of Earth's water back to their own home planet as well as the preserved bodies of all human beings which are to be eaten as food by the Visitors. Beyond their fantastic technological breakthroughs, they also possess the power to brainwash human beings and ultimately to control and then to destroy all human life. As the series unfolds, we are told that the home planet of the Visitors has become uninhabitable and thus the Visitors plot to take over the Earth, using its water and human inhabitants for their physical survival. The problem or pollution guiding this myth, then, deals with the highest of stakes. The future of the entire human race is at stake. The problem is truly a universal one.

In a very fundamental sense, blame cannot be attached to any particular and individual agent for this condition. Certainly, human beings are not to be faulted for initially welcoming those who appear to be friends. Similarly, although more difficult to accept, even the Visitors are without blame. Similar to the motives guiding humans, the Visitors want to survive as a race. Although their choice of food might be otherwise, instinct guides them. In a similar vein, although domination and control of the Earth may not be necessary, we are led to believe that not all of the Visitors are militaristic; some of the Visitors seek the friendship of human beings and would prefer that a more accommodating set of interactions define their relationships with humans. In one sense, then, the responsibility for the conflict is a function of circumstances, instincts, and civilizations which are beyond the control of any single individual or group of individuals.

Purification of this problem functions on two levels.

On a more personal and social level, Donovan and Julie lead the Freedom Fighters against the alien Diana and her colleagues. In episode after episode of this series, these two forces engage in a life-and-death struggle which is intended to represent the struggle of the two species. Both forces are committed, clever, and perceive their struggle as an ultimate objective. Yet, on this level, purification seems to reveal only a sense of the mundane, if inherently destructive, nature of all wars.

Yet, purification also occurs on a second level within this series. We are led to believe that a new, completely reordered, and totally unexpected world may emerge because of this conflict. The symbol of this new social system is Elizabeth, the "Star Child," who is the child of a human mother and an alien father. Although Elizabeth is the first offspring of the two races, she is more than a "hybrid." She does represent both races, she is part of both races, but she also possesses characteristics which transcend both species. Her growth rate, for example, is far more rapid than either race, and her major life cycle changes are the result of metamorphoses which are capable of dramatically altering her entire physiological and mental character. In the end, Elizabeth possesses new kinds of absolute powers which neither race understands nor can control. When absolute conflicts have occurred between the two races, or when either race is threatened by annihilation, Elizabeth intervenes to reduce the level of conflict or to sustain the race which is threatened by extinction. In this sense, Elizabeth constitutes a vision of what the new world might be, a group of creatures more humane and more powerful than either of the original two races. The ultimate purification, then, would seem to reside, not with the humans and not with the Visitors, but with Elizabeth, the Star Child. Thus, in its own way, a message of this series appears to be that interspecies cohabitation will produce a more beneficial world for all.

Yet, the final redemptive phase of V remains unclear. The nature of this "new" world or even the final consequences of fighting an alien force are unclear. We do not know if Elizabeth is a prototype of what is to come nor do we know what kind of social order she symbolizes. Even if Elizabeth is not a prototype of a "new" order, we do not know if the humans will destroy the aliens. We do not know if the aftermath of a "final resolution" will create a united global community. The final vision remains unclear in this series. Yet, the series suggests that such a vision can be expected. As is true of all myths, the series posits the existence of a universal problem which is not easily attributed to the actions of any single person or group of people. Certainly, the resolution requires that extraordinary, if not supernatural, powers be employed. Yet, a future is embedded in such a drama. In V, Liberation Day is celebrated by all human beings throughout the world. Similarly, Elizabeth continues to change and to develop. Thus, although we may not know which future is before us, certainly a future is promised, a future which will at least unify the human race, perhaps create a framework for living with other kinds of intelligent species, and possibly produce a new evolutionary leap in the development of the human race. The excitement of the mythical drama resides, in part, in wondering what a totally unexpected but reconceived future could be.

Popular Television Series as Communication Systems, 1974–1975 to 1984–1985

Having defined and illustrated the communication matrix proposed here, the 1984–1985 television series are now appropriately classified into the matrix. Table 2 provides the results of such a classification. Once the nature of this classification system is understood, there is reason to believe that others are likely to classify these popular television series into the same categories of this matrix.[2]

During the last eleven years, popular television series have undergone changes in their communicative emphasis. Table 3 details these changes on a year-by-year basis. Table 4 provides a compilation of these changes, highlighting the changes from 1974–1975 to 1984–1985.[3]

Using Tables 3 and 4 as our base, we can come to five major conclusions.

First, ironic communication has been consistently underrepresented during the last eleven years, accounting for as little as 4 percent of all television series in some years and only for 11 percent at the peak during one season. Compared to some of the more extreme variations which have occurred in other forms of communication, ironic communication systems are relatively constant and stable feature of prime time television. Yet, these series—such as *All in the Family, The Jeffersons,* and *Three's Company*—were some of the most popular television series. Insofar as the ironic series have been successful modes of communication, and insofar as the ironic forms reflects "the rhetoric of the loser," viewers apparently find such symbolic explorations and modes of interaction significant. The ironic form apparently functions as a temporary corrective, creating the opportunity to enjoy a moment of cynicism in which the central and controlling characters in life are cast as the cause of the problems that "minor" characters must correct. Overall, ironic communication systems must be viewed as important. Yet, ironic symbols do not appear to be a numerically dominant feature in the world of television. While finding ironies important, Americans are an apparently more optimistic people, who do not find this cynical mode of communication a desirable, persistent, and central feature of the communication systems they respond to and wish to share in on either a short-term or long-term basis.

Second, perhaps balancing the excesses of the ironic form, given its similar numeric significance, mythical communication has also remained relatively stable as a percentage of all television series. Although mythical series have ranged from 4 to 10 percent of all television series during the last eleven years, they have clearly remained between 5 and 7 percent of all

Table 2. 1984–1985 television season*

Irony: 3–6%	Romance: 18–34%
The Jeffersons	Hardcastle and McCormick
Three's a Crowd	Knight Rider
It's Your Move	Scarecrow and Mrs. King
	The A Team
Mime: 9–17%	Remington Steele
The Love Boat	The Fall Guy
Diff'rent Strokes	Matt Houston
Alice	Riptide
Newhart	Cover Up
The Facts of Life	Jessie
Cheers	Hunter
Benson	Airwolf
Webster	Hawaiian Heat
Kate & Allie	Glitter
	Mickey Spillane's Mike Hammer
Leader: 21–40%	Street Hawk
T.J. Hooker	Murder, She Wrote
Hill Street Blues	Hot Pursuit
Gimme A Break	
Trapper John, M.D.	Myth: 2–4%
AfterMASH	V
Hotel	Highway to Heaven
St. Elsewhere	
Magnum, P.I.	
Simon and Simon	
Family Ties	
The Dukes of Hazzard	
Miami Vice	
E/R	
Night Court	
Charles in Charge	
Finders of Lost Loves	
Dreams	
Partners in Crime	
The Cosby Show	
Who's the Boss?	
Cagney & Lacey	

*As defined by *TV Guide,* 32 (September 8–14, 1984), p. A-1. Total number of series = 53 (rounding off accounts for total of 101 percent). Final compilation does not include soap operas *(Dynasty, Paper Dolls, Knots Landing, Dallas,* and *Falcon Crest),* news and semidocumentaries *(TV's Bloopers & Practical Jokes, Foul-Ups, Bleeps & Blunders, People Do the Craziest Things,* and *20/20),* movies, or sports.

television series for during eight of the last eleven years. In contrast to the ironic mode, mythical communication apparently provides an opportunity for viewers to fantasize and to escape from life's harsh realities. The mythical form introduces novelty into television's prime-time hours. Human

Table 3. Changes in the communication patterns of popular television series

	Irony		Mimetic		Leader		Romantic		Mythical		Total*	
Season	N	%	N	%	N	%	N	%	N	%	N	%
1974–75	3	6	13	28	18	38	10	21	3	6	47	99
1975–76	4	7	23	40	22	39	5	9	3	5	57	100
1976–77	3	5	25	45	17	31	7	13	3	5	55	99
1977–78	3	5	27	48	12	21	10	18	4	7	56	99
1978–79	2	4	21	47	10	22	9	20	3	7	45	100
1979–80	6	10	23	41	9	16	16	29	2	4	56	100
1980–81	3	7	23	55	9	21	4	10	3	7	42	100
1981–82	3	6	25	50	12	24	7	14	3	6	50	100
1982–83	6	11	18	32	17	30	12	21	4	7	57	101
1983–84	4	8	13	26	15	30	13	26	5	10	50	100
1984–85	3	6	9	17	21	40	18	34	2	4	53	101
Total	40	7	220	39	162	29	111	20	35	6	568	101

*Rounding off accounts for differences above and below 100%.

bionics and technological innovations (*The Six Million Dollar Man* and *The Bionic Woman*), animal intelligence (*Planet of the Apes* and *Mr. Smith*), the occult and magic (*The Night Stalker* and *Just Our Luck*), the supernatural (*Jennifer Slept Here* and *Highway to Heaven*), the future (*Buck Rogers in the 25th Century*), human transformations (*The Incredible Hulk* and *Manimal*), extraterrestrial life *(V)*, and wish fulfillment (*Fantasy Island)* have all constituted dimensions of the popular mythology in these series.

Thus, the ironic and the mythical forms do function as important modes of communication on television. However, the fact that these systems of communication are underrepresented compared with other categories may indicate that although people do need a sense of the cynical and the godly, daily life cannot pragmatically be controlled by these modes of interaction.

Third, mimetic communication has experienced an overall decline when

Table 4. Changes in the communication patterns of television series

Communication System	1974–1975 Season (%)	1984–1985 Season (%)	% Shift from 1974 to 1984 (%)
Irony	6	6	0
Mime	28	17	−11
Leader	38	40	+2
Romance	21	34	+13
Myth	6	4	−2

series aired during the 1974–1975 season are compared to those televised during the 1984–1985 season. Yet, this overall pattern should not ignore the fact that mimetic series rose from roughly one-quarter of all series in 1974–1975 to over half of all series during the 1980–1981 season and then began to decline by some 38 percentage points to constitute less than 20 percent of all series in the 1984–1985 season. Conception of everyday life, then, seemed to constitute a period of interest, if not celebration, in later half of the 1970s but it no longer seems to be able to generate such excitement as the 1980s have thus far emerged.

These changes in the mimetic form coincide with national changes in popular self-conceptions among Americans. The Gallup poll organization, on a rather irregular basis, has asked samples of Americans how "satisi-fied" they are with their "personal life" during the last eleven years. When asked at five different points during the last eleven years, Americans have expressed the following degrees of satisfaction:

August 1974	35 percent satisfaction
February 1978	57 percent satisfaction
February 1979	77 percent satisfaction
December 1981	81 percent satisfaction
August 1983	77 percent satisfaction

We cannot determine if national opinions about the personal life perfectly correspond to every change in television series on a year-by-year basis. However, national personal life satisfaction attitudes and changes in mimetic television series appear to mirror each other. As people reported increased satisfaction about the personal life in the last half of the 1970s, mimetic television series also increased. As people reported declining rates of satisfaction about the personal life in the early part of the 1980s, mimetic television series also declined. Certainly, the *direction* of the correlation appears to be related. However, the *rate* of change does differ in the first part of the 1980s. Declines in television series are occurring at a more rapid rate than national opinions would suggest. If it is true—as I suggested at the completion of the seven-year study (Chesebro, 1982, p. 510)—that "major changes in popular television series signify basic transformations in American life," we might expect increasing rates of dissatisfaction to be nationally reported by Americans in the latter part of the 1980s.

Fourth, television series containing leader-centered communication systems appear to have only modestly increased (some 2 percent) from the 1974–1975 to the 1984–1985 season. However, a more careful examination of this eleven-year period indicates, with only a modest 1 percent increase during one year, that leader-centered television series consistently declined from the 1974–1975 season to the 1979–1980 season. Since the

1979–1980 season, leader-centered television series have consistently increased some 24 percentage points during the last five years.

If one remembers the dissatisfaction with government that was generated by events such as the Watergate affair and the Iranian crisis, the decline in leader-centered conceptions on television is understandable. Indeed, a similar pattern is evident in terms of how Americans viewed "the way in which Congress is handling its job" (Gallup Report, 1981, p. 15):

August 1974	40 percent satisfaction
April 1975	38 percent satisfaction
September 1978	29 percent satisfaction
June 1979	19 percent satisfaction
June 1981	38 percent satisfaction

Although data are only available from 1979, the Gallup poll organization reports that national satisfaction with "the way things are going in the U.S. at this time" appears to parallel this trend in leader-centered television series:

November 1979	19 percent satisfaction
December 1981	27 percent satisfaction
August 1983	35 percent satisfaction
February 1984	50 percent satisfaction

If other trends in national satisfaction are employed, an even more striking parallel between leader-centered television series and popular sentiments emerges. In his November 19, 1984 article, "Americans in Poll View Government More Confidently," *New York Times* reporter Adam Clymer integrates the results of three polls: (1) the 1964–1982 results of the National Election Studies Series of the Center for Political Studies of the University of Michigan, (2) the November 18–22, 1983 *New York Times* patriotism survey, and (3) the *New York Times* and CBS News Poll of November 8–14, 1984 (pp. A1 and B10). An overall and long-term view of the nation's varying degree of satisfaction with "the government" is created. If these results are compared to the data obtained here regarding leader-centered television series, the following relationships emerge:

Table 5

Year	New York Times Integration (%)	Chesebro's Leader-Centered Television Results (%)
1964	63	—
1965	—	—
1966	53	—

Table 5 (*continued*)

Year	New York Times Integration (%)	Chesebro's Leader-Centered Television Results (%)
1967	—	—
1968	51	—
1969	—	—
1970	42	—
1971	—	—
1972	38	—
1973	—	—
1974	26	38
1975	—	39
1976	25	31
1977	—	21
1978	24	22
1979	—	16
1980	22	21
1981	—	24
1982	29	30
1983	30	30
1984	40	40

An examination of these two patterns of change indicates some limitations which must affect our interpretations. The Chesebro results appear some ten years after the first measure of national confidence reported in 1964. Similarly, the *New York Times* data have not been gathered every year. Moreover, there *may*, depending on the type and kind of statistical measures employed, be some variations in the two sets of data in terms of 1974 and 1976. Nonetheless, if one allows for the typical kind of statistical error rates involved in all poll data results, when the data are compared for a specific year when *both* the *New York Times* surveys and the Chesebro studies are available (as they are for seven of the last eleven years), the yearly level as well as overall directions and rates of change of these two measures are virtually identical.

Overall, strong evidence exists to suggest that the level as well as the direction and rate of change of national popular opinion about the government coincide with the decline and now the rise in leader-centered television series. Such findings argue for a synoptic placement of television within the American culture: network television series do not function as an external agency influence on the rest of society; these programs are an integral part of our society, subject to the same changes in national opinion as any other societal institution.

Fifth, romantic television series have apparently increased some 13 percentage points from the 1974–1975 television season to the 1984–1985 season. Yet, as was true of the leader-centered series, romantic television series have only recently—since the 1980–1981 season—experienced a consistent increase. Prior to the 1980–1981 season, romantic television series were neither persistent nor stable.

During the 1974–1980 period, romantic television series were extremely volatile, shifting up and down by as much as 12 percentage points from one year to the next. During this period, the volatile nature of romantic television series coincided with the nation's sporadic and rapidly shifting periods of idealism. The landslide election that put Richard Nixon in the White House in 1972 collapsed in three months in 1974. The antigovernment sentiment that elected Jimmy Carter in 1976 was directed against Carter by the end of his administration. With the ever-present "eye" of the media exposing the slightest blemish and mistake, it is doubtful that any person, institution, policy, or action can sustain the kind of glorification associated with a romantic conception. Yet, every nation must celebrate its ideals. During the 1974–1980 period, the United States appeared to be desperately searching for its ideals, rapidly shifting from one ideal to another, seeking a sense of permanence in a world of ever-increasing rates of change. Romantic television series reflected, or perhaps caused, this neurotic quest for a humanly attainable vision and goal for the nation.

If the changes in romantic television series from the 1980–1981 to 1984–1985 season are any indication, Americans have apparently found romantic conceptions increasingly satisfying and reliable. Although only 10 percent of television series were romantic at the beginning of the 1980–1981 season, romantic series had consistently increased some 24 percentage points by the beginning of the 1984–1985. Perhaps the vision proposed by Ronald Reagan, himself associated with the romance images of the "big silver screen," affected the faith Americans have placed in romantic symbols. While this four-year period indicates an undeniable growing involvement and interest in the use of romantic symbols, the 1974–1980 period also indicates that such romantic visions may easily collapse at the first sign of a dramatic crisis. It is questionable whether or not any romantic conception can sustain itself when life's realities undergo a major change.

Overall, the leader-centered and romantic communication systems have dominated popular television series since 1980. As the sitcom has been replaced by the adventure series, leader-centered and romantic symbols are increasingly controlling American television, accounting for almost 75 percent of all television series on the air during the 1984–1985 season. The focus of America's attention appears to be concentrated on those who can guide others and provide a vision for the future. If this frame of mind continues, I would suspect that the image of the romantic leader will undoubtedly capture the imagination and attention of Americans. At the same time, such a frame of reference places greater reliance on others for our own destiny. In this sense, the perspective is basically conservative, requiring a commitment to forms of idealism, and the belief that the epic struggles of others somehow represents our own personal endeavors (see Chesebro, 1982b, p. 509). Although such visions are certainly necessary, they do turn our attention, if not distracting us, from developing a more comprehensive symbol system in which cynicism and faith, romance and leadership, and the personal life are all equally relevant frames of reference.

Popular Television Series as Value Systems

At the outset of this reading, the word *value* was used as a standard of worth, utility, importance, and excellence that controls specific attitudes and daily behaviors. Values are the basis for endorsing or rejecting experiences and phenomena encountered in everyday interactions. Remembering the stated intentions of the producers of television series and Miller's observation that "every communicative act involves, by necessity, a value judgment," we have noticed that popular television series appear to be sources of value orientations which are broadcast daily into the ongoing life experiences of television viewers. Comstock has concluded, after examining some 2500 social scientific research reports on the effects of television, that "entertaining programs can maintain or alter behavior" (1980, p. 495). Accordingly, it becomes appropriate to identify the explicit relationship which exists between the types of television series we have discussed and value orientations themselves.[4]

Treating each of the five communication dramas as forms of subtle persuasion, and relying upon the manifest content defining each of these dramas, the following set of "equations" emerges:

Ironic Communication = Existentialism
Mimetic Communication = Individualism
Leader-centered Communication = Authority
Romantic Communication = Idealism
Mythical Communication = Theology

The primary value associated with each of these communication systems was initially explored by Northrop Frey when he first defined each category. His conception functions as our point of departure as we consider the nature of each of these equations one at a time.

In equating ironic communication with an existential value orientation, we should first note that irony is characterized by a sense of disparity or inconsistency. The ironic figure says one thing but means another. The ironic character may (Socratic irony) or may not (dramatic irony) intend to create the disparity, but the disparity or inconsistency is a minimum condition for irony to exist. Moreover, for irony to exist, an "audience" must be aware of the disparity—the disparity is not "announced" in the ironic form itself but relies on the discerning "eye" of the audience. In this sense, the ironic figure is "out of control" while the "knowing audience' functions as an "inner group" which knows the "real" meaning behind the baffling exterior of the disparity.

Second, the tragic ironic character possesses a sense of being randomly set aside or isolated from the rest of society. As Frye (1957, p. 41) has noted, the ironic character "is innocent in the sense that what happens to him [or her] is far greater than anything he [or she] has done provokes, like the mountaineer whose shout brings down the avalanche." This "sense of arbitrariness," according to Frye (p. 41), "casts the victim as having been unlucky, selected at random or by lot, and no more deserving of what has happens to him [or her] than anyone else would be. If there is a reason for choosing him [or her] for catastrophe, it is an inadequate reason, and raises more objections that it answers." Even if the ironic character is comic, the audience still possesses the sense that the ironic figure (even if he or she created the catastrophe) is "innocent," for who would want true disaster to befall George Jefferson, Jack Tripper, or Matthew Burton. In such cases, the needs or conditioning of these ironic characters "forces" them to create the disparities. The audience is aware, then, of the source or motive of the inconsistency. Nonetheless, there remains a sense in which the ironic character is isolated from society, particularly when other characters in the series are aware of the discrepancy and must correct the disparity. In such cases, the realism of the act itself stands out regardless of the intent of the ironic figure. What actually happened—a true sense of realism—controls, not what is intended. In more tragic forms, when the ironic character senses the isolation, "melancholy," perhaps to the point "where the individual is so isolated as to feel his [or her] existence a living death" can emerge (Frye, 1957, p. 29). In more comic forms, the ironic character experiences the isolation by virtue of his or her sense of embarrassment, stupidity, or desire to ignore the inconsistency. In either case, this sense of isolation scapegoats the ironic character.

Third, the ironic act is completely objective. As we have already noted, the arbitrariness of the catastrophe faced by the ironic character is part of the audience's response. Technically, the ironic form itself makes no such statement. The form itself is, in this sense, completely objective. Socrates, for example, "pretends to know nothing, not even that he is ironic. Complete objectivity and suppression of all explicit moral judgments are essential to his method" (Frye, 1957, p. 62). Thus, concludes Frye (1957, p.

40), "pity and fear are not raised in ironic art: they are reflected to the reader from that art." In our culture, this sense of an ironic objectivity emerges when it becomes the norm to believe that human actions cannot be evaluated as good or bad; evaluative assessments are avoided: actions are viewed only as mere acts, devoid of any moral implication. As Frye (1957, p. 62) aptly observes in terms of literature, "In our day a ironic provincialism, which looks everywhere in literature for complete objectivity, suspension of moral judgments, concentrating on pure verbal craftsmanship, and similar virtues, is in the ascendant." In its extreme form, then, the ironic form actually "passes through a dead center of complete realism, a pure mime representing human life without comment and without imposing any sort of dramatic form beyond what is required for simple exhibition" (Frye, 1957, p. 285).

The joining of the sense of disparity, isolation, arbitrariness, and objectivity creates the existential quality. For our purposes here, existentialism can be conceived as a philosophy that is centered on the analysis of existence and of the way the human being finds himself or herself existing in the world, that regards human existence as not exhaustively describable or understandable in scientific terms, and that stresses freedom and responsibility of the individual, the irreducible uniqueness of an ethical or religious situation, and usually the isolation and subjective experiences (such as anxiety, guilt, dread, and anguish) of the individual. This philosophical view carries with it, then, a profound sense of the ironic which easily lends itself toward the use of satire, parody, ridicule, burlesque, and even the casting of paradoxes, potentially functioning as a rationalizing value for the political tactics of the radical revolutionary or reactionary who, feeling isolated and removed, finds it "natural" to invoke violence in the name of peace.

In equating the mimetic communication system with individualism, the equation gains power insofar as everyday life is captured or our own personal experiences are portrayed. The emphasis here is on the routine drama of everyday interactions. Accordingly, the visions of the gods, the extraordinary personality, symbols of authority, and the cynical are diminished—the life of "Everyman" and "Everywoman" are highlighted. The unique and esoteric features of the personal life emerge. In this context, Frye (1957, p. 59) has observed that mimetic forms "deal with an intensely individual society." Accordingly, the appeal of the mimetic resides in pathos. "Pathos," in Frye's (1957, p. 38) words, "presents its hero as isolated by a weakness which appeals to our sympathy because it is on our own level of experience." Frye (1957, p. 39) concludes his train of thought by noting that, "The root idea of pathos is the exclusion of an individual on our own level from a social group to which he [or she] is trying to belong. Hence the central tradition of sophisticated pathos is the study of the isolated."

When the entire social system is cast as mimetic, one has the sense of a world of diverse and unique individuals, each proclaiming his or her own identity. As Frye (1957, p. 347) has put it, "mimic wars" are "made out of 'points of view.'" Accordingly, mimetic television series seem to have little in common if life-styles are emphasized. Life for Bob Newhart in his Vermont inn has little to do with the issues affecting the girls and Mrs. Garrett in their gourmet shop and is far removed from what occupy the attention of Diane and Sam in *Cheers*, which is, of course, completely distinct from the life-style being forged by Kate and Allie. Yet these series do find a common and unifying theme—they all emphasize the individuality and uniqueness of people living "everyday" lives. We are drawn to these unique worlds out of curiosity, because we want to see what others like us are dealing with and how they are dealing with it, and perhaps because there is a style for dealing with everyday life that can be recognized, if not modified and used. In this sense, the appeal of a style emphasizes the means, agency, pragmatics, and conventions of life. To focus on a particular style, to examine it in detail, and to allow one style to characterize all, are ways of knowing that are technically identified as synecdoche and metonymy. But, we need not emphasize such serious overtones here, for the mimetic is profoundly individualistic and therefore avoids the common "group-think" required for political action. In fact, the effort to achieve social identification with others is, in many ways in these series, cast as a comic but enjoyable experience.

In sharp contrast, the leader-centered communication system places symbols of authority, influence, and power over others as necessary, effective, and useful modes of human interaction. Authority can be viewed as a set of skills, resources, and so forth that allows one to control. Or, authority can be viewed as a relationship in which one agent's behavior causes or is allowed to cause another's behavior. In either case, those in authority examine the situation or scene, consider the materials available and the material outcomes of decisions, and attempt to develop and secure support for an idiom that will allow one to move "logically" from one issue to the next in proper syllogistic order until the solution emerges. Others may have to be coached to accept certain precepts—a form of the didactic—if the necessary concerted actions are to be taken. The goals, aims, or solutions toward which these steps are taken may require the use of metaphors. In the end, the voice of the political liberal can function as a model for such modes of authority. Thus, Dr. Trapper John, night court judge Harry Wapner, and emergency room Dr. Howard Sheinfeld are individuals, but they also wield authority, authority directed toward a liberal end.

The romantic communication system, as an idealistic value system, highlights the extraordinary features of the almost unbelievable personality—

those few "geniuses" among us are emphasized in this form. In Frye's (1957, pp. 60, 62, 59, and 186) words, romance is a "rhetoric of personal greatness" which looks "everywhere for genius and evidences of great personality." This romantic character, beyond being "an extraordinary person," also "creates his [or her] own world," exists "in a state of pantheistic rapport with nature" and lives with "adventure." The quest defines the universal pattern of the romantic figure. As Frye (1957, p. 187) has put it:

> The complete form of the romance is clearly the successful quest, and such a completed form has three main stages: the stage of the perilous journey and the preliminary minor adventures; the crucial struggle, usually some kind of battle in which either the hero or his [or her] foe, or both, must die; and the exaltation of the hero.

An understanding of the quest is very likely to take the form of a proverb, "a secular or purely human oracle" whose "wisdom is the tried and tested way" with the accompanying "virtues" of "prudence and moderation" (Frye, 1957, p. 298). Proverbs are often designed to create a state of mind in which one's initial predisposition leads to yet another and then to another until the final state of mind adheres to a quality quite different from the original predisposition. Burke (1931/1968, pp. 124–128) has identified such symbolic forms as qualitative. Before leaving the romantic form, however, we should note that its implicit class and political emphasis. As Frye (1957, p. 306) has noted, "The social affinities of the romance, with its grave idealizing of heroism and purity, are with the aristocracy." More directly, Frye (1957, p. 186) observes that, "In every age the ruling social or intellectual class tends to project its ideals in some form of romance, where the virtuous heroes and beautiful heroines represent the ideals and the villains the threats to their ascendancy." Frye argues that this class bias accounts for the character of chivalric romance in the Middle Ages, aristocratic romance in the Renaissance, bourgeois romance since the eighteenth century, and revolutionary romance in contemporary Russia. Although there is a sense in which the "commoner" identifies with the struggles of the romantic hero or heroine, the conservative appeal of the romantic system may be more than an accidental feature of the form, for inherent within the romantic scheme is an essential belief in a superiority of some to many by virtue of genius or extraordinary personality. Such characteristics are not learned or acquired—the romantic hero or heroine is "born, not made"— and protected and insulated by the social institution they have created. Despite this political dimension, the romantic frame of reference nonetheless inspires, idealizes, and offers hope. *Hardcastle and McCormick* introduces us to the importance of the personal commitment to law and order; *Jessie* reveals the power of the trained, yet sensitive, expert in dealing with the disturbed; *Murder, She Wrote* symbolizes the importance of thoughful, incisive, inductive reasoning.

As we shift to our final mode of communication, the mythical system, a theological value scheme emerges. Theologies are associated with the class of religious communities, but the essence of a theology is its reliance on some kind of god or divinity. Whether the divinity be religious or otherwise, its will is assumed to create and to regulate the natural, human, and ethical laws controlling all human beings. Such systems are easily transformed into fate-control systems: one's purpose in life is externally imposed. In rather blunt terms, Frye (1957, p. 64) argues that, "Mythology projects itself as theology." As a form of theology, a myth can therefore carry with it the sense that a commandment, a parable, an aphorism, or a prophesy is involved in the meaning of the myth. As an "inspired" oracle, for example, the future may be foretold. Thus, the myth functions, in Frye's (1957, p. 136) words, "near or at the conceivable limits of desire." It does not, however, "mean that it necessarily presents its world as attained or attainable by human beings." Nonetheless, by virtue of the divine purpose and mysticism associated with myth, human actions are compelled. Moreover, the divine purpose will repeat itself as a form in virtually all dimensions of human and natural experience—the divine will is cast as "everywhere," permeating and reflected in all things, and is therefore commonly identified with a repetitive form. When used for political ends, the divinely inspired leader is cast as inspired directly by God—he or she is superb and godlike in some way, if not supremely good. Under such conditions, democracy is unnecessary, for who would use a popular vote to determine the good when the word of a god is immediately available through the divinely inspired leader. Such reasoning is reactionary in essence and often destructive in practice. Yet, the mythical scheme need not possess such negative connotations. On *Highway to Heaven*, wishes—even the most impossible ones—come true. On *V*, a form of absolute evil, linked with the most advanced technology, is posited, but it challenges and unifies human beings to become all that they can, ultimately promising even to eliminate evil. A mythical framework does, however, determine the good and the evil; others must abide by the values contained within these myths.

These five values—existentialism, individualism, authority, idealism, and theology—are promoted in varying degrees in popular television series. Existentialism (ironic communication systems) and theology (mythical communication systems) are seldom promoted in popular television series. The extremes—the coldly objective and the religious—are virtually ignored in the world of television. In contrast, in the latter half of the 1970s, popular television series emphasized the life-style of the individual (mimetic communication systems), casting individualism as exciting, enjoyable, and personally rewarding. As we have moved into the 1980s, television's commitment to individuality has given way to a kind of celebration in the usefulness, if not raw power, of authority (leader-centered communication systems). When coupled with an idealistic conception of human beings (romantic communication systems), the raw power of authority is recast and becomes a force for the good. Rather than functioning as "mere sources of entertainment," selective life-styles are promoted on popular television series. These life-styles contain commitments to certain types of actions, behaviors, and beliefs. When cast as problem-solving techniques, they implicitly suggest that certain life-styles and their concomitant values are more effective, useful, and desirable than others. Granted, viewing a single show from one television series is unlikely to affect us. However, the vast majority of our entertainment—some 75 percent of all series broadcast during the current year—promote the same two values. The repetition of these same values—particularly when placed in the elegantly produced settings and as enacted by actors and actresses who have already captured the public's imagination—is likely to leave its influence, if not overtly change our attitudes, beliefs, and actions.

Conclusion

Television is a part of our homes. Most of us do not know what our homes would be like without television. Beyond being a permanent feature of the home, television also constantly bombards us with information and images on a regular basis. These messages are entertaining, but they also contain persuasive messages. Moreover, these persuasive messages are patterned rather than random; they selectively reinforce certain types of communication rather than others. These communication systems contain values, values which promote certain life orientations and not others. There is, indeed, an intimate relationship among the popular television series we watch, the ways in which we communicate, and the values which govern our lives.

Notes

1. When measured by the number of hours scheduled to be devoted to series, series function as the dominant type of television program on prime time network television. The following table provides the base for this conclusion.
2. During the last eleven years, multiple reliability tests of this classification scheme have been carried out under various testing conditions employing both graduate and undergraduate students (for detailed descriptions of these tests, see Chesebro, 1979, pp. 558–559; Chesebro, 1982, p. 517). These reliability tests have produced agreement ratings ranging from 72.4 percent to 84.4 percent. More recently, twelve undergraduate students—familiar with previous classifications

Types of network programs, 1974–present[a]

Premiere Week[b]	Series[c]		Soaps[d]		Movies[e]		Variety[f]		Sports		News and Semi-documentaries[g]	
	N	%	N	%	N	%	N	%	N	%	N	%
1974[h]	43	68	0	0	15	24	2	3	2	3	0	0
1975	45	71	0	0	12	19	3	5	3	5	0	0
1976	39.5	63	0	0	15.5	25	6	10	2	3	0	0
1977	44	70	0	0	13	21	4	6	2	3	0	0
1978	39	62	1	2	17	21	3	5	2	3	1	2
1979	43	68	1	2	14	22	0	0	2	3	3	5
1980	36.5	58	4	6	14	22	5	1	2	3	6	10
1981	37	59	6	10	12	19	2	3	2	3	4	6
1982	43	68	4	6	11	17	0	0	2	3	3	5
1983	38	60	8	13	12	19	0	0	2	3	3	5
1984	43	68	5	8	10	16	0	0	2	3	3	5

[a] N = total hours devoted to this type of program between 8:00 P.M. and 11:00 P.M. EST. Rounding off accounts for differences above and below 100% for each season.

[b] "Premiere Week" as defined by *TV Guide* each season. The "Primiere Week" is the lineup of regularly scheduled or planned activities by the three national networks for each season, but not necessarily what programs are actually broadcast each week during any particular week. Planned and actual programming may differ significantly. During the actual broadcast week of September 13–19, 1982, for example, series constituted 38% of prime-time network broadcasting whereas movies constituted 44.4% of this time period. For additional details, see James W. Chesebro, "Communication, Values, and Popular Television Series—A Seven Year Assessment," in *Inter/Media: Interpersonal Communication in a Media World*, by Gary Gumpert and Robert Cathcart, 2nd ed. (New York: Oxford University Press, 1982), footnote 75. Nonetheless, the broadcasting of a miniseries (such as *Shogun*, which accounts for the disparity between the planned and actual broadcast programs for the week of September 13–19, 1980) remains relatively exceptional and unique. The planner schedule remains, then, the basic definition of network intentions and investments for each season.

[c] See Chesebro (*op. cit.*) for a definition of a series, particularly Table 2.

[d] Soap operas include *Dallas, Secrets of Midland Heights, Knots Landing, Dynasty, Flamingo Road, Falcon Crest, The Yellow Rose, Emerald Point, N.A.S., For Love and Honor, Bay City Blues,* and *Paper Dolls*. For an analysis of the distinction between series and soap operas, see James W. Chesebro and John D. Glenn, "The Soap Opera as a Communication System," in *Inter/Media: Interpersonal Communication in a Media World*, ed. by Gary Gumpert and Robert Cathcart, 2nd ed. (New York: Oxford University Press, 1982), pp. 250–261.

[e] Movies include all films, made-for-TV movies, and miniseries.

[f] Variety includes regularly scheduled shows such as *The Carol Burnett Show, Sonny and Cher Revue, Cher, Tony Orlando and Dawn, Redd Foxx, Mary, Dick Clark's Live Wednesday, The Tim Conway Show, Barbara Mandrell and the Mandrell Sisters,* and *The Nashville Palace*.

[g] News and semidocumentaries includes regularly broadcast shows such as *60 Minutes, Prime Time Sunday, 20/20, Real People, That's Incredible, Games People Play, Speak Up America, NBC News Magazine with David Brinkley, TV's Bloopers & Practical Jokes, Foul-Ups, Bleeps & Blunders,* and *People Do the Craziest Things*.

[h] During the 1974–1975 season, one hour of prime time was "turned over" to the local stations thus reducing the number of total prime-time hours from 63 to 62 during this season.

of television series employed in this design—independently classifed all 57 television series which constituted the 1982–1983 television season. A standard of "perfect agreement" was employed; each member of the verification team had to classify each series into exactly the same category as it had been previously classified by this researcher. This standard and procedure produced an overall agreement rating of 79.8%, with the following agreement ratings achieved for each category:

Irony = 87.5%
Mime = 81.1%
Leader = 75.0%
Romance = 80.9%
Myth = 97.4%

3. A "television series" is defined as a prime-time (8:00 P.M.–11:00 P.M.) national network production, regularly scheduled to be broadcast (thereby excluding movies, made-for-TV movies, and specials), of a dramatic nature involving conflict-resolution (thereby excluding sports, news specials, regularly scheduled news programs, variety programs, and semidocumentaries) in which the major or central plot of each show is completed within the time frame in which it begins (thereby excluding serials or soap operas). For a detailed description of nonseries, see footnote 1 above. Whereas 1974–1975 season series seldom changed during the season, by the middle of the 1977–1978 season, almost 50 percent of all series broadcast at the beginning of the season had been replaced. This replacement rate has been sustained or increased each year since the 1977–1978 season, frequently beginning some two weeks after the beginning of a new season. Accordingly, an arbitrary definition of each season was required. *TV Guide's* listing of the series defining each new season in September of each year (The "Fall Preview" issue) has thus been employed as the definition of each of the seasons employed in this survey. *TV Guide's* conception of the new season constitutes a popular definition of the new season as well as coinciding with the first major Neilsen rating of the year.

4. For a detailed and formal conception of the communication-value relationships suggested in this analysis, see Table 5, "Substantive and Strategic Variables Associated with the Value Orientation of Each of the Five Communication Dramas" (Chesebro, 1982, p. 509).

GAYE TUCHMAN

Women's Magazines: Marry, Don't Work

Professor Tuchman, in this excerpt from her recent book Hearth and Home: Images of Women in the Mass Media, *looks at the way so-called "women's magazines" present sex roles for women. She views the popular magazine medium as creating narrow, stereotyped roles for women, primarily to satisfy advertisers who sell products to women. Her concern is that these roles, repeated in all media, become models which women are compelled to follow. She does, however, find hope in the fact that some magazines are responsive to the changing roles of liberated women.*

What changes have you noticed in women's roles on TV, in magazines, on the radio? Do you agree with Tuchman that most media portrayals of women place a higher value on the role of housewife and mother than other roles?

Read "Dissociation in a Hero: Superman and the Divided Self," by Arthur Asa Berger and "Double Play and Replay: Living Out There in Television Land" by Ron Commings for some thoughts about how male roles are influenced by the mass media.

As the American girl grows to womanhood, she, like her counterpart elsewhere in industrialized nations, has magazines available designed especially for her use. Some, like *Seventeen,* whose readers tend to be young adolescents, instruct on contemporary fashions and dating styles. Others, like *Cosmopolitan* and *Redbook,* teach about survival as a young woman—whether as a single woman hunting a mate in the city or a young married coping with hearth and home.

This section reviews portrayals of sex roles in women's magazines, seeking to learn how often they too promulgate stereotypes about the role their female readers may take—how much they too engage in the symbolic annihilation of women by limiting and trivializing them. Unfortunately, our analyses of images of women in magazines cannot be as extensive as our discussion of television. Because of researchers' past neglect of women's issues and problems, few published materials are available for review.

Like the television programs just discussed, from the earliest content analyses of magazine fiction (Johns-Heine and Gerth, 1949) to analyses of magazine fiction published in the early 1970s, researchers have found an emphasis on hearth and home and a denigration of the working woman.

From *Hearth and Home: Images of Women in the Mass Media,* by Gaye Tuchman, Arlene Kaplan Daniels, and James Benet. Copyright © 1978 by Oxford University Press, Inc. Reprinted by permission.

The ideal woman, according to these magazines, is passive and dependent. Her fate and her happiness rest with a man, not with participation in the labor force. There are two exceptions to this generalization: (1) The female characters in magazines aimed at working-class women are a bit more spirited than their middle-class sisters. (2) In the mid-1970s, middle-class magazines seemed less hostile toward working women. Using the reflection of hypothesis, particularly its emphasis upon attracting readers to sell advertisements, we will seek to explain the general rule and these interesting exceptions to it.

Like other media, women's magazines are interested in building their audience or readership. For a magazine, attracting more readers is *indirectly* profitable. Each additional reader does not increase the magazine's profit margin by buying a copy or taking out a subscription, because the cost of publication and distribution per copy far exceeds the price of the individual copy—whether it is purchased on the newsstand, in a supermarket, or through subscription. Instead a magazine realizes its profit by selling advertisements and charging its advertisers a rate adjusted to its known circulation. Appealing to advertisers, the magazine specifies known demographic characteristics of its readership. For instance, a magazine may inform the manufacturer of a product intended for housewives that a vast proportion of its readership are homemakers, while another magazine may appeal to the producer of merchandise for young working women by lauding its readership as members of that target group. Women's magazines differentiate themselves from one another by specifying their intended readers, as well as the size of their mass circulation. Additionally, they all compete with other media to draw advertisers. (For example, *Life* and *Look* folded because their advertisers could reach a larger group of potential buyers at a lower price per person through television commercials.) Both daytime television and women's magazines present potential advertisers with particularly appealing audiences, because women are the primary purchasers of goods intended for the home.

Historically, middle-class women have been less likely to be members of the labor force than lower-class women. At the turn of the century, those married women who worked were invariably from working-class families that required an additional income to assure adequate food, clothing, and shelter (Oppenheimer, 1970). The importance of this economic impetus for working is indicated by the general adherence of working-class families to more traditional definitions of male and female sex roles (Rubin, 1976). Although middle-class families subscribe to a more flexible ideology of sex roles than working-class families, both groups of women tend to insist that the man should be the breadwinner. The fiction in women's magazines reflects this ideology.

Particularly in the middle-class magazines, fiction depicts women "as creatures . . . defined by the men in their lives" (Franzwa, 1974a, p. 106; see also Franzwa, 1974b, 1975). Studying a random sample of issues of *Ladies' Home Journal, McCall's,* and *Good Housekeeping* between the years 1940 and 1970, Helen Franzwa found four roles for women: "single and looking for a husband, housewife-mother, spinster, and widowed or divorced—soon to remarry." All the women were defined by the men in their lives, or by their absence. Flora (1971) confirms this finding in her study of middle-class (*Redbook* and *Cosmopolitan*) and working-class (*True Story* and *Modern Romances*) fiction. Female dependence and passivity are lauded; on the rare occasions that male dependence is portrayed, it is seen as undesirable.

As might be expected of characterizations that define women in terms of men, American magazine fiction denigrates the working woman. Franzwa says that work is shown to play "a distinctly secondary part in women's lives. When work is portrayed as important to them, there is a concomitant disintegration of their lives" (1974a, p. 106). Of the 155 major female characters depicted in Franzwa's sample of magazine stories, only 65, or 41 percent, were employed outside the home. Seven of the 65 held high-status positions. Of these seven, only two were married. Three others were "spinsters" whose "failure to marry was of far greater importance to the story-line than their apparent success in their careers" (pp. 106–7). One single woman with a high status career was lauded: She gave up her career to marry.

From 1940 through 1950, Franzwa found, working mothers and working wives were condemned. Instead, the magazines emphasized that husbands should support their spouses. One story summary symbolizes the magazines' viewpoint: "In a 1940 story, a young couple realized that they couldn't live on his salary. She offered to work; he replied, 'I don't think that's so good. I know some fellows whose wives work and they might just as well not be married'" (p. 108). Magazines after 1950 are even less positive about work. In 1955, 1960, 1965, and 1970 not one married woman who worked appeared in the stories Franzwa sampled. (Franzwa selected stories from magazines using five-year intervals to enhance the possibility of finding changes.)

Since middle-class American wives are less likely to be employed than their working-class counterparts, this finding makes sociological sense. Editors and writers may believe that readers of middle-class magazines, who are less likely to be employed, are also more likely to buy magazines approving this life-style. More likely to work and to be in families either economically insecure or facing downward mobility, working-class women might be expected to applaud effective women. For them, female dependence might be an undesirable trait. Their magazines could be expected to cater to such preferences, especially since those preferences flow from the readers' life situations. Such, indeed, are Flora's findings, presented in Table 1.

Table 1. Female dependence and ineffectuality by class, by percentage of stories *

	Working Class	Middle Class	Total
Female Dependence			
Undesirable	22	18	20
Desirable	30	51	41
Neutral	48	31	40
Female ineffectuality			
Undesirable	38	18	28
Desirable	4	33	19
Neutral	58	49	53

* Adapted from Flora (1971).

However, this pattern does not mean that the literature for the working-class woman avoids defining women in terms of men. All the women in middle-class magazines dropped from the labor force when they had a man present; only six percent of the women in the working-class fiction continued to work when they had a man and children. And Flora explained that for both groups "The plot of the majority of stories centered upon the female achieving the proper dependent status, either by marrying or manipulating existing dependency relationships to reaffirm the heroine's subordinate position. The male support—monetary, social, and psychological—which the heroine gains was generally seen as well worth any independence or selfhood given up in the process" (1971, p. 441).

Such differences as do exist between working-class and middle-class magazines remain interesting, though. For they indicate how much more the women's magazines may be responsive to their audience than television can be. Because it is the dominant mass medium, television is designed to appeal to hundreds of millions of people. In 1970, the circulation of *True Story* was "only" 5,347,000, and of *Redbook,* a "mere" 8,173,000. Drawing a smaller audience and by definition, one more specialized, the women's magazines can be more responsive to changes in the position of women in American society. If a magazine believes its audience is changing, it may alter the content to maintain its readership. The contradictions inherent in being women's magazines may free them to respond to change.

A woman's magazine is sex-typed in a way that is not true of men's magazines (Davis, 1976). *Esquire* and *Playboy* are for men, but the content of these magazines, is, broadly speaking, American culture. Both men's magazines feature stories by major American writers, directed toward all sophisticated Americans, not merely to men. Both feature articles on the state of male culture as American culture or of male politics as American politics. Women's magazines are designed in opposition to these "male magazines." For instance, "sports" are women's sports or news of women breaking into "men's sports." A clear distinction is drawn between what is "male" and what is "female."

Paradoxically, though, this very limitation can be turned to an advantage. Addressing women, women's magazines may suppose that some in their audience are concerned about changes in the status of women and the greater participation of women in the labor force. As early as 1966, before the growth of the modern women's movement, women who were graduated from high school or college assumed they would work until the birth of their first child. Clarke and Espositio (1966) found that magazines published in the 1950s and addressed to these women (*Glamour, Mademoiselle,* and *Cosmopolitan*) stressed the joys of achievement and power when describing working roles for women and identifying desirable jobs. Magazines addressed to working women were optimistic about these women's ability to combine work and home, a message that women who felt that they should or must work would be receptive to. Indeed, in 1958 Marya and David Hatch criticized *Mademoiselle, Glamour,* and *Charm* as "unduly optimistic" in their "evaluation of physical and emotional strains upon working women." Combining work and family responsibilities may be very difficult, particularly in working-class homes, since working class husbands refuse to help with housework (Rubin, 1976). But even working-class women prefer work outside the home to housework (Rubin, 1976, Vanek, forthcoming) since it broadens their horizons. Wanting to please and to attract a special audience of working women, magazine editors and writers may be freed to be somewhat responsive to new conditions, even as these same writers and editors feature stereotyped sex roles in other sections of their magazines.

Additional evidence of the albeit limited responsiveness of women's magazines to the changing status of women in the labor force is provided by their treatment of sex-role stereotypes since the advent of the women's movement. The modern women's movement is usually said to begin in the mid-1960s with the founding of the National Organization for Women. The data is of consequence for the study of sex roles in women's magazines because of Betty Friedan's involvement in the National Organization for Women. Her book, *The Feminine Mystique,* published in 1963, provided much of the ideology for the young movement. And, its analysis of sexism ("the problem with no name") was based in part on an analysis of the portrayal of sex roles in women's magazines. In an undated manuscript cited in Busby (1975), Stolz and her colleagues compared the image of women in magazines before and after the advent of the women's movement. Like others, they found no changes between 1940 and 1972. However, a time lag ("culture lag") is probably operating since nonmaterial conditions (ideas and attitudes) change more slowly than do material conditions (such as participation in the labor force).

Several very recent studies affirm that women's magazines may be introducing new conceptions of women's sex roles that are more conducive to supporting the increased participation of women in the labor force. Butler and Paisley [1] note that at the instigation of an editor of *Redbook*, twenty-eight women's magazines published articles on the arguments for and against the Equal Rights Amendment, a constitutional change prompted by the women's movement and the increased participation of women in the labor force. Franzwa's impression of the women's magazines she had analyzed earlier is that they revealed more sympathy with working women in 1975. [2] Sheila Silver (1976) indicates that a "gentle support" for the aims of the women's movement and a "quiet concern" for working women may now be found in *McCall's*. By the terms "gentle support" and "quiet concern," she means to indicate that the magazine approves equal pay for equal work and other movement aims, although it does not approve of the women's movement itself. That magazine and others, such as the *Ladies' Home Journal*, continue to concentrate upon helping women as housewives: They still provide advice on hearth and home. The women's magazines continue to assume that every woman will marry, bear children and "make a home." They do not assume that every woman will work some time in her life.

In sum, the image of women in the women's magazines is more responsive to change than is television's symbolic annihilation and rigid typecasting of women. The sex roles presented are less stereotyped, but a woman's role is still limited. A female child is always an eventual mother, not a future productive participant in the labor force.

Notes

1. Matilda Butler and William Paisley. Personal communication, Fall 1976.
2. 1976, personal communication.

PAUL MESSARIS

Parents, Children, and Television

This essay, like many others, is concerned with the effects of television on children, but what is different is the consideration of the role of parent within child-medium interaction. Paul Messaris deals with some intriguing issues such as the role of television in shaping our perceptions of reality and the role of parents in shaping our perceptions of television reality. Think of your early childhood experiences with this medium. How did you learn to distinguish the make-believe from the real, the commercial from the program, the drama from the news? Can you remember at what age? Are you still sometimes unsure? Did your parents use television characters and situations to teach you about the "real" world? Professor Messaris tells us the answers given by mothers to these and similar questions.

One of the things that make the effects of television on children so complicated to study is the fact that children don't respond to television in a social vacuum.[1] A child's social relationships—in particular, the relationship between parents and children—can influence the child's response to television in a variety of ways. For example, parents' opinions about violence have been found to make a difference in children's reactions to violence on TV. On the other hand, relationships between parents and children may themselves be influenced in several ways by television. In particular, as we will see below, situations and issues that a child has been exposed to on television can become important topics of parent-child discussions. In view of these complications, perhaps the most adequate way to summarize the situation is to say that what a child gets out of his or her relationship with TV depends on a broader set of relationships including not just the medium and the child but also, at the very least, the child's parents. The aim of this chapter is to investigate some consequences of the parent-child-television relationship.

This investigation will be divided into two parts, corresponding to two kinds of things children may learn as a result of their joint relationship with television and their parents: on the one hand, how to perceive the world; on the other hand, how to behave toward it. More specifically, our first concern will be with the various ways in which parents and television together may contribute to a child's developing stock of knowledge about

This article was written expressly for the second edition of *Inter/Media*. Copyright © 1982 by Paul Messaris.

the real world and, in particular, the child's sense of the nature of society and social relationships. Second, we will sift through some of the evidence on a question that many writers about television have examined: To what extent can children's imitation of violence or other kinds of behavior seen on TV be influenced by their parents?

In addition to drawing on past research where appropriate, our discussion of these issues will be based to a great extent on a recent study whose aim was to find out what kinds of things parents and children talk about in reference to television.[2] The study consisted of a series of exploratory, open-ended interviews with mothers of grade-school-age and younger children. A total of 119 mothers were interviewed, all of them residents of the Philadelphia area. Each interviewee was asked some thirty questions about various kinds of TV-related talk. For example: "Do you ever tell your children that something on TV is unrealistic, that things wouldn't happen like that in real life?" "Do your children ever ask you to explain something they didn't understand in a TV program?" "Do you ever find it convenient to use an example from TV to teach your children how they should act— or how not to act?" Whenever a mother said that a particular kind of discussion had occurred in her own family, our interviewers would ask for detailed examples of the incidents in question. In an exploratory study like this one, the examples themselves are what counts, of course, rather than the initial "yes" or "no." Several of these examples will be used to flesh out the discussion that follows.

Parents, TV, and Children's Perceptions of Reality

Through television, a child can be exposed to a constant stream of images about things outside his or her own experience. It is often assumed that these images make important contributions to children's notions of what the world is like. However—contrary to popular assumptions—the learning process involved here may rarely be simply a matter of believing everything one sees. Rather, it seems that parents are often crucially involved in this learning process and that children themselves actively rely on parents in using material from television to construct a picture of the real world. There are at least three important ways in which parents may contribute to their children's formation of television-based world-views: First, parents may have to teach a child the distinction between various categories of programming—e.g., fantasy, "realistic" fiction, news, documentaries, etc.— each of which has a different kind of relationship to the real world. Second, once a child has learned this general distinction, parents may be called upon to perform a more specific task: since there is wide variation within program types in the degree to which any one program accurately reflects some aspect of reality, parents may play the role of validators of specific portrayals. Finally, a parent may supplement information provided on television, by giving the child background data, pointing out connections between events, and so forth. We will examine each of these three possibilities separately.

Categories of Programming and Their Relationship to Reality
One of the mothers in our interviews described the following problem: Her five-year-old son had noticed that actors who "die" in one TV program often "come back to life" in other programs, commercials, or reruns. So, when one of the family's dogs was killed in a fight, the son wanted to know when the dog was going to come back. By her own account, this mother had found it very difficult to clear up her child's confusion. The reason for this difficulty may perhaps be clear: merely telling the child that in real life people or animals don't return from the dead could not have been enough to "set him straight" on all aspects of his misconception of the situation. Unless a child already knows that there is such a thing as a distinction between "real life" and "fiction," the statement that a particular event doesn't occur in real life must be meaningless. Learning this distinction itself, then, may be a prerequisite to any discussion of whether something observed on TV can occur in real life or not. But there is also another aspect to this child's confusion. As the example makes clear, the child did not understand the distinction between one program and the next or between fiction, commercials, etc. Consequently, a blanket statement about the difference between "fiction" and "reality" would also have been bound to mislead him, since it is more than likely that he would have had no notion of which aspects of TV are fictional and which are not.

The general point that this example should make clear is that a child's mastery of the relationship between TV and reality must begin with the formation of categories: one kind of program must be distinguished from another, and, for each type, the appropriate distinction between its contents and reality must be learned. How does this learning occur? On the one hand, the child's general cognitive development appears to play a role.[3] On the other hand, the specific intervention of parents—or older siblings, when they are available—also seems to be a crucial part of this process.

From our interviews with mothers, it is possible to derive a rough estimate of the stages that children go through in learning about these matters. There are obviously many distinctions to be learned, but all of these can be subsumed under two overriding principles, namely, that TV as a whole is distinct from reality and that TV programming itself can be subdivided into various categories. Our interviews indicate that these two general principles are frequently learned in connection with the following more specific distinctions: first, an initial distinction between the "fantasy" part of TV and the real world; second, within TV, a distinction between fictional and "reality" programming (news, documentaries, etc.).

The first of these distinctions appears to be the earliest one that parents try to impress on their children, and the reasons for its urgency are clear: first, parents are often anxious about the possibility that a child will hurt himself or herself by trying to imitate some of the impossible feats shown in "superhero" programs or cartoons. For example, one mother told us that she was repeatedly trying to impress on her children (ages two and five) that, "in real life, you could never run over someone with a car and they bounce back up, you know, after being flattened like a pancake." Another made the following familiar point: "I'm always telling him that Spiderman and Superman can't fly because I don't want him leaping out of any windows on me. 'If your daddy can't do it, it can't be done!' " (The child in this case was a five-year-old). A second reason for parents' concern over the TV-reality distinction is the frequent need to soothe children's fears of monsters, vampires, and other nonexistent creatures. In the following case, for example, a mother explains how she and her husband tried to deal with her six-year-old son's fear of the Wicked Witch's cackle in *The Wizard of Oz,* which the child had seen on TV:

> So what we would do is cackle. You know, try to, uh, show that it's—it's just, um, a play put on or an act, that there aren't any witches, you know, around, that *I* can cackle and make myself look like a witch just like she can. You know, we try to deal with it that way.

The crucial lesson that a child presumably derives from such discussions is that the things shown on TV are of a different kind from the rest of his or her experience. Much remains to be learned, of course, about the precise nature of the relationship between these two realms, but this basic distinction seems to be the starting point for all subsequent learning. However, a second essential building block is also necessary for this kind of learning, namely, the notion that TV programming itself is divided into various categories. From our interviewees' accounts, it appears that the way in which this second notion is introduced is frequently as a partial "retraction" of the lesson that children derive from the kinds of discussions cited above. In other words, what seems to happen is that children are often left with the impression that *all* of TV is fantasy or fiction, so that the first step toward distinctions between programming types is the realization that some of TV is not fictional at all. This situation is illustrated in the following example of a mother's reminiscence about an event that occurred when her oldest child was about six or seven and her youngest about two or three:

I remember during the Viet Nam war getting very upset: We were watching television, the news, while we were eating dinner. And they were showing the children and women dead in the village and I—I started crying, and I couldn't eat my dinner. And the kids got very upset. It wasn't the thing to watch at dinnertime, actually. . . . I explained to them that everything that you see on television isn't make-believe. The news is real. And . . . it hit cold to them that this was real that they were looking at. And it upset them terribly.

In ways like this, then, children learn that there are different categories of TV programming, each with its own relationship to the real world. Many specific distinctions have to be constructed on the basis of this general principle; and, in view of the subtlety of some of them (for example, "docudrama" vs. "regular" drama vs. documentary; "live" broadcasts vs. videotapes[4]), it is probably safe to say that at some point many parents are themselves faced with situations that they don't fully comprehend.

The Accuracy and Representativeness of TV Portrayals of Reality

Once a child has grasped the basic notion of a distinction among categories of programs, a different kind of problem presents itself to him or her. This is the problem of the degree to which a specific program or portrayal is accurate or representative in its depiction of reality. In other words, the issue is no longer one of constructing categories but, instead, that of judging specific items within any one category. For example, a child may want to know whether conditions under slavery were really as bad as shown on *Roots;* whether big-city life is really as dangerous as it seems to be on various police shows; and so forth. According to the mothers in our interviews, questions of this sort are a frequent topic of parent-child discussions. By providing answers to such questions, parents may play a significant role in their children's use of television as an instrument for exploring the nature of the real world.

As one might expect, children seem particularly likely to ask their parents questions about images that have troubled them in some way. Portrayals of evil characters, of human or animal suffering, of various kinds of dangers were often mentioned by our interviewees as topics of children's questions. However, the things that children found disturbing weren't always negative in themselves. Quite frequently, children also seemed threatened by images of wealth or happiness that contradicted their own circumstances in life. In cases like these, too, parents would be asked to comment about the accuracy of the troubling image. We will look at some instances of this kind of situation first, before discussing how parents deal with more negative portrayals.

Many observers have pointed out that the population of the "television world" tends to be wealthier than its real-life "counterpart"[5] and that less well-to-do TV viewers, in particular, may be confronted with a considerable disparity between their own life-styles and what they see on the screen.[6] Furthermore, aside from the issue of wealth, the quality of parent-child relationships in many family shows—especially the calm rationality of parents—can also be enviably different from the real-life home environment of many younger viewers. Accordingly, many of our interviewees described instances in which they had felt the need to emphasize to their children that such images are exaggerations and that one shouldn't expect real life to be as glamorous, pleasant, etc. For example, one mother described her reaction to hearing her eleven-year-old daughter wish for a life and a job like that of the "bionic woman":

> I do remember then going into a discussion of, you know, things always being pretty nice and the jobs on TV always being famous and adventurous and that, and I told them that, you know, that that just is not so all the time. Everything looks glamorous on TV, but in real life it's not like that every day.

The program our interviewees mentioned most often in this vein was *The Brady Bunch,* which was being shown in reruns every weekday afternoon during the period in which these interviews were being conducted. These are some of the things mothers said about this program:

> You know, like the Brady Bunch . . . it's so, uh, gingerbready, that show, you know. They don't make—really make it real, you know. Everything is like fluffed over, like Ozzie and Harriet. The father's always in a suit and the mother's always dressed up with her hair done. I mean, who does their housecleaning like that, you know? And you try to point out to them that that's not really real life.

> Their rec room was so clean. There were never any dishes in the sink. You never see anybody vacuuming. You never see anybody wearing old clothes, jeans, and a sweatshirt.

What seems to be happening in these cases, then, is an attempt by mothers to dampen possible unrealistic expectations that a program might create for a child, although a touch of resentment also appears to be operating here, particularly in the *Brady Bunch* examples. Both of these ingredients are apparent in mothers' comments about how their children respond to programs like *The Brady Bunch:* "I think that at one point he must have felt very deprived because he wasn't living in a house like the Brady Bunch." "The children seem to feel that that's reality and what they're living in is somehow a mistake." Whether these perceptions on the part of the mothers are accurate or not is, of course, an open question, although mothers did say that their children ask them such things as "How come you don't solve things like Mrs. Brady?" or complain that "Mrs.

Brady wouldn't do it like that." In other words, mothers who tell their children that portrayals like that of the *Brady Bunch* are exaggerated or false may be doing more than protecting their children from painful disillusionment with reality. They may also be protecting their own families from the strain that can be caused by a child's resentment.[7]

We can now turn to cases in which parents and children confront the darker side of the world of television: portrayals of evil and crime, suffering and danger. Here, too, mothers' comments to their children about these troubling visions contained a clear element of protectiveness. In these cases, however, this protectiveness typically led to confirmation, rather than negation, of the accuracy of the images in question. In other words, in apparent attempts to warn their children about the dangers of the real world— or, at least, that aspect of it that appears on TV—mothers would typically tell their children that TV's troubling portrayals of a cruel and dangerous reality were true. In both of the examples that follow, the children were entering adolescence:

> Well, when you see, uh, if you'll excuse the expression, a real bastard, um, you know, uh, I guess something like—like that fellow on *Dallas*, not that they watch it, uh, "Well, can people really be that rotten and mean?" And, uh, they've seen it on television and it is true. It does happen. Yeah, we've referred to that. People do get murdered.

> Like these, this thing they had on the runaway kids: We had a big discussion about that because I told him that, you know, the kids, like, they do run away, they do get in trouble, and, you know, they do get in things like this white slavery stuff. You know, I said they do abuse them and all, you know, like we've had a good discussion about that. . . . Well, he wanted to know if it was really true there, you know, if that does really happen to kids. . . . I told him that stuff is true, that, you know, boys, they do get into, you know—or they sell their bodies. I said, I call that white slavery that you have to do things for other people, you know, with sex and all. I says, it's not like you're cleaning, you know, it's that kind of thing. I said, and this stuff really does happen when kids run away.

As this second example shows, warnings of this kind may also contain implicit statements about the advantages of one's own family life. This element is present more explicitly in the following example, from the mother of a ten-year-old girl:

> They had a special on child abuse and, uh, I let them watch it, you know, and—I mean, this really sounds terrible, but, like, I told her, I said, "You are really lucky, 'cause there are parents that treat their children like that." You know, so I mean, I have done things like that, which probably sounds cruel to you.

In other words, these comments also seem to have the double element which we saw in parents' dealings with "positive" programs like *The Brady*

Bunch: One the one hand, the parents appear to be trying to make sure that their children will develop adequate images of the good and bad sides of the outside world. At the same time, however, the parents also appear to be concerned with strengthening their own families, either by playing down a threatening difference between TV and their own circumstances or by playing up a difference which is to their advantage.

Parental Supplementation of TV Information

TV programming is typically designed to be compatible with even the most impoverished stock of information on the part of the viewer. Nevertheless, younger TV viewers are bound to encounter situations with unfamiliar premises from time to time. When that does happen, parents are likely to be the ones turned to for an account of the "background" information that the child doesn't have—although older brothers or sisters are also pressed into this kind of service. In our interviews with mothers, this kind of TV-related discussion—providing supplementary information—turned out to have been a very common experience. Four-fifths of the mothers described detailed incidents of this sort.

The kinds of information that mothers said they had provided in connection with TV varied widely, but it is possible to make a rough distinction between two general categories: on the one hand, information that all—or almost all—people acquire as they grow up; and, on the other hand, more "specialized" information, either of a "scholarly" kind (historical, scientific, etc.) or having to do with specific occupations, ethnic groups, etc. The first of these two categories includes such issues as human reproduction (where babies come from, how they are born), death, sex (and rape, adultery, prostitution, venereal disease, etc.), marriage and divorce, illness and drug addiction, delinquency and crime, etc. For example, one mother told us that, when a program on childbirth had been shown on television, her seven-year-old daughter had watched it with her and "she literally asked me everything from beginning to end about the show." Another mother remembered that, after her children had seen a funeral on television, "they wanted to know, you know, 'Does everybody die? When do they die?'" and she had to "explain it all to them." A third mother told us that her children had assumed, because of the prevalence of divorced parents on TV shows, that divorce is a standard part of marriage and wanted to know when their own parents were going to get divorced.

Naturally, parents vary in the degree to which they are willing to answer questions on some of these topics, especially when sex is somehow involved. Whereas one mother told us that her ten-year-old daughter's questions about sex on TV were always answered fully ("We don't hide anything or hold anything back"), another described the following "non-answer" to a sex-related question:

> Once he saw a comic show and there was a line that said something like, "Sex is like peanuts. Once you start eating them you can't stop." And everyone laughed. . . . He repeated it a couple of times . . . "peanuts . . ." and he asked me, "What does that really mean?" And I said, "I can't really explain it but it's as being though something you start and it's hard to stop. It's like when you start eating a cracker. Sometimes you want to keep eating some crackers." But that's as far as it went.

What difference does it make how a parent answers this kind of question? More generally, what is the consequence of children's questions and parents' answers on these "adult" topics?[8] At first blush, it might seem that, to the extent that parents do in fact give their children full details on such topics, they are "speeding up" the children's entry into the informational world of adulthood. From this point of view, one could say that television, by injecting these "adult" topics into parent-child discussions, is causing children to "grow up" before their time.[9] However, one should be cautious in drawing such a conclusion. Once children are in school, information (and misinformation) on sex and other "adult" topics can be transmitted "horizontally" among children of the same age, so that any one child's reliance on information from "above" (parents, older siblings, "adult" media) is lessened considerably. In this kind of situation, a parent's refusal to deal with a certain topic at home may be of little consequence to the child's stock of information on that topic. This situation is illustrated in the following quotation from our interviews:

> I told her that it was something I didn't think she was old enough to understand or really comprehend. And I said, there is so much in some of these sex movies . . . the shame of it is they leave nothing to the imagination. I think it's a mystery that should be left a mystery to some people. Leave a little bit to be desired. They show everything. I just said I didn't think at that time she was old enough. She thought I was ridiculous. She said she understands and other children have seen it and her friends watch this and that. . . .

In cases of this sort, then, television and the parent may not be important sources of information on a particular issue. This is not to say, of course, that the nature of the interaction between parent and child is a trivial matter in such cases. As the above example suggests ("She thought I was ridiculous"), such interactions can have important consequences for the parent-child relationship itself.

Aside from asking TV-inspired questions about "adult" topics, children also question their parents about matters that are unfamiliar in a different way: distant times and places, unencountered religious practices or ethnic groups, scientific principles and findings. For example:

I was watching *Dr. Zhivago* and my eleven-year-old son was with me, and he was discussing—he wanted to know how they could do certain things, uh, take over their houses in Russia and capture him and take him to the army, and I had to explain to him the difference in cultures, and what democracy is and what communism is, and he understood what I was telling him.

Other mothers described discussions of such things as the American Western migration (in connection with *Little House on the Prairie*), the economic system of the South under slavery (in connection with *Roots*), the meaning of the Jewish Seder (in connection with *Holocaust*), etc.

This kind of parental involvement in children's television viewing is often encouraged by people concerned with the educational potential of television. Experiments in which an adult watches television with a group of children and supplies interpretive commentary suggest that children absorb televised information better under such circumstances than when they are viewing alone.[10] But the benefits to the child of this kind of behavior may extend far beyond the specific information gleaned from a particular program or set of parental comments. It can be argued that, when a parent responds positively to a child's request for this kind of "specialized" information about a TV program, two "lessons" are being conveyed to the child: in addition to gaining the specific information requested, the child is also being reinforced in his or her use of TV as a "springboard" for the intellectual mastery of new areas of knowledge. Indeed, this reinforcement can probably occur even if the parent does not have the information herself, so long as the child's intellectual curiosity is rewarded. A good example of this in our interviews was the case of a mother who watches *Nova* with her grade-school son and helps him dig through the encyclopedia for explanations of things which neither of them may have understood. To the extent that it successfully reinforces a child's tendencies for intellectual exploration, parental behavior of this kind must have far greater consequences for a child's view of the world than any specific item of knowledge would be likely to have. What this behavior can cultivate in the child is a view of the world as a realm to be conquered through the exercise of one's mind. Few particular aspects of reality can be more important than this general view.

Research in progress by several scholars indicates that the kind of TV-related behavior described above is most likely to be found, not surprisingly, in families in which there is a more general tendency to support intellectual flexibility and an uncompromising pursuit of knowledge.[11] Related work by other researchers has also supported a connection between this kind of family environment and a more information-seeking (rather than entertainment-oriented) approach to television.[12] It is also worth noting that sociologists concerned with the ultimate consequences of this general style of parental behavior have argued that it is particularly likely to facilitate achievement in children's later lives, since the pursuit of intellectual mastery is an adaptive trait in a society which places high value on professional occupations.[13] However, these broader implications of the behavior we are examining here are mere speculation at this point.

Parents, TV, and Children's Behavioral Learning

Do children learn to behave in one way or another by imitating what they see on television? This question has occupied communication researchers for some twenty years. Most of this research has dealt with the imitation of aggression, although investigators have increasingly been looking at the subject of "prosocial" behavior too: helping other people, sharing things, etc. The most common interpretation of all of this research is that television can indeed—at least in principle—affect children's behavior, although the actual extent of this effect may not always be large and is, in any case, difficult to measure. As for the possible influence of parents on children's responses to TV, the consensus seems to be that parents can modify or block the effects of TV if they make an active effort to that end,[14] but that otherwise children are "at the mercy" of the medium. In the following discussion, however, a somewhat different position will be presented.[15] What will be argued here is that the common view of these matters may have got things the wrong way around: In other words, it may be the case that imitation doesn't occur at all unless parents (or other people) have previously encouraged a child—knowingly or not—to engage in the kind of behavior being imitated. According to this position, then, parental involvement is a prerequisite for imitation, rather than simply a possible modifier of its occurrence. Although this position certainly represents a minority view, there is much evidence that points in its direction.

In examining this position, we will be drawing primarily on findings from past research, rather than on the interviews that we have used up to this point. In particular, because of the considerable detail that has been covered in research on aggression, we will focus our discussion on that aspect of imitation, with the understanding that what is said about aggression should be taken to apply, in many respects, to other kinds of behavior as well. The starting point in any discussion of visually mediated aggression is usually the work of Albert Bandura and his colleagues.[16] In a series of experiments beginning in the early 1960s, these investigators demonstrated that children who have seen a small-screen, TV-like film of a man assaulting a Bobo doll in various ways are more likely to do the same kinds of things to a Bobo doll themselves than children who haven't seen the film. The conclusion that is usually drawn from these experiments is that the children learned the aggressive behavior from the film. In other words, it is concluded on the basis of this kind of evidence that children can pick up behavioral patterns purely from visual presentations. The implication, of course, is that, unless parents intervene, children who watch a lot of violence on TV may turn into violent people themselves.

One of the reasons for the stir caused by findings of this sort is that they seem to go against a long- and widely-held psychological principle according to which children cannot learn new forms of behavior unless their environment actively reinforces what they are learning.[17] The experiments described above appear to contradict this principle, since the children in the experiments seem to be learning to be aggressive without any environmental reinforcement: a TV or movie screen cannot respond to them, no matter what they do. However, this contradiction may be an illusion. To begin with, we must remember that the children who participated in these experiments obviously had past histories, which would have included their parents' responses to previous aggression on their own part. To what extent did these past experiences with aggression influence their behavior in the experimental setting? Many violence researchers would argue that such previous influence couldn't be operating in the experiments, because the kinds of aggression that children were being tested on (lassoing a Bobo doll with a hula-hoop, for example) were too unlikely to have occurred in a child's previous experience. But this argument is less impregnable than it may sound: it could well be that the learning of one kind of aggression carries over into another kind too—in other words, that what one learns is "aggression" in general. It is worth pointing out, for example, that in experiments in which children were tested on forms of aggression that were deliberately different from what they had seen on TV, strong relationships between exposure and subsequent aggression were found all the same.[18] In order to find out what role prior experience could have played in these experiments, then, we must go to studies that have examined these things directly.

One set of studies has looked at the connection between a child's past history of aggressiveness and his response to aggressive TV in an experimental setting. These studies did not examine the role of parents in the children's previous experiences with aggression, but it is probably safe to assume that, where parents did exist, they were an important source of influence in the development of the child's aggressive tendencies.[19] In any case, what these studies show is that a child's pre-existing aggressive tendencies appear to make a considerable difference to the child's response to an aggressive TV "diet." The less aggressive a child was initially, the less likely he was to respond aggressively to the televised aggression—and, in fact, in some cases the less aggressive children didn't respond aggressively at all.[20] What this tells us, in other words, is that previous environmental reinforcement does indeed seem to be necessary for imitation, and that the movies or TV programs used in these experiments were probably triggering behavior that had already been learned, rather than teaching children something new.

As to the role of parents in the development of the tendencies that a violent TV program can then operate upon, several studies provide relevant evidence. Each of these studies has looked at the influence of family environment on the relationship between adolescents' real-life aggressiveness and their real-life exposure to aggressiveness on TV. In each case, what has been found is that this relationship becomes weaker or stronger depending on various aspects of parental behavior: for example, how strongly parents emphasize nonaggression,[21] how clear a picture they have conveyed to their children of their stance on aggression,[22] what kinds of means (aggressive or otherwise) they use to discipline their children,[23] and so forth. These studies give us grounds for concluding, therefore, that children's aggressive responses to violence on TV depend on tendencies developed in the course of a child's interactions with his or her parents.

More generally, the thrust of this whole argument has been that parents are probably much more intimately involved in their children's imitative responses to TV than most people think. Whereas the typical assumption is that parents influence their children's imitations only when they make a deliberate effort to do so, the position outlined above is that prior parental reinforcement of behavior may be indispensable to subsequent imitation from TV, regardless of any deliberate parental intervention in the child's experience with TV itself. In other words, even if a parent's behavior toward the child is never explicitly concerned with television, a child's imitation of television may depend crucially on previous parental influence on the child's behavior. It goes without saying, of course, that these conclusions are tentative, since the findings we have examined were concerned exclusively with aggressive behavior and since, moreover, the amount of space available to us has not permitted us to examine possible counterarguments[24] in detail.

Nothing that has been said so far should be taken to imply that parents cannot—or do not—control their children's behavioral responses to TV through deliberate intervention as well—in other words, through comments, advice, etc., referring directly to TV, as opposed to the more general kind of influence we have examined above. Our own interviews with parents yielded numerous examples of attempted control of this sort. Among other things, parents described warning their children not to imitate the behavior of "the Fonz" (in this parent's words, "he's such a creep!"); the fictional character played by Gary Coleman ("that little guy

Gary Coleman is just . . . he's rude. I don't care what anybody says, but if any kid ever talked to me the way he did, he'd be wearing his teeth on the back of his head"); the nose-picking teenagers in *Saturday Night Live* ("you're trying to teach children not to do it and they make a joke out of it"); or the phrase "Watch it, sucker!" from *Sanford and Son*. On the other hand, many parents also described instances in which they had encouraged imitation, rather than the opposite. For example, one mother told us that she often used characters from *Romper Room* as behavioral models for her three-year-old daughter:

> If she'll stick out her tongue or spit, I'll tell her, "Now, do the children in Miss Nancy's classroom spit and stick out their tongues?" . . . Um, I use that a lot with my middle one because on "Romper Room" they're all good. They're all goodies.

Another mother described a long pep talk aimed at getting her son to imitate the hard work which must have been involved in the achievements of a certain winter Olympics champion:

> These people were not born, uh, jumping off cliffs and mountains and, uh, on skates and what have you. A lot of hard work, a lot of desire, a lot of push, and that's the end result.

How effective is this kind of advice in encouraging or discouraging children's imitations of TV? The question has been studied systematically in a pair of related experiments.[25] In these experiments, an adult member of the experimental team would sit with a child during the screening of a violent film and would make either disapproving comments ("He shouldn't do that"; "That's wrong"; "That's awful"), approving comments ("Boy, look at him go"; "He sure is a tough guy"; "That's really something"), or no comments at all. The victim in these films was a Bobo doll, shown being hit with a hammer, kicked around, etc. After the screening, the child would be allowed to play in a room containing, among other things, a Bobo doll and various likely weapons. The object of the experiments, of course, was to determine if the adult's comments had any influence on the child's imitative aggression. The findings turned out to depend on the children's age. With younger children (five-year-olds), the adult's comments seemed to make a difference only if the adult stayed with the child in the playroom during the period in which imitation was being measured. With older children (ten-year-olds), however, the influence persisted even after the departure of the adult "commentator." In both age groups, the direction of the influence was what one would expect: the adult's approving comments appeared to encourage imitation, while the disapproving comments discouraged it.

These results suggest fairly clearly that parental control of imitation through direct involvement in a child's TV viewing is feasible. In view of the rudimentary "commentary" used in these experiments, it should be added that there is some indirect evidence that more extensive attempts to reason with a child are also effective means of controlling responses to TV in the parents' absence, whereas authority-based commands are not.[26] It need hardly be added, of course, that a fool-proof way of preventing imitation is to block exposure in the first place. Although studies have indicated that parents do not generally exercise much direct control over their children's program choices,[27] some specific programs are exceptions to the rule. For example, many of the mothers in our interviews told us that they prevented their children from watching *Three's Company* because of its presentation of cohabitation and, in one mother's view, the fact that "it's promoting gaiety." To the extent that parents succeed in preventing their children's exposure to such material, they are also by definition precluding the possibility of imitation.

Summary

The aim of this chapter has been to show that parents may play a crucial role in determining what children learn from television. Two aspects of learning were examined: first, the development of the child's perceptions of reality; second, behavioral learning through imitation. With regard to the first of these, the following points were made: (1) Parental instruction appears to be a vital ingredient in the process by which children come to grips with the distinction between categories of programming and with the relationship of each category to the real world. (2) By conforming or denying the accuracy of specific programs or portrayals, parents may add a filter of their own to the world-view that a child extracts from television. (3) Since parents are often called upon to supplement the information provided in a television program, the final lesson that a child extracts from the viewing experience may be a joint product of what was shown on the screen and what was provided by the parent. With regard to children's behavioral learning through the imitation of things seen on television, the following argument was made: there is considerable evidence in favor of the notion that children's imitation of visual images does not occur at all unless the behavior in question has already been reinforced by parents (or other people with whom a child has had a substantial history of interaction). Consequently, previous parental encouragement or discouragement of a certain kind of behavior may crucially determine whether that behavior will be imitated when a child observes it on TV. This encouragement or discouragement may be made with explicit reference to TV, but it need not be explicit to be effective. Both with regard to the perception of reality and with regard to overt behavior, then, what a child learns from television may in fact be a product of the broader relationship among medium, child, and parent.[28]

Notes

1. For other perspectives on this general point, see Steven H. Chaffee, "The Interpersonal Context of Mass Communication," in *Current Perspectives in Mass Communication Research,* eds. F. G. Kline and P. J. Tichenor (Beverly Hills: Sage Publications, 1972), pp. 95–120; J. A. Anderson, P. J. Traudt, S. R. Acker, T. P. Meyer, and T. R. Donohue, "An Ethnological Approach to a Study of Televiewing in Family Settings," Paper presented to the Western Speech Communication Association, Los Angeles, 1979; James Lull, "The Social Uses of Television," *Human Communication Research,* 6:197–209 (1980), reprinted in this volume.

2. For further details on this study, see Paul Messaris and Sari Thomas, "Social-Class Differences in Mother-Child Discussions about Television," Paper presented to the Speech Communication Association, Anaheim, 1981.

3. Leona Jaglom and Howard Gardner, "Decoding the Worlds of Television," *Studies in Visual Communication,* 7(1):33–47 (Winter 1981). See also D. B. Wackman and E. Wartella, "A Review of Cognitive Developmental Theory and Research and the Implications for Research on Children's Responses to Television," *Communication Research,* 4:203–224 (1977).

4. For a discussion of some of the complexities involved here, see Gary Gumpert, "The Ambiguity of Perception," *Et cetera,* 34 (June 1977), reprinted in this volume.

5. B. S. Greenberg, K. W. Simmons, L. Hogan, and C. K. Atkin, "The Demography of Fictional TV Characters," in *Life on Television,* ed. B. S. Greenberg (Norwood, N.J.: Ablex, 1980), pp. 35–46.

6. T. R. Donohue, T. P. Meyer, and L. L. Henke, "Black and White Children: Perceptions of TV Commercials," *Journal of Marketing,* October 1978:34–40.

7. On these points, see also Dennis Kerr, "Family Discussions about Depictions of Families on Television," Paper presented to the Conference on Culture and Communication, Philadelphia, 1981.

8. For another point of view on these issues, see Catherine E. Kirkland, "Televised Portrayals of Sexual Topics as the Basis of Parent-Child Interaction," Paper presented to the Conference on Culture and Communication, Philadelphia, 1981.

9. Joshua Meyrowitz, "Television and the Obliteration of Childhood," Paper presented to the Conference on Culture and Communication, Philadelphia, 1981.

10. C. Corder-Bolz and S. L. O'Bryant, "Can People Affect Television? Teacher vs. Program," *Journal of Communication,* 28(1):97–103 (1978); C. Corder-Bolz, "Mediation: The Role of Significant Others," *Journal of Communication,* 30(3):106–118 (1980). See also W. Andrew Collins, Brian L. Sobol, and Sally Westby, "Effects of Adult Commentary on Children's Comprehension and Inferences about a Televised Aggressive Portrayal," *Child Development,* 52:158–163 (1981).

11. Carla Sarett, "Socialization Patterns and Children's Television- and Film-Related Play," Ph.D. Dissertation, University of Pennsylvania, 1981; Avishai Soudack, "Social Class and Parent-Child Television-Related Interaction," M. A. Thesis, Annenberg School of Communications, University of Pennsylvania, 1981.

12. Steven H. Chaffee, Jack M. McLeod, and Charles K. Atkin, "Parental Influences on Adolescent Media Use," in *Mass Communications and Youth*, eds. F. G. Kline and P. Clarke (Beverly Hills: Sage Publications, 1971). See also James Lull, "Family Communication Patterns and the Social Uses of Television," *Communication Research*, 7:319–334 (1980).

13. M. L. Kohn, *Class and Conformity* (Chicago: The University of Chicago Press, 1977).

14. A. D. Leifer, N. J. Gordon, and S. B. Graves, "Children's Television: More than Mere Entertainment," *Harvard Educational Review*, 44:213–245 (1974).

15. The author has made the same argument in Paul Messaris, "Family Processes and the Social Functions of Television," Paper presented to the Conference on Culture and Communication, Philadelphia, 1981.

16. For an overview, see Albert Bandura, "Social-Learning Theory of Identificatory Processes," in *Handbook of Socialization Theory and Research,* ed. D. A. Goslin (Chicago: Rand McNally, 1969).

17. B. F. Skinner, *Science and Human Behavior* (New York: The Free Press, 1953); J. L. Gewirtz, "Mechanisms of Social Learning: Some Roles of Stimulation and Behavior in Early Human Development," in Goslin, *op. cit.*

18. R. M. Liebert and R. A. Baron, "Short-term Effects of Televised Aggression on Children's Aggressive Behavior," in *Television and Social Behavior,* Vol. 2, eds. J. P. Murray, E. A. Rubinstein, and G. A. Comstock (Washington, D.C.: U.S. Government Printing Office, 1972).

19. Michael E. Roloff and Bradley S. Greenberg, "TV, Peer, and Parent Models for Prosocial and Antisocial Conflict Behaviors," *Human Communication Research*, 6:340–351 (Summer 1980).

20. C. K. Friedrich and A. H. Stein, "Aggressive and Prosocial Television Programs and the Natural Behavior of Preschool Children," *Monographs of the Society for Research in Child Development*, 38(4), Serial No. 151 (1973); R. D. Parke, L. Berkowitz, J. P. Leyens, S. West, and R. J. Sebastian, "Some Effects of Violent and Nonviolent Movies on the Behavior of Juvenile Delinquents," in *Advances in Experimental Social Psychology,* Vol. 10, ed. L. Berkowitz (New York: Academic Press, 1977).

21. Jack M. McLeod, Charles K. Atkin, and Steven H. Chaffee, "Adolescents, Parents, and Television Use: Adolescent Self-Report from Maryland and Wisconsin Samples," in *Television and Social Behavior,* Vol. 3, eds. G. A. Comstock and E. A. Rubinstein (Washington, D.C.: U.S. Government Printing Office, 1972); Jack M. McLeod, Charles K. Atkin, and Steven H. Chaffee, "Adolescents, Parents, and Television Use: Self-Report and Other-Report Measures from the Wisconsin Sample," *Ibid.*

22. J. R. Dominick and B. S. Greenberg, "Attitudes toward Violence: The Interaction of Television Exposure, Family Attitudes, and Social Class," in G. A. Comstock and E. A. Rubinstein, *op. cit.*

23. F. Korzenny, B. S. Greenberg, and C. K. Atkin, "Styles of Parental Disciplinary Practices as a Mediator of Children's Learning from Antisocial Television Por-

trayals," in *Communication Yearbook 3,* ed. D. Nimmo (New Brunswick, N.J.: Transaction Books, 1979).

24. R. M. Liebert, L. A. Cohen, C. Joyce, S. Murrel, L. Nisonoff, and S. Sonnen-schein, "Effects of Television: Predispositions Revisited," *Journal of Communication,* 27(3):217–221 (1977).

25. D. J. Hicks, "Effects of Co-observer's Sanctions and Adult Presence on Imitative Aggression" *Child Development,* 39:303–309 (1968); J. E. Grusec, "Effects of Co-observer Evaluations on Imitation: A Developmental Study," *Developmental Psychology,* 8:141 (1973).

26. V. K. Prasad, T. R. Rao, and A. A. Sheikh, "Can People Affect Television? Mother vs. Commercial," *Journal of Communication,* 28(1):91–96 (1978).

27. P. J. Mohr, "Parental Guidance of Children's Viewing of Evening Television Programs," *Journal of Broadcasting,* 23:213–228 (1979).

28. For a discussion of other aspects of this issue, see Paul Messaris and Carla Sarett, "On the Consequences of Television-Related Parent-Child Interaction," *Human Communication Research,* 7:226–244 (Spring 1981).

ELLEN WARTELLA

Getting to Know You: How Children Make Sense of Television

Today children begin watching television as early as 6 to 12 months. But, what are they seeing and what does it mean to them? Wartella has reviewed the observational studies of children and television along with her own research findings, and concludes that for children to make sense of TV requires an ongoing practice with TV form and content accompanied by ongoing interpersonal communication. She makes her case by first analyzing television as communication and then connects that with the interpersonal context in which television watching is done to establish how children learn to make sense of television.

DAVID (aged 22 months, pointing at morning news show on TV screen): Dat football.

MOTHER: No David, that's a basketball—see they're inside—see the hoop.

DAVID: Dat football, Mommy.

MOTHER: No David, not football, that's a basketball—see it's big and round.

DAVID: Hockey—dat hockey, Mommy.

MOTHER: No David, that's not hockey—that's basketball. See they're talking about basketball news.

DAVID: Football—hockey—dat ball, Mommy, dat ball.

My son, David, is just learning how to make sense of television—indeed he's just learning how to make sense of most of his environment. Television, in particular, is not a very important part of his world. He never asks to have it turned on; he's as likely to turn away when the set is on as he is to watch it. When he does watch television, he uses the experience to tell me all the vocabulary words he knows—man, woman, ball, baby, map, Steve. There are times, such as in the foregoing interchange, when television is something more. Television is both an object David must learn to understand and it is a mechanism for me to teach him about television and about the world and to distinguish footballs from basketballs from hockey pucks. It is this interpersonal context of children's television watching that is reviewed here. It is in this context that the work of making sense of television goes on.

This article was written expressly for the present volume. Copyright © 1986 by Ellen Wartella.

The following discussion examines the interpersonal context of children's television use—that is, how children watch television. It reviews observational and participant observational studies of children and television. The thesis of this review is that the work of sense-making about television and about the world through television is an ongoing practice occuring in children's everyday interchanges with television. This argument has two steps: first, an analysis of television as a communication medium and second, the interpersonal context of television watching.

Television Is a Communicative Medium

Fifteen or so years ago most researchers of television effects on children didn't even consider what today is taken for granted—that children of different ages see television in different ways. Studies of the psychology of child viewers have detailed the ways in which children come to make sense of television and to interpret television messages as they grow older (see Wartella, 1979). Certain trends in this research are readily apparent. First, information processing studies share a belief that the study of television's influence on children requires attention to the nature of children and their developing cognitive capacities. Thus, much of this research is developmental in nature. That is, it attempts to describe how children of different ages attend to and interpret specific television messages, such as dramatic plotlines, advertisements, or television characters as people (see Ward, Wackman, and Wartella, 1977; Wartella, 1980, Collins, 1982, Singer and Singer, 1983; Bryant and Anderson, 1983). Second, most of these studies are concerned not just with the content of television (is it violent? is it arousing?) but also with *how* television packages the content, or its *form*. Huston and Wright (1983), write that "television is distinguished from other media by its forms, not its content." By forms they mean visual and auditory production and editing techniques which characterize television. The use of slow motion, cuts, pans, zooms, pacing, auditory distortion, and animation, are all formal characteristics of TV's messages. These forms influence both what is communicated and how the child interprets that message. Form can be distinguished from content, say Huston and Wright (1983). They offer the example of the use of dialogue (a formal characteristic of television) which can be analyzed separately from what is said on the program (a content characteristic of the message). Forms and content are both part of the communicative context of television.

But children do not watch television forms and message content separately. Television watching is a communication experience for children. Children attend to television *in toto* as a medium of communication (Rice and Wartella, 1981). From the perspective of the viewer, form and content are intertwined into an audiovisual, meaningful experience. For the viewer television is made up of people, objects, events, and stories. This content of television, however, does have a distinctive characteristic—it is patterned. Patterns reside in the representational codes or ways of packaging television's messages which connect forms and content. These codes interact in a communicative interchange between the child viewer and the television representation. Children actively and interactively interpret the representational codes of television. Before looking at how children come to make sense of television, first we must examine how television communicates to the child.

Because television does not literally present the world as we perceive it, the representational codes it uses to present events involves the selection, editing, and re-presentation of events in some sequence connected through media conventions. For instance, zooms are used to direct our attention to some aspect of an object—to highlight that one aspect of the larger object. For instance, when a burglar enters a room we see the room in wide angle, but as the camera zooms into a picture on the wall, we "know" the thief will go there to look for the wall safe. As adults we often do not consciously notice the ways in which production techniques guide and influence our sense making of the program; we learn to take for granted television forms. Thus, we can accept a television drama which condenses 40 years in a person's life into the space of one hour. Such re-presentation in television is done through the use of three kinds of representational codes: iconic codes, medium-specific production codes, and the generic codes such as language. These three codes interact in the production of a message.

Iconic codes refer to the literal presentation of a visual image. Many of those studying the psychology of television watching believe that the visual code of television is the most overpowering aspect of the medium. The fact that television can show the *Challenger* landing from space, children playing in a playground, a frog jumping in a pond—these visual images, according to some, suggest that television, is "a string of pictures" (Postman, 1979). Indeed, television's novelty as a medium of broadcasting was its ability to add pictures to radio sound—and this iconic ability is frequently the focus of commentary about the medium (Singer and Singer, 1983). But the iconic representational code of television is certainly not the only way in which television conveys its messages.

Iconic representations or visual images are packaged in particular patterns of production and editing conventions, the *medium-specific production codes* of television. Television is not just a string of pictures; it is a carefully selected and packaged presentation of images which tends to involve distortion and manipulation of events and objects in ways that cannot be duplicated by human perception. Such techniques as cuts, fades, zooms, flashbacks, instant replays, and other special effects manipulate and present iconic images in novel ways. Time and space are distorted through these codes. And these medium-specific codes are patterned. Observers of television, particularly of children's television, have commented on the particular kinds of medium-specific codes used in American television. In a series of studies, Huston and Wright and colleagues (1981, 1983) have distinguished between *perceptually salient* forms and *reflective* forms.

Perceptually salient forms of production characteristic of television are those that have their greatest influence in eliciting children's attention. They involve intensity, change, novelty, surprise and contrast (Huston and Wright, 1983). Included in the definition of perceptually salient forms are such production techniques as fast pace, strange voices, high levels of visual and auditory special effects. On the other hand, more reflective production forms include singing, zooms and moderate action levels. These are reflective forms because they encourage repetition and elaboration of the content of the programming. According to one study of children's television programs (Huston, Wright, Wartella, Rice, Watkins, Campbell, and Potts, 1981), Saturday morning network television shows, particularly animated shows, use the more perceptually salient forms. These shows are the quickly changing, fast-paced, high-action, visual "onslaught" that critics characterize as "hype." In contrast, educational television such as *Sesame Street* and *Mister Rogers* contain lower levels of the perceptually salient forms of television and higher levels of reflective forms such as high amounts of child dialogue which has been found to maintain attention and and aid in rehearsal, reflection and comprehension of the program's message (Rice, Huston, and Wright, 1982).

Children must come to interpret the nonliteral messages associated with these medium-specific production codes of television. It is clear that as children grow older they become more adept at decoding these medium-specific representation codes. For instance, Huston and Wright (1983) argue that perceptually salient features serve as *markers* signalling to the children that certain kinds of content are coming up. For example, when children hear child characters or sound effects, or see animation, these features may signal to the child that something which would be entertaining to them as children is on the set and they should pay attention. On the other hand, other features such as adult voices on adult news shows may signal content which would be above the children's heads. Moreover, Huston and Wright argue that as children grow older they become increasingly adept at using these medium-specific forms as markers to direct their attention to programming. And the greater the children's abilities to interpret such medium-specific production codes, the more "media literate" the child is said to be.

A third set of representational codes available on television and which require interpretation are the more generic codes which are neither medium-specific nor iconic. Perhaps most important to the generic codes of television is language. As Rice (1984) has demonstrated there is a wide variation in how language is used in children's television. Moreover, she found that there were three packages of consistent patterns of language associated with both iconic and medium-specific representational codes. In her analysis of children's educational and commercial television programs Rice found three relationships: first, programs which used little language but highly salient production forms (such as *Road Runner* cartoon shows); second, programs which use a moderate amount of dialogue and linguistic features, such as the moderate use of immediate references to novel words used on *Mister Rogers;* and finally, a group of programs which use high amounts of dialogue and linguistic features such as many grammatically incomplete comments and comments for which the content is not immediately present with low use of formal production characteristics. An example of the latter package of linguistic and generic production codes is *Gilligan's Island,* a program often found on late-afternoon commercial stations and known to attract child viewers. Moreover, in this analysis, Rice found that these different packages of generic and media-specific codes demonstrate differences in how children's programs attempt to adapt language to meet the needs of child viewers. She suggests that through dialogue simplications, through the use of focusing such as recasting and repeating novel words or words used in novel contexts, the generic codes of television interact with other iconic and production codes to influence children's attention and comprehension. Moreover, educational show producers adjust generic codes to the more limited language ability of younger children. When *Sesame Street,* for instance, mimics commercial programming by saying "today's show is brought to you by the letter H" and then introduces and repeats "H" words throughout the show, it is using a technique to aid children's language learning. Moreover, adjustments, such as using repeated rephrasings of novel words with referents immediately visible, are comparable to the sorts of adjustments adults make when speaking to children (Rice 1984).

Thus, it is clear that television is not just a visual medium—a visual onslaught or a string of pictures. The three representational codes of television—iconic, medium-specific forms and generic codes such as language—interact with each other to produce the television communication. Children must draw on their knowledge of each of these representational codes in order to interpret TV messages. We know from research that this "knowledge" changes as children grow older. Children's abilities to identify visual images seem to make the iconic code the easiest to interpret.

Although even here there are times when children have to learn to interpret novel images, as in the case of David's inability to distinguish between basketball and football. Medium-specific codes, many of which are probably more difficult to interpret, are nevertheless learned as children become more familiar with the nature of television production. We aren't born with the ability to understand an instant replay or flashback, but as we watch television and encounter their use we come to identify and understand their meanings. Generic codes like language are part of the child's real-world communicative experiences. What the child is learning outside of the television context can be brought to bear in interpreting television. Thus as children's language increases they can better interpret TV's language, and television can aid in their language learning.

Finally, in addition to the codes which are used to communicate television content, there are the varying sorts of content available to children on TV. Much of the content of television—the stories of dramas and comedies, the persuasive appeals of advertisements, the discourses of news programs as well as the overt educational content of public television—is novel, particularly for young children. Children not only need to learn how to decode the representation codes of television but they need to acquire an understanding of the content of television's world. Children's limited social experiences and knowledge about people and events will affect their interpretations of the media content as well as their abilities to interpret televisions codes. Collins (1982), in reviewing children's cognitive processing of television messages, for instance, notes that children's real-world social knowledge influences their abilities to comprehend television dramatic narratives. For example, 6-year-olds pay relatively little attention to romantic love scenes because they have no real-world significance for them. Not so for a 13-year-old viewer.

Across a variety of studies, evidence has accumulated that children's comprehension of television's messages—their understanding of dramatic narratives, of advertising content, and of news content—increases as children grow older. Such developmental improvements in children's comprehension ability mean that children gradually acquire the ability to comprehend television stories in an adult manner, to correctly infer character motivations, and to understand and infer the logical connection among scenes of a plot and correctly interpret the persuasive aspect of advertising appeals (see Collins, 1982 for a review). The more complex the social content depicted on television, the greater and the more abstract the representational codes used to convey that content, the greater the difficulty young children have in comprehending television.

The communicative context of children's television watching, then, refers to the constant interaction of the codes and content of television with children's interpretations of the codes and content. These elements—the child and the codes and contents of television—have been the primary focus of studies of children's processing of television (see Bryant and Anderson, 1983). Furthermore, how codes, content, and the cognitive abilities of children interact to influence how television is viewed has led to a number of developmental descriptions of *what* children attend to and *what* they understand of television's messages as they grow older. For instance, the comic book nature of *Dukes of Hazzard* is more appealing to young elementary school children than to many teenagers. On the other hand, *Hill Street Blues,* with its complex interweaving of plot, episode, and character, is beyond the understanding of younger viewers. The process of going from a regular viewer of *Sesame Street* to a fan of *Dukes of Hazzard* to a devotee of *Hill Street Blues* involves not just a maturation from 3 to 18 years. It involves *learning how* to make sense of and appreciate televisions codes and differing contents. Unfortunately, *how* children learn to interpret the codes and social content of television is not well specified in many descriptions of children and television. Getting to know television involves the *social context* of television's use and observational studies of children watching television are accumulating which suggest that the work of sense-making is often an *interpersonal process* for young viewers.

The Interpersonal Context of Television Watching

A number of studies, including laboratory studies and surveys, have demonstrated that the presence of adults in the viewing situation aids young children's comprehension of TV programs (Stevenson, 1972; Ball and Bogatz, 1971, Watkins, 1970, Calvert, Huston, and Wright, 1982; Collins, Sobol, and Westby, 1981). Stevenson (1972) suggested that adults are able to focus young children's attention on particular objects and events on a TV program. Similarly, the *Sesame Street* research (Ball and Bogatz, 1970, 1971) suggested that the greatest learning of cognitive skills from *Sesame Street* was among those preschoolers who were *encouraged during* viewing; among the children who viewed the program in small groups with monitors and observers (Ball and Bogatz, 1970, 1971; Cook, Appleton, Conner, Shaffer, Tamkin, and Weber, 1975). Although we aren't sure what the monitors said to the children, presumably they focused the young children's attention to the set and repeated or elaborated on the TV content. More recently, in laboratory studies Watkins, Calvert, Huston, and Wright (1982) and Collins, Sobol, and Westby (1981) have been able to demonstrate that when adult coviewers directly focus children's attention on implicit relationships between scenes of a plot or on scenes central to under-standing the pilot line, they can aid children's understanding and improve children's interpretation of the program.

These studies all suggest the importance of the interpersonal context of television viewing as the locus of children's learning about the medium of television. More recent observational research demonstrates that it is in-deed in interpersonal interactions with parents and siblings that children get to know television.

Ethnographic or observational data provide examples and evidence of the sort of interactions that occur in the viewing situation and how these interactions aid children's decoding of television messages. As Messaris and Kerr (1984) recently noted, global measures of parental viewing practices do not predict children's sophistication with interpreting television pro-grams. It is in the more microscopic and specific context of individual in-stances of television watching that both direct and indirect learning occurs.

One way to begin to understand how children understand television is to look at children's earliest encounters with the medium. In an often-cited study, Hollenback and Salby (1979) found evidence of babies as young as 6 to 12 months visually and vocally responding to television an average of one to two hours a day. Carew (1980) reported a developmental trend in the amount of time infants spend with television. Television was found to occupy less than 1 percent of a baby's time at 12 months, 2 percent at 18 months, 3 percent at 24 months and 8 percent at 30 months. Anderson and Lorch (1983) suggest that by 2½ years of age children are regularly watching television. And why? According to Hollenbeck and Slaby, it is visual and auditory stimulating, and infants are responsive to stimulation in their environment. In other words, infants attention is turned toward television merely because parents turn the set on.

A recent participant observational study of infants watching *Sesame Street* suggests there is complexity in toddlers' early interactions with television. Lemish (1984) conducted a year-long participant observational study of 16 familics with babies between 6½ months and 2½ years of age. In addition to observing the children watching television, she interviewed the parents about their recollection of the development of the children's interest and attention to television.

Several important observations have been made in this study. First, Lem-ish (1984) finds that toddlers who are just beginning to talk, ask to have their favorite show, typically *Sesame Street* turned on for them, or they turned it on and off by themselves. Second, she observed children in the 18- to 24-month range watching *Sesame Street* at nearly full attention for as long as 30 to 40 minutes. During these attentive moments the children sang along with the *Sesame Street* themes, pointed out characters they knew ("that's Big Bird"), pointed and labeled animals on the set ("a lamb, a dog"), and generally showed involvement and active processing of the television program. This active view of the child watching television is very much a part of developmental accounts of how children come to know television (see e.g., Anderson and Lorch, 1983). However, whereas most other attention studies have been conducted in laboratories, Lemish's study demonstrates active attention in a home-viewing context and with children much younger than previous studies suggested.

What goes on in the interactions in the viewing context? Lemish provides evidence of a considerable number of examples of imitative learning from television; toddlers learning to throw a ball after watching a baseball game on television, a 24-month-old baby trying to snap his fingers as he saw Mister Rogers do, innumerable examples of children learning numbers and concepts of big and small and letters from watching *Sesame Street*. Perhaps the most interesting evidence of the importance of television in young children's learning, both about the medium and about the world, comes from an examination of children's language learning from television.

Lemish and Rice (1984) conducted detailed analyses of how children between 6 and 30 months decoded the generic code of language on television and how television was used by the parents of these children to teach the children language. They found four main categories of children's verbalizations while watching television. Remember, they were observing babies who are just in the process of acquiring language. (1) The babies designated objects, characters, and animals on the screen such as pointing to a dog, or pointing to television characters they knew ("that's Ernie, that's Bert"). (2) The babies frequently questioned coviewing mothers about the television content. "What's Grover doing, Mommy?" asked a 20-month-old or "Where is Susan?" asked a 30-month-old as Susan was under a car and difficult to see. Mothers in the process of answering these questions help the children identify both confusing images on the set and interpret the narrative and programming content. (3) The babies frequently repeated television dialogue or parental comments about the television content such as when a 23-month-old was watching a commercial about repeating "Coke is it, coke is it, coke is it" or the 20-month-old who blurted out in the kitchen when the television was off, "Sesame Street is a production of the Children's Television Workshop." (4) Finally, Lemish and Rice report evidence of babies using language to describe the television content they are watching. Such description occurred among the children with more advanced language skills who frequently were noticed expanding and elaborating on the television content as when a 22-month-old while watching *Sesame Street* commented, "They are playing with the dog." Children were thus providing a verbal narrative of the ongoing action.

Of most importance in these studies were observations of mothers and fathers interracting with the children. Lemish and Rice (1984) call this using television as a "talking picture book." The children talk to, label, repeat, and elaborate the action on the television set. The parents encourage the children's "reading" of the television and faciliate the children's learning of language and concepts. They do this by designating objects on the set, by answering the babies' questions about what is happening on the television (Who is that? Bert or Ernie?), and by responding to the children's questions about the codes and content of television. My conversation with David at the beginning of this reading is prototypical of toddler-parent talk during TV viewing. A particularly good example of how early training about television's conventions occurs is provided by Lemish and Rice (1984) when they describe the mother of a 33-month-old child explaining the ideas of program schedules in the following interchange:

CHILD: Where did Smurfs go?
MOTHER: They are all over.
CHILD: Why?
MOTHER: They'll be back next week.
CHILD: Why?
MOTHER: Because we see them on Saturday morning.

It is clear from the observations made of toddlers that even very young children are learning to make sense of the television codes and content. Also, television is a means for parents to teach children about language and a source of information about the world. The interpersonal context within which toddlers watch television is an active and interactive one: children overtly interact with the television set as well as with their parents about the television set.

There are several other studies of older preschool and young elementary school children which demonstrate the importance of parental interaction with the television set. For instance, Messaris and Sarett (1981) noted in a study of this age group that parent-child communication involves parental interpretations of television content for the child. This is the age span that survey and experimental researchers identify as the period in which children's understanding of television advertising develops. For instace, Ward, Wackman, and Wartella (1977) suggest that the development of children's understanding that television advertising is trying to sell products (the persuasive impact of advertising messages) and, therefore, that advertisements differ from television programs (which are intended to entertain) develops during these years. Comprehension moves from rudimentary understanding of persuasive intent among preschoolers to an understanding that advertisements are trying to get you to buy products around ages 5 or 6. Some argue that true comprehension of the importance of being "wary" or "skeptical" of advertisement's claims because of the self-interest of the advertiser trying to sell his product probably doesn't develop until children acquire the ability to take the role of the other—a more general cognitive skill which develops in late childhood or after about age 10.

L. Reid (1979) conducted a study of the impact of family group interaction on children's understanding of advertising messages. He engaged in a participant observation study of nine children who ranged in age from 5 to 11 years of age.

What Reid's limited evidence (he did only observe nine children) suggests is that children, even those as young as 5, learn about the persuasive appeal of advertising and learn to distinguish advertisement claims while watching TV with their family at home. He cites the example of a 5-year-old who, while watching a commercial for a Six Million Dollar Man doll which can perform amazing feats (like Steve Austin in the program) comments, "but my Six Million Dollar Man (doll) don't do that—'cause! That's on TV. . . . That's just stuff in a commercial." Reid notes that parent's talk to the children both while watching television and in other contexts about television commercials. Parents explain how ads want you to buy their products and they comment on the truth value of the commercial claims. He notes, for instance, children asking their parents, "Can you do that in real life?" Such questions are ongoing commentaries one can observe when watching television with a young elementary or preschool child. The question itself signals a budding awareness that television is make-believe, that the visual images of television are manipulated, that they are constructed, and that television is not a representation of real life. Reid believes that young children, even 5-year-olds, understand better the purposes of advertising than is indicated by the developmental descriptions derived from interviews with such children outside the viewing situation. He argues that when you watch children watch television you observe their ongoing interpretations of the TV content, and that under such circumstances even 5-year-olds can demonstrate an understanding of the purpose of advertising. Unfortunately, Reid's observational data derive from a very small sample and they have not been demonstrated more widely. However, his evidence is not totally at odds with the developmental descriptions. The wholeness and completeness and import of the knowledge that advertisements try to sell products probably is a notion which is gradually developed as children grow older. The rudimentary understanding of the 5-year-old as demonstrated by Reid and described in the developmental literature is a less formed understanding than older children demonstrate both in and out of the viewing context. Also, as Wartella (1980) has observed, the developmental description deals with estimates of *how many* children at different ages have clear understanding: even in survey data about half of 5-year-olds were able to verbally articulate an understanding of the selling intent of commercials. But the other half were not.

Such distinguishing of different kinds of content on television continues past the age of 5. In the early elementary years children's program preferences are shifting from child-oriented shows to more adult-oriented fare, such as situation comedies and prime time programming (Comstock, Chaffee, Katzman, McCombs, and Roberts, 1978). With this shift children are exposed to social content beyond their social experiences but the ongoing desire to interpret and elaborate on the material is still present.

Two recent studies suggest that the ongoing interaction which describes how children interpret television messages occurs among siblings as well as between parents and children. Alexander, Ryan, and Munoz (1984) observed 9- and 7-year-old siblings watching television in their home over five months. They also made shorter observations of children in 24 households over a 15-week period averaging 50 hours of observation per family sibling group (either two or three siblings per household).

Their ethnographic data on siblings watching television suggest that, as with parents, siblings' ongoing interactions while watching television are important in how younger children learn about the codes and content of television. Alexander, Ryan, and Munoz analyzed the sibling talk during television watching. They observed, for instance, the majority of talking in the television context was nontelevision related talk (63.5 percent). Such talk includes discussions of planning of future events (when to eat or play) as well as comments about everyday occurrences (what happened at school). This is clear evidence that the children were not always giving their full attention to the program. But television-related talk did occur and it was patterned. Alexander, Ryan, and Munoz found three television talk categories: television characters, production conventions of the television medium, and the ongoing action.

Through a question-answer pattern of talking the younger children in the sibling pair learn to decode the messages of television with help from their older brother or sister. Children asked questions to identify television characters. "That's Dr. Strange, right? No. Odin? No, That's not Odin." Just like the toddler watching *Sesame Street,* in this case, 7-year-old children need help in identifying people and some events on television. As suggested earlier the presumably more easily interpreted iconic codes of television sometimes are ambiguous for children and they need help in identifying the visual image—particularly the people of TV programs.

Second, Alexander observed multiple instances of siblings reasoning out production and editing changes, or how things are done on television. "How do they make characters disappear?" "How does slow motion work?" She observed a sibling pair (ages 8 to 10) creating explanations of how special effects on television are created. Moreover, she observed older siblings who were more knowledgeable of programming production techniques "explaining" and "labeling" flashbacks and other special effects tricks for their younger siblings.

Third, sibling talk while watching television included discussions of how the program would unfold—"predicting" the story narrative. Siblings would frequently "guess" and talk about how they think things will happen. Children talk about the "bad guys" on television adventure shows, and how the "good guys" are likely to win, the heroes never die, and that the "good guys" are always saved in the nick of time. Children learn the patterns and conventions of television stories; things are tidy and neat on television.

Finally, there were comments about the truth of the television program. Elementary school children are uncertain about what can and can't be done on television, what is real and can happen in real life, and what is not real. A frequent comment observed was "Can you do that in real life? For real?" Alexander, Ryan, and Munoz (1984) found that siblings frequently comment about commercials, particularly about how commercials say things that aren't true. It would seem that in this age period children are acquiring the ability to distinguish the purpose of advertising messages. They are participating in ongoing discussions about the truth value of advertisements. As previous survey research indicated, skepticism about television truthfulness is highly correlated with understanding persuasive intent of commercials (Ward, Wackman, and Wartella, 1977). Indeed, understanding persuasive intent may be the result of the frequent and ongoing comments about the truthfulness of advertising.

Talk with parents and siblings is clearly the interpersonal context through which children learn to make sense of television and learn to use television to learn about the world.

Developmental studies show that children only gradually come to understand and interpret television in an adult manner. But *how* that sense making is conducted—the work of learning about television—is not *solely* the result of larger, more abstract cognitive development during childhood. It's not just that children's cognitive maturing outside of television, in school, and in other interactions affects how they interpret television. Instead, the interpersonal context of television watching and the talk that occurs there creates the context within which siblings, parents, and perhaps peers as well facilitate children's developing understanding of the medium. Children then can use the medium for acquiring knowledge about the nontelevision world.

Thus, getting to know television is the result of general cognitive development, growth in social or real world knowledge, and interpersonal experience with watching television. Talking about television leads to learning about television and the medium's messages are interpreted in a rich and varied interpersonal context.

RONALD J. FABER, JANE D. BROWN, and JACK M. McLEOD

Coming of Age in the Global Village: Television and Adolescence

Adolescence is a period of intense cognitive development, of preoccupation with future roles, and of struggles with sexual relationships. It is also a time of increased freedom of choice of media involvement. These factors, according to the authors of this essay, make adolescents' use of television a particularly important area of study. Although there is much public concern over the effects of television on very young children, little has been done to study adolescent use of the medium.

The subject of this essay is adolescent crises and tasks and the role of television in their resolution. What is discussed tells us much about how the mass media in general and television in particular affect the way individuals resolve issues related to their life stage.

Julie is a junior in high school. She is planning to take the college entrance examinations in a couple of weeks and has been studying hard in preparation for them. She becomes nervous, however, and grows increasingly unsure of her ability to score high enough to get into college. Her mother Ann, her sister Barbara, and the building superintendent Schneider are looking through college catalogues suggesting schools and potential majors for Julie. However, for Julie this only increases her fear of failing and she finally threatens them that maybe she won't go to college at all. This threat leads to an argument over the advantages and disadvantages of a college education. During the argument Julie accuses her mother of trying to run her life. She says she hasn't had time to decide what she wants to do for herself. Eventually both Julie and her mother give in a little and Julie decides to take the exams to avoid closing any options, yet does not make a commitment that she will go to college as her mother desires.

Each week, about 40 million television viewers tune in to view an episode of *One Day at a Time,* from which this storyline was taken. Each week they witness the interpersonal drama (and comedy) of a three-person household made up of a young divorced woman and her two adolescent daughters. This show, and numerous other top rated programs like it, frequently focuses on the difficult and painful problems people face in their own lives. These shows, designed primarily as entertainment, have dramatized such serious problems as death, running away from home, falling in love for the first time, and coping with the stigma of a physical handicap. Do all viewers "take away" the same information and perceptions from this viewing experience? What is it they learn from watching such shows?

In this [essay] . . . we will argue that different viewers learn different things from such portrayals of life issues. We will develop a model of assessing mass media effects which suggests that the critical factor lies not just in how the program focuses on the problem, but rather in where the individual viewer is in relation to the problem. For example, an adolescent watching the episode of *One Day at a Time* just described may focus on how Julie deals with resolving the dilemma of future educational and career choices. The adolescent might also learn more about the specific kinds of educational options Julie is considering, as well as the arguments in favor of or against going to college. On the other hand, a mother of adolescent children would probably be more interested in the dilemma Julie's mother faces: how to persuade her daughter to take the tests and not limit her future options. However, another mother whose children are grown up and is considering what to do with the rest of her life may be most sensitive to the arguments for going to college or going to work even though they are discussed by an adolescent in the television presentation. A younger viewer might be expected to find Julie's problem interesting in that it points to issues they will soon have to grapple with themselves. Perhaps yet another viewer is currently involved in an argument with his or her own parents about an entirely different topic. This viewer might be most sensitive to Julie's discussion tactics as an example of strategies that might be used with his or her own parents.

These differences in perspective or issue salience brought with the viewer to the specific content will affect what that viewer takes away from his or her exposure. A number of other factors will intervene in the process of learning from television portrayals about life issues. Some of these factors will be discussed as important to an understanding of individual differences in media effects. A viewer who has had little personal experience with a range of occupations, for example, may more readily accept the television portrayal of various occupations, while a viewer who has had personal experience with persons in the occupation will compare the television portrayal with his or her prior understanding of the occupation. An individual's ability to think abstractly or to understand the underlying roles being portrayed will also affect what is learned from the presentation. The direction and pattern of influence of other socialization agents will also influence how an individual perceives specific media portrayals.

Before describing in more detail how these factors are interrelated, we will examine the issue of central concern here: how the resolution of developmental tasks may be related to media exposure. It is our intent here to develop a research model which may account for individual differences in mass media effects. The basis of the model is that we cannot assume that the media audience is similarly motivated to attend to the same attributes of particular presentations. The audience differs on a number of factors, but a critical difference is their current set of life issues. These life issues or tasks may be linked to various stages of human development. We argue that, if we can assess the salience of these life tasks at any one point in time, we will be able to predict which aspects of the media presentation will be attended to and will affect subsequent levels of knowledge, values, and behaviors of that individual.

Although any life stage can be examined similarly, we will focus here on the adolescent life stage for three reasons. First, a number of adolescent researchers and theorists (Havighurst, 1972; Erikson, 1968) have clearly specified certain developmental tasks which most adolescents are faced with between the ages of 12 and 22. These tasks include such things as choosing an occupation and other future roles, learning how to interact with the opposite sex, developing a sex-role identity, and achieving independence from the family. Second, adolescence is a period of increased activity oriented toward gathering information about the future. Such activity should increase the importance of television as an important source of information. Third, adolescents are generally in the final stage of cognitive development, unlike younger children whose thought processes are still progressing. Thus, the behavior of adolescents is less a function of what they *can* do and more a matter of what they *actually* do. They are also a more active audience than younger children because they have more control over how their individual needs for information will be satisfied. Thus, we might expect adolescents to understand more complex portrayals and perhaps even seek out such portrayals since they are relevant to their own lives.

Developmental Task Resolution Strategies

The central elements of the research model described here are what we have called internal constraints. These are factors which are generated within the individual and are directly related to the specific tasks of the life stage. As the individual grows older and faces critical life decisions, he or she may adopt different strategies for dealing with the resolution of these life conflicts, e.g., what job to choose, what sort of political ideology to adhere to. The strategies a person develops for coping with these decisions vary along two dimensions. First, persons differ in the degree to which they have made a commitment to or personal investment in particular alternatives (choosing to be a doctor rather than a lawyer or nurse). Second, individuals differ in the degree to which this commitment (or lack of commitment) is based on active exploration of the range of alternatives. These dimensions are derived from Erikson's (1968) argument that firm commitments which are preceded by periods of crisis or consideration of alternative options are necessary conditions of successful decision-making regarding life tasks. Marcia (1966) has based a program of research on Erikson's theory. He has labeled these two dimensions of decision-making "commitment" and "crisis." By dichotomizing the dimensions, he has developed a four-fold typology which may be thought of as four different strategies of life task/conflict resolution (see Figure 1). Presence or absence of crisis and the extent of commitment in any life task serves to define the decision strategy.

The *achievement* strategy is one in which the individual has experienced a crisis period and has invested in or commited him or herself to a particular choice. The *moratorium* strategy refers to those individuals who are currently engaged in decision-making, but have not yet been able to make a commitment. Individuals who adopt a *foreclosure* strategy have not experienced a crisis but have firm, often parentally or externally imposed or determined commitments. Those with a *diffusion* strategy have almost no strategy at all. The diffusion individual is not currently involved in trying to make a decision and has not made a commitment to any alternative, unlike the foreclosure who has made a commitment, but, similarly, has not experienced crisis.

An individual may be characterized by different strategies depending on what life task is being examined. For instance, an adolescent may have successfully made a commitment to being a lawyer after many days of looking at alternative occupational choices. The person would be labeled

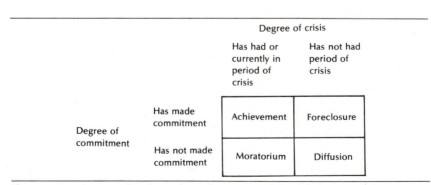

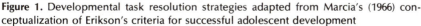

Figure 1. Developmental task resolution strategies adapted from Marcia's (1966) conceptualization of Erikson's criteria for successful adolescent development

as in an achievement strategy—having made a commitment after experiencing a crisis. At the same time, he or she may have adopted a diffusion strategy for dealing with the problem of autonomy from his or her parents. The adolescent is either comfortable in the current situation or not yet ready to cope with the anxiety of examining alternatives.

Marcia (1976) has found that decision-making strategies may also change in a rather logical sequence culminating in the achievement strategy. In a longitudinal study he found some evidence for a progression from the diffusion or foreclosure strategy to the achievement strategy through moratorium. Thus, as an adolescent moves into a period of actively seeking alternatives from which to choose (crisis) and begins to make tentative commitments (commitment), he or she moves out of the passive strategy of diffusion into moratorium. As the individual begins to firm up those commitments and narrow them down to particular, finite choices, he or she moves into the achievement strategy. The individual who begins with a foreclosure strategy (at adolescence, generally simply accepting the parents' commitments) might be pushed into a moratorium strategy by the critical change toward seeking alternatives. He or she might then conceivably get frightened by too many alternatives and either resort to the diffusion strategy or retreat back to the original foreclosure strategy. He or she could also, however, cope with the moratorium strategy of exploration of alternatives and move in the direction of adopting an achievement strategy.

Adolescent Developmental Tasks

A review of the literature on adolescent development indicates that these crises or tasks which an adolescent may be dealing with can be condensed and synthesized into five distinct areas. These tasks, in the chronological order that they are usually encountered during adolescence, are: (1) accepting changes in one's body and developing a positive body image; (2) developing more completely defined sex roles and learning about cross-sex relationships; (3) beginning to achieve economic and emotional independence (freedom from authority); (4) preparing for future occupational and family roles; and (5) developing civic competence. It is our belief that television, while not the sole socializing agent, can contribute to the way an individual resolves each of these tasks. Furthermore, we feel that Marcia's categories of decision strategies can be applied to each of the tasks to help determine what information from television will be most important to an adolescent using different decision strategies.

Body Image

The beginning of adolescence is usually defined by the onset of puberty and the development of changes in body shape (Campbell, 1969; Douvan and Gould, 1966). For girls, physical changes generally start around 10 years of age and last until 12½. For boys, the growth spurt usually starts to develop around 12 and these changes continue until approximately 14½ (Matteson, 1975; Tanner, 1964; Douvan and Gould, 1966).

These physical changes in early adolescence have been shown to affect also adolescents' attitudes toward themselves and their peers. Adolescents are highly self-conscious about their looks. Frazier and Lisonbee (1971) found that 50% of male and 82% of female adolescents were concerned about some aspect of their facial appearance. Jones and Bayley (1950) found that two-thirds of the adolescents they interviewed expressed a desire to change some component of their physique.

Physical attractiveness also seems to be an important factor in acceptance by peers during early adolescence. Research has shown that most young adolescents rate physical attractiveness as more important than similarity of ideas in choosing friends of either sex (Gronlund and Anderson, 1957; Cavior and Dokecki, 1973). These physical and attitudinal changes combine to form the first major task of adolescence—the development of a positive body image.

Entertainment television may play an important role in helping adolescents work through this task. Preadolescents and those people first entering adolescence have neither resolved nor thought much about their own concept of beauty or attractiveness. In Marcia's terms, these adolescents may be labeled as in diffusion in regard to their body image. For these people, television may serve as an informational device for learning what society's standards of beauty and attractiveness are. Television provides many examples of the ideal male and female bodies (for example, *Charlie's Angels,* a show starring three beautiful women detectives who solve cases at the direction of their unseen boss Charlie. *The Six Million Dollar Man* and the *Bionic Woman,* both shows starring physically attractive persons who have superior bionic powers which they use to solve crimes and avert disasters). These characters, representing the extreme stereotypes of masculine and feminine beauty, are often placed in action-adventure programs. Thus, not only are these characters beautiful, they also display excellent control over their bodies.

Situation comedies may also be useful to adolescents who are concerned with learning society's values of beauty. Situation comedies are more likely to provide both ideal and nonideal types. For example, *Happy Days,* a comedy set in the 1950s and centered around a middle-class American family, shows both the ideal (Fonzie) and the average (Richie, Potsie, and Ralph). *Welcome Back Kotter,* a show about a high school teacher's relationship with his class of ne'er-do-wells, provides an even greater range of examples from Vinnie Barbarino (the ideal type) to Arnold Horshack. Thus, adolescents in diffusion may learn both the ideals and the range of acceptable body types from television.

Adolescents who are already concerned with their appearance, but who have not yet decided on how they can make the most of what they have, can be described as being in moratorium. These adolescents already know what society's values are and are concerned with living up to these values or learning to accept themselves as they are. For these adolescents, television may serve to provide a different type of information. These teenagers may pay particular attention to specific attributes of a wide range of characters. For example, the hair styles of the women on *Charlie's Angels,* and *Bionic Woman,* and other characters may be compared and contrasted by these adolescents to determine which they think are the best styles and/or which would most suit them. The same thing may also be done for other attributes of attractiveness such as make-up, clothes, physical builds, and walking styles. Thus, adolescents in moratorium are likely to use television to compare specific options they have open to them and to help decide which specific characteristics will most benefit themselves.

Foreclosure and achievement adolescents have already determined how they plan to resolve this task. For these young people, television may be useful only insofar as it presents characters who exhibit the particular style the adolescent has chosen for him or herself. These characters may be attended to in order to learn more detailed information. For example, an adolescent who views himself as very similar to Vinnie Barbarino may adopt some of Vinnie's mannerisms or copy his walk. These adolescents may pick up some of the more subtle information about body image, such as the importance of self-confidence in attractiveness, from a specific character. However, characters who do not fit with the adolescent's own self image are likely to be ignored or ridiculed, especially among foreclosure adolescents.

Sex Roles
Although evidence shows that much sex-role learning has already occurred before adolescence, this is the stage during which increased awareness of the biological determinants of sex differentiated behavior and increased interaction with age mates of both sexes leads to increased pressure to conform to sex "appropriate" behaviors. Nonstereotypical sex role behaviors are frequently accepted prior to adolescence on the ground that "this is just a stage which the individual will grow out of." If the person still

wants to pursue these nontraditional behaviors into adolescence, however, they will often face ridicule from peers. This may be especially true for boys because they generally seek support from the full peer group while girls typically seek out a few close friends for support.

We assume that foreclosure is the most typical strategy for the sex role task in adolescence. Learning from parents, peers, and the media all combine to push the average adolescent toward sex-stereotyped roles before the adolescent or preadolescent has made any attempt to consider alternative forms. These adolescents will probably reject or ridicule television portrayals of nontraditional behaviors. While the vast majority of television content reinforces stereotyped behaviors, adolescents who are considering alternative roles may find their greatest (if not their only) source of support from those few, sensitively handled, nonstereotypical portrayals in the media.

Recent research on the concept of androgyny, or the blending of roles based on gender, suggests that sex roles are not a unidimensional construct. Individuals adopt patterns of behavior which are typically associated with their own gender along with attributes which have been traditionally associated with the opposite sex. Societal norms are slowly shifting toward greater acceptance of androgynous behaviors by both males and females. It appears that a greater degree of sensitivity in men and assertiveness in women, for example, is now acceptable.

These changes in societal norms may be encountered in the media before they are found among peers or parents. It is also now more acceptable for men to cry in some situations and for women to be less helpless and more athletic. Even a character who embodies the macho male toughness as much as the Fonz is now able to cry when his best friend is seriously injured. Action-adventure programs with female leads such as *Charlie's Angels* and *Wonder Woman* show women as competent and successful in difficult and dangerous situations. Women's sports have also gained greater respectability and wider television coverage. These programs may encourage women to continue in sports when they previously may have been discouraged by those around them. Television is even showing that women can compete with men in sports with programs like *Challenge of the Sexes* in which both male and female television stars compete in a variety of sports events. These shows may provide support for those adolescents currently considering what their options are as well as change the expectations and norms for younger viewers.

Another area of sex role learning which occurs during pre- and early adolescence is in regard to cross-sex relationships. Dunphy (1963), using participant observation, found that peer groups move from unisex groups to heterosexual cliques during adolescence. Those adolescents who are still in unisex peer groups and have not yet begun to date may be characterized as in diffusion on this task. These adolescents are aware that they will begin to date at some point and may be engaged in anticipatory socialization to prepare for this occurrence. Matteson (1975) has proposed that cross-sex behaviors are learned via the media before adolescence. During adolescence when sexual feelings begin to emerge, adolescents may express these feelings in the ways they have seen them portrayed on television and in films.

What an adolescent will attend to during cross-sex encounters on television may differ depending on the adolescent's own prior experiences. Preadolescents who have not started to date may be most concerned with how their same sex characters are expected to act, what one does on a date, or what the sexual expectations are. Adolescents closer to beginning to date may be more concerned with specific strategies for getting dates. Entertainment television may provide examples for these adolescents. For example, strategies for asking someone out on a date have been explored in *James at 15* (the story of a young boy's adolescence), *Happy Days,* and *Welcome Back Kotter.* The appropriateness of girls asking boys for dates has been discussed on *Laverne and Shirley* (two young working-class women on their own in the 1950s), and *One Day at a Time.* More subtle (and traditional) ways for girls to attract boys have been portrayed on *One Day at a Time, Laverne and Shirley, Three's Company* (two single women who have a male roommate), and *Rhoda* (a single, now divorced, woman on her own in New York City). Ways for women to turn down dates they do not want have also been shown on several of these shows. These portrayals may be the only way for adolescents to learn these strategies other than by trial and error. This may be especially true among males where one may feel compelled to pretend to have more experience than one does in order to obtain status within the peer group.

Television can also provide useful information to those adolescents who have already begun dating. These adolescents may use entertainment television programs to reinforce the behaviors they have already learned. Gerson (1966) found that while adolescents' use of media for norm acquisition about dating behavior is more common (42.4% report doing this sometimes or more frequently), media use for reinforcement was also fairly common (35.2%). Not surprisingly, nondaters in Gerson's study used media almost solely for acquiring norms and strategies, while those adolescents already dating reported greater usage of media for reinforcement.

Another way in which television's portrayal of cross-sex interactions can help adolescents involved in dating is by allowing them a glimpse of what life is like for the opposite sex. Girls who watch *Happy Days* or *James at 16* (the same adolescent boys one year older), for example, may be able to gain a greater understanding of the fears boys may experience in getting up the courage to ask a girl out. Similarly, boys watching shows like *One Day at a Time* may gain greater insights into adolescent girls' fears and expectations. Research studies have found that adolescent males stress eroticism over romanticism while adolescent females stress romanticism first (Ehrmann, 1959). Entertainment television may enlighten viewers of each sex about the values of the opposite sex. One episode of *One Day at a Time* recently centered around an adolescent girl's decision over which type of boy was more important to her: an attractive and popular boy who was interested in her only as a sex object versus a less physically desirable boy who was more sincere and cared for her as a person. Shows like this may help adolescents recognize these values and priorities in themselves and those around them.

Independence

Another task of adolescence is to begin to achieve emotional and economic independence from one's family. Three factors combine to make this task somewhat easier. First, strong peer groups exist during this period. During adolescence, the values of the peer group may for the first time begin to conflict with those of the family, thus giving the adolescent an alternative viewpoint (Bowerman and Kinch, 1959). Second, the adolescent is given greater opportunity to spend time outside of the home, making family relations less crucial. This also acts to prepare the adolescent for the future emotional break from home. However, studies have generally shown that adolescents use peer group norms for less important decisions such as clothing styles and music tastes, while the family's influence is still stronger for more important and long range decisions (Kandel and Lesser, 1969; Brittain, 1969). The final contributing factor is the acquisition of part-time or summer employment. These jobs make the first dent in the adolescent's economic dependence on the family.

Television may act as an anticipatory socialization agent for this task. Initially, adolescents in diffusion may be attracted to strong, independent characters who appear to have control over their own lives and successfully defy authority figures. However, as this task gains salience for adolescents and they become more concerned with actually making a break from their parents (greater crisis), the type of portrayal which is most likely to influence them changes. At this stage adolescents may attend to young adult characters on television who have or are in the process of making a break from their families. Shows like *Laverne and Shirley, Busting Loose,* and *Three's Company* show young adults out on their own for the first time, and the problems they experience.

Some programs have portrayed the difficulties in leaving home and have shown the more negative aspects of life on one's own within individual episodes. *The Waltons* (a show which portrays an extended family in rural Virginia during the Depression) showed the difficulties of the oldest son's attempt to break from home to go to college. An episode of *Happy Days* depicted Richie leaving home to live with his older brother so that he could have more freedom. *One Day at a Time* ran a four-part episode where Julie ran off to live with her boyfriend. In the last two examples, the episodes ended with the major characters returning home after discovering the problems of life on their own. This may be functional in keeping those viewers who are not yet prepared from making the break from home too soon, or it can be dysfunctional in reducing the adolescent's confidence in his or her own ability to "make it" away from the family. Either way, these shows can alert the adolescent to potential problems in making the separation, as well as provide those adolescents who have already decided with specific strategies for making the break from home.

Autonomy in decision-making is also a recurrent theme on many family dramas and situation comedies. These presentations may alert the diffusion and some foreclosure adolescents to the impending task of making a separation from parental influence. For adolescents with other decision strategies, these programs may provide specific arguments and strategies they can use to gain greater decisional autonomy from their parents. However, these shows may provide the greatest benefit to those adolescents who watch them with their parents. These programs may lead to discussions of autonomy within the context of the viewer's own family. These discussions can be brought up in a less threatening and argumentative atmosphere than might have occurred without the televised presentation. These programs and/or the ensuing discussions may also serve to alert parents to the fact that their children are growing up.

Future Roles

During adolescence the individual is expected to begin preparing for the roles he or she will take on in adulthood. One of the most important future roles the adolescent will assume is the occupational role. While some search and thought about occupations occurs in childhood, there are usually large increases on both the crisis and commitment dimensions during later adolescence in regard to occupations (Ginzberg et al., 1951).

The process of occupational choice can be divided into three distinct stages. In the first stage, the individual searches through all of the possible options. Television presentations can affect this stage of the process in two ways. Normally adolescents cannot view or even know about all the potential occupations available in a modern industrial society. Technology and societal fads can invent new jobs overnight. Many potential occupations remain unknown to the majority of the population. The media can expose some of these possibilities to the adolescent. McLuhan first suggested such a sequence when he described television as serving as a global village, showing people the options they cannot come into contact with in their own lives. Even though television has been criticized for portraying only a limited range of occupations, this range may still be broader, or at least different from, those occupations the adolescent comes in contact with in his or her own environment.

Current programs on television are also beginning to present a wider range of occupational alternatives than have existed in the past. Previously, entertainment television has been characterized as presenting only a few possibilities (primary doctors, lawyers, and police officers) primarily at the upper end of the occupational status categories (DeFleur, 1964). While these occupations are still prevalent, there is now a wider range of characters in less prestigious occupations such as a garage mechanic (Fonzie), maintenance man (Schneider on *One Day at a Time*), waitress (*Alice*), and factory workers (*Laverne and Shirley*). The middle range of occupational status positions is also represented by characters such as Archie Bunker (bar owner on *All in the Family*), Howard Cunningham on *Happy Days* and Walter on *Maude* (store owners), the characters on the *Mary Tyler Moore* show and *Lou Grant* (television and newspaper reporters, editors, and producers), Rhoda and Julie on *One Day at a Time* (designers), and Ann Romano on *One Day at a Time*, Julia and Maria on *On Our Own*, and J.J. on *Good Times* (various jobs in advertising). This list represents only major characters on long running series. The number of occupations represented by characters appearing on just one episode of a program is even greater. At this stage of occupational decision, where the adolescent is merely looking at the possible options, these one-shot appearances are just as important as characters in recurring roles.

The way in which an occupation is presented may also affect whether or not it will be considered as an option. Traditional portrayals, in terms of sex appropriateness, may cause an adolescent to close out options, while nontraditional portrayals may increase the possibilities a person will consider. For example, the depiction of Jack on *Three's Company* as studying to be a chef, or of Angie Dickinson as a police officer in the show *Police Woman*, may lead adolescents to consider sex-stereotyped jobs as open to both sexes. Additionally, if an occupation is consistently shown as being dull or undesirable, it is not likely to get much consideration. DeFleur and DeFleur (1967), for example, found that children (6–13 years old) appear able to learn the prestige of various occupations from television. High television viewers were much closer to matching the status ratings parents and experts gave for occupations highly visible on television than less frequent viewers. However, at this first stage of occupational choice, the individual is more interested in what occupations are available rather than focusing on the merits of any particular job.

The second stage of occupational choice involves narrowing down all of the potential choices to those which are most desirable. Media presentations can affect this decision process. Adolescents are generally in the formal stage of logical operations. According to Piaget, one aspect of formal operations is the ability to think in terms of abstract, hypothetical reasoning (Piaget, 1972). The individual can now integrate different pieces of information in new ways. Therefore, adolescents should be able to extract different portrayals of an occupation and mentally put them together to provide increased knowledge of the differing rewards and requirements of each job. The degree to which the individual perceives televised portrayals of these occupations as realistic will obviously play an important part in determining whether this televised information is used to narrow the possibilities. If occupational portrayals are viewed as realistic, this should result in the elimination of some of the possibilities and the enhancement of others.

The last stage in the occupational decision-making process is to narrow the alternatives even further until a final decision is made. This is the process of moving from moratorium to achievement. This requires more specific information about the rewards, routines, and requisites of each occupation, as well as an awareness of the individual's own goals and values. Because televised portrayals rarely go into extensive depth in presenting occupations, it is unlikely that television will have a very large impact at this stage. However, it is possible that some televised portrayals may aid adolescents at this stage as well as those adolescents who have already made an occupational decision (foreclosure and achievement). For these people, subtle variations in their considerations may be influential.

The brother of one of our colleagues provides an example of how these subtle considerations may work. This particular adolescent had already decided that he wanted to become a chef. Upon watching an episode of *Love Boat*, a comedy about short-term relationships evolving on short ocean cruises, he realized for the first time that chefs would be needed on ocean liners. Thus, he could combine his choice of vocation with his enjoyment of boats by seeking this type of employment. This possibility may never have occurred to him without his viewing of this program. This additional information may not seem very important to us, but could prove crucial to his future happiness.

Civic Competence
The final task of adolescence is the development of civic competence, a minimally informed participation in the affairs of the community. While

this area, like most of the others already discussed, has its foundations in childhood, change continues through late adolescence when the legal age of voting becomes imminent and community issues become more pertinent. Not only are these changes manifested by the accumulation of specific pieces of political knowledge, but later adolescence shows a difference in the frames of reference used to evaluate political action. Our political socialization research, utilizing the category system of Adelson and O'Neil (1966), found that 16 year olds compared to those three years younger saw problems of community conflict in rather different terms: they were more likely to consider future implications rather than just the present situation; they used impersonal as well as personal standards; they viewed the whole problem beyond its parts; they concentrated on the positive aspects of the situation rather than simply the negative facets; and they more often invoked a force of principle in analyzing conflict. All these attributes should affect the intake of television content.

Along with the growth in civic competence, older adolescents also begin to use the public affairs content of the media more (Jennings and Niemi, 1974; McLeod and Brown, 1976). There is also a growing awareness that the media may play an important role in developing political competence. Public affairs media use has been linked to the learning of specific information by adolescents during election campaigns (Chaffee et al., 1970), and our research also suggests that use of this type of content may develop more mature political frames of reference as well.

Information about politics and our legal system can also be gathered by watching entertainment television. Certainly the fact that most adolescents know that a person being arrested must be read their rights is a direct result of watching police programs on television. Most adolescents have never been in court yet they can pick up some information about the workings of the judicial system from shows like the *Tony Randall Show* where the main character plays a judge. However, entertainment television programs may be dysfunctional in this area by providing a distorted view of the judicial system for the sake of dramatic presentation.

Civic competence also includes developing one's own morals and values. Erikson, Marcia, and Kohlberg all discuss the period of adolescence as an important point in developing these values. Kohlberg's work (1976) in moral development shows that as a person moves through the moral judgment stages there is a change in who they consider when making a moral decision. There is a movement from an egocentric orientation to a consideration of relevant others, to a societal orientation, and finally to a prior-to-society orientation.

At the beginning of adolescence individuals are usually at stages two or three in Kohlberg's hierarchy. These stages are concerned with what relevant other people will think of the individual. At stage three, for example, people determine what is morally right on the basis of what friends and peers will think. Stage four is the beginning of a societal orientation. Here, morality is based on what the law says is right. At the end of adolescence some people may reach stage five. This stage is based on a social contract philosophy. Rules and laws are seen as necessary for a smooth running society, but they are also seen as arbitrary and changeable. There is an awareness that certain principles may be more important than specific laws. This is the first stage of the prior-to-society orientation.

Kohlberg has found that most American adults never go beyond stages three or four. Additionally, the longer a person remains at a given stage the less likely he or she is to go beyond that stage. Thus, if people are going to reach the more principled levels (stages five and six), they generally do so at the end of adolescence or early adulthood.

Entertainment television presentations of the reasoning behind the action in decision-making situations can help or hinder social development. Kohlberg and Turiel state that stage growth occurs when a person begins to see the flaws in his or her own reasoning. This causes cognitive disequilibrium, which eventually produces stage change. Lorimer (1971) has shown that exposure to films can produce these changes. He used two experimental conditions. In one, subjects were taught how to reason through dilemmas and were given opportunities to try. The second group saw the movie *Fail-Safe* and two weeks later held an informal discussion about it. A control group was also used. In a 10-day post-test the instruction group showed the greatest amount of stage increase. However, on a 50-day post-test most of these subjects reverted back to their original stage. The film group, on the other hand, had a smaller increase on the 10-day posttest, but showed even greater increase on the 50-day posttest. Puzzled by these results, Lorimer reinterviewed several of the subjects. They indicated that the training group considered the instruction like school work—something to be memorized, regurgitated, and then forgotten. Subjects who saw the movie, however, were confronted with alternative forms of reasoning which they compared to their own decisions. This led to actual disequilibrium which, in turn, led to true stage growth. Therefore, it seems that some television presentations, coupled with interpersonal communication, can lead to stage change. However, given the current television content and the time constraints for presenting decisions in depth, it seems probable that stage growth beyond the conventional level (stages three and four) is more likely to be inhibited than enhanced. Nonetheless, the present trend toward mini-series like "Roots" and "Rich Man, Poor Man" and more feature-length televised movies may allow for greater depth in presentations which could contain the type of content necessary to stimulate stage growth.

Aside from an overall moral orientation, specific values are also undergoing examination during adolescence. These specific values appear in many individual episodes of the current television shows. *One Day at a Time*, *What's Happening* (three adolescent black boys), and *Happy Days* have explored the issue of cheating in school. Lying or keeping silent to protect a friend has been dealt with on *James at 15*, *One Day at a Time*, and *Good Times* (a show depicting the life of an urban black family). Doing or not doing things which are against one's personal values for the sake of acceptance by peers has frequently been shown on shows like *James at 15*, *Good Times*, and *Eight is Enough* (a family of eight children and their parents). These are just a few of the possible examples. These programs may help adolescents to think about and clarify their own values and ethics, and eventually help them to achieve their own sense of morality.

External Constraints

Until this point we have argued that the stage of resolution and the content of the task currently being resolved by individuals will affect what kinds of effects television presentations will have on their audiences. We have generally assumed that, except for the stage of resolution of the specific task, adolescents are similar in how they will perceive television shows. But even adolescents in similar resolution stages probably do not perceive the same portrayals similarly. At least three kinds of factors intervene or serve as constraints on the linkage between developmental task resolution and the effect of exposure to television. Adolescents differ in terms of prior relevant experience with the content matter, cognitive and social abilities, and social-cultural norms. We have labeled these factors external constraints because they are external to the task resolution process. We will describe each set of external constraints in turn.

Experiential Constraints

Varying amounts and diversity of personal experience provide individuals with more or less information with which to evaluate media portrayals in relation to their own perceptions of social reality. These evaluations will play a part in determining the extent to which an individual uses media to help resolve the various life cycle tasks. Pingree (1978), for example, found that when children were told that actresses in television commercials actually hold jobs they represented in the commercials, the children showed less stereotypical attitudes than other children exposed to the same commercials.

Amount of experience is an important variable since we hypothesize that television will have a greater effect when individuals do not have personal experiences to use as a yardstick, to measure the accuracy of the television portrayal. Noble (1976) describes television as a necessary extension for learning for modern man. In village societies all potential options are available for observation within a person's everyday encounters. However, due to the complexity of modern industrial societies, many alternatives now lie outside an individual's normal experiences. Thus, television may help to provide information about these unobservable possibilities. We would expect, for example, that urban adolescents who have had relatively little opportunity to be exposed to occupations located primarily in rural areas, such as farming or taking care of animals, would attend to portrayals of such activities in a less judgmental way than rural adolescents who have had the opportunity to observe such activities first-hand.

Cognitive and Social Ability Constraints

Adolescents differ developmentally in terms of both cognitive and social skills. We have already discussed briefly how cognitive variables may limit what adolescents can take away from media exposure. These cognitive variables are important during adolescence in at least two ways. First, adolescents who have achieved a higher level of reasoning (formal operations), and thus the ability to think abstractly, would be expected to be able to take parts of different portrayals across different shows and mentally manipulate and integrate them in different applications in their own lives. Adolescents who have not achieved this more abstract reasoning ability would be less likely to be able to assimilate diverse portrayals and thus in a qualitative sense would be learning quite different things from their exposure to television. We would expect, for example, that adolescents who have not achieved formal operations would be less likely to move into the moratorium or achievement stages of task resolution since they lack the ability to integrate different pieces of information into a coherent pattern. Pre-formal-operations adolescents might be expected to accept more readily the full role portrayal rather than only certain aspects or attributes of the portrayed role.

Second, cognitive variables are important in that they serve as a constraint on an adolescent's orientation toward the future. Concrete operational individuals have been found to be primarily limited to a "here and now" orientation, rooted in the present. The development of formal operations, on the other hand, allows the person to move beyond the present to a more future planning orientation. With the onset of formal operations, the adolescent is able to project him or herself into the future and speculate what different roles might be like. Until this time television portrayals may not seem relevant except in a very specific, short-term sense.

However, in relation to some of the tasks, such as body image and interpersonal relations, the ability for future projection may not be as important as with some of the other tasks such as the development of civic competence and the selection of occupational roles, which require consideration of future, relatively unpredictable situations.

Social skills or role-taking ability may also act as a constraint on learning from the media. Generally, role-taking, or the ability to put oneself mentally in the place of the other, has been found to change with age (Selman, 1971; Flavell et al., 1968). To comprehend fully the demands and constraints on a television character, that viewer must be able to place him or herself in the character's position. This sort of comprehension is not possible until higher stages of role-taking ability have been reached. Generally, the study of role-taking has been concerned with the understanding of only one relevant constraint on another's viewpoint. However, the process of role-taking can also involve understanding multiple roles which have conflicting demands. The few studies which have investigated conflicting role presentations have found that the ability to cope with the conflicting information changes during adolescence. Gollin (1958), for example, studying how children of different ages resolve inconsistencies in role portrayals (i.e., the character is helpful in one situation and nasty in another), found that younger children (10½ year olds) focused on only one of the behaviors in describing the character. Viewers who were 13½ years old mentioned both the good and bad aspects of the behaviors, but still used only one of them in describing the character's personality. Subjects who were 16½ years old, however, were able to discuss both behaviors and to attribute motivations to account for both of them. These results have implications for both interpersonal interactions and for what an adolescent can and will comprehend in media presentations.

Persons with higher levels of role-taking ability may also be more likely to comprehend the difference between attributes of an individual character and the attributes of the role that character occupies. This is a crucial aspect of gathering accurate information about sex, occupational, and familial roles. For example, one must be able to discriminate between attributes which are due to Kojak's personality and those which are general attributes of all police officers. This ability to separate attributes allows the viewer to determine more appropriately how he or she might "fit in" to a given role. For example, in making choices about occupational roles, the adolescent must be able to match his or her own values, abilities, interests, desires, and so forth with attributes of the occupation such as the potential rewards, the requirements for entrance to the occupational category, and the various routines of the job. Without higher levels of role-taking ability, this process of objective comparison is not possible.

Societal and Cultural Constraints

Factors in the adolescent's environment may also influence to what extent media are used in task resolution and which aspects of media presentations are found relevant. Previous research on such variables as social class, family communication patterns, and degree of peer group integration has found that these factors influence both the pattern of media use and the kinds of effects exposure has on the individual.

For example, a large number of studies have found a positive relationship between an adolescent's social class standing and his or her occupational aspirations and expectations (Leifer and Lesser, 1976; Wylie, 1963). Social class has also been found to be related to patterns of media use. Greenberg and Dominick (1969) found that blacks and adolescents from lower social class backgrounds watch more television than adolescents from higher social strata. Lower income adolescents have also been found to perceive television as being more like real life than adolescents from higher income families.

A series of studies (summarized in McLeod and Chaffee, 1972) have shown that the patterns of communication emphasized in the family influence the adolescent's subsequent usage of the mass media. These studies have shown, for example, that adolescents who have been constrained by the need to maintain harmony in interpersonal communication situations are the heaviest users of television and spend the most time with entertainment rather than public affairs—oriented content on television. This suggests that adolescents learn patterns of communication from the interpersonal situation which they may then generalize to the mass communication situation as well. It also suggests that they may approach the mass communication situation with compensatory motives. For example, adolescents in families that emphasize the maintainence of harmony and discourage the exploration of controversial issues have been found to use entertainment television as a source of aggression. Here then, they may be able to find an outlet for those repressed desires they are not allowed to express in their family environment. Thus, we might expect that adolescents who approach the viewing situation with different motives as well as different communication expectations will attend to different aspects of the media content and will learn different things from the exposure.

The cultural context of the adolescent can influence the relationship between media exposure and task resolution in still another way. Television, or the media environment, is only one of a variety of sources of information about the larger social environment. As adolescents grapple with the tasks of their life stage, they are influenced not only by their parents, their teachers, and perhaps their church, but also by their age mates. Although most research on the influence of peers during asolescence suggests that parents retain their status as the more influential socialization agent, other research suggests that regardless of influence, simply the process of being involved with the peer group is an important part of adolescence. Johnstone (1974) found, for example, that adolescents who aspired to be accepted as members of specific peer groups, but were not fully integrated with the chosen group, were the heaviest viewers of television. Horrocks (1965:20) writes: "In addition to providing emotional bulwarks for the adolescent in the form of security, prestige and so on, the peer group has the further function of acting as a proving ground—a place to test oneself, to try things out, and to learn to cope with others."

Perhaps when the adolescent does not have the "security" of the peer group in which to test these things out, he or she may turn to another kind of proving ground—that of the world of television. Perhaps with television the adolescent may find learning about interpersonal relationships less threatening than in the peer group, which may ridicule or ostracize the adolescent for deviant "testing out" behaviors. Thus, we would expect to find greater use of the media for learning about things which are threatening or taboo in the peer group, as well as greater use of the media by adolescents who are not well-assimilated in the peer group with which they desire to be associated. Although somewhat less likely, adolescents may also use television as a third standard of comparison when the values proposed by their parents and friends are in conflict.

In sum, a number of other factors operate as constraints on the relationship between the adolescent and his or her use of television in the resolution of life tasks. We have discussed some which we consider most relevant. As more research in conducted on the use of television by adolescents other

External constraints	Internal constraints	Media constraints	Media uses	Effects
A. *Experiential*	Developmental task	Media content	Attributes of	A. Knowledge
B. *Cognitive and*	resolution strategy		content attended	B. Values
social abilities		(Breadth and	to and used in:	C. Behaviors
C. *Societal and*		depth of por-		
cultural	a. Diffusion	trayal of	a. Direct learning	Regarding
	b. Foreclosure	relevant task)	b. Stimulation of	developmental tasks
	c. Moratorium		fantasies	of life stage
	d. Achievement		c. Stimulation for	
			interpersonal	(in adolescence:)
			discussion/	
			consideration	a. Body image
				b. Sex role
				c. Independence
				d. Future roles
				e. Civic competence

Figure 2. Model of life-span developmental approach to mass media uses and effects

constraints will certainly emerge. At this point, however, these are some of the other factors which should be taken into account. The full research model we have been describing here is diagrammed in Figure 2.

Media Constraints

We have discussed the first two sets of constraints (internal and external) diagrammed in the model. A third set of constraints, those within the media content per se, remain. Obviously, media can be a factor in adolescent development only if portrayals relevant to life tasks are available. In our previous discussion we have provided anecdotal evidence which suggests that, at least on prime time entertainment television of recent seasons, issues centered on adolescent tasks have been portrayed. Existing content analyses of television unfortunately do not provide us with adequate information regarding the extent and diversity of such portrayals. We do not know, for example, how often and in what way issues relevant to the resolution of the task of achieving independence from the family are presented. However, we do know that, although a variety of occupations are portrayed on television, television characters are most likely to be in professional occupations and women are underrepresented in occupational roles of any kind (DeFleur, 1964). We also know that a great deal of television content is devoted to the analysis of interpersonal relationships as well as the discussion of public affairs, which suggests that television is a potential source of learning about such tasks as developing a sex role and civic competence, but also that such portrayals may be highly stereotypical or inaccurate, thus serving to limit options.

We also know, however, that television has begun to explore more taboo subjects (masturbation on *Mary Hartman, Mary Hartman*), alternative lifestyles (homosexual marriage, also on *Mary Hartman*; trans-sexualism on *Medical Center*), and nontraditional occupations (female lawyers and police officers). These presentations may broaden the range of options perceived by adolescents. In fact the media may play its most important role in presenting information about nontraditional lifestyles and options because these may be the most threatening topics for an adolescent to bring up in interpersonal communication. Their only source of information about these possibilities may be media presentations.

Television presentations may be an important factor in the resolution of life tasks for still another reason. Television presents a strong visual image of the outcomes of different problems and resolution strategies. Janis (1980) and Abelson (1976) argue that when a person has a particularly strong visual image of an upcoming event or outcome, it will exert an inordinately strong influence on their decision-making regarding that event. This visual image is called a script. Janis believes that people can easily develop personal scripts from television, because the vivid visual image is presented there for the individual. Repetition of a specific image can add to its likelihood of being adopted as a personal script. If television can facilitate the development of personal scripts, and these scripts do influence decision-making, then media content may be of central importance in resolving many of our developmental tasks.

Media Uses

The three types of constraints just discussed are expected to influence media usage. Media uses are defined here as the specific content attended to and recalled, as well as the ways in which such content is used in the process of resolving specific life tasks. We have hypothesized three ways in which television content can be used in the process of task resolution.

First, television content may be used for direct learning of information relevant to the task. Adolescents may learn directly from media presentations about societal norms and ideals of female beauty, for example, from watching televised beauty pageants or commercials for beauty products. Direct learning is likely to be most important to people who feel that their considerations about a task are likely to be ridiculed or rejected in an interpersonal communication situation. For example, adolescents who mature physically earlier than their age mates may feel embarrassed about discussing the changes in their bodies with parents or peers. Similarly, an adolescent who is considering a nontraditional sex role or occupation which does not conform to peer or parental expectations may be highly fearful of discussing these topics. Therefore, much of their learning about such topics may come from the media, which is a less threatening source of information.

Second, the media can affect the resolution of life tasks through the stimulation of fantasies. Singer (1973) has found that day-dreaming is most frequent during adolescence. Adolescent fantasies tend to focus on romance, sex, achievement, and the future. Adults, on the other hand, tend to fantasize about more concrete, real life situations (e.g., where to spend a vacation, job promotions). Because adolescents are day-dreaming about future possibilities, media content relevant to the tasks of their life stage may act as a springboard for these fantasies.

Third, media content may serve as a stimulus for interpersonal discussion and consideration of options relevant to the issues of adolescence. Television has been found to be a topic of conversation in interpersonal communication between adolescents and their parents and friends (Foley, 1968; Lyle and Hoffman, 1972). Television presentations may help to raise subjects which might otherwise be hard to bring up. It may also be less threatening to discuss these issues in terms of the television character rather than as directly relevant to one's own self.

Media Effects

Finally, the model predicts that each of the constraint sets as well as the uses made of the media content (generation of fantasies, interpersonal communication, direct learning) will affect knowledge, values, and behaviors regarding each of the life tasks. We hypothesize that adolescents will gain information about the task area, will learn and apply new values, and finally will exhibit patterns of behavior based, at least in part, on observation of media presentations. Changes in knowledge should occur all during the task-resolution process. Changes in basic values and behaviors are more likely to occur at the point of reaching stable achievement on the task, although some exhibition of different behaviors may occur during periods of experimentation with various options (e.g., wearing make-up for a period of time to see what it looks like because women on television wear make-up).

We have presented a rather speculative look at how the mass media in general and television content in particular may affect how individuals resolve issues related to their stage in the life cycle. The focus has been on the adolescent life stage as an example of how this model may be applied. We believe this model provides a useful framework for a better understanding of the effects of the mass media on individuals.

NANCY WOOD BLIESE

Media in the Rocking Chair: Media Uses and Functions Among the Elderly

Have you thought about getting old? Do you picture the aged "you" surrounded by family and friends or alone in a room with a television set? It
cannot be denied that we all age and that an increasing proportion of our
society falls into the "aged" category each year. The United States Census
Bureau states, in its latest report, that the number of Americans sixty-five
years of age and older doubled between 1950 and 1980. Nancy Bliese has
been involved in ongoing research on the elderly and their changing cognitive and communicative patterns. This essay presents her findings on how
the elderly use the media.

   After reading the essay, reflect upon your image of the elderly and evaluate
your present media patterns. Are your media uses different than those of the
elderly interviewed in this study? In what ways do you expect your media
involvement to change as you join the ranks of the elderly?

Irma watches a lot of television. Her "friends" are the hosts of game and
talk shows and the characters on soap operas. She writes long letters to
her favorites, speaking to them as though the friendship were a mutual
and longstanding one, and speaks to her acquaintances of these people at
great length and using a familiar tone. One might say she has lost touch
with reality. Sarah, on the other hand, has little time for television. She
usually watches one or two programs a day, which she chooses for their
informative or cultural enrichment characteristics. She says that she is too
busy to bother watching "trash" programs, and she is right. She has a very
busy schedule of volunteer work during the day and her evenings are spent
catching up on correspondence with friends, doing necessary housework,
engaging in her hobby of needlepoint, or curling up with a good book.
Both of these women are real, though their names have been changed to
protect their identities. One of them is forty-two years old, the other is
eighty-four. Which is which?

   If you guessed that Sarah is the elderly person, you chose correctly. Yet
Irma more nearly fits our stereotypes about elderly persons and their uses
of media. As you read this article, you will find out more about the myths
and realities surrounding media use by elderly persons. The myths come

from a number of sources including the media themselves and, unfortunately, some scholarly literature. The realities come from interviews with 214 individuals over age seventy and from twelve panel interviews with groups of eight to thirteen men and women over age sixty-five. The sample includes persons from both urban and rural environments, from all levels of the socioeconomic spectrum, and from several different cultural backgrounds. It also includes both homebound elderly and persons who are able to get about freely. It does not include any persons living in nursing homes, because the small proportion of the elderly population living in nursing homes (about 5 to 10 percent) is not representative of the elderly population in general.

Defining Media

Defining mediated communication is a problem. Just as Gumpert and Cathcart say that, "Every type of human communication . . . is still basically an interpersonal communicative act,"[1] it is equally possible to define every human communication act as being mediated. It is probably more appropriate to speak of degrees of mediation than to draw a black-and-white distinction between mediated and unmediated communication. Even a face-to-face interaction between two people, probably the most unmediated form of communication, is affected by such physical factors as distance and ambient noise levels. The more removed the source from the receiver and the smaller the possibilities for feedback, the greater the amount of mediation.[2]

Rather than pursue an exact definition of mediated communication, an exercise with a high probability of failure, let us instead talk about the behaviors that were surveyed and the relationships among them. In the individual interviews the respondents were asked about a wide range of communication activities including face-to-face interaction, attendance at meetings, use of radio and television, use of the telephone and citizen's band radio, and use of both printed and personal written communications such as books, magazines, newspapers, and personal cards and letters. In the panel (or group) interviews, most of the time was spent on uses of mass media such as television, radio, and various print media. The results of these interviews, as you will see, show that some of the popular beliefs about the uses and functions of media among elderly persons are true, some are questionable, and some are plainly wrong.

Old People and the Media

The first thing that we learned about old people and the media is that making generalizations is almost impossible. The elderly differ widely in their uses of media and in the functions that those uses serve. Some older persons, like Sarah, are so busy that they do not have much time for television or other media use; others, especially the homebound, use media to fill time. The range of types of media used, functions of those uses, and amount of usage seems to be very similar to the range for all adults over age thirty-five. While the variety is about the same, the intensity or amount of uses varies considerably from that of younger adults and the distribution of use is different. (For example, older people tend to read fewer newspapers because more of them have problems of either eyesight or budget that limit this activity.)

The interviews indicate that there are several categories of media usage. The functions served by the categories are the same as those for the general population, but a particular function may take on more or less importance as a person ages. The categories are not listed in order of importance. You must also understand that they were derived from the answers to open-ended interview questions rather than being given as a checklist. The latter method might have been an easier way to gather data, but it could have left out some important uses that would not have occurred to us in creating the questionnaire. The ten functions, each of which will be discussed individually, are:

(1) To supplement or substitute for interpersonal interactions
(2) To gather content for interpersonal interactions
(3) To form and/or reinforce self-perceptions and to gather information about societal perceptions of various groups of people
(4) To learn appropriate behaviors (including age-appropriate ones)
(5) For intellectual stimulation and challenge (e.g., game shows)
(6) As a less costly substitute for other media (e.g., television news instead of a newspaper)
(7) For networking and mutual support
(8) For self-improvement (e.g., exercise programs, language lessons)
(9) For entertainment
(10) For "company" and safety.

Below we define each of these functions and talk about their relative importance to the elderly.

To supplement or substitute for interpersonal interaction. Two of the most individuous hypotheses regarding use of media by the elderly are the disengagement hypothesis[3] and the substitution hypothesis[4] The disengagement hypothesis holds that it is inevitable that older persons will desire to disassociate themselves from increasingly larger portions of their environments. The consequence of this desire for disengagement is withdrawal from both social interaction and exposure to other sources of stimulation, including the media. Fortunately, even before the present study was done the disengagement hypothesis had come into considerable question.[5] Our study shows these doubts to have been valid. Not one of our subjects *desired* disengagement, though a few had even become "de facto" disengaged because of psychological trauma. All of these people wished that they had the ability to interact with others.

Disengagement implies lack of psychological ability to interact. Isolation implies lack of others with whom to interact. Many of our subjects were isolated to some degree. In fact, some could be classified as quite isolated (one to two face-to-face interactions per month). Both they and the disengaged subjects partially confirmed the substitution hypothesis. This hypothesis says that older persons will tend to substitute mass media communication for interpersonal communication when the latter is unavailable or extremely difficult. Eighty-nine percent of our subjects engaged in substitution all or part of the time. Forty percent used substitution occasionally (during illness, when friends or relatives were away); 32 percent used it moderately (to compensate for loneliness created by the deaths and moves of friends and relatives rather than making new friends); and 17 percent used it extensively (mass media were almost a total replacement for interpersonal contact). Most of this last group were homebound; however, most of the homebound persons in our sample used substitution only occasionally or moderately. In other words, most of the homebound persons dealt with their situations by having friends come in or by visiting on the telephone. If the telephone is classified as a substitution, which it is not in the original literature on the hypothesis, then all of our subjects used substitution to some degree. However, as we will see later, it seems more appropriate to treat telephoning separately.

Several studies have indicated that substitution increases life satisfaction.[6] While it is probably true that persons who use substitution are more satisfied than those who use absolutely none, it is also true that 93 percent of our subjects who found themselves forced to substitute mass media communication for interpersonal communication were moderately to extremely dissatisfied with the substitution. Their attitudes are summarized by one homebound woman, age ninety-three, who said: "I watch a lot of television and listen to the radio because I have no one to talk to. All my friends are dead and the relatives I have left don't care. But every time I turn the set on it reminds me that I have no one and that is very depressing. Sometimes I don't bother because I don't want to be reminded of my situation." [7] When we measured life satisfaction in a subsample of two groups of homebound persons that were matched for amount of face-to-face and telephone contact, we did not find a significant correlation between amount of mass media use and satisfaction. Thus, our conclusion is that while it is certainly true that mass media use is substituted for direct interpersonal interaction, the substitution is far from satisfying.

To gather content for interpersonal interactions. This was a rather surprising use of media. It did not occur to us before beginning the interviews. However, 43 percent of our sample volunteered that they used television, radio, and newspapers in this way. Both specific and general information-gathering were used. About 29 percent of the sample mentioned watching specific programs that their friends also watched so that they could use the program as a topic of conversation. Forty percent also mentioned general information-gathering (e.g., "I like to keep up with the news so I won't seem stupid."). The total is more than 43 percent because many people engaged in both specific and general information-gathering.

Self and societal perceptions. There is considerable literature that shows that television is an important influence on our perceptions of ourselves and on our understanding of societal stereotypes and opinions.[8] Though no one in the sample mentioned watching television or using any other medium intentionally for this purpose, almost everyone mentioned the impact of media portrayals on their own behaviors and opinions. Many also mentioned a great deal of irritation at the negatively stereotypic portrayals of older persons in both electronic and print media. They were particularly displeased by the portrayals of older people in commercials and print advertisements. One man, age eighty-four, said: "To see the ads on TV these days a body would think that old folks spend all their time worrying about constipation, loose dentures, and arthritis. And look at that old geezer on the [name deleted] lemonade commercial! They make him out to be deaf and stupid, besides. The whole thing gives old people a bad name."[9] In the panel interviews we talked about whether media portrayals affected the participants' views of themselves and their reactions toward others. Everyone agreed that with few exceptions the effect on their own self-images was negative, something to be overcome. When asked what they would like to see more of in the media, the second choice (after less sex and violence) was more programs specifically for and about old people and more realistic portrayals of the elderly in other programming. In general, both the panels and the individual interviewees felt that the negative stereotype of the elderly presented in the media reflected a societal opinion that older people were useless, infirm, crochety, senile, and a burden. Unless evidence to the contrary is given, most feel that younger people have such attitudes toward them as individuals and behave accordingly. This may lead to a sort of self-fulfilling prophecy in which escalating degrees of negative feelings are displayed between the generations.

Learning appropriate behaviors. This function is related to those discussed in the previous section. Whenever we are called upon to learn new roles, we gather information from a variety of sources. The media, both print and electronic, certainly serve this function for older persons. Seventy-three percent of the respondents said that they follow advice given in the print and electronic media regarding appropriate role behavior (e.g. how to be a good mother-in-law), etiquette, and relations toward others. The problem with following such advice is that the youth-oriented bias mentioned in the previous section may lead to inappropriate behavior and/or interpersonal discomfort. Even though senior citizens find this situation obnoxious, they may follow the models or advice given for lack of more appropriate options.

Intellectual stimulation and challenge. This was another surprising finding. Seventy-six percent of the respondents said that they watch game shows requiring skill or memory in order to challenge themselves. In other words, they play against the players. In general, they find harder games more desirable and prefer not to watch games in which the primary element is luck. They believe that engaging in the mental exercise provided by difficult games preserves intellectual functions. Thirty-eight percent of the sample also work crosswords, acrostics, or other word games at least twice a month for the same reason. Still others work mathematical puzzles, play postal chess, or see Shakespeare to "keep the brain working." There is a very great fear among older people of losing their mental faculties. There is no scientific evidence to indicate that any of the activities mentioned serve a prophylactic function, but there is a widespread belief among the elderly that they do.

As a less costly substitute for other media. One thing that elderly persons have in common with young people is that both groups usually have to function on relatively strict budgets. Among the economies mentioned, the most common was "waiting until the movie comes on television." For the older person in the city this action serves a double function—economy and safety. However, this particular economy is practiced in rural areas with approximately the same frequency as it is in the city. In addition, 56 percent of the sample said that television and the very inexpensive or free entertainments provided by senior centers, religious groups, museums, and the like constituted their *only* forms of entertainment. Other economies included using television and radio news as a cheaper substitute for a daily newspaper, watching public television instead of going to a live performance ("Live from Lincoln Center" appears to be quite popular), writing letters instead of telephoning, and (mostly in the city) taking advantage of free films offered by various groups. There is often an effort to economize even on those media for which one pays by exchanging printed matter with friends, taking advantage of senior citizen discounts, and using libraries and public reading rooms instead of buying books and newspapers.

For networking and mutual support. Though the telephone is a less immediate form of communication than face-to-face conversation, it plays an important role in the lives of the elderly. Unlike substitution of mass media for interpersonal communication that most of the people surveyed found to be unsatisfactory, 97 percent thought that telephone conversations were as good as or better than face-to-face interaction. Eighty-eight percent of the sample participated in some form of formal or informal telephone networking system designed to check to see whether people are in good health. One of these involved no actual interaction. If the person picked up the telephone after three rings and immediately hung up, that was the signal that all was well. Most of the networks involve extensive communication among the members. Thus they serve the functions of friendship and support as well as giving the reassurance that someone will check regularly to see that each person is alive and well. Though there has been no previous research to document whether telephone conversations serve the same functions as personal visits in maintaining cognitive function and psychological health, there is good reason to suppose that they would, at least if supplemented with occasional personal visits.[10] The primary ingredients necessary to maintaining cognitive function and psychological health are feedback and emotional support. Both of these functions are served by the telephone. As mentioned earlier, some older people actually prefer telephone visits to personal ones because telephone conversations do not require dressing, house-cleaning, getting out of bed, or providing refreshments. There is also less feeling of obligation because a telephone call is perceived as requiring less effort on the part of the caller than a personal visit. Of course, no one indicated a desire to completely replace personal interactions with telephone visits, but almost everyone felt that a telephone call was as good or better than a visit in many cases. Everyone interviewed indicated that the telephone was crucial to feeling secure and independent and it appeared that almost everyone would give up nearly every other convenience and necessity before giving up the telephone if economy measures were necessary. In fact, such is the fear among the elderly that they will become ill out of reach of the telephone that those who are able to afford it have one in each room or a cordless portable model. One popular device is a battery-operated medallion that will ring "911" when a button is pressed.

For self-improvement. Our culture instills in us the value of constant self-improvement. This is no less true among elderly persons than among other groups. In fact, they may have a greater need to engage in activities that lead to self-improvement because they do not have the excuse of too much work to assuage their guilt. Almost everyone in the sample engaged in hobby, volunteer, self-improvement or other "work." Twenty-one percent of the sample used television or radio self-improvement programs for purposes of maintaining health (mainly exercise programs) or learning something (cooking, a language, carpentry, gardening). Thirty-nine percent used print media for systematic learning or self-improvement. A part of this thirty-nine per cent overlaps the 21 percent who used television and radio, but a total of 51 percent of the entire sample used identifiable media sources for self-improvement of some sort. In addition, a large number of people—about 62 percent of the sample—regularly listened to phonograph or tape recordings of music or other materials for purposes of learning something or improving themselves in some way and 12 percent of the sample had made a telephone call to a tape-recorded medical information library in the previous year.

For entertainment. Everyone in the sample used media for entertainment at rates which ranged from twice per week to almost constantly. From the participation figures given by the subjects, it seems reasonable to believe that some of what was listed as "pure entertainment" had already been listed elsewhere (gathering content for interpersonal interactions, self-improvement, etc.) by the coders because some of the busier subjects seem to have had no room for sleeping and eating in their schedules. This category was originally meant to reflect recreational communication, but it seems to have been contaminated along the way. Despite this problem in coding, it seems reasonable to conclude that elderly people, like everyone else, spend a certain amount of time using the media recreationally. For the same reasons that differences occur among younger adults—cultural values, time taken by other activities, psychological needs, and so on—there is a wide range in recreational activity levels.

For "company" and safety. All of our subjects lived alone in their own homes or apartments. Thus it is not surprising that, like younger people, many of them play the television, radio, or phonograph so that they will not seem so "alone" in the house. Fifty-four percent of the sample used the media for "company" at least part of the time. We have not been able to find any corresponding data for younger adults, but the fact that most who used media in this way said that they had either done it all their lives or at times when they had been alone would lead us to believe that such usage by younger people would be similar. For some reason, 34 percent of our sample (some overlap with the "company" figures) also believed that having the television or radio on gave them an additional measure of safety from intruders when they were in the house alone. Police have indicated to us that while additional protection from intruders is afforded by playing a radio or television when one is away because it makes the dwelling seem to be occupied, there is no extra protection if someone is already in the house.[11] Perhaps the sounds make these people (mostly women) feel less alone, or perhaps they have misunderstood the police advice about home protection, but for some reason they feel safer if the television or radio is playing.

Content Preferences of Older Persons

Although the kinds of media use by older people are similar to uses found among younger groups, their content preferences are markedly different. Nearly everyone in our sample felt that there was too much explicit sexual activity (some of what they defined as explicit is defined as innuendo by others) and too many "dirty" jokes on prime time television and in films. Ninety-four percent of the sample expressed disapproval of such television programs as "Three's Company," "Charlie's Angels," "Mork and Mindy," "M.A.S.H.," and other popular programs. Many of them watched the soap operas but tended to think that they had "gone downhill since they started to get dirty." Approximately 15 percent refused to watch soap operas any longer, though they had been ardent fans at one time, because of the increased explicitness and sexuality. They tended to prefer dramas with little sex or violence and bland humor such as "Little House on the Prairie" or "The Waltons." Lawrence Welk's musical show was also a great favorite. In short, the older audience is much more conservative about sex and somewhat more conservative about violence than the younger generation.

Conclusions

The catalogue of media uses and functions is the same for both older and younger adults. The primary differences occur in the relative importance of the various uses and in preferred content for such media as radio, television, and films. But to describe the similarities and differences in use between older and younger generations is not to tell the whole story. The media serve as a source of both the substance and the form of our interpersonal interactions. Our only other models are our own and others' real-life interactions. It would be very tidy if the media and real-life models did not interact. But they do. Each modifies the other in innumerable and not easily definable ways.

We cannot blame the media for our dread of growing old. That dread has led many persons to risk life and limb in search of a "Fountain of Youth." We can ask the media to present old age realistically—neither ignoring it, nor debasing it, nor glorifying it. We can also ask the media to serve the needs of the older population more adequately than they are now doing. Currently most prime-time programming has been aimed at the magical eighteen to thirty-four-year age group, which advertisers are only now beginning to realize is rapidly shrinking in both numbers and monetary resources.[12] As the older groups grow in numbers and monetary resources, advertisers may begin to listen to their demands and the balance may be restored. Then the media and real-life interactions may become reasonably similar in substance and form. At least one can hope.

Notes

1. Gary Gumpert and Robert Cathcart, eds., *Inter/Media: Interpersonal Communication in a Media World.* New York: Oxford University Press, 1979, p. 154.
2. The idea of degrees of mediation is suggested by many perceptual psychologists; see Fritz Heider, *The Psychology of Interpersonal Relations,* New York: John Wiley, 1957; and by media specialists; see Wilbur Schramm, "Channels and Audiences," in Ithiel de Sola Pool, et al., eds., *Handbook of Communication,* Chicago: Rand McNally, 1973.
3. E. Cumming and W. E. Henry, *Growing Old.* New York: Basic Books, 1961.
4. M. J. Graney and E. E. Graney, "Communications Activity Substitutions in Aging," *Journal of Communication,* 1974, 24(4), 88–96.
5. There are many problems with disengagement theory. Several articles surrounding the issue appear in L. R. Goulet and P. B. Baltes, eds., *Life Span Developmental Psychology: Research and Theory,* New York: Academic Press, 1970.
6. M. J. Graney, "Happiness and Social Participation in Aging," *Journal of Gerontology,* 1975, 30, 701–706.
7. Interview with subject #17336, October, 1980, New York, N.Y.
8. For a good review of this literature see Melvin DeFleur and Edward Dennis, *Understanding Media,* Chicago: Scott-Foresman, 1981.
9. Interview with subject #22748, December, 1980, New York, N.Y.
10. The same interviews that served as the basis for the study reported here also included a number of tests of cognitive functioning and questions about direct interpersonal communication levels. The results of these questions indicate that cognitive functioning level and psychological well-being are strongly associated with levels of feedback and support.
11. Personal communication, Senior Citizen Protection Program, New York City Police Department, May, 1981.
12. "Oldsters Grow More Numerous," *Active Aging,* Wichita, Kansas: Wichita State University, May, 1981, p. 4.

MICHAEL NOVAK

Television Shapes the Soul

This essay makes two points: (1) that television affects our perception of reality and (2) that television effects spring from a "class bias." Michael Novak points out a fascinating but often overlooked point about the television industry: that the writers, producers, network executives and others in positions of authority represent the ten percent of our population who have had four or more years of college. They are the intellectual elite. He believes that this educated, affluent and, for the most part, liberal elite is imposing its perceptions and values on the rest of society. Even though you might not agree with Novak, depending on the motives you attribute to those who produce television, you will have to admit that it is not the uneducated who have control of the electronic media. Read the Chesebro article on values and popular TV series to see how values are manipulated through television.

For twenty-five years we have been immersed in a medium never before experienced on this earth. We can be forgiven if we do not yet understand all the ways in which this medium has altered us, particularly our inner selves, the perceiving, mythic, symbolic—and the judging, critical—parts of ourselves.

Media, like instruments, work "from the outside in." If you practice the craft of writing sedulously, you begin to think and perceive differently. If you run for twenty minutes a day, your psyche is subtly transformed. If you work in an executive office, you begin to think like an executive. And if you watch six hours of television, on the average, every day . . . ?

Innocent of psychological testing and sociological survey, I would like to present a humanist's analysis of what television seems to be doing to me, to my students, to my children, and, in general, to those I see around me (including those I see on television, in movies, in magazines). My method is beloved of philosophers, theologians, cultural critics: try to *perceive,* make *distinctions, coax into the light* elusive movements of consciousness. It goes without saying that others will have to verify the following observations; they are necessarily in the hypothetical mode, even if some of the hypotheses have a cogency that almost bites.

Two clusters of points may be made. The first, rather metaphysical, concerns the way television affects our way of perceiving and approaching reality. The second cluster concerns the way television inflicts a class bias on

From *Television as a Social Force,* Praeger Special Studies, 1975. Copyright © 1975 by the Aspen Institute for Humanistic Studies. Reprinted by permission of Michael Novak and the Aspen Institute for Humanistic Studies.

the world of our perceptions—the bias of a relatively small and special social class.

Television and Reality

Television is a molder of the soul's geography. It builds up incrementally a psychic structure of expectations. It does so in much the same way that school lessons slowly, over the years, tutor the unformed mind and teach it "how to think." Television *might* tutor the mind, soul, and heart in other ways than the ways it does at present. But, to be concrete, we ought to keep in view the average night of programming on the major networks over the last decade or so—not so much the news or documentaries, not so much the discussions on public television or on Sundays, not so much the talk shows late at night, but rather the variety shows, comedies, and adventure shows that are the staples of prime-time viewing. From time to time we may allow our remarks to wander farther afield. But it is important to concentrate on the universe of prime-time major network programming; that is where the primary impact of television falls.

It is possible to isolate five or six ways in which television seems to affect those who watch it. Television series represent genres of artistic perfomance. They structure a viewer's way of perceiving, of making connections, and of following a story line. Try, for example, to bring to consciousness the difference between the experience of watching television and the experience of learning through reading, argument, the advice of elders, lectures in school, or other forms of structuring perception. The conventions of the various sorts of television series re-create different sorts of "worlds." These "worlds" raise questions—and, to some extent, illuminate certain features of experience that we notice in ourselves and around us as we watch.

Suppose that you were a writer for a television show—an action-adventure, a situation comedy, even a variety show. You would want to be very careful to avoid "dead" spots, "wooden" lines, "excess" verbiage. Every line has a function, even a double or triple function. Characters move on camera briskly, every line counts, the scene shifts rapidly. In comedy, every other line should be a laugh-getter. Brevity is the soul of hits.

Television is a teacher of expectations; it speeds up the rhythm of attention. Any act in competition with television must approach the same pace; otherwise it will seem "slow." Even at an intellectual conference or seminar we now demand a swift rhythm of progressive movement; a leisurely, circular pace of rumination is perceived as less than a "good show."

But not only the pace is fast. Change of scene and change of perspective are also fast. In a recent episode of *Kojak,* action in three or four parts of the city was kept moving along in alternating sequences of a minute or less. A "principle of association" was followed; some image in the last frames of one scene suggested a link to the first frames of the new scene. But one scene cut away from another very quickly.

The progression of a television show depends upon multiple logics—two or three different threads are followed simultaneously. The viewer must figure out the connections between people, between chains of action, and between scenes. Many clues are *shown,* not *said.* The viewer must detect them.

The logic of such shows is not sequential in a single chain. One subject is raised, then cut, and another subject is picked up, then cut. Verbal links—"Meanwhile, on the other side of the city . . ."—are not supplied.

In teaching and in writing I notice that for students one may swiftly change the subject, shift the scene, drop a line of argument in order to pick it up later—and not lose the logic of development. Students understand such a performance readily. They have been prepared for it. The systems of teaching which I learned in my student days—careful and exact exegesis proceeding serially from point to point, the careful definition and elucidation of terms in an argument and the careful scrutiny of chains of inference, and the like—now meet a new form of resistance. There has always been resistance to mental discipline; one has only to read the notebooks of students from medieval universities to recognize this well-established tradition of resistance. But today the minds and affections of the brighter students are teeming with images, vicarious experiences, and indeed of actual travel and accomplishments. Their minds race ahead and around the flanks of lines of argument. "Dialectics" rather than "logic" or "exegesis" is the habit of mind they are most ready for. I say this neither in praise nor in blame; pedagogy must deal with this new datum, if it is new. What are its limits and its possibilities? What correctives are needed among students—and among teachers?

The periodization of attention is also influenced by the format of television. For reasons of synchronized programming the ordinary television show is neatly divided into segments of approximately equal length, and each of these segments normally has its own dramatic rhythm so as to build to dramatic climax or sub-climax, with the appropriate degree of suspense or resolution. Just as over a period of time a professor develops an instinct for how much can be accomplished in a fifty-minute lecture, or a minister of religion develops a temporal pattern for his sermons, so also the timing of television shows tutors their audience to expect a certain rhythm of development. The competitive pressures of television, moreover, encourage producers to "pack" as much action, intensity, or (to speak generally) entertainment into each segment as possible. Hence, for example, the short, snappy gags of *Laugh-In* and the rapid-fire developments of police shows or westerns.

Character is as important to successful shows as action; audiences need to "identify" with the heroes of the show, whether dramatic or comic. Thus in some ways the leisure necessary to develop character may provide a counter-tendency to the need for melodramatic rapidity. Still, "fast-paced" and "laugh-packed" and other such descriptions express the sensibility that television both serves and reinforces.

Television tutors the sensibilities of its audience in another way: it can handle only a limited range of human emotions, perplexities, motivations, and situations. The structure of competitive television seems to require this limitation; it springs from a practiced estimation of the capacity of the audience. Critics sometimes argue that American novelists have a long tradition of inadequacy with respect to the creation of strong, complicated women and, correspondingly, much too simple and superficial a grasp of the depths and complexities of human love. It is, it is said, the more direct "masculine" emotions, as well as the relations of comradeship between men, that American artists celebrate best. If such critical judgments may be true of our greatest artists working in their chosen media, then, a fortiori, it is not putting down television to note that the range of human relations treated by artists on television is less than complete. The constraints under which television artists work are acute:the time available to them, the segmentation of this time, and the competitive pressures they face for intense dramatic activity. To develop a fully complicated set of motivations, internal conflicts, and inner contradictions requires time and sensitivity to nuance. The present structure of television makes these requirements very difficult to meet.

This point acquires fuller significance if we note the extent to which Americans depend upon television for their public sense of how other human beings behave in diverse situations. The extent of this dependence should be investigated. In particular, we ought to examine the effects of the growing segregation of Americans by age. It does not happen frequently nowadays that children grow up in a household shared by three generations, in a neighborhood where activities involve members of all generations, or in a social framework where generation-mixing activities are fairly common. I have many times been told by students (from suburban environments, in particular) that they have hardly ever, or never, had a serious conversation with adults. The social world of their parents did not include children. They spent little time with relatives, and that time was largely formal and distant. The high schools were large, "consolidated," and relatively impersonal. Their significant human exchanges were mostly with their peers. Their images of what adults do and how adults think and act were mainly supplied by various media, notably television and the cinema. The issue such comments raise is significant. Where *could* most Americans go to find dramatic models of adult behavior? In the eyes of young people does the public weight of what is seen on television count for more than what they see in their private world as a model for "how things are done"? Indeed, do adults themselves gain a sense of what counts as acceptable adult behavior from the public media?

If it turns out to be true that television (along with other media like magazines and the cinema) now constitutes a major source of guidance for behavior, to be placed in balance with what one learns from one's parents, from the churches, from one's local communities, and the like, then the range of dramatic materials on television has very serious consequences for the American psyche. While human behavior is to a remarkable extent diverse and variable, it tends to be "formed" and given shape by the attraction or the power of available imaginative materials: stories, models, symbols, images-in-action. The storehouse of imaginative materials available to each person provides a sort of repertoire. The impact of new models can be a powerful one, leading to "conversions," "liberations," or "new directions." The reservoir of acquired models exerts a stong influence both upon perception and upon response to unfamiliar models. If family and community ties weaken and if psychic development becomes somewhat more nuclearized or even atomized, the influence of television and other distant sources may well become increasingly powerful, moving, as it were, into something like a vacuum. Between the individual and the national source of image-making there will be little or no local resistance. The middle ground of the psyche, until recently thick and rich and resistant, will have become attenuated.

The point is not that television has reached the limit of its capacities, nor is it to compare the possibilities of television unfavorably with those of other media. It is, rather, to draw attention to television as it has been used in recent years and to the structures of attention that, by its presentations, it helps to shape.

The competitive pressures of programming may have brought about these limits. But it is possible that the nature of the medium itself precludes entering certain sorts of depths. Television may be excellent in some dimensions and merely whet the appetite in others.

Television also seems to conceive of itself as a national medium. It does not favor the varieties of accent, speech patterns, and other differences of the culture of the United States. It favors a language which might be called "televisionese"—a neutral accent, pronunciation, and diction perhaps most closely approximated in California.

Since television arises in the field of "news" and daily entertainment, television values highly a kind of topicality, instant reflection of trends, and an effort to be "with it" and even "swinging." It values the "front edge" of attention, and it dreads being outrun by events. Accordingly, its product is perishable. It functions, in a way, as a guide to the latest gadgets and to the wonders of new technologies, or, as a direct contrary, to a kind of nostalgia for simpler ways in simpler times. Fashions of dress, automobiles, and explicitness "date" a series of shows. (Even the techniques used in taping shows may date them.)

Thus television functions as an instrument of the national, mobile culture. It does not reinforce the concrete ways of life of individual neighborhoods, towns, or subcultures. It shows the way things are done (or fantasized as being done) in "the big world." It is an organ of Hollywood and New York, not of Macon, Peoria, Salinas, or Buffalo.

I once watched television in a large hut in Tuy Hoa, South Vietnam. A room full of Vietnamese, including children, watched Armed Forces Television, watched Batman, Matt Dillon, and other shows from a distant continent. Here was their glimpse of the world from which the Americans around them had come. I wanted to tell them that what they were watching on television represented *no place,* represented no neighborhoods from which the young Americans around them came. And I began to wonder, knowing that not even the makers of such shows lived in such worlds, whose real world does television represent?

There are traces of local authenticity and local variety on national television. *All in the Family* takes the cameras into a neighborhood in Queens. The accents, gestures, methods and perceptions of the leading actors in *Kojak* reflect in an interesting and accurate way the ethnic sensibilities of several neighborhoods in New York. The clipped speech of Jack Webb in *Dragnet* years ago was an earlier break from "televisionese." But, in general, television is an organ of nationalization, of homogenization—and, indeed, of a certain systematic inaccuracy about the actual, concrete texture of life in the United States.

This nationalizing effect also spills over into the news and the documentaries. The cultural factors which deeply affect the values and perceptions of various American communities are neglected; hence the treatment of problems affecting such communities is frequently oversimplified. This is especially true when matters of group conflict are involved. The tendency of newsmen is subtly to take sides and to regard some claims or behavior as due to "prejudice," others as rather more moral and commendable.

The mythic forms and story lines of the news and documentaries are not inconsonant with the mythic forms represented in the adventure stories and Westerns. "Good" and "evil" are rather clearly placed in conflict.

"Hard-hitting" investigative reporting is mythically linked to classic American forms of moral heroism: the crimebuster, the incorruptible sheriff. The forces of law and progress ceaselessly cut into the jungle of corruption. There is continuity between the prime-time news and prime-time programming—much more continuity than is detected by the many cultivated Cyclopses who disdain "the wasteland" and praise the documentaries. The mythic structure of both is harmonious.

It should prove possible to mark out the habits of perception and mind encouraged by national television. If these categories are not decisive, better ones can surely be discerned. We might then design ways of instructing ourselves and our children in countervailing habits. It does not seem likely that the mind and heart tutored by many years of watching television (in doses of five or six hours a day) is in the same circumstance as the mind and heart never exposed to television. Education and criticism must, it seems, take this difference into account.

The Class Bias of Television

Television has had two striking effects. On the one hand, as Norman Podhoretz has remarked, it has not seemed to prevent people from reading; more books are being published and mass marketed than ever before in American history. It is possible that television stimulates many to go beyond what television itself can offer.

Secondly, television works, or appears to work, as a homogenizing world to a national audience. In many respects, it could be shown, the overall ideological tendency of television productions—from the news, through the talk shows, to the comedy hours, variety shows, and adventure, crime, and family shows—is that of a vague and misty liberalism: belief in the efficacy of an ultimate optimism, "talking through one's problems," a questioning of institutional authorities, a triumph of good over evil. Even a show like *All in the Family,* beneath its bluster and its violation of verbal taboos, illustrates the unfailing victory of liberal points of view: Archie Bunker always loses. A truly mean and aggressive reactionary point of view is virtually non-existent. There is no equivalent on national television to *Human Events* and other right-wing publications, or to the network of right-wing radio shows around the nation. While many critics of right and left find prime-time television to be a "wasteland," few have accused it of being fascist, malicious, evil, or destructive of virtue, progress, and hope. Television's liberalism is calculated to please neither the new radicals nor the classic liberals of the left, nor the upbeat, salesmanlike exponents of the right. In harmony with the images of progress built into both liberalism and capitalism, television seems, however gently, to undercut traditional institutions and to promote a restless, questioning attitude. The main product—and attitude—it has to sell is the new.

This attachment to the new insures that television will be a vaguely leftist medium, no matter who its personnel might be. Insofar as it debunks traditions and institutions—and even the act of *representing* these in selective symbolic form is a kind of veiled threat to them—television serves the purposes of that large movement within which left and right (in America, at least) are rather like the two legs of locomotion: the movement of modernization. It serves, in general, the two mammoth institutions of modern life: the state and the great corporations. It serves these institutions even when it exalts the individual at the expense of family, neighborhood, religious organizations, and cultural groups. These are the only intermediate institutions that stand between the isolated individual and the massive institutions.

Thus the homogenizing tendencies of television are ambivalent. Television can electrify and unite the whole nation, creating an instantaneous network in which millions are simultaneous recipients of the same powerful images. But to what purpose, for whose use, and to what effect? Is it an unqualified good that the national grid should become so pre-eminent, superior to any and all local checks and balances? The relative national power and influence of state governors seems to have been weakened, for example; a state's two senators, by comparison, occupy a national stage and can more easily become national figures.

But in at least five other ways national television projects a sense of reality that is not identical to the sense of reality actual individuals in their concrete environments share. Taken together, these five ways construct a national social reality that is not free of a certain class and even ethnic bias. The television set becomes a new instrument of reality—of "what's happening" in the larger, national world, of "where it's at." In some sense what isn't on television isn't quite real, is not part of the nationally shared world, will be nonexistent for millions of citizens. Three examples may suggest the power of this new sense of reality.

Experiments suggest (so I am told) that audiences confronted with simultaneous projection on a large movie screen and on a television set regularly and overwhelmingly end up preferring the image on the smaller set. The attraction of reality is somehow there.

On the political campaign, or at a sports event, individuals seem to seek to be on camera with celebrities, as if seeking to share in a precious and significant verification of their existence. A young boy in Pittsburgh exults, "I'm real!" as he interposes himself between the grinding cameras and a presidential candidate in the crowd. Not to be on television is to lack weight in national consciousness. Audience "participation" (the ancient platonic word for being) fills a great psychic hunger: to be human in the world that really counts.

Finally, anyone who has participated in a large-scale event comes to recognize vividly how strait and narrow is the gate between what has actually happened and what gets on television. For the millions who see the television story, of course, the story is the reality. For those who lived through a strenuous sixteen-hour day on the campaign trail, for example, it is always something of a surprise to see what "made" the television screen—or, more accurately, what the television screen made real. That artificial reality turns out to have far more substance for the world at large than the lived sixteen hours. According to the ancient *maya*, the world of flesh and blood is an illusion. And so it is.

Television is a new technology and depends upon sophisticated crafts. It is a world of high profit. Its inside world is populated by persons in a high income bracket. Moreover, television is a world that requires a great deal of travel, expense-account living, a virtual shuttle between Los Angeles and New York, a taste for excellent service and high prestige. These economic factors seriously color television's image of the world.

The glitter of show business quickly spread to television. In the blossomy days when thinkers dreamed of an affluent society and praised the throwaway society, the shifting and glittering sets of television make-believe seemed like a metaphor for modern society. Actually, a visit to a television studio is extraordinarily disappointing, far more so, even, than a visit to an empty circus tent after the crowd has gone. Cheaply painted pastel panels, fingerprints sometimes visible upon them, are wheeled away and stacked. The cozy intimacy one shares from one's set at home is rendered false by the cavernous lofts of the studio, the tangle of wires, the old clothing and cynical buzzing of the bored technicians, crews, and hangers-on. Dust and empty plastic coffee cups are visible in corners where chairs compete for space. There is a tawdriness behind the scenes.

In a word, the world of television is a radically duplicitous world. Its illusions pervade every aspect of the industry. The salaries paid to those who greet the public remove them from the public. The settings in which they work are those of show business. Slick illusion is the constant temptation and establishes the rules of the game.

Moreover, the selling of products requires images of upward mobility. The sets, designs, and fluid metaphors of the shows themselves must suggest a certain richness, smoothness, and adequacy. It is not only that writers and producers understand that what audiences desire is escape. (One can imagine a poor society in which television would focus on limited aspiration and the dramas of reality.) It is also the case, apparently, that an inner imperative drives writers, producers, and sponsors to project their *own* fantasies. Not all Americans, by far, pursue upward mobility as a way of life. A great many teach their children to have modest expectations and turn down opportunities for advancement and mobility that would take them away from their familiar worlds.

The myths of the upwardly mobile and the tastes of the very affluent govern the visual symbols, the flow, and the chatter of television.

The class bias of television reality proceeds not only from the relative economic affluence of the industry and its personnel. It springs as well from the educational level. "Televisionese" sends a clear and distinct message to the people, a message of exclusion and superiority. (George Wallace sends the message *back;* he is not its originator, only its echo.) It is common for a great many of the personnel connected with television to imagine themselves as anti-establishment and also perhaps as iconoclastic. Surely they must know that to men who work in breweries or sheet metal plants, to women who clean tables in cafeterias or splice wires in electronic assembly plants, they must seem to be at the very height of the Establishment. Their criticisms of American society—reflected in *Laugh-In,* in the nightclub entertainers, and even in the dialogue of virtually every crime or adventure show—are perceived to be something like the complaints of spoiled children. There seems to be a self-hatred in the medium, a certain shame about American society, of which Lawrence Welk's old-fashioned, honeyed complacency and the militant righteousness of Bob Hope, John Wayne, and *Up With America!* are the confirming opposites. To confuse the hucksterism of television with the real America is, of course, a grievous error.

Television is a parade of experts instructing the unenlightened about the weather, aspirins, toothpastes, the latest books or proposals for social reform, and the correct attitudes to have with respect to race, poverty, social conflict, and new moralities. Television is preeminently a world of intellectuals. Academic persons may be astonished to learn of it and serious writers and artists may hear the theme with withering scorn, but for most people in the United States television is the medium through which they meet an almost solid phalanx of college-educated persons, professionals, experts, thinkers, authorities, and "with it," "swinging" celebrities: i.e., people unlike themselves who are drawn from the top ten percent of the nation in terms of educational attainment.

It is fashionable for intellectuals to disdain the world of television (although some, when asked, are known to agree to appear on it without hesitation). Yet when they appear on television they do not seem to be notably superior to the announcers, interviewers, and performers who precede them on camera or share the camera with them. (Incidentally, although many sports journalists write or speak condescendingly of "the jocks," when athletes appear as television announcers—Joe Garagiola, Sandy Koufax, Frank Gifford, Alex Karras, and others—the athletes seem not one whit inferior in intelligence or in sensitivity to the journalists.) Television is the greatest instrument the educated class has ever had to parade its wares before the people. On television that class has no rival. Fewer than ten percent of the American population has completed four years of college. That ten percent totally dominates television.

It is important to understand that the disdain for "popular culture" often heard in intellectual circles is seriously misplaced. Television, at least, more nearly represents the world of the educated ten percent than it reflects the world of the other ninety percent. At most, one might say in defense, the world of television represents the educated class's fantasies about the fantasies of the population. To say that *kitsch* has always required technicians to create it is not a sufficient route of escape. Do really serious intellectuals (i.e., not those "mere" technicians) have better understandings of where the people truly are? What, then, are those better understandings?

The interviews recorded by Robert Coles, for example, tend to show that persons of the social class represented by Archie Bunker are at least as complicated, many-sided, aware of moral ambiguities, troubled and sensitive, as the intellectuals who appear on television, in novels, or in the cinema. Artists who might use the materials of ordinary life for their creations are systematically separated from ordinary people by the economic conditions of creativity in the United States.

The writers, producers, actors, and journalists of television are separated from most of the American population not only by economic standing, and not only by education, but also by the culture in which their actual lives are lived out. By "culture" I mean those implicit, lived criteria that suggest to each of us what is real, relevant, significant, meaningful in the buzzing confusion of our experience: how we select out and give shape to our world. The culture of prime-time television is, it appears, a serious dissolvant of the cultures of other Americans. The culture of television celebrates to an extraordinary degree two mythic strains in the American character: the lawless and the irreverent. On the first count, stories of cowboys, gangsters, and spies still preoccupy the American imagination. On the second, the myth of "enlightenment" from local standards and prejudices still dominates our images of self-liberation and sophistication. No doubt the stronghold of a kind of priggish righteousness in several layers of American history leads those who rebel to find their rebellion all too easy. It is as though the educated admonish one another that they "can't go home again" and that the culture against which they rebel is solid and unyielding.

But what if it isn't? What if the perception of culture on the part of millions is, rather, that chaos and the jungle are constantly encroaching and that the rule of good order is threatened in a dozen transactions every day—by products that don't work, by experts and officials who take advantage of lay ignorance, by muggings and robberies, by jobs and pensions that disappear, by schools that do not work in concert with the moral vision of the home?

Television keeps pressing on the barriers of cultural resistance to obscenities, to some forms of sexual behavior, and to various social understandings concerning work and neighborhood and family relationships. A reporter from the New York Times reports with scarcely veiled satisfaction that Deep Throat is being shown in a former church in a Pennsylvania mining town, as though this were a measure of spreading enlightenment. It might be. But what if our understanding of how cultural, social, and moral strands are actually interwoven in the consciousness of peoples is inadequate? What if the collapse of moral inhibition in one area, for a significant number of persons, encourages a collapse at other places? What if moral values cannot be too quickly changed without great destructiveness? The celebration of "new moralities" may not lead to the kind of "humanization" cultural optimists anticipate.

Television, and the mass media generally, have vested interests in new moralities. The excitement of transgressing inhibitions is gripping entertainment. There are, however, few vested interests wishing to strengthen the inhibitions which make such transgressions good entertainment. Television is only twenty-five years old. We have very little experience or understanding proportionate to the enormous moral stakes involved. It is folly to believe that laissez-faire works better in moral matters than in economic matters or that enormous decisions in these matters are not already being made in the absence of democratic consent. When one kind of show goes on the air others are excluded during that time. The present system is effectively a form of social control.

I do not advocate any particular solution to this far-ranging moral dilemma; I do not know what to recommend. But the issue is a novel one for a free society, and we do not even have a well-thought-out body of options from which to choose. In that vacuum a rather-too-narrow social class is making the decisions. The pressures of the free market (so they say) now guide them. Is that so? Should it be so?

Because of the structure and history of the social class that produces prime-time television, group conflict in the United States is also portrayed in a simplistic and biased way. The real diversity of American cultures and regions is shrouded in public ignorance. Occasional disruptions, like the rebellion of West Virginia miners against certain textbooks and the rebellion of parents in South Boston against what they perceived as downward mobility for their children and themselves, are as quickly as possible brushed from consciousness. America is pictured as though it were divided between one vast homogeneous "middle America," to be enlightened, and the enlighteners. In fact, there are several "middle Americas."

There is more than one important Protestant culture in our midst. The Puritan inheritance is commonly exaggerated and the evangelical, fundamentalist inheritance is vastly underestimated (and under-studied). Hubert Humphrey is from a cultural stream different from that of George Wallace or of John Lindsay. There are also several quite significant cultural streams among Catholics; the Irish of the Middle West (Eugene McCarthy, Michael Harrington) often have a quite different cultural tradition from the Irish of Philadelphia, Boston, or New York. Construction workers on Long Island are not offended by "pornography" in the same way as druggists in small midwestern towns; look inside their cabs and helmets, listen to their conversations, if you seek evidence. There is also more than one cultural stream among American Jews; the influence of the Jews of New York has probably misled us in our understanding of the Jewish experience in America.

It seems, moreover, that the social class guiding the destiny of television idealizes certain ethnic groups—the legitimate minorities—even while this class offers in its practices no greater evidence of genuine egalitarianism than other social classes. At the same time this class seems extremely slow to comprehend the experiences of other American cultures. One of the great traumas of human history was the massive migration to America during the last 100 years. It ought to be one of the great themes of high culture, and popular culture as well. Our dramatists neglect it.

Group conflict has, moreover, been the rule in every aspect of American life, from labor to corporate offices to neighborhoods to inter-ethnic marriages. Here, too, the drama is perhaps too real and vivid to be touched: *these* are inhibitions the liberal culture of television truly respects. Three years ago one could write that white ethnics, like some others, virtually never saw themselves on television; suddenly we have had *Banacek, Colombo, Petrocelli, Kojak, Kolchack, Rhoda, Sanford,* and *Chico.* Artists are still exploring the edges of how much reality can be given voice and how to voice it. These are difficult, even explosive matters. Integrity and care are required.

It must seem odd to writers and producers to be accused of having a "liberal" bias when they are so aware of the limitations they daily face and the grueling battles they daily undergo. But why do they have these battles except that they have a point of view and a moral passion? We are lucky that the social class responsible for the creative side of television is not a reactionary and frankly illiberal class. Still, that it is a special class is itself a problem for all of us, including those involved in it.

JAMES LULL

Ideology, Television, and Interpersonal Communications

In this essay Lull links the macro and microsocial elements of the public's relationship to media. He weaves an intricate pattern in which interpersonal behavior manifests roles and values elaborated in the mass media. Within the context of using and participating with the media, Lull examines the nature of the rules which govern media participation. What communication rules govern your media habits? Which set of rules seem to predominate—parametic, habitual, or tactical?

There is an intimate liaison between the varied and highly specialized communications media in society and the intricate modes of unmediated, human interaction that are created in everyday life. This isomorphism obviates the distinction often made between "mass" and "interpersonal" communication. These descriptive formulations are more productively viewed as counterparts in a larger phenomenon—the ongoing, purposive construction of social meaning and the attendant fashioning of cultural artifacts that express social relations.

The approach to understanding human communication recommended here requires close examination of the environments where mediated communications are received, interpreted, and used. Social members communicate verbally and nonverbally in those locations. Their interactions often focus directly on and are influenced significantly by the mass media. The influence involves not only television, but also film, print media, and especially music transmitted via radio, records, tapes, concerts, and video.

The major points to be made in this writing can be summarized thusly: First, the mass media are operated in the United States fundamentally to help perpetuate selected ideologies that represent particular concerns of media owners, managers, and financial backers—the commerical advertisers. Second, audience members engage in imaginative, sometimes elaborate uses of mass media—both their technical properties and symbolic content—to accomplish a wide variety of personal and social objectives. Third, the uses of media made by audience members are patterned and are governed by identifiable rules of social order. Finally, systematic effects of the mass media can be observed by analyzing the intepersonal communication of au-

This article was written expressly for the present volume. Copyright © 1986 by James Lull.

dience members in their rule-governed uses of communications technologies.

Ideological Features of Television Content

Access to television for the authorship of ideas is not random or democratically determined in the United States and other capitalist countries. There is a pecking order that favors sponsors with the greatest degree of influence (i.e., those with the largest advertising budgets) even among those who are financially qualified to present images on television. This highly selective process understandably contributes to a loading of media content with messages supportive of organizational entities that can purchase time. Persons who control these institutions have become not only members of the nation's economic elite but also its "information elite," because the flow of information in a capitalist economy reflects the priorities of those who own the major business interests. This central fact should never be ignored or downplayed in any analysis of media systems and has been a major focus of criticism of American media by researchers and theorists from around the world.

Some mass communication researchers have examined those institutions that are in favorable positions for access and their media activities. Advertising, entertainment, and information (or "news") industries have been studied in relation to our nation's military priorities, international communications, and the domination of world commerce by Western powers, especially the United States (e.g. Schiller, 1969, 1973, 1976; Tunstall, 1977; Gerbner and Gross, 1973; Real, 1977; Boyd-Barrett, 1977; Smith, 1980; Hamelink, 1983). The influence of media organizations on international economic activity and on world cultures has been criticized by scholars concerned not only with television but also film (Guback, 1969; Wasko, 1983) and music (Firth, 1981; Wallis and Malm, 1984).

Concerning television, one point of view suggests that all programming—the medium's entire agenda—is a fundamental and powerful contributor to the way audience members conceive of their own culture (Gerbner, 1973). In other works, selected aspects of television content such as advertising (Ewen, 1976; Ewen and Ewen, 1982), news (Molotch and Lester, 1973; Tuchman, 1974, 1978) or entertainment programming including soap operas, prime-time television, miniseries, and virtually everything else has been addressed critically in this regard (Wander, 1976, 1979; Kellner, 1979; Gitlin, 1983). The research community has become much more aware and active in recent years in a critical dimension. The widespread concern with television's proven behavioral effects has perhaps helped stimulate insightful and condemning analyses of television content. Numerous analyses of the manipulative capabilities of television have systematically demonstrated that the medium affects public perceptions of racial characteristics, sex-role behaviors, vocational circumstances, and images of the elderly. Evidence of television's ability to introduce or sustain stereotypes is clear. The common use of "flat" (stereotypical, one-dimensional) characters in television (advertising, entertainment, and news) reflects a belief on the part of television's producers and writers that audience members must be given uncomplicated heroes and heroines who have thoroughly predictable attitudes and behaviors.

These ordered categories of content on television suggest a highly subjective and often misleading picture of the world. These weighted presentations may help foster or reinforce attitudes held by audience members toward the entire range of cultural objects and events they encounter personally and some they receive *only* in mediated form. Systematic treatment of these partisan domains produces television's most basic and repeated messages. The cumulative effect is a profile of the social and cultural world in which citizens live. This has been termed "cultural indicators" (Gerbner, 1973; Gerbner and Gross, 1976). The abundance of studies undertaken to assess television's institutional processes and content generally show that these symbolic protrayals do not change much from year to year, decade to decade. Although the technology of television (both production formulae and improvements in sets) has undeniably improved throughout the history of the medium, content of the medium is no more culturally enlightened or fair than it was when the medium was first introduced. In fact, some observers lament that the content of television is of inferior quality now. Despite popular and academic criticism, for instance, the amount of television violence has remained stable or actually increased in recent years. Similarly, the medium's presentation of womens' roles reflects endurance of traditional stereotypes even in the face of a serious, national movement to erase predictable and degrading media images of women.

Audience Members' Uses of Television

A notable research tradition in mass communication has developed in response to the empirically verified belief of many scholars that audience members are not simply the passive recipients of media imagery. Research has demonstrated extensively that people use television and other media—both the formal properties of communications technologies and their symbolic content—in the resolute construction of their daily lives. Known as the "uses and gratifications" perspective, this theoretical approach has framed numerous studies conducted in many countries around the world, especially during the past 15 years. Published reports resulting from this work have been summarized and debated in the mass communications literature (Blumler and Katz, 1974; Rosengren, Wenner, and Palmgreen, 1985).

Uses and gratifications research has been strongly criticized (Elliott, 1974; Swanson, 1977). A major concern of the critics is how to conceptualize the point of departure in uses and gratifications analyses of audience activity. What stimulates audience members to attend to television and employ the medium for various purpoes? What motivates audience behavior?

Some uses and gratifications researchers have boldly described audience activity as attempts on the part of humans to *gratify particular needs.* These hypothesized needs (a concept raised here as a problematic rather than a given) are typically said to be grounded in theories of motivation such as Maslow's self-actualization approach (1954; 1962) or the psycho-sexual/psychosocial synthesis of Erikson (1982). Because needs are not directly observable, communication researchers can only speculate about their origin and existence, if indeed they exist at all. Furthermore, uses and gratifications research is commonly regarded as part of the functionalist tradition (Laswell, 1948; Merton, 1957; Wright, 1960), a theoretical construct that is also highly controversial.

Despite the substantial criticism leveled at uses and gratifications research, an impressive number of sophisticated empirical studies have been conducted from this perspective. Putting aside the question of what motivates people to attend to media, accumulated research dating back more than 40 years clearly shows that audience members employ the mass media purposively. Uses and gratifications research might more accurately be labeled "media use research" because this dimension of human involvement with media is more self-evident than is the gratifications side. When a researcher inquires as to the gratifications that supposedly result from contact with television and other media (and, presumably motivates the contact as well) there is justifiable concern regarding the accuracy with which the mental orientations of audience members can be described. To interpret particular uses of television as attempts to gratify human needs adds a serious level of psychologizing to the supposedly empirical process of documenting audience activity.

Uses of television and other media are numerous and involve a wide variety of behaviors. Even the early studies of radio and newspapers were able to detect subtle uses of media in audience members' construction of their daily routines (Lazarsfeld, 1940; Herzog, 1944; Berelson, 1949; Riley and Riley, 1951). The early empirical studies helped define mass media as resources for daily living. Media were found to be connected not only to the personal lives of audience members in isolation, but also to the social networks in which they live. Their uses included topics for conversation, agents of entertainment, and resources for the creation of desired familial relations. Content was used for its peer group utility, personal advice, and for role models to imitate. An early ethnographic study documented television's ability to help people define their sex roles and family roles, develop middle-class problem-solving strategies, and to act as a cathartic agent for chastizing oppressive institutions (Gans, 1962).

Systematic recent research has categorized the various uses of television and other media by audience members. Perhaps the most well known of these typologies is that proposed by McQuail, Blumler, and Brown (1972). Their schema was based on survey data collected in England and found that television is useful for information purposes, for diversion, for personal identity, and for assistance in the development and maintenance of satisfactory personal relationships.

In the United States there has been a recent flurry of observational studies of the relationship between television and human behavior, particularly the contribution of the electronic media to goal-oriented interpersonal interaction. Among the foci of these various research projects are the uses of television for communicative purposes by families (Reid and Frazer, 1980), the interpersonal rules of the viewing experience (Reid, 1979; Lull, 1982), childrens' uses of media themes and characters in play (Sarett, 1981; James and McCain, 1982), families' educative uses of television (Bryce, 1980), the incorporation of television content into vocational routines (Pacanowsky & Anderson, 1982), uses of television in public viewing situations (Lemish, 1982), the facilitative contributions of television to the maintenance of marital and friendship relations (Wolf, Meyer, and White, 1982), and the decision-making processes that lead to the selection of television programs (Lull, 1982).

A few years ago I published an article that reported many uses of television undertaken by audience members in family settings (Lull, 1980). The findings were observations collected over three years in Wisconsin and California. An analysis was made of the role of television at home extending into a wide range of activities undertaken by parents and children. Television was found to be used by audience members for background noise, companionship, entertainment, punctuation of time and activity, regulation of talk patterns, experience illustration, establishing common ground, entering conversations, reducing anxiety, clarifying values, providing an agenda for talk, creating patterns of physical and verbal contact and neglect, family solidarity, family relaxant, reduction of conflict, maintenance of relationships, decision making, behavior modeling, solving problems, transmitting values across generations, legitimizing opinion, disseminating information, substitute schooling, role enactment, role reinforcement, substitute role portrayal, intellectual validation, exercise of authority, gatekeeping, and for the facilitation of arguments. This long list is presented here together with the overview of the early "uses" literature to make a central point of this reading: Television and other mass media are used frequently and imaginatively by audience members for a great many purposes. Some of these purposes are more personal than social, but nearly all have interpersonal consequences. No attempt has been made here to describe the origins that may impel media use or the alleged gratifications that they provide for their users. For purposes of this writing it is important only to make the point as clearly as possible: Television is a pervasive resource that is absolutely central to the construction of everyday life by its millions of viewers.

Rules of Television Viewing

There are regularities in human communication processes. These activities are not lawful in the sense that scientific phenomena are. Unlike other forms of behavior, human communication is affected by the remarkable tendency of its participants to transcend their environments through learning and to travel curious, idiosyncratic paths in the formation of their social worlds. Furthermore, communication is dramatically influenced by the everchanging contexts in which it occurs. Human communication episodes commonly are patterned but not determined or invariant. Regularities in human interaction, therefore, may more accurately be described as "rulelike" than lawful.

The patterns of human interaction that occur in relation to the presence of television can be addressed by scholar and students from the emerging "communication rules" perspective (Lull, 1982; Shimanoff, 1980; Pearce, 1980; Cushman, 1977; Cushman and Whiting, 1972). There is little agreement as to exactly what constitutes a rule. Few would disagree, however that whereas communication in its many forms is the expedient by which social actors transfer meaning, rules inhere in patterns of interpersonal and mediated human interaction. Social members create, then follow, modify, or break communication rules.

Communication rules inhabit two basic social domains. They exist in the lived interpersonal habitats of audience members and in the symbolic, mediated world that exists between sources and consumers of media content. In the first case, humans communicate with each other directly, person to person, and do so according to rules. This unmediated interaction takes place in what can be termed "microsocial environments." These contexts include families, but also work groups, peer groups, friendship networks, and any other natural, informal social aggregations. In the second case, messages are transmitted to audience members who are parasocially connected to media sources and encouraged to respond to televised imagery in a rule-governed manner. The product of this exposure is collective social action that leads to cultural norms. This patterning takes place at the "macrosocial" level since it reflects the attitudes and actions of people throughout society. Although the manifestation of these rule systems differ, communication that takes place in both spheres has common characteristics.

Habitual Rules

Habits are frequently repeated social activities that typically take place in situations where some authority figure prescribes or endorses routine forms of behavior. Some habits are formalized and articulated; others may simply be the patterns that develop as a result of routine communication.

At the microsocial level, there are definite rules in many families about the time, amount, and content of television viewing that is permitted and the relationship of viewing to domestic responsibilities. These central activities are habits in most homes where parents exercise control. The rules may or may not be stated.

Some habitual behaviors involving television result from repeated actions that originate with or are sanctioned by the more powerful or imaginative family members. Older siblings may control Saturday morning television viewing because of their age and size. Their favorite shows are watched habitually because the original selection process was controlled by them. Others who desire to watch the same program on the same set must abide by the established viewing routine. In other cases, the very youngest family members can sometimes influence family television viewing habits by their energetic interaction with television. They have sophisticated knowledge of program content and scheduling and are often willing to sit directly in front of the set and change the channel until they find something they like. Also, young children often notice the times when other family members are not watching or paying attention to the television set. During these times (late afternoon, after school, for instance), they control the selection of programs and help establish viewing routines favorable to them. These are a few examples of microsocial habits that have something to do with television.

Macrosocial habits take the form of national patterns of exposure to television. Viewer routines are habitual when particular kinds of programming are aired at the times deemed appropriate (e.g., profitable) by programming executives at the networks. Commercial television presents a fairly inflexible agenda wherein particular times of the day are associated with types of television programs. Furthermore, the presentational format of network television—the rhythm of program segment/commercial/program segment/commercial, etc.—is a prescribed habitual mode of commercial programming. The formula is so ingrained in the medium and its audience that even noncommercial television systems and stations have had to adopt similar breaks in their programming, filling the interruptions with public service announcements, news briefs, or appeals for funds. Although ratings feedback may influence decisions about when to telecast various programs, media managers ultimately place programs at their discretion. Broad patterns of social behavior are stimulated in the process as audience members typically adjust their routines to fit television schedules.

Parametric Rules

Like habits, parametric interaction often reveals an unequal distribution of power between and among interlocutors. This rule type is more complicated than habits, however, because here a wider latitude of acceptable behavior and usually distinct options are permitted. Parameters refer to the boundaries of human action. In the study of television, they are the choices that authority figures tolerate having to do with viewing behavior and the content of the medium itself.

Parametric rules of television viewing at the microsocial level are more complicated than habits because they are more spontaneous, more varied, and typically involve interpersonal negotiations. Parametric rules constructed by families include the choosing of shows for group viewing and fabrication of the interpersonal activities that accompany exposure to the medium. Viewers may choose to talk to each other, engage in roughhouse play, and reposition themselves in front of the set during commercial breaks. But families and other viewing groups typically have expectations about the length and intensity of these disruptions. Viewers ongoingly choose the programs and create the interpersonal atmosphere that surrounds viewing through their parametric, rule-based communication.

To briefly contrast habitual and parametric rule types at the microsocial level, consider this example: Parents in a particular family may require the children to be home by a certain time on school nights. After that time, activities in which the children may engage are limited to options that the parents allow (e.g., watching television, doing schoolwork, playing with the home computer, and so forth). The first condition—being home at a specified time—has a binary quality. There is but one "correct" behavior. Compliance with an understood expectation is required by a power figure, a parent. It is a habit.

In the second instance there are numerous activities that fall into the range of acceptability. Although the parents may suggest a set of preferred behaviors, they will tolerate a range of actions. All the interactants understand what constitutes appropriate behavior. As long as they care to keep the peace, construction of the social world takes place within the boundaries. It is a microsocial parametric rule. Parameters function as guidelines and limits.

Sometimes there is an intermingling of rules. Habits sometimes collide with parametric rules. To illustrate this, children may be permitted to play a video game among other leisure-time options (parametric rule) after they finish their chores at home (habitual rule). When playing the game, however, older children are not allowed to dominate the amount of playing time of the younger siblings (habitual rule). There is an impractical intersection of communication rules here that causes confusion and requires supervision. This sorting-out process is a complicated process in and of itself that has been discussed by rules theorists but goes beyond what is being discussed here.

Macrosocial parametric rules are of particular interest because they reflect the concerns of critical theorists raised in the early paragraphs of this chapter. These rules can generally be considered cultural norms—overarching characteristics of a society that define it internally and externally. True to the rules conception, television viewers choose to watch varying program content. However, only a tightly controlled range of program elements, each of which helps teach the language of the socioeconomic system and its corresponding cultural assumptions, is available for viewing.

There is considerable evidence to indicate that the audience collectively responds to television in ways the controlling interests desire. It is true that audience members have the option to turn off the television set, to disregard or refute the content of themes portrayed on television, to escape the influence of national advertising through alternative consumer activity, and to elect political candidates who have not appeared regularly on the visual medium. Every television set has an off switch; every audience member has potential access to streams of information that conflict with television's messages; most stores carry products that are not advertised on television; and electoral ballots bear the names and party affiliations of candidates who do not receive much attention from the media. Still, Americans watch television now more than ever before; the medium effectively sets the agenda for a great deal of conversation and behavior that takes place during viewing and following exposure; national advertising campaigns frequently achieve enormous financial success in direct relation to sponsored imagery; and mainstream political parties and their candidates continue to dominate the American political system (Comstock, Chaffee, Katzman, McCombs, and Roberts, 1978).

Individual audience members cannot alter television's agenda, they can only choose to accept or reject the messages that are offered. The proven tendency is for most people to stay within the prescribed parameters and exercise choices from the range of allowable alternatives. As a result, domination of commercial markets by large corporations and maintenance of the two-party system (where the basic ideologies of both parties are extremely similar compared to choices that can be made in many other nations) are facts of life in the United States. Although television is not the only contributor to this process of social control, its impact on the public consciousness is enormous. Coordination of these "choices" at the macrosocial level represents parametric, rule-governed communication that partly accounts for the success of institutions to win and maintain ideological hegemony in what is advertised as a free and open society.

Tactical Rules

The third fundamental communication rule type is tactical. These are methodical interactions that people create in order to accomplish interpersonal goals. They are coordinated communication srategies. Tactical rules can be very simple or very complex. They are patterned behaviors designed to use media in some way that furthers the interests of at least one of the interactants. They may follow the logic of the practical syllogism (Von Wright, 1962; Cushman and Pearce, 1977).

Beginning with the basic understanding that communication can be used as a resource to create desired social relations, tactics that are invented in this spirit are boundless in their particular forms but generalizable in their type. Sometimes by using extremely complicated interpersonal methods, interactants develop highly complex patterns or routines of interaction design to satisfy some objective.

Tactical rules of human communication inhabit countless aspects of family life with television. Tactical rules can be found in the form of communication strategies designed to facilitate effective interaction, to create desired interpersonal distance, to apply information learned from television to family and peer group life, and to demonstrate one's personal competence. Tactical rules, therefore, regulate conversational styles and agendas, facilitate attempts at interpersonal affiliation and avoidance, systematize media learning, and frame efforts to establish and reaffirm personal identities. In their patterned efforts to achieve these objectives, social members use television and other media as resources in their verbal and nonverbal communication.

Tactical rules refer to behavioral patterns that emerge from the efforts of audience members to construct social circumstances they desire. Generally, these strategies are implicit and unarticulated. Proxemic patterns between children may develop, for instance, when one child positions himsel or herself in front of the television set in order to share time with an admired sibling or parent. An adult may enter a discussion about a television program that aired the previous night in order to talk easily with her or his associates at work. A husband may encourage his wife to watch television shows centered around a particular profession toward which the woman is drawn, thereby encouraging vicarious participation in a vocational setting that marriage and child raising may have denied her. A young viewer may achieve status as an opinion leader on modern music by referring regularly to Music Television (MTV) when conversing at school. These are a few examples of the ways in which television is woven into the interpersonal relationships of its viewers. When these "uses" of television have a strategic and repeated quality, they may be tactical rules at the microsocial level. In this context, tactical communications are fashioned by viewers who respond to problems or goals they have at home or in other familiar surroundings.

Tactical communication rules operate at the societal level, too. At the macrosocial level, the sources of television programming "communicate" information to an entire nation of viewers, millions of people. These cultural lessons are assimilated to some degree by audience members throughout the country who then incorporate elements of the sponsored imagery into their everyday interpersonal relations. In this way, patterns develop across the country that are often first suggested and later reinforcd by television. These lessons advocate special ways of thinking. Consumerism may be the most pervasive case in point because the creation of a climate for consumption is fundamental to commercial broadcasting. Television endlessly cultivates the notion that through the display of material wealth, or at least the appearance of it, a person can find self-esteem, collect friends, and be happy. The first step in macrosocial, tactical communication is the effective transmission of values through television programming. The second step is the employment of these suggestions by viewers as they construct their daily lives.

An illustration may help make the point: A recent national television commercial campaign showed a young man standing next to his new Toyota automobile while several attractive young women walked past him adoringly. Noticing the female attention, the man asks rhetorically: "Is it me or my Toyota?" At the conclusion of the commercial one of the admirers answers: "It's your Toyota, silly." Clearly, the advertisement was designed to sell much more than personal transportation. The viewer who is influenced by this message may regard the purchase of the new car as a strategy that can facilitate personal or interpersonal objectives. If this behavior is patterned across the culture—and it very often is—advertising sources and viewer-consumers have engaged in large-scale, mediated, tactical interactions that may also help promote consumption-dependent values in everyday, unmediated social interaction.

Advertising examples are only the most obvious representatives of tactical rules at the societal level that involve television content. Practical methods suggested by television for personal or social success are also evident directly in the story lines of dramatic programs, in occurrences that are selected for treatment in news programming, and in the subtle, subtextual lessons of television's programming generally. The visual medium's symbolic content is one version of the normative constitution of culture—its rules—that is transmitted to a larger audience than is regularly exposed to any other centralized message source. Elements of the reality portrayed on television subsequently become resources for determining boundaries within which society should proceed, for choosing popular courses of social action, and for calculating specific means-to-ends strategies such as the rule-based, problem-solving activity just discussed. Large-scale social consensus is achieved in the process and the result, in the traditional sociological sense, is mass communication.

Ideological Consequences of Television-Related Interpersonal Interaction

Audiences for television can be regarded simultaneously as occupants of thousands of microsocial enclaves such as family homes and as a national group of millions of viewers who all receive essentially the same mediated imagery. Rules of communication govern human interaction in both situations. Habitual, parametric, and tactical rules are present in small social groups and in the society at large.

The three circumstances discussed so far—purposive content, purposive use, and patterned use—are further empowered by the way they interact. The link that unites these components into a larger cultural process is interpersonal communication in its various forms, particularly conversation. Simply put, dominant ideologies are spread effectively throughout society by the creative and systematic uses made of television by audience members in their routine communicative interaction.

Consider this example: A woman who desires to spend time with her husband on Monday nights during the fall in the United States may find it necessary to sit in front of the television set while he watches the football game. In doing so, she is immediately exposed to the values of competition inherent in the game itself and in the dozens of commercials that interrupt action. Her use of television as an agent of interpersonal unity has exposed her to the medium's one-way flow of value-laden information.

Furthermore, the husband and wife may use television content to settle an argument. In an actual example from ethnographic research, a disagreement between a married couple took place one afternoon regarding the estimated gasoline mileage that one of the new automobiles was reported to have. That night, the husband's opinion on the mileage estimate was confirmed by information in a commercial advertisement that appeared on television. He gloatingly made certain that his wife who was sitting in the same room learned the "correct" information. Television was used by him as a resource for demonstrating his personal competence on the topic.

This little episode has larger implications. By controlling television's agenda, the economic elite profit from interpersonal uses such as this. When people incorporate television selected agenda into their goal-oriented interpersonal communication, ideologies present in the medium's content are concretized socially. In this case, the automobile commercial stimulated conversation that is consistent with the desire of the automobile industry to perpetuate the belief that private forms of transportation are to be preferred to public transportation. Interpersonal uses of television, especially when they involve conversation, contribute to maintenance of ideological imperatives supportive of the value system of media sources and their financeers. Analyses of audience activity help demonstrate how the ideological features of the dominant economy are spread throughout society as influential symbols received and interpreted by individual viewers, then used by them in interpersonal communication.

Audience members talk about television in dozens of ways at home. They often use television examples to explain feelings or to clarify situations. By referring to television's stories and characters, for instance, it is possible to disambiguate confusion. To say, for example, "you know, he's a real Archie Bunker type" is an effective way to describe a personality in a way that nearly everyone in the United States understands. Similarly, children may tell their mothers that life at their friends' houses is "just like the Brady Bunch." In cases like these, television's content becomes the common referents that facilitate effective interpersonal communication. Television becomes the ultimate standard by which private situations are compared and evaluated. The television world is also sometimes invoked in conversation by persons who believe their lives are not as satisfactory as those portrayed on the screen. Arthur Bremer, the would-be assassin of George Wallace, wrote in a school essay: "I would like to think that I was living with a television family and there was no yelling at home and no one hit me" (Carpenter, 1973).Television supplies low-risk topics that facilitate discussions between new acquaintances. Its content helps youngsters enter adult conversations and establishes an agenda for casual conversation at home, school, and work. The medium provides opportunities for the clarification of values through interpersonal discussion of what happens on the screen. Television's themes inhabit the decision-making processes of families, their problem-solving activities, and the social roles they imitate and learn from. Television furnishes themes for conflict too, stimulating discussions and arguments.

Television's content is reproduced through interpersonal relations in all social environments. Children base much of their playtime activities at school and in their neighborhoods on the lives of characters from television and film (Sarett, 1981; James and McCain, 1982). Sometimes children create elaborate games based on television drama. At other times they use bits and pieces of characterizations for spontaneous, inventive purposes. Since the appearance of the "Mr. T" character, for instance, young people from preschool to college age call each other "Fool!", the most famous of this television personality's characteristic lines. As humorous and innocent as this may appear, it glorifies and gives credibility to a manner of human interaction that is nonempathetic and hostile. Television's stylistic devices such as the predictable utterances of flat characters often gain fast and widespread appeal. These characterizations typically emphasize conflict and competition. Incorporation of these and other subjective program elements into interpersonal communication is commonplace.

Conclusion

The content of commercial television in the United States is organized in ways that reflect the values of economic forces that control the flow of information around most of the world. Audience members use television to construct a wide range of goal-directed activities. The psychological, sociological, and cultural conditions that are said to motivate human uses of television may never be well understood. Nonetheless, abundant empirical evidence indicates that the convenient visual medium is woven purposefully into the intricate tapestry of audience members' complicated lives. Uses of television, and the construction of communication in general, is patterned at the microsocial and macrosocial levels of analysis.

Human involvement with television introduces, extends, and reinforces its messages. When audience members merge mediated content into their own interaction, values implicit in programming are distributed through family and friendship networks to all of society. Therefore, human uses of television that supposedly demonstrate evidence of control over the medium by "active" audience members (Blumler and Katz, 1974), are actually integral elements of economic and cultural domination. From this perspective, some of television's uses are also some of its most powerful effects. This is an ironic twist in mass communication theory that hopefully will not be lost in future thinking and research about this ubiquitous, yet sometimes subtle, instrument of influence.

SARI THOMAS

Mass Media and the Social Order

To what extent do the mass media initiate and stimulate social change? In this provocative essay, Thomas describes how the media may also provide stability and order for the maintenance of the status quo. Examine the class structure messages of which you are aware and link them with the multi-class-coded and single class-coded media which you attend. Compare the Thomas position with that of James Lull in their description of "ideology" as a fundamental force in developing those media which affect each of us.

From its formal beginnings, one of the hallmarks of communication research has been an emphasis on studying change. For example, scholars have always documented "new" technologies to determine how economics and international relations are altered by such developments. Similarly, researchers have been demonstrating how mass-media images of various events and persons seemingly change over the years, usually in conjunction with societal upheaval, political movements, the actions of activist groups, and so forth. Most notably, communication scholars have always shown a profound interest in studying how mass media change people—in terms of their attitudes and values as manifested, for example, in voting behavior. Certainly, then, no one can argue that change is not a relevant part of studying mass-media institutions, message systems, and behavior. However, this emphasis on change may sometimes cause us to overlook another very vital function of the mass media. This other, overlooked function may be expressed with such words as maintenance, stability, and order. It could be argued that one of the most important processes to which the mass media contribute heavily is the maintenance of the social order.

What It Means to Maintain the Order

All living systems, individual organisms as well as societies, require a considerable amount of stability to survive. Our bodies, for example, can handle occasional trauma and serious irregularity, but not if that trauma is too prolonged or that irregularity is too severe. Based on their historical antecedents, human societies vary amongst themselves in terms of their specific requirements for stability. Although the specifics may vary from society to society, we can say that on the whole, social stability requires that the desires and needs of society members must be calibrated to what their society has to offer. Specifically, one can distingish between two closely related areas of life that must be shaped according to social conditions: (1) positioning in class structure and (2) concomitant life expectations. In other words, every society must, in order to sustain itself, have a fairly stable economic order and class structure and "appropriate" life expectations among its citizenry. In addition to these things, a society must have mechanisms by which change introduced into either of these areas is prevented from happening *too* quickly. For, most organic systems—our bodies, our societies—cannot survive radical change. For example, when history books relate that a revolution took place on such and such a date, what we have is a mere convenience for memorization and citation. We remember a particular act or the culmination of a set of events and pinpoint it in time for reference. In fact, however, revolutions occur as extended processes over a number of years, if not centuries. Given all the above, let us examine some ways in which the mass media in U.S. society contribute to the maintenance of the social order.

Class Structure

When examining the "shape" of U.S. class structure, a simple question inevitably emerges: How is it that a lot of people seem to act against their own self-interests? Regardless of one's personal political views, it is objectively the case that in the United States, wealth and power are not evenly distributed; a very small number of people have a great deal and most everyone else has relatively little. Yet, the masses with relatively little, work very hard to support this overall system which results in inequitable distribution of material wherewithal. Why is that? Or, more specifically, what role do the mass media play in helping to contain this system?

There are three interrelated messages promulgated throughout the popular U.S. media which may be interpreted as serving to make this system of imbalanced conditions acceptable to those who might otherwise find cause to react.

Message 1: There's Room at the Top

This first message emerges in the mass media's distorted portrayal of the socioeconomic structure; that is, real-life statistics are distorted. Anyone who watches a fair amount of television can observe what content-analysis research has borne out time and time again—that proportionately, the world of television characters is dominated much more by middle- to upper-class "people" than is American real life. Poorer people are simply not represented very often. Similarly, the occupations of television characters tend to lean far more to the professional, if not glamorous side of the employ-ment spectrum, whereas the masses of everyday workers who are needed for the overall real-life system are not proportionately portrayed.

For decades, scholars and critics have been explaining these "misrepre-sentations" in three ways. First, they claim the need for television to excite dramatically and, by extension, they suggest that the lives of the rich and glamorous are more exciting than those of others. Perhaps. But it might be argued that even if this is the case, it is a cultivated aesthetic. Second, the need for everyday people to relax and escape has also been cited in this context. Again, perhaps people do have (learned) inclinations toward seeing life-styles much different from their own. On the other hand, research has also indicated that people like to see characters with whom they *can* iden-tify. Finally, some have argued that since upper-middle-class writers create what we see and hear, we are merely getting a reflection of the writers' world. If it is true that we are getting such reflections, then we should also presume a most doubtful fact: That the lives of the real rich and famous are similar to the lives of their character-counterparts on TV. None of these explanations would seem thoroughly to explain television's distorted shape of class structure, so we might consider another possibility—that the rela-tively heavy-viewing American public is being taught indirectly that wealth is more plentiful than it really is. High school seniors might be more in-clined to apply to Harvard if they believe there are 5000 openings rather than 800. In the maintenance of the social order, widespread belief in a roomier upper echelon might also suggest that the possibilities of upward social mobility are good. This sort of message, then, sets the stage for Mes-sage 2.

Message 2: Anyone Can Achieve
Another theme common to the popular U.S. media is that, given the wide-open arena suggested by Message 1, anyone has a decent chance of accom-plishing upward social mobility. Classic examples of this message occur in our literature (e.g., Horatio Alger stories), our films (e.g., *Rocky*) and on television (e.g., *The Jeffersons*). In case one might think that the messages with which we're dealing are limited to mass-media fiction, it can usually be demonstrated that "real-life" media coverage (news, documentary, etc.) is also quite active in the maintenance process. For example, it is not only Rocky's story, but that of Sylvester Stallone's climb from Hell's Kitchen which is disseminated. Similarly, we need only to recall the kind of media attention paid to once-poor lottery winners.

In considering the "anyone-can-make-it" myth, we must also think about the frequency of and emphasis on such portrayals in comparison to other possibilities. That is, although it would be inaccurate to claim that people *never* "make it," we should remember that for every person who *does* accomplish this sort of radical achievement, there are hundreds, thousands, if not millions of others (depending on the goal) who *have tried* and failed. Except in brief statistical reports, we generally do not hear about the failures; even though the "failures" are most of us, we are infrequently documented and almost never portrayed.

The traditional explanation of this second "misrepresentation" usually insists that people like to see, hear, or read "uplifting" stories, that the average truths are too grim. In response, it might be said that because we've been raised on "uplifting" tales—that such tales are familiar and, thus, understandable to us—we may have developed such a preference. However, as suggested in the discussion of the "room-at-the-top" message, we must question *why* we have been familiarized with such stories. We must not jump to the conclusion that what we have (and possibly enjoy) automatically reflects what is innate or universally natural. The "anyone-can-make-it" myth, in our society, is taught so as to give hope to the many hopeless; but this hope is *not* for their individual, psychiatric well-being. Instead, the message is a *culturally* stabilizing one. Hope is *societally* functional; it keeps people keeping on—the essence of maintenance.

Does this mean that we never see any negative portrayals—that we never see people fall? Absolutely not. However, the third of our class-structure messages makes the equation complete by indicating where trouble may be found.

Message 3: It's Not So Great at the Top

Let us review in simplified form our messages on class structure stated thus far: There's a wide-open arena for upward social mobility and everyone has a decent chance to move up. These myths are good as far as they go; they allow people to believe in, and thus, support the system. But people are neither completely blind nor ignorant. Some of the people who struggle for something considerably better but still don't succeed appreciably can get disillusioned. A lot of people are well aware that it's a lot easier to get rich if one is born that way. Hope for the *future,* as provided in the first two messages may sometimes be comforting, but it's not always enough for the *present.* A message which can temper immediate hostility is required. It is in this context that the mass media provide the third message: that "it's not so great at the top." This message is often translated in several ways, for example, as "money doesn't buy happiness," "you can live on love," or "wealth/power corrupts."

In the world of mass-media fiction, we see this general message often. The Cratchits are essentially happy, whereas Ebenezer Scrooge, whose lust for wealth has overcome him, must suffer. In daytime-television serials, the poorer families usually display a loving harmony which is in stark comparison to the interpersonal conflict within the very wealthy families. In prime-time television, we see misery and constant trauma awaiting the Ewings, Carringtons, and so forth, but the Waltons are essentially at peace. In fact, one may wonder why night-time serials seem to concentrate on the rich. In addition to serving the "room-at-the-top" myth, another reason probably is that serialization requires "running" problems—serious complications that can continue from episode to episode. Such problems in the mass media are largely confined to the wealthy. Poorer or middle-class people are usually placed in contexts (often comedic) in which their problems can be *resolved* in a half hour or one hour.

American fiction films have also kept this myth alive for decades. The perennial classic *It's A Wonderful Life,* for example, tells us that wealth is not the answer, and, in the present, as we watch Rocky progress through various Roman numerals, we also see a man who is increasingly encumbered by worries as he climbs that ladder of success. Our popular novels, plays, and films often replay these morals for us in a variety of ways—by showing us characters who cannot find happiness in supposed success (e.g., Sammy Glick, Duddy Kravitz) or simply by taking us inside the world of glamor, power, and wealth and showing it to be pretty treacherous terrain (e.g., novels by Harold Robbins, Jacqueline Susann, or Judith Krantz.) Similarly, the Beatles echoed or foretold sentiments repeated throughout the lyrics of popular music when they sang "All You Need Is Love" or "Can't Buy Me Love."

Again, the message in question is not limited to mass-media fiction but appears quite regularly in our news and documentary. Unfortunately, there are too many murders that occur every day in the U.S. Technically, Sunny Von Bulow was not even murdered, but this wealthy, high-society matron's sad destruction allegedly by the hands of her baron husband received coverage hundreds of times more powerful and lengthy than that given to the numerous other victims of violent crime. In recent years, the murder of the wealthy "Scarsdale Diet Doctor," Herman Tarnower, by the headmistress of a socialite school is the only story which could compete with the Von Bulow saga. Barbara Walters interviews *these* people, Shana Alexander writes books about *them,* they are "covered" in national, network news, but the "little" people who similarly suffer or die are "fortunate" to receive the barest of public attention. Some might argue that our values are quite topsy-turvy here—that all human life should be treated with equal significance. However, the social value of these major stories far exceeds the value of any individual life. It is not that we are especially taught to mourn Sunny Von Bulow, Herman Tarnower, or the like, but that we are taught the unseemly side of wealth and power, no matter how atypical those unseemly instances might be.

The autobiographies of our rich and glamorous movie stars may be interesting on a variety of levels, but the majority of them tell the same story: you might think it's all limousines, parties, and fantasies fulfilled, but it's really (as Joan Fontaine so aptly entitled her tome) "no bed of roses." Indeed, a major role played by our huge celebrity-gossip industry is to let us know how difficult it is "up there."

Collectively, what such messages provide for us is a rationalization for our less than glamorous, powerful or wealthy lives. Though we are taught that we should have hope if wealth and its concomitants are what we *really* desire, we are simultaneously instructed to be grateful for the prices we *don't* have to pay.

"Appropriate" Expectations

That any little boy [sic] can grow up to be president is a classic "American dream." Awake, however, we know that with every generation, there will be only a handful of grown-up boys who will suffer real disappointment when this dream isn't realized. In other words, most of us know fairly early in life what our general limitations will be. It's not so much that we consciously have to figure these limitations out; instead, the "sense" of our possibilities is constantly bred in us from childhood. Usually, by the time we're teenagers, our goals and aspirations are pretty much in line with the reality of our circumstances.

The reason we must (at least tacitly) understand and accept such limitations is, again, a stability issue. American society has never been calibrated so as to provide all its citizens with the same advantages. It would be destabilizing were people to be regularly and strongly provoked by the clash of fantasy and reality. Our fantasies, then, must be tempered and given perspective. However, the mass media's role in helping to cultivate appropriate life expectations is not all that simple. For, within the *mass* audience, different groups of people must be taught different things. To understand how this is accomplished, we need to consider the concept of specialized *coding*.

Those systems that constitute the mass media vary in a number of ways—technologically, sensorily, aesthetically, etc. A mass-media system may also be classified in terms of its primary audience. Any system that is basically directed toward a demographically homogenous audience is *single class coded*. Within a single-class-coded system, there will usually be an ideological uniformity to the messages, promoting ideology that is "appropriate" to its fairly uniform audience. For example, weekly national tabloids (e.g., *The National Enquirer, The Star*) are primarily geared to a working-class readership. As one might predict from previous discussion, these tabloids densely concentrate on stories of "little people making it" or "coping successfully with life's hardships" counterposed with articles describing the problems of celebrity life.

Clearly, certain mass-media systems are oriented toward a more diverse or heterogeneous audience. Such systems are *multiclass coded;* that is, there are special subdivisions catering to special groups within the given mediated form. Moving across subdivisions, one can see ideological shifts that are sometimes dramatic. The cases of "women's" reading material as well as popular erotica are interesting examples of variations in coding.

With the case of romance/confession magazines, we have an instance of very narrow single-class coding. Here, the primary audience is not only working class, but women within that group. Thus, the material in these artifacts needs to "make sense" of very specialized social-adjustment problems. Were we to consider the traditional category of "women's" magazines (to include only publications such as *Good Housekeeping, McCall's, Ladies' Home Journal,* etc.) we again see a narrow, single-class orientation: middle-class, female homemakers. Such magazines had the role of rationalizing, if not glorifying, the conditions of domestically confined women who were and, in fact, remain, central to the reproduction of a male-dominated labor force. It would seem that more recently, relatively small changes have occured in the social structure along gender lines. Thus, new, more specialized periodicals evolved for women who still have to contend with a male-dominated order, but not necessarily in a domestic context. If we expand our category, "women's" magazines, to include the traditional as well as newer periodicals (e.g., *Ms.*), one might begin to identify a class coding within this system. However, in this case, the ideological variations are moderate, to say the least. For the differences in messages required by single-working versus married-homemaking women are relatively minor compared to the larger understanding to which all "women's" magazines must arrive: how to be content and function peacefully under male domination. Ironically, even the more "radical" of these magazines may be interpreted as teaching this message.

If we turn our attention to erotica magazines (those publications designed to titillate sexually, such as *Playboy* or *Hustler*), a more clear-cut example of multiclass coding emerges. With erotica designed for heterosexual men, two classes of magazines may be noted. The first group, directed toward upwardly mobile men *(Playboy* and *Penthouse),* presents many articles and advertisements recommending the "good life" in terms of high-priced cars, designer clothing, fancy technology, luxurious travel, fine dining, and so forth. More importantly, perhaps, these upwardly mobile magazines present uncommonly beautiful, "perfect-bodied," seductively posed women as female standards to fit in with the other artifacts of the "good life."

The second category of erotica is designed for working-class men and includes such magazines as *Cheri, Gallery,* and *Hustler.* Overall, these publications contain little written material; articles, if any, are typically geared toward graphic documentation of sexual events and experiences, and advertisements are almost exclusively for sexual paraphernalia and services. The women populating the pages of these magazines, although boldly sexual, are typically "imperfect" physical specimens who are lacking the somewhat ethereal qualities of their counterparts in the upwardly mobile publications.

From even these brief descriptions of the two classes of heterosexual-male-oriented erotica, it shouldn't require extensive explanation to see how standards and expectations are differentially cultivated along social-class lines. However, the coding within popular erotica does not end with these two cases, and in exploring this subject further, we may return with an interesting twist to the subject of "women's" reading material.

As the feminist movement gained momentum in demanding sexual equality, it seemed only natural that women, too, might be accorded their own slice of the erotica pie, so to speak. At one point, several publications featuring naked males, ostensibly for female appreciation, were launched. Of these initial efforts, only *Playgirl* magazine survived as the single example of popular print erotica designed for women. Now, overall, *Playgirl's* written material is more sexually oriented than that published in other magazines for women (including *Cosmopolitan*), but still, its articles have more in common with all other "women's" magazines than with written material in "men's" magazines. Specifically, *Playgirl* articles, like those generally found in "women's" publications, usually deal with the condition of being female (e.g., "how to deal with sexual harassment" or "how to cope when his salary is less than yours"). Another way to look at this is as follows: There really is no such thing as "men's" magazines or, for that matter, "white" magazines in the same way that there *are* such things as "women's" magazines or "black" magazines (e.g., *Ebony* or *Jet.*) For although it is functional to have specialized media which quite specifically rationalize social subordinancy to disempowered groups (e.g., women and blacks), the empowered orders of the population do not require such services. *Playboy, Esquire,* or even *Gentleman's Quarterly* don't need to teach men how to survive with their maleness because being male is not a handicap in our society. Thus, so-called "men's" magazines tend to publish general "American culture" material.

Advertisements in *Playgirl* are often for "exotic" garments (ostensibly to excite men in intimate situations) and even for paraphernalia that supposedly will heighten a man's sexual reactions in these intimate contexts. Of course, the male-oriented erotica (particularly that of the working class) also features advertisements for the same paraphernalia (i.e., to enhance *men's* sexual experiences). Such advertising patterns subtly set an agenda as to "appropriate" expectations for seduction and pleasure-giving "responsibilities" in our culture.

The photographs in *Playgirl* are also quite telling in terms of a gender-class code. Unlike the physically perfect models appearing in *Playboy* and *Penthouse,* and even unlike the physically imperfect (but, often physically exceptional) models appearing in men's working-class erotica, the male models appearing in *Playgirl* (with the frequent exception of the center-fold) are pretty much average guys. That is to say, the men's faces, musculature, and sexual attributes are typically of the sort that the average woman might find among most of the under-35 men she might meet. Therefore, the first thing we might say is that although ordinary women have to "compete" with some pretty powerful fantasy images, *Playgirl* does not provide parallel competition for men. This, of course, is very much in keeping with the maintenance of a male-power order. What is also exceedingly interesting is that, unlike the sensual or blatantly sexual texture common to most all photographs in male-oriented erotica, the pictures in *Playgirl* are nonsexual. That is, unlike the women models in male-oriented erotica, the men in *Playgirl* are rarely coy, beckoning, or sexually exhibitionistic in their body positioning, eye gaze, or general demeanor. They are almost never shown in a state of sexual arousal. What they *are* is naked—a wallet snapshot minus clothes. This lack of sexuality is also important in the maintenance process. Despite the lip service to sexual democracy paid by the existence of *Playgirl* magazine, *male*-objectified erotica is something that is rarely created for women simply because it would be inappropriate to train women to have the same expectations as men. In the imbalance of power, it would be similarly inappropriate for men to have to expect to satisfy women in the way that women are expected to satisfy men. All in all, then, one should begin to see how specialized coding within the mass-media system provides various sectors of the population with standards and expectations appropriate to their existing status in the established social order.

Controlling Change

Although maintenance of the prevailing order is something with which all living systems are preoccupied, this by no means implies that systems can't

and don't change. Change doesn't occur simply because maintenance procedures have failed, but because change and maintenance are interlocking
aspects of life. In one sense, maintenance occurs *because* of the inevitability of change, that is, maintenance processes prevent change from causing
critical or fatal injuries to systems.

Change can be either existential or purposeful. Existential change results
quite naturally and inevitably from living; it is the result of the present
compounding the past. Existential change is that to which Heraclitus referred when he said "a man can never step in the same river twice." Any
living event is different (changes) every moment of its existence because
time is de facto an agent of change. Purposeful change is the intentional
effort by a person or persons to manipulate the present so as to alter the
seeming course of the future. Political revolutions are obvious examples of
purposeful change. However, a possible explanation for the failure of so
many political revolutions to bring about what was originally intended is
that existential change was not accounted for in the overall revolutionary
scheme. Indeed, social scientists know very little about how time, alone,
operates as an independent agent. In any case, social change of either type,
especially of the sometimes-radical purposeful variety, must be regulated
so that a livable order prevails. The mass media seem to help regulate change
through at least five mechanisms: (1) preparation, (2) "culture"-lagging,
(3) counteraction, (4) diversion, and (5) discrediting.

The mediated portrayal of possible change to come is what is meant by
preparation. Idiomatically stated, mass-media preparation is a way of softening the blow before the boom is lowered. Although popular science fiction typically speaks more to contemporary issues than to the future, a second function of science fiction is to introduce anticipated change. Similarly,
for example, print or broadcast journalism might provide a segment dealing with ongoing genetic research that seems on the verge of a "break-
through." Such stories prepare the public for change and, thereby, make
the process of change-introduction lengthier so as to provide more time for
the diffusion of a new condition or idea.

Although preparation helps lengthen the change process by introducing
something new *before* it actually emerges, "culture"-lagging helps lengthen
that process *after* the emergence of a new event or idea. More specifically,
it is often the case that the mass media will give attention ("agendize") an
issue long after it has been a more-than-passing concern on a grass-roots,
interpersonal level. For example, the feminist movement was well under
way for many years before movies, television shows and traditional "wom-
en's" magazines began dealing with it in any substantial way.

The fact that the mass media *do* eventually deal with change-provoking
public issues should not be taken to mean that the treatment of such issues

is always, or even typically, evenhanded and accurate. That is, "substantial" *attention* does not mean that the media are positively promoting a given change. On one hand, it might be argued that *any* attention given to an issue, positive or negative, is promotional by virtue of the publicity per se. On the other hand, the media are capable of providing this kind of promotion while at the same time diffusing the power (and thus, the change-producing potential) of the issue. This diffusion of power primarily occurs through counteraction, diversion, and discrediting.

Counteraction is the process of giving vent to a change-producing issue while simultaneously "lobbying" against it adoption. More often than not, the public airing of the issue is performed straightforwardly while the reactive lobbying is subtly disseminated. On television, for example, it is common for talk shows, made-for-TV movies, and many situation-comedy series to treat consciously (often on a "culture"-lagged basis) a contemporary public issue such as the case of married, familied women dedicatedly pursuing a full-time, out-of-home career. The programs may even provide a sympathetic treatment of the issue. However, in keeping with the example, one might simultaneously examine aspects of violence and sex on television to see a different portrait painted. For example, if married-homemaking women are continuously portrayed as much less likely to be victims of violent crime than their working counterparts, or if marriage-and-family-oriented women are continuously shown to be more desirable to men, then counteractive messages can be said to exist.

Whereas counteraction involves the placement of a change-related issue amid messages of contrary suggestion, diversion refers to the treatment of the relatively nonthreatening aspects of a controversial issue. In the process of diversion, two interrelated things may be accomplished in terms of regulating change. First, attention is drawn away from the potentially radical (and often, most important) element(s) of the controversy, and second, some peripheral and/or safe issue is spotlighted in its place. Concentration on a peripheral or safe issue sets an agenda with respect to "what is important" about the controversy and thereby helps deflect future public debate from getting close to the more threatening problem. In light of the theme of this reading, it might be interesting to consider examples of "media self-examination" to illustrate such diversion.

Considerable critical acclaim greeted the release of the movie *Network*. In addition to aesthetically oriented praise, the film was hailed as a brutal and scathing drama/satire on the condition of mass-network television. Although receiving a bit less attention, a slightly later film, *S. O. B.*, was similarly acclaimed, this time for offering a hard-hitting satire on the condition of the mass-oriented film industry. There seemed to be a uniform delight engendered by these two movies as a sort of retributional "high"; the guys who have been "sticking it to" the public for so long (as the movies, themselves, asserted) have finally been exposed, and even better, hoisted on their own petards, as it were.

What exactly *did* these movies say about mass-media industry? About what were they so scathing and brutal? In truth, the films offered only one central criticism—that mass-media executives and entrepreneurs will do pretty much anything for ratings, ticket buying . . . money. Is this big news? Does this really go against the grain of the American ethos, or, put another way, don't the mass media provide countless counteractive messages suggesting that competition, entrepreneurism, indeed capitalism are good? Might not these films be just full-spectrum portrayals of the major class-structure myths—a lot of people trying to achieve, making it, and being corrupted and crazied in the process? In fact, *Network* is ironically and precisely the kind of film that *television* might have made about television. Most importantly, what neither *Network, S. O. B.* or a host of self-reflexive media presentations rarely take into consideration is the criticism that may come from concern over the kinds of ideas that our mass media promote. Diverting attention away from analysis of mass-media ideology and focusing instead on industrial greed helps to diffuse a potential powderkeg.

Although diversionary tactics might orient public attention to *safer* aspects of a potential change-producing issue, discrediting (Gerbner, 1978) that issue implies directing attention to only or mostly its "negative" or vapid aspects. For example, through a good part of the 1960s antiwar movement, protesters were often characterized by the media more in terms of their sloppy appearances and too-liberal life-styles than in terms of their views on United States Southeast Asian policy. Similarly, to a person whose only contact with feminism in the early 1970s was through the mass media, it might have appeared that "bra burning" was the central aim of the women's movement. Clearly, discreditation of this sort may help considerably in weakening the force of a change-producing issue.

Intentionality

In examining the issues discussed in this reading, it might be easy to jump to a dangerous conclusion: That those in the roles of creating and disseminating mass-media messages are somehow consciously engineering our society's maintenance. This is far from the case. Clearly, in particular instances, writers, producers, and so forth are aware of the ideological implications of certain features of their creations. However, by and large, people write what has been written, produce what has been produced, create what is "appropriate," and a great deal of contemplation and reflection is not required to so reproduce a functional reality. People who create or attempt to create functionally "inappropriate" work are either relegated to the confines of relative anonymity in some small subcultural pocket or, even more typically, they "fail" as creators. In any case, such individuals will not likely become *agents provocateurs* of the popular culture (unless, of course, their work becomes "appropriate"). Those identified as the "radicals" in the *mass* system are typically the "safe" creators who take on controversy in a diversionary form.

In fact, it might be argued that there is a safety net attached on the audience's side. The occasional "inappropriate" or even radical production that slips through into the mass-public sphere usually either blends into the more conservative background or, when standing alone, does not meet with much appreciation. It is difficult to cite examples in this category because they are few, but the 1977 film, *Blue Collar*, may be a case in point. This film which uncompromisingly and heavy-handedly portrayed corruption and futility as characteristics of the system rather than of individuals did terribly at the box-office despite excellent performances by Richard Pryor and others. Who's to say exactly why this film failed? Bad marketing strategies? Poor release-timing? "Inappropriate" ideology?

The point is that no matter what business we work in, *all* businesses (including those attached to the mass media) are only subsidiaries of the larger industry of culture production. This argument will be elaborated shortly; it is sufficient for the present to advance a position contrary to the dogma of rationalism embodied in the phrase *cogito ergo sum*. As William Graham Sumner aptly reversed this concept, ". . . the first task of life is to live. Men begin with acts, not with thoughts" (1971, p. 112).

Mass Media

Over the past few decades there have been many attempts to define what a *mass* medium actually is. Many scholars seem to view the *mass* medium as something emerging from the Industrial Revolution. Consequently, events they call mass media are relatively recent technological systems. Admittedly, the terms "mass," "popular," etc., have been rather casually employed here to refer to those message systems and subsystems that are dominant in this society because they reach huge numbers of people . . . because they are pervasive. Although pertinence of this terminology to foregoing discussion was minimal, there remains one outstanding point to which this matter is relevant.

It would be inaccurate to view postindustrial, technological, message-producing systems as the *only* types of message systems to have major impact on social-order maintenance. For, throughout history, it would appear that the dominant (most pervasive) modes of human symbolic creation have always served in the general process of cultural integration. Thus, examining the social function of ancient Egyptian bas-relief, Gothic stained-glass windows, Renaissance painting, and so forth, would show such artifacts to have both taught and reinforced the reigning values and beliefs in the societies from which they emerged.

Certainly, no one can claim that postindustrial technology was an inconsequential development in the history of the social functions of symbolic artifacts. Indeed, the consequences of industrialization is the topic of countless publications. However, for our purposes here, the *continuity* of the order-regulating role played by symbolic artifacts—whether or not such artifacts conform to a stringent definition of "mass"—is the more useful perspective.

The Mass Media and Interpersonal Forces

The discipline of communication has, for a long time, produced debate over whether the mass media or interpersonal forces are the more powerful in governing behavior. On one hand, people may have families, peers, formal education, work situations, religious affiliations, etc., all of which sociologists and anthropologists have shown to be influential in determining behavior. On the other hand, in addition to communication research showing mass-media "effects," U.S. statistics indicate that the only activity in which the average citizen engages more than television viewing (let alone combined media use) is sleeping! Thus, it's hard to imagine that the mass media are anything but influential. The problem with *either* argument is that the theoretical distinction between interpersonal and mass-media activities separates that which is not, in practice, separable.

As suggested earlier, culture production (i.e., the interdependent creation and regulation of material artifacts, standardized activity, and worldview) is the overarching industry for which all other systems and institutions are supposed to work and to which they all are supposed to contribute. From this perspective, it might be further suggested that all "subsidiary industries" (including interpersonal and mass-media activities) can best be identified as interdependent rather than independent social forces.

The nature and extent of this system interdependence has also been debated for a long time in the social sciences. From the general perspective of this reading, there would seem to be three variations on the integration of social systems.

Interdependence Yielding Ideological or Behavioral Uniformity
With regard to any given behavioral or ideological issue in a society, one might find several spheres of activity that are contributing to a coherent

version of reality on that issue. For example, despite all the clamor over *mass-media* violence, it is exceedingly difficult to identify the mass media as a single or even central force in this matter. When we consider, among other things, that our cultural norms include corporal punishment of children (family), physically ferocious sport (peer-group leisure), capital punishment, and war (government), it seems clear that the teaching of violence for purposes of catharsis and problem solving is a topic in the "lesson plans" of various systems.

Interdependence Yielding Appropriate *Ideological or Behavioral Variance*
As suggested earlier in the discussion of specialized coding, different groups of people are taught different things. What is important to remember here is that these differences are usually functional to the operation of society as a whole. In this context, then, it must be emphasized that specialized coding does not occur exclusively in the mass media, but in interpersonal spheres as well.

In the case of popular erotica, we saw that upwardly mobile men, working-class men, and women (as a general class) were offered distinctly different versions of sexual fantasy. It was further argued that this delivery of different sexual perspectives is useful in maintaining the social structure with reference to social-class and gender relations. One can similarly turn to Protestant theology and teaching as an interpersonal example of this general process.

If, instead of sexual-fantasy images, we look at the issue of salvation, it can be noted that different versions of salvation are taught to different Protestant denominations. Here, a crucial factor is that most Protestant denominations are linked to specific socioeconomic classes. Thus, if fundamentalists and Pentecostals (predominantly composed of "lower" classes) are typically taught that personal piety through belief and prayer will yield salvation, whereas Episcopalian and Presbyterians (generally composed of "middle and upper" classes) receive a greater emphasis on the salvational value of world improvement through vocational or professional achievement, we can see again how people are taught *different* things that are appropriate to the overall functioning of the order. With the latter example, it is suggested that for poorer classes, "salvation through personal faith and devotion" is not only a method within their reach, but one that doesn't encourage striving for upward mobility. Conversely, the upwardly mobile condition is rationalized though the instruction of "salvation by worldly acomplishment."

Certain scholars have sometimes labeled differing versions of reality— particularly those leading to conflicts between groups—as "dysfunctional." This assumption—that variance (and its resulting conflict) are unilaterally "bad" for a society—seems to confuse the scientific term "functional" with the value term "good." However, being "functional" is being "good" only insofar as it is good to stabilize and maintain the existing social structure. For example, hostility between working-class whites and blacks is morally "bad," but this *doesn't* mean that it's dysfunctional. The maintenance of the present order in the United States depends on disjunction in the "lower" classes so that workers will remain subordinated. Similarly, it is neither surprising nor dysfunctional (except perhaps for Norman Lear) that the character of Archie Bunker was seen by some as a disgusting buffoon and by others as an unsung hero. Such variations in response are perfectly complementary to the ideological divisions required in the uniform functioning of contemporary U.S. society.

Independence Yielding Dysfunction and Change

To the extent that a society is stable, all of its systems (interpersonal and mass) will have a consonance based on either uniformity and or *functional* variance. However, societies are living systems subject to mutation and modification, and, as a result, dysfunctional interrelationships may arise. When dysfunctional change is introduced into the social system that change may be either diverted, counteracted, or discredited, it may (in extreme cases) destroy the society, or it may (usually through processes of prolonging its effects) be ultimately absorbed and, thus, alter the social order. The last possibility (including the ramifications of "existential" change) suggests that *complete* cultural integration (a *perfectly* functional social order) never exists entirely at any given point in time. However, it does not seem that "perfection" in this regard is a requirement. Instead, an operating society will preponderantly evince a functional integration of its systems and institutions.

The foregoing discussion illustrated how various social systems and institutions (involving both interpersonal *and* mass communication) are interdependent parts of the social order as a whole. In this context, then, it is difficult to delineate precisely what functions, if any, the mass media *exclusively* perform in the sphere of social-order maintenance. However, although it may not be possible to demarcate some clear-cut territory belonging to the mass media, it may be useful to regard the development of mass communication as a social imperative in certain conditions.

In societies where oral, face-to-face interaction is the dominant carrier of the social order—where the teaching and reinforcement of worldview is transmitted through interpersonal means—large-scale organization breaks down or never becomes possible. For example, in ancient Mesopotamia prior to the use of papyrus, the attempt to establish royal/priestly control over a wider area ended in failure because of the incompatibility of resulting local variations of the "order." That is, if 10 different priests are sent to 10 different places to establish control, 10 different "stories" may emerge. However, the story can be kept straight if the priests remain in one place.

Innis (1951) pointed out that the integration of societies over large areas of space went hand and hand with the emergence of media capable of widespread distribution. In the earlier cases, the course was served by papyrus and writing utensils. But, as we can see, this process has never ceased in societal evolution. In fact, the extensiveness of mass mediation may be even more vital presently because, in significant respects, societal integration is becoming increasingly global. Whether such globalism is a cause and/or effect of mass communication, it is no accident that the ideological themes mentioned earlier are becoming increasingly universal.

The temporal corollary to this spatial expansion is interesting in terms of social order maintenance. Goody and Watt (1962) have argued that in cultures where the dominant mode of communication cannot adeptly transverse space (in oral cultures), tradition and order are better maintained because anything from the past that does not adapt to the present is pretty much left by the wayside. In other words, in preliterate cultures, the past remains only in human memory which is considerably more prone to adaptation and death than technologically stored records. Thus, in cultures where pervasive mass media permit not only spatial distribution, but preservation *over time,* a destabilizing tendency may result from the public's exposure to messages from the past which are incompatible with present conditions. If this is accurate, then mass-mediated society is inherently less stable than a non-mass-mediated society. In this light, the pervasive conservatism of mass-media content makes even more sense; because the mass media are requisite in spatially expanded society, they must guard the order from without and within.

Note

This essay was originally delivered as a lecture at the Department of Communication Arts and Sciences, Queens College, CUNY, November, 21, 1984. For that purpose and for the purposes of this volume, the attempt was not to present a densely annotated review, but an overview and integration of a culturalist-functionalist approach to mass-communication study. Nonetheless, the theory in this essay is much indebeted to an enormous amount of earlier work in sociology and anthropology— particularly that of the British and American functionalist "schools." Because many of the ideas here are synthesized from positions taken by others (usually with respect to a different range of questions), particular point-by-point citation is rare. The Bibliography suggests those works that were most important in this effort. The author apologizes for any violence done to these works in their reapplication and incorporation.

Postscript

Every medium of communication connects human beings to forces existing outside their personal environment. Each new medium redefines a person's relationship to the knowledge which is unique to a particular time and place.

The acquisition of knowledge is an inherent part of human development, a development which, in the broad cultural perspective, cannot be curtailed or short circuited. Some individuals acquire more or less knowledge, but none can exempt themselves from a world bent on the acceleration of amassed information and data. The result is that we want to know more and more about all facets of existence. It could be said that we know more and understand less. Nonetheless, the direction of the knowledge generating process always thrusts us forward.

The connection of knowledge and media technology is symbiotic. Each media innovation, each step in the process of the absorption of knowledge spawns and stimulates further need for knowledge which promotes changes in technology. Knowledge stimulates knowledge. Technology creates technology and technology generates knowledge. As each increment occurs the relationship of one person to another is altered and the relationship of person to technology is altered as well.

Walter Ong explores the restructuring of human personality and values in the symbiotic process of knowledge acquisition and technological advancement. We have selected this provocative essay to close our anthology because it synthesizes a number of perspectives intrinsic to our theme of the media-interpersonal connection. Ong has taken the vantage point of history and linked it with the pschological and sociological reverberation of knowledge, media, and person, leaving us to ponder our choices in a world of exploding knowledge and technology.

WALTER J. ONG

Knowledge in Time

Man is a venture in knowledge. The story of knowledge and its uses, good and bad, is the story of man. Man's knowledge is essentially incremental. It not only accumulates but also metabolizes and grows, feeding on other things and on itself. Its potential is unlimited, which means that when it is true as true can be, and certain beyond the shadow of a doubt, it is also incomplete.

Knowledge did not always grow so fast as it does now. Its growth has accelerated from an extremely slow start. Insofar as quantitative statements about knowledge have meaning, we can be fairly certain that there was a time toward the beginning of man's history when knowledge took 10,000 years—perhaps even 100,000 years—to double, and that at a later period it doubled in 1000 years, and still later in 500 years. It has been estimated that today man's knowledge doubles every 15 years. We are used to this tempo of development of knowledge and find it hard to believe how slowly knowledge advanced before the development of writing. In some stone-age cultures, the same pattern for a hand axe or spear point persisted for thousands upon thousands of years. In such cultures massive social and psychological structures evidently almost immobilized knowledge.

But virtual immobilization was necessary. It insured against loss. Before the invention of writing (only some 5500 years ago, around 3500 B.C.) knowledge was not only in short supply but also devastatingly insecure. In cultures without records, it could easily leak away. Gargantuan efforts were needed simply to conserve knowledge by keeping it fixed either through recitative formulas for such knowledge or, for nonverbalized knowledge, through such cultural institutions as the tradition of unvarying spear-point design. Without writing, mere retention of the knowledge that had accumulated (no one knew quite how) proved so formidable a task that even apart from the risk of loss if set patterns were varied, the subsistence economies of early mankind could afford neither the time nor the energy for planned knowledge expansion. This state of affairs persisted to a greater or lesser degree for centuries after the invention of writing and even beyond the invention of print until the implications of print for storing and shaping knowledge were digested into the social consciousness and individual psychological structures.

Until print was thus interiorized, cultures remained largely what David

From *Knowledge and the Future of Man*, edited by Walter J. Ong, S.J. Copyright © 1968 by Holt, Rinehart and Winston. Reprinted by permission of Holt, Rinehart and Winston, Publishers.

Riesman has well labeled "tradition-directed." In such cultures, when expansion of knowledge actually did occur, it was likely to pass with little notice. Thus medieval European thinkers, for example, went far beyond Aristotle in the development of formal logic, moving toward modern symbolic logic (though without the symbols or variables of modern logic, so that the movement was all the more arduous). But they appear to have been aware hardly at all that they had made vast new discoveries. The essential intellectual need was still felt to be holding onto what was known. Eric Havelock's intriguing *Preface to Plato* and Frances A. Yates's seminal work on *The Art of Memory* have made it clear how early world views and thought structures inherited from antiquity and still widely operative as late as the seventeenth century were in great part determined by the need to hold knowledge in patterns that served ready recall. You knew the things that lent themselves to memory schemes.

Memorization and the iconographic imagination, which memorization encourages, constituted a style of life. The Ramist "method" or way of abstractly organizing knowledge and communication, which swept the most technologizing parts of Europe in the sixteenth and seventeenth centuries, was in great part of tantalizingly simple memory system, disguised as science and made plausible by diagrams that could be given ready currency by print. The method proved short-lived, for the new invention of printing, which Ramism exploited, was actually making mnemonic systems in the mind less necessary, as our various computing machines have finally made them obsolete. Knowledge storage was effected more and more outside the mind, first by writing, then by print, finally by our electronic circuitry. But those living through the changes induced by new knowledge storage and retrieval and communication developments are never entirely aware of what the changes are. Hence of necessity they lean on obsolescence and even find obsolescence exciting.

For the advancement of learning, storage of knowledge is essential, but insofar as knowledge is mere "information" or "structure" its storage and retrieval are not truly intellectual tasks. As artificial extramental information storage and retrieval systems (writing, print, and electronics) evolved, the mind was freed more and more to do its proper work of thinking, and the acceleration of knowledge got under way. To store and organize knowledge, oral cultures had to devote vast amounts of time to reciting it. Learning *was* in effect memorizing. Early chirographic cultures recorded knowledge and began to analyze it. Late chirographic cultures, such as that of medieval Europe, codified it. The typographical culture of the Renaissance indexed it; indexes were not unknown in manuscripts, but they remained relatively inefficient until print could produce hundreds of copies of a text with all the words in exactly the same place on the page, at which time indexing became a major selling point for learned works. Today we have computerized knowledge, which is to say that not merely have we set up outside the mind exponentially more effective information storage and retrieval systems but also, more basically, that we are actually breeding knowledge outside the mind. The computer is a special milieu in which knowledge can be cultivated outside its normal habitat.

Of course, the computer breeds knowledge only insofar as knowledge involves structures of "information"—that is, insofar as it can be quantified, directly or indirectly. This means that the computer can do almost anything with knowledge except think about it, which is to say it can do everything but decide with reference to an actual, existing situation whether something is true or false. An actual, existing situation is always one in which there are nonquantified and even nonconceptualized factors. It is, in other words, a noncomputerized situation. Computer verdicts concerning "truth" or "falsity" are vacuities. Either before or after they are arrived at, they have to be applied by someone who *really* knows. But the computer frees the mind to apply knowledge (to judge truth and falsity) in many situations more complex and sweeping than any the mind could compass without computerization.

Not only do new knowledge storage, retrieval, and communication systems (the "media") accelerate the growth of knowledge, but the growth of knowledge also of course accelerates the development of new media. Scripts grow out of the knowledge accumulated in oral culture, the alphabet out of greater knowledge accumulated in a pictographic script culture, alphabetic letterpress typography out of structures of knowledge favored by a chirographic or manuscript culture, and electronic circuitry out of the vast store of knowledge which typography made possible and put at the service of modern science.

When we look to the speed with which the media develop, we find that here, too, there is a spectacular acceleration. Only after being on earth some 500,000 years (to take a fairly good working figure) did man move from his original oral culture, in which written records were unknown and untought of, to literacy. The first script appeared around 3500 B.C. In another two thousand years the alphabet put in its appearance, around 1500 B.C. By the mid-1400s of the Christian era alphabetic letterpress printing appeared in west central Europe. In another four hundred years the telegraph was devised. Within another sixty years, the wireless. Thirty-five years more brought television. A few decades later we had the whole panoply of spacecraft, Telstar, electronic computers in vast quantity, and countless related devices. Each advance exploited antecedently existing knowledge more efficiently than had the advances that went before, for new knowledge does not simply layer itself onto existing knowledge but interacts with it. It is not an additive but a multiplier.

The total pattern of acceleration in knowledge is thus a complex one. Of itself, knowledge grows and accelerates its own growth. This growth also produces new media, which further accelerate growth (and of course change the structure of knowledge and of the psyche, as will be seen later). The new media themselves, finally, appear in an accelerating sequence, more and more of them faster and faster as time moves on.

II

We have reached a period today when the accumulation of knowledge has made possible insights of new clarity and depth into the history of knowledge itself. Growth of knowledge soon produces growth in knowledge about knowledge, its constitution, and its history, for knowledge is of itself reflective. Given time, it will try to explain not only the world but itself more and more.

What has happened and is happening to knowledge can be considered under several more or less distinct headings: (1) growth in knowledge of the physical universe; (2) growth in knowledge of man and his life world, including his sense of history; (3) increased exteriorization of knowledge (connected with the development of "objective" science); (4) interiorization of knowledge; (5) thrust into the future and growth in responsibility; (6) the permanent limitations of growth. We can take these up in order.

Knowledge of the Physical Universe

When marveling about growth in knowledge, many persons focus immediately on our increase in knowledge of the physical universe during the past hundred years (since Darwin) or perhaps three hundred years (since Newton). Here results of increased knowledge are indeed striking. Discoveries in the physical sciences often lead to the production of "hardware" or other products that are highly visible and palpable and that enable man to dominate his physical environment spectacularly: steam engines, telegrams, radar, jet-propelled spacecraft, plastics, television. Knowledge is power. In the early 1600s Francis Bacon gave this old commonplace its best publicized utterance, and Thomas Hobbes soon reiterated Bacon's cosmopolitan Latin in plain English. But Bacon and Hobbes only stated the aphorism. We have lived it, particularly regarding the physical sciences.

Even at his imaginative best, early man could not quite foresee what we have lived through. Bacon had thought of better organizing or "methodizing" the knowledge already on hand and of exploiting nature by achieving a better grasp of "forms." He hardly conceived of breaking through the kinds of frontiers that Newton, Darwin, and Planck have put behind us.

The breakthroughs began with two seventeenth-century developments: the application of mathematics to the physical sciences and an intent and minute observation of nature unknown to earlier ages, which, contrary to the still popular persuasion, had not consciously thrown out induction in favor of deduction but had simply supposed that ordinary observation sufficed for inductive purposes and which thus had not troubled with controlled experiment. Anyone could tell immediately that a heavy body "naturally" falls faster than a light body because when stones and feathers were thrown out a high window at the same time, the stones reached the ground first. Despite Newton's laws of gravitation, they still do.

Experimentation to prove they do not or should not had to do less with ordinary experience than with pure science. But physical science seldom stays pure, and the new sciences in the seventeenth century and later made themselves felt in practical ways very soon. Indeed, post-Newtonian science was in alliance with practical craftsmanship from the very beginning. The closely controlled observations called for by the new mathematization and experimentation themselves demanded finely constructed tools, such as telescopes and microscopes and vacuum pumps. The new sciences used knowledge-producing tools more than earlier science had ever done, and it was a natural thing for the artisans who could make delicate machines for research purposes to make scientifically designed machines for practical purposes. A new breed of thinker arose, the "inventor." "Projectors" the eighteenth century still called them disdainfully, with little sympathy for the Thomas A. Edison syndrome.

We have long ago passed the stage where "inventors" seem intruders on the intellectual scene. The physical sciences have paid off in practical contrivances and processes so abundantly as to make us even discredit science that does not have immediate application. Systematized, formalized knowledge has penetrated the whole of life. In a technologized society not only automobiles and television sets but even soap and apples cannot be produced effectively without a store of systematized, formalized knowledge. Artisan's rule-of-thumb skills have largely yielded to science and are yielding more and more daily.

The result has been a new texture for life itself. Man is dealing constantly with complex, formalized structures rather than with "nature," whether it be in planting corn specifically designed for his region's rainfall and temperatures or crossing a neighborhood street intersection, which he must do by following traffic lights programmed to the city-wide diurnal flow of traffic. It is misleading to imply, as Jacques Ellul and others do, that these formal patterns are something alien to man, a self-subsistent intrusion on his life. They are in fact very human structures devised by human beings in order to make their lives bareable, to give them more security, privacy, and personal independence than early man ever knew. (Philippe Ariès has shown in *Centuries of Childhood* how lacking in security, privacy, and independence were living conditions for even the well to do through the eighteenth century and later. The crowding in our slums today was normal to earlier urban life; it has become intolerable because now for the first time it can be avoided and indeed is avoided by most city dwellers.)

It is not the inhuman effects of technological living—our being "dominated" by machines, whatever that may mean—but the human effects that pose our problem. The science that underlies technological living has given a new shape to the contents of the human mind. In earlier ages abstract, formalized thought was dominantly philosophical and religious. Knowledge of the physical universe, while it was not so thin as the popular imperssion today would have it, was still relatively jejune and unsatisfying. Today the physical sciences have become so rich and fecund that the mind can lose itself in them for a lifetime.

The mere bulk of learning in the physical sciences is overwhelming. Devising systems to abstract, store, and retrieve the results of each year's new research has become a major problem. Even with the best of such systems, it is occasionally less time consuming to repeat certain bits of research than it would be to comb the vast float of extant literature for needed information.

The overwhelming weight of detailed knowledge regarding the physical world carried within technological cultures calls for a special balance in man's consciousness as he learns to address himself and the world around him. Technological man has a personality structure different from that of non-technological man. The stages of culture described by David Riesman as successive tradition-directed, inner-directed, and other-directed are relevant here. Tehcnological man may be inner-directed or other-directed or on the border line between the two, but he cannot be tradition-directed as primitive peoples are. (This is by no means to say that technological man has no traditions; he does have in great number, but he is also likely to reflect on them and analyze them.) To move a nontechnologized culture into the scientific, technological world demands far more than supplying those in such a culture with "information." It demands a restructuring of personality which inevitably forces the painful psychological, political, and ideological dislocations seen in the developing countries today. We can hope to understand and to deal with these dislocations better than we now do. But we can hardly hope to eliminate them totally.

Meanwhile, it is defeatist to suppose that man's attention to the physical world is some kind of degradation. There are dangers here, of course, dangers of total absorption, but of itself man's present managerial position over some of the natural world (some of it only a tiny fraction, for there is no question of managing the galaxies) means that the material world is being more spiritualized by being more subjugated to the mind.

Knowledge of Man and His Life World

If advance in the physical sciences has been spectacular, it has, nevertheless, in fact not been conclusively greater than advance in knowledge elsewhere. A little attention to library acquisitions and bibliographies today as compared with 150 or even 10 years ago makes it patent that insofar as increments in various knowledges are comparable, the humanities and the social and behavioral sciences are growing seemingly as fast as the physical sciences. By far, most of the intellectual and literary and cultural history on library shelves today had not been written 150 years ago. A hundred and fifty years ago most of our linguistic knowledge concerning the thousands of languages man speaks or has spoken did not exist. Neither did most of sociology, anthropology, psychology, and countless other subjects dealing with the human life world as such.

Moreover, in these fields knowledge often grows geometrically because here, perhaps more than in the physical sciences, different and even remote areas of knowledge have a way of interacting with one another today to form new and productive configurations. Psychology and linguistics yield the composite field of psycholinguistics, itself closely allied to cultural anthropology. Analysis, especially historical analysis, of literary forms, of scientific discoveries, of styles in painting, and of political institutions daily throw more and more light on one another.

In addition, the humanities are automatically enlarged by growth of knowledge in the sciences. Every science, not only the social and behavioral sciences, has a history, which is a matter for humanistic study. And the humanities seize on technological interventions for their own specific purposes and thus extend themselves into new areas. Opposition between technology and the humanities is more imaginary than real. The printing press, a technological device, was developed largely under Renaissance humanist auspices, and the use of computers for textual study and other humanistic purposes is already becoming commonplace.

Advances in the humanities and social and behavioral sciences have combined with advances in the physical sciences to affect radically man's sense of his life world and sense of identity, if we take sense of identity to mean the sense of where one comes from and how one relates to those other than oneself, how one fits into what one knows of the universe.

Changes here have been too vast to enumerate, but some of their forces can be seen in the changes regarding man's sense of time. Until quite recent years man had no very effective idea of the real time scales applying to the universe of which he was a part. Today our frames of reference have been brought more into accord with actuality, the macroscale frames largely by the natural sciences and the (relatively) microscale frames by the humanities and social sciences. We know that it took the universe some five to ten billion years of active evolution to produce the conditions making life possible on our earth. We know that social structures and psychological structures have evolved irreversibly over periods of tens of thousands and hundreds of thousands of years. Even though it is not always explicitly attended to, the past is a massive fact in the sense of identity of any well-educated man today, that is to say, of any man thoroughly in touch with his surroundings. We no longer think of ourselves as beings who inhabit a cozy (but savage) universe that began some 6000 years ago, as Western man often used to do, nor do we think of time in terms of unreal cyclic patterns such as the Hindu kalpa (4,320,000,000 years), an imaginative projection having nothing to do with researchable fact and indeed running counter to such fact. Today we know the past as something with which we are in publicly and circumstantially verifiable contact, and as affecting the real present in ways that are matter for scientific, cosmological, and historical study.

The immensity of space has likewise lately become known to us and affected our sense of identity, but it has done so less directly, for space is mostly beyond us, in a real sense . . . [A man on the moon] will be roughly only $\frac{1}{400}$ of the distance to the sun and an infinitesimal fraction of the distance to the nearest star outside the solar system. Most of space is permanently remote from us. We feel little kinship with Betelgeuse or with galaxies millions of light years away. But time is in us: the material in our own bodies is five to ten billion years old. Our modern sense of measured time has revolutionized all knowledge dealing with man's life world at least as drastically as Planckian and Einsteinian discoveries have revolutionized modern physics. The appearance of studies such as Martin Heidegger's great work entitled *Being and Time (Sein und Zeit)* signals the overwhelming sense of time in which modern man is plunged. From antiquity man has speculated philosophically about the nature of time, but only in recent generations have his philosophy and his whole life world become immersed in it. This immersion in time is what commits modern man to change and propels him irresistibly into the future.

Knowledge concerning man and his life world, which includes his artistic and literary productions, also is power, quite as much as knowledge of physical science is. It is most obviously power in the social and behavioral sciences, which lend themselves readily to use, moral or immoral as the case may be, aiding in the solving of human problems or implementing manipulations of human beings as though they were things. Knowledge in the humanities is power, too, for the humanities give us greater insight into the nature of man, and this insight provides ground for greater control over man's behavior, again for good or evil. To understand a people's psychology in order to deal with them on a practical footing, it is advisable to study their literature and art. Such study can be undertaken more productively today than ever before because of the immense advances, effected over the past few generations, in comparative literary and art history and in criticism.

Humanistic knowledge grows in complex fashion because what is new mixes constantly with what is very old. The humanities draw directlty on knowledge that is rooted in pre-history, and even the newest discoveries in the humanities are likely to have antique counterparts: psychological literary criticism may draw on Freud's description of the Oedipus complex, but Freud himself is rooted in Euripides, who in his drama put his finger directly on Freud's problem two thousand years earlier. Still, Euripides is not Freud. Freud knew more, even about Oedipus, and so does the competent present-day critic. Even when we fully avow how much our present knowledge of man derives from the ancients, we must still be aware that what we today know about man in terms of his whole life world immeasurably exceeds what earlier man could get at. We have the advantage both of the general accumulation of learning and also of the greater penetration of time and space which has made cross-cultural studies possible.

Exteriorization of Knowledge

As knowledge has grown, it has become both more exteriorized and more interiorized. Early man's knowledge tended to merge the exterior and interior worlds. Even in a technologized culture, the child's consciousness must first be formed in an intersubjective world of personal relationships—mother, father, other human beings. Primitive man remained close to this world in his adult cosmology, too. The universe was anthropomorphic in a myriad of ways. Lonely for his own kind on an earth that was underpopulous, early man commonly filled the empty forests and air and waters with living beings—wood nymphs, gnomes, spirits of all sorts, nereids—not entirely unlike himself. Totemic systems blended the animal and human in ways that still enchant and puzzle anthropologists and philosophers down to

Maurice Merleau-Ponty and Claude Lévi-Strauss. Even so sophisticated a cosmology as that of Aristotle and Ptolemy was basically animistic and anthropomorphic: the putative celestial spheres surrounding the earth and bearing the planets were taken to be living, intelligent beings. Only through their mediation did change take place in our dull sublunary world. We can see these early constructs of physical science as partly projections from man's own interior, minimally "objective." They connect in part with early man's proclivity for interiorizing, auditory syntheses (the music of the spheres) rather than objective, visual syntheses (the universe held together by measurements).

At the same time, early cultures often exteriorized man's own interior to a degree that would make us acutely uncomfortable. Tribal patterns of thought and activity overpowered the individual. Visitors from technologized cultures living with the people in nontechnologized society often find themselves unnerved by the almost total lack of privacy: life is lived as a kind of total exposure, with almost no opportunity for withdrawal into oneself. Of course, before writing was invented, individual study of a subject was impossible. Thought advanced either obscurely in the gradual evolution of social institutions and language or by being publicly talked out, which is to say it advanced communally. Oral cultures had no Aristotles or Scotuses or Newtons or Einsteins. To a degree, morality itself consisted in external arrangements: touching a dead body even inadvertently could render one ritually impure and vaguely guilty, even though it was not strictly a prohibited action.

Post-Copernian, post-Newtonian man has in great part (not entirely, as he often thinks) foresworn allegiance to these primitive views that half-humanized and thus half-interiorized the external world and at the same time half-exteriorized man's interior consciousness. The interior and exterior are thought of as separate—all too much so, particularly since Plato and Descartes. The external world is now conceived of more typically as a visual synthesis, a set of things defined by surface, a congeries organized not by sound and resonance but by a certain structured disposition in space, something essentially picturable. Although the world in which we live presents itself to all the senses, we habitually consider it as something that is, above all, seen, and perhaps touched (but here only to a degree: touch works for stones but not for clouds). Essentially, the world is "objects," things with surfaces abutting on one another. Our knowledge has progressed, in the physical sciences particularly, when we have thought of the world only this way, keeping ourselves and all interiority out of the focus of attention. Technology has to do with objective things, apprehended from outside, devoid of personal resonance. Eventually, our knolwedge has become focused on exteriority so intently that we have tended more and more to regard man himself and perhaps even God as a thing. We are by now actuely aware of the corner we have been painting ourselves into. We talk incessantly of the dangers of depersonalization. We fear being reduced to a mere Social Security number, a computerizable quantity.

Interiorization of Knowledge

But all the while that knowledge was in a sense being exteriorized and depersonalized, a counter movement has also been under way. Ours is not only an exteriorizing, depersonalizing age but also an interiorizing, personalizing one. No other age has been so explicitly conscious of the human person as ours is. Although early society was deeply personal in some ways, its organization communal and feudal, based on personal ties rather than on issues and analytically conceived programs, it was also in other ways terribly impersonal, and unavoidably so. Often it showed little respect for human life. Capital punishment for crimes such as stealing or even for what we would consider misdemeanors took a staggering toll every day in the most civilized countries of Europe as late as the sixteenth century and beyond, when crowds comparable to those attending professional baseball and football games today still regularly assembled to view hangings and the subsequent savage mutilation of the body of the victim (drawing and quartering) carried out, in accordance with the law, before the victim expired. Punitive mutilation was common: one met on the streets men and women whose ears or noses had been cut off or who had been branded for punishment. In this general context of unprogrammed and programmed violence, religious persecution, which strikes us today as so horrible when seen in isolation and which was indeed horrible enough, shows itself also as almost incidental—a manifestation in one particular life area of patterns of savagery accepted everywhere.

In such a world it is not surprising that philosophical thought, too, attended relatively little to the person as person. The good life of the Greek philosophers simply wrote off the slaves and lower classes as not worth consideration. The higher ranges of speculation in the Greek tradition were largely concerned with "forms" and grew much more directly out of the physics of the time than out of explicit attention to the humane. The term "metaphysics," that is, post-physics, which was used for the highest reaches of philosophical thought, suggests the general state of affairs. Deep interest in the human as human was of course discernible in philosophy from the start, but when abstract thought moved in on man's life world, somehow or other it atomized this world into a congeries of virtues and vice. The richness of human life was caught in something of its integrity by early art and literature, but even here, we are now beginning to understand, the economy of knowledge inherited from primitive oral culture tended to dissolve human complexities in abstract virtue-and-vice polarities. Oral modes of thought persisted long after the arrival of writing and even print, losing their dominance only when the Romantic movement overwhelmed the ancient rhetorical and dialectical educational tradition.

Major intellectual developments focusing explicitly on the person as person can be traced directly to early Christian theology in the first ecumenical councils through the Second Council of Constantinople (A.D. 553), as Denis de Rougemont has suggested in *Man's Western Quest*. Here the early Church thoroughly thrashed out problems concerning the person of Christ and the difference between Father, Son, and Holy Spirit precisely as persons, further elaborating the Scriptural insistence on the personal relations of each individual human being to God. Philosophy, however, picked up little of the theological concerns centered around the Trinity of Persons. Only in the nineteenth century (that is, during the industrial revolution) did philosophy become highly anthropologized, centering itself more explicitly on man as man. In our own day this anthropologizing has culminated in the personalist philosophy of Gabriel Marcel, Karl Jaspers, and others. Personalist philosophy (and complementary reverse personalism, such as Sartre's) are just as typical of twentieth-century civilization as technology is.

Interiorizing, personalizing trends in thought are too diffuse and too numerous to be listed here in detail, but something of what they come to can be seen in the history of literature. Literature, of course, always personalizes its matter in the sense that it has somehow to do with man in his lived experiences, with human problems and hence with the interior, human consciousness. But its personalizing potential has been progressively intensified as the focus of plotting has moved over the ages from the more exterior world of fixed social institutions, exteriorized adventure, or episodic exploit, to the human interior directly realized through stream-of-consciousness or interior monologue and related techniques. Such a movement can be traced variously in Greek tragedy from Aeschylus through Euripides, in Elizabethan drama from its crude para-academic beginnings through Shakespeare, or again in the history of the novel, which in two centuries evolved from the relatively externalized machinations of Fielding's eighteenth-century *Tom Jones* to the baroque interiority of Joyce's twentieth-century *Finnegans Wake*. Indeed, the novel itself as a genre comes into being late because it depends on advanced interiorization of attention, if we accept Lionel Trilling's well-founded view that a novel is essentially a critique of a complex society which sees through the obvious, exterior, somewhat fraudulent surface of that society to some deeper (interiorly realizable) truth. As a personalized critique of society, though far less interiorized than

Joyce, Fielding's work is more interiorized than is John Lyly's *Euphues* of nearly two centuries earlier.

Something similar to what has happened in literature has also happened in art, as José Ortega y Gasset has explained in *The Dehumanization of Art and Other Essays:* the focus has moved from representations of the exterior world to more and more concern with representations of inner states of mind. Obvious parallels suggest themselves in music.

Perhaps the most pervasive interiorization of knowledge today is coming about in our understanding of history. In place of what used to be more or less standard history, consisting of accounts of military and political ventures, we are developing a sense of history as basically cultural and psychological. We know now that psychological structures change as cultures change: much of the current popular interest in the "media" feeds on a vague awareness of this fact, which has been the concern of scholars quite clearly since Freud's *Civilization and Its Discontents* and indeed from the time of Giovanni Battista Vico (1668–1744). External historical events are shaped by personality structures, which themselves are the result of external historical events and cultural patterns, all these interacting with a certain amount of incalculability insofar as free human decisions (always in very limited existential fields) are also in play.

To the best of modern historians the world is not simply a series of external happenings so much as it is a concatenation of interior states of consciousness: both exterior and interior need to be accounted for, but the principal focus is on the latter. Personalist philosophies of intersubjectivity have their effect here in showing how interpretation of exterior reality itself demands and builds on relations of persons to persons. The Jesuit paleontologist and cultural historian, Pierre Teilhard de Chardin, has gone further in interpreting personal, interior consciousness as the focus of the entire evolutionary process, cosmic, organic, and historical. In *The Phenomenon of Man,* in *The Future of Man,* and in others of his works, Teilhard attends to the way the physical universe evolves toward "inwardness" and consciousness and to the way consciousness itself evolves as man fills and organizes the earth.

Looking to historiography in these perspectives and with the eyes of the future, we might say that history is deposited as personality structure. You and I in our own particular consciousness are our own history, and collectively we are the history of mankind. History is the way we are. It is why we confront ourselves and other men and the world the way we do. To say this is not to imply any kind of fatalism or total determinism. Man is free, and history itself involves free choice. But man must make choices within situations that are actually presented to him and that he does not choose. History is a fabric woven by choice out of necessity. In such a fabric, choice regards the present and the future. The necessities, interior as well as exterior, in which choice asserts itself often derive from the past.

What we are beginning to learn about the effects of history in the organization of consciousness and personality structures has almost limitless implications for our understanding of knowledge itself and its development. For knowledge exists in dependence on given personality structures. A tradition-directed culture cannot produce highly original speculative thought because the personality structured to such a culture cannot function independently of accepted tribal patterns and, indeed, cannot even want to experience itself as "original." Tradition-directed cultures are, roughly, oral cultures or cultures in which script has not been sufficiently interiorized to change psychic organization. Eric Havelock has shown in his *Preface to Plato,* mentioned earlier, how Plato's highly speculative philosophy, and in particular his "ideas," were dependent on an attitude toward the world made possible only by writing, which prepares the psyche for the fixity and remoteness from the human life world that the "ideas" stand for.

Our growing awareness of the variant psychological structures produced by different cultures and in particular of the need for knowledge to be detribalized in the sense of personally interiorized (as in David Riesman's "inner-directed" character) in order to produce a technological thinker is affecting our sense of global understanding. We are reaching the point where we may no longer regard "elections" in which a predictable winner piles up 99 percent of the vote as frauds managed so naïvely as to be merely quaint. We can begin to appreciate that such more or less enforced patterns of publicly manifested conformity found in neotechnological cultures are doubtless due in great part to old tribal or tradition-directed personality structures, which cannot be eradicated in a day. The divisions of opinion on which a democracy thrives could paralyze a personality formed in a newly technologized or half-technologized milieu, in which the older tribal organization of consciousness calling for nondeviance is still operative.

We are also, or should be, long past the stage where we label members of still earlier, pretechnological, oral cultures "lazy" because their members do not take enthusiastically to the ethic of "hard work" which technological cultures automatically structure into their successful members' psyches. We know that persons in pretechnological cultures are perfectly capable of doing things that are quite as difficult and demanding as the tasks of an assembly-line worker or a junior business executive but that their outlook on existence is at root so communal that the idea of "making something of yourself" will necessarily appear to them unrealistic and even unmanly. Man, they feel, is supposed to live in a world of human events, not in constant traffic with such things or abstractions as technological life demands. To make a fetish of work is to dehumanize oneself, to become a machine. The problem facing developing nations, as an increasing number of psychological studies shows, is not a problem of exhorting lazy people to work hard, but more profoundly, that of restructuring personalities or of structuring young, forming personalities in the ways that technological life requires for its members if they are to survive as human beings. Our growing knowledge of knowledge is making us more adept at describing socially determined differences in personality structures. But we are as yet far from knowing how to change them.

Thrust into the Future and Growth in Responsibility

The growth of knowledge is certainly one of the factors thrusting modern man into the future. Very primitive peoples tend to live from hand to mouth more than more developed civilizations do. Growth into a planned economy has come about gradually. Manufacture of clothing and weapons showed planning for the future, which the planting of crops further intensified. Later the large civil governments developed in antiquity relied on intensive planning, as in the elaborate irrigation work along the Nile in ancient Egypt. At first governmental planning had been largely to maintain the precarious status quo, but with colonization and empire it meant also plotting major changes for individuals and regions, though seldom avowed changes in style of life. Yet even in style of life, some programmed change was possible as early as among the ancient Romans, for example, because these peoples had enough knowledge of climate, natural resources, engineering (particularly for their roads), and writing (an absolute essential, as Harold Innis has made clear) to have some control over the future.

Today, however, programming the future has entered a new stage. Earlier time scales, related more or less to the duration of a few generations, have been superseded. We think habitually of the future of the human race on earth a hundred years from now, or five hundred years, or two thousand years. In the control of natural resources—the soil and its products, food crops, forests, fisheries, water power—we already effectively plan in ways that will determine conditions of life in the next few centuries, and it is in part our ability to do this which gives our life the future pitch it has. But the principal reason for the thrust into the future which makes our state of mind today different from that of earlier man is our knowledge of cosmic and organic evolution. We are aware that we live in an evolving universe, pitched into the future. The world is structured in patterned change. Not only can man change things; he can change the very pattern of change as well.

Our awareness of patterns of development extends beyond the exterior universe into knowledge itself. As time goes on, we learn more and more about how knowledge comes into being, about learning processes and processes of discovery, about how knowledge can be not merely stored and communicated but also brought into existence as well as increased. We engineer knowledge itself in advance, as the Rockefeller Foundation helped do a few decades ago when it found the increment of knowledge in the life sciences inadequate and hence made the decision to divert large funds into stepping up the increment here, a decision that helped produce within a few years our new understanding of DNA and the genetic code of living organisms. The ability to program knowledge gives man a kind of exponential control over nature. If knowledge is power, knowledge of how to generate knowledge is power over power.

With his present sense of an evolving universe, his store of knowledge, and his awareness of knowledge as power, man today quite naturally feels his life role to be largely that of a manager. Of course, not every man and woman even in a highly technologized society thinks of himself or herself as an active global planner, but everyone knows that this is now the role of the human race taken as a whole. From national planning commissions of all sorts down to science fiction and comic strips, the mythology of global and, to a very limited extent, cosmic management permeates all levels of society and all economic levels.

We know that if we are responsible today more than ever before for the conditions we live in, we shall also be still more responsible in the future. In the past when civil disorders occurred or wars broke out, man could put it down to the inescapable state of human affairs, to vices bred into men. No one in his right mind would deny that today we have our share of real vices, but we are at the same time aware that breakdowns in society must be accounted for by a great many things other than vice—lack of education, of economic opportunity, the revolution of rising expectations, the unthinking use of the mass media of communication, and a great many other social developments over which we can exercise control even though we may not yet have learned how to do so very effectively.

The buildup of knowledge and the proliferation of means for storing and communicating knowledge that makes man's managerial role possible and imperative also, of course, creates severe strains in society. There is a great deal of illusion in loose talk about "turnover" in knowledge, which mistakes knowledge for a commodity and thus confuses it with agglomerates of "information," forgetting that true knowledge in human beings cannot "replace" earlier knowledge but must somehow be integral with earlier knowledge in order to be functional or even psychologically possible at all. Nevertheless, even when we write off the cheap equations such talk relies on, we must still note that the rapid increase in knowledge divides the generations. The mode of assimilating the store of human knowledge, and particularly the "image field" used in managing it, probably differs considerably between those who are twenty years old and those who are fifty. Such differences should not be minimized. But neither should they fill us with despair. The are not unbridgeable but simply take work to bridge. A good many persons in their fifties and beyond are doing the best work interpreting just such differences between the generations. It is paradoxical that only a relative oldster such as Marshall McLuhan can interpret the younger generation to themselves and that to many of his own generation his interpretation remains incomprehensible. It would be more paradoxical if all the younger persons understood and none of the oldsters did. Such is not the case. Some of both groups do. His interpretations and those of others like him in fact do bridge the chasm.

A more serious problem created by proliferation of knowledge and man's resulting managerial responsibility is that of withdrawal. Withdrawal symptoms show up more and more in technologically advanced societies. Often they are factitious and even meretricious: the beatnik or hippie is not really "dropping out" but looking desperately for an in-group that will satisfy his own demands. Often, seeming withdrawal is merely a way of securing attention without responsibility. Nevertheless, it creates real problems, and the withdrawal syndrome is certainly connected with the pressures of managerial expectations. The sociological studies show that hippies come typically not from the underprivileged but almost entirely from among the relatively well to do or the very wealthy, where the pressures of responsibility in one way or another make themselves felt. Withdrawal, real or simulated, will probably be a major problem with us for a long time.

The countervailing factor to withdrawal is the possibility of cooperation which modern technological society offers and indeed has to a great extent implemented. We fail all too often to be aware of the fantastic cooperative ventures that the human race has by this time achieved, despite the dissensions that still tear at the national and international fabrics. Man is a cooperating animal, and the earliest human traces on earth show the results of joint action. By the time of the Old Empire in Egypt, shortly after 3000 B.C., cooperative endeavor (not all of it voluntary, by any means) could raise the pyramids. The organization evident in such early works is overwhelmingly impressive, given the conditions of communication and transport under which it was achieved. But in intricacy of detail, it is negligible compared to the cooperation required today for airing a single television program, if one considers all of what is really involved in bringing together the persons and equipment as well as the actual operation of the latter: the skills going into the design and manufacture of television apparatus, the intricacies of program planning, the transportation systems needed for moving personnel to and from the studio (carefully engineered automobiles, subways, freeways patroled by helicopter, traffic-light engineering, and so on ad infinitum). And if the cooperative effort in producing a pyramid or even a medieval Gothic cathedral is, for all its wonder, small compared to that needed for a single television broadcast, it is infinitesimal compared to that required to launch a rocket to the moon. Massive cooperation is the hallmark of technological society. Even the routine cooperative activity of a single metropolis in the course of one day surpasses all powers of conceptualization. No one can really disengage himself from the cooperative network of modern living, and in point of fact, few ever really want to.

Bibliography

ELIZABETH S. WHITE **Interpersonal Bias in Television and Interactive Media**

"Another Woe for Videotex," *Electronic Media* (November 8, 1984): 6.

Arlen, G. "Videotex Goes On-Line," *Channels* (November/December 1983): 40.

——. "Teletext Takes to the Air," *Channels* (November/December 1983): 41.

Boorstin, Daniel J. *The Republic of Technology.* New York: Harper & Row, 1978.

Bradshaw, J. "The Shape of Media Things to Come" in G. Gumpert and R. Cathcart (eds.), *Inter Media: Interpersonal Communication in a Media World,* 2nd ed. New York: Oxford University Press, 1979.

Carey, J. "Videotex: The Past as Prologue," *Journal of Communication* 32 (Summerl 1982): pp. 241–249.

Carey, J. and Kreiling, A. "Popular Culture and Uses and Gratifications: Notes Toward an Accomodation," in J. Blumler and E. Katz (eds.), *The Uses of Mass Communication: Current Perspectives in Gratifications Research.* Beverly Hills, Cal.: Sage, 1974, p. 232.

Dozier, David M., Hellweg, Susan A., and Ledingham, John A. "Implications of Interactive Cable Systems: Reduced Consumer Contact" in R. Bostrom (ed.), *Communication Yearbook 7.* Beverly Hills, Cal.: Sage, 1984.

Fowler, Gene D. and Wackerbarth, Marilyne E. "Audio Teleconferencing versus Face-to-Face Conferencing: A Synthesis of the Literature." *Western Journal of Speech Communication* 44 (Summer 1980):252–259.

Fredin, Eric S. "The Context of Communication— Interactive Telecommunication, Interpersonal Communication, and Their Effect on Ideas," *Communication Research* 10 (October 1983): 118–124.

Greenberg, B. (1974) "Gratifications of Television Viewing and Their Correlates for British Schoolchildren," in Blumler and Katz, 1974, p. 88.

"Interactive Cable Television—Three Studies," *Telecommunications Policy* 18 (September 1979): 414–418.

Johansen, R. and DeGrasse, R. "Computer-Based Teleconferencing: Effects on Working Patterns." *Journal of Communication* 29 (Summer 1979).

Nordlund, J. "Media Interaction" in Gumpert and Cathcart, 1979.

Page, C. "CATV: Two'Way Access to City Hall," *Nation's Cities* 44. (May 1978). pp. 22–28.

Philips, Amy F. "Computer Conferences: Success or Failure?" in R. Bostrom, (ed.), *Communication Yearbook 7.* Beverly Hills, CA: Sage, 1984.

Salem, P. and Gratz, R. "High Technology and Social Devolution." Paper presented to the World Conference on Systems, Caracas, Vanezuela, 1983.

Schudson, M. "The Ideal of Conversation in the Study of the Mass Media," *Communication Research* 5 (July, 1978).

Swank, C. "Media Uses and Gratifications—Need Salience and Source Dependence in a Sample of the Elderly," *American Behavioral Scientist* 23 (September/October, 1979).

Tan, A. "Why TV Is Missed," *Journal of Broadcasting* 21 (Summer 1977).

GERALD R. MILLER A Neglected Connection: Mass Media Exposure and Interpersonal Communicatie Competency

Berger, C. R., Gardner, R. R., Parks, M. R., Schulman, L., and Miller, G. R. "Interpersonal Epistemology and Interpersonal Communication," in G. R. Miller (ed.), *Explorations in Interpersonal Communication*. Beverly Hills, Cal.: Sage, 1976.

Blumer, J. G. and Katz, E. (eds.). (1974) *The Uses of Mass Communication: Current Perspectives on Gratifications Research*. Beverly Hills, Cal.: Sage, 1974.

Bunders, R. W. The Effects of Type of Information, Dogmatism, and Sex of Dyad on Predictive Accuracy. Unpublished masters thesis, Michigan State University, 1980.

deTurck, M. A. and Miller, G. R. A Scale for Measuring Propensity for Psychological-level Prediction. Unpublished paper, Michigan State University, 1981.

Katz, E. and Lazarsfeld, P. F. *Personal Influence*. Glencoe, Ill.: The Free Press of Glencoe, 1955.

Katz, E., Gurevitch, M., and Haas, H. "On the Use of Mass Media for Important Things," *American Sociological Review* 38 (1973): 164–181.

Kelly, G. A. *The psychology of Personal Constructs*. Vol. 1. New York: W. W. Norton, 1955.

Lazarsfeld, P. F., Berelson, B. R., and Gaudet, H. *The People's Choice*. New York: Duell, Sloan and Pearce, 1944.

McLuhan, N. *Understanding Media: The Extensions of Man*. New York: McGraw-Hill, 1964.

Miller, G. R. "Communication in the Third 100 Years: Can Humanity and Technology Coexist Peacefully?" *Centennial Review* 21 (1977): 176–193.

Miller, G. R. and Steinberg, M. *Between people: A new analysis of interpersonal communication*. Chicago: Science Research Associates, 1975.

Miller, G. R. and Sunnafrank, M. "All is for one, but one is not for all: A conceptual perspective of interpersonal communication." In F. E. X. Dance (ed.) *Human Communication Theory*. New York: Harper & Row, 1982.

Nordenstreng, K. "Comments on Gratifications Research in Broadcasting," *Public Opinion Quarterly*, 34 (1970): 130–132.

JAMES A. DANOWSKI Interpersonal Network Structure and Media Use: A Focus on Radiality and Non–Mass Media Use

Atkin, C. K. "Anticipated Communication and Mass Media Information Seeking," *Public Opinion Quarterly* 36 (1972): 188–199.

Cathcart, R. and Gumpert, G. "Mediated Interpersonal Communication: Toward a New Typology," *Quarterly Journal of Speech* 69 (1983): 267–277.

Cook, J. B., "Public Relations Roles and Organizational Communication Behaviors." Master's thesis, School of Journalism and Mass Communication, University of Wisconsin, 1982.

Danowski, J. A. "An Uncertainty Model: Friendship Communication Networks and

Media Related Behaviors." Paper presented to the International Communication Association, New Orleans, 1974.

————. "An Information Theory of Communication Functions: A Focus on Informational Aging." Doctoral dissertation, Department of Communication, Michigan State University, 1975.

————. "Informal Communication Network Centrality and Individual's Formal Organizational Authority." Monograph, Annenberg School of Communications, University of Southern California, 1976.

————. "Cognitive Complexity of Radial and Interlocking Interpersonal Network Nodes." Monograph, School of Journalism and Mass Communication, University of Wisconsin, 1981.

————. "Network Structure and Use of Organizational Computer-Mediated Communication and Teleconferencing." Monograph, School of Journalism and Mass Communication, University of Wisconsin, 1982.

————. "Interpersonal Communication Network Radiality and Long Distance Telephone Behaviors and Attitudes." Paper presented to the International Communication Association, Honolulu, 1985.

————. and Adler, I. "Charitable Health Organization Donor Profile." Monograph, School of Journalism and Mass Communication, University of Wisconsin, 1983a.

————. and Adler, I. "Wisconsin Union Communication System Assessment." Monograph, School of Journalism and Mass Communication, University of Wisconsin, 1983b.

————. and Van Engen, M. "Readership of Employee Publications as a Function of Interpersonal Communication." Monograph, School of Journalism and Mass Communication, University of Wisconsin, 1983.

Gumpert, G. "The Rise of Uni-Comm," *Today's Speech* 23 (1975): 34.

Hughey, J. D. "Media Preference and Empathy." Paper presented to the International Communication Association, Honolulu, 1985.

Johansen, R. *Electronic Meetings*. Reading, Mass.: Addison Wesley, 1979.

Meyer, J. R. "Cognitive Abstractness and Person Memory." Paper presented to the International Communication Association, Honolulu, 1985.

Rogers, E. M. and Argarwala-Rogers, R. *Communication in Organizations*. New York: Free Press, 1976.

Schomish, T. P. "The Effect of Personal Communication Networks on Members' Voting in a Merger of Agricultural Cooperatives." Doctoral dissertation, School of Journalism and Mass Communication, University of Wisconsin, 1983.

Short, J., Williams, E., and Christie, B. *The Social Psychology of Telecommunications*. New York: Wiley, 1976.

KARL ERIK ROSENGREN AND SWEN WINDAHL **Mass Media Consumption as a Functional Alternative**

Blumler, J. G., Brown, J. R., and McQuail, D. The Social Origins of the Gratifications Associated with Television Viewing. Mimeo, 1970.

Brown, J. S. "Acquired Drives," *International Encyclopedia of the Social Sciences*, vol. 4. New York: Macmillan, 1968.

Dysinger, W. S., and Rucknick, C. A. *The Emotional Responses of Children to the Motion Picture Situation*. New York: Macmillan, 1933.

Emmett, B. P. "A New Role for Research in Broadcasting," *Public Opinion Question* 32 (1968): 654–656.

Horton, D. and Wohl, R. R. "Mass Communication and Para-Social Interaction," *Psychiatry* 19 (1956): 215–229.

Lundberg, D. and Hultén, *Individen och Massmedia*. Stockholm: Nordstedt & Soner. (in Swedish), 1968.

Noredenstreng, K. "Consumption of Mass Media in Finland." *Gazette* 15 (1969): 249–259.

Merton, R. K. *Social Theory and Social Structure*. New York: Free Press, 1963, pp. 34ff.

Theodorson, G. A. and Theodorson, A. G. *A Modern Dictionary of Sociology*. London: Methuen, 1970.

Turner, M. A. News-reading Behavior and Social Adjustment, *Journalism Question* 35 (1958): 199–204.

Zetterberg, H. L. *On Theory and Verification in Sociology*. Bedminster Press, 1965, pp. 72ff.

ROBERT CATHCART   **Our Soap Opera Friends**

Adler, Renata. "Afternoon Television: Unhappiness Enough, and Time, in Horace Newcomb (ed.), *Television: The critical view*, 2nd ed. New York: Oxford University Press, 1979.

Davis, K. D. and Baran, S. J. *Mass Communication in Everyday Life*. Belmont, Cal.: Wadsworth, 1981.

Meyrowitz, Joshua. "Television and Interpersonal Behavior: Codes Perception and Response," in Gary Gumpert and Robert Cathcart (eds.), *Inter/Media: Interpersonal Communication in a Media World*, 2nd ed. New York: Oxford University Press, 1979.

Porter, Dennis. "Soap Time: Thoughts on a Commodity Art Form," in Newcomb, 1979.

Rosengen, K. E. and Windahl, S. "Mass Media Consumption as a Functional Alternative," In Denis McQuail (ed.), *Sociology of Mass Communication*. London: Penguin, 1972.

Timberg, Bernard. "The rhetoric of the camera in television soap opera," in Horace Newcomb (ed.), *Television: The Critical View*, 3rd ed. New York: Oxford University Press, 1982.

PETER MOSS AND CHRISTINE HIGGINS   **Radio Voices**

Avery, Robert K. "A Functional Analysis of Talk-Radio: A Case Study." Unpublished paper, delivered at the Broadcast Education Association Convention, Las Vegas, Nevada, 1978.

Brown, Ray. *Characteristics of Local Media audiences*. London: Saxon House, 1978, p. 125.

Burke, K. *A Grammar of Motives*. New York: Prentice-Hall, 1945.

Burns, Elizabeth. *A Study of Convention in the Theatre and in Social Life*. London: Longman, 1972.

Ebbesen, K. "Radio Access: The Danish Approach," *Journal of Broadcasting* 19, 3 (Summer 1975): 358–362.

Enzensberger, Hans Magnus. "Constituents of a theory of the Media," *New Left Review* 64 (1970): 331–347.

Enzensberger, Hans Magnus, interviewed on *The Stick Together Show* for the Combined Trades Union Broadcasting Committee, Melbourne, May 1981.

Goffman, E. *Interaction Ritual.* London: Allen Lane, 1972.

———. *Forms of Talk.* Philadelphia: University of Pennsylvania Press, 1981.

Halliday, M. A. K. *Language as Social Semiotic.* London: Edward Arnold, 1978.

Higgins, C. S. and Moss, P. D. "A Discourse Analysis of Talk-Back Radio: Some Cultural Implications," *Australian Review of Applied Linguistics* 4 (1981): 173.

———. *Sounds Real: Radio in Everyday Life,* St. Lucia: University of Qeensland Press, 1982.

Hood, S. "Brecht on Radio," *Screen* 20, 3/4 (Winter 1979/80): 28.

Horton, Donald and Wohl, R. Richard. "Mass Communication and Para-Social Interaction: Observations on Intimacy at a Distance," *Psychiatry* 19, 3 (1956): 215.

Losito, Orozo: "La "Nuova" Radio ed il Pubblico," *R.A.I. Informazione radio TV* 1 (1978): 14–18.

Macdonald, J. Fred (quoting an NBC vice president). *Don't Touch That Dial.* New York: Nelson Hall, 1980, p. 88.

Mendelsohn, H. "Listening to Radio," in L. Dexter and D. White (eds.), *People, Society and Mass Communications.* Glencoe: The Free Press, 1964.

Radio Marketing Bureau. *The Time People Spend with Commercial Air Media.* Findings of the Association of Radio Broadcasting: Sydney, Australia, 1983.

Radio 2GB, *The Foreground Factor,* Sydney, Australia, 1983.

Smith, David M. "Some Uses of Mass Media by 14 Year Olds," *Journal of Broadcasting* 16, 1 (Winter 1971–72): 37–50.

Troldahl, Verling C. and Skolnik, Roger. "The Meanings People have for Radio Today," *Journal of Broadcasting* 12, 1 (Winter 1968): 57–67.

Turow, Joseph. "Talk Show Radio as Interpersonal Communication," *Journal of Broadcasting* 18 (Spring 1979): 115–128.

ROBERT CATHCART AND GARY GUMPERT   **The Person-Computer Interaction: A Unique Source**

Aronson, S. "The Sociology of the Telephone," *International Journal of Comparative Sociology* 12 (September 1971): 12–28.

Carey, J. "The Mass Media and Critical Theory: An American View," In M. Burgoon (ed.), *Communication Yearbook* 6. Beverly Hills, Cal.: Sage, 1982.

Cathcart, R. and G. Gumpert. "Mediated Interpersonal communication: Toward a new typology," *Quarterly Journal of Speech* 69 (August 1983): 267–277.

Covvey, H. D. and McAlister, N. H. *Computer Choices.* Boston: Addison-Wesley, 1982.

Dizard, W. P. *The coming Information Age: An Overview of Technology, Economics, and Politics.* New York: Longman, 1982.

Ducey, R., and R. E. Yadon. "Computers in the Media: A New Course in the Curriculum," *Feedback* 23 (Spring 1983) 6.

Gauffenic, A. "Nineteen Eighty-four: From Fiction to Reality," *Impact of Science on Society* 2 (1983): 133–138.

Horton, D. and Wohl, R. Mass Communication and Para-Social Interaction: Observation on Intimacy at a Distance," *Psychiatry* 19 (1956): 215–229.

Levy, S. Travels in the Network Nation," *Technology Illustrated* (February 1983): 56–61.

Millar, F. E. and Rogers, L. E. "A relational approach to interpersonal communication," in G. R. Miller (ed.), *Explorations in Interpersonal Communication*. Beverly Hills, Cal.: Sage, 1976.

Miller, G. R. and Steinberg, M. *Between People*. Chicago: Science Research Associates, 1975.

Papert, S. *Mindstorms*. New York: Basic, 1980.

Phillips, G. M. *"The Rhetoric of Computers."* Paper presented at the meeting of the Eastern Communication Association, Ocean City, Md., April 1983.

Turkle, S. "Computers as Rorschach," in G. Gumpert and P. Cathcart (eds.), *Inter/Media: Interpersonal Communication in a Media World,* 2d ed. New York: Oxford University Press, 1982.

Vail, H. "The Home Computer Terminal—Transforming the Household of Tomorrow," *The Futurist* 14, 6 (December 1980): 52–58.

CHARLES TURNER   **Music Videos and the Iconic Data Base**

Becker, S. *Discovering Mass Communication*. Glenview, Ill.: Scott, Foresman, 1983.

Budd, R. and Ruben, B. *Beyond Media: New Approaches to Mass Communication*. Rochelle Park, N.J.: Hayden, 1979.

Carpenter, E. *They Became What They Beheld*. New York: Outerbridge and Dienstfrey, 1970.

Eliot, T. S. *The Waste Land and Other Poems*. New York: Harvest Books, 1934.

McLuhan, M. *The Medium is the Massage*. New York: Bantam Books, 1967.

Neumann, E. *The Origins and History of Consciousness*. Princeton, N.J.: Princeton University Press, 1954.

Schwartz, T. *The Responsive Chord*. Garden City: Anchor Books, 1973.

Toffler, A. *The Third Wave*. New York: Morrow, 1980.

Trow, G. W. S. *Within the Context of No Context*. Boston: Little, Brown, 1981.

SHERRY TURKLE   **Computer as Rorschach**

Armer, P. "Attitudes Towards Intelligent Machines," Edward A. Feigenbaum and Julian Feldman (eds.), *Computers and Thought*. New York: McGraw-Hill, 1963.

Neisser, U. "Computers as Tools and as Metaphors," in Charles Dechert (ed.), *The social impact of Cybernetics*. Notre Dame, Ind. The University of Notre Dame Press, 1966.

Weizenbaum, T. *Computer Power and Human Reason: from Judgment to Calculation*. San Francisco: W. H. Freeman, 1976.

ANTHONY SMITH   **The Self and Postindustrial Society**

Baxandall, Michael. *Painting and Experience in Fifteenth Century Italy*. Oxford: Oxford University Press, 1972.

Berger, John. *About Looking*. New York: Pantheon Books, 1980.

Burgin, Victor, ed. *Thinking Photography*. London: Macmillan, 1982.

Lowe, Donald M. *History of Bourgeois Perception*, Brighton, England: Harvester Press, 1982.

Ong, Walter. *The Presence of the Word*. New Haven and London: Yale University Press, 1967.

Panoisky, Erwin. *Studies in Iconology*. London: Harper & Row, 1939, 1972.

Pierce, J. R. *Symbols, Signals and Noise*. London: Hutchinson, 1961.

Sontag, Susan. *On Photography*. New York: Farrar, Straus and Giroux, 1977.

Turkle, Sherry. *The Second Self—Computers and the Human Spirit*. Cambridge: MIT Press, 1984.

Yates, Frances. *The Art of Memory*. London: Pengiun Books, 1966.

JAMES W. CHESEBRO **Communication, Values, and Popular Television Series— An Eleven-Year Assessment**

A. C. Nielsen Company. *1982 Nielsen Report on Television*. Northbrook, Ill.: Nielsen Media Research, 1982.

Agena, K. "The Return of Enchantment," *New York Times Magazine*, Section 6 (November 27, 1983): 67–68, 72, 74, 76, 78.

Bitzer, L. F. The Rhetorical Situation. *Philosophy and Rhetoric* 1 (January 1968): 1–14.

Burke, K. *A Grammar of Motives and a Rhetoric of Motives*. Cleveland, Ohio: Meridian Books/The World Publishing Company (original works published in 1945 and 1950), 1962.

Burke, K. *Counter-Statement*. Berkeley and Los Angeles, Cal.: University of California Press (original work published in 1931), 1968.

Burke, K. *The Rhetoric of Religion: Studies in Logology*. Berkeley, Cal.: University of California Press (original work published in 1961), 1970.

Chesebro, J. W. "Communication, Values, and Popular Television Series—A Four-Year Assessment," in G. Gumpert and R. Cathcart (eds.), *Inter/Media: Interpersonal communication in a Media World*. New York: Oxford University Press, 1979, pp. 528–560.

———. (1982). "Communication, Values, and Popular Television Series—A Seven-Year Assessment," in G. Gumpert and R. Cathcart (eds.), *Inter/Media: Interpersonal communication in a media world*, 2nd ed. New York: Oxford University Press, 1982, pp. 468–519.

Chesebro, J. W. and Hamsher, C. D. "The Concession Speech: The MacArthur-Agnew Analog," *Speaker and Gavel* 11 (January 1974): 39–51.

———. "Communication, Values, and Popular Television Series," *Journal of Popular Culture* 8 (Spring 1975): 589–603.

Chira, S. "What Children 'See' When Watching TV," *New York Times* (January 6, 1983): C1 & C6.

Collins, G. "Assessing TV Impact on Young," *New York Times* (August 2, 1982): A13.

Comstock, G. "Television and Its Viewers: What Social Science Sees," in G. C. Wilhoit and H. de Bock (eds.), *Mass Communication Yearbook*, Vol. 1. Beverly Hills, Cal: Sage, 1980, pp. 491–508.

Davidson, B. "Forecast for Fall: Warm and Human," *TV Guide* 22 (February 16, 1974): 5–8, 10.

Efron, E. "What Makes a Hit?" *TV Guide* 22 (April 27, 1974): 2–4, 6–7.

Frye, N. *Anatomy of Criticism* (1971 ed.). Princeton, N.J.: Princeton University Press, 1957.

Gallup Report. "Leisure Time Activities," *The Gallup Report* (Report No. 146) (March 1977): 14–15.

———. "Outlook toward Nation," *The Gallup Report* (Report No. 173) (December 1979): 13.

———. "Congress Popularity," *The Gallup Report* (Report No. 189) (June 1981): 15.

———. "Outlook toward Nation," *The Gallup Report* (Report No. 197) (February 1982): 13.

———. "Outlook toward Personal Life," *The Gallup Report* (Report No. 197) (February 1982): 12.

———. "Relationship between Television Violence and Crime," *The Gallup Report* (Report No. 200) (May 1982): 36.

———. "Outlook toward Nation," *The Gallup Report* (Report No. 216) (September 1983): 16.

——— "Outlook toward Personal Life," *The Gallup Report* (Report No. 216) (September 1983): 17.

———. "Outlook toward Nation," *The Gallup Report* (Report No. 222) (March 1984): 4.

Gardella, K. "Why TV Viewing Is on the Increase," [New York] *Daily News* (February 1, 1984): 60.

Gunther, M. "Why Sitcoms Are Running Out of Laughs and Viewers," *New York Post* (July 13, 1984): 93.

Heffner, R. D. "Television: The Subtle Persuader," *TV Guide*, 21 (September 15, 1973): 25–26.

Hinckley, D. "It's Nothing to Smile About: The Decline of TV Sit-coms," [New York] *Daily News* (May 6, 1984): 1, 7.

Marshall, G. "Our Happy Days Together," *TV Guide*, 32 (April 28, 1984): 4–9.

Miller, G. R. *An Introduction to Speech Communication* (2nd ed.). Indianapolis, Ind.: Bobbs-Merrill, 1972.

Murphy, M. "Hollywood's Forbidden Subjects," *TV Guide*, 31 (August 13, 1983): 2–6.

Nord, D. P. (1983). "An Economic Perspective on Formula in Popular Culture," in E. Wartella and D. C. Whitney (eds.), *Mass Communication Review Yearbook* vol. 4. Beverly Hills, Cal.: Sage, pp. 287–301.

O'Connor, J. J. "Last of 'Happy Days,' " *New York Times*, (May 8, 1984): C17.

Reinhold, R. "An 'Overwhelming' Violence-TV Tie," *New York Times* (May 6, 1982): C27.

Roper Organization, Inc. *Trends in Attitudes toward Television and Other Media: A Twenty-four Year Review*. New York: Television Information Office/Roper Organization, Inc. (April 1983).

Schwartz, T. "Do the Networks Need Violence?" *New York Times*, Section 2 (May 23, 1982): p. 1.

Simons, H. W. "A Conceptual Framework for Identifying Rhetorical Genres." Paper presented at the meeting of the Central States Speech Association, Kansas City, Kans., April 1975.

Smith, S. B. "Average Family Viewing Passes 7 Hours a Day," *New York Times* (January 28, 1984): 47.

Snow, R. P. *Creating Media Culture*. Beverly Hills, Cal.: Sage, 1983.

Wildmon, D. "Big Fuss of Little House," *TV Guide,* 31 (June 4, 1983): A-2.

Wilson, J. F. and Arnold, C. C. *Dimensions of Public Communication.* Boston, Mass.: Allyn and Bacon, 1976.

Wrage, E. J. "Public Address: A Study in Social and Intellectual History," *Quarterly Journal of Speech,* 33 (December 1947): 451–457.

GAYE TUCHMAN **Women's Magazines: Marry, Don't Work**

Busby, Linda J. "Sex-Role Research on the Mass Media," *Journal of Communication* 25, 4 (1975): 107–31.

Clarke, P. and Esposito, V. "A Study of Occupational Advice for Women in Magazines," *Journalism Quarterly* 43 (1966): 477–485.

Davis, Margaret. "The *Ladies' Home Journal* and *Esquire:* A Comparison." Unpublished manuscript. Stanford University, Department of Sociology, 1976.

Flora, Cornelia. "The Passive Female: Her Comparative Image by Class and Culture in Women's Magazine Fiction," *Journal of Marriage and the Family* 33 (August 1971): 435–444.

Franzwa, Helen. (1974a) "Working Women in Fact and Fiction," *Journal of Communication* 24, 2 (1974a): 104–109.

———. "Pronatalism in Women's Magazine Fiction," in Ellen Peale and Judith Senderowitz (eds.), *Pronatalism: The Myth of Motherhood and Apple Pie.* New York: Thomas Y. Crowell, 1974b, pp. 68–77.

———. (1975) "Female Roles in Women's Magazine Fiction, 1940–1970." In R. K. Unger and F. L. Denmark (eds.), *Woman: Dependent or Independent Variable.* New York: Psychological Dimensions, 1975, pp. 42–53.

Johns-Heine, P. and Gerth, H. "Values in Mass Periodical Fiction, 1921–1940," *Public Opinion Quarterly* 13 (Spring 1949): 105–13.

Oppenheimer, Valerie Kincaid. "The Female Labor Force in the United States: Demographic and Economic Factors Governing Its Growth and Changing Composition." Population Monograph Series No. 5. Berkeley: University of California, Institute of International Studies, 1970.

Rubin, Lillian. *Worlds of Pain. Life in the Working-Class Family.* New York: Basic Books, 1976.

Silver, Sheila. "Then and Now—Content Analysis of *McCall's* Magazine." Paper presented at the annual meeting of Association for Education in Journalism. College Park, Marland, August, 1976.

Vanek, Joann. *Married Women and the Work Day: Time Trends.* Baltimore, Md.: Johns Hopkins University Press, 1980, chap. 4.

ELLEN WARTELLA **Getting to Know You: How Children Make Sense of Television**

Alexander, A., Ryan, M. S., and Munoz, P. "Creating a Learning Context: Investigations on the Interaction of Siblings during Television Viewing," *Critical Studies in Mass Communication* 1, 4 (1984).

Anderson, D. R. and Lorch, E. P. "Looking at Television: Action or Reaction?" in J. Bryant and D. R. Anderson (eds.), *Children's Understanding of Television: Research on Attention and Comprehension.* New York: Academic Press, 1983, 1–33.

Ball, S. and Bogatz, G. A. *The First Year of Sesame Street.* Princeton, N.J.: Educational Testing Service, 1970.

————. *The Second Year of Sesame Street*. Princeton, N.J.: Educational Testing Service, 1971.

Bryant, J. and Anderson, D. R. *Children's Understanding of Television: Research on Attention and Comprehension*. New York: Academic Press, 1983.

Carew, J. "Experience and the Development of Intelligence in Young Children at Home and in Day Care," *Monographs of the Society for Research in Child Development* 45 (1980): 1–89.

Collins, W. A. "Cognitive Processing in Television Viewing," in D. Pearl, L. Bouthilet, and Lazar, J. (eds.), *Television and Behavior: Ten Years of Scientific Progress and Implications for the Eighties*, vol. 2. Washington, D.C.: U.S. Government Printing Office, 1982, pp. 9–23.

Collins, W. A., Sobol, B., and Westby, S. "Effects of Adult Commentary on Children's Comprehension and Inferences about a Televised Aggressive Portrayal," *Child Development* 52 (1981): 158–163.

Comstock, G., Chaffee, S., Katzman, N., McCombs, M., and Roberts, D. *Television and Human Behavior*. New York: Columbia University Press, 1978.

Cook, T. D., Appleton, H., Conner, R. F., Shaffer, A., Tamkin, G. A., and Weber, S. J. *Sesame Street Revisited*. New York: Russell Sage Foundation, 1975.

Hollenback, A. R. and Slaby, R. G. "Infant Visual and Vocal Responses to Television," *Child Development* 50 (1979): 41–45.

Huston, A., Wright, J., Wartella, E., Rice, M., Watkins, B., Campbell, T., and Potts, R. "Communicating More than Content: Formal Features of Children's Television Programs," *Journal of Communication* 31 (1981): 32–48.

Huston, A. C. and Wright, J. C. "Children's Processing of Television: The Information Functions of Formal Features," In J. Bryant and D. R. Anderson (eds.), *Children's Understanding of Television: Research on Attention and Comprehension*. New York: Academic Press, 1983, pp. 35–68.

Lemish, D. (1984) The Pampered *Sesame Street* viewer." Unpublished manuscript. University of Wisconsin, Madison.

Lemish, D. and Rice, M. "Toddlers, Television and Talk: Observation in the Home." Paper presented at the International Communication Association Convention, San Francisco, 1984.

Messaris, P. and Sarett, C. "On the Consequences of Television-related Parent-Child Interaction," *Human Communication Research* 7 (1981): 226–244.

Messaris, P. and Kerr, D. "TV-related Mother-Child Interaction and Children's Perceptions of TV Characters," *Journalism Quarterly* 61 (1984): 662–666.

Postman, N. "The First Curriculum: Comparing School and Television," *Phi Delta Kappan* (November 1979): 163–171.

Rice, M. "The Words of Children's Television," *Journal of Broadcasting* 28 (1984): 445–461.

Rice, M. and Wartella, E. "Television as a Medium of Communication: Implications for How to Regard the Child Viewer," *Journal of Broadcasting* 25 (1981): 365–372.

Rice, M., Huston, A., and Wright, J. C. "The Forms of Television: Effects on Children's Attention, Comprehension and Social Behavior," In D. Pearl, L. Bouthilet, and J. Lazar (eds.), *Television and Behavior: Ten Years of Scientific Progress and Implications for the Eighties*, vol. 2. Washington, D.C.: U.S. Government Printing Office, 1982, pp. 24–38.

Reid, L. "The Impact of Family Group Interaction on Children's Understanding of Television Advertising," *Journal of Advertising* 8 (1979): 13–19.

Singer, J. L. and Singer, D. J. "Implications of Childhood Television Viewing for Cognition, Imagination and Emotion," in J. Bryant and D. Anderson (eds.), *Children's Understanding of Television: Research on Attention and Comprehension.* New York: Academic Press, 1983, pp. 265–296.

Stevenson, H. W. "Television and the Behavior of preschool children." In J. P. Murray, E. A. Rubinstein, and G. A. Comstock (eds.), *Television and Social Behavior,* vol. 2. Washington, D.C.: U.S. Government Printing Office, 1972.

Ward, S., Wackman, D., and Wartella, E. *How Children Learn to Buy.* Beverly Hills, Cal.: Sage, 1977.

Wartella, E. "The Developmental Perspective," in E. Wartella (ed.), *Children Communicating.* Beverly Hills, Cal.: Sage, 1979, pp. 7–19.

———. "Children and Television: The Development of the Child's Understanding of the Medium," in G. Wilhoit and H. DeBock (eds.), *Mass Communication Review Yearbook,* vol. 1. Beverly Hills, Cal.: Sage, 1980.

Watkins, B., Calvert, S., Huston, A., and Wright, J. "Children's Recall of Television Material: Effects of Presentation Mode and Adult Labeling," *Developmental Psychology* 16 (1982): 672–674.

RONALD J. FABER, JANE D. BROWN AND JACK M. MCLEOD   **Coming of Age in the Global Village: Television and Adolescence**

Abelson, R. "Script Processing in Attitude Formation and Decision Making," in J. Carroll and A. Payne (eds.), *Cognition and Social Behavior.* Hillsdale, N.J.: Lawrence Erlbaum, 1976.

Adelson, J. and O'Neil, R. "Growth of Political Ideas in Adolescence: The Sense of Community." *Journal of Personality and Social Psychology* 4 (1966): 295–306.

Bowerman, C. and Kinch, J. "Changes in Family and Peer Orientation of Children between the Fourth and Tenth Grade." *Social Forces* 37 (1959): 206–211.

Brittain, C. "Adolescent Choices and Parent-Peer Cross-pressures," in R. Grinder (ed.), *Studies in Adolescence.* Toronto: Macmillan, 1969.

Campbell, E. "Adolescent Socialization," In D. Goslin (ed.), *Handbook of Socialization theory and Research.* Chicago: Rand-McNally, 1969.

Cavior, N., and Dokecki, P. R. "Physical Attractiveness, Perceived Attitude Similarity, and Academic Achievement as Contributors to Interpersonal Attraction among Adolescents," *Developmental Psychology* 9 (1973): 44–54.

Chaffee, S., Ward, S., and Tipton, L. "Mass Communication and Political Socialization," *Journalism Quarterly* 47 (1970): 647–659, 666.

DeFleur, M. "Occupational Roles as Portrayed on Television," *Public Opinion Quarterly,* 28 (1964): 57–74.

——— and DeFleur, L. "The Relative Contribution of Television as a Leaning Source for Children's Occupational Knowledge," *American Sociological Review,* 32, 5 (1967): 777–789.

Douvan, E. and Gould, M. "Modal Patterns in American Adolescence," in M. Hoffman and L. Hoffman (eds.), *Review of Child Developmental Research,* vol. II. New York: Russell Sage Foundation, 1966.

Dunphy, D. "The Social Structure of Urban Adolescent Peer Groups," *Sociometry,* 26 (1963): 230–246.

Ehrmann, W. W. *Premarital Dating Behavior.* New York: Holt, Rinehart and Winston, 1959.

Erikson, L. H. *Identity: Youth and Crisis.* New York: Norton, 1968.

Flavell, J., Botkin, P., Fry, C., Wright, J., and Jarvis, P. *The Development of Role-taking and Communication Skills in Children.* New York: Wiley, 1968.

Foley, J. "A Functional Analysis of Television Viewing." Unpublished doctoral dissertation, University of Iowa, 1968.

Frazier, A., and Lisonbee, L. K. "Adolescent Concerns with Physique," in R. Muss (ed.), *Adolescent Behavior and Society: A Book of Readings.* New York: Random House, 1971.

Gerson, W. "Mass Media Socialization Behavior: Negro-White Differences," *Social Forces,* 45 (1966): 40–50.

Ginzberg, E., Ginsburg, S. W., Axelrad, S., and Herma, J. L. *Occupational Choice: An Approach to a General Theory.* New York: Columbia University Press, 1951.

Gollin, E. "Organizational Characteristics of Social Judgment: A Developmental Investigation," *Journal of Personality* 26 (1958): 139–154.

Greenberg, B., and Dominick, J. "Racial and Social Class Differences in Teenager's Use of Television," *Journal of Broadcasting* 12 (1969): 331–344.

Gronlund, N., and Anderson, L. "Personality Characteristics of Socially Accepted, Socially Neglected and Socially Rejected Junior High School Pupils," *Educational Administration and Supervision,* 43 (1957): 329–338.

Havighurst, R. *Developmental Tasks and Education.* New York: Longmans, Green, 1972.

Horrocks, J. "Adolescent Attitudes and Goals," in M. Sherif and C. Sherif (eds.), *Problems of Youth.* Chicago: Aldine, 1965.

Janis, I. "The Influence of Television on Personal Decision Making," in S. Withey and R. Abeles (eds.), *Television and Social Behavior.* Hillsdale, N.J.: Lawrence Erlbaum, 1980.

Jennings, M. and Niemi, R. *The Political Character of Adolescence: The Influence of Families and Schools.* Princeton, N.J.: Princeton University Press, 1974.

Johnstone, J. (1974) "Social Integration and Mass Media Use among Adolescents: A Case Study," in J. Blumler and E. Katz (eds.), *The Uses of Mass Communications: Current Perspectives on Grafitications Research.* Beverly Hills, Cal.: Sage, 1974.

Jones, M. C. and Bayley, N. "Physical Maturing among Boys as Related to Behavior," *Journal of Educational Psychology* 41 (1950): 129–148.

Kandel, D. and Lesser, G. "Parental and Peer Influence on Educational Plans of Adolsecents," *American Sociological Review* 34 (1969): 212–222.

Kohlberg, L. "Stages and Moralization: The Cognitive-Developmental Approach," in T. Lickona (ed.), *Moral Development and Behavior: Theory, Research and Social Issues.* New York: Holt, Rinehart and Winston, 1976.

Leifer, A. and Lesser, G. "The development of career awareness in young children." Washington, D.C.: National Institute of Education Papers in Education and Work: Number one, H.E.W., 1976.

Lorimer, R. "Change in Development of Moral Judgments in Adolescence: The Effect of a Structured Exposition versus a Film and Discussion," *Canadian Journal of Behavioral Science,* 3, 1, (1971): 1–10.

Lyle, J. and Hoffman, H. "Children's Use of Television and Other Media," in E. Rubinstein, G. Comstock, and J. Murray (eds.), *Television and Social Behavior, Vol. IV, Television in Day-to-Day Life: Patterns of Use.* Washington, D.C.: U.S. Government Printing Office, 1972.

Marcia, J. "Development and Validation of Ego Identity Status," *Journal of Personality and Social Psychology* 3 (1966): 551–558.

———. (1976) "Identity Six Years After: A Follow-up Study," *Journal of Youth and Adolescence,* 5:145–160.

Matteson, D. *Adolescence Today: Sex Roles and the Search for Identity.* Homewood, Ill.: Dorsey, 1975.

McLeod, J. and Brown, J. "The Family Environment and Adolescent Television Use," in R. Brown (eds.), *Children and Television.* Beverly Hills, Cal.: Sage, 1976.

McLeod, J. and Chaffee, S. H. "The Construction of Social Reality," in J. Tedeschi (ed.), *The Social Influence Process.* Chicago: Aldine-Atherton, 1972.

Noble, G. *Children in Front of the Small Screen.* Beverly Hills, Cal.: Sage, 1976.

Piaget, J. "Intellectual Evolution from Adolescence to Adulthood," *Human Development* 15 (1972): 1–12.

Pingree, S. "The Effects of Nonsexist Television Commercials and Perceptions of Reality on Children's Attitudes about Women," *Psychology of Women Quarterly* 2 (1978): 262–277.

Selman, R. "Taking Another's Perspective: Role-Taking Development in Early Childhood," *Child Development* 42 (1971): 1721–1734.

Singer, J. *The Child's World of Make-believe.* New York: Academic Press, 1973.

Tanner, J. M. "The Adolescent Growth-Spurt and Developmental Age," in G. T. Harrison, J. S. Weiner, J. M. Tanner, and N. A. Barnicot (eds.), *Human Biology: An Introduction to Human Evolution, Variation, and Growth.* Oxford: Clarendon, 1964.

Wylie, R. "Children's Estimates of Their Schoolwork Ability as a Function of Sex, Race, and Socioeconomic Level," *Journal of Personality* 31 (1963): 203–224.

JAMES LULL   **Ideology, Television, and Interpersonal Communication**

Berelson, B. "What 'Missing the Newspaper' means," in P. F. Lazarsfeld and F. N. Stanton (eds.), *Communications Research: 1948–49.* New York: Harper, 1949.

Blumler, J. G. and Katz, E. *The Uses of Mass Communications.* Beverly Hills, Cal.: Sage, 1974.

Boyd-Barrett, O. "Media Imperialism," in J. Curran, M. Gurevitch, and J. Woolacott (eds.), *Mass Communication and Society.* Beverly Hills, CA: Sage, 1977, pp. 116–135.

Bryce, J. "Families and Television: An Ethnographic Approach." Doctoral dissertation, Columbia University, 1980.

Carpenter, E. *Oh! What a Blow that Phantom Gave Me.* New York: Holt Rinehart and Winston, 1973.

Comstock, G., Chaffee, S., Katzman, N., McCombs, M., and Roberts, D. *Television and Human Behavior.* New York: Columbia University Press, 1978.

Cushman, D. and Whiting, G. C. "An Approach to Communication Theory: Toward Consensus on Rules," *Journal of Communication* 22 (Spring 1972): 217–238.

Cushman, D. "The Rules Perspective as a Theoretical Basis for the Study of Communication," *Communication Quarterly* 25 (Fall 1977): 30–45.

Cushman, D. and Pearce, W. B. "Generality and Necessity in Three Types of Communication Theory, *Human Communication Research* 3 (1977): 344–353.

Elliott, P. "Uses and Gratifications Research: A Critique and a Sociological Alternative," in J. G. Blumler and E. Katz (eds.), *The Uses of Mass Communications*. Beverly Hills, Cal.: Sage, 1974.

Erikson, E. *The Life Cycle Completed*. New York: Norton, 1982.

Ewen, S. *Captains of Consciousness*. New York: McGraw-Hill, 1976.

Ewen, S. and Ewen, E. *Channels of Desire*. New York: McGraw-Hill, 1982.

Frith, S. *Sound Effects: Youth, Leisure, and the Politics of Rock and Roll*. New York: Pantheon, 1981.

Gans, H. *The Urban Villagers*. New York: Free Press, 1962.

Gerbner, G. "Cultural Indicators: The Third Voice," In G. Gerbner, L. Gross, and W. Melody (eds.), *Communications Technology and Social Policy*. New York: Wiley, 1973, pp. 555–573.

Gerbner, G., Gross, L., and Melody, W. (eds.), *Communications Technology and Social Policy*. New York: Wiley, 1973.

Gerbner, G. and Gross, L. "Living with Television: The Violence Profile," *Journal of Communication* 26 (1976): 173–199.

Gitlin, T. *Inside Prime Time*. New York: Pantheon Books, 1983.

Golding, P. and Elliott, P. *Making the News*. London: Longman, 1979.

Guback, T. *The International Film Industry*. Bloomington, Ind.: Indiana University Press, 1969.

Hamelink, C. J. *Cultural Autonomy in Global Communications*. New York: Longman, 1983.

Herzog, H. "What Do we Really Know about Daytime Serial Listeners? in P. F. Lazarsfeld and F. N. Stanton (eds.), *Radio Research: 1942–43*. New York: Duell, Sloan and Pearce, 1944.

James, N. C. and McCain, T. A. "Television Games Preschool Children Play: Patterns, Themes and Uses," *Journal of Broadcasting* 26 (1982): 783–800.

Katz, E., Blumler, J. G., and Gurevitch, M. "Uses of Mass Communication by the Individual," in W. P. Davision and F. T. C. Yu (eds.), *Mass Communication Research*. New York: Praeger, 1974, pp. 11–35.

Kellner, D. "TV, Ideology, and Emancipatory Popular Culture," *Social Review* 9 (1979): 13–53.

Laswell, H. D. "The Structure and Function of Communications in Society," in L. Bryson (ed.), *The Communication of Ideas*. New York: Harper, 1948.

Lazarsfeld, P. F. *Radio and the Printed Page*. New York: Duell, Sloan and Pearce, 1940.

Lemish, D. "The Rules of Television Viewing in Public Places," *Journal of Broadcasting* 26 (1982): 757–781.

Lull, J. "The Social Uses of Television," *Human Communication Research* 6 (1980): 197–209.

———. "A Rules Approach to the Study of Television and Society," *Human Communication Research* 9 (1982): 3–16.

———. "How Families Select Television Programs: A Mass-Observational Study," *Journal of Broadcasting* 26 (1982): 801–811.

Maslow, A. *Motivation and Personality*. New York: Harper, 1954.

———. *Toward a Psychology of Being*. Princeton, N.J.: Van Nostrand, 1962.

McQuail, D., Blumler, J. G., and Brown, J. R. "The Television Audience: A Revised Perspective," In D. McQuail (ed.), *Sociology of Mass Communication*. Harmondsworth, England: Penguin Books, 1972, pp. 135–165.

Merton, R. K. *Social Theory and Social Structure*. Glencoe, Ill.: Free Press, 1975.

Molotch, H. and Lester, M. "Accidents, Scandals and Routines: Resources for Insurgent Methodology," *The Insurgent Sociologist* 3 (1973): 1–11.

Pacanowsky, M. and Anderson, J. "Cop Talk and Media Use," *Journal of Broadcasting* 26 (1982): 741–756.

Pearce, W. B. "Rules theories of Communication: Varieties, Limitations and Potentials." Paper presented to the Speech Communication Association, New York, 1980.

Real, M. *Mass Mediated Culture*. Englewood Cliffs, N.J.: Prentice-Hall, 1977.

Reid, L. "Viewing Rules as Mediating Factors of Children's Responses to Commercials," *Journal of Broadcasting* 23 (1979) 15–26.

Reid, L. and Frazer, C. "Children's Use of Television Commercials to Initiate social Interaction in Family Viewing Situations," *Journal of Broadcasting* 24 (1980): 149–158.

Riley, M. W. and Riley, J. W. "A Sociological Approach to Communication Research," *Public Opinion Quarterly* 15 (1951).

Rosengren, K. E., Wenner, L. A., and Palmgreen, P. *Current perspectives on Media Gratifications Research*. Beverly Hills, Cal.: Sage, 1985.

Sarett, C. "Socialization Patterns and Preschool Children's Television- and Film-related Play Behavior." Doctoral dissertation, University of Pennsylvania, 1981.

Schiller, H. *Mass Communications and American Empire*. Boston: Beacon Press, 1969.

———. *The Mind Managers*. Boston: Beacon Press, 1973.

———. *Communication and Cultural Domination*. White Plains, N.Y.: International Arts and Sciences Press, 1976.

Shimanoff, S. *Communication Rules*. Beverly Hills, Cal.: Sage, 1980.

Smith, A. *The Geopolitics of Information: How Western Culture Dominates the World*. New York: Oxford University Press, 1980.

Swanson, D. L. "The Uses and Misuses of Uses and Gratifications," *Human Communication Research* 3 (1977): 214–221.

Tuchman, G. *The TV Establishment*. Englewood Cliffs, N.J.: Prentice-Hall, 1974.

———. *Making News. A Study in the Construction of Reality*. New York: Free Press, 1978.

Tunstall, J. *The Media Are American*. New York: Columbia University Press, 1977.

Von Wright, G. H. "Practical Inference," *Philosophic Review* 72 (1963) 159–179.

Wallis, R. and Malm, K. *Big Sounds from Small Peoples: The Music Industry in Small Countries*. London: Constable, 1984.

Wander, P. "The Waltons or How Sweet Adversity Really Was," *Journal of Communication* 29 (1976): 85–88.

———. "Daytime Television: The Angst of the Upper Class," *Journal of Communication* 29 (1979): 146–154.

Wasko, J. *Movies and Money: Financing the American Film Industry*. Norwood, N.J.: Ablex, 1983.

Wolf, M., Meyer, T. P., and White, C. "A Rules-based Study of Television's Role in the Construction of Social Reality," *Journal of Broadcasting*, 26 (1982): 813–829.

Wright, C. R. "Functional Analysis and Mass Communication," *Public Opinion Quarterly* 24 (1960): 605–620.

SARI THOMAS   **Mans Media and the Social Order**

Adorno, T. W. "Television and the Patterns of Mass Culture," in B. Rosenberg and D. M. White (eds.), *Mass Culture: The Popular Arts in America*. Glencoe, Ill.: Free Press, 1957.

Bell, D. "The Disjunction of Culture and Social Structure: Some Notes on the Meaning of Social Reality," in G. Holton (ed.), *Science and Culture: A Study of Cohesive and Disjunctive Forces:* Boston: Addison Wesley, 1965.

Bensman, J. and Vidich, A. *The New American Society*. Chicago: Chicago University Press, 1971.

Berger, P. and Luckmann, T. *The Social Construction of Reality: A Treatise on the Sociology of Knowledge*. Garden City, N.Y.: Doubleday, 1967.

Bodanza, L. L. "A Content Analysis of Three Mass-Culture Tabloids." Unpublished manuscript, Temple University, 1981.

Brinton, C. *Ideas and Men*, Englewood Cliffs, N.J.: Prentice-Hall, 1950.

Callahan, B. P. "A Content Analysis of Top Ten Songs from 1948 to 1980." Master's thesis, Temple University, 1983.

DeFleur, M. L. "Occupational Roles as Portrayed on Television," *Public Opinion Quarterly* 37 (1973): 138–151.

Durkheim, E. *The Division of Labor in Society*. New York: Macmillan, 1964.

———. *The Elementary Forms of the Religious Life*. Glencoe, Ill.: Free Press, 1947.

Elkin, F. "The Value Implications of Popular Film," *Sociology and Social Research* 38, no. 1 (1954): 53–63.

Gentile, F. and Miller, S. M. "TV and Social Class," *Sociology and Social Research* 45, no. 2 (1961): 202–209.

Gerbner, G. "The Social Role of the Confession Magazine," *Social Problems* 6 (1958): 118–126.

———. "The Dynamics of Cultural Resistance," in G. Tuchman, A. K. Daniels, and J. Benet, (eds.), *Hearth and Home: Images of Women in the Mass Media*. New York: Oxford University Press, 1978.

Gerth, G. and Mills. C. W. *Character and Social Structure: The Psychology of Social Institutions*. New York: Harper 1953.

Goldenweisser, A. A. "The Autonomy of the Social," *American Anthropologist* 19 (1917).

Goody, J. *Literacy in Traditional Societies*. Cambridge: Cambridge University Press, 1968.

——— and Watt, I. "The Consequences of Literacy," *Comparative Studies of Society and History*, 5 (1962–3): 238–250.

Greenberg, B. S. *Life on Television: Content Analysis of U.S. TV Drama*. Norwood, N.J.: 1980.

Harvey, J. "The Content Characteristics of Best-Selling Novels," *Public Opinion Quarterly* 17 (1953): 247–258.

Hauser, A. *The Social History of Art, Vols. I and II*. New York: n.d.

Innis, H. *Empire and Communication*. London: Oxford University Press, 1950.

———. *The Bias of Communication*. Toronto: University of Toronto Press, 1951.

Johns-Heine, P. and Gerth, H. H. "Values in Mass Periodical Fiction, 1921–1940," *Public Opinion Quarterly* 13 (1949): 303–316.

Kerr, W. A. and Remmers, H. H. "The Cultural Value of 100 Representative American Magazines," *School and Society* 54 (1941): 305–316.

Kroeber, A. L. "On the Principle of Order as Exemplified by Changes of Fashion," *American Anthropologist,* 21 (1919).

———. "The Superorganic," *American Anthropologist,* 49 (1947).

Larsen, O. "Social Effects of Mass Communication," in R. E. L. Faris (ed.), *Handbook of Modern Sociology.* New York: Prentice-Hall 1964.

Lazarsfeld, P. F. and Merton, R. K. "Mass Communication, Popular Taste and Organized Social Action," in L. Bryson (ed.) *The Communication of Ideas.* New York: Harper, 1948.

Leach, E. R. "Culture and Social Cohesion," in G. Holton (ed.) *Science and Culture: A Study of Cohesive and Disjunctive Forces.* Boston: Addison-Wesley, 1965.

Malinowski, B. "Culture," *Encyclopaedia of the Social Sciences.* 4.

———. *Magic, Science and Religion, and Other Essays.* Glencoe, Ill.: Free Press, 1948.

Marx, K. *A Contribution to the Critique of Political Economy.* Chicago: University of Chicago Press, 1904.

Mead, G. H. *Mind, Self and Society: From the Standpoint of a Social Behaviorist.* Chicago: University of Chicago Press, 1934.

Mead, M. "Public Opinoin Mechanisms among Primitive People," *Public Opinion Quarterly* 1 (1937): 3–16.

Merton, R. K. *Social Theory and Social Structure.* New York: Free Press, 1963.

Murdock, R. K. *Social Structure.* New York: Macmillan, 1979.

Niebuhr, H. R. *The Social Sources of Denominationalism.* New York: Holt, 1929.

Parsons, T. *The Social System.* New York: Free Press, 1951.

Radcliffe-Brown, A. R. *Structure and Function in Primitive Society.* Glencoe, Ill.: Free Press, 1953.

Rainwater, L. "The Problem of Lower Class Culture," *Journal of Social Issues* 26 (1976): 1–19.

Riesman, D., N. Glazer, and R. Denney. *The Lonely Crowd.* New Haven, Conn.: Yale University Press, 1950.

Seggar, J. and Wheeler, P. "World of Work on TV: Ethnic and Sex Representations in TV Drama," *Journal of Broadcasting* 17 Winter (1973): 97–104.

Smith, M. D. and Matre, M. "Social Norms and Sex Roles in Romance and Adventure Magazines," *Journalism Quarterly* 52 (October 1975): 213–18.

Spencer, H. *The Principles of Sociology* New York 1898.

Sumner, W. G. "Fundamental Notions of the Folkways and of the Mores," in E. A. Schuler, T. F. Hoult, D. L. Gibson, and W. B. Brookover, *Readings in Sociology.* New York: Macmillan, 1971.

Thomas, S. "Learning What People Learn from the Media: Some Problems with Interviewing Techniques," *Mass Comm Review* 8 (1981): 410–415.

———. "Some Problems of the Paradigm in Communication Theory," *Philosophy of the Social Sciences* 10, (1980).

———. "The Relationship between Daytime Serials and Their Viewers." Doctoral dissertation, University of Pennsylvania, 1977.

———. "The Route to Redemption: Religion and Social Class," *Journal of Communication,* 35 (Winter 1985): 111–122.

———. "Gender and Social-Class Coding in Popular Photographic Erotics," Paper presented at the Eastern Communication Association Convention, Philadelphia, PA, 1984.

Thomas, S. and Callahan, B. "Allocating Happiness: Television Families and Social Class," *Journal of Communication* 32 (Summer 1982): 67–77.

Thomas, S. and Harenza, D. T. "No Bed of Roses: An Analysis of Autobiographies of American Film Stars," research in progress.

Thomas, W. Z. and Znaniecki, F. *The Polish Peasant in Europe and America*. N.Y.: 1927.

Tuchman, G. "The Symbolic Annihilation of Women by the Mass Media," in G. Tuchman, A. K. Daniels, and J. Benet, *Hearth and Home: Images of Women in the Mass Media*. New York: Oxford University Press, 1978.

Veblen, T. I., *The Theory of the Leisure Class: An Economic Study of Institutions*. New York: Macmillan 1899.

Warner, W. L. and Henry, W. E. "The Radio Day Time Serial: A Symbolic Analysis," *Genetic Psychology Monographs* 37 (1948): 161–175.

Weber, M. *The Protestant Ethic and the Spirit of Capitalism*. New York: Free Press, 1958.

White, L. A. "Culturological vs. Psychological Interpretation of Human Behavior," *American Sociological Reveiw*, 12 (1947) *Review* 12, no. 1 (February 1947): 8.

———. *The Science of Culture: A Study of Man and Civilization*. New York: 1949.

Wright, C. R. *Mass Communication: A Sociological Perspective*. New York: Random House, 1959.

Znaniecki, F. *Cultural Reality*. Chicago: Chicago University Press, 1919.